THE 2005 WORLD CHAMPION
CHICAGO
WHITE SOX:
GRINDERS & GAMERS

Edited by Eric Conrad, Mark Morowczynski,
Bill Nowlin, and Don Zminda
Associate editors Len Levin and Carl Riechers

Society for American Baseball Research, Inc.
Phoenix, AZ

The 2005 World Champion Chicago White Sox: Grinders and Gamers
Edited by Eric Conrad, Mark Morowczynski, Bill Nowlin, and Don Zminda
Associate editors Len Levin and Carl Riechers

Design: Rachael Sullivan
Front cover photographs: Ron Vesely / Chicago White Sox
All interior photographs are by Ron Vesely / Chicago White Sox, unless otherwise noted.
Back cover images: Courtesy of Ken Smoller

ISBN 978-1-960819-36-9 ebook
ISBN 978-1-960819-37-6 paper
Library of Congress Control Number: 2025902707

CONTENTS

MANAGER

COACHING STAFF

The Championship Moments sculpture in front of the stadium capturing key moments from the 2005 playoffs.

Courtesy of Ken Smoller

INTRODUCTION

Chicago is a city with many nicknames. Its "Windy City" moniker originated in the late 1800s as a comment on the city's long-winded politicians, but if you stand on the corner of Jackson and Wabash downtown today, you might beg to differ when that wind comes off the lake. Famous poet Carl Sandburg called Chicago the "City of Big Shoulders" for its hard-working blue-collar citizens – a characterization that is still connected to many current South Side residents. Chicago was also called "The Second City," a term first used as an insult that Chicago was "lesser than" New York by journalist A.J. Liebling of the *New Yorker*. Chicagoans now use the term with pride.

The White Sox are the Second City's second team. We have a chip on our shoulder and for good reason. When you say you are a baseball fan from Chicago, many people assume you are a Cubs fan. The Cubs had the longest World Series drought, 108 years; the White Sox rank second at 87 years, but much less was made about *that* fanbase's long suffering. When it comes to baseball curses, the curse of The Black Sox or the curse of Shoeless Joe is lesser known than the Curse of the Bambino, which the Red Sox allegedly suffered for selling Babe Ruth to the New York Yankees. When Shoeless Joe Jackson was portrayed by Ray Liotta in the film *Field of Dreams*, they had him bat right-handed and throw left-handed. Jackson actually batted lefty and threw righty. Imagine any of the movies showing the great Ruth hitting and throwing from the right side! But this movie's mistake went unnoticed.

In over 100 years of major-league baseball, only 10 teams have led their division from the first day to the last day of the season. This is frequently referred to as going wire-to-wire. Of those 10, only five went on to also win the World Series: the 1927 Yankees, the 1955 Brooklyn Dodgers, the 1984 Detroit Tigers, the 1990 Cincinnati Reds, and the 2005 White Sox. That is a rare group to be included in. The 2005 White Sox also went 11-1 in the playoffs, which is tied with the 1999 New York Yankees for the best postseason record in the wild-card era that began in 1995. Whether generally known or not, those are impressive accomplishments.

Finally, after coming up short in the playoffs in 1959, 1983, 1993, and 2000 – not to mention having the 1994 season lost while sitting with the second-best record in the AL – there was a championship baseball team in Chicago. The Cubs had come close in 2003 before their painful and famous collapse. The city was ready to celebrate the White Sox World Series victory with a parade that started at US Cellular Field and wound through many South Side neighborhoods including Bridgeport, Bronzeville, Chinatown, Pilsen, and Little Italy, eventually making its way to the Loop, where members of the team spoke in front of the Chicago Board of Trade. The players rode in double-decker buses waving to what seemed like half the city. Attendance at the White Sox victory parade was estimated at 1.75 million. Like all larger gatherings of people, estimate is a kind way to say they have really no idea. Don't mention that number in earshot of a Cubs fan, though. They will remind you that when the Cubs finally won their elusive World Series title 11 years later, attendance at *their* parade was estimated at *five* million. Of course it was.

The Sox' 2005 World Series title was truly a team win. Frank Thomas, at age 37, was, to date, the only future Hall of Famer on this team. And Thomas was only a minor contributor to the 2005 crown, limited to just 34 games that year in June and late July before refracturing the same left ankle that he had surgery on the previous year. Mark Buehrle, Jon Garland, and Paul Konerko were named All-Stars. Scott Podsednik won the "All-Star Final Vote" in the first year text-message voting was allowed.

As a team, the 2005 White Sox did the little things right. They played "Ozzie ball." Singles and bases on balls magically turned into runs with steals and sacrifices. The team's pitching staff was fourth in the league in ERA and third in complete games. They had 35 one-run victories. The team's average bWAR was 1.2, slightly better than an average player. But as a team, they were great.

With such a dominant regular and postseason performance, surely now the White Sox would get their due. An odd thing happened, however: The team seemed to disappear from baseball fans' minds like a ghost returning to the cornfield. Would you believe ESPN, the worldwide leader in sports (so ESPN says), forgot to mention them as the 2005 World Series winner, not once, but twice, in back-to-back years, no less? If you are a White Sox fan, you believe it. We are used to it.

Twenty years after that memorable season, it's time to give the 2005 White Sox their due. The contributions of 57 SABR members to this book produced many new SABR biographies, more than a dozen new games recapped, and a number of essays. This was truly a team effort on the part of the SABR Chicago chapter, as well as by members of many other SABR chapters. A big thanks goes to co-editor Bill Nowlin, for kick-starting the investigation into this project and finding time to guide this book, as he's done for countless other SABR projects.

Completing this book would have been a much more difficult—if not impossible—task without the extraordinary support we received from the Chicago White Sox. Particular thanks go to Chairman Jerry Reinsdorf, who contributed the heartfelt and personal Foreword. Special thanks also go to Scott Reifert, Vice President of Communications for the

White Sox, and to Megan Biasotti, Darren Georgia, Billy Russo, and the other members of the White Sox staff who provided us with photos and contact information, and who generously supported our project from beginning to end. Thanks also to SABR member Ken Smoller for allowing access his own White Sox photos for use in the book.

This book was produced over the course of another historic White Sox season, but for the wrong kind of history. The 2024 White Sox set the modern-day record of losses with a 41-121 record, surpassing the hapless 1962 Mets. Many franchises' worst records were broken, but that will have to wait for a different SABR project. After a season like 2024, the 2005 team doesn't feel 20 years away, it feels much closer to 87 years.

With every spring training, there is always hope. A fresh season lies ahead; what if things break right this year? In 2005 they surely did for the White Sox. Here they were first, and this book is to make sure they are not forgotten. We hope you enjoy looking back on this truly unique season as you do looking ahead, where anything can happen.

Mark Morowczynski, Eric Conrad, and Don Zminda
October 2024

CHAMPAGNE TOASTS & CEMETERIES

By Jerry Reinsdorf

You saw the evidence across every cemetery in Chicago. White Sox flags draped graves. Baseballs, family photos, jerseys, and other memorabilia sat atop headstones, along with half-full beer cans and empty champagne bottles.

With so many powerful memories from that magical 2005 World Series-winning season, it may seem strange that one of my strongest recollections starts in a graveyard, but if you truly know Chicago and White Sox fans, it actually makes all the sense in the world.

For many Sox fans – raised from birth to love their team – it was only natural to celebrate the city's first World Series victory since 1917 with those very people who first made them into White Sox fans, who shared the highs and lows of the franchise, over lifetimes.

As the team finished its four-game sweep of the Astros that October, Chicago's cemeteries took on a unique,

decorated look. Living Sox fans wanted to share this very special celebration with the generations who came before them, the generations of hard-working fans who made them into Sox fans, teaching them to love this team. Undying love for your team doesn't even come close to describing how Sox fans feel.

"My father died minutes after the last out," one fan stopped me in the parking lot the next April. "And he died happy. He knew."

It was proof that that White Sox baseball was so much more than a game. It's the seemingly limitless thread that connects us.

Chicago, the spirit of Chicagoans, the power of baseball and the passion of White Sox fans never cease to amaze me, even after five decades. This is a very special franchise with very special fans.

The Duke with the 2005 World Series Trophy

THE 2005 WORLD CHAMPION CHICAGO WHITE SOX

The story of the 2005 White Sox is filled with awe-inspiring moments, funny coincidences and of course, heroes whose exploits will never die.

Home runs by Paul Konerko and then, shockingly, by Scott Podsednik to win a damp Game Two. Truly amazing starting pitching performances by José Contreras, Freddy García, Mark Buehrle, and Jon Garland lead us past the Angels in the American League Championship Series and then the Astros in the World Series. Bobby Jenks and his sizzling, ninth-inning fastball are supported by stellar bull-pen performances by Cliff Politte, Dámaso Marté , Neal Cotts, and Luis Vizcaíno . El Duque's bases-loaded, magic-trick escape in Boston to win Game Three in the Division Series. Jermaine Dye, World Series MVP who drove in the game winner in Game Four's 1-0 decision, Carl Everett's leadership, Tadahito Iguchi's clutch fielding and ability to shoot ball after ball into right field behind the runner. Geoff Blum's late-night heroics to cap Game Three. And of course, Joe Crede, Aaron Rowand, and A.J. Pierzynski, who not only stood out night after night on the field, but also somehow created a rallying cry for the 2005 team one night in Baltimore when a dive-bar cover band played "Don't Stop Believin.'"

All of this was built brilliantly by general manager Ken Williams and orchestrated on a nightly basis by manager Ozzie Guillén, the master motivator/energizer/instigator.

Baseball, the people who work in the industry, the people who play it and the people who watch it with all the passion in the world, are notoriously superstitious. We were no different in 2005.

With a large midsummer lead slowly and precipitously narrowing, I must admit I fell under sway. A friend gifted me a ceramic, hand-painted figure of John Wayne. It measured maybe 18 inches high. I noticed that receiving the gift coincided with a winning streak, so I did something that was obvious and natural for any sports fan. For road games, I positioned "The Duke" on the living-room couch with the television set to the channel where our game would air. He couldn't miss a pitch. And for home games, well, he attended them all, sitting with guests and fans alike. I am still not sure how much credit we want to give him for our dominating 11-1 playoff run, but we were not taking any chances that October.

After two stunning plays by shortstop Juan Uribe to complete the sweep, we celebrated together -- teammates, friends, family – shedding tears on the infield in Houston. The moments from the final out until Ozzie, Kenny, and I were holding the Commissioner's trophy seemed a dream. I am not sure my feet touched the ground, but I know a cigar never tasted so good.

The parade in Chicago was one of our proudest moments as 2 million Chicagoans came together to celebrate without a single incident or arrest. The route from the ballpark to downtown was lined with Sox fans. You could feel the love for this team.

Important milestones in life, events like weddings, births and graduations, generate powerful, overwhelming emotions in people. This parade absolutely delivered all of that for those of us on the double-decker buses, but it also was different because of its length and intensity as we drove through neighborhood after neighborhood toward downtown. School students lined the streets with signs saying, "I've waited my whole life for this!" Nuns cheered us. Office workers held up signs and waved. Construction workers flew Sox flags from unfinished buildings and street overpasses. Fans, many cheering, others weeping, stepped toward the buses holding up photos of long-dead relatives. They wanted our players to see, and wanted their predecessors to share in, history. The intersection of Michigan Ave. and Wacker Drive was filled with love, happiness and so much positive energy. You could feel the pride.

Then Paul Konerko spoke to the crowd.

"Everybody kept asking me the last couple of days what I did with that last ball, the last out," he said, leaning into the microphone. "Well, it's going to this man right here because he earned it."

Turning to me, Paulie handed me the single, most touching gift anyone has ever given me.

The 2005 White Sox, the leadership, the team, the players, and even that cherished baseball, don't belong to me or to any one person. Those moments, those emotions, those memories belong to all White Sox fans, those living, those yet to come and even those who celebrated our World Series victory with a midnight champagne toast in a cemetery, surrounded by love.

HOW THE 2005 WHITE SOX WERE BUILT

By Jim Margalus

During their 11-1 run through the postseason that followed a wire-to-wire regular season for their first World Series title in 88 years, the 2005 White Sox used the same 25-man roster in all three series, and nearly half of the players on that roster became a part of the organization only over the previous year.

Seeking to shake up a team coming off a third consecutive runner-up finish to the Minnesota Twins in the AL Central Division, general manager Kenny Williams turned over 11 roster spots from the end of the 2004 season through the July 31 trade deadline in 2005, but nobody could accuse him of buying a title.

The White Sox opened the 2005 season with the 13th-highest payroll in the major leagues, but Williams made his biggest splash the previous summer. He traded three players for Seattle All-Star starting pitcher Freddy García, then signed him to a three-year, $27 million extension in July.[1]

Other moves to land brand-name players fell through. Randy Johnson refused to lift his no-trade clause to consider a trade to the White Sox,[2] and hopes of signing Omar Vizquel were dashed when the San Francisco Giants added an extra year to their contract offer.[3]

Williams was forced to test his resourcefulness. He traded from a surplus to address other needs when he sent Carlos Lee and his $8 million salary to Milwaukee for Scott Podsednik and Luis Vizcaino. Neither player matched Lee's production, but the money saved created some operating room for a series of smaller bets. Over the course of the winter, Williams signed a starting catcher, starting second baseman, starting right fielder, fifth starter, and eventual closer. None of the contracts guaranteed more than two years or an annual salary exceeding $5 million.

And in a sense, the White Sox got what they paid for, because none of the veteran acquisitions had a career year. They all had decent to good years, however, and what made the sum greater than the parts was exceptional health. Every starting position player on the Opening Day roster played in at least 128 games; only six pitchers were required to make a start for the White Sox because four starting pitchers eclipsed 200 innings; and only one reliever lost his job over the course of the season. That stability carried over into the postseason, as White Sox starting pitchers threw at least seven innings in 11 of 12 games, including four consecutive complete-game victories in the American League Championship Series.

It proved to be a formula that was impossible for the White Sox repeat – and for that matter, the major leagues may never see four consecutive complete games in October again – but for one season, hitting on a series of modest wagers led to one incredible payoff.

PLAYERS ACQUIRED FOR OR DURING THE 2005 SEASON:

A.J. Pierzynski: Signed a one-year, $2.25 million contract on January 6, 2005, after the San Francisco Giants nontendered him a month earlier.

Jermaine Dye: Signed a two-year, $10.15 million contract on December 9, 2004, after the Oakland Athletics declined a $14 million option, instead buying him out for $1.5 million. The contract also included a $6 million option for 2007.

Tadahito Iguchi: Signed a two-year, $4.95 million contract on January 27, 2005, after playing the previous eight seasons with the Fukuoka Daiei Hawks in Japan.

Dustin Hermanson: Signed a two-year, $5.5 million contract on December 9, 2004, after splitting time between the Giants rotation and a closer role the previous season.

Scott Podsednik and **Luis Vizcaíno** Acquired from the Milwaukee Brewers in a trade for Carlos Lee on December 13, 2004.

Bobby Jenks: Claimed off waivers from the Anaheim Angels for $20,000 on December 17, 2004, and assigned to Double-A Birmingham.[4]

Orlando Hernández: Signed a two-year, $8 million contract on December 22, 2004, after spending his first six major-league seasons with the New York Yankees.

Chris Widger: Signed a minor-league contract with an invitation to free agency on January 19, 2005, after spending the 2004 season playing for the independent Camden Riversharks of the Atlantic League.[5]

Pablo Ozuna: Signed a minor-league contract with an invitation to spring training on January 19, 2005, after he was released from the Philadelphia Phillies organization.

Geoff Blum: Acquired from the San Diego Padres in a trade on July 31, 2004, for Ryan Meaux.

THE 2005 WORLD CHAMPION CHICAGO WHITE SOX

HOLDOVERS:

In order of longevity:

Joe Crede: Selected in the fifth round of the 1996 draft out of Fatima High School in Westphalia, Missouri.

Aaron Rowand: Drafted by the White Sox out of Cal State Fullerton in the first round (35th overall) of the 1998 draft, signed on June 12, 1998.[6]

Jon Garland: Acquired in a trade with the Chicago Cubs for Matt Karchner on July 29, 1998.

Paul Konerko: Acquired in a trade with the Cincinnati Reds for Mike Cameron on November 11, 1998.

Mark Buehrle: Signed with the White Sox in May of 1999 for $150,000 as a draft-and-follow pick after being selected out of Jefferson College in Missouri in the 38th round of the 1998 draft.

Willie Harris: Acquired in a trade with the Baltimore Orioles for Chris Singleton on January 29, 2002.

Dámaso Marté: Acquired alongside Ruddy Yan in a trade with the Pittsburgh Pirates for Matt Guerrier on March 27, 2002.

Neal Cotts: Acquired as a player to be named later in a trade with the Oakland Athletics on December 3, 2002. The White Sox traded Keith Foulke, Mark Johnson, Joe Valentine, and cash for Billy Koch and two players to be named later. Daylan Holt was the other.

Juan Uribe: Acquired in a trade with the Colorado Rockies for Aaron Miles on December 2, 2003.

Cliff Politte: Signed a one-year, $800,000 contract with the White Sox on January 7, 2004, with a $1.3 million club option for 2005.

Timo Pérez: Acquired in a trade with the New York Mets for Matt Ginter on March 27, 2004.

Freddy García: Acquired alongside Ben Davis in a trade with the Seattle Mariners for Michael Morse, Miguel Olivo and Jeremy Reed on June 27, 2004.

Carl Everett: Acquired in a trade with the Montreal Expos for Jon Rauch and Gary Majewski on July 18, 2004.

José Contreras: Acquired in a trade with the New York Yankees for Esteban Loaiza on July 31, 2004.

OTHER NOTABLE CONTRIBUTORS:

Frank Thomas: Drafted by the White Sox in the first round (seventh overall) in 1989, but he was limited to 34 games due to ankle and foot problems and played his last game for the White Sox on July 20.

Shingo Takatsu: Signed with the White Sox on January 22, 2004, after spending the previous 13 seasons with the Yakult Swallows in Japan. He saved 19 games for the White Sox in 2004 and opened the 2005 season as the closer, but lost the job to Hermanson in May, and was optioned to Triple-A Charlotte in July to open a spot for Jenks in July. He was released on August 1.

Brandon McCarthy: Drafted by the White Sox in the 17th round in 2002, McCarthy made his major-league debut against the Chicago Cubs on May 22, and made 12 appearances over three stints during the season. He was the only pitcher outside the original five-man rotation to start a game for the 2005 White Sox, making 10 starts in all, but was left off the postseason rosters in favor of Hernandez.[7]

FRONT OFFICE AND COACHING STAFF:

Ken Williams: Became the 11th general manager in White Sox history on October 24, 2000, after being promoted from vice president of player development. He was drafted by the White Sox in 1982, and after six major-league seasons joined the White Sox front office in 1992.

Ozzie Guillén: Became the 37th manager in White Sox history on November 11, 2003, after 16 major-league seasons as a shortstop – 13 of them with the White Sox – and three seasons serving as a third-base coach, first for the Expos in 2001, then with the Marlins in 2002 and 2003.

Don Cooper: Promoted to White Sox pitching coach on July 22, 2002, after spending the previous 15 seasons as a coach and coordinator in the organization, including a two-month midseason stint as White Sox pitching coach in 1995.

Greg Walker: Promoted to hitting coach on May 19, 2003, after the midseason firing of Gary Ward. He rejoined the organization as the hitting coach at Triple-A Charlotte after spending nearly his entire nine-year career as a first baseman for the White Sox from 1982 to 1990.

SOURCES

In addition to the sources cited in the notes, the author consulted the Chicago White Sox media guide for transaction histories and Baseball-Reference.com for statistics.

NOTES

1   "Pitcher Garcia Signs Deal for $27 Million," *Los Angeles Times*, July 7, 2004. The three players traded were Miguel Olivo, Jeremy Reed, and Michael Morse; the White Sox also received catcher Ben Davis in the deal, but he did not play for the White Sox in 2005.

2   "Randy Says No to White Sox," *Chicago Tribune*, December. 7, 2004: 12.

3   Scot Gregor, "Vizquel Joining Giants Stuns Sox GM Williams," *Arlington Heights* (Illinois) *Daily Herald*, November 16, 2004: 4.

4   John Romano, "The Fast Life," *Tampa Bay Times*, October 25, 2005.

5   Kevin Minnick, "S.J.'s Widger Signs with White Sox," *Cherry Hill* (New Jersey) *Courier Post*, January 20, 2005.

6   Scot Gregor, "Young White Sox Testing Manuel's Patience," *Arlington Heights Daily Herald*, June 14, 1998: 3.

7   Thomas Boswell, "The Stuff of Legend," *Washington Post*, October 7, 2005.

GRINDING AND BELIEVING

A RECIPE FOR SUCCESS ON A HISTORIC 2005 WHITE SOX JOURNEY

By Jeff Allan Howard

Driving along the oft-congested Chicago expressways in 2005, one might occasionally pass a wayside billboard that featured a White Sox player in full uniform with a random-seeming catchphrase. If you drove the same route, you saw it every day and during those rush-hour traffic jams, the image lasted longer, leaving a lingering impression.

The seeds for the sundry slogans were planted before the 2005 season even started. It was part of a campaign to bring the Southside Chicago baseball team to the forefront of the general populace of the city of Chicago.

There was baseball magic in the air. The Boston Red Sox had won the 2004 World Series with a record-setting drive that culminated with their first title in 86 years. That accomplishment perhaps fostered belief in the notion that similar dreams could come true in Chicago, where a White Sox championship had not been seen since 1917.

The White Sox marketing department sat down with Chicago's Two by Four ad agency to create a vision of what an ideal baseball team might look like. Ozzie Guillén, the team's second-year manager, was invited to the table and, of course, Ozzie delivered. For about an hour, he was on a roll and his ramblings filled the pages of an entire notepad.

A recurring theme emerged: "I want grinders. I want to grind out runs. I want to grind out wins. I want guys that play every game." The result became known as "Grinder Ball."[1]

"Win Or Die Trying" ended up being Grinder Ball Rule #1.[2] Random in their message and random in their numeric assignment, the Grinder Rules popped up randomly across the Chicago city landscape on billboards, buses, trains, and radio spots, spreading the message of all that was good about White Sox baseball.

The 60-second White Sox Grinder Rule #1 dramatic voice-over radio pitch sounded like this:

"Grinder Baseball Rule number 1. 'Win or die trying.' Not a complicated rule but a basic one. It's simple. You go out there and grind out a win every day.

That's why we play by a certain set of rules.

Never walk, even when you walk. That's rule number 37.

Advance a runner at all costs. Rule 62.

Never be late for the National Anthem no matter what nation you're from. Rule 18.

Fans deserve a team relentlessly focused on winning doing whatever it takes to win. That's what being a Grinder is all about. "Win or die trying." Yeah. That's Sox rule number one!"[3]

Did it work? The Two by Four ad agency website lauds the campaign as "Best.Case.Study.Ever."

"Chicago White Sox – The team hadn't won a World Series in 88 years. Then they hired us.

Nine months later they won the World Series. END OF CASE STUDY."[4]

Grinder Rules emerged during a significant series in the 2005 season when the White Sox visited Baltimore from Friday, July 29, through Monday, August 1, to culminate a seven-game road trip. The four-game weekend series drew 165,172 fans to Camden Yards.

The White Sox convincingly won the first three July games of the series. They launched two home runs under Friday night lights to claim a 7-2 victory. They added three more home runs in the Saturday afternoon game to catapult them to a 9-6 victory. For the Sunday night TV game of the week, two White Sox batters were hit by pitches and the Orioles hit two home runs, but the White Sox won again, 9-4.

Tensions were running as high as the 87-degree August heat on the Chesapeake Bay for that 12:38 P.M. Monday matinee in Baltimore. AJ Pierzynski was hit by a Daniel Cabrera pitch in the top of the sixth inning.[5] With two outs in the bottom of the sixth, Mark Buerhle was ejected when he plunked B.J. Surhoff during a close game which the White Sox were leading, 2-1.[6]

The White Sox rallied for four runs on seven hits in the final three innings after the Buerhle ejection to record a 6-3 victory. Pierzynski led the way with an eighth-inning leadoff home run to spark the attack.[7] "They won that one for Buehrle," said manager Guillén after the game.[8] The team departed the Charm City with a 69-35 record after the four-game sweep, reaching their pinnacle Central Division lead of 15 games. The victory also marked the first time the

White Sox recorded two four-game road sweeps in the same season since 1954.[9]

While assorted and varied, the Grinder Rules did not include "Don't Stop Believing." That one was born in Baltimore during this very series. It became a theme that extended right through the championship celebration parade before millions on the streets of Chicago in October 2005.

It happened in a hotel bar.[10] According to the legend, Pierzynski, Joe Crede, and Aaron Rowand, who were self-proclaimed as "The Three Stooges," gathered at the establishment, blending with the regular crowd that shuffled in. Likely it was after the Saturday afternoon game.

A singer in a smoky room provided lounge-singer-styled entertainment while beverages were sipped and stories were shared. As this story goes, at some point during a set that lacked satisfactory song-selection, the normally reserved Crede, who was indeed just a small-town boy, spontaneously urged the singer to "Play Some Journey!" Certainly, the other two Stooges supported the suggestion and piled on until the troubadour ultimately consented.

The singer sang "Don't Stop Believin'" – likely the only Journey song on his playlist. The Stooges loved it. The song stuck and evolved into a theme song as the 2005 season progressed.[11]

It was not until September when the message of the song would serve as inspiration after the White Sox had seen their 15-game plunge to just 1½ games. They hosted their Central Division nemesis Minnesota Twins for a four-game weekend series with just 11 games left in the season beginning Thursday, September 22.

The White Sox lost the Thursday night game. It was a dramatic 11-inning defeat. But they rebounded to sweep the remaining three games of the series. They went on to claim the AL Central Division title. "Hold on to that feeling."

Afterward, the White Sox blitzed though the AL play-offs, winning 11 games while losing just one with "Don't Stop Believin'" playing along the way. The song surfaced over the loudspeakers during home playoff batting practice; and White Sox DJ Christopher Hubble played a riff during a playoff game with the Angels in Chicago to seemingly invoke a game-winning rally. Heck, it resonated for the whole plane ride home from Los Angeles after the White Sox secured a berth in the 2005 World Series, defeating the Los Angeles Angels of Anaheim.[12] (Anaheim, the home of Disneyland, "where dreams come true.")

Pierzynski was on a mission to include singer and songwriter Steve Perry for the World Series experience and succeeded. Perry hopped aboard the bandwagon and came along for the ride.[13]

Like a leprechaun, he popped up at random spots along the historic path during the White Sox' journey to history. He was there in Chicago for Game One of the World Series.

He was in Houston for the Game Four clincher when the White Sox won the pot of gold. Perry was even on stage on the city streets in downtown Chicago singing his song to streetlight people up and down the boulevard.

For that one, he called on backup singers in front of the millions who gathered for the revelry of the celebration. "I need some help up here," said Perry. "I want Crede, I want AJ, I want Rowand, I want everyone around." At 5-feet-7, he was dwarfed by the Three Stooges, all of whom stood at least 6-feet-1. It embodied the leprechaun illusion.[14] Despite oh so many Journey arena concerts, there were surely none that numbered the millions on that celebratory day in downtown Chicago.

The Stooges have fond recollections. Said Crede on his 2013 induction into the Missouri Sports Hall of Fame, "Hanging out with Steve Perry, always makes me laugh. It was a great time in my life."[15]

NOTES

[1]   Scott Merkin, "How the Sox Grinder Ball Rules Came to Be," MLB.com, January 8, 2021. https://www.mlb.com/news/white-sox-grinder-ball-rules-origin.

[2]   The billboard image showed Paul Konerko, clad in White Sox home pinstripes, swinging for the fences.

[3]   Two by Four website: https://www.twoxfour.com/work/white-sox (contains "White Sox Grinder Rule #1" radio audio link).

[4]   Two by Four website. https://www.twoxfour.com/work/white-sox.

[5]   Grinder Rule 54: If you can't take the heat get out of the batter's box.

[6]   Home-plate umpire Daniel Gorman deemed Buerhle's errant throw to be intentional and ejection-worthy. It ended a most impressive streak that Buerhle had taken quite some time to develop. Until then he had worked at least six innings in 49 consecutive starts. He was just an out away from 50 when he got the thumb.

[7]   Grinder Rule 26: Your hitting should serve as a warning. To low flying aircraft.

[8]   Mark Gonzalez, "Plunked, Not Dunked; Ump Tosses Buerhle," *Chicago Tribune.* August 2, 2005: 4.1.

[9]   Grinder Rule 88: Make history history.

[10] Likely, it was after the 1:26 P.M. Saturday, July 30, game since that was the only game that left some evening downtime.

[11] Stacy St. Clair, "Hit Parade White Sox Players Particular about Intro Music Blasted Before Each At-Bat: *Arlington Heights Daily Herald,* October 23, 2005: 16.

[12] St. Clair.

[13] Grinder Rule 11: When jumping on the White Sox bandwagon, do not, I repeat DO NOT, keep your hands and arms inside the wagon at any time.

[14] Steve Perry, lead singer of Journey, is listed as a generous 5-feet-7. Crede and Pierzynski log in at 6-3 while Rowand is 6-1. The YouTube video is available for viewing: https://www.youtube.com/watch?v=504B3iR5M_8.

[15] Bill Pollack, "World Series Champ Still Misses the Game," February 1, 2013, podcast. World Series Champ still misses the game (PODCAST) - Missourinet

GRINDERS AND GAMERS

THE GRINDER RULES

Baseball-fever.com/forum/American-league/
chicago-white-sox/2709-white-sox-grinder-rules

The Grinder Rules were a marketing campaign throughout the 2005 season with new rules being added throughout the year capturing the spirit of the team and the fanbase. Rules were not done in numerical or sequential order, gaps or missing rules in the Grinder Rules list below is expected. Here are the World Champion White Sox Grinder rules to live by.

1) Win. Or die trying.

2) Be MVP, M T W T F S S

3) Bite worse than your bark.

4) Knowing what's coming and hitting what's coming--not the same thing.

5) Every pitch is full count. Every inning, the ninth. Every game, game seven.

6) The best seat in the house is often determined by the best players in the house.

7) Grinder ball requires speed, defense, and discipline. And immigration.

8) Play every game like it's your last.

9) Be realistic, expect miracles.

10) Only one statistic matters: W

11) When jumping on the White Sox bandwagon, do not, I repeat DO NOT, keep your hands and arms inside the wagon at any time.

12) There is only one acceptable reason not to hold onto the ball: Amputation

13) There is only one thing more valuable than ability. The ability to recognize it.

14) It's a mother's right to yell at her boys.

15) Be a highlight reel.

16) Level the playing field Preferably while the other team's on it.

17) Never be satisfied with what you have achieved. It pales in comparison to what you can achieve.

18) NEVER be late for the National Anthem. No matter what nation you're from.

19) A reputation is not built on what you are going to do.

20) Hot dog vendors don't take credit.

21) Thieves will be punished. Swiftly, harshly and repeatedly.

22) When attending a Chicago White Sox game, don't blink.

23) When all is said and done, make sure you've "done" more than you said.

24) Play like there are no rules.— like gravity for instance.

25) A good outfielder doesn't see the wall. He tastes it.

26) Your hitting should serve as a warning. To low flying aircraft.

27) If the fence won't come to you, go to the fence.

28) Always give fans something they can take away from the game. Like the other team's pride.

29) Play like a star. Never act like one.

30) Good enough, isn't.

31) Never swing at foolish pitches. Unless they're foolishly belt high, right down the middle.

32) Respect respect.

33) The best way to get out of a hole is to dig deeper.

34) For some, it's not a choice. It's genetic.

36) You can't spell "win" without a few "k's".

37) Never walk. Even when you walk.

38) You're either counted on or counted out.

39) Be a man. Play like a boy.

41) Never underestimate the power of power.

43) Step up to the plate even if you're not stepping up to the plate.

44) There is more to baseball than peanuts and cracker jacks.

45) The best defense is a good win.

46) Respect the past, people that are shoeless, and anyone named Joe.

47) Flying does not make you superman. Getting up and making the throw to first for the force out, now that makes you Superman.

49) There are no starting pitchers. Only finishing pitchers.

50) Be head and shoulders and arms and legs and spine and torso above the competition.

53) There are always willing players: Those willing to do whatever it takes to win. And those willing to watch them.

54) If you can't take the heat get out of the batter's box.

55) It's called stepping up to the plate for a reason.

57) There's power in numbers. Like #14, #23, #5, #24, #15, #25...

58) Never throw back a home run ball, even if it from the other team.

59) GO. GO. GO.

61) There is no "I" in team. But there is one in quit.

63) You don't have to be a coach to coach.

65) Do not sit in the leftfield bleachers, home to Scott Podsednik.

66) There is nothing loveable about losing.

69) There's always this year. (Well, and last year.)

71) If at first you succeed, repeat.

73) When bringing the family to a White Sox game know your limits.

74) Believe in magic. Not magic numbers.

75) Heroes aren't made. They're rotated.

76) Pitch. Hit. Win. Repeat.

78) Ixnay on talkin' about the ayoffsplay

88) Make history, history.

89) Taste victory and be hungry forever.

92) Interpretive dance at 101 M.P.H.

95) Be more than a one hit wonder.

96) Expect the unexpected at U.S. Cellular field, home of the White Sox.

98) Batters should fear your fast ball. Not because it can get them out. Because it can knock them out.

99) Intimidation can come in the form of a screaming 99 MPH fastball or a screaming 9 year-old.

162) Crying in baseball is acceptable only if champagne burns your eyes.

174) Hoist the city up on your shoulders. They'll return the favor.

CHICAGO AND NATIONAL MEDIA COVER THE BREAKING OF ANOTHER SO-CALLED CURSE

By Tom Shaer

In 2005 I was a sports anchor and talk show host at ESPN Radio in Chicago after decades on television and radio in that city.

When the 2005 White Sox began play, virtually no one noted that the franchise was entering the 88th season since it last won a World Series – and there was certainly no talk of a "curse," though the scandal of the 1919 Black Sox still somewhat haunted the franchise's history.

The crosstown Cubs had two seasons earlier blown a three-games-to-one lead in the NLCS and their championship drought now stood at 96 years, continuing the "Billy Goat Curse," which the media furthered.[1] Only months earlier, fans across the world were breathlessly caught up in the Boston Red Sox finally ending the media-created "Curse of the Bambino" with their first fall classic triumph in 86 years.[2] But the longer starvation of the other Sox? Not newsworthy.

In the preceding 15 seasons, the White Sox had almost always finished with more wins than the Cubs, usually by a wide margin. That period also began with White Sox Chairman Jerry Reinsdorf finally getting his team's television broadcasts on equal footing with the Cubs as each team was carried on free TV by WGN and the same regional [cable] sports channel. The better records and vastly-improved exposure created new fans and more-equitable daily coverage. The Sox were slowly narrowing the popularity gap with the Cubs; a title-winning step forward would rapidly accelerate that progress.

Coming off a mediocre 83-79 record, the White Sox were definitely not expected to win the division. A wild-card consolation prize? Maybe. Manager Ozzie Guillén made few promises, but we sports reporters sensed an implicit promise that he and his team would be interesting. While the not-yet-ready-for-the-Hall of Fame Dusty Baker dodged and whined during media sessions for the disappointing Cubs, Ozzie, who never met a microphone he didn't like, was a breath of fresh air. He combined blunt comments with just enough wacky things. The man got our attention daily, and the Sox could always use more attention.

I had known Ozzie since his rookie year of 1985, so none of this was a surprise. But it was interesting to see him grow as a leader, brilliantly taking the daily pulse of his team and finding a way to use his sizable ego and the spotlight to maintain a somewhat positive image for his team as its lead in the American League Central Division shrank from 15 games on August 1 to only a game-and-a-half over the Cleveland Indians with just eight games left to play.

Veteran Chicago baseball reporter Bruce Levine is the only person to broadcast pregame and postgame coverage for the flagship radio stations of both the White Sox and Cubs championship teams. He witnessed the manager's daily performances for the growing print and broadcast horde.

"Ozzie did his best Casey Stengel impression and regaled everyone for an hour each pregame," Levine recalled. "His players said he kept the pressure off them, especially when they blew most of that big division lead. Ozzie was always, in his own mind, honest after games. If he thought his guys needed to be better, he said so. He complimented both his team and opponents. He famously called the 2004 Minnesota Twins 'piranhas.'"[3]

White Sox General Manager Ken Williams had a decent relationship with reporters but there existed a healthy mutual skepticism over four years of averaging only 83 wins. However, Williams aggressively made many, many acquisitions for 2005 that we would later praise, as those players contributed so much.[4] He retooled with speed, pitching, and toughness instead of plain power.

Among the five – yes, five – new starting position players, A.J. Pierzynski was always a fun interview. Of six new pitchers, my personal favorite was the modest Cliff Politte, whose wry humor and self-deprecating manner belied his spectacular success in middle relief (67⅓ IP, 2.00 ERA). When Bobby Jenks took over the closer role, another character emerged.

To the surprise of everyone, the White Sox broke from the gate strong and were 53-24 through June. With the North Side Cubs barely above .500, the NBA Bulls contending but disappointing, the NFL Bears lousy for three straight seasons, and the NHL Blackhawks even worse, the South Siders owned Chicago's sports coverage.

Space in newspapers was allotted more to the winning team, nightly TV highlights were Sox-heavy, and talk shows focused on them – with not winning a World Series in the previous 87 years becoming more a part of the reporting. Walk-off home runs and other game-winning base hits plus a few strokes of luck provided plenty of highlights to fuel the media bandwagon hurtling forward.

ESPN-1000 was the network-owned all-sports station and flagship of the White Sox Radio Network. I spent a lot of time at games and off the job with play-by-voice John Rooney, one of the best in the business, who is now going on two decades as lead radio voice of the St. Louis Cardinals. The excitement in the broadcasts of "Roons," who had been doing the Pale Hose for 18 seasons, really hit home with the fans. They were caught up in this resurgent team.

There remains an age-old rule of "no cheering in the press box," but while we all stayed professional, the quiet pleasure of covering a winner was unmistakable. For some, there was also a measure of emotion because only cold, uncaring people would not want the best for players or coaches they'd known for years. We all encountered more than our share of jerks but there are more good people than bad in baseball. On the 2005 White Sox, I pulled for Paul Konerko, Frank Thomas, and hitting coach Greg Walker.

Though not a publicity hound, "Paulie" was as classy as they came. Still very unassuming, he now smiled more after games. It was cool to see him have another great year (40 HR, 100 RBIs) and finally reach the pinnacle in his seventh season in Chicago and approaching a decade in the major leagues.

Thomas could be difficult but he was really just a big kid and I knew his sensitive side. The often-ignored sad fact of the magical 2005 season is that the greatest hitter in the history of the franchise was limited by injuries (including another fractured bone in his foot) to only 34 games and didn't play after July 20. Still, "The Big Hurt" slugged 12 homers and drove in 26 runs – fantastic numbers in a mere 105 at-bats as the White Sox went 24-10 with him in the lineup.

Before an interview during a postseason celebration, Thomas had tears in his eyes and said to me, "I'm not really part of this. I didn't do much." I assured him that in a season when the team found itself barely hanging on with little more than a week remaining, his teammates and smart fans knew his numbers had been vital. I hoped he believed me.[5]

Months later, the White Sox released Thomas and he got nasty, criticizing the front office numerous times. For a good while, GM Williams never responded but finally blew his stack after still more knocks from the departed slugger during the next spring training.[6] The rancor then and in earlier years was all on Thomas but Reinsdorf, the owner, later had a statue of the Hall of Famer installed at the ballpark, retired his number, and brought him back to the Sox payroll as a team ambassador.

"These players belong to the fans," Reinsdorf said privately. "Frank's achievements were not lessened because he got mad about the contracts he signed. He was a truly great hitter."[7]

Walker was a gutty, hard-working man. Quiet, he appeared to have little to say but interviews with him included excellent insight ever since he was a key contributor on the 1983 division-dominating White Sox team that brought the organization out of the amateur eras of previous owners. "Walk" told me often during 2005 why particular hitters were succeeding but he wouldn't take any credit. In an on-field interview after the final World Series game in Houston, he surveyed the celebration around him and proclaimed his "blind loyalty"[8] to the White Sox. The love was not unrequited.

After the locals lost 10 of 14 games including two of three at home against the second-place Cleveland Indians and had only that slim 1½-game lead, I arrived early to cover the home contest vs. Minnesota on Friday, September 23.[9] The Jerry Reinsdorf I encountered on the field obviously realized his team did not then look World Series-capable.

"If we don't at least go deep into the playoffs, all the good things from this season will be forgotten," he volunteered.[10] It seemed he was looking to just hang on and somehow find an improbable path to the ALCS.

However, the White Sox stormed back to retake control of the pennant race with eight wins in their last 10 games. In contrast, the Indians lost all but one of their last seven and the first-place Chicagoans finished with a six-game cushion.

Veteran sportswriter Mark Gonzalez came to Chicago in 2005 as the *Chicago Tribune*'s White Sox beat writer.

"The biggest thing was they never lost their hold on first place. ... Some people were waiting for Ozzie Guillén to explode, but he took a lot of pressure off his players. I recall him sending Dámaso Marté home early but brought him back four days later to get big outs in a key win. [Later] Ozzie did his best managing in the playoffs but I think that got overlooked," Gonzalez said.[11]

41-year Chicago sportscaster and lifelong Sox fan Rich King felt, "Some fans and media gave up but most kept their heads. Good thing, because the team rallied when it mattered and never looked back."[12]

The fans, now in off the ledge, were downright giddy. The media reflected that, even behind the scenes. An episode in the newsroom of my old Chicago TV station, WMAQ-Channel 5, is memorable.

On Sunday, September 25, the White Sox were still leading by only 1½ games. While they continued their series with the Twins, the Indians were in Kansas City. One of those lucky breaks for the Sox occurred when Cleveland's Grady Sizemore (2024 interim manager of the South Siders) lost a fly ball in the sun which scored the winning run in

Courtesy Tom Shaer

ESPN Radio Chicago Sports Anchor and Talk Show Host Tom Shaer and Hall of Famer Carlton Fisk after Shaer MC'd the August 7, 2005 unveiling of the White Sox' statue of Fisk at then-U.S. Cellular Field.

the bottom of the ninth inning.[13] I was visiting friends in the Channel 5 newsroom and was astonished to see everyone, including nonfan types, on their feet screaming at TVs, cheering for Kansas City!

In Chicago, stations that week began assigning news reporters to augment their sports staff in covering the team. All outlets added to their coverage with each passing day; that continued through the victory parade. Front-running news management can sense a winner – when it hits them over the head. Nationally, the *New York Times* and others rediscovered the Chicago White Sox.

"Don't Stop Believin'" by Journey (1981) accidentally became the 2005 team's de facto theme song after Pierzynski and others had mockingly requested it during a July night out in Baltimore. White Sox Senior Vice President Scott Reifert found Journey frontman Steve Perry, by then 56 years old, and invited him to the postseason.[14]

But a fan-favorite tune from long ago actually emerged first that season. "Let's Go-Go-Go White Sox," the song by Captain Stubby and the Buccaneers for the 1959 American League pennant winners, was resurrected by ballpark scoreboard operations director Jeff Szynal with editors Justin Tuazon and Roman Farias. They created a music video and used it at the right time: the walk-off June 18 victory in the Dodgers' first series in a White Sox ballpark since that '59 Fall Classic.[15] The Sox scored four runs with two out in the ninth inning including Pierzynski's two-run homer as exclamation point.

The song preceded another last-at-bat win the next day and was thereafter played at big in-game moments. Soon, "Let's Go-Go-Go White Sox" was heard on radios in Chicagoland and sung by fans too young to have originally known it. National and local media covered the story and

people grabbed every remaining record from the sole store owner who had bought them up years before.[16]

The playoffs and World Series were a blur. The 11-1 record was so unexpected, at once exhilarating and mystifying. Remember, the Red Sox team that these Sox swept in the first round was the defending World Series champion.

After the final game in Boston, two broadcasting colleagues and I happened upon an impromptu party thrown together for White Sox staff following the unexpected sweep. Executive Advisor and former GM Roland Hemond and Senior Executive Vice President Howard Pizer invited us in. I'll never forget the diminutive Roland shouting to the room, "Tonight, Boston belongs to the White Sox. The Chicago White Sox!"

Major League Baseball issued more than 1,300 credentials for the World Series.[17] I and other local reporters were sought by national television as guest "experts." All of a sudden, this 87-year dry spell was sexy; most of us wisely did not call it a "curse."

When the even more unexpected sweep of the Houston Astros ended with a groundout to shortstop, John Rooney exclaimed on radio, "Out, out – for a 'White Sox winner' and a WORLD CHAMPIONSHIP!"[18] Everything had come together.

One of the many warm moments from the on-field celebration and aftermath came when Reinsdorf quietly asked Paul Konerko's father, Hank, "Isn't it nice when we see our kids do well?"[19]

The parade was surreal. All six Chicago TV stations and two cable channels aired live, continuous coverage, as did numerous AM radio stations. I was positioned at a tremendously crowded intersection – all downtown blocks on the route were teeming with humans, countless rows deep. People everywhere. Incredibly, I made direct eye contact with Greg and Carman Walker as their bus passed.

Later, I high-tailed it to the podium site near the Chicago River and happened to be standing next to the executives' bus as Reinsdorf and his son Michael disembarked.

"Eighty-seven years," the chairman said. "Eighty-seven years is no curse but it is a long time. We bought the team 25 years ago and it feels like we've all carried those years, especially the fans. I'm happy for them."[20]

The media got it right when the Baseball Writers Association of America named Guillén American League Manager of the Year. But as Gonzalez still notes, "It was a slap in the face when the other general managers voted Mark Shapiro of Cleveland as *The Sporting News* Executive of the Year over Williams."[21]

So the White Sox had finally come in from the cold. At last, at long last, they were full partners. It was nice to see. The little secret no one admits in the relationships between sports teams and media is that each side needs the other. Teams crave free publicity and media outlets need content every day. Reporters shouldn't be cheerleading but it sure is better when everybody can enjoy an outcome.

NOTES

1   When his pet goat was denied entry to Wrigley Field for the 1945 World Series, owner Sam Sianis of the Billy Goat Tavern claimed a hex on the Cubs, saying they would never win it all as long as his goat remained banned. But, in fact, the Cubs did let Sianis family goats into the ballpark numerous times beginning in 1982 (for ABC-TV's *Real People*) and including multiple postseason appearances through the 1998 playoffs (covered on local TV news). Still, the "Billy Goat Curse" was perpetuated for 34 years into the 2016 World Series by the media, which helped the publicity-wise Sianis family grow their tavern business to six locations. They have since added two for a total of eight.

2   There sometimes is confusion about the language and number of years involved in droughts, streaks, and "first since" events. The last Red Sox World Series title had been in 1918. Thus, 85 years passed *before* the season when Boston, in the 86th year, finally won its next World Series championship. Otherwise, that drought would have extended to 86 years without a title. See SABR's book on the 2004 Red Sox season: *Sox Bid Curse Farewell: The 2004 Boston Red Sox*, edited by Bill Nowlin (Phoenix: SABR, 2004).

3   Email and text-message interviews with Bruce Levine, November 2024.

4   See Jim Margalus on "How the 2005 White Sox Were Built," in this volume.

5   Author interview with Frank Thomas, October 16, 2005.

6   Mark Gonzalez, "He's an Idiot," *Chicago Tribune*, February 26, 2006; Associated Press, "GM: 'He Better Stay Out of White Sox Business,'" ESPN.com, February 27, 2006.

7   Author interview with Jerry Reinsdorf, July 31, 2011.

8   Pat Boyle interview with Greg Walker, Comcast SportsNet Chicago, observed by the author, October 26, 2005.

9   See Michael Marsh's writeup of the September 23 game elsewhere in this book.

10 Author conversation with Jerry Reinsdorf, September 23, 2005.

11 Email interviews with Mark Gonzalez, November 2024.

12 Interview with Rich King in Scottsdale, Arizona, November 26, 2024.

13 Staff writers, "AL Beat: Sizemore Loses Fly Ball in Sun; Cleveland Falls," *Seattle Times*, September 26, 2005; Associated Press, "White Sox Extend Lead," *Los Angeles Times*, September 26, 2005; Andy Call, "Indians Try Not to Think About Great Collapse of '05," *State Journal-Register* (Springfield, Illinois), September 13, 2007.

14 Interview with Scott Reifert, October 17, 2024; email interviews with Scott Reifert, October 2024. Jeff Howard's article "Grinding and Believing" in this volume offers more on the subject.

15 Email interview with Jeff Szynal via Scott Reifert, October 18, 2024; Andrew Pentis, "Stadium Songs: Chicago White Sox," ESPN.com, July 24, 2012.

16 Interview with Scott Reifert, October 17, 2024; email interviews with Scott Reifert, October 2024.

17 Interview with Scott Reifert, October 17, 2024.

18 WMVP-AM recording of the broadcast. Surprisingly, the *Chicago Tribune* substantially misquoted Rooney when printing it across two pages in its special coverage the next day.

19 Author real-time observation, October 26, 2005, and author review of postgame videotape, September 2024.

20 Interview with Jerry Reinsdorf, October 28, 2005.

21 Email interviews with Mark Gonzalez, November 2024.

JON ADKINS

By J.P. Garrett

On his 1960s radio show, White Sox owner Bill Veeck once declared, "A ballclub is no better than its scouts."[1] One former White Sox player who found his true calling not on the field, but as a scout for one of the best teams in baseball, is pitcher Jon Adkins.

Born on August 30, 1977, in Huntington, West Virginia, to parents Doug and Peggy Adkins, Jonathan Scott Adkins grew up in the nearby town of Wayne with his older brother, Mark. Doug Adkins taught ornamental horticulture and turf grass management at Wayne High School and ran a community greenhouse where students, including those with special needs, could learn about working and interacting with people. (As of 2024 the greenhouse still operated.)

In high school Jon played basketball and baseball. As a freshman he pitched on the state championship team alongside his cousin, Tim Adkins. Tim later signed with the Toronto Blue Jays and spent 12 years in the minors as a left-handed pitcher. Though he never made it to the major leagues, Tim's experience gave Jon his first glimpse of a possible major-league career.

Jon Adkins   2005

The high-school baseball team won the state championship again his junior and senior years, and in the summers he played on the Lexington Dixie travel team, for which he faced better hitters and honed his game. Between travel ball and help from his high-school coach, George Brumfield, Jon, who pitched right-handed, was attracting interest from college programs and pro scouts. Upon graduation, he chose to attend Oklahoma State University and play for coach Gary Ward.

"I knew I would have an opportunity pitch early," Adkins said about choosing Oklahoma State. "And coming from a small town in West Virginia, I felt comfortable in a smallish town [like Stillwater]."[2]

After Adkins' freshman year, he pitched for the Orleans Cardinals of the Cape Cod League, alongside college teammate and roommate Josh Holliday. Starting with the 1997 season, Josh's father, Tom Holliday, Oklahoma State's pitching coach and recruiting coordinator, took over as coach of the OSU Cowboys. While Tom Holliday led Oklahoma State to the College World Series in 1999, Adkins wasn't part of that team. In June 1998 he was selected by the Oakland Athletics in the ninth round of the amateur draft, though injury kept him out of the rookie leagues that year.

And so began Adkins' journey through the A's minor-league system as a starting pitcher in Modesto, Midland, and Sacramento. His first assignment was in 1999 to the Class-A Modesto A's (California League), where he appeared in 26 games (15 starts) and worked 102 innings with a record of 9-5 and a 4.76 ERA. "They did a good job developing and nurturing players," Adkins said, "and they have a lot of continuity. When I go back as a scout or to the instructional league, I see a lot of the same coaches."

In 2000 Adkins spent some time with the Arizona League A's, pitching 15 innings with a 3.00 ERA and a 1-1 record. He then went back to Modesto, where his 1.81 ERA and 5-2 record in nine games jumped him from high-A to Triple A at the end of the season. With the Sacramento River Cats, he pitched in only one game; the resulting 9.00 ERA prompted his start at the beginning of the 2001 season in the Double-A Texas League with the Midland Rockhounds.

Adkins started 24 games in Midland, pitching 137⅓ innings and finishing 8-8 with a 4.46 ERA. Again at the end of the season he was sent to Sacramento, where he fared a bit better. He appeared in three games and started two, his ERA was 4.26 at the end of the season.

GRINDERS AND GAMERS

Adkins began the 2002 season back in Sacramento, where he started 20 games with a 6.03 ERA. He was traded on July 25 to the White Sox for second baseman Ray Durham and cash. Durham was a fan favorite and an All-Star in 1998 and 2000, but he was also in the last year of his contract.

"The decision to trade Ray was not an easy one," White Sox general manager Ken Williams told ESPN. "Ray has been part of our family since 1990, [however,] in Adkins, we are getting a young pitcher with a live, quick power arm."[3]

After the trade, Adkins was assigned to the White Sox' Triple-A affiliate, the Charlotte Knights, for the remainder of the 2002 season. He immediately contributed to the team, starting seven of the eight games in which he appeared and finishing with a 3.69 ERA.

He began the 2003 season with the Knights as well. Adkins started 19 of 26 games through mid-August, pitching 122⅔ innings with a 3.96 ERA. He was called up to the White Sox in August when right-handed reliever Billy Koch was injured.

Adkins had been a starting pitcher until the big leagues, but his major-league debut came in relief when he came out of the bullpen on the road against the Anaheim Angels on August 14, 2003. "That day was a whirlwind of emotions," he said. "It was a lot of grind to get to that point, but it was a very fulfilling, special day, especially being able to share it with my family."

Adkins entered the game for manager Jerry Manuel in the bottom of the seventh inning, in a game the Angels were winning 4-0. There were two outs and a runner on first base. Adkins walked designated hitter Tim Salmon, then yielded a ground-rule RBI double to third baseman Scott Spiezio. After Adkins walked Bengie Molina, Manuel took the ball from him and gave it to Scott Schoeneweis, who struck out Adam Kennedy.

It was an inauspicious debut, but Adkins was given another shot the next night, against the Rangers in Texas. He worked 2⅓ innings, charged with four runs in an 11-5 loss.

Adkins appeared in two late September games, the second one in Kansas City, where he worked the final four innings, allowing just one hit.

For the 2003-2005 seasons, Adkins bounced between Charlotte and Chicago, continuing to answer the call from the bullpen, appearing in four games for the White Sox in 2003. He spent the entire 2004 season in Chicago, pitching 62 innings in 50 games and amassing a 2-3 record with a 4.65 ERA.

"Whenever I think about [moving from starter to reliever], I kind of say, I'd like it in the bullpen," Adkins told the *Chicago Sun-Times*. "It's an adrenaline rush that you get going. … Whatever they need me to do, that's what I'll go out and do."[4]

Adkins made the 40-man roster for what became the World Series season in 2005. But with an already loaded bullpen that would finish the year with a 3.23 ERA, he didn't make the team out of spring training. He did come up for about a month, however, pitching 8⅓ innings in five games during the team's drive to the AL Central Division title. He did not make the postseason roster, but did earn a World Series ring.

Released after the season, Adkins signed with the San Diego Padres, spending almost all season with the major-league club, where he appeared in 55 games and finished with a 3.98 ERA. It might be just a coincidence, but he joked in his interview that his year with the Padres was the last time they won the NL West.

At the end of the 2006 season, the Padres traded Adkins and outfielder Ben Johnson to the New York Mets for Heath Bell and Royce Ring. After his brief stint with the Mets and some time with Yaquis de Obregon of the Mexican Pacific Winter League, he signed with the Cincinnati Reds as a free agent in late 2007.

"That was a really cool couple of years," Adkins said of his time with Cincinnati. "Growing up in West Virginia, which is Reds country, they were at their peak in 1990 when I was an impressionable eighth-grader."[5] He pitched in only four games for the Reds, though, in the 2008 season, spending most of his time with Triple-A Louisville. Released before the 2009 season, and after pitching in both the Mexican Pacific Winter League and the Venezuelan Winter League, signed with the Lotte Giants of the Korean Baseball Organization.

"That was a cool experience," he said of his time in the beachfront city of Busan, where the Giants played. The team "has a really good fan base and are a good organization to play for. The manager was Jerry Royster and the pitching coach was Fernando Arroyo, who I knew from the A's minor-league system." Though some of the coaching staff were familiar, playing in Korea was an eye-opening experience, starting with spring training in Sai-Pan. "My grandfather told me how Sai-Pan was a strategic island during World War II, and that's something I would normally never get to see, being from a small town." Another new aspect of the KBO was the length of the season – 10 months vs. the six-month US major-league season. Adkins thrived there, leading the league with 26 saves.

His performance garnered another call from the Reds. They signed Adkins again for the 2010 season and sent him to Triple-A Louisville, where he pitched in 34 games before being released right before the All-Star break. At that point, a rookie named Chris Sale was pitching in the bullpen for Triple-A Charlotte and was called up to the White Sox. With a slot to fill, the White Sox signed Adkins and he finished the year (and his playing career) there.

"I wanted to go out on my own terms," Adkins said. "I didn't want to bang around Triple A a long time, eating up innings." He thought he might want to transition to scouting, so he had a conversation with John Farrell, another pitcher from Oklahoma State who later coached there and had just been named manager of the Toronto Blue Jays.

"He advised me to develop my evaluation skills in order to get back on the field," Adkins said, which he did, and as a result, "I love scouting."

By the end of the 2010 season, Adkins was hired by the Boston Red Sox as an area scout, the first two years for the Ohio Valley and then three years in South Texas and South Louisiana. He signed Travis Shaw, whom the Red Sox selected in the ninth round of the 2011 draft. In 2015 he was hired by the Los Angeles Dodgers for whom, as of 2024, he was the Northeast regional cross-checker working out of Lexington, Kentucky.

He also went back to school, using MLB's college scholarship plan. As a native of West Virginia, he chose Marshall University, which many members of his family had attended. In 2010 he earned a bachelor's degree in liberal arts. As for his master's degree, "I've had that since I was 20 years old, with all of my life experiences in baseball."

In his spare time, he said in his 2024 interview, he enjoyed hunting, working out, and spending time with his girlfriend, Jen. They attend football games at the University of Kentucky and of course Oklahoma State, where Jen's son is on the football equipment staff.

But the majority of his time is spent scouting, where his philosophy is, "If you dominate the job you're in and be where your feet are, good things will happen."[6] As a high-school pitcher in a small town in West Virginia, he may not have predicted where life would take him, but it seems to be going in the right direction. "I've been lucky to be around a lot of good baseball people," Adkins said. "It's been a good ride so far."

SOURCES

In addition to the sources cited in the Notes, the author consulted Baseball-Reference.com, Baseball Almanac.com, ESPN.com, the *New York Times*, and a number of other publications, as well as the Korean Baseball Organization website at

https://www.koreabaseball.com/record/player.asp?player_id=79596.

NOTES

1   Paul Dickson, *Bill Veeck Baseball's Greatest Maverick* (New York: Walker Brooks, 2012), 536.

2   Author interview with Jon Adkins on February 20, 2024. Unless otherwise indicated, all direct quotations in this biography come from this interview.

3   "Athletics Acquire Durham for Stretch Run," ESPN.com, July 26, 2002, accessed October 4, 2024. https://www.espn.com/mlb/news/2002/0725/1410102.html.

4   Doug Padilla, "Ex-Starter Adkins Having Fun in Bullpen," *Chicago Sun-Times*, May 18, 2004. Suntimes.com, accessed February 17, 2024. https://www.espn.com/mlb/news/2002/0725/1410102.html.

BRIAN ANDERSON

By Eric Conrad and Mark Morowczynski

Twenty-two regular-season tiebreaker games were played in the National and American Leagues from 1946 to 2018. The 18th took place on September 30, 2008, between the Minnesota Twins and the Chicago White Sox or, as it's better known in Chicago, "The Blackout Game." The White Sox won the game 1-0 on a Jim Thome home run in the bottom of the seventh, but the image that is burned into many fans' minds is the final out. A fly ball into short right-center by Alexi Casilla was caught by Brian Anderson, who had to make a headfirst dive. Celebration ensued. Anderson played one more season for the White Sox before being traded to the Boston Red Sox on July 28, 2009, for Mark Kotsay. He tried to remake himself as a pitcher before retiring in 2015. The Blackout Game catch would become one of Anderson's most memorable moments. Looking back on that play, Anderson said, "You dive, and you can feel the volume, you feel the place shaking. It's crazy."[1]

Brian Nikola Anderson was born on March 11, 1982, in Tucson, Arizona. His parents were Dana and Leslie Anderson, and he had a younger half-sister, Brooke, and a half-brother, Christopher. He described his father as a "typical California laid-back guy," and said his parents met in Arizona, were married young, and divorced early.[2] Dana worked for the D'amore Group Home, a place for kids who faced domestic or mental challenges, by providing mentorship, supervision, transportation, and staying over-night if needed. Leslie sold media advertising. Leslie later married Dave Holmes, who worked construction in marble and ceramic tile.[3] Brian always had an easy and outgoing personality with jovial streak; teammates once described him as a surfer dude from the desert.[4] He grew up a "diehard Dodger fan" with his father and described a transformation-al experience when Dodgers pitching coach Ron Perranoski threw him a baseball in the stands: "I flipped my lid."[5] He recalled once trash-talking Larry Walker during a game, said his father yelled at him, and he vowed to never speak ill of another baseball player again.[6] As a child he signed his name "Brian Anderson, Los Angeles Dodgers."[7]

Anderson attended Canyon del Oro High School, a base-ball powerhouse that won three state titles in the 1990s[8] and has produced major-league players Shelley Duncan, Chris Duncan, Ian Kinsler, Jason Stanford, Colin Porter, and Scott Hairston.[9] Anderson, Kinsler, Hairston, and Chris Duncan were all teammates.[10] Kent Winslow, who coached Anderson for his final two years at the high school, said Anderson set the record for punishment drills. "He'd show up for a game with one cleat," Winslow said. "And no jersey."[11] Anderson was named 5A state player of the year.[12]

Anderson then attended the University of Arizona with coach Andy Lopez. He started as a pitcher and moved to center field as a freshman.[13] He described assistant coach Jerry Stitt as "the best hitting guru."[14] Anderson landed on a scout's radar with an impressive junior season: .375, 14 home runs, 61 RBIs, and 17 steals.[15]

Anderson played for the collegiate Cape Cod Baseball League during summers. He said, "That was the place you wanted to go."[16] He recalled playing for the Bourne Braves in 2001, along with future major leaguers Conor Jackson, Joe Blanton, and Ryan Speier.[17] He returned to the Cape Cod League in the summer of 2002, playing for the Cotuit Kettleers.[18]

Selected by the White Sox as an outfielder 15th overall in the 2003 free-agent draft, Anderson was labeled a five-tool player by White Sox scouting director Doug Laumann.[19] He joined the Rookie league Great Falls White Sox, playing

Brian Anderson   2005

in 13 games in 2003 before his season ended due to a wrist injury that required surgery in the offseason to repair.[20]

At the start of the 2004 season, Anderson was moved up to the Winston-Salem Warthogs of the Advanced-A Carolina League for 69 games with a .319/.394/.532 slash line. Promoted to the Double-A Birmingham Barons, he played in 48 games, batting .270/.346/.416. He made only two errors the entire season, an indicator of his defensive prowess.

Anderson was moved up to the Triple-A Charlotte Knights at the start of the 2005 season, where he slashed .294/.358/.470 in 117 games with 16 home runs.

On August 16, 2005, Chicago's Scott Podsednik was placed on the 15-day disabled list with a strained left hip muscle.[21] Anderson was promoted to the team to face the Minnesota Twins, where he started in right field and batted ninth. His first hit came in the seventh inning off starter Brad Radke, a line drive to left field. Anderson later scored on a double by Timo Perez. The White Sox lost the game 9-4 in 16 innings. "It was fun, but a long game," said Anderson, who ended the game with a strikeout. "That first hit was a load off my shoulders. If I had gone 0-for-7, it would have hurt a little bit."[22]

Anderson played in 12 other games that season, with his best performance coming 10 days after his debut, on August 26 at Seattle against the Mariners. He went 3-for-4 with two home runs, the first of his career, off Félix Hernández, with three RBIs and a stolen base, and the White Sox won 5-3. He finished the season with a slash line of .176/.176/.382 and was left off the playoff roster.

Aaron Rowand, Daniel Haigwood, and Gio González were traded to the Philadelphia Phillies for Jim Thome during the 2005 offseason. Anderson was slated to take over the day-to-day responsibilities of center field.[23] This was a lot of responsibility for the 24-year-old, who still didn't have a place of his own. Anderson was living with college friend Lindsay Tamblyn's mother in the Lincoln Park neighborhood.[24] He said it was "a lot easier to deal with a bad game when a nurturing mom figure makes you a meal."[25]

Anderson began the 2006 season with the White Sox, starting most games in center field. He struggled to find his footing at the plate: This would be a trend throughout his career. "I'm a guy that feeds off success. I'm trying to get something going, but I'll go 1-for-3, and then the next game I do just crappy. This is by far the biggest challenge of my career, to have to battle through this."[26]

Anderson was involved in another infamous White Sox moment of this era on May 20, 2006, in a game against the Chicago Cubs. He hit a fly ball to left field in the bottom of the second inning. A.J. Pierzynski tagged from third and collided with Cubs catcher Michael Barrett. Pierzynski emphatically slapped home plate after the collision, and Barrett took offense. As Pierzynski walked back to the dugout, Barrett exchanged words and punched him in the face. Both

benches cleared and Anderson tackled Cubs player John Mabry.[27] Barrett, Mabry, Pierzynski, and Anderson were all ejected. This was the only ejection of Anderson's career. Barrett was suspended for 10 games and Anderson for five, and Pierzynski was fined an undisclosed amount.

Anderson continued to play excellent defense, which kept him on the team.[28] He made his first error of the season on August 18 against the Twins, breaking a 111-game errorless streak. While Anderson improved in the second half, the season ultimately ended with disappointment at the plate; he batted .225/.290/.359, with 8 home runs and 33 RBIs.

In the 2006-2007 offseason, Anderson played in the Venezuelan Winter League at the White Sox' request. "I'm going to go there for a month and work on a better approach to my ballgame," he said.[29] He described the experience as "crazy," and said it occurred while his relationship with manager Ozzie Guillén was the tensest: "Ozzie wanted the best for me, to get more exposure. He wanted me to get more at-bats."[30] Anderson only last two weeks in Venezuela after losing 20 pounds because of a severe stomach illness. "It's my career; it's my swing. I better figure this out or I'm gonna be bagging groceries soon," he said.[31]

With spring training getting underway, the message from Guillén was clear: Anderson was promised nothing for the 2007 season. In fact, Guillén said the former first-round pick would have to win his starting job all over again.[32] Anderson would make the team in the fourth outfield spot, providing relief for Darin Erstad and Scott Podsednik.[33]

Anderson once again struggled at the plate at the start of the season. After just 19 plate appearances over the month of April with a .118/.211/.176 slash line, he was optioned to Triple-A Charlotte on April 30 to get more at-bats.[34] His season ended after 57 games with an injury to his left wrist.[35] His .255/.318/.435 slash line was slightly worse than when he was there in 2004.

In 2008 Anderson made the White Sox out of spring training, once again as a fourth outfielder.[36] He continued his strong defensive play while playing in 98 games, 59 of them in the later innings as a defensive replacement. His new approach to coming off the bench was noticed by Guillén and showed Anderson's maturity. "Last year, it was sitting long stretches, combined with the poor attitude I had," Anderson said. "I was bitter because I wasn't starting, and I was negative about it. Now, I'm a lot more positive about what I do, and that helps."[37]

Anderson again mirrored his 2006 season at the plate: a slash line of .232/.272/.436 with 8 home runs and 26 RBIs. The White Sox finished the season 88-74, tied with the Minnesota Twins for first in the AL Central Division.

Game 163 took place on September 30 in Chicago. The fans arrived in their black gear – black shirts, black pants, black hats, black jackets, and looks of fierce determination. Even the White Sox brass was dressed in black T-shirts with the words "SOX PRIDE BLACKOUT" on them.[38]

Anderson came in to pinch run in the bottom of the seventh for Ken Griffey Jr. and then replaced him in center field. This set up an Anderson swan dive catch to end the game and send the White Sox into the postseason to face the Tampa Bay Rays, who defeated them in the Division Series three games to one.

Anderson once again found himself in a backup outfield role behind Dewayne Wise to start the 2009 season as the fourth outfielder. A week into the season Wise suffered a separated right shoulder, creating playing time for Anderson.[39] He continued to struggle at the plate and after 65 games on July 20 he was sent to Triple-A Charlotte after Carlos Quentin was recalled from his rehab assignment.[40] On July 28 Anderson was traded to the Boston Red Sox for Mark Kotsay and was sent to Triple-A Pawtucket.[41] Anderson was soon called back up, but he mostly played as a defensive replacement late in games, appearing in 19, pinch-running in two games, and had only 21 plate appearances. "I take a lot of pride playing defense," Anderson said. "I've struggled offensively to stay consistent, but with some at-bats, I can put together some quality at-bats and help this team win some games."[42] On December 12 he was released.

Anderson signed with the Kansas City Royals, and he let the team know that he wanted to try becoming a pitcher.[43] He made his pitching debut on July 4, striking out two and allowing a single in one inning for the Arizona Rookie League Royals.[44] He was released at the end of the year and signed with the Yankees. Anderson pitched in Double A until he suffered an arm injury in May 2011.[45] He also had a rib removed under his collarbone to try to alleviate arm pain.[46] He signed with the Los Angeles Dodgers on February 26, 2012, but was released on March 31. He caught on with the Colorado Rockies on April 7 but was released on the 15th.

Anderson spent 2013 and 2014 working in the medical supply industry.[47] He said he was "seeing the handwriting on the wall." Nick Arroyo, a friend who was the company's CEO, told him that he was good with people and taught him some talking points. Anderson excelled at selling to doctors, saying it was "not easy when they're 10 times smarter than you."[48]

In 2015 an older and wiser Anderson attempted one last comeback as an outfielder with the White Sox. "If I could talk to these young kids in camp," Anderson said, "I would tell them to stay focused on the job. Don't get me wrong, when I was on the field I made sure I did my work and took it seriously. But I guess you could say I had too much fun with other things. I was young and could have handled it better."[49] He was released before the season began.

Anderson joined Chip Hale's staff at the University of Arizona in 2022 as an undergraduate assistant coach focusing on outfielders and coaching first base as well as providing guidance to younger players.[50] "Once I'd reached the major leagues, that was kind of enough; I had reached that pinnacle. I lacked the discipline, the maturity at that time to handle certain situations. When I should have gone right, I was going left, and that caused me to lose the drive to keep playing. And then ultimately, you don't perform, they don't want you to be on the field anymore."[51]

In August Anderson joined the coaching staff of Pima College in Tucson, Arizona.[52] He then moved to Northwestern University, where in 2023 he became interim coach after Jim Foster was fired following allegations of abusive behavior.[53] He stayed for the 2024 season under new head coach Ben Greenspan. He left Northwestern after his second season. He described it as a great experience working with young players and said that it gave him a chance to move back to Chicago. In mid-2024 he was pursuing head coaching opportunities.[54]

Anderson and his wife, Danielle, have a daughter, Scarlett. Of his wife, Anderson said, "I would not be coaching without Danielle. Going every which way, every direction, mostly down. She's the reason I got into coaching. She did all of this while she was pregnant."[55]

SOURCES

In addition to the sources cited in the Notes, the authors consulted Baseball-Reference.com and Retrosheet.org.

NOTES

1   Michael Lev, "After 'Underachieving' Pro Career, Ex-UA Star Brian Anderson Reinvents Himself as Coach," *Arizona Daily Star* (Tucson), February 19, 2022: 1.

2   Brian Anderson telephone interview with Eric Conrad, June 19, 2024. Unless indicated otherwise, all direct quotations come from this interview (Anderson interview).

3   Anderson interview with Mark Morowczynski, October 19, 2024.

4   Tom Verducci, "Brian Anderson, OF-Turned-Pitcher-Turned-OF, Wants One Last Chance," *Sports Illustrated*, February 24, 2015.

5   Anderson interview.

6   Anderson interview.

7   Patrick Finley, "White Sox Good Fit for Star from CDO, UA," *Arizona Daily Star*, March 1, 2006: A1.

8   Greg Hansen, "Ex-Wildcats in NBA to Play in All-Star Game," *Arizona Daily Star*, June 8, 2003: C2.

9   Greg Hansen, "Welcome to Big Leagues, Stefen," *Arizona Daily Star*, March 30, 2019: B02.

10 Tom Verducci.

11 Patrick Finley.

12 Chris Davis, "White Sox Rookie Well-Schooled as Tucson Amateur," *Arizona Daily Star*, March 20, 2005: C3.

13 Patrick Finley.

14 Anderson interview.

15 Chris Jackson, "Fullerton Regional Team Capsules," *Arizona Daily Star*, May 27, 2003: C3.

16 Anderson interview.

17 Anderson interview.

18 Sue Horton, "All-Time Major League Baseball Players from the Cape Cod Baseball League," https://capecodbaseball.org.ismmedia.com/ISM3/std-content/repos/Top/2012website/archives/Current%20Year/All_Time_MLB_CCBL_Alumni.pdf.

19 Doug Padilla, "First Choice a 'Five-Tool Player,'" *Chicago Sun-Times*, June 4, 2003: 139.

20 Doug Padilla, "Anderson Feeling at Home in Sox Camp – Tucson Resident, 22, Not Putting Pressure on Himself to Succeed," *Chicago Sun-Times*, March 11, 2004: 145.

21 Toni Ginnetti, "Sox Want 'Disabled' Podsednik Health for Stretch," *Chicago Sun-Times*, August 16, 2005: 109.

22 Dave Dyck, "Anderson a Hit in Debut with Sox," *Chicago Tribune*, August 17, 2005: 4.

23 Doug Padilla, "Sox Get Thome for Rowand: GM Williams Adds Injury-Plagued Big Bat, Loses Fan Favorite," *Chicago Sun-Times*, November 24, 2005: 134.

24 Nina Metz, "Life's a Ball with 2 Homes and 2 Moms," *Chicago Tribune*, February 26, 2005: 15.

25 Anderson interview.

26 Joe Crowley, "Anderson's Struggles Will Cost Him ABs," *Chicago Sun-Times*, May 3, 2006: 113.

27 Mike Kiley, "Mabry Injured after Brawl with Anderson," *Chicago Sun-Times*, May 21, 2006: A97.

28 Toni Ginnetti, "Ozzie: Great Expectations Will Be Met," *Chicago Sun-Times*, June 10, 2006: 77.

29 Joe Cowley, "Anderson Winter Plan: Small Ball," *Chicago Sun-Times*, September 19, 2006: 101.

30 Anderson interview.

31 Patrick Finley, "Showtime Is Now for Ex-CAT Anderson," *Arizona Daily Star*, February 20, 2007: C4.

32 Joe Cowley, "Life of Brian on the Upswing: Changes at Bat Keep Anderson in Sox' CF Picture," *Chicago Sun-Times*, February 27, 2007, 92.

33 Joe Cowley, "Ozzie says B.A. Gets to Stay: Anderson Given Spot," *Chicago Sun-Times*, March 28, 2007: 106.

34 Toni Ginnetti, "Struggling Anderson Sent Down," *Chicago Sun-Times*, April 30, 2007: 105.

35 Joe Cowley, "Painful Pen Collapse – Orioles 7, White Sox 6," *Chicago Sun-Times*, July 15, 2007: A74.

36 Joe Cowley, "Springboard to Success? – No-Nonsense Camp Might Be First Step in Turning It Around," *Chicago Sun-Times*, March 29, 2008: 49.

37 Joe Cowley, "Cabrera Says Scioscia 'Is on Another Level,'" *Chicago Sun-Times*, May 12, 2008: 77.

38 Rick Telander, "Thome, Danks, Pierzynski … Heroes Aplenty in Win," *Chicago Sun-Times*, October 1, 2008: A3.

39 Joe Cowley, "Won, Lost, Record – White Sox 10, Tigers 6 Sox Win," *Chicago Sun-Times*, April 14, 2009: 58.

40 Joe Cowley, "Anderson Demotion Stirs Usual Emotion," *Chicago Sun-Times*, July 21, 2009: 57.

41 Amalie Benjamin, "Learning Curve for Buchholz: He's Well-Adjusted This Time Around," *Boston Globe*, July 29, 2009: C3.

42 Michael Silverman, "Red Sox Notebook – Newcomers in Lineup – Anderson in Right for Drew," *Boston Herald*, August 16, 2009: B4.

43 Greg Hansen, "Dough Rising Fast for Coaches," *Arizona Daily Star*, April 4, 2010: C2.

44 Patrick Finley, "Ex-Cat Gets the Royal Treatment," *Arizona Daily Star*, July 12, 2010: B7.

45 Greg Hansen, "Hansen's Sunday Notebook: Miller Is Fine Doing Quiet, Dirty Work," *Arizona Daily Star*, December 4, 2011: B2.

46 Greg Hansen, "Hansen's Sunday Notebook: Recruiters Like Cochise," *Arizona Daily Star*, February 19, 2012: B2.

47 "CDO Grad, ex-Cat Anderson Working on a Comeback," *Arizona Daily Star*, February 28, 2015.

48 Anderson interview.

49 Tom Verducci, "Brian Anderson, OF-Turned-Pitcher-Turned-OF, Wants One Last Chance," *Sports Illustrated*, February 24, 2015.

50 Michael Lev, "After 'Underachieving' Pro Career, Ex-UA Star Brian Anderson Reinvents Himself as Coach," *Arizona Daily Star*, February 19, 2022: 1.

51 Michael Lev.

52 "Pima Adds Ex-Wildcat Brian Anderson, Tucson High's Oscar Romero to Coaching Staff," *Arizona Daily Star*, August 19, 2022: 1.

53 Michael Lev, "Arizona OF Mac Bingham Headed to LSU; Ex-Wildcat Brian Anderson Named Interim coach at NU," *Arizona Daily Star*, July 14, 2023: 1.

54 Anderson interview.

55 Anderson interview.

JEFF BAJENARU

By Bill Pruden

Jeff Bajenaru achieved the dream of every little boy who has ever played baseball seriously – he made the big leagues. And while his time in the majors was short, derailed by injuries, he not only achieved the ultimate prize – being a part of a World Series champion – but he used his playing days as a springboard to a career as a pitching coach, a vocation that had him working in 2024 with the Triple-A Reno Aces.

Jeffrey Michael Bajenaru was born on March 21, 1978, in Pomona, California, about 30 miles east of Los Angeles. The oldest of three children born to Ed Bajenaru, a firefighter, and his wife, Debbie, a teacher, Jeff was initially unhappy about his father initially signing him up for Little League.[1] According to one story, at 8 years old he would hide under the table and refuse to play.[2] Only when his father said he had to try it, that he had to play one season – at which point if he did not like it he did not have to play again, did he give it a try.[3] In a telephone interview with the author, he acknowledged his initial reluctance, recalling that having never played before, and not being sure he would like it, he had very real reservations. But looking back, he said almost ruefully that it took no time at all for him to "absolutely fall in love with it."[4] He had found his passion, and through ups and downs it would be the centerpiece of his life for the next two decades.

As much as Bajenaru loved the game, the idea of playing in the big leagues was not something he initially imagined. He played high-school baseball at Senator Ruben S. Ayala High School in Chino Hills, a school that boasted an outstanding program. Indeed, Bajenaru recalled that in his junior year Ayala High was ranked number two in the country in preseason polls, a ranking it could not maintain but which nevertheless reflected both the team's talent and the aspirations of the program.[5] In the midst of such a talent-laden squad, Jeff, who had skipped the fourth grade, was an undersized but driven competitor.[6] And displaying his characteristic approach to the game – "I would simply outwork everybody"[7] – he responded to the challenge in fine form, crafting a solid career for a talented team. But in the end, while he aspired to win a college scholarship to continue his career, despite his best efforts he was "overlooked in high school and did not get any offers for anything."[8]

Bajenaru was disappointed but he was also determined to continue playing baseball and so after graduating at age 17 in 1995, he walked on at the University of California, Riverside, making the team as an outfielder.[9] However,

before the season started, he hurt his shoulder, had to have surgery, and missed the season. Happily, he was able to play summer ball and with the extra year allowing him to get stronger, he transferred to Riverside City College.[10] In the end a more mature Jeff Bajenaru took RCC by storm, turning in a performance that in 2015 earned him induction into the school's hall of fame.[11] In his two years at RCC, he hit .380 with 153 hits, 115 runs scored, 111 RBIs, 35 doubles, and 202 total bases. He was a critical cog in the team's 74-24 record and one conference title.[12] In addition he became a pitcher when, early in his sophomore year, while messing around throwing in the outfield he caught the eye of one of the coaches and the idea of his possibly pitching was born.[13] Despite compiling a 1-1 record with 20 strikeouts in 10 innings, he never imagined that the experiment would become his ticket to the pros.[14] But first there was the big-time college baseball to which he had long aspired. While his RCC record caught the attention of the Oakland Athletics, who selected him in the 13th round of the 1998 amateur draft, it had also attracted the attention of big-time

Jeff Bajenaru   2005

college programs; and having finally gotten the scholarship offer he had long desired, Bajenaru opted to stay in school, heading to the University of Oklahoma.

The versatile right-hander crafted an impressive college career in Norman, Oklahoma, earning first team All-American honors as a utilityman as well as first team Big 12 honors as an outfielder while also being selected to the second team as a relief pitcher. He left Oklahoma having set both school and conference records for the most saves.[15] At one point he converted 19 save opportunities in a row.[16] While he had been selected by the White Sox in the 36th round of the June 1999 draft, he again opted to continue his education, returning to Oklahoma for his senior year, but in the aftermath of an outstanding 2000 collegiate season, Bajenaru signed with the White Sox before the 2000 draft. Comfortable with John Kazanas, the White Sox scout who had pursued him, and unsure of what the draft would yield, the admittedly "naïve" Bajenaru decided to take the sure thing and begin his professional career.[17]

While Bajenaru loved being fully involved in the game and missed hitting, as he embarked on his professional career it was clear that being a reliever represented the quickest route to the big leagues.[18] In that quest, his first stop was the Bristol White Sox, Chicago's Rookie League affiliate. The 6-foot-1 right-hander pitched in 12 games, all in relief, compiling a record of 1-1 with an ERA of 3.77 in 14⅓ innings. He struck out 31 batters while picking up five saves before he was promoted to the Winston-Salem Warthogs in the high A Carolina League. There Bajenaru posted a 2-0 record with two saves in 10 games out of the bullpen. In 12⅓ innings his ERA was 4.38 and he struck out 15.

Bajenaru returned to Winston-Salem for the start of the 2001 season and in 35 appearances he was 2-4 with 10 saves, an ERA of 3.35, and 51 strikeouts in 40⅓ innings. This performance earned him a promotion to the Birmingham Barons of the Double-A Southern League. But after only two appearances and 4⅓ innings, Bajenaru was shut down, had Tommy John surgery and missed all of the 2002 season. The 2003 season saw Bajenaru back in Birmingham where he turned in a performance that showed he had made a full recovery from the surgery. Appearing in 50 games and pitching 64⅔ innings, he went 4-2 with a 3.20 ERA, 62 strikeouts, and 14 saves.

While Bajenaru's 2003 season reflected clear progress, he was nevertheless back in Birmingham at the start of the 2004 campaign. However, after chalking up 12 saves in 32 games with an ERA of 1.34 and 51 strikeouts, he was promoted to the Triple-A Charlotte Knights (International League). There he was no less impressive. He finished 15 of the 16 games in which he pitched while earning 10 saves in 20 innings with an ERA of 1.80. All of this led to a late season call-up by the White Sox.

On September 4, 2004, against the Seattle Mariners at U.S. Cellular Field, Bajenaru made his major-league debut. Looking back, he remembered coming out on the

field before the game, looking around the ballpark, seeing Ichiro Suzuki among others, and feeling "in awe of it all." Like so many, making the majors was, he said, "always my dream, but I never thought it would happen." Then it was game time, and sitting in the bullpen, every time the phone rang, he hoped it was for him. Finally, with the White Sox holding a commanding 8-4 lead, Bajenaru took the mound in the top of the ninth following Neil Cotts, who had surrendered one run in the top of the eighth in relief of starter Mark Buehrle. It was he said, "a dream come true," but at the same time "kind of scary." But once the first pitch was thrown, he recalled, it was no different from any other time. It all narrowed down to him and the batter.[19]

With his wife, Alysa, and his parents in the stands cheering him on, Bajenaru got off to a strong start, retiring the first batter he faced, Mariners shortstop José Lopez, on a groundout to the third baseman. But things quickly went awry as the number-nine batter, Willie Bloomquist, hit a groundball single. He was followed by Ichiro Suzuki, who grounded a single to right field that advanced Bloomquist to third. With runners on first and third, Bajenaru gave up a line-drive single to right to Randy Winn that scored Bloomquist while moving Suzuki to third base. Suddenly the Mariners had the tying run at the plate and White Sox manager Ozzie Guillén brought in Shingo Takatsu from the bullpen in an effort to blunt the Mariners' momentum and seal the victory. Takatsu struck out Mariners DH Edgar Martínez for the second out, but he walked Bret Boone to load the bases. Raúl Ibañez followed Boone and he lined Takatsu's 3-and-2 pitch to right field, scoring Suzuki and Winn. However, the White Sox escaped with a victory when Boone was thrown out at third trying to advance after the runs had scored. For Bajenaru, a rookie too excited to notice that his name was misspelled on his first White Sox jersey, it was a memorable if inauspicious debut; he was charged with three earned runs in one third of an evening, leaving him with an ERA of 81.00.[20]

But now that he was on the major-league roster, Bajenaru had a number of chances to show he truly belonged. He pitched in eight more games, logging a total of 8⅓ innings and being charged with one loss, while reducing his ERA to a 10.80. He struck out eight.

With a taste of the big leagues behind him, Bajenaru wanted more but he started the 2005 season back in Charlotte. He was a stalwart for the Knights, pitching in 61 games and earning 19 saves while posting a 1.41 ERA with a 4-6 record. He pitched 70⅓ innings, striking out 83 batters and walking 29. This effort earned him a spot in the Triple-A All-Star game and a late-season call-up to the White Sox. He pitched 4⅓ innings of mop-up duty in four losses and had a 6.23 ERA as the White Sox finished 99-63 to lead the Central Division of the American League by six games over the Cleveland Indians. While Bajenaru was disappointed at not being on the postseason roster, he understood the realities of big-league baseball by this time in his career.[21] In an effort to be better positioned for the future, he went to Mexico after the regular season to get in some additional work. He followed the postseason on Spanish-language television as the White Sox defeated the defending champion Boston Red Sox in the Division Series and the California Angels in the Championship Series before sweeping the Houston Astros in the World Series to claim their first World Series championship since 1917. He watched the World Series victory on a Mexican version of ESPN, joyful for his teammates and knowing that he was part of that championship team.[22]

For Bajenaru, the euphoria of being a part of a World Series championship team was tempered a bit when early in spring training, on March 8, 2006, as the White Sox prepared to defend their crown, he was traded to the Arizona Diamondbacks for infielder Alex Cintrón. But Bajenaru said he initiated a "good conversation" with White Sox GM Kenny Williams, letting him know that if he was not in the White Sox' future plans he would appreciate being traded to a place where he might have more of an opportunity – and that was what happened.[23] He was "appreciative of the trade" – one that could not have been easier since both teams shared the Kino Sports Complex, a multiple-use sports complex in Tucson, Arizona, for spring training. Bajenaru had to simply cross to the other side of the parking lot.[24]

It was an easy transition. He remained in Tucson after quickly switching teams and started the 2006 season with the Diamondbacks' Triple-A affiliate, the Tucson Sidewinders. He pitched 80 innings in 52 games for Tucson with an ERA of 4.50 before getting a call-up during which he made what proved to be his final appearance in the big leagues, throwing a single inning on August 7 against the San Francisco Giants. Entering the game in the top of the sixth with the Diamondbacks leading 3-2, Bajenaru gave up four hits, three of them home runs, and four runs, to take the loss.

Bajenaru did not anticipate that the outing against the Giants would be his last effort. But unable to continue due to a rotator cuff injury and a torn labrum – injuries that he had tried to pitch through, but which resulted in having two surgeries as well as a third cleanup operation – he missed all of the 2007 season while undertaking a rigorous rehab program in hopes of saving his career.

It was not to be. He said his arm and throwing "never felt the same" after the surgery.[25] At one point he took a bucket of balls and just went out to throw, wanting to just let it all go and see how it felt.[26] But ultimately after the "long year of rehab," with the hope that it would feel right and he could "come back, it was still hurting," and he just walked into the Diamondbacks offices and told A.J. Hinch, the team's director of player development, that he was retiring.[27] In a professional baseball playing career that had spanned seven seasons, he had played parts of six seasons in the minor leagues, earning 79 saves with a 2.91 ERA and a 20-18 record. His major-league career, curtailed as it was by injuries, was significantly less robust as he appeared in just 14 games, spread out over three seasons. He pitched a total of 13⅔ innings, lost two games, and posted an unsightly ERA of 11.20.

Given how things had unfolded, the end of Bajenaru's playing career came quickly and yet as he looked back, "it was a slow progression."[28] It was not easy, for while he recognized that physically he could no longer compete, he "was not ready to be done, [he] did not want to be done." He had "hoped to play longer."[29] And while it was an end he knew would eventually arrive, he was unsure of what lay ahead. Almost a decade later he acknowledged that he still "didn't kn[o]w if he knew what he was doing," but unable to play, he nevertheless did know that he "wanted out of the game for a little while, at least."[30]

Almost 30 years old, unsure of what the future held but with a growing family, after his retirement he got a job on the staff of the family's church. Passionate about his faith, he thought the job was a way to give back while he tried to figure out what came next.[31]

He quickly discovered that he really enjoyed the work at his church, and recognized that "helping … kids live this difficult life" was not only something he found very rewarding, but that it was something he realized could also be done at the same time that he taught the game, "which I love."[32] The two-year hiatus away from baseball ultimately left Bajenaru, a rare player who loved the game's history so much that he had, at the urging of the legendary baseball executive Roland Hemond, joined SABR while he was playing, anxious to get back into the game.[33] He realized that not only did he miss the game a lot, but he came to feel that, while in working for the church he was, in a sense working for God, being out of baseball he was not doing what God had intended him to do, so he determined to see about getting back into the game.[34] Looking back, both he and Alysa said it was "a weird two years" and Jeff and his wife, who had weathered the frequent moves alongside him, recalled that "being settled felt very unsettling." After two years they were, in Alysa's words, "ready to jump back in."[35] At the same time, they were grateful for the break, one during which their two children were born.

Once he decided to return to the game, Bajenaru began the search for an appropriate position and after a brief appointment as an assistant baseball coach and physical fitness instructor at his alma mater, Riverside City College, at the end of 2010, he joined the Diamondbacks organization, where as of 2024 he had been a pitching coach of one form or another ever since. His rise up the ladder has mirrored that of many young coaches and former players. Bajenaru did three stints on the back lots of the Arizona Summer League for the Diamondbacks before he was named pitching coach of the team's Rookie League affiliate, the Missoula Osprey of the Pioneer League, at the start of the 2014 season, a post he held for two seasons with the team winning the Pioneer League championship in 2015. Bajenaru then spent three seasons (2016-18) with the Class-A Visalia Rawhide (California League) before moving to the Triple-A Reno Aces in 2019. While he lost the 2020 season when the schedule was canceled during the pandemic, he was back with the Aces in 2021, before moving to the Hillsboro Hops (High-A Northwest League) in 2022. He was back with Reno in 2023 and remained a part of their staff in 2024.

Central to his career is the fact that for Bajenaru professional baseball has always been a family proposition. Jeff met Alysa when they were both students at the University of Oklahoma but just a few weeks before he signed his first pro contract in the spring of 2000. They were married in 2002 just before Jeff headed to spring training, while Alysa finished at Oklahoma, earning her degree in nutritional science and starting work as a clinical dietician.[36] However, when he began the 2003 season with the Double-A Birmingham Barons, Alysa put her professional aspirations aside and jumped headfirst into the baseball world. A grateful Jeff, who unabashedly said that "she's way smarter than me," recognized the sacrifices she has made, observing that "she could be doing so many more things."[37] But she has happily been at Jeff's side throughout his professional baseball odyssey, even at one point serving beer at the games in Birmingham where she had a beer stand on the stadium concourse, a location that allowed her to both watch the game and make additional money – enough in tips to pay their rent.[38]

A trained dietician, as well as a skilled photographer, Alysa has been nothing but a supportive baseball wife, but she has also recognized and worked to address some of the challenges that come with that life. In helping found the online community "Our Baseball Life," she has sought to help others deal with those same challenges.[39] The idea came to her when she was, as she remembered "sitting in nowhere, Montana, when I realized that I couldn't be the only baseball wife or girlfriend feeling alone at that moment."[40] Acting on the thought, she started an Instagram account called WAGS in Real Life, designed "to connect women in baseball, and over the years it has grown into a vibrant community, a place to share stories and meet other women who get this life."[41] As the organization grew, she got help from Paige Murphy and in the late 2010s they joined forces with Lory Ankiel, who since 2010 had been running "Our Baseball Life," a resource guide for professional baseball families in an effort to help serve this distinctive community.[42]

These efforts shine an even greater spotlight on the way that family has been a critical factor in Jeff and Alysa's relationship from the start. With the early months of their marriage being a distance relationship they determined to try not do that again, vowing to sacrifice financially to stay together as best they can and as they have had children that has only reinforced their determination to stay together and do things as a family, whether it is Alysa's home schooling the children when they were younger or now that they are living in Arlington, Texas, working to take advantage of their surroundings like visiting Sequoia when Jeff was with Visalia or simply going to visit him during the children's spring break from school or during the summer. Their son has often joined Jeff on the field before the game and he has even had some time as a batboy, while Alysa and their daughter regularly attend games. Too, Alysa takes the kids on at least one road trip a year where they get to see Jeff as well as experience the area where the team is playing.

It is against this backdrop that Jeff Bajenaru pursues this second phase of his professional journey. His work as a coach has drawn praise and attention. After helping make the Rawhide staff statistically one of the best in the league in his second year, Bajenaru was named the 2017 California League Coach of the Year, an honor he also received in 2018.[43] And it wasn't just the locals who noticed his good work. Over the winter before the 2018 season, Bajenaru had an interview for the Philadelphia Phillies' assistant pitching coach position, and he has subsequently interviewed with the Diamondbacks and the Texas Rangers about MLB jobs.[44] But he is not in a rush. In 2018 he stayed in Visalia, an area he was familiar with and enjoyed, and while he appreciated the interest from the Phillies, as well as the subsequent interest from other teams, he said he is no rush to move up, saying it was different from being a player when it was all about advancing to the next level.[45] At the same time, he has no interest in moving in another direction. He says he once thought about it, but he has come to see that coaching pitching is his "niche."[46] While he admits he would love to be able to do it at the major league level, he says he finds it tremendously rewarding to be able to work with a young pitcher and help them take the next step towards achieving their dream. In fact, he says he had not anticipated the satisfaction that he says come from "the chance to see someone else get their dream."[47] And Jeff Bajenaru knows about dreams. While he "wishes his playing career had been longer," the part of him that is still the 8-year-old who fell in love with the game, the kid who was able to not only achieve his big-league dream but also win a World Series ring has found that every time he gets to tell a young pitcher that he is being called up it is special. You can hear it in his voice as he notes, "to be a part of someone's dream, there's nothing like that!!" Jeff Bajenaru has clearly found his niche!

GRINDERS AND GAMERS

SOURCES

In addition to the sources cited in the Notes, the author consulted baseball-almanac.com and Baseball-Reference.com.

NOTES

1   Author telephone interview with Jeff Bajenaru, July 26, 2024; Unless otherwise indicated, all direct quotations attributed to Bajenaru come from this interview.

2   Ryan Chamberlain, "SABR Nine: Chicago White Sox's Jeff Bajenaru," December 22, 2005; https://sabr.org/latest/sabr-nine-chicago-white-soxs-jeff-bajenaru/; Bajenaru interview.

3   Chamberlain; Bajenaru interview.

4   Bajenaru interview.

5   Bajenaru interview.

6   Bajenaru interview.

7   Bajenaru interview.

8   Chamberlain.

9   Email, Jeff Bajenaru to author, August 12, 2024.

10 Bajenaru interview; email, Jeff Bajenaru to author, August 12, 2024.

11 "Jeff Bajenaru," Riverside City College Sports Hall of Fame; https://www.rccathletics.com/alumni/hof/bios/Jeff_Bajenaru.

12 "Bajenaru," RCC Sports Hall of Fame.

13 Bajenaru interview.

14 "Bajenaru," RCC Sports Hall of Fame.

15 "Bajenaru," RCC Sports Hall of Fame.

16 John E. Hoover "Bajenaru's Breakdown Is Unusual," *Tulsa World*, May 2, 2000.

17 Bajenaru interview; email from Rod Nelson, SABR Scouts Committee, September 24, 2024.

18 Bajenaru interview.

19 Bajenaru interview.

20 Sydney Daniel, "Touching Home with Alysa Bajenaru – Our Baseball Life," *AATB: All About That Base*, July 14, 2020; https://allaboutthatbasedotcom.wordpress.com/category/interviews/touching-home/.

21 Bajenaru interview.

22 Bajenaru interview.

23 Bajenaru interview.

24 Bajenaru interview.

25 Bajenaru interview.

26 Bajenaru interview.

27 Benjamin Hill, "On the Road: Marriage, Kids and Baseball," Milb.com, September 9, 2016, https://www.milb.com/news/gcs-200292520; Bajenaru interview.

28 Hill.

29 Bajenaru interview.

30 Hill.

31 Bajenaru interview.

32 Hill.

33 Email, Jeff Bajenaru to author, July 26, 2024.

34 Bajenaru interview.

35 Hill.

36 Hill.

37 Hill.

38 Hill.

39 See the website at Our Baseball Life.com.

40 Daniel.

41 Daniel.

42 Daniel.

43 Email, Jeff Bajenaru to author, August 12, 2024.

44 Vongni Yang, "Jeff Bajenaru Leads Visalia Rawhide's Attack-Minded Pitching Approach," *Visalia* (California) *Times-Delta*, April 5, 2018, https://www.visaliatimesdelta.com/story/sports/2018/04/05/jeff-bajenaru-leads-rawhides-attack-minded-pitching-approach/484306002/; Bajenaru interview.

45 Yang.

46 Bajenaru interview.

GEOFF BLUM

By Don Zminda

Geoff Blum's baseball life has featured many highlights, but he will always be best remembered for one dramatic at-bat. In Game Three of the 2005 World Series between Blum's Chicago White Sox and the Houston Astros, he belted a home run in the top of the 14th inning to break a 5-5 tie and propel the White Sox to a three-games-to-none lead. Chicago closed out the Series with a 1-0 win the next night. The Game Three homer proved to be the final plate appearance of Blum's 87-day (regular and postseason) White Sox career – but it made him an immortal hero to South Side fans. A monument outside Guaranteed Rate Field celebrating the 2005 World Series championship includes an image of Blum in his home-run swing.

Born on April 26, 1973, in Redwood City, California, about 25 miles south of San Francisco, Geoffrey Edward Blum moved with his family to Chino in Southern California's San Bernardino County when he was three years old. His father, Bill, held a number of jobs during his working career; his mother, Connie (née Johnson), worked as an office manager, first for a construction company and then at junior high schools in the Inland Valley near their home. Bill and Connie's other child, Greg, was born in 1978, and both Blum brothers were star athletes at Chino High. A catcher and first baseman, Greg Blum played ball at the University of Arkansas and then spent four seasons (2000-03) in the Montreal Expos and Minnesota Twins' farm systems, never advancing past the Class-A level.

Geoff Blum played both baseball and basketball at Chino High before attending the University of California in Berkeley. Cal's longtime baseball coach, Bob Milano, was a major influence on both Blum's career and life. One of Milano's key moves was to turn Blum, who previously had batted exclusively from the right side, into a switch-hitter. "I owe everything to that man when it comes to baseball, switch-hitting and becoming a better human being," said Blum.[1] With Blum at shortstop in 1992, his freshman year, the Golden Bears reached the College World Series in Omaha, but were eliminated in the first round. Blum also played amateur ball for the Mat-Su Miners in the Alaska Baseball League and the Brewster Whitecaps in the Cape Cod League.[2]

After his junior year at Cal, Blum was selected by the Montreal Expos in the seventh round of the 1994 amateur draft. Assigned to Vermont of the Class-A New York-Penn League, he made an impressive debut, batting .344, the second-highest average in the league, in 63 games. *Baseball America* chose him as shortstop on the league's all-star team. Blum steadily advanced up the Montreal farm system over the next five years, including parts of three seasons (1997-99) with the Expos' top farm team, the Ottawa Lynx of the Triple-A International League. When Expos shortstop Orlando Cabrera sprained his ankle in August of 1999, Blum was summoned to Montreal. Blum was surprised by the call-up. "(Director of player development) Don Reynolds called me at 11 (Sunday) night," he told the *Montreal Gazette*. "I wanted to know who was crank calling."[3]

He made his major-league debut against the San Diego Padres at Stade Olympique on August 9, 1999, batting eighth as the starting shortstop against right-hander Matt Clement. "I was nervous as hell and excited as hell," Blum recalled about that first plate appearance. "Everything was moving pretty fast. He struck me out on a curveball and I went back to the dugout with a smile on my face." He fared better against Clement the next time up, doubling to right-center to drive in two runs; he also singled in the sixth inning against

Geoff Blum   2005

GRINDERS AND GAMERS

Carlos Almánzar as the Expos went on to an 8-0 victory. Four days later, at Denver's Coors Field, Blum hit the first of his 99 regular-season major-league home runs, a fly ball down the right-field line against Colorado Rockies right-hander Mike DeJean. He hit two more homers at Coors Field the next night. Blum finished his rookie season for the Expos with 8 home runs in 45 games, and his .504 slugging percentage that year was his highest for a single season.

Blum was the starting shortstop for 40 of the Expos' 54 games after joining the club in 1999, but with Cabrera healthy again in 2000, he became more of a utility player, starting games at all four infield positions. He also pinch-hit in 26 games. This would become a familiar role for Blum. Over the course of his career, he qualified for the league batting title only once (in 2001), and more than 20 percent of his games (297 of 1,389) came in a pinch-hitting role. He appeared in the starting lineup at seven different positions (including designated hitter) during his career, but never started more than 94 games at a single position in any season. His versatility and ability to contribute after coming off the bench helped him last in the majors until he was 39 years old. Though Blum was never a big-time slugger, his power was also an asset, as he posted five seasons with 10 or more home runs. Blum described himself as a "line-drive, gap-to-gap hitter. A lot of my at-bats were late in games against closers, so I just tried to make do with what I have. I knew I was going to be an asset the more contact I made, so I focused more on line drives with occasional power."

Blum batted .283 in 124 games for the Expos in 2000, his first full major-league season, then played in a career-high 148 games the next year while starting games at third base, second base, first base, and left field. However, his batting average dropped to .236, and in March of 2002 he was traded to the Houston Astros for third baseman Chris Truby. "I'm obviously shocked," Blum said after learning of the trade. "I was born and raised a Montreal Expo."[4] It was the first of two stints (2002-03, 2008-10) in Houston for Blum, which would prove to be his favorite major-league stop. "The fan base embraced me when I played here," Blum said of Houston, "and I just saw the ball good at Minute Maid Park. It was also kind of cool getting to play with the likes of Jeff Bagwell, Craig Biggio, Billy Wagner, and a group of veteran, All-Star type players who had a history of winning. I gleaned a lot of information from those guys that helped me throughout my career." Blum hit 10 home runs with 52 RBIs for Houston in both 2002 and 2003. He matched his career high with a .283 batting average in '02, followed by a .262 mark the next year.

Although Blum had played well in his two seasons with Houston, the Astros were looking to reduce payroll, and they also wanted give more playing time to Morgan Ensberg, who had shared third base with Blum in 2003. In December of 2003, the team traded Blum to the Tampa Bay Devil Rays for pitcher Brandon Backe. The trade saved the Astros more than $1 million in salary.[5] Blum spent one year in Tampa Bay, batting .215. Handed his release by the Devil Rays after the 2004 season, he signed a free-agent contract with the San Diego Padres.[6] The signing marked a homecoming for the California native, whose house in San Clemente was about 60 miles north of Petco Park, the Padres' home park. At the time Geoff's wife, Kory, was pregnant, and in May of 2005, she gave birth to triplets: daughters Audrey, Ava, and Kayla. The Blums also have a daughter, Mia, who is 16 months older than her three sisters.

Blum got into 78 games for the Padres in 2005 before being dealt to the White Sox at the July 31 trade deadline for minor-league pitcher Ryan Meaux.[7] "I met the team on the road in Baltimore," Blum recalled. "And having been traded a couple of times, I knew that some of these environments could be tough. There could be guys that say, why is this guy here, we don't want him. And there'd be other guys that would just ignore you because you weren't there to start the season. But it was unique in Chicago because, to a man, they all came up to me and shook my hand and said welcome to the ballclub. I really appreciated how they all took me in, from Paul Konerko to Pablo Ozuna. That made it really easy."

At the time of the trade, the White Sox were leading the Cleveland Indians by 14½ games in the American League Central Division race, and the versatile Blum's primary role was to fill in for the regular infielders, along with occasional pinch-hitting assignments. Blum got into 31 games over the final two months of the season (95 at-bats), hitting .200 with one home run. He was a member of the team's postseason roster, but prior to Game Three of the World Series, he'd had only one postseason at-bat. "I had faced Bronson Arroyo in a Division Series blowout [Game One] against the Boston Red Sox," Blum recalled. "That was my only at-bat until 21 days later, when the World Series moved to Houston for Game Three. The four of us who were on the bench – myself, Chris Widger, Pablo Ozuna, and Willie Harris – had hardly played up to then. But with the Series now in a National League park, pitchers would have to bat. We were going to be ready, because we knew there would be some opportunities for us now."

Blum entered Game Three with the score tied 5-5 in the bottom of the 13th inning, taking over for Tadahito Iguchi at second base as part of a double switch. When the Astros failed to score and the game moved to the 14th, Blum was scheduled to bat third in the inning against Astros right-hander Ezequiel Astacio. "Jermaine Dye got on base with a hit," Blum recalled, "and I'm sitting on deck thinking that if Paul Konerko gets on as well, I'm gonna have to bump Jermaine and Paul over in my only World Series at-bat. I felt a little bit of trepidation because I couldn't remember the last time I'd bunted [Blum's last successful sacrifice bunt had come in August of 2004]. Konerko hits the ball, third baseman Morgan Ensberg makes a great backhand stop, [second baseman] José Vizcaíno makes a crazy good turn and they turn the double play. And there was almost a sense of relief because I was like, I don't have to bunt."

Freed from worrying about having to lay down a bunt, Blum relaxed. "I had a good relationship with Jerry Layne, the home-plate umpire, and the Astros catcher, Brad Ausmus, was a former teammate and a great friend," he recalled. "Digging in and talking to him kind of settled me down." When Astacio missed with his first two pitches, Blum thought, "I'm just gonna try to hit a line drive to left field, maybe shoot the gap in left-center and get to second base. But, as luck would have it, Astacio missed his spot by a good foot and a half down and in. I squared it up."[8] Blum's fly ball cleared the right-field fence for a home run that put the White Sox ahead, 6-5. They scored another run before the half-inning ended, then set down the Astros in the bottom of the 14th to finish off the win. Less than 24 hours later, the White Sox were World Series champions for the first time in 88 years.

The team's victory parade in downtown Chicago on October 28, Blum said, "was absolutely incredible. I drank in every possible moment. I remember standing up there with Joe Crede and Aaron Rowand; Ed Farmer, the White Sox radio announcer, was next to me. We kept looking at each other going, 'This is unbelievable.' It was remarkable to see the turnout and how grateful everybody was to have us be World Series champions. That's something I'll never forget."

Three days after the parade, Blum became a free agent, and on November 16 he rejoined the San Diego Padres for a two-year stint.[9] "I loved my time in San Diego," said Blum. "It was another ballclub that was established. They were winning. There was a good mix of older and young talent. Guys like Trevor Hoffman, who'd been around for more than a decade, and Adrián González, who was just breaking in. The environment there was very good, and of course the weather was beautiful." With Blum getting into 109 games – 60 as a starter – and batting .254 in his usual handyman role, the Padres won the National League West title in 2006; however, they lost the Division Series to the St. Louis Cardinals, three games to one. Blum was the Padres' starting shortstop in all four games, going 1-for-8 but drawing four walks and posting a .385 on-base average. Blum had a similar season in 2007, hitting .252 in 122 games while playing five different defensive positions, as the Padres dropped to third place.

A free agent after the 2007 season, Blum rejoined the Astros.[10] In 2008 he had his major-league highs in home runs (14) and RBIs (53), despite playing in only 114 games. "It helped to come back from Petco Park, which is a graveyard for hitters, to a more hitter-friendly ballpark in Minute Maid Park," said Blum. "I also liked being in the NL Central." He followed up with 10 homers and 49 RBIs in 120 games – most of them at third base – in 2009. His playing time dropped to 93 games, only 42 of them as a starter, in 2010, the year in which he turned 37. Blum spent his final

two seasons (2011-12) with the Arizona Diamondbacks;[11] hampered by a knee injury that required surgery in April of 2011, he appeared in only 23 games in 2011 and 17 in 2012. He was a member of the Diamondbacks' postseason roster in 2011, when the team won the National League West title under Kirk Gibson, and was hitless in two pinch-hitting appearances in the team's Division Series loss to the Milwaukee Brewers. Blum played his final major-league game on July 17, 2012, singling as a pinch-hitter against José Arredondo of the Cincinnati Reds. He was released by the Diamondbacks three days later.

Although Blum's career numbers – 99 regular-season homers, a .250 career batting average, career OPS+ of 81 in 1,389 games over 14 seasons – were not those of a major star, his ability to handle a number of roles helped make him a player whose skills were always in demand. "He's a valuable commodity," said one of Blum's managers, Bruce Bochy. "Everything he does, he does well, which is a bigger plus for someone who can play shortstop. And a switch-hitter in that utility role, he's the perfect double-switch candidate and pinch-hitter."[12] Blum was also regarded as a positive influence on a club. "It's tough to say goodbye to a guy like Geoff," Astros general manager Gerry Hunsinger said after Houston traded Blum to Tampa Bay in 2003. "Geoff is a terrific person and a good player who was well-liked by his teammates."[13]

"I never went into a season where I didn't feel like I belonged in the starting lineup," Blum said about his major-league career. "As much as it can create some disappointment, I think that attitude helped me be a good role player. I had a good work ethic and a good mentality, and I was always prepared when the manager called on me, whether to come off the bench or to start that day." The list of managers whom Blum played for includes such successful skippers as Bochy, Felipe Alou, Lou Piniella, Jimy Williams, Bud Black, Kirk Gibson, and Ozzie Guillén. Asked to name his favorite manager, Blum selected Alou, who gave him his first major-league job, but he also has fond memories of playing for Guillén with the White Sox in 2005. "I had played against Ozzie after coming to the big leagues, and then he was my third-base coach in Montreal, so I knew who he was," said Blum. "There was a brutal honesty about Ozzie both as a player and as a manager. On your best day, he was gonna say you were an All-Star; on your worst day he was gonna say you didn't belong on the team, but I didn't mind that that mentality in a manager. I thought he did a great job with the group he had in '05."

Blum said he's thought at times about taking on the responsibility of managing a team. "I think you get to the point, maybe a little bit later in your career, where you wonder if you could have an impact and be able to lead a team," he said. "It would be a pretty daunting task, but I think it's something that I wouldn't shy away from if the opportunity came about." In the meantime, Blum settled into a successful post-playing career as a member of the Houston

Astros' broadcast crew. After retiring as a player in 2012, he said, "I wanted to stay inside the game, and I told my agent that if he knew of any openings in coaching, scouting, media, or whatever, I would love an opportunity." The 2012 season happened to be the final season for longtime Astros broadcaster Milo Hamilton; another veteran member of the team's broadcast crew, Bill Brown, was interested in reducing his schedule to home games only. Blum landed a spot as a television color analyst for Astros road games beginning with the 2013 season, and became the team's full-time TV color analyst four years later. He has been awarded two Lone Star Emmy awards for his work.

As a player, Geoff Blum played in more games (580), recorded more hits (440), and hit more home runs (46) for the Houston Astros than for any of the other six major-league teams he played for. He has continued to represent the Astros as a broadcaster for more than a decade since his retirement as a player in 2012. By contrast, Blum's entire White Sox career consisted of those 87 days in 2005. Yet Blum will always be remembered for the World Series home run he hit *against* the Astros – as a member of the White Sox. Two decades after his dramatic homer, Blum said that White Sox fans still stop and thank him at games, card shows and offseason events for his vital contribution to the team's only World Series championship in the last 100-plus years. "You know, maybe the only reason I was on that team was for that swing in Game Three," he said. "If you're going to write a script where you're only in town for three months, and you're able to have an impact like I did, I don't think you could write a better script."

SOURCES

Statistics and play-by-play are from baseball-reference.com and Retrosheet.com.

NOTES

1   Unless otherwise indicated, all quoted material is from the author's interview with Geoff Blum, February 5, 2024.

2   Geoff Blum Howe Sportsdata questionnaire, National Baseball Hall of Fame Geoff Blum file.

3   "Expos Story," *Montreal Gazette*, August 10, 1999: 10.

4   Stephanie Miles, "Minaya Makes His First Trade," *Montreal Gazette*, March 13, 2002: 11.

5   Jose De Jesus Ortiz, "Astros Deal Blum to Rays," *Houston Chronicle*, December 15, 2003: 48.

6   Bernie Wilson, "Williams Headed Back to San Diego, *Palm Springs* (California) *Desert Sun*, December 9, 2004: 29.

7   Mark Gonzales, "All-Purpose Blum Will Come in Handy," *Chicago Tribune*, August 1, 2005: 3-3.

8   www.mlb.com/news/geoff-blum-world-series-home-run; accessed August 28, 2024.

9   Mark Gonzales, "Sox Series Hero Blum Goes Home to Padres," *Chicago Tribune*, November 17, 2005: 4-3.

10 "Astros Bring Back Geoff Blum," *Victoria* (Texas) *Advocate*, November 21, 2007: 17.

11 Nick Percoro, "D-Backs Finalize 2-Year Deal with Infielder Blum," *Arizona Republic* (Phoenix), November 16, 2010: 17.

12 Bill Canter, "A Super Sub," *San Diego Union-Tribune*, April 29, 2005: 13.

13 Ortiz, "Astros Deal Blum to Rays."

JOE BORCHARD

By Christopher Kamka

In the 2001 *Baseball Prospectus* annual, this comment was penned for a White Sox prospect:

"He's credited with a strong arm and the athleticism to play center field and has been compared to Larry Walker and Dale Murphy."[1]

Joe Borchard didn't have a career on the level of those greats, but still managed to put together a noteworthy athletic résumé.

Joseph Edward Borchard was born on November 25, 1978, in Panorama City, California, to Joseph and Janice (Beckman) Borchard. Joe the elder was drafted by the Kansas City Royals out of Moorpark (California) College in the 48th round of the 1969 major-league amateur draft, though he didn't sign. He is a descendant of German immigrants who arrived in the Ventura County area in the 1860s.[2] Janice was born in Guam; her family moved to California when she was in the sixth grade.[3] Janice and Joe, who ran a farm growing tomatoes and strawberries in Camarillo (California), had three children, Julie, Joe, and Jill.[4]

Joe Borchard   2005

Young Joe was a three-sport athlete at Camarillo High School, playing football and baseball as well as basketball. He finished as Camarillo's all-time leading passer, with over 6,000 yards and 51 touchdowns, including 2,906 yards and 30 TD as a senior.[5] He was named the 1996-97 Ventura County High School Male Athlete of the Year by the Ventura County Sports Hall of Fame. On the hardwood, he suffered torn ligaments in his left ankle during a layup drill in midseason, which shortened his senior season.[6]

Borchard was a switch-hitter; "I started switch-hitting when I was 12," he told a sportswriter. "My dad was also a switch-hitter. He taught me how to do it. He just saw a lot more advantages than disadvantages with it, and I agreed with it."[7]

As a junior, Borchard hit .341 with 31 RBIs for Camarillo, adding a 3-1 record and a 2.48 ERA on the mound.[8] As a senior he was even better, with a .415 batting average, 11 home runs, and 42 RBIs.[9]

On January 3, 1997, Borchard committed to Stanford over California; he had also considered UNLV, San Jose State, and Oregon State.[10] The Baltimore Orioles took a flier on Borchard in the 20th round of the June 1997 amateur draft, presenting him with a dilemma – sign with the Orioles or accept the football scholarship at Stanford, where he would continue to play baseball, admittedly his favorite sport. However, he did have the option to change his scholarship to baseball if he decided to drop football.[11] Ultimately, Borchard chose Stanford.

Borchard, a history major, was a legitimate two-sport star for the Cardinal, following in the footsteps of Stanford legend John Elway. In three seasons on the diamond, he hit .346/.446/.594 with 40 homers and 187 RBIs in 186 games. He was First-Team All-Pac 10 in 1999 (.372 BA, 11 HR, 56 RBIs) and 2000 (.333 BA, 19 HR, 76 RBIs).[12]

On the gridiron, he tossed 10 touchdowns vs. one interception in 16 games at Stanford. A redshirt as a freshman in 1997, he first saw game action in 1998 as backup to Todd Husak. On September 19, Borchard entered the game in the fourth quarter of a 34-34 game with 34 seconds left, after Husak was injured on a sack on the North Carolina 43-yard line. The Tar Heels had just turned the ball over and were looking to hold on and send the game to overtime, but Borchard had other ideas. On his first play of the game, Borchard scrambled for a 41-yard gain all the way to the two-yard line, which set up a game-winning field goal.[13]

GRINDERS AND GAMERS

On September 25, 1999, he came off the bench to throw for 324 yards and five touchdown passes in a 42-32 win over UCLA.

Borchard has the distinction of appearing in both the Rose Bowl (2000) and the College World Series (1999 and 2000). He juggled baseball and football – even occasionally on the same day. On April 29, 2000, he played a few series in a Stanford football spring scrimmage, then jumped on a golf cart and went over to the baseball field, where he rapped a few hits against Cal.[14]

Three football scouts contacted by White Sox GM Ron Schueler projected Borchard as a late first-round or a second-round NFL draft pick as a quarterback. White Sox scouting director Duane Shaffer said Borchard had "the best power from a college player since Mark McGwire."[15]

In the 2000 draft, the White Sox took a gamble on Borchard with the 12th overall pick. There was uncertainty as to whether Borchard would play for the White Sox or be the starting quarterback for Stanford in his senior season. Otherwise, he would have gone even higher in the draft, as scouts from at least three teams reportedly ranked him the top player in the draft.[16]

Borchard finished his Stanford baseball career in the College World Series on June 17, 2000, failing to collect a hit in four at-bats in the 6-5 loss to LSU, though he was named an outfielder on the All-Tournament team. In total, he went 7-for-14 with a home run, four RBIs, and five runs scored in four tournament games.

Borchard signed with the White Sox on August 8 for a $5.3 million bonus, the largest ever given to a player acquired through the draft, at the time. The next largest bonus was given to the first overall pick, Adrián González ($3 million). Borchard's record bonus stood until Justin Upton's $6.1 million topped it in 2005.

According to Borchard's agent, Jim McDowell (brother of former major-league pitcher Jack McDowell), "The White Sox asked what it would take, we gave them a range and they responded. There was NFL interest in Joe, the extent of which would have been clearer after the upcoming season. Joe loves football, but when you talk about this kind of money, it's a business decision. All signs point to taking this and going to the diamond."[17]

The White Sox bonus was contingent on Borchard's commitment solely to baseball. His career as Stanford quarterback was over. According to McDowell, the record bonus would be paid over 2½ years, with payments ceasing if Borchard returned to football.[18]

Borchard's professional baseball career started on August 9, 2000, in Tucson in the Arizona Rookie League. He hit .414 (12-for-29) in a brief seven-game showing. He was quickly promoted to the Advanced-A Winston-Salem Warthogs of the Carolina League. Starting at DH, he collected an RBI double batting fifth for manager Brian Dayett in his first game, on August 17, despite not getting to the ballpark until 4:30 P.M.[19]

Borchard's first pro home run came on August 25, off right-hander Steve Bechler of the Frederick Keys, one of two homers he would get in 14 games at Winston-Salem.[20] He hit .289 for the Warthogs before moving on yet again, this time to Double-A Birmingham, where he went 5-for-22 (.227) in six games, filling in because of injury.[21]

Borchard struggled in the spring of 2001, and ended up spending the entire season with Birmingham, where the 6-foot-4 center fielder started on his road to the majors. At the Southern League all-star game on June 20 in Kodak, Tennessee, Borchard won a pregame home-run derby (his pitcher was none other than Tommy John, then a radio analyst for the Charlotte Knights, who often tossed batting practice),defeating Corky Miller in the finals. Then in the actual game, Borchard hit a two-run walk-off homer in the 10th inning of a 4-3 win West Division victory, garnering game MVP honors.[22]

On July 8 Borchard went 1-for-2 with a single for Team U.S. in the MLB Futures Game at Safeco Field in Seattle. For the season he had a slash line of .295/.384/.509 with 27 homers (second in the league) and 98 RBIs (leading the league) in 133 games. A high number of strikeouts (158) and errors (12) may have prevented a late-season call-up, but the highly touted prospect was on his way.

After the season, Borchard participated in the 2001 Baseball World Cup, playing for Team USA. He hit a two-run homer in a 4-1 semifinal win against Chinese Taipei, though Cuba won it all with a 5-3 win over the US team.

Entering 2002, Borchard was 12th overall on the *Baseball America* top 100 prospect list – in between Austin Kearns and Nick Johnson. (Josh Beckett topped the list.) He made a strong bid to make the White Sox roster out of spring training, hitting .375, but a hairline fracture suffered when he fouled a pitch off his foot sealed his fate.[23] Borchard played in the 2002 MLB All-Star Futures Game in Milwaukee on July 7, going 0-for-3 with three strikeouts. Through August, in 117 games with Charlotte, he hit .272/.349/.498, with 20 home runs (fifth in the International League), though he still had a high strikeout total (139).

On September 1 Borchard was pulled in the fourth inning of Charlotte's game against Durham. The White Sox were bringing him up to the majors.

"It was a huge surprise," Borchard said. "The way things have gone this year, it just seemed like it wasn't going to be the right time."[24]

Borchard hit sixth in the White Sox lineup the next day, starting in right field for manager Jerry Manuel. He fouled out against the Blue Jays' Corey Thurman in the second inning. Then he followed a Carlos Lee double with a home run in the fourth inning. He became only the fourth player in White Sox history (after Russ Morman, Craig Wilson, and Lee) to hit a home run in his major-league debut. Miguel Olivo would join that list less than two weeks later. Matt Skole has the only such White Sox debut home run since (May 28, 2018). Career base hit number two – and career homer number two came a week later in Kansas City, of the inside-the-park variety off Paul Byrd. It was the first White Sox inside-the-parker since Chris Singleton on September 29, 2000.

After that, Borchard had six starts and seven games where he came in off the bench, finishing his 16-game introduction to the majors with a .222/.243/.389 slash line, 2 homers, and 5 RBIs. He got a few reps after the season, appearing with Mayaguez in the Puerto Rican Winter League.[25]

Borchard started the 2003 season at Triple-A Charlotte. He earned another 16-game taste of "The Show" following a May 23 promotion, but took a step back, hitting .184/.246/.265 with one home run and 18 strikeouts in 57 plate appearances. (The homer was off the pitcher who went on to win the Cy Young Award, Roy Halladay.) In early June, Borchard was sent back to Charlotte, where he finished his Triple-A season with a .253/.307/.398 slash line, 13 homers, and 53 RBIs in 114 games.

Borchard began the 2004 season at Charlotte, where he regained some of his power stroke, batting .266/.333/.495 with 16 home runs in 82 games. On May 17 he homered from both sides of the plate, including a grand slam in 13-5 rout of the Scranton/Wilkes-Barre Red Barons.

On July 9, the White Sox placed Frank Thomas on the disabled list with an ankle injury; he was done for the year. Magglio Ordoñez returned after missing 37 games with a knee injury. Borchard was called up, but not for long. Nine days later, the White Sox made a deadline deal with the Rangers for Carl Everett, and Borchard was the odd man out. He headed back to Charlotte after going 3-for-19 (.158).

However, Ordoñez's knee still wasn't quite right, and after just 10 games back, he was done for the season (As it turned out, his White Sox career was over; he left for Detroit for 2005.) Borchard ended up with his first long look in the majors, taking over as the primary right fielder for the remainder of 2004.

Big-league pitching baffled Borchard; he posted a meager .174/.249/.338 line with nine home runs and 57 strikeouts in 222 plate appearances (25.7 percent strikeout rate; well above the major-league average of 16.9 percent) in 63 games for the South Siders. However, he did finish the season on a bit of a power surge, homering four times in his final eight games.

It might be considered that Borchard's signature major-league moment came on August 30, 2004, as he etched his name in the White Sox record book. He launched a Brett Myers offering 504 feet to the right-field concourse. It surpassed the previous ballpark record of 495 feet by Frank Thomas in 2002. When told of his record-setting achievement, his reaction was "complete shock."[26] As of 2004, it remained the longest home run in what since 2016 has been called Guaranteed Rate Field.

After the 2004 season wrapped up, Borchard played for Mazatlán in the Mexican Winter League, but struggled mightily in 14 games, hitting .140 (7-for-50).

While the White Sox went wire-to-wire in 2005, Borchard hit .265/.338/.484 with 29 home runs … in Charlotte. Despite hitting .261 with five home runs in spring training, there wasn't a spot on the roster for him, with Scott Podsednik, Aaron Rowand, and Jermaine Dye holding down the three starting outfield spots. Timo Pérez was the backup outfielder, with Ross Gload and Willie Harris as additional bench depth.

Borchard was a September call-up, going 5-for-12 in what proved to be his last action with the White Sox. He made one start – on September 30, the day after the White Sox clinched the AL Central Division championship – and went 1-for-6 with a double and four strikeouts in a 13-inning 3-2 win over Cleveland. It was his last regular-season hit in a White Sox uniform.

Borchard was dealt to the Mariners in exchange for lefty reliever Matt Thornton on March 20, 2006. He was barely given a chance in Seattle, logging only six games and nine plate appearances (he went 2-for-9) before being designated for assignment on April 23. The Marlins claimed him off waivers on May 3. The White Sox did well in the trade with Seattle; Thornton through 2024 is the White Sox franchise leader in relief appearances, with 512.

Borchard finished 2006 with 114 games (108 with Florida) and hit .230/.319/.393 with 10 home runs. It was the only time he played in as many as 100 major-league games in a season. He was used 51 times as a pinch-hitter; 49 times with the Marlins for 2006 NL Manager of the Year Joe Girardi. He hit a respectable .250 (11-for-44) with a solid .353 on-base percentage in pinch-hit plate appearances in 2006.

A fun piece of trivia: Borchard is the last player to homer off Greg Maddux, Tom Glavine, and John Smoltz in the same season, although only Smoltz was still pitching for the Braves at the time. Glavine was now with the Mets and Maddux had returned to the Cubs. On September 6, 2006, Borchard hit a solo homer to give the Marlins a 1-0 lead. It would be all they needed, as Anibal Sánchez completed a no-hit, 2-0 win against the Diamondbacks that day.

In 2007 Borchard was the Marlins' Opening Day starting right fielder – the only time he made an Opening Day starting lineup. He went 0-for-3 with a pair of walks, one with the bases loaded. He appeared in 85 games (41 as a pinch-hitter), putting together a .196/.287/.313 slash line. The strikeouts remained a problem, with 60 in 202 plate appearances; he was designated for assignment on August 8. His most recent hit had been a single on July 25 off reigning NL Cy Young Award winner Brandon Webb. It wound up being his final major-league hit.

Borchard finished the 2007 season with Triple-A Albuquerque, where he hit a torrid .355/.452/.711 with 8 home runs and 28 RBIs in 22 games, collecting Pacific

Coast League Player of the Week honors August 20-26, when he hit .520 with four home runs and 14 RBIs.

Borchard signed with the Braves for 2008 and ended up starting the season at Triple-A Richmond, where he hit .274/346/.453 in 33 games before undergoing Tommy John surgery in May. Borchard had struggled with elbow pain since the spring of 2006, but as he battled for roster spots, he kept quiet on his injury and fought through it.[27] Hoping for a pain-free fresh start, Borchard began 2009 playing for the Braves Triple-A affiliate Gwinnett. He was released in May, though he quickly signed with the Giants, where he reported to Triple-A Fresno.

On May 3, 2010, in Colorado Springs, Borchard became the second player in Fresno Grizzlies history to hit for the cycle (after Nate Schierholtz in 2008). He played in 125 games for Fresno in 2010, hitting .263/.340/.469 with 17 home runs.

In 2011 Borchard signed with the Bridgeport (Connecticut) Bluefish of the independent Atlantic League. He played in 24 games for manager Willie Upshaw, hitting .229 before announcing his retirement in June.

"You do this for 12 years and really see every end of the spectrum, it seems like," Borchard said. "I really gave it every chance possible. At the end of the day, you really have nothing to be ashamed of. It's just things go a certain way and that's it and it's time to move on and get into whatever's next."[28]

In 301 major-league games over six seasons, Borchard batted.205 with 26 home runs and 77 RBIs. He never attained All-Star status, but his career had some memorable moments. College World Series and Rose Bowl in the same season. Record-setting bonus. Th longest home run hit at a major-league ballpark. Not too many players can boast a 500-foot home run AND an inside-the-park home run on their résumé.

After his playing career Borchard worked as a financial representative for Northwestern Mutual in Charlotte and for several years served as the director of sales at Ventura Coastal LLC, which sells citrus juices, pulps, oils, purees, and more.[29]

Borchard was inducted into the Ventura County Sports Hall of Fame in 2012. In 2019 he was inducted into the Charlotte Knights Round Table of Honor. As of 2024 he was the Knights' career leader with 78 home runs and 227 RBIs. The Stanford Athletic Hall of Fame came calling next, in 2023 – for both baseball and football.

SOURCES

In addition to the sources cited in the Notes, the author consulted Baseball-Reference.com.

NOTES

1   *Baseball Prospectus* 2001 Edition (Washington, D.C.: Brassey's, 2001), 314.

2   Steve Henson, "Borchard: Despite a Relatively Low Passing Percentage, He Shows He's No Average Joe," *Los Angeles Times*, December 13, 1996: C9.

3   Jose Cepeda, "ChiSox Draft Borchard, Chamorro Taken With 12th Pick Overall in First Round," *Pacific Daily News* (Agana Heights, Guam) June 7, 2000: 56.

4   Earl Gault, "Not Your Ordinary Joe: Son of Farmer Hasn't Forgotten Working-Class Roots," *Rock Hill* (South Carolina) *Herald,* May 30, 2002: 4C.

5   David Lassen, "They're First Class All the Way," *Ventura County Star* (Camarillo, California), January 19, 1997: 19.

6   Jim Parker, "Borchard Ponders *the* Question," *Thousand Oaks* (California) *Star,* July 12, 1997: B5.

7   George Castle, "Borchard Happy With Switch to Baseball," *Hammond* (Indiana) *Times,* March 16, 2001: 123.

8   Jim Parker, "Borchard to Stanford, Nielsen Chooses USC," *Los Angeles Times*, January 4, 1997: C11.

9   Parker, "Borchard Ponders *the* Question."

10   Parker, "Borchard to Stanford, Nielsen Chooses USC."

11   Parker, "Borchard Ponders *the* Question."

12   https://gostanford.com/news/2013/04/17/player-bio-joe-borchard-3.

13   Steve Elling, "Triangle's Three-Sided Fall; Heels Let Another One Slip Away," *Raleigh News and Observer,* September 20, 1998: C1.

14   Dave Newhouse, "No Ordinary Joe: Stanford's Borchard a Two-Sport Success," *Oakland Tribune*, April 30, 2000: 14.

15   Phil Rogers, "No. 1 Pick Borchard Gets Big Bonus," *Chicago Tribune*, July 29, 2000: 51.

16   Jack Magruder, "Borchard's Big Bonus," *Arizona Daily Star* (Tucson), August 6, 2000: 38.

17   "Borchard Signs for Record Bonus," *Los Angeles Times*, July 29, 2000: 121.

18   "Borchard Signs for Record Bonus."

19   "Borchard Gets Hit in Debut," *Ventura County Star*, August 19, 2000: C7.

20   "Warthogs' Homers Too Much for Keys," *Winston-Salem Journal*, August 26, 2000: 33.

21   Paul Sullivan, "Sox's Pitching Staff Turns Things Around," *Chicago Tribune*, August 31, 2000: 51.

22   Nick Gates, "West Is Best In 10: Borchard Has Final Swing in Home Run Duel," *Knoxville News-Sentinel*, June 21, 2001: 39, 43.

23   Bob Buttitta, "Minor Delay," *Ventura County Star*, March 19, 2002: 27.

24   Associated Press, "Borchard's No Ordinary Joe: Rookie's HR Powers Sox," *Hammond Times*, September 3, 2002: 37.

25   https://www.mlb.com/player/joe-borchard-400021.

26   Associated Press, "Sox Ride Borchard's Blast," *Chicago Tribune*, August 31, 2004: 33, 19.

27   Bob Buttitta, "Borchard Hopes to Make Pain-Free Bid for the Bigs," *Ventura County Star*, January 24, 2009: 29

28   Rich Elliott, "Bluefish's Borchard, Missing His Family, Retires From Baseball," *Connecticut Post* (Bridgeport), June 2, 2011. https://www.ctpost.com/news/article/bluefish-s-borchard-missing-his-family-retires-1407525.php.

29   Scott Merkin, "Where Are They Now? Get to Know Joe Borchard," MLB.com, May 19, 2020. https://www.mlb.com/news/where-are-they-now-white-sox-joe-borchard.

MARK BUEHRLE

By Jeremy Gibbs

Left-hander Mark Buehrle pitched in 518 games, starting 493 of them, over a 15-year career. He finished his career with a 214-160 career record with a 3.81 ERA and 1,870 strikeouts in 3,283⅓ innings pitched. Buehrle was a five-time All-Star, and won four Gold Gloves and one World Series championship. He pitched two no-hitters, one of them a perfect game.

Mark Alan Buehrle was born on March 23, 1979, in St. Charles, Missouri to John and Pat Buehrle. John was an ex-Marine who became a paramedic, then the manager of the St. Charles City Water Department. Pat worked in the lunchroom at Barnwell Junior High, where her children attended school. Mark was the youngest of the three boys; they had a younger sister. St. Charles is about 30 minutes northwest of Busch Stadium in downtown St. Louis. Mark grew up rooting for the Cardinals, watching them make the World Series three times before he turned 9 years old and admiring pitchers John Tudor and Joe Magrane, both lefties, and closer Todd Worrell, who was his favorite even though he threw right-handed.

Mark Buehrle   2005

Buehrle played a lot of baseball in his youth. "Just like any kid playing baseball, I loved everything about it," he said. "Waiting for school to end to get dressed into the uniform and get out on the field. I just really enjoyed the competition involved with it."[1]

Unlike most kids, Buehrle had superior control. His sister, Amy Buehrle English, fondly remembered:

A story I've heard a lot my whole life is when he was like one or two (years old), my parents took him to a church picnic or fair. He played one of those games where you throw a ball and knock something over. He just sat there and threw the ball over and over and over hitting the target each time. People would stop to watch because he was so young and so good. So, I'm pretty sure it was known since he was little that he would be a great ballplayer.[2]

His control even impressed 1983 Cy Young Award winner John Denny, who agreed to coach him privately. Denny was drafted by the Cardinals in 1970 and was a starting pitcher for them for five seasons before being traded to Cleveland.

In an era before travel ball, the first real test a young man will pass is to make his high-school baseball team. However, Buehrle did not make his freshman baseball team at Francis Howell North high school.

English teacher Neil Berry was the freshman baseball coach. He explained: "The only thing I can tell you is that FHN had a program wide pitching coach who loved Mark from his first day as a freshman. I remember his evaluation of Mark was glowing, and he was so impressed that Mark had pinpoint accuracy. The problem was that he was only 5 feet tall and his pitches were hit back harder than he threw them. The reason he didn't make the team as a freshman was that he was a pitcher only and threw batting practice speed. He also had a bit of an attitude problem as a freshman."[3]

Buehrle tried out again his sophomore year, but still did not make the team even with the new coaching from John Denny. "After I got cut those first two years, I pretty much decided I was done," Buehrle said. "I just felt like getting cut, not being able to make your freshmen and sophomore teams, then there was going to be no way I'd make the varsity team. I basically just decided that I was done, baseball wasn't going to be my thing and I should move on."[4]

Incidentally, it wasn't Mark Buehrle who was supposed to be cut from the junior varsity team that year. It was another Mark B. instead. This led to the creation of the "Mark Buehrle rule" at Francis Howell North that declared all cuts in the baseball program had to go through the head coach before being finalized.

However, after his father scolded him for his defeatist attitude, letting him know that he did not raise a quitter, Mark found redemption his junior year after growing nearly a foot during the offseason. During his junior year, he worked out of the bullpen as a lefty specialist and put up a 2-0 record with a 0.60 ERA.

Buehrle worked as a starter his senior year, gaining the attention of local scouts as he continued to fill out and gained velocity on his fastball and stronger bite in his curveball. He chose to attend nationally ranked Jefferson College in nearby Hillsboro, Missouri.

"It was a pretty easy sign," said Dave Oster, former Jefferson College baseball coach, of landing Buehrle as a recruit. "We saw him play one day, asked him to come down for a visit and the next day he came down, he liked the place and committed, and then it kind of went from there."[5]

The scouts quickly took notice. "I remember the first tournament we had was down at Southwest Missouri State," Buehrle said. "I threw a couple of innings down there and the next thing I knew, there were a few scouts handing me index cards asking me to fill out information on myself. At first I thought someone was playing a joke on me. At the time, there was another lefty who pitched for us that threw harder than I did and was a sophomore. I had thought they mistook me for him."[6]

After that first year, the Chicago White Sox selected Buehrle in the 38th round of the June 1998 amateur draft with the 1,139th overall pick. Buehrle did not sign initially. The White Sox used the "draft and follow" strategy, which allowed them to retain his rights for a year. Buehrle was undeterred. He underwent a more rigorous offseason training program, becoming the ace of the Jefferson College pitching staff the following season. Just before their draft rights expired, the White Sox made him an offer of $150,000, and he signed.

Buehrle did not spend much time in the minor leagues. In 1999 he started 14 games for the Burlington Bees of the Class-A Midwest League and went 7-4 with 91 strikeouts in 98⅔ innings. The next season Buehrle started 16 games for the Birmingham Barons of the Double-A Southern League and was 8-4 with a 2.28 ERA. That production was good enough to get a call to the big leagues.

On July 16, 2000, Buehrle made his major-league debut, pitching the ninth inning of a blowout win for the White Sox over the Milwaukee Brewers. He allowed two hits and one earned run. He made his first start three days later against the Minnesota Twins in Minneapolis. Over seven innings

he allowed six hits and two earned runs and earned his first major-league victory, 3-2.

Buehrle spent the first 12 years of his career with the White Sox. He mostly worked out of the bullpen his rookie season, After defeating the Twins, he started two more games. However, after getting knocked around by the California Angels in the second of those starts, his next 24 appearances were all in relief.

The White Sox won the American League Central Division title in 2000 but were swept by the Seattle Mariners in the Division Series. Buehrle pitched in one game, getting the call in the top of the ninth inning of Game Two and allowing an inherited runner to score.

Buehrle made the starting rotation in 2001 and became a steady presence on the pitching staff, starting 362 games and going 157-118 with a 3.82 ERA (120 ERA+) over an 11-year period (2001-2011). He was named to four All-Star Games and finished fifth in the Cy Young Award vote in 2005.

Buehrle made his first All-Star Game appearance in 2002, having started 19 games with a 12-7 record while producing a 3.57 ERA in the first half of the season. He pitched two innings, allowing one run. In what ended up being one of the strangest All-Star Games, the game ended in a tie after both teams ran out of pitchers in the 11th inning.

In 2003 Buehrle's 14-14 record with a 4.14 ERA was better than average (112 ERA+), but not as good as his career average (117 ERA+). In 2004 he led the American League in innings pitched (245⅓) while producing a 16-10 record with a 3.89 ERA (121 ERA+). This was his fourth consecutive season with at least 200 innings pitched, an achievement that would become the norm for him rather than the exception.

Buehrle was a major contributor to the White Sox in 2005, with a record of 16-8. His 3.12 ERA was the best among White Sox starters. Only Jon Garland, with 18 wins, topped Buehrle in victories. Buehrle started the All-Star Game and earned the win for his two innings pitched as the American League scored in the bottom of the second and never gave up the lead, winning 7-5.

Beginning in 2001, Buehrle started each of the remaining 490 games of his career, with one notable exception: On October 25, 2005, after throwing 100 pitches over seven innings in Game Two of the World Series two days before, Buehrle was called upon to close out Game Three. He needed only three pitches to induce the Houston Astros' Adam Everett to pop out and end the game.

That appearance was notable because of what happened before the event. Assuming that he would not be needed during the game, Buehrle had a few beers.

"Yes, I did have a few beverages on the bench, and I went up to (pitching coach) Don Cooper in the sixth, seventh, or eighth inning. I don't remember what it was," Buehrle said. "They were starting to use the bullpen. This guy came in for a third of an inning and this guy came in for a third, so it was getting thinner and thinner there. "I'm like, 'Will you need me?' and Coop said, 'No.' So I go get another beer. I did that a few times, and it was like, when he said, 'Yeah, get [your] crap on,' I thought he was just saying it because he was sick of me asking him. I got ready and went down there."[7]

Buehrle's 2006 season was reminiscent of the tale *Strange Case of Dr. Jekyll and Mr. Hyde*. He was good in the first half, putting up a 9-4 record in 16 games started with a 3.22 ERA through June. His final three months was a completely different tale. He finished 3-9 with a bloated 7.12 ERA. Overall, he finished 12-13 with a 4.99 ERA, the highest of his career. The White Sox missed out on the playoffs, finishing five games behind the Detroit Tigers for a wild-card spot..

On April 18, 2007, Buehrle was virtually perfect when the Texas Rangers came to town. The only blemish on his record that day was a walk to Sammy Sosa. Nonetheless, two pitches later, Buehrle caught Sosa leaning in the wrong direction and threw to first baseman Paul Konerko to pick him off, and didn't allow another baserunner. In a book published in 2008, he said, "When I see my name connected to a no-hitter, it seems unreal. You see "last no-hitter pitched in the Major Leagues" and you see my name. It's kind of overwhelming."[8]

In 2007 Buehrle had 201 innings pitched in 30 starts, producing a 10-9 record with a 3.63 ERA. The White Sox, on the other hand, were the worst they would be in Buehrle's time with them, going 72-90 and finishing fourth in the AL Central Division with only the Kansas City Royals faring worse.

The White Sox got back to their winning ways in 2008, finishing first in the division with an 89-74 record. Buehrle went 15-12 with a 3.79 ERA. He started Game Two of the American League Division Series against the Tampa Bay Rays at Tropicana Field. Buehrle threw seven-plus innings and was the losing pitcher, giving up five runs and 10 hits in a 6-2 loss.

On July 23, 2009, at US Cellular Field, Buehrle was perfect against the Rays. Notoriously a quick worker, he mowed through the Tampa Bay lineup almost effortlessly. He breezed through the first inning, using only 10 pitches to induce two groundouts and a strikeout. He used 18 pitches in the second, the most he required for an inning, but was able to get Carlos Peña to pop out, Ben Zobrist to strike out, and Pat Burrell to fly out. (Peña did push him into a full count.) Buehrle settled back down in the third inning, retiring the Rays with only 11 pitches. In the fourth, B.J. Upton worked a full count before striking out. Buehrle quickly retired the next two batters, Carl Crawford and Evan Longoria, getting through the inning having thrown just 11 pitches. He was even better in the fifth, needing only 10 pitches. After getting through the first two batters in the sixth without much trouble, Jason Bartlett pushed him into a full count before grounding out to shortstop. Buehrle needed only nine pitches to get through the seventh inning,

inducing two groundouts and a fly ball. In the eighth inning, Buehrle struck out Peña, then Zobrist worked a full count before fouling out to the third baseman, Gordon Beckham, requiring seven pitches. Buehrle needed seven more pitches to retire the next batter as well, retiring Pat Burrell on a lineout to Beckham.

Statcast has a statistic called Tempo, which measures the median time between pitches. Their data exists since 2010. With the bases empty, no one has a faster tempo equivalent to throwing a pitch every 5.9 seconds. Fast pitchers keep defenses on their toes. That proved to be necessary during the ninth inning. Manager Ozzie Guillén brought Dewayne Wise into the game in the ninth inning to help shore up the defense, moving Scott Podsednik from center field to left field while sending bad-fielding Carlos Quentin to the bench. Guillén's move proved to be the right one. The first batter Buehrle faced in the ninth inning was Gabe Kapler. On a 2-and-2 pitch, Kapler hit a drive to deep left-center field. It looked like the ball was headed over the wall. However, Wise raced back diagonally to the wall, leapt up, and caught the ball, robbing Kapler of a home run. Broadcaster Ken Harrelson described the play as "(u)nder the circumstances, one of the greatest catches I have ever seen in 50 years in this game."[9]

Buehrle cinched the major leagues' 18th perfect game by striking out Michel Hernandéz and getting Jason Bartlett on a weak grounder to shortstop.

"I can't believe that happened to me," Buehrle recalled. "I'm not a guy who should be throwing perfect games, with not striking guys out, not hard throwing. Just the same thing with the no-hitter. I said I would never throw a perfect game, or a no-hitter, and I ended up doing both of them. So, it was, 'No way. That just didn't happen.'"[10]

(Coincidentally, the home-plate umpire for the perfect game was Eric Cooper, who worked behind the plate for Buehrle's no-hitter against the Rangers.)

In his next start, Buehrle retired the first 17 batters he faced. Combining his final out in Baltimore on July 18 with his perfect game and those 17 Twins batters on July 28 summed up to 45 straight batters retired. This was a major-league record, later broken by San Francisco Giant Yusmeiro Petit over a course of eight games in 2014.

In 2010 the White Sox finished with an 88-74 record, seven games behind the New York Yankees for a wild-card spot. Buehrle was 13-13 with a 4.28 ERA, the second worst of his career. This ERA was exactly league average, something that Buehrle was not accustomed to, producing an average ERA+ of 117 during his 15 seasons as a starter with only two seasons below 100.

Buehrle did have one notable moment in the sun that season. On June 19 a poll was conducted by the MLB Twitter account asking "Which pitcher made the best play?" The poll offered the following options: Greg Maddux (2008), Mark Buehrle (2010), Bartolo Colon (2015), and Vince Velasquez (2018) with videos showcasing each pitcher's impressive defensive play. While this was not a scientific poll since the respondents were self-selected, Buehrle was the winner for his kick save on April 5, 2010 – a through-the-legs glove flip to prevent Cleveland Indians catcher Lou Marson from legging out a single up the middle.[11]

Buehrle's defensive prowess was widely recognized. The play on Marson came in one of his four straight Gold Glove years (2009 to 2012). Only 11 pitchers have won the award more often.

Part of good defense in the pitching position is picking off baserunners. According to MLB.com, Buehrle was the best at it, getting 100 pickoffs in his career, one better than Steve Carlton.[12] It should be noted that pickoffs did not become an official statistic until 1974. It is widely recognized that Carlton accumulated some 45 more pickoffs in his full career.[13]

Info Solutions developed a defensive runs saved statistic in 2003. Since that year, the only pitcher who saved more runs than Buehrle is Zack Greinke – 98 to 88. The next closest is Jake Westbrook with 62.[14]

Buehrle became a free agent after the 2011 season. He signed a four-year contract with the Miami Marlins worth $58 million.[15] In 31 starts for the Marlins in 2012, Buehrle posted a 13-13 record with a 3.74 ERA and won a Gold Glove for the fourth consecutive year. His time in Miami was short-lived. After finishing in last place with a 69-93 record, the Marlins decided it was time to trim the fat reminiscent of their post-championship sells of 1997 and 2003. Along with shortstop José Reyes, starting pitcher Josh Johnson, John Buck, and Emilio Bonifacio, Buehrle was traded to the Toronto Blue Jays in what appeared to be a salary dump.

"I'm upset with how things turned out in Miami," Buehrle said in a statement issued through his agent, Jeff Berry." Just like the fans in South Florida, I was lied to on multiple occasions. But I'm putting it behind me and looking forward to moving on with my career."[16]

In his three seasons in Toronto, Buehrle started 97 games and produced a 40-28 record with a 3.78 ERA. He was selected to the All-Star team in 2014.

On October 2, 2015, two days before the end of the regular season, Buehrle threw 6⅔ innings against Tampa Bay and picked up his 15th victory. Many, including Buehrle, thought that this might be the final game of his career. He saved the game ball.

Manager John Gibbons had other ideas. Buehrle had pitched 198 innings. Two more would put him at 200 innings pitched for the 15th consecutive year, a feat that only four other pitchers – Gaylord Perry, Don Sutton, Warren Spahn, and Cy Young – had accomplished. On October 4, the last day of the regular season, Buehrle started against the Rays again. He did not survive the first inning, giving up eight runs (all unearned, thanks to two Blue Jays errors), getting just two outs and giving up five hits and a walk.

"Sad thing, I felt better today than I did on Friday, better than I've felt in the last month, month and a half," Buehrle said afterward. "This game is crazy. I didn't feel great on Friday and went 6⅔, and today I felt great and they had to take me out in the first inning."[17]

After the game, Buehrle was informed that he had not made the Blue Jays' postseason roster. The Blue Jays decided to carry just four starting pitchers – David Price, R.A. Dickey, Marcus Stroman, and Marco Estrada along with seven relief pitchers. Those 45 pitches thrown on a pleasant day in Tampa Bay would prove to be his final major-league tosses.

"I was told I was retiring," Buehrle said. "I got about 400 text messages today from friends who are, 'Sad to see you go, to be retiring.' And I'm like, 'What's going on here?' Apparently I'm done, and what a way to go out. Nowadays we don't have a decision. It's what people tell us."[18]

In 2017 the White Sox retired Buehrle's number 56. It is one of 12 numbers retired by the team. Nine of the players have been inducted into the Baseball Hall of Fame.

"It's an amazing feeling," said the 38-year-old Buehrle, who was flanked by his wife, his two children, and his mother and father at the 30-minute ceremony. "I really can't put it into words how I feel. ... It's a special day."[19]

In retirement Buehrle devoted himself to being the best father he could be to his two children. Said his sister, Amy Buehrle English, "He is a dad first and foremost."[20] Buehrle spent time hunting, traveling, and woodworking. Buehrle has always enjoyed the outdoors. His sister cited an article from when he was a player that said, "Whenever he has time, sometimes around the All-Star break in July, Buehrle races back to St. Charles to laze around the 18-acre pond on his property. He might take out a boat or just sit on shore with a fishing pole and a worm for bait, watching his bobber."[21]

Buehrle and his wife, Jamie, displayed a passion for dogs. While living in Chicago, they provided public service announcements for animal rescue facilities, appeared on pet adoption billboards, and headed a Sox for Strays promotion at US Cellular Field.

When Buehrle signed his contract with the Marlins in 2012, he bought a house in Broward County approximately 30 minutes from the Marlins Stadium in Miami-Dade County because pit bulls are prohibited in the county.[22] Once he was traded to the Blue Jays, things got even more complicated since pit bulls are banned in the Province of Ontario. The Buehrles opted to keep their family in the St. Louis area, living with their four dogs while Mark lived by himself during the baseball season.

Since 2000, no one has approached Buehrle's consistency in producing 14 seasons of at least 200 innings pitched and falling four outs short of a 15th. As of 2024, Justin Verlander was the closest to this level of production, posting 12 seasons of at least 200 innings pitched. Nine of the 10 pitchers with more than 14 (Don Sutton, Greg Maddux, Phil Niekro, Warren Spahn, Bert Blyleven, Steve Carlton, Tom Seaver, Gaylord Perry, and Grover Cleveland Alexander are in the Hall of Fame; the sole exception is Roger Clemens.

Since 2000, Buehrle ranks seventh among all starting pitchers in WAR (as of 2024). The top four – Verlander, Clayton Kershaw, Max Scherzer, and Zack Greinke – were active in 2024. The sixth, CC Sabathia, was elected to the Hall of Fame in 2025.

In his book *One Hundred Years of White Sox Baseball*, author Mark Pienkos summarizes Buehrle the player: "Mark Buehrle is one of those rare breeds of pitchers that only comes around once in a lifetime. He was special in so many ways: reliable, great fielder, didn't waste time between tosses, great command of his pitches so as not to allow lots of walks, yet able to strike out batters without having a great deal of velocity."[23]

SOURCES

In addition to the sources cited in the Notes, the author consulted Baseball-Reference.com, Retrosheet.org, and a number of other sources including the following:

Chicago Sun-Times, White Sox: 2005 World Series Champions (Chicago: Sports Publishing, LLC. 2005).

Lee Jenkins, "Miracle on the South Side," *Sports Illustrated*, August 3, 2009.

Colleen Kane, "Mark Buehrle on His Quiet Retirement: 'I Wanted to Sneak My Way Out,'" *Chicago Tribune*, February 24, 2017. Retrieved September 10, 2024, from https://www.chicagotribune.com/2017/02/24/mark-buehrle-on-his-quiet-retirement-i-wanted-to-sneak-my-way-out/.

Elliot Lee, *Red-Tagged: Dirty Diamonds* (CreateSpace Independent Publishing Platform), 2015.

Mark Buehrle | MLB Contracts & Salaries. (n.d.). Spotrac.com. Retrieved September 10, 2024, from https://www.spotrac.com/mlb/player/_/id/169/mark-buehrle.

Tom Stone, *Now Taking the Field: Baseball's All-Time Dream Teams for All 30 Franchises* (Chicago: ACTA Publications, 2017).

NOTES

1   Jeff Strange, "From Being Cut in High School to an MLB All-Star Team: Mark Buehrle Shares His Story," Patch.com (St. Peters, Missouri), March 6, 2011. https://patch.com/missouri/stpeters/from-being-cut-in-high-school-to-an-mlb-all-star-teamab0e9608ea.

2   Amy Buehrle English, interview by author, September 19, 2024.

3   Neil Berry, interview by author. December 15, 2021.

4   Strange.

5   James Fegan, "Before Mark Buehrle Made the Hall of Fame Ballot, White Sox Scouts Saw Potential," *New York Times*, November 22, 2020. https://www.nytimes.com/athletic/2191063/2020/11/22/mark-buehrle-hall-of-fame/.

6   Strange.

7   Scott Merkin, "Remembering Mark Buehrle's Perfect Game," MLB.com, July 22, 2019. https://www.mlb.com/news/remembering-mark-buehrle-s-perfect-game.

8   Lew Freedman, *Game of My Life: White Sox: Memorable Stories of Chicago White Sox Baseball* (Chicago: Sports Publishing, 2008), 199.

9   Scott Merkin, "Oral History of Mark Buehrle's Perfect Game," MLB.com. Retrieved October 10, 2024, from https?//www.mlb.com/news/mark-buehrle-perfect-game-2009-an-oral-history.

10 Scott Merkin, "Remembering Mark Buehrle's Perfect Game."

11 Video can be seen on YouTube at: https://www.youtube.com/watch?v=ujUdP7H81no.

12 MLB.com stats. https://www.mlb.com/stats/pitching/pickoff/all-time-totals?expanded=true.

13 Kevin Czerwinski, "The Pickoff Artist," *BallNine*, September 27, 2022. https://ballnine.com/2022/09/27/the-pickoff-artist/.

14 Bill James, "Fielding Bible," Fielding Bible, n.d.. Accessed November 20, 2024. https://archive.fieldingbible.com/DRSLeaderboard.

15 The 2012 Marlins were managed by Ozzie Guillén.

16 Associated Press, "Mark Buehrle: Marlins Lied to Me," ESPN.com, November 21, 2012. https://www.espn.com/mlb/story/_/id/8661291/mark-buehrle-says-miami-marlins-lied-multiple-occasions.

17 G. Chisholm, "Buehrle Falls Short of eat, Postseason Roster Spot," MLB.com, October 4,2015 Retrieved November 14, 2024, from https://www.mlb.com/news/mark-buehrle-falls-short-of-feat-alds-roster/c-153295414.

18 Chisholm.

19 Associated Press, "White Sox Retire Mark Buehrle's No. 56 Jersey," *USA Today*, June 24, 2017. https://www.usatoday.com/story/sports/mlb/2017/06/24/white-sox-retire-former-star-pitcher-buehrles-no-56-jersey/103167590/,

20 English interview.

21 English interview.

22 Jerry Crasnick, "Outlawed Pit Bull Will Keep Buehrle Away From His Family," ESPN.com, February 7, 2013. Retrieved September 17, 2024, from https://www.espn.com/mlb/story/_/id/8921726/outlawed-pit-bull-keep-mark-buehrle-away-family.

23 Mark Pienkos, *1917-2017: One Hundred Years of White Sox Baseball: Highlighting the Great 1917 World Series Championship Team* (Sarasota, Florida: Pepperpot Press, 2017), 90.

JAMIE BURKE

By Bob Webster

"An average day in the minors is far superior to the best day pulling green chain and risking life and limb in a stifling sawmill," said Jamie Burke, commenting on his first seven years in the minors. "It's my job; I'm getting paid for something I love to do."[1]

That attitude is what kept Burke in professional baseball for 18 seasons.

James Eugene Burke was born in Roseburg, Oregon, on September 24, 1971, to Walter and Marilyn Burke. Walter worked in the timber industry.[2] Marilyn was a secretary at Douglas Community Hospital in Roseburg for many years.[3] Walter and Marilyn were both involved in church activities while raising Jamie and his three older sisters; Julie, Gina, and Jodi.[4]

Jamie honed his baseball skills at an early age. He played wiffle ball[5] in a neighbor's backyard which helped his hand-eye coordination and as an 8-year-old he skipped summer school classes to practice baseball with the older kids before going to his own practice later. His mother was not happy when she was told that he skipped summer school 37 times that summer.[6]

Jamie played baseball and football at Roseburg High School, and helped lead both programs to the state title games three times before he graduated in 1990. In the 1988 state quarter-final game, Burke kicked a 27-yard field goal in overtime to give Roseburg a 10-7 victory over Barlow High School.[7] Roseburg lost the state title game to Benson (Portland). Burke was a first-team all-state defensive back and a third-team selection at kicker for the 1989 team that lost to Ashland (Oregon) in the state title game. Thurman Bell, Burke's high school football coach said of Burke, "Jamie was a coach's player because he loved to compete and he dedicated all of his time and energy into whatever sport he was playing."[8] He was the starting shortstop for the 1990 Roseburg High School baseball team that made it to the state championship game before losing to Klamath Union High School, 5-2. His baseball coach, Ron Goodell, said of Burke, "Not only was he talented, but he was also the hardest working kid on the team." Goodell continued, "Jamie was serious about being as good of a player as he could be."[9]

Burke was second-team all-state in baseball (shortstop) in 1990, Roseburg Legion MVP in 1990, all-conference place-kicker in 1988-89, all-league safety in 1989, all-state free safety in 1989, and third-team all-state placekicker in 1989.[10] He received an athletic scholarship to Oregon State University.[11]

Burke's scholarship at Oregon State was in baseball, but he walked on the football team with the understanding with the coach that if he didn't win the job he would go right into fall baseball. Burke won the starting kicker job.[12] This kept him busy. Burke's schedule consisted of taking 15 credit-hours of classes as well as football and baseball practices. "I'm keeping busy," Burke said. "Right now there is a lot of stress – I'm either studying or playing sports."[13]

Burke red-shirted the 1991 baseball season and played his freshman season in 1992. He switched from shortstop to third base at Oregon State because he had a good arm and the Beavers already had a shortstop. In a game on April 14 against Linfield College, Burke broke a little finger sliding into home in the seventh inning.[14] After missing 14 games, Burke returned and was hot. In his first five games back, he was 8-for-20 with 9 RBIs.[15] He finished the season batting .333 in 39 games.

Jamie Burke   2005

With the 1992 football season approaching, the Oregon State football coach was presented with a pleasant surprise. Burke was the placekicker and Tim Kollas was the punter for the coming season. The pleasant surprise was that Kollas could back up Burke and Burke could back up Kollas in case of injuries. The backups from the previous season graduated and transferred, thus leaving the two juniors with enough experience to back up each other. That came in handy during road games when the team could take a maximum of 60 players, per league rules. Instead of taking 56 position players and four kickers, the Beavers could take 58 position players and two kickers.[16]

Burke finished the 1992 football season with 13 extra points and five field goals made.[17]

While back at third base for the Oregon State University Beavers in 1993, Burke improved on his 1992 batting average of .333 by hitting .346. On June 3 Burke was drafted by the California Angels in the ninth round of the amateur draft. Burke signed the following day, finished his finals as a redshirt freshman at Oregon State, and after a week at the Angels' camp in Mesa, Arizona, he reported to the Boise Hawks of the short-season Class-A Northwest League.[18] After 30 games, Burke ranked fifth in the league in hitting (.311) and was starting to play third base on an everyday basis.[19]

Even though Burke had a hard time sleeping on the long bus rides of the Northwest League, he was very positive about his experience in minor-league baseball. He said, "It's a boy's dream to play baseball every day, and it really is fun. It's so fun it's hard to explain. It's such a different life than ever before." He added, "You eat, sleep, and just play baseball … and get money for it. There really is no bad part to this, it's a dream come true."[20]

The Angels were concerned about Burke playing football and the possibility of getting injured. "They told me I'm a prospect and don't want anything to happen to me," said Burke. It turned out that the Angels won, and Burke would not be playing football at Oregon State that fall. He finished the season at batting .301, third best in the league.[21]

Burke was promoted to the Angels Low-A affiliate Cedar Rapids Kernels of the Midwest League for the 1994 season and batted .264 with one home run and 47 RBIs in 127 games. He split time at first base (64 games) and third base (61 games).

In 1995 Burke played for the Lake Elsinore Storm of the High-A California League, batting .274 with 2 home runs and 56 RBIs in 106 games while appearing in 89 games at third and 21 games at first. He survived the early season concern when the major-league teams reduced their rosters from 40 to 25 players. When the players are reassigned, there is a trickle-down effect. "The only thing that hurts us is, in two weeks from now, we're going to have a different team," said Storm manager Mitch Seoane.[22] "I really don't know what's going on," said Burke. "It's not going to bother me. Some of my teammates were talking about it today,

but it's something I'm not going to worry about."[23] From 1996 through 1998, Burke moved back and forth between Midland of the Double-A Texas League and Vancouver of the Triple-A Pacific Coast League. He started to catch in 1996, with five games behind the plate in Vancouver and eight games catching for Midland. The coaches saw his soft hands and throwing ability as a catcher in spring training and decided to move him to the catcher position to add to his versatility.[24]

In 1996 Burke hit .319 with 2 home runs and 16 RBIs in 45 games with Midland and .250 with one home run and 14 RBIs in 41 games with Vancouver. He spent most of 1997 with Midland, batting .329 with 6 homers and 72 RBIs in 116 games. His batting average dropped in 1998: .244 with Midland, and .216 with Vancouver.

After the Angels switched Triple-A affiliates from Vancouver to Edmonton for the 1999 season, Burke played for the Edmonton Trappers and hit .336 in 46 games. He was sidelined after getting hit by a pitch on June 13, shattering his left elbow and sidelining him for the remainder of the season.[25] Before his injury, Burke had a 16-game hitting streak, and a 28-game on-base streak.

Burke played 56 games at third base and caught 19 games for Edmonton in 2000, hitting .240. He returned from his broken elbow but sustained multiple injuries including fouling a ball off his foot, landing him on the disabled list on June 1. He was activated on June 16.[26]

This was the 28-year-old Burke's fourth year in Triple A and his attitude and work ethic were what kept him going. He said of his time in the minor leagues, "It's my job; I'm getting paid for something I love to do. I'm having a great time here, day in and day out, 138 games a year." "We just got done with a stretch of 52 straight games, and just got a day off yesterday. But I'll tell you this much, I'd rather do that, playing baseball seven days a week, than actually sitting behind a desk or going out there to work in the lumber mills or something like that. This is something that happens once in a lifetime, so I'm going to give it my all."[27]

Burke believed he was close to a call-up because of his versatility; he could catch and play third base, first base, and the outfield. "Right now it is important to have a third catcher who can play a lot of other positions," said Edmonton manager Gary Templeton. "A lot of rosters carry three catchers, but the third catcher is a very versatile guy. If a guy like Burke can prove he can do the job catching – the Angels already know he can play third and first – there's a spot for him. They're finally realizing he's one heck of a catcher."[28]

The Angels moved their Triple-A affiliation to Salt Lake for the 2001 season and became the Stingers. Burke caught 36 games for the Stingers in 2001 and played first, third, and outfield in 21 games. On May 9 he finally got his big break. Angels catcher Benji Molina strained his right hamstring and was placed on the 15-day DL. Molina was expected to miss two or three weeks. Burke was called up and made his major-league debut on May 9 against the White Sox in Chicago, when he came into the game in the ninth inning to catch. His next appearance was on May 13, when he pinch-hit for David Eckstein in the ninth inning and collected his first big-league hit, off the Tigers' Matt Miller. He stayed in the game and played first base. Burke was sent back down to Salt Lake for a brief time on May 31. He was back up a few days later and finished three more games at catcher before Molina was activated from the disabled list. He finished his brief first year in the majors playing in nine games and collecting one hit in five at-bats.

Burke was back in Salt Lake for the 2002 season. In 88 games he hit .304. On October 15 Burke was granted free agency by the Angels and on October 31, he signed with the White Sox.

Sent to the Triple-A Charlotte Knights in 2003, Burke played in 94 games and batted .322. On August 9 he was summoned to join the White Sox. He served as a backup for catchers Sandy Alomar and Miguel Olivo. Olivo had hurt his shoulder in a home-plate collision and was day-to-day. Burke's call-up was to buy time with hopes of Olivo not having to go on the disabled list.[29]

Alomar caught on August 8, so it would be Olivo's turn on August 9. Since he was still hurting, Burke got the call. He responded by going 1-for-2 with his first major-league RBI. On the 11th, in a game against his former team in Anaheim, Burke entered the game to catch in the eighth inning. The 31-year-old Burke was finally caught up in some real major-league excitement. With the White Sox down 10-4 in the top of the ninth against the Angels and star reliever Troy Percival, Carlos Lee singled. Frank Thomas homered to make the score 10-6. Singles by Magglio Ordñez and Carl Everett and an RBI single by Paul Konerko made the score 10-7. José Valentin flied out to center, the first out. Tony Graffanino was hit by a Percival pitch. Burke singled to center, driving in Everett from third, Konerko advancing to third and Graffanino to second to make the score 10-8. Roberto Alomar struck out looking and Carlos Lee popped out to short to end the rally and the game.

Burke was sent back to Charlotte when pitcher Neal Cotts was called up to make his major-league debut the next night. "I was really encouraged with the way he handled himself and the pitching," manager Jerry Manuel said. "And he looked like a professional hitter."[30]

Burke was back with the White Sox as a September call-up and played in four games. In his brief call-up, he was 3-for-8 with 2 RBIs.

Burke started the 2004 spring-training campaign with a bang. In mid-March, he was hitting .385 in 13 at-bats, but after some roster juggling, Burke was sent back to Charlotte.[31] The 32-year-old Burke played 37 games with Charlotte and a career-high 57 games with the White Sox in 2004, batting .333 with 40 hits in 120 at-bats. His versatility enabled Burke to catch 45 games and play right field, first base, third base, and designated hitter two games each.

On January 6, 2005, A.J. Pierzynski was signed as a free agent by the White Sox. He remained with the White Sox for eight seasons. The White Sox also picked up free agent catcher Chris Widger over the offseason, blocking Burke from becoming a White Sox mainstay for the 2005 season. He was called up from Charlotte on May 4 and in the eighth inning of the May 5 game against the Royals, Burke pinch-hit for Pierzynski and grounded out. Burke was designated for assignment on May 8 and returned to Charlotte for the rest of the 2005 season, appearing in 101 games with the Knights before he was granted free agency on October 5. In November he signed with the Texas Rangers.

Burke spent the 2006 season with the Rangers' Triple-A affiliate Oklahoma RedHawks, where he hit .278 with 10 home runs and 49 RBIs while dividing his time as a catcher (55 games), third baseman (24 games), and first baseman (18 games). He became a free agent on October 15 and signed with the Seattle Mariners.

After beating out Rene Rivera for the backup catcher position, Burke played in 50 games with the Mariners in 2007, of which 48 were behind the plate. He was primarily the backup to starting catcher Kenji Johjima. Burke hit .301 (34-for-113) with 8 doubles, a homer, and 12 RBIs.

In the last game of the season, the 36-year-old Burke hit his first major-league home run, off A.J. Murray of the Texas Rangers in the second inning. He also executed a sacrifice squeeze bunt in the fourth inning. The Mariners did not make the playoffs, but they did manage to crack open cans of beer and sprayed the beer on Burke in a postgame celebration.[32]

With Johjima the starting catcher in 2008, Burke shared the backup catcher position with Jeff Clement. Burke hit .261 (24-for-92) and made an appearance on the mound. In the eighth inning on July 6 against the Detroit Tigers, after reaching on an error, starting catcher Johjima was lifted for pinch-runner Jeremy Reed. In the top of the ninth, Burke replaced Reed and stayed in the game to catch. The ninth inning ended with the score tied, 1-1. With the score still 1-1 going into the 15th inning and the Mariners already having used six pitchers, Mariners manager Jim Riggleman called on Burke to switch from catcher to pitcher. It did not go very well for Burke; he gave up a leadoff double to Miguel Cabrera, who advanced to third on a wild pitch and scored on Marcus Thames's sacrifice fly. Burke did retire Iván Rodríguez and Edgar Rentería, but the one run given up by Burke was the difference as the Mariners did not score in the bottom half of the 15th inning.

The 37-year-old Burke was granted free agency by the Mariners on December 12, 2008, and signed a minor-league deal with the team on December 23.

Burke started the 2009 season with the Tacoma Rainiers, but on April 15 the Mariners' Johjima suffered a hamstring strain. Burke was called up to back up catcher Rob Johnson. Manager Don Wakamatsu said of Burke's call-up, "I've known Jamie from three different organizations and I trust his ability to call a game and his relationship with the pitching staff. He's a good fit to bring up. He was in competition all spring to make the club and it's nice to bring up somebody who I know personally and trust."[33]

Burke hit .284 with Tacoma in 22 games and .122 with Seattle that season before being sold to the Washington Nationals on September 18. Three Nationals catchers were injured and the team needed help. Burke played in six games for the Nationals and was granted free agency on October 29 before signing a minor-league deal with the club three weeks later.

The 38-year-old played most of the 2010 season with the Syracuse Chiefs of the Triple-A International League, batting .234 in 47 games, and was granted free agency on October 5, 2010. He had been called up once, on June 6 when catcher Carlos Maldonado was placed on the 15-day disabled list with a fractured left thumb. As the third-string catcher, Burke got into only one game, with no at-bats. Burke retired as a player after the 2010 season, and after taking a year off from baseball, managed the Cedar Rapids Kernals in 2012 and the Burlington Bees in 2013, both Single-A affiliates of the California Angels.

Burke retired from baseball after the 2013 season to be with his family. Burke is now divorced and is the father of three teenage boys – Parker, Paxton, and Payson. Burke finished his degree at Oregon State in 2005 and received a teaching degree in 2024. He teaches physical education in the Oakland, Oregon, School District, where he also coaches football for the middle school and baseball at the high school.[34]

SOURCES

The author used Retrosheet.org and Baseball-Reference.com for stats and game information, and had a phone interview with Jamie Burke on December 8, 2024.

NOTES

1   Brooks Hatch, "A Few Minor Details," *Albany* (Oregon) *Democrat-Herald*, July 23, 2000: 11.

2   Walter Eugene Burke obituary, *Roseburg* (Oregon) *News-Review, August 28, 2022 ???? date??* www.nrtoday.com/obits/walter-eugene-burke/article_c5960402-ef8d-586f-9e7d-5ea09f28729c.html.

3   Telephone interview with Jamie Burke on December 8, 2024.

4   Walter Burke obituary.

5   Wiffle ball is a scaled-back version of baseball. "The Wiffle Ball Inc. – A Brief History," www.wiffle.com.

6   Jamie Burke interview.

7   Associated Press, "Prep Teams Steam Toward State Grid Championships." *Albany* (Oregon) *Democrat-Herald*, November 28, 1988: 13.

8   "DC Greats," www.douglascountysportsonline.com/dc-greats/15-dc-greats/dc-greats/700-jamie-burke. (DC is Douglas County.)

9   "DC Greats."

10   Brooks Hatch, "A Few Minor Details."

11   "DC Greats'" Brooks Hatch, "Getting the Skinny on New Posts," *Corvallis* (Oregon) *Gazette-Times*, August 21, 1991: 9.

12   Capi Lynn, "Freshman Has Toehold on Starting Kicking Spot," *Salem* (Oregon) *Statesman-Journal*, August 30, 1990: 3D.

13   Jason Quick, "OSU's Burke Gets Kicks in Two Sports," *Corvallis Gazette-Times*, November 7, 1990: 13.

14   "Beavers Lose Ballgame, Burke," *Corvallis Gazette-Times*, April 15, 1992: 13.

15   "Hot Spot: Pac-10 North Baseball," *Salem Statesman-Journal*, May 14, 1992: 27.

16   Brooks Hatch, "OSU's Kickers Ready to Back Each Other Up," *Corvallis Gazette-Times*, August 26, 1992: 11.

17   https://www.sports-reference.com/cfb/players/jamie-burke-1.html.

18   Phil Smith, "Angels Sign Oregon St. Third Baseman," *Idaho Statesman* (Boise), June 10, 1993: 3B.

19   Jason Quick, "Runnin' Down a Dream," *Corvallis Gazette-Times*, July 18, 1993: 9.

20   Quick, July 18, 1993: 12.

21   Brooks Hatch, "Burke Return Possible, but Not Likely," *Corvallis Gazette-Times*, September 13, 1993: 9.

22   "Storm Watch," *The Californian* (Salinas, California), April 13, 1995: 10.

23   "Storm Watch."

24   Jamie Burke interview

25   "Solid Redbirds Bring Drew to Town," *Edmonton* (Alberta) *Journal*, June 26, 1999: 41.

26   Norm Cowley, "Jamie Burke Getting His Swing Back After Pitch Drilled Him on the Elbow," *Edmonton Journal*, June 17, 2000: 42.

27   Brooks Hatch, "Burke: Hopes His Versatility Will Get Him to 'The Show,'" *Albany* (Oregon) *Democrat Herald*, July 23, 2000: 13.

28   "Burke: Hopes His Versatility Will Get Him to 'The Show.'"

29   Bill Jauss, "Sox Summon Burke as Olivo Insurance," *Chicago Tribune*, August 9, 2003: 3-4.

30   Teddy Greenstein, "Quick Hook Keeps Snagging Garland," *Chicago Tribune*, August 13, 2003: 4-4.

31   https://www.rotowire.com/baseball/player/jamie-burke-6682.

32   Gregg Bell, "Burke's First Career HR Leads M's," *Corvallis Gazette-Times*, October 1, 2007: 11.

33   Ryan Divish, "Burke to Replace Injured Johjima," *Tacoma* (Washington) *News Tribune*, April 17, 2009: C3.

34   Jamie Burke interview.

RAÚL CASANOVA

By Tony S. Oliver

Thanks to Giacomo Girolamo's lecherous lifestyle, "Casanova" has become shorthand for a lotario prone to incorrigible womanizing. The term, however, literally translates "new house" or "new home" in Italian. This meaning is much more adequate for Raúl Casanova, whose 21-year professional career included stints with nearly 30 teams in the major, minor, Puerto Rican, Dominican, and Mexican leagues.

Raúl Casanova was born on August 23, 1972, in Humacao, a town on Puerto Rico's eastern coast. Casanova and his older brother were raised in Ponce by his maternal grandmother, Bertha Irizarry, after their mother, Silvia Pou, left the island to pursue better economic opportunities in New York City.

Raúl would hurry home after school to watch the New York Mets on television. His New York City-raised grandmother was a devoted fan, thanks to the abundance of telecasts on cable television, and together they cheered the 1980s Mets.

When he was about 8 years old, Casanova attended a clinic by former Ponce Leones player Enrique "Quique" Rivera, who promptly assigned the skinny, tall kid to catching duties.[1] Casanova took to the position quickly: "Since then, I only played as a catcher. I liked it because you're always in the action, receiving the pitches, paying attention to the manager's signals … and giving signals to my own teammates."[2] Irizarry would attend her grandson's baseball practice and avidly cheer from the sidelines: "I remember one time I hit a long home run and she almost fainted, she was so happy. They had to bring her water! She was famous in the parks we played, everyone could her rooting, 'C'mon Raúl, hit it in the hole!'"[3]

Casanova idolized Rubén Sierra, with whom he would later play with the Santurce Cangrejeros (Crabbers) in 1994-1995 and the Detroit Tigers (in 1996). Montréal Expos scout Pepito Centeno took Casanova under his wing and encouraged him to play with a team in the San Juan metropolitan area. Casanova would play Saturday and Sunday and then return to his grandmother's house on Sunday evenings. He credits the 90-minute car ride with facilitating his career, as "baseball was more competitive in the San Juan area than in the southern portion (of the island). That helped me develop as a player … and to be determined about improving my skills."[4] In 1989, he played for the Río Piedras 134 team, which lost in the title game against Woodland Hills in the American Legion Baseball tournament.[5]

By his late teens, Casanova had grown to 6-feet and 200 pounds. Besides Centeno and the Expos, Kansas City Royals birddog Johnny Ramos scouted the prospect. Shortly after Casanova's Ponce High School graduation, Luis Rosa and Rosendo "Junior" Román persuaded the New York Mets to choose the youngster in the eighth round of the 1990 amateur draft.

Casanova was shocked by the news: "I was young, so I didn't know how (the baseball business) worked. My grandmother was very emotional, since it was her team. … It was a great blessing. I ran out to the streets and told everyone I had been drafted!"[6] The $40,000 signing bonus, paltry by today's standards, greatly helped the family, which lived in Section 8 housing and received additional government assistance.

Within a week of signing, Casanova reported to the instructional league. Away from his family for the first time, he struggled in 23 games with the Gulf Coast League

Raul Casanova   **2005**

Mets (5-for-65, no extra-base hits). Cuban American John Tamargo and Puerto Rican Román, Casanova's first two managers in the Mets organization, helped him transition to the new culture.

In 1991 Casanova improved to .243 in 32 games in the GCL but managed only one hit in 18 at-bats for Kingsport in the Appalachian League. He improved to .270/.401/.438 for Kingsport in 1992 and enjoyed a five-game call-up with Class-A Columbia. More importantly, he tried switch-hitting: "I had finished my batting cage routine and started messing around from the left side. Our catching instructor, John Gibbons, saw me and said, 'Wait a second, let me get the hitting coach.' A few swings later, they suggested I try it, reasoning I had nothing to lose since it was still the instructional league."[7]

On December 7, 1992, the Mets sent Casanova to San Diego as the player to be named later to complete a trade for infielder Tony Fernández.[8] Casanova hit .265 in 76 games with the Class-A Waterloo Diamonds in 1993. He played with Santurce in the 1992-1993 and 1993-1994 Puerto Rico Winter League (PRWL) seasons.

Casanova enjoyed his finest professional campaign in 1994 with the Class-A Advanced Rancho Cucamonga Quakes. Minor-league hitting coach Tom Robson, who had worked with Sierra in the Texas Rangers organization, altered Casanova's batting stance to unlock his power. Because of a nagging injury to his throwing elbow, he was the primary DH in the first half of the season, which allowed him to concentrate on hitting. By July 14, he had broken the team's single-season home-run record and had driven in 87 runs. However, he also excelled behind the plate and threw out four baserunners in the first three innings of a June 11 game.[9]

Casanova was chosen as the Padres' minor-league player of the year, made the California League all-star team, and won the batting title. He did not go two straight games without a hit in last the 56 games of the season to finish at .340 with a team-high 23 home runs and 120 RBIs.[10] He was even more dominant in the postseason (.485, 3 home runs, 12 RBIs in eight games) as the Quakes won the California League title. League managers named him the "Most Dangerous Hitter" and the runner-up in the "Hitter with the Best Power," "Best Batting Prospect," and "Best Defensive Catcher" awards.[11]

Teammate Bill Anderson singled out Casanova as the player who awed him the most: "What an unbelievable presence in the locker room and on the field."[12] The Padres added him to the 40-man roster after the season, and manager Tim Flannery was effusive in his praise: "You build ballclubs around guys like him. In my mind, he has made himself the top prospect in the organization."[13] Casanova was grateful for Flannery's vote of confidence: "He fought for me to be the DH … and he helped me to better understand the game. He was very positive, always keen on the little things. He greatly boosted my confidence and was key

in my development."[14] Casanova returned to Puerto Rico and played with Santurce in the 1994-1995 season but saw sporadic playing time as Junior Ortiz's backup.[15]

In 1995 *Baseball America* ranked Casanova the 60th best prospect in the minor leagues (and second-best in the San Diego system).[16] He was solid with Double-A Memphis, but not spectacular, slashing .271/.330/.448 in 89 games. Since the Padres had Brad Ausmus, a capable young catcher, as their starter, they felt no need to rush Casanova. He played with the Caguas Criollos under Sandy Alomar Sr., whom he credited as his best PRWL manager: "He gave me the opportunity as a rookie. He always taught and spoke about the positive aspects of the game. I learned a lot from him, and my confidence grew. I only played for a year with him, but afterwards, whenever he'd see me, he would continue to give me advice."[17]

On March 22, 1996, San Diego traded Casanova to the Tigers in a six-player transaction. The Padres received Cade Gaspar, Sean Bergman, and Todd Steverson while Detroit also obtained Richie Lewis and Melvin Nieves. Tigers GM Randy Smith, newly hired from San Diego, was well-versed in the Padres farm system. He called the swap a "foundation for the future" despite "a lot of inexperienced players on both ends."[18]

Casanova played eight games with Double-A Jacksonville (10-for-32) and was soon promoted to Triple-A Toledo. He was 3-for-4 with a double and a home run in a May 20 exhibition game between Toledo and the Tigers, prompting a call-up to the major leagues. According to Casanova, manager Bill Plummer "called me a few days later and asked me to come to the park very early … so I arrived, and I'm told, 'You're going to the big leagues.' I got goosebumps … started crying, and my mind raced to memories of those who helped me get to this stage, but first and foremost was my grandmother, who raised me. In Detroit, my locker was next to Cecil Fielder's. … All I did was listen to him, Alan Trammell, Lou Whitaker."[19] Sadly, Casanova's grandmother had died and was unable to see their dream fulfilled.

Casanova debuted for the Tigers on May 24, 1996, against the Cleveland Indians as the designated hitter. He fought the customary nerves: "Even though people couldn't see it, my knees were shaking, but I settled down after that first at-bat. Detroit was predominantly an African American city and I was given a Barry White song ("Casanova") that stuck with me. The fans liked the song and started singing along when I came to the plate."[20] He struck out on three pitches against Brian Anderson in his first at-bat and was hitless in the next three, but almost got a hit in his last appearance with a line drive that Albert Belle, a notoriously poor fielder, caught before it hit the grass. He was the starting catcher the next day and walked in his last plate appearance.

Casanova started 0-for-10 as *Baseball Weekly* fretted that he "might represent management's first premature call-up," though it noted "[G]ood defensive mechanics but needs work at the plate."[21] He broke through against Kansas City with a single off Tim Belcher on May 27 for his first major-league hit. Two days later, a seventh-inning solo home run off Kevin Appier tied the game before Nieves drove in the winning run in the eighth.

On June 6 Casanova became the 73rd player to homer from both sides of the plate in the same game.[22] Both his third-inning shot against right-hander Jimmy Haynes and his seventh-inning blast against left-hander Rick Krivda were in vain as the Orioles bested the Tigers, 13-6.[23] It was be the only time in his major-league career that Casanova hit two home runs in one game, and the feat may have bought him some additional time on the big-league roster. But a freak injury derailed his rookie season. While swinging a bat in the clubhouse, Casanova fractured a bone in his left wrist and spent two months on the disabled list. In his absence, Smith traded for Ausmus, but Detroit recalled Casanova in September. He ended the season with a .188 batting average in 25 games.

Detroit traded Ausmus to Houston during the winter meetings. While the Tigers envisioned Casanova as their future catcher, they optioned him to Toledo to begin the 1997 season. After 12 games in Triple A, he was called up when Matt Walbeck broke his wrist. Despite trepidation given his struggles the prior year, Bell and Smith "would rather see Casanova get at-bats every day, but they didn't want to send a message that would affect his confidence."[24] Casanova caught a career-high 92 games (and appeared in nine others). He enjoyed a trio of three-hit games and a nine-game hitting streak in late May to early June but cooled off in July to end the season with .243/.308/.332 averages.

In 1998 a poor start (.143 in April) and injuries limited Casanova to 16 games with the Tigers and 50 with Toledo. Detroit had signed veteran Joe Oliver to "push Casanova a little bit," but Paul Bako ended up catching most of the team's games.[25]

A rib fracture sidelined Casanova in the first half of 1999. He appeared in 44 games with Toledo, a pair with the GCL Tigers, and four with Class-A Advanced Lakeland. He became a free agent on October 15, and two months later signed with the Colorado Rockies.

Casanova hit .331 and won the 1999-2000 PRWL batting title for his hometown Leones.[26] At the time, he was the fifth catcher to pace the league in hitting.[27] He cherished the opportunity to play at home: "The stadium was five minutes away from my house. The owners (the Muñoz family) treated me very well, with a lot of respect. Those years were spectacular. ... I had a lot of fun and developed greatly as a player."[28] Santurce added him to its roster for the Caribbean Series, which the Crabbers dominated (unbeaten in six games) as Casanova hit .313 with 6 RBIs.[29]

Despite his winter-league success, the Rockies released Casanova at the end of spring training. He signed with Milwaukee and had a strong comeback year in 2000. He played in 86 games and drove in a career-high 36 runs while sharing catching duties with Henry Blanco, a better defender but weaker hitter.

On June 12 Casanova had three hits and three RBIs against the Montréal Expos. He hit his first career grand slam a day later, the only runs Milwaukee scored in a 9-4 defeat. On August 2 he doubled to break a 4-4 tie against the San Francisco Giants in a 6-4 Brewers victory. Manager Davey Lopes lauded his catcher, noting, "He's been doing an outstanding job ever since we brought him up the big leagues. He's had several chances before but has failed. ... This is a new lease on life for him. ... Right now, he's a guy you like to see at the plate on these situations."[30]

In the last game at Milwaukee County Stadium, on September 28, 2000, Casanova had the team's last two hits and last run, the lone Brewer to cross the plate in an 8-1 loss to San Diego.

In 2001 Casanova slashed .260/.303/.484 in 71 games with a career-high 11 home runs but missed the last two months of the regular season with cartilage damage in his left knee. The Brewers re-signed him for $800,000 during the offseason.

Before the 2002 season, the Brewers traded Blanco to the Atlanta Braves for Bako, but Casanova endured his worst year since 1998. A rare highlight came on April 7, a single off Curt Schilling in the third inning of a scoreless game. Schilling allowed no other safeties, walking two and striking out 17 for his second career one-hitter.

Casanova hit a grand slam on May 12 against the Cubs but suffered a miserable start (16-for-87). After a three-month stint on the disabled list with a torn UCL, Milwaukee released him on September 3. Eight days later, he signed with Baltimore and appeared in two games but struck out in his sole plate appearance. The club released him on October 1.

Casanova spent the next two years in the minors with the Rockies (2003), Orioles (2003), Red Sox (2004), and Royals (2004) organizations. Though he hit .296 in 2003 and .310 in 2004, he was not promoted to the major leagues. In 2004 he led the PRWL in RBIs as the primary DH (sharing catching dues with José "Cheo" Molina) for the title-winning Ponce team, managed by José Cruz Sr.

The White Sox signed Casanova to a minor-league deal on February 17, 2005. He was solid in 70 games with Triple-A Charlotte (.266/.326/.489) but the parent club, which led the AL Central wire-to-wire, was set at catcher with A.J. Pierzynski (18 home runs in 460 at-bats) and capable backup Chris Widger (.241 in 45 games). On the last day of spring training, GM Ken Williams had told Casanova, "Raúl, if you do a good job, I'll bring you up."[31]

The club called up Casanova in September once rosters expanded. He appeared in six games, five as a defensive replacement and one as a pinch-hitter. Behind the plate, he fielded nine chances without an error in 14 innings. Chicago was 5-1 in his appearances and Casanova went 1-for-5 at the plate, his lone hit being a single against the Angels on September 10.

Casanova recalled his White Sox experience fondly: "It was a wonderful learning experience. I had the opportunity to be surrounded by many talented teammates. It was an unforgettable year. Once the game started, we were unbeatable. Ozzie Guillén kept the team relaxed and with a good attitude."[32] The manager "did not pressure us, he gave us good advice. ... Whenever he would get upset with us, it was with the goal of improving our play."[33]

Casanova enjoyed the camaraderie with Guillén, third-base coach Joey Cora, and pitchers Orlando "El Duque" Hernández, José Contreras, and Freddy García. Though he was not on the postseason roster, he was on the reserve list, capable of being activated in case of injuries to the White Sox catchers, and received a World Series ring.

Granted free agency after the World Series, Casanova signed with the Oakland Athletics on January 5, 2006. He played eight games in the minors (9-for-34). Oakland did not call him up and did not re-sign him at the end of the season. Casanova won the MVP award in 2006-07, this time with Caguas.[34]

Casanova agreed to terms with Tampa Bay on January 12, 2007. He was solid with Triple-A Durham (.291/.346/.461) and received a midseason promotion to the major leagues when backup receiver Josh Paul sprained his left elbow. Casanova appeared in 21 games in June and July and hit six home runs. He returned to the majors in mid-September but managed only one extra-base hit in 24 at-bats. In 89 plate appearances with Tampa Bay, he hit .253/.315/.519.

Casanova played in the Dominican Republic Winter League during the 2007-08 season. His .355 on-base percentage was solid, but he had only four extra base-hits among his 28 singles for the Leones (Lions) del Escogido.

Casanova signed with the New York Mets organization on December 4, 2007, coming full circle to his first professional franchise. He broke camp with the parent club in 2008 and played in 20 games through early June. In his last major-league game, on June 8 against the San Diego Padres, he was 1-for-3 with a single and a walk. His last home run, off John Smoltz, was memorable: "I went 3-for-4 with two RBIs. ... I thought, 'Hey, today I'll be the Player of the Game ... but then Carlos Delgado hit two home runs!'"[35]

Although Casanova's .344 OBP was respectable for a catcher, the Mets optioned him to Triple-A New Orleans given his anemic power output (one home run, two doubles in 61 plate appearances). He hit .295 with the Zephyrs in 44 games but did not return to the major leagues, despite

lackluster numbers from Brian Schneider, Ramón Castro, and Robinson Cancel with the parent club.

The Mets granted Casanova free agency on September 30, and he ended his major-league career with 387 games played, 255 hits, 98 runs scored, and a .236 batting average. Though he wished his career had been more successful, he nevertheless "gives thank to God. When a player suffers a lot of injuries, he is typically sent down to the minors and eventually released. I had many opportunities as people saw my talent, the sacrifices I made, and how seriously I approached the game."[36]

Casanova played in the (summer) Mexican League in 2009 with the Tigres (Tigers) of Quintana Roo. After 64 games (.267/.373/.403) the club released him on June 15. He signed with Reynosa for the stretch run 10 days later and was spectacular in 31 contests for the Broncos (.342/.418/.513). He went 6-for-22 as Reynosa fell in the first round of the playoffs to Saltillo.[37]

Casanova retired from the PRWL after the 2010-11 season, which he split between Mayaguez and Ponce. To Casanova, the PRWL "was everything. It helped me develop as a player. I worked at all of things I need to improve, especially hitting from the right side and throwing to second base. ... When you play against such fine competition, it's imperative to learn as otherwise you'll be on the bench."[38]

Casanova concluded his playing career with the Patillas Leones of the Puerto Rico semiprofessional league (Liga Béisbol Doble-A de Puerto Rico) in 2010. A year later, he managed the Maunabo Jueyeros (Crabbers) to the championship, and led the Las Piedras Artesanos (Artisans) in 2014 and the Fajardo Cariduros in 2022.

In 2021 Casanova served as an envoy to Ecuador as part of the US State Department's sports diplomacy program.[39] As of 2024, he lived in the San Juan metropolitan area with his second wife, Mariela González, and five sons. He accepted Jesus Christ as his Savior in 2011 and operates two businesses named El Shaddai (a name for God found in the Book of Genesis): a restaurant and a hitting center that offers batting and catching instruction. The latter, a lifelong ambition, is a source of pride and joy: "I love what I do. I understand the need to teach. ... Puerto Rico lags in the production of baseball players. I met with Commissioner (Rob) Manfred (and others) and was asked, 'How come Puerto Rico is not producing many players?' My answer was that Puerto Rico has a lot of talent ... but the coaching from ages 8-14 is lacking. You can't expect a young kid who does not get the right training to suddenly become a stud at 15. I'd love to run seminars for coaches."[40]

GRINDERS AND GAMERS

ACKNOWLEDGMENTS

Raúl Casanova for answering the author's questions via text message.

SOURCES

In addition to the sources cited in the Notes, the author consulted baseball-reference.com, thebaseballcube.com, and beisbol101.com.

NOTES

1   Rivera played eight seasons in the minor leagues, mostly with the St. Louis Cardinals.

2   "Raúl Casanova, un maestro con el bate que comparte la palabra de Dios en el mundo del béisbol," *Baseball Ahora,* YouTube, July 6, 2020, https://www.youtube.com/watch?v=8GKCavDjW58.

3   "Raúl Casanova, un maestro con el bate que comparte la palabra de Dios en el mundo del béisbol."

4   "Raúl Casanova en vivo," Baseball Fogueo PR, https://www.facebook.com/watch/live/?ref=watch_permalink&v=280342146414113.

5   American Legion Baseball National Champions, https://www.legion.org/documents/baseball/national_champions.pdf.

6   "Raúl Casanova en vivo," Baseball Fogueo PR.

7   "Raúl Casanova, un maestro con el bate que comparte la palabra de Dios en el mundo del béisbol," *Baseball Ahora.*

8   Casanova was the player to be named later; Wally Whitehurst and D.J. Dozier had been originally included in the transaction.

9   Back of 1996 Bowman Foil #352 baseball card, https://www.tcdb.com/GalleryP.cfm/pid/20195/Raul-Casanova?ColType=0&sYear=0&sTeam=&sCardNum=&sNote=&sSetName=&sBrand=&PageIndex=4#google_vignette.

10 Bruce Chick (.372) and Jason Thompson (.360) had fewer than 300 plate appearances.

11 "Quakes' Casanova Wins Honor," *San Bernardino* (California) *Sun,* September 21, 1994: C2.

12 David Blow, "Blow by Blow," Lulu Publishing Services, 2013: 157.

13 *Baseball Digest,* March 1995, https://www.baseball-almanac.com/players/trades.php?p=casanra01.

14 "Raúl Casanova en vivo," Baseball Fogueo PR.

15 After winning the 1994-1995 PRWL title, Santurce outscored its opponents, 55-15, in the Caribbean Series, winning all its six games.

16 The Baseball Cube, Raúl Casanova page, https://www.thebaseballcube.com/content/prospects_team_year/1995~24~BA/.

17 "Raúl Casanova, un maestro con el bate que comparte la palabra de Dios en el mundo del béisbol," *Baseball Ahora.*

18 Associated Press, "Tigers Swap with A's, Padres," *Kokomo* (Indiana) *Tribune,* March 23, 1996: B4.

19 "Mi primera tacita de café (My first cup of coffee)," February 2023, https://open.spotify.com/episode/3QF3vK7lMP9kuohxjPthKw.

20 "Mi primera tacita de café."

21 Reid Creager, "Detroit Tigers, A.L. East," *USA Today Baseball Weekly,* June 3, 1993: 31.

22 "Home Runs from Both Sides of the Plate in One Game," Baseball Almanac, https://www.baseball-almanac.com/feats/feats20.shtml.

23 Baltimore Orioles 13, Detroit Tigers 6, June 6, 1996, https://www.retrosheet.org/boxesetc/1996/B06060BAL1996.htm.

24 Redi Creager, "Catch-22: Casanova Gets Reluctant Call," *The Sporting News,* April 28, 1997: 34.

25 Tom Gage, "Baseball: Tigers," *The Sporting News,* January 5, 1998: 68.

26 Jorge Colón-Delgado, "Valores del año 2020-21," *Béisbol101,* January 11, 2021, https://beisbol101.com/valores-del-ano-2020-21-johneshwy-fargas-hace-historia/.

27 He was preceded by *Josh Gibson* (1941-42), *Brian Harper* (1982-83), *Orlando Sánchez* (1984-85), and *Héctor Villanueva* (1990-91). Jonathan Morales (2020-2021) was the sixth (and last through 2023).

28 "Raúl Casanova, un maestro con el bate que comparte la palabra de Dios en el mundo del béisbol," *Baseball Ahora.*

29 Tom Van Hyning, "Comparing the February 1995 'Dream Team' to February 2000 Santurce Cangrejeros," *Béisbol 101,* March 8, 2019, https://beisbol101.com/comparing-the-february-1995-dream-team-to-february-2000-santurce-cangrejeros/.

30 Associated Press, "When Good Road Tips Go Bad: Giants Lose Finale," *Santa Cruz* (California) *Sentinel,* August 3, 2000: D1.

31 "Raúl Casanova en vivo," Baseball Fogueo PR.

32 Text message conversation between Raúl Casanova and the author, May 4, 2024.

33 "Raúl Casanova, un maestro con el bate que comparte la palabra de Dios en el mundo del béisbol," *Baseball Ahora.*

34 Jorge Colón-Delgado, "David Vidal: Jugador Más Valioso 2018," *Béisbol 101,* January 27, 2018, https://beisbol101.com/david-vidal-jugador-mas-valioso-2018/.

35 "Raúl Casanova en vivo."

36 "Raúl Casanova en vivo."

37 https://www.milb.com/es/mexican/stats/games/2009/postseason-cumulative?page=2&sortState=asc.

38 "Raúl Casanova en vivo."

39 "Raúl Casanova," Sports Diplomacy, U.S. Department of State, https://sportsenvoy.org/cpt_alumni/raul-casanova/

40 "Raúl Casanova en vivo."

JOSÉ CONTRERAS

By Tony S. Oliver

"Pressure-tested." The label suited José Contreras, the ace of the formidable Cuban national team of the 1990s that dominated international competition. Fidel Castro himself had deemed the pitcher *"el titán de bronce"* (the bronze titan), a nickname first bestowed upon Cuban Revolutionary hero Antonio Maceo, one of the country's founding fathers.

How could José Contreras wilt under pressure? "People would tell me, 'Wow, you pitched in a sold-out Yankee Stadium.' But I'd already pitched in a full park, the Estadio Latinoamericano. I trained for three months to go to Atlanta and win the Gold Medal in a 10-game competition. If you get off to a bad start, if you lose two games, you're out of the tournament. … You have to wait four more years … (and) cost you four years of work."[1]

José Ariel Contreras Camejo was born on December 6, 1971, in Las Martinas, an agricultural town in the western-most Cuban province, Pinar del Río. As the youngest child, he helped his parents, Florentino and Modesta, and eight siblings grow tobacco on the family farm, which lacked electricity until his late teens. Contreras, who rode his horse

Jose Contreras   2005

to school, dreamed of becoming a veterinarian until he was discovered by former Cuban national team pitcher Jesús Guerra Hernández in a sandlot game.

Barefoot and shirtless, Contreras played third base and threw a perfect strike to first – from his knees. Impressed, Guerra Hernández said, "Come with me to the Youth Academy, and in two years you'll be on the Cuban national team."[2] Until then, Contreras preferred volleyball to the Cuban national pastime.

Two years later, the 6-foot-4, 255-pound Contreras debuted in the Cuban *Serie Nacional* (National Series)1991-1992 season. Under the tutelage of Guerra Hernández (whom Contreras considered a second father) and Juan Carlos Oliva (Tony Oliva's brother), Contreras blossomed into the top starter of his hometown *Vegueros* (Tobacco Growers) and a formidable one-two punch with fellow flamethrower Pedro Luis Lazo.

Coach Maximiliano Gutiérrez suggested a new pitch: the forkball. A quick study, Contreras fanned contact hitter Lourdes Gurriel Sr. twice. The stunned batter asked Contreras about the pitch. "Oh, that's a forkball I'm learning," said Contreras. "Learning it? That's your pitch!" replied Gurriel. Contreras, who had "heard the bat blowing in the wind" in the two at-bats, marveled at the praise from one of Cuba's all-time greats.[3]

Now blessed with two devastating pitches, Contreras appeared in 232 games from 1991 through 2002 and posted a 117-50 record with a 2.82 ERA in 4,419 innings.[4] The team won the National Series Championships in 1996-1997 and 1997-1998.

Contreras represented Gold Medal-winning *selección nacional* in the 1998 and 2001 World Baseball Cup, the 1996 Olympic Games, the 1995 Intercontinental Cup, the 1998 Central American & Caribbean Games, and the 1999 Pan-American Games. Only twice, in the 1997 Intercontinental Cup and the 2000 Olympics, did the squad finish as runners-up.

In the 1999 Pan-American games, Contreras pitched six innings in a Saturday semifinal game against the Dominican Republic and fanned 13 Americans in eight innings two days later.[5] Perhaps his finest amateur hour was in the 2000 Summer Olympics, when he struck out 13 opponents in 12 innings in the first round.[6] The Cubans thought Japan was their toughest opponent and opted to start Contreras, who tossed a six-hit, nine-strikeout shutout in the semifinal.

But it meant he was not available for the final, won by the Tommy LaSorda-managed Team USA. As Contreras recalled, "We were in shock. … At that time we were beating everybody easily. … We had that streak. We had a very good team. And the US was playing with minor leaguers. The Cuban National Team wasn't prepared to lose that game."[7]

Fans wondered how Contreras would fare against US major-league talent. A relative thaw in US-Cuba relations under President Bill Clinton presented the opportunity to use baseball as a diplomatic tool, and the Baltimore Orioles agreed to take part in a two-game series. In the Havana opener on March 28, 1999, the Orioles chased Cuban starter José Ibar after two innings. Contreras, in relief, dominated the major leaguers, striking out 10 in eight shutout frames. Although Baltimore won, 3-2, in 11 innings, stateside press was awed by his performance.[8] Milton H. Jamail noted that it "may have been the most widely seen tryout camp in the history of baseball."[9] A 56-minute rain delay and demonstrations by Cuban exiles (including one who ran onto the field in the fifth inning and tussled with a Cuban-born umpire) marred the second game, held in Baltimore on May 3, 1999. While Contreras struggled (three runs, two earned, in 1⅓ innings), the Cuban team outslugged the Orioles, 12-6.

Contreras was constantly approached by well-meaning agents as well as charlatans. He was stoic in his determination: "For this sum ($50 million), not any other, would I turn my back on my family, on my people, or on my homeland? I have a lot of respect, confidence, and admiration for Fidel."[10] *El Comandante* had a soft spot for his bronze titan and gifted him a Peugeot 406, a veritable luxury in 1990s Cuba, when the island's economy sputtered after the disintegration of the Soviet Union and the disappearance of economic subsidies.

Although officially the Cuban socialist government believes in equality, athletes receive "considerations" for their feats. Contreras, who lived in a "sports hotel" (essentially a dormitory), was promised a home but it was much delayed. Additionally, it was in dire need of repairs, and for two years he waited for the promised assistance. When his car broke down in the summer of 2002, Contreras asked sports Minister Humberto Rodríguez for money to pay for its repairs. Not only was the plea rebuffed but Rodríguez nonchalantly told Contreras to find his own way home. The humiliation was too much to bear for a proud man who had nothing left to prove in amateur baseball.

Contreras resolved to defect but was torn about losing the support of his countrymen: "Cubans love baseball and I would see how not the people but the government would insult those who 'deserted' via the state media."[11] Before he departed for Saltillo, Mexico, for the American Series in October, his father told him to stay loyal. He could not tell his family, an unfathomable burden.

On October 1 Contreras tossed a complete-game, six-hit, one-run victory against the Dominican Republic.[12]

Only he knew it would be the last of his 14 wins for the national team. Contreras and coach Miguel Valdés eluded their chaperones at their hotel and traveled over 1,300 miles to Tijuana, near the US border. They hid for a week amid rumors that Castro was offering a reward for his kidnapping and return to the island.

By then news spread quickly in Cuba, and the government bitterly castigated its one-time star. Contreras spoke with his siblings over the phone but was concerned about the reaction of his wife, Miriam Murillo-Flores, and his father. The elder Contreras assuaged him: "You were my José in Cuba and you will be my José in the United States."[13]

Had Contreras stayed in the United States, he would have been subject to a nine-month wait before the amateur draft. By moving to Nicaragua, he was deemed an international free agent. Teams skipped the traditional tryout and jumped into negotiations. Agent Jaime Torres counseled his client to be calm, but the pitcher, who had earned $1 a month in Cuba, could hardly believe his ears. When Torres rebuffed Pat Gillick's Toronto offer, Contreras screamed. "I jumped from the chair. … I asked 'Jaime, what did he say?' … He told me to remain calm, but I answered, 'How can I be calm? I heard $19 million, and that's the same in English, Spanish, or Russian!'"[14]

The acrimonious bidding war led Boston Red Sox President Larry Lucchino to comment, "The evil empire extends its tentacles even into Latin America" as the Yankees signed Contrera to a $32 million, four-year contract.[15]

Introduced to the New York press in early February, Contreras sought to avoid politics and concentrate on baseball: "I could talk about Cuba. I could talk about Cuban baseball, but I am not here as a politician, to talk about politics."[16] During a difficult spring training (10.38 ERA),[17] Orlando Hernández counseled him "Don't read the New York press too much or else it'll drive you crazy."[18] As if the tabloid frenzy were not enough, his father, Florentino, suffered a stroke in Cuba, and Contreras did not see him again before his death in 2004.[19]

Contreras debuted in the major leagues on Opening Day, March 31, 2003, against the Toronto Blue Jays. He relieved Roger Clemens and allowed a leadoff double to Eric Hinske to start the seventh inning but struck out Orlando Hudson, Chris Woodward, and Ken Huckaby to escape the jam. In the eighth inning, he left the bases loaded with two outs. Two runs scored, charged to Contreras, but the Yankees won, 8-4.

By mid-April, Contreras's 10.80 ERA prompted the Yankees to send him to the minor leagues. GM Brian Cashman noted, "We can't afford for long stretches of time to provide the learning curve at the major-league level. If it's best for him to go down, so be it."[20] After merely six games (2-0, 41 strikeouts, seven walks in 27⅔ innings), Contreras rejoined New York but a sore shoulder sidelined him most of the summer. He finished the season with a 7-2 record, one hold, one blown save, and a 3.30 ERA. More importantly, the Yankees won 13 of his 18 appearances.

Contreras did not pitch in the AL Division Series against the Minnesota Twins and struggled against the Red Sox in the Championship Series (four appearances, 5.79 ERA) and the Marlins in the World Series (four games, 5.68 ERA). Pressed into emergency relief in Game Five after starter David Wells suffered back spasms, he allowed four runs in three innings and took the loss.

Contreras was uncomfortable in the bullpen: "All my career, I was a starter. … When I went to the bullpen to relieve, I thought it would be easy, but it wasn't. I thought I'd throw two innings and just try to get outs. I did that, but it wasn't that simple. To prepare yourself psychologically, it's not the same. To prepare yourself physically, it's not the same."[21]

A revamped Yankee starting rotation in 2004 opened a spot. Contreras contributed eight victories in 18 starts, but puzzled pitching coach Mel Stottlemyre with his inconsistency: "From the windup, I'm really happy with him," Stottlemyre said. "From the stretch, he still rushes a little bit."[22] Contreras acknowledged that he "would go to the mound and (I) would load myself up with too many thoughts. … In the past, I was never like that."[23]

Contreras, in fact, battled more than just hitters. It had been more than 18 months since he had last seen Miriam and daughters Naylenis and Naylan. Contreras would "come (home) after a game and often cry. I'd come back to an empty sofa, an empty house."[24] As is customary when athletes desert, the Castro government made life difficult for relatives left behind. Contreras bitterly remembered that "[t]hey were making life very difficult, accusing her or just thinking of leaving. They threatened not to give her an exit visa for five years, and I'm sure they threatened to put her in jail on whatever trumped-up charges they could come up with."[25] Contreras believed Castro himself was behind the decision: "I think he's disappointed in the decision I made, and he's taking it out on my family. It bothers me. During eight years, I gave all I had to the team and the country. If (the Cuban government) thought about that, they would think to release my family."[26]

In June 2024 Miriam, the girls, and 18 other Cubans escaped on a speedboat that landed on Big Pine Key, about 100 miles southwest of Miami.[27] At the time, under the so-called "wet foot, dry foot" policy, Cubans who reached the mainland would be allowed to apply for political asylum, while those intercepted at sea would be returned to the island. The reunited couple welcomed a third child, José Florentino, in 2006.

On June 27, 2004, with his wife and daughters in attendance, Contreras pitched six shutout innings in the Yankees' 8-1 victory over the New York Mets. Catcher John Flaherty remarked, "It actually seemed like he was having more fun doing his job today. Obviously, his family has a lot to do with that. But there have been more smiles in that corner the last three days than we've seen in the last year and a half."[28] Ominously, Torre told reporters, "When things aren't going well, there's a tendency to think of all the bad things in your life. That's a huge thing that hadn't been settled. Now it has been. That should help. But he still has to go out and pitch."[29]

The Yankees traded Contreras to the Chicago White Sox on July 31, 2004, for Esteban Loaíza. Cashman was diplomatic: "José Contreras has a great deal of talent and a ceiling, and you see it and you get excited. But we just felt that, right now, in our situation, Esteban Loaíza would be more reliable for us in accomplishing what we're trying to accomplish."[30] The *New York Post*, not known for its tact, proclaimed, "[T]he Yankees got rid of a big headache. … This club has designs too grand to keep playing camp counselor to Contreras. … And he still is battling all kinds of cultural and language differences, even with his wife and children now by his side."[31] Few questioned the decision-maker: "George (Steinbrenner) got tired of Contreras, plain and simple," wrote one newsman.[32]

Although heartbroken about the trade, Contreras understood the rationale, saying, "Any team would have traded me for two sacks of oranges because I was not doing well."[33] Contreras was warmly welcomed by his new White Sox teammates, and despite his uneasiness, he shared a tequila shot with manager Ozzie Guillén the night before his first start.[34] Guillén told him, "I'm sticking with you because you are going to give me what I need," boosting his confidence.[35]

Contreras was 4-1 in August for the White Sox despite allowing 15 earned runs in 38⅓ innings. He struggled in September (three losses, three no-decisions) before an impressive eight scoreless innings against the Royals in the season finale.

Orestes "Minnie" Miñoso, Chicago's Cuban ambassador, was a huge supporter. When Contreras first met him, "I started crying. It was history. That smile too. I will never forget that smile. Minnie is our Jackie Robinson. He was one of the first Latinos in the big leagues."[36] While in the United States Miñoso is rightly recognized as a pioneer, Cubans on the island were admonished for mentioning his name: "It was a crime to watch (major-league) baseball. I learned about (Miñoso, Luis Tiant, Atanasio "Tony" Pérez) when I got here in 2002."[37]

Though not seen as preseason favorites, the 2005 White Sox won an AL-leading 99 games and 11 more in the postseason. Starters Mark Buehrle (16-8), Freddy García (14-8), Jon Garland (18-10), and Contreras (15-7) reached double-digit victories and Orlando Hernández added nine.

On August 9 Contreras handcuffed the Yankees in seven innings, yielding only three singles and two walks for a 2-1 victory. Derek Jeter noted, "Contreras (has) done it for us before. He pitched well. … He didn't do it as consistently as he probably would have liked to, but he's got great stuff and he mixes it up."[38] Contreras began to throw side-arm more often: "I had that angle in Cuba, but I hadn't thrown with it much here. Being around El Duque (Hernández) so much, I've gotten to work at it and gotten results from it."[39]

After an August 15 loss against Minnesota to drop his record to 7-7, Contreras won his next eight games and was named the AL Pitcher of the Month for September. To Contreras "[T]he biggest adjustment was the strike zone. It's larger in amateur (Cuban) baseball. I also had to study the hitters, which I didn't do in Cuba. There, I knew what I had to throw. … But here (in the majors) there are 30 teams, and sometimes they call up someone from Triple A and you wonder where he came from."[40] His streak couldn't have come at a better time. Chicago's 15-game lead over Cleveland in the Central Division had shrunk to a mere game and a half by September 24.

Contreras was superb in the postseason and started each series opener. He allowed two runs in 7⅔ innings against Boston in the Division Series. In the Championship Series against the Angels, he lost the first game, 3-2. After the White Sox hurlers tossed three consecutive complete-game victories, Contreras won the clincher, 6-3, going the distance despite an hourlong rain delay in the fifth inning. After the interruption, Contreras retired the last 12 Angels in a row. He won Game One of the World Series as Chicago swept Houston.

Contreras said of the Windy City: "Chicago is home. … I feel like this is where I belong, and this is my forever home."[41] Among his professional feats, "the best moment was 2005, when we won the World Series. … It'd been 89 years since the city had last won, and we were able to win with a team no one thought was capable."[42]

Contreras started strong in 2006. He won his first nine decisions and was named the AL Pitcher of the Month for April. His July 14 loss snapped a streak of 17 consecutive victories that dated back to the prior August. Although he missed two weeks in May with a pinched nerve in his right leg and his ERA increased to 4.27, Contreras won 13 games and was named to the All-Star Team, his sole appearance in the midsummer classic. Pitching coach Don Cooper marveled: "I've never seen anyone improve that much. Thank God he did, because we've all got rings."[43]

Contreras regressed in 2007 (5.57 ERA, 10-17) and 2008 (7-6, 4.54 ERA). He struggled in 2009 (0-5, 8.19 ERA) and was briefly demoted to the minors. Upon his return, he won two straight starts (16 shutout innings) but by the end of August, he fell out of favor with a 5-13 record and a 5.42 ERA.

The White Sox traded Contreras on August 31, 2009, to the Colorado Rockies for minor leaguer Brandon Hynick. For the Rockies, Contreras contributed 17 strong innings (3 runs, 17 strikeouts, 8 walks) in seven games during the stretch run. The surprising Rockies finished 92-70 but lost in the Division Series to the Philadelphia Phillies. Contreras tossed two innings in the postseason (two walks, three strikeouts, one run) but Colorado declined to offer him a contract for 2010.

Philadelphia was impressed by the 37-year old's performance and signed him in February 2010. As a middle reliever, Contreras was 6-4 in 67 games with a 3.34 ERA and tossed four scoreless innings in the postseason, but the Phillies lost to the World Series champion San Francisco Giants. Contreras returned to Philadelphia in 2011 (3.86 ERA) and 2012 (5.27 ERA) in 34 games and won his last major-league decision on May 16, 2012, against the Chicago Cubs. Pitching against the Miami Marlins, he suffered a torn ulterior cruciate ligament and a torn flexor pronator tendon in his pitching elbow in a game on June 1 that was his last appearance with the Phillies.[44] He underwent Tommy John surgery shortly thereafter.

Contreras signed with the Pittsburgh Pirates on February 23, 2013. He was released after seven games (five runs in five innings). Though he inked a deal with the Boston Red Sox the next day, he struggled in Triple-A Pawtucket and was released.

In 11 years in the major leagues, Contreras pitched in 299 games (175 starts, 78-67). Although his 4.57 ERA, 4.29 FIP, and 100 ERA+ reflect an average performance, one must consider that he debuted in the major leagues at age 31 after many years of overuse. He was better in the postseason (4-3, 3.49 ERA, 38 strikeouts, 11 walks in 49 innings). Contreras also played in Mexico, Taiwan, and the Dominican Republic.

In 2024 Contreras and his second wife, María Isabel Silva, lived in Atlanta with their teenage son, Joseph, a coveted baseball prospect who played in the 2024 Double Duty Classic, a showcase of the nation's best inner-city baseball talent.[45] (The name honors Ted "Double Duty" Radcliffe, a Negro League player who would routinely pitch both games of a doubleheader.)

Contreras is also a proud stepfather to Walter Lenys and Kevin, María Isabel's children from a prior relationship. In 2024 the elder Contreras also played in the Cooperstown East-West Game, a tribute to the pioneers that included 30 former big-leaguers.[46]

Contreras has served as an assistant to the White Sox general manager and mentors young Cuban talent, such as Yoán Moncada, Luis Robert, Bryan Ramos, and Oscar Colás.[47] In his free time, he helps aspiring young hurlers through Contreras 52 Pitching & Consulting. More than a business, he considers it a calling: "Baseball has given me a lot."[48] His desire to "pay it forward" was shaped by his relationship with Miñoso.[49]

ACKNOWLEDGMENTS

José Contreras for graciously agreeing to a phone interview with the author on October 10, 2024.

Michael Marsh for sharing his research on José Contreras with the author.

Don Zminda, whose contacts with the Chicago White Sox helped the author connect to José Contreras.

SOURCES

Besides the sources referenced in the Notes, the author consulted Baseball-reference.com and retrosheet.org.

Unless otherwise noted, quotations are from the author's telephone interview with José Contreras on October 10, 2024.

NOTES

1   "The Global Game Podcast: Episode 1," World Baseball and Softball Confederation, April 16, 2021, https://open.spotify.com/show/4yY2L3mJmPzuFT3aGkypFe.

2   "Capítulo 30: José Contreras," *Modo Béisbol,* July 31, 2021, https://www.youtube.com/watch?v=8PFVn_aOux4

3   Daniel de Malas, "Nunca antes contando: Mano a mano con José Contreras, de Pinar a Chicago," *FepCuba Canal Oficial de YouTube,* July 4, 2024, https://www.youtube.com/watch?v=F8yjLdw1QNo.

4   "Estadísticas José Contreras," *Béisbol Cubano,* accessed October 6, 2024, https://www.beisbolcubano.cu/estadisticas/Jugador?idJugador=3201.

5   Associated Press, "Plus: Pan American Games; Cuba Beats U.S. for Baseball Gold," *New York Times,* August 3, 1999, https://www.nytimes.com/1999/08/03/sports/plus-pan-american-games-cuba-beats-us-for-baseball-gold.html.

6   "Baseball: Official Report of the XXVII Olympiad-Results," LA84 Foundation, accessed October 6, 2024, https://digital.la84.org/digital/collection/p17103coll8/id/50011/rec/6.

7   Adam McCalvy, "Baseball's 'Miracle on Grass': An Oral History," MLB.com, September 27, 2024, https://www.mlb.com/news/featured/oral-history-team-usa-wins-gold-at-2000-olympics.

8   Richard Justice, "Orioles Leave Cuba With a Win," *Washington Post,* March 29, 1999: D1, https://www.washingtonpost.com/wp-srv/sports/orioles/daily/march99/29/os29.htm.

9   Milton H. Jamail, *Full Count: Inside Cuban Baseball* (Carbondale, Illinois: Southern Illinois University Press, 2000), 145.

10   Wright Thompson, "Jose Contreras' Long Road from Las Martinas, Cuba," *Kansas City Star,* March 30, 2003, https://www.kansascity.com/sports/mlb/article73764467.html.

11   Aliet Arzola, "Contra Reloj: José Ariel Contreras, el Titán al descubierto," *OnCuba News,* May 10, 2021, https://www.youtube.com/watch?v=9axPOd7U4u8Ierto.

12   Associated Press, "Contreras Confirmed as Defector, Coach Valdés Missing," ESPN.com, October 4, 2022, https://www.espn.com/oly/news/2002/1004/1441357.html.

13   Thompson, "Jose Contreras' Long Road from Las Martinas, Cuba."

14   Alfre Alvarez, "Qué Pasa MLB: José Ariel Contreras: Así fue como me escapé de CUBA para jugar GRANDES LIGAS." *Que Pasa MLB/Amor beisbolero,* March 14, 2022, https://www.youtube.com/watch?v=8G8UEHLBhkc.

15   Murray Chass, "Baseball: What's $32 Million More? Yanks Sign Contreras," *New York Times,* December 25, 2002, https://www.nytimes.com/2002/12/25/sports/baseball-what-s-32-million-more-yanks-sign-contreras.html.

16   "'El Titán' llega finalmente al estadio de los Yanquis," *Laredo* (Texas) *Morning Times* (LMT Online), February 5, 2003, https://www.lmtonline.com/lmtenespanol/article/El-Tit-n-llega-finalmente-al-estadio-de-los-10367562.php.

17   Charlie Nobles, "Baseball: Like That, Contreras Ends Talk of Slump," *New York Times,* March 15, 2003, https://www.nytimes.com/2003/03/15/sports/baseball-like-that-contreras-ends-talk-of-slump.html.

18   Rafael Hermoso, "Baseball: Hernández Counsels Contreras," *New York Times,* March 12, 2003, https://www.nytimes.com/2003/03/12/sports/baseball-hernandez-counsels-contreras.html.

19   Buster Olney, "Baseball: Yankees React to Contreras's Slump with Caring," *New York Times,* March 10, 2003, https://www.nytimes.com/2003/03/10/sports/baseball-yankees-react-to-contreras-s-slump-with-caring.html.

20   "Baseball: Contreras May Go to Minors," *New York Times,* April 19, 2003, https://www.nytimes.com/2003/04/19/sports/baseball-contreras-may-go-to-minors.html.

21   Bill Finley, "Baseball: How to Get to Rivera? Go Right with Contreras." *New York Times,* October 11, 2003.

22   Tyler Kepner, "Baseball: Contreras Trying to Carry On Without Family," *New York Times,* June 20, 2004, https://www.nytimes.com/2004/06/20/sports/baseball-contreras-trying-to-carry-on-without-family.html.

23   Kepner, "Baseball: Contreras Trying to Carry on Without Family."

24   Tyler Kepner, "Baseball: A Reunited Contreras Is Ready to Settle Down," *New York Times,* June 24, 2004, https://www.nytimes.com/2004/06/24/sports/baseball-a-reunited-contreras-is-ready-to-settle-down.html.

25   Kepner, "Baseball: A Reunited Contreras Is Ready to Settle Down."

26   Associated Press, "Contreras' Family Not Allowed to Leave Cuba," ESPN.com, February 19, 2004, https://www.espn.com/mlb/news/story?id=1739263.

27   Jack Curry, "Baseball: Contreras Eager to Pitch With Family on Hand," *New York Times,* June 26, 20024, https://www.nytimes.com/2004/06/26/sports/baseball-contreras-eager-to-pitch-with-family-on-hand.html.

28   Jack Curry, "Baseball: Contreras's Big Victory: His Family," *New York Times,* June 28, 2004, https://www.nytimes.com/2004/06/28/sports/baseball-contreras-s-big-victory-his-family.html.

29   Curry, "Baseball: Contreras's Big Victory: His Family."

30   Tyler Kepner, "Unable to Acquire a Cy Young Winner, Yanks Settle for All-Star," *New York Times,* August 1, 2004, https://www.nytimes.com/2004/08/01/sports/baseball-unable-to-acquire-cy-young-winner-yanks-settle-for-all-star.html.

31   Joel Sherman, "Yankees Sending Jose on His Way; Trade Value: Addition by Subtraction," *New York Post,* August 1, 2004, https://nypost.com/2004/08/01/yankees-sending-jose-on-his-way-trade-value-addition-by-subtraction/.

32   George A. King III, "Yankees Deal Contreras to White Sox For Righty Loiza," *New York Post,* August 1, 2004, https://nypost.com/2004/08/01/deal-contreras-to-white-sox-for-righty-loaiza/.

33   Scott Merkin, "White Sox Legend Returns to Chicago," *White Sox Beat Newsletter,* MLB.com, April 20, 2023, https://www.mlb.com/news/white-sox-legend-jose-contreras-returns-to-chicago.

34   Author's interview with José Contreras, October 10, 2024.

35   Merkin, "White Sox Legend Returns to Chicago."

36   José de Jesus Ortiz, "José Contreras Honored by Hall's Invite to East-West Classic," *Our Esquina,* February 15, 2024, https://ouresquina.com/2024/jose-contreras-honored-by-halls-invite-to-east-west-classic/.

37 Clemson Smith Muñiz, "José Contreras: A ChiSox Ambassador with Stories to Tell," *La Vida Baseball,* March 27, 2018, https://www.lavidabaseball.com/jose-contreras-cuba-journey/.

38 Tyler Kepner, "Yankees Blinded by Flashy Contreras," *New York Times,* August 10, 2005, https://www.nytimes.com/2005/08/10/sports/baseball/yankees-blinded-by-flashy-contreras.html.

39 Kepner, "Yankees Blinded by Flashy Contreras."

40 Daniel de Malas, "Nunca antes contando: Mano a mano con José Contreras, de Pinar a Chicago."

41 Merkin, "White Sox Legend Returns to Chicago."

42 Rubén Castro, "José Contreras pensó en el retiro."

43 Andrew Seligman, "Contreras Finally Displaying All His Talent on the Mound," *Pocono Record* (Stroudsburg, Pennsylvania), June 25, 2006.

44 Kevin Cooney, "Elbow Tear Leaves Future in Doubt for Contreras," *Phillyburbs,* June 3, 2012, https://www.phillyburbs.com/story/sports/columns/2012/06/03/elbow-tear-leaves-future-in/17856474007/.

45 "Hijo del lanzador Cubano José Ariel Contreras firma contrato con importante agente de MLB," *CiberCuba,* April 25, 2024, https://www.cibercuba.com/noticias/2024-04-26-u1-e208933-s27066-nid280996-hijo-lanzador-cubano-jose-ariel-contreras-firma.

46 Dan Cichalski, "East West Classic a True Throwback Celebration at Cooperstown," MLB.com, May 25, 2024, https://www.mlb.com/news/hall-of-fame-2024-east-west-classic-recap.

47 James Fegan, "White Sox Great José Contreras Mentors Cuban Pitching Prospect Norge Vera: 'This Is Personal to Me,'" *New York Times,* November 17, 2021, https://www.nytimes.com/athletic/2960899/2021/11/17/white-sox-great-jose-contreras-mentors-cuban-pitching-prospect-norge-vera-this-is-personal-to-me/.

48 Author's interview with José Contreras, October 10, 2024.

49 Tyler Kepner, "Baseball Gets Another Chance to Honor a Legend," *New York Times,* November 15, 2021, https://www.nytimes.com/2021/11/15/sports/baseball/minnie-minoso-hall-of-fame.html?searchResultPosition=2.

NEAL COTTS

By Bill Pruden

While the highlight of southpaw reliever Neal Cotts' pitching career was undoubtedly being a contributing part of the 2005 World Series champion White Sox, his career was so much more than that memorable experience. He returned to college to complete his degree and fulfill a promise to his mother more than two decades after he had left to pursue his big-league dream. And in returning to pitch in the majors after an absence of almost four seasons, Cotts' baseball journey offers lessons about determination, dedication, and resilience that transcend the game of baseball while serving as both an inspiration and an example for any aspiring professional athlete.

Neal James Cotts was born on March 25, 1980, in Lebanon, Illinois, a town of less than 3,200 in southwest Illinois about 25 miles from St. Louis. His father, Jack, worked for US Steel and his mother, Jane, was a high-school math teacher.[1] The older of two boys, he was fortunate to have "hyper-supportive parents" as he grew up.[2] Cotts attended Lebanon High School, graduating in 1998. He was a strong student, regularly earning a place on the

honor roll. He earned membership in the National Honor Society and was one of two students at the school who were awarded honorable mention honors from the American Legion at graduation.[3]

Unsurprisingly, Cotts was a star athlete, playing soccer (until an injury ended that pursuit), basketball, and baseball, where he shined most brightly. In his senior year he pitched both a no-hitter and a perfect game, struck out 105 in 62 innings, and posted an ERA of 1.92. His efforts earned him numerous accolades, including selection to the *Belleville* (Illinois) *News-Democrat*'s 1998 Class A All-Area Baseball team as both a pitcher and an outfielder.[4] His future as a big-league pitcher notwithstanding, Cotts also won the Illinois Class A state hitting derby in the spring of 1998 when his point total more than doubled that of the runner-up. His hitting prowess was no surprise; as he batted .557 and drove in 25 runs during his senior year at Lebanon High School.[5]

But despite his Lebanon High accomplishments, efforts reinforced by his play in American Legion ball, where he received the Most Valuable Player Award, Cotts had never really envisioned his baseball career amounting to anything big.[6] He received little attention from colleges, and Illinois State University gave him a look only because the Lebanon coach knew the team's pitching coach, Tim Johnson.[7] But once Cotts arrived, he developed impressively and by the start of his sophomore year he was the top hurler on a squad that included three other major-league prospects.[8]

Cotts earned the attention of major-league scouts, being named first team all-Missouri Valley Conference after leading the team to a 31-22 mark in 2001. He finished his college career with an 18-9 record and an ERA of 3.58.[9] Cotts was selected in the second round of the 2001 amateur draft by the Oakland Athletics. Deciding to forgo his senior year, the young southpaw signed with the A's and split the summer between the Vancouver Canadians of the Class-A Northwest League and the Visalia Oaks of the high A California League. Pitching in 16 games (14 starts), he had a combined record of 4-2 with an ERA of 2.73. Cotts spent all of 2002 with the Modesto A's of the California League, logging 137⅔ innings in 28 appearances, all as a starter. He went 12-6, 4.12, striking out 178.

Cotts' fortunes took a decided turn in December of 2002 when he was traded to the Chicago White Sox, one of two players to be named later in a deal that brought Billy Koch to the White Sox while sending Keith Foulke, Mark

Neal Cotts　　　　**2005**

GRINDERS AND GAMERS

Johnson, Joe Valentine, and cash to Oakland. Joining a team in transition, Cotts was initially assigned to the Birmingham Barons of the Double-A Southern League. After going 9-7, 2.16 in 21 starts and giving up only 67 hits in 108⅓ innings pitched, and with the White Sox struggling to find a fifth starter, he was brought up to the big-league team.[10]

Cotts made his major-league debut on August 12, starting against the Anaheim Angels in Anaheim. Staked to a 2-0 first-inning lead, the 23-year-old left-hander retired the Angels' leadoff batter, Chone Figgins, gave up a single to Alfredo Amezaga, and got Garret Anderson to hit into an inning-ending double play. After the White Sox upped their lead to 3-0, Cotts struggled with his control in the second, walking the first two and giving up a run-scoring single before a double play and a strikeout ended the inning. Cotts' control issues worsened in the third as he walked the first two batters, who moved up on a sacrifice. Cotts then walked the next two, forcing in a run, whereupon White Sox manager Jerry Manuel removed the lefty, who had walked six and given up two hits in 2⅓ innings. (The White Sox won the game, 10-4.)

Cotts started three more games, in one of which, on August 22, he went five innings and earned his first major-league victory. He finished the season with a big-league record of 1-1. The White Sox determined that Cotts could be a contributor to the team out of the bullpen. In 2004, under new manager Ozzie Guillén, Cotts pitched 65⅓ innings in 56 games (all but one in relief), went 4-4 with an ERA of 5.65.

Cotts played an important role on the 2005 World Series winners, emerging as a central figure out of the bullpen. While compiling a 4-0 record with an ERA of 1.94, he gave up only 38 hits in 60⅓ innings. He was no less impressive in the postseason as the White Sox won 11 of 12 games to win their first World Series crown since 1917. Pitching in all four World Series games as the White Sox swept the Houston Astros, he was the winner of Game Two, when he got the final out in the top of the ninth to squelch an Astros rally, then was the beneficiary of Scott Podsednik's ninth-inning walk-off home run. He was named Setup Man of the Year in an MLB poll.[11]

Neither the White Sox nor Cotts were able to duplicate the magic of 2005 the following season. The team got off to a strong start, only to fade, and Cotts' performance dropped across the board. He posted a record of 1-2, but more telling was the ballooning of his ERA to 5.17. He made a career-high 70 appearances, but pitched only 54 innings. He gave up 33 runs, more than twice as many as he had in 2005, and the 12 home runs he yielded represented a painful contrast with the single blast he surrendered in 2005.

Barely a year removed from earning his championship ring, on November 16, 2006, Cotts was traded across town to the Chicago Cubs for minor-league pitcher Carlos Vasquez and reliever David Aarsdsma.

Cotts started strong with the Cubs in 2007, starting the season with 11 straight scoreless appearances (10⅔ innings) during the first month of the season. But after allowing runners to score in four of what proved to be his final five appearances with the Cubs in 2007, all of which sent his ERA to 4.86, he was sent down to the Triple-A Iowa Cubs in the Pacific Coast League. His effort to regain his form in Iowa was hampered by injuries as he spent a month, from June 20 to July 21, on the disabled list with a left hamstring strain. Overall, his record with Iowa was 2-2 with a 4.83 ERA in 24 games, six of which he started. Despite the ups and downs, in December of 2007, the Cubs re-signed Cotts, giving him a one-year deal. While he started the season back in Iowa, he was recalled in May and assumed the role of primary left-handed reliever after the team traded away Scott Eyre. Overall, he appeared in 50 games for the Cubs, all in relief, posting a record of 0-2 and an ERA of 4.29 in 35⅔ innings pitched.

Cotts started the 2009 season with the Cubs, and while he pitched less than an inning in 11 of his first 19 appearances, he gave up only one run in his first eight outings. However, his effectiveness diminished and on May 27 he was sent back to Iowa. While he was scored upon in only two of his 12 appearances with the Iowa Cubs, he suffered an injury and on July 2 he underwent Tommy John surgery on his elbow, ending his 2009 season and beginning a medical nightmare that at one point seemed poised to end his pitching career.

The problem for Cotts was not the surgery, which by all accounts went just fine, but what came next. Released by the Cubs at season's end, he signed a free-agent contract with the Pittsburgh Pirates at the end of December. But things got complicated when he injured his left hip while rehabbing, aggravating an old high-school injury, a broken leg from a "cheap shot," Cotts recalled, but one that had not been set right.[12] It resulted in hip surgery and the insertion of a rod in his leg.[13] The surgery left his right leg "microscopically shorter" than the left, which put more stress on his hip, causing a labrum tear during his rehab efforts. Another surgery followed but it was complicated by a staph infection that led to a month on antibiotics and one more surgery.[14] To no one's surprise after his medical marathon, the Pirates released Cotts but the New York Yankees offered him an invitation to spring training in 2011. However, when he flunked the physical immediately upon reporting to camp, the Yankees released him.[15]

Thus began an unceasing effort to get one more chance, an effort marked by more failed physicals, numerous conversations that ended abruptly upon the disclosure of Cotts' medical records and countless unreturned phone calls. Among teams that worked him out and were impressed by what they saw there was still the overriding fear that another injury could result in a career-ending injury.[16] It reached a point where his agent, Joe Bick, candidly told Cotts that he had done all he could and that Cotts' career was probably over. Bick recalled that Cotts "had been through hell and back medically and he had come so far. The thought of not being able to get that last opportunity was just heart-wrenching. We felt like we had failed him."[17] Cotts took the news stoically, figuring he would go back to school, finish his degree, and do some pitching instruction as a sideline.[18]

Cotts did find some consolation in being out of the game, for while the whole process made for a real-life medical drama, it did afford him a chance he had never previously had to spend extended time in season with his wife, Jaime, and their two young children. But he remained determined to give baseball another try. It was a determination that Jaime understood. Recognizing that Neal had "baseball in his heart," she said she "didn't think of other options, because when you have that drive … it's easy to support."[19] She added, "He made it easy for me to say, 'Keep going, keep going.'"[20]

And keep going Cotts and Bick did. Finally, perhaps because Bick was also the agent for the Rangers' star young outfielder Jurickson Profar, as 2012 spring training was about to start, the Texas Rangers' GM, Jon Daniels, a man known for being willing to take a risk, agreed to give Cotts a chance despite his medical history.[21]

After all the surgeries and all the rehab, doubts remained, but they were quickly erased when Cotts was "so impressive after arriving in minor league camp that he joined the major leaguers within a week and was contending for a spot in the bullpen."[22] Reflective of his recent history, on the last day of spring training, Cotts tore his left lat muscle.[23] But he had shown the Rangers enough that they assigned him to their Triple-A club in Round Rock where he rehabbed the injury, finally returning to the mound for the first time in three years on June 11, 2012. Cotts spent the 2012 season in Round Rock. By his own account he pitched "here and there decently," but overall he did "not throw great."[24] But while he did not get a late-season call-up, his performance in compiling a record of 2-1 with an ERA of 4.55 in 25 games and 31⅔ innings pitched was enough to warrant an offer of a contract for 2013.

Cotts started the 2013 season back in Round Rock, but an impressive early start brought inquiries from other teams and the promise by the Rangers of an imminent call-up.[25] The long and winding road back to the big leagues, one marked by the anxiety, the frustration, and the questions about whether he would ever pitch again, all came to a head on May 21, 2013, when, with six pitches, he got three straight outs against the Oakland Athletics, completing his first inning in the major leagues since May of 2009.[26] It was the beginning of a storybook season. In 58 games and 57 innings Cotts gave up only 7 earned runs for an ERA of 1.11, the best on the Rangers staff, and the fifth best among American League relievers who pitched at least 20 innings. He compiled a record of 8-3 with his victory total topping

all AL relief pitchers. And it earned him a new one-year, $2.2 million contract with the Rangers.

The distinctive nature of Cotts' comeback was recognized when the now Chicago resident and former White Sox and Cubs hurler was given the Chicago-Area Major League Player of the Year Award by the Pitch and Hit Club, a local group that promotes baseball in the area.[27]

Cotts did not enjoy the same level of success in 2014. Like the Rangers, whose win total plummeted from 91 in 2013 to 67 in 2014, Cotts finished at 2-9 with an ERA of 4.32 in 73 appearances and 66⅔ innings pitched. Once again a free agent, Cotts signed with the Milwaukee Brewers in January 2015. However, his time in Milwaukee was short-lived when, after 51 appearances in which he had a 3.26 ERA in 49⅔ innings, on August 21 Cotts was traded to the Minnesota Twins for a player to be named. He finished the season pitching in 17 games with the Twins, getting no decisions and posting a 3.95 ERA in 13⅔ innings. He made what proved to be his final major-league appearance on October 3, 2015, in Minnesota against the Kansas City Royals, when, in the top of the seventh with two outs and the Twins trailing 2-1, Cotts replaced Blaine Boyer, who had just given up the tiebreaking run. Cotts walked Eric Hosmer before Jonny Gomes reached on an error by shortstop Eduardo Escobar. Cotts then gave up a two-run double to deep right-center field by Mike Moustakas and was removed from the game.

In the summer of 2015 it had been announced that Cotts had been elected to the Illinois State Athletics Percy Family Hall of Fame. The 2016 baseball season was a series of trials as Cotts sought to keep his major-league career alive.[28] Again a free agent, he was signed by the Houston Astros in late February, only to be released on March 25. Over the course of the season he appeared in 41 games for Yankees, Angels, and Rangers' Triple-A farm clubs, compiling an overall record of 2-2 with an ERA of 3.83 in 44⅔ innings. In January 2017, Cotts, again a free agent, signed with the Washington Nationals. He appeared in 52 games for the Triple-A Syracuse Chiefs where he was 1-3 with an ERA of 3.94 in 48 innings. He was released on November 6, 2017. His professional career was over.

With his playing career definitely over, the 37-year-old Cotts turned his attention to some long- overdue business – the completion of his college degree. When he left Illinois State after being drafted by Oakland in 2001 after his junior year, he was on track to graduate. During his playing career he had "tried to chip away at the remaining credits," but did not have the time to make any real progress.[29] However, with the daily rigors of baseball now behind him, and encouraged by a conversation he had had with Illinois State athletic director Larry Lyons at his Hall of Fame induction in 2015, Cotts took the plunge, taking advantage of online offerings and working with the university to make it happen.[30]

In the early going, he did his studying and his work on school projects during the day when his children were at school and things were quiet. In the after-school hours and evenings he would work at a baseball school with which he signed on when he retired.[31] When Covid arrived in the spring of 2020, Cotts had only an internship to complete and while he was able to do it, he, like countless others, was deprived of a spring graduation ceremony. But much to the delight of his mother, a longtime teacher, and his wife and children, he had earned his degree, a Bachelor of Applied Science in General Studies.

As of 2025, Cotts and his family resided in Chicago, where they have lived since his early days with the White Sox. Cotts worked with the Slammer Illinois Baseball & Softball Academy in Lake Forest, a Chicago suburb. Cotts is one of a number of former professional ballplayers on the academy's staff. The organization's website touts the number of professional prospects it has developed, but speaks of using baseball as the vehicle for "Developing Future Athlete Leaders."[32] As a staff member, Cotts can describe for his students the way he overcame the physical challenges he faced on his road back to achieving a second act in his baseball career. He offers them a vivid reminder of the human dimension in athletics.

SOURCES

In addition to the sources cited in the Notes, the author consulted MLB.com, baseball-almanac.com, and Baseball-Reference.com.

NOTES

1   David Haugh, "Help Was Lying in the Weeds," *Chicago Tribune*, October 25, 2005.

2   George Castle, "The Award Cotts Doesn't Yet Have Is the One That Really Marks the Man," Chicago Baseball Museum, January 28, 2014; https://chicagobaseballmuseum.org/wp-content/uploads/CBM-Neal-Cotts-20140128.pdf.

3   "High School Honor Roll," *Lebanon* (Illinois) *Advertiser*, April 16, 1997, February 11, 1998; "The Lebanon High School Seventy-Seventh Annual Commencement Program," *Lebanon Advertiser*, June 3, 1998.

4   Haugh; Rod Kloeckner, "Lebanon Senior Named as Pitcher, Fielder," *Belleville* (Illinois) *News-Democrat*, July 7, 1998.

5   "Neal Cotts Is Champion of Hitting Derby," *Lebanon Advertiser*, June 10, 1998.

6   "Cotts Shows Promise for Pro Baseball," *Lebanon Advertiser*, July 25, 2001; Kevin Bersett, "Former Redbird Star Makes Unlikely Return to the Big Leagues," *Illinois State News* (campus newspaper), February 17, 2014; https://news.illinoisstate.edu/2014/02/former-redbird-star-makes-unlikely-return-big-leagues-2/

7   Bersett.

8   Bersett; Jeremy Accardo, Eric Eckenstahler, and Brian Forystek were all members of the Illinois State team that Cotts joined; the first two went on to play in the major leagues. "Redbirds in the Pros," Illinois State Redbirds; https://goredbirds.com/sports/2014/4/30/Pros_baseball.aspx.

9   Bersett; Randy Reinhardt, "Cotts Making His Pitch," *Bloomington* (Illinois) *Pantagraph*, May 16, 2001; Nick Carta, "Little-Known ISU Baseball Great Is White Sox Hero," *Normal* (Illinois) *Vidette,* February 5, 2021; https://www.videtteonline.com/blogs/carta-little-known-isu-baseball-great-is-white-sox-hero/article_6c0c1a4c-67db-11eb-bbb0-23d3346605ec.html.

10 "Cotts Strong in Loss," *Bloomington Pantagraph*, August 18, 2003.

11 Bersett.

12 Evan Grant, "How Neal Cotts Went from the Brink of Baseball Oblivion to Key Cog in Rangers Bullpen," *Dallas Morning News*, July 1, 2013; https://www.dallasnews.com/sports/rangers/2013/07/02/grant-how-neal-cotts-went-from-the-brink-of-baseball-oblivion-to-key-cog-in-rangers-bullpen/.

13 Grant.

14 Grant.

15 Castle.

16 Bersett.

17 Grant.

18 Grant.

19 Castle.

20 Castle.

21 Bersett; Grant.

22 Grant.

23 Castle.

24 Castle.

25 Grant.

26 Bersett.

27 Castle.

28 Tim Van Duyne, "2015 Hall of Fame Class Announced," *Illinois State News*, July 9, 2015; https://news.illinoisstate.edu/2015/07/2015-hall-fame-class-announced/.

29 Mike Williams, "Cotts Completes Degree at ISU After Long MLB Career," Illinois State Redbirds, May 9, 2020; https://goredbirds.com/news/2020/5/9/baseball-cotts-completes-degree-after-long-mlb-career.

30 Williams.

31 Williams.

32 "Slammers Baseball & Softball Training Academy; https://www.slammersillinois.com/.

JOE CREDE

By Jim Margalus

If the major leagues awarded an MVP for an entire post-season, rather than separate honors for the Championship Series and World Series, Joe Crede built one of the 2005 White Sox' strongest cases.

At the plate, he hit .289/.327/.622 with 4 homers and 11 RBIs, with one of those runs driven in coming at the White Sox' most vulnerable point of the postseason. In the field, he provided lockdown defense at third base that drew comparisons to World Series legends like Brooks Robinson and Graig Nettles.

Until August of that year, it would have been hard to see it coming, because Crede's climb to being a key component of a World Series champion wasn't a straightforward one.

Crede was born on April 26, 1978, in Jefferson City, Missouri, and raised in Westphalia, a city 15 miles away with a population of around 300. The Crede family was an athletic one. His father, David, played for a US Air Force baseball team, the Weisbaden Flyers, in Germany, and tried out for the Dodgers in consecutive springs before turning to fast-pitch softball upon returning home.[1] A Crede cousin,

Joe Crede   2005

Dennis Higgins, played in the major leagues from 1966 to 1972, including time with the White Sox in 1966 and 1967.[2]

David and Debbie Crede had four children: a daughter, Leigh Ann, and three baseball-playing sons – Brad, Joe, and Josh, all of whom starred at Fatima High School. Brad, five years older than Joe, played college baseball at Central Missouri State University. Josh, five years younger than Joe, saw his baseball career cut short by a car accident in 1999.[3]

The two older Crede brothers were both selected in the 1996 draft. The White Sox selected Joe out of Fatima High in the fifth round on the recommendation of scouts Doug Laumann and Paul Provas, while the Phillies drafted Brad in the 19th round. Brad Crede played two years of professional ball, topping out at Class A before going into teaching. Joe's playing days lasted considerably longer.

Joe played rookie-level ball with the Gulf Coast League White Sox in 1996, batting .299 in 56 games. In 1997 he hit .271 for the Hickory Crawdads (Class-A South Atlantic League).

Crede established his bona fides in 1998, hitting .315 with 20 homers, driving in 88 and winning the Class-A+ Carolina League MVP with Winston-Salem as a 20-year-old. A toe injury hampered him in 1999, but in 2000 he was the Southern League MVP with the Birmingham Barons, with a 306 average, 21 homers and 94 RBIs in 2000.

The White Sox called Crede up that September, giving him a handful of late-game appearances and a couple of starts after the White Sox clinched the division championship. He debuted on September 12 and got his first major-league hit in his second plate appearance, on September 17 against Toronto's Paul Quantrill. Crede's first career start came at third base against the Kansas City Royals on September 29, during which he recorded his first career RBI on a sacrifice fly.

When it came to regular playing time, the 6-foot-3-inch righty's path over the next two seasons was blocked by a cluster of veterans including José Valentin, Herbert Perry, Royce Clayton, and Tony Graffanino. Crede was exclusively a third baseman, which made him a poor fit for a bench role.

The logjam finally broke at the trade deadline in 2002. The White Sox trailing the Minnesota Twins by 14 games in the AL Central Division in late July, traded stalwart second baseman Ray Durham to Oakland and turned their attention to the following season, which included playing

Crede regularly at third base the rest of the way. Crede, then 24, immediately validated the minor-league accolades by hitting .285/.311/.515 with 12 home runs in 53 games, including a stretch of six homers over seven games to close out August.

But as Crede became a major-league regular, he was prone to slumps that could last weeks, and sometimes months. He had dealt with slow starts in the minors, and *Baseball America's* 2002 scouting report said Crede "expects so much from himself that he's too critical at times."[4] White Sox coaches tried to get the taciturn Crede to lighten up,[5] but over time they came to accept the ups and downs for the combination of above-average defense and 20-homer power, especially when the White Sox surged out of the gate and built a seemingly insurmountable division lead during the first half of 2005.

Two injuries in the 2005 season jeopardized Crede's standing. One would rear its ugly head down the road, but one was credited with rejuvenating his season.

He went into the All-Star break with a sore back, determined to be due to herniated discs, but he planned to play through the discomfort for the rest of the season.[6] In late August he suffered a hairline fracture on the tip of his right middle finger during a bunt attempt. That required a trip to the disabled list.

The rest might have turned out to be a blessing. Crede was mired in an 0-for-21 slump before the finger injury, but he returned after the minimum 15-day stay by starting a six-game hitting streak. He said he used the time off to study tape and make tweaks to his swing,[7] and the adjustments stuck. He hit .371/.409/.726 with six homers over the final 19 games of the regular season. His resurgence couldn't have been timelier, because the Cleveland Indians had whittled the White Sox' 15-game lead down to a few games over the final fortnight of the season.

Crede provided a preview of his heroics to come on September 20, the middle game of a critical three-game series against Cleveland. The Indians won the opener to narrow the White Sox lead to 2½ games, and then tied the second game by tagging Bobby Jenks with a blown save in the top of the ninth, which sent the game into extra innings. After Dustin Hermanson pitched a scoreless top of the 10th, Crede led off the bottom of the inning. He had already homered earlier in the game, and he turned David Riske's 1-and-0 fastball into his second homer, a no-doubt blast that gave the White Sox some welcome breathing room.

That turned out to be the second-biggest hit of Crede's 2005 season, as it was trumped by his walk-off double in Game Two of the ALCS against the Angels. He came to the plate after A.J. Pierzynski extended the ninth inning of a 1-1 game by running to first base after swinging over Kelvim Escobar's low splitter that may or may not have hit the dirt. After pinch-runner Pablo Ozuna stole second, Crede roped a hanging splitter off the left-field wall for a 2-1 victory that tied the Series at one win apiece.

The White Sox won their final eight games of the post-season, beating the Angels in five games before sweeping the Astros, and Crede was a major factor in both Series.

He and Pierzynski teamed up to victimize Escobar again in Game Five of the ALCS. With two outs in the eighth, Escobar walked Aaron Rowand, and then Pierzynski reached on an Escobar error when Escobar fielded a nubber along the first-base line, but tagged Pierzynski with his glove while his bare hand held the ball. Once more that brought Crede to the plate with two outs in a tie game, and he hit Francisco Rodriguez's full-count slider back up the middle. Adam Kennedy smothered the fourth hop in shallow center field, but his throw home on one knee didn't have enough on it to get Rowand, and the White Sox took a 4-3 lead they held the rest of the way.

When the White Sox advanced to the World Series, Crede continued to collect important hits. He put the White Sox ahead 4-3 in Game One with a fourth-inning solo shot off Wandy Rodriguez, which held up as the game-winning run thanks to six scoreless innings by the White Sox bullpen. He contributed an RBI single early in Game Two, then hit a solo shot off Roy Oswalt in Game Three that started a five-run fifth that erased Houston's 4-0 lead.

Crede paired the clutch hits with clutch defense. In Game One he made three outstanding plays to his right, including a pair of diving stops in the sixth and seventh innings, both times preventing a runner on third from scoring the tying run. He followed it up with a diving catch of Adam Everett's liner in Game Two. The steady stream of highlight plays evoked comparisons to Brooks Robinson, and the Orioles Hall of Famer offered his praise when asked about Crede's October reel.

"He gets down in the dirt, he looks like one of those blue-collar workers," Robinson told the *Chicago Tribune*. "I was really impressed with his play in the World Series, the way he moves around. He's terrific."[8]

Crede's all-around excellence and high-leverage heroics over both Series gave him a strong case as the White Sox' most important player in October, but he missed out on both MVP honors. Though Crede went 7-for-19 with two homers, two doubles, and seven RBIs in the ALCS against the Angels, Paul Konerko took home the MVP. Crede went 5-for-17 with two homers and a double against the Astros, but Jermaine Dye took the honors by hitting .438 and delivering the Series-winning single in Game Four.

Crede had to settle for being a local hero, including a starring role in the championship parade, during which he, Pierzynski, and Rowand sang "Don't Stop Believin'" with Journey frontman Steve Perry. The trio had adopted the 1981 hit as a rally song after hearing it in a Baltimore bar,[9] and Crede's participation was the culmination of a years-long attempt to show his personality.

Unfortunately for Crede, his time at the top of his game was limited. He sustained the breakout form well into 2006, reaching his typical 20 homers by the final week of July and carrying a .300 average into September, but the herniated discs flared up shortly after Labor Day, and while he avoided a trip to the disabled list, it sapped his offense the rest of the season, as he finished with just seven hits in his last 62 plate appearances. Despite the fizzle at the finish, he batted .283/.323/.506 with 30 homers and earned a Silver Slugger Award at third base.

Back problems defined the rest of Crede's Chicago career. He opted against surgery after the 2006 season, choosing a strength and conditioning program to build up the muscles around the troublesome discs.[10] After two months of struggles, Crede underwent a procedure, a "microdiscectomy to remove herniated disc particles that were putting pressure on a sciatic nerve."[11] It cost him the rest of the season, and White Sox manager Ozzie Guillén criticized Crede for delaying the procedure.

"When you have surgery right now, it's like nothing," Guillén said. "You go through a couple months of rehab on your way back and sometimes you feel better. It's a shame we had to wait this long to make that happen because if he did it when he was supposed to do it, then right now we'd have a different surgery."[12]

Crede's recovery, both physically and in terms of his relationship with the franchise, wasn't that simple. He returned to the lineup for Opening Day in 2008, and while he opened the season by hitting .253/.314/.516 with 7 homers and 22 RBIs over 25 games in April, the encouraging start revealed further friction between the player and the organization. Crede, an impending free agent represented by Scott Boras, said the White Sox had not made him a compelling offer to consider signing an extension before reaching free agency.[13] The two sides had talked past each other in the run-up to the regular season. White Sox general manager Kenny Williams said Boras told the team that there was no interest in discussing an extension,[14] while Boras said he didn't want to negotiate a contract for a player while he was injured.[15]

Crede's hot start turned into his first All-Star nod, as he hit .252/.323/.463 with 16 homers and 49 RBIs during the first half, but shortly after the second half started, the debate was moot. His back problems returned, and two trips to the injured list limited him to just 11 games the rest of the season.[16]

Crede played his last game for the White Sox on September 2, 2008. He watched from the bench as the Sox outlasted the Minnesota Twins for the division title in a tiebreaking Game 163 at Guaranteed Rate Field. He had a second back surgery in October 2008, which prolonged his inability to find his next contract.

Shortly after spring training started in February 2009, Crede signed a one-year, $2.5 million deal with the Twins.[17]

His contract included incentives worth upward of $7 million, but the move to the artificial turf of the Metrodome didn't agree with the 31-year-old Crede. He played in just 90 games around an assortment of injuries – right shoulder, bruised hand, bruised knee, sore hamstring – before another flare-up with his back effectively ended his season in late August. He played in just two games in September, striking out in all four plate appearances in what turned out to be his final major-league game on September 13, and underwent a third back surgery after the season.[18]

Crede missed all of the 2010 season in recovery, but although he signed with the Colorado Rockies on a minor-league deal with an invitation to spring training in January 2011, he never reported.

"The bottom line was the back was just not responding to what treatment I was getting," Crede said. "I'd hate to say how many cortisone shots I've had in my back. I don't think I want to know how many cortisone shots in my back. With the three surgeries and the last one, I felt it went well, it just didn't go as well as I thought it would."[19]

Crede returned to Missouri after his playing days to tend to his farm and help raise his three children – Anna, Lucy, and Jace – with his wife, Lisa. His jersey was retired by Fatima High School, and he was inducted into the Missouri Sports Hall of Fame in 2013, but while his back has improved with distance from his playing days, it limited his ability to coach the next generation of Credes.

"I helped out my youngest boy, who is in eighth grade now, with his team," Crede said in 2022. "I realized I can't do it anymore from hitting groundballs and pitching to him. Everything starts hurting. I hate getting old."[20]

Crede finished his career hitting .254/.304/.444 with 140 homers and 470 RBIs in 888 major-league games, but the herniated discs truncated what could have been a more storied career, and it also continued the White Sox' decades-long trend of career-altering injuries to third basemen.

Pete Ward finished top 10 in MVP voting in 1963 and 1964 but suffered whiplash in a car accident and wasn't the same. Bill Melton won the White Sox' first-ever home-run crown in 1971, but he fell off a ladder and injured his back. Robin Ventura wrecked his ankle on a slide at home plate in 1997, shortening his run as the franchise's greatest third baseman.

Crede's career took a little too long to get going, and ended too soon after that to fulfill the expectations from his prospect days of being Ventura's heir apparent, but because he peaked at the right time, he has something that no other White Sox third baseman in 88 years could boast: a World Series ring.

GRINDERS AND GAMERS

SOURCES

In addition to the sources cited in the Notes, the author consulted Baseball Reference.com and MLB.com.

NOTES

1   John Mullin, "'Real' Crede Answering Call," *Chicago Tribune.* March 19, 2004: A9.

2   Melissa Isaacson, "Sheds Shell, Raises Game," *Chicago Tribune*, August 7, 2005: 3, 12.

3   Joshua Crede Obituary, *Gasconade County Republican* (Owensville, Missouri), October 11, 2023.

4   https://www.baseballamerica.com/players/676811-joe-crede/.

5   "'Real' Crede Answering Call."

6   Mark Gonzales, "Crede Not Backing Down," *Chicago Tribune*, July 15, 2005: 4, 3.

7   "Tale of the Videotape a Good One for Crede," *Chicago Tribune*, September 16, 2005.

8   Melissa Isaacson, "Outstanding in His Field," *Chicago Tribune*, July 2, 2006: 17, 5.

9   Tim Rohan, "With Giants in Series, One Rock Song Goes On and On and On and On," *New York Times*, October 27, 2014. https://www.nytimes.com/2014/10/27/sports/baseball/with-sf-giants-in-world-series-2014-one-rock-song-goes-on-and-on-and-on-and-on.html.

10   Mark Gonzales, "Happy Camper: No Surgery, Pain," *Chicago Tribune*, February 21, 2007: 4, 5.

11   Mark Gonzales, "White Sox Losing Crede, Not All Hope," *Chicago Tribune*, June 13, 2007. https://www.chicagotribune.com/2007/06/13/white-sox-losing-crede-not-all-hope/

12   Scot Gregor, "Crede to Miss Rest of Season," *Arlington Heights* (Illinois) *Daily Herald*, June 13, 2007: 2-3.

13   Jack Curry, "Crede Returns to the White Sox, but for How Long?" *New York Times*, April 25, 2008. https://www.nytimes.com/2008/04/25/sports/baseball/25whitesox.html.

14   Mark Gonzales, "Crede's Back – for Now," *Chicago Tribune*, February 17, 2008: B6.

15   Scot Gregor, "Crede's Back – for How Long?," *Arlington Heights Daily Herald*, February 16, 2008: Sports 1.

16   Associated Press, "Crede Depending on Second Opinion for His Return," *New York Times*, September 13, 2008.

17   "Twins Add 3B Crede to Lineup," ESPN.com, February 21, 2009. https://www.espn.com/mlb/news/story?id=3923604.

18   Associated Press, "Crede to Have 3rd Back Surgery," ESPN.com, September 20, 2009. https://www.espn.com/mlb/news/story?id=4489679.

19   Doug Padilla, "Crede Back in Chicago, Talks Glory Days," ESPN.com, September 13, 2011.

20   Mark Gonzales, "Joe Crede Says Playing Through Back Pain Hasn't Hurt Him Today," *Chicago Sun-Times*, August 28, 2022.

JERMAINE DYE

By Sean Kolodziej

For a professional athlete, it takes perseverance and courage to come back from an injury and play again at an elite level. Jermaine Dye had to do this many times during his baseball career. Despite having to overcome injuries at almost every stop during his 14 years in the majors, the 6-foot-4, 210-pound right fielder with a powerful bat and a great arm succeeded when most others would have failed. Beginning with a home run in his first major-league at-bat, he was able to add a Silver Slugger Award, a Gold Glove Award, and a World Series MVP Award to his résumé before retiring.

Jermaine Trevell Dye was born on January 28, 1974, in Oakland, California, to Bill and Neda (Morgan) Dye. He grew up in San Pablo, 14 miles north of Oakland, where his father drove a bus for the city. On some summer mornings, Jermaine and his sister Angie would be dropped off by their father at Candlestick Park in San Francisco. They watched the Giants take batting practice from the bleacher seats, and would be joined later on by their father after he completed his route.

Jermaine Dye   2005

Dye's father was also his coach in various youth leagues throughout his childhood. After he made it to the big leagues, Dye's father was still there for him. "He calls when he sees something wrong, and I call him when I need to tell him what I think," Jermaine told the *San Francisco Chronicle*. "He's been my coach all my life."[1]

Dye went to Will C. Wood High School in Vacaville, California. He was the quarterback for the football team and a small forward for the basketball team, and pitched for the baseball team. He received scholarship offers to play football (from Brigham Young) and basketball (from the University of Nevada at Las Vegas)), but ultimately chose to pursue baseball. "He was a good all-around player, a good student, everything," said Don Trolinger, Dye's high-school batting coach. "We knew he had (talent). We just didn't know where he would go with it."[2]

Dye was drafted by the Texas Rangers in the 43rd round (1,210th overall) of the June 1992 amateur draft. Opting to not sign with the Rangers, he chose to go to Cosumnes River College in Sacramento, California, to play for coach Rod Beilby. Instead of pitching, Beilby recommended that Jermaine become a hitter. The coach's suggestion turned out to be good advice. Dye finished his freshman year leading the team with a .397 batting average with a .480 on-base percentage and a .744 slugging percentage. He was second on the team in runs scored (29). He had nine assists as an outfielder. He was named Bay Valley Conference Most Valuable Player for the 1993 season.

Dye was drafted again, this time by the Atlanta Braves in the 17th round (488th overall) of the June 1993 draft. Brave scout Dave Wilder signed him on June 6.

Dye, 19 years old, started the 1993 season playing for the Braves affiliate in the Rookie-level Gulf Coast League (later known as the Florida Complex League). After batting .347 in 31 games, he was moved up to the Danville (Virginia) Braves of the Appalachian League. Dye hit his first professional home run at Danville. He finished the season batting .277 in 25 games.

After making a good impression playing rookie ball, Dye was promoted to the Macon (Georgia) Braves of the Class-A South Atlantic League for 1994 and continued to hit well, clocking 15 home runs with 98 RBIs while batting .298 in 135 games with a league record 41 doubles.

Another year brought another promotion, and Dye opened the '95 season playing for the Double-A Greenville

Braves (Southern League). He again proved he was capable of hitting professional pitching, turning in 15 home runs with 71 RBIs while batting .285 in 104 games. He had an impressive 22 assists playing the outfield.

Once the season ended in Greenville, Dye played in the Arizona Fall League for the Sun Cities Solar Sox. The Braves sent Hall of Famer Willie Stargell, a special assistant, to Arizona to work with Dye. He hit well again, leading the league with 41 RBIs. The Braves added Dye to their 40-man major-league roster to prevent their losing him in the Rule 5 draft. The move gave Dye an automatic invite to spring training for the 1996 season.

After batting .364 with 12 RBIs in 25 spring-training games, Dye started the 1996 season with Richmond Braves of the Triple-A International League. This was not a controversial move, as the Braves already had three very good outfielders in Ryan Klesko, Marquis Grissom, and David Justice. "This spring Dye showed the kind of all-around natural ability that he had shown in previous years in the minors," Braves assistant general manager Dean Taylor said. "We feel he has a solid future as an everyday outfielder at the major-league level."[3]

Justice dislocated his left shoulder on May 15. The Braves needed an outfielder to replace him on the roster, and Dye was called up. Dye made his major-league debut on May 17. On a 1-and-0 count, he homered in his first at-bat off Reds pitcher Marcus Moore. He was the first Atlanta player to accomplish the feat, and the first Brave to do so since Chuck Tanner did it for Milwaukee in 1955.

Dye went on to win the starting right fielder job for the rest of the season, hitting .281/.304/.459 with 12 home runs in 98 games. Justice continued to travel with the team as he recovered from his injury, and he formed a bond with Dye. Said Justice, "I didn't have anybody to show me what I needed to do to be successful when I first came into the majors. That's why I'm going to do my best to help Jermaine become the best player that he can be."[4]

The Braves went 96-66 that season, finishing first in the NL East Division, and swept the Los Angeles Dodgers in the best-of-three Division Series. Dye only had two hits in 11 at-bats in the series, but one of the hits was a seventh-inning home run in Game Two that broke a 2-2 tie. After beating the St. Louis Cardinals in the Championship Series four games to three (Dye was 6-for-28), the Braves faced the New York Yankees in the World Series. After winning the first two games, the favored Braves lost the next four. Dye struggled in the series, going 2 for 17 (.118) with one RBI.

After losing the World Series, the Braves looked to revamp their outfield for the 1997 season. They traded Justice and Grissom to Cleveland for Kenny Lofton. They also traded Dye, along with pitcher Jamie Walker, to the Royals for outfielder Michael Tucker and infielder Keith Lockhart. The Royals were looking for a right-handed outfielder, and Dye fit the role perfectly. The trade was not received well in Kansas City, however, as Tucker was viewed as an up-and-coming prospect.

The 1997 season turned out to be a disaster for the Royals. Manager Bob Boone was fired in July and the club finished 67-94, in last place in the AL Central Division. Dye was plagued by injury. He ended up playing only 75 games, as he dealt with a severe bone bruise in his left foot. Later he suffered a strain in his right quadriceps. His offense declined, too, and at one point in the season, he was sent down to Triple-A Omaha to work on his hitting.

The Royals (72-89) moved up to third place in 1998. Dye played in only 60 games for the Royals. He had played poorly in spring training, largely because of his still sore right quadriceps, and he started the year at Omaha. He was recalled by the Royals in early May, but was again demoted to Omaha on June 29. He returned to the majors on August 11 when the Royals traded Jermaine Allensworth to the New York Mets. After seeming to get into a hitting groove, Dye tore cartilage in his right knee while getting into his car on September 1. The injury put an end to his season. In KC, he hit just .234, with 5 homers and 23 RBIs.

Because Dye was struggling at the plate and was injury-prone, expectations were probably low for his 1999 season. But he arrived fully healthy for spring training, although without a guarantee of making the big-league roster. He played well enough in spring training that when the Royals traded outfielder Jeff Conine to the Baltimore Orioles, Dye was named the starting right fielder to begin the season. He made the most of the opportunity. Finally playing fully healthy, he hit .294 with 27 home runs and 119 RBIs. The fans took to him, too, chanting "Dye-no-mite!" when he made a good play.

Dye continued his excellent hitting in 2000, establishing career highs in batting average (.321) and home runs (33), to go along with 118 RBIs. The numbers were good enough for him to be voted to start the All-Star Game. Dye's fielding was outstanding too; he won the AL Gold Glove for right fielders. He was the first Royals outfielder to win the award since Willie Wilson in 1980. Alongside teammates Johnny Damon and Carlos Beltrán, the Royals outfield seemed destined for great things.

That outfield was soon broken up. Damon, in the last year of his contract, was traded to the Oakland A's on January 8, 2001. Kansas City, a small-market team, had many players due for contract extensions, including Dye, whose contact was expiring at the end of 2002.

The 2001 season started out strong for Dye. He continued his solid hitting and great defense. Then, on July 25, he was traded to the Oakland A's in a three-team trade that sent Neifi Pérez to the Royals. As part of the trade, the Colorado Rockies received José Ortiz, Mario Encarnación, and Todd Belitz. Joe Posnanski, a columnist for the *Kansas City Star*, wrote, "Dye is everything that we want Kansas City baseball to be about. He's modest, works hard, keeps to himself, plays well, and now he's gone because the Royals simply can't afford him. Or won't afford him. Only (Royals owner) David Glass knows for sure."[5]

With the addition of Dye, the Athletics were sending a message that they were going all in on reaching the play-offs. With the help of Dye's bat (.297 batting average, 13 home runs, and 59 RBIs in 61 games), the A's finished the season with a record of 102-60, in second place in the AL West (the Seattle Mariners finished with a historic 116-46 record), and earned a wild-card spot in the postseason. In the AL Division Series, Dye fractured his tibia by fouling a ball off his left leg in Game Four. The A's lost that game, and the series.

Dye signed a three-year, $32 million extension to stay with the A's on January 16, 2002. The deal was the richest in team history at the time. The contract also included a $14 million team option for the 2005 season. Dye started the season on the injured list, still recovering from his broken leg. He made his season debut on April 26. He ended up batting .252 with 24 home runs and 86 RBIs in 131 games. The A's finished in first place in the AL West with a record of 103-59. But like the year before, they lost in the AL Division Series, this time to the Minnesota Twins, three games to two. Dye hit .400 for the series but had only one RBI.

Dye struggled with injuries for most of the 2003 season. He landed on the injured list twice. On April 24 he slipped and injured his knee while fielding a ball. On July 6 he separated his right shoulder in a home-plate collision with Anaheim catcher Bengie Molina. He played in only 65 games, hitting an abysmal .172 with 4 home runs and 20 RBIs. The A's again finished in first place in the AL West with a record of 96-66, and again lost the Division Series in five games, this time to the Boston Red Sox. Dye was 3-for-13 in the series with a home run and 3 RBIs.

Coming into the 2004 season, Dye was in the last year of his three-year contract with the A's. He was set to make over $11 million, and the A's had a $14 million option for 2005. He needed a great season for the team to justify the team's picking up that option. He started the year off strong. At the All-Star break, he was batting .285 with 16 home runs and 54 RBIs. In early August, Dye sprained his thumb while trying to make a sliding catch on the artificial turf in Minneapolis. Instead of taking time off, he insisted on playing through the pain. But the injury clearly affected his swing, and he cooled off in the second half of the season. He finished the year batting .265 with 23 home runs and 80 RBIs. The A's declined to exercise Dye's $14 million option. He became a free agent for the first time in his career.

Dye signed with the Chicago White Sox on December 9, 2004. The two-year deal was for $10.15 million, with a $6.75 million option for 2007. Dye turned down more lucrative offers to play for the White Sox, saying, "I felt Chicago was going in a good direction and with the pitching staff, I felt I had a better chance of helping the team out and

getting into the playoffs. … I just wanted to be somewhere I could be happy."[6]

Dye replaced Magglio Ordóñez for the 2005 season. Ordóñez had spent the first eight seasons of his career with the White Sox, making the All-Star team four times and putting up power numbers. Dye matched that performance, hitting .274 with 31 homers and 86 RBIs in the regular season. The postseason, though, was when Dye truly earned his contract.

The 2005 White Sox finished in first place in the AL Central Division with a record of 99-63. They bulldozed their way through the postseason, sweeping the Red Sox in the Division Series, ousting the Angels, four games to one in the Championship Series, then sweeping the Houston Astros in the World Series. Dye was named the World Series MVP after hitting .438 with a home run and 3 RBIs, including the game-winning RBI in the deciding Game Four.

The next year, 2006, proved to be the monster year for Dye. He hit .315 with 44 home runs (second only to David Ortiz in the AL) and 120 RBIs. He made his second All-Star Game and won a Silver Slugger Award. He finished fifth in AL MVP voting. The White Sox, however, could not make it back to the World Series. They finished with a record of 90-72 and were third in the AL Central Division. On October 30 they exercised their $6.75 million option for Dye's 2007 season.

The 33-year-old Dye struggled in the first half of the season. He came back stronger in the second half, finishing the year with a respectable 28 home runs and 78 RBIs. His name came up in trade rumors all season, but on August 18 he signed a two-year extension with the White Sox worth $22 million, with a mutual option for 2010. Chicago struggled as a team and finished the year in fourth place in the division with a 72-90 record.

Dye returned to form in 2008, hitting .292 with 34 home runs and 96 RBIs. He tied for second in the AL with 77 extra-base hits. He finished second in the All-Star final vote to Evan Longoria, who made the last spot on the team. The White Sox returned to their winning ways and finished in first place in the AL Central Division, but lost in the Division Series to the Tampa Bay Rays three games to one. Dye batted .375 in the series, including a home run in Game Four.

Dye hit his 300th career home run on April 13, 2009. Making it extra special, the next batter, Paul Konerko, also hit his 300th home run. Dye hit well in the first half of the season. At the All-Star break, he had a .302 average with 20 home runs and 55 RBIs. However, his output severely declined after the break: just .179 with 7 home runs and 26 RBIs. According to Dye, the problem was that "he received less regular playing time after the White Sox's out-field became more 'crowded.'"[7] Left fielder Carlos Quentin returned from plantar fasciitis on July 20 and center fielder Alex Ríos was claimed off waivers on August 10. From then on, Dye got fewer at-bats and his slump continued into

September. "Having everyone rotate between the outfield and DH, doing all that, I think it made it that much tougher than being in the lineup every day, trying to work your way out of a slump," he said. "It just kind of piled up and piled up."[8] On November 6 the White Sox bought out his $12 million mutual option for $950,000, making him a free agent again.

Dye entered the 2009-2010 offseason as a 35-year-old, two-time All-Star veteran with a World Series MVP to his name. Expectations were that he would have to take a pay cut from his previous year's $11.5 million salary. However, the offers that came in were surprisingly low. The Chicago Cubs offered him a one-year, $3 million contract. "No doubt, I've probably slowed down a little bit (defensively), but not enough to not be getting (attractive) offers," Dye said. "I just want to be treated fairly. I know the market is down, but there are still guys getting money that I feel I'm better than."[9] Dye decided to turn down all the low offers and wait until a good situation arose. He stayed in shape all season and set his sights on signing with a team for the 2011 season.

In 2010 Dye was inducted into the Cosumnes River College Hall of Fame. He said that being inducted was "one of the top three awards I have received. I played baseball in high school, but CRC is where I learned how and what it would take to play professional baseball."[10]

As the 2011 major-league season approached, Dye still had not received an offer he liked, and he was not interested in signing a minor-league contract. On March 31, 2011, he announced his retirement from baseball.

Retiring from baseball allowed Dye to spend more time with his wife, Tricia, and take a more active role in raising his three children, Devin, Tiara, and Jalen. Because he no longer had to travel during the baseball season, he was able to watch his kids play youth sports. He became an avid golfer, appearing in many pro-am tournaments. He began hosting an annual golf tournament benefiting Fresh Start, which provides surgeries and medical care to children in need. "Every year we come together and see what we are able to provide for these children through this one event, which is happiness, it's incredible," said Dye. "I'm very grateful to be a part of Fresh Start for so many years, providing life-changing work to so many."[11]

SOURCES

Unless otherwise indicated, all statistics and team records were taken from baseball-reference.com.

NOTES

1 Michelle Smith, "Dad Still Coaching Dye/Muni Driver Helped Steer His Career," *San Francisco Chronicle*, June 20, 2004: 31.

2 Tim Casey, "Everybody Loves Jermaine, a Nice Guy Who Finished First," *Sacramento Bee*, October 28, 2005: 17.

3 Bill Zack, "Braves Happy to Leave Florida, Spring Training," *Anderson* (South Carolina) *Independent Mail*, March 29, 1996: 27.

4 Terrence Moore, "Dye May Make Tutor Justice Expendable," *Atlanta Constitution*, May 18, 1996: 49.

5 Joe Posnanski, "Reality Is, Royals Can't Afford Anyone," *Kansas City Star*, July 25, 2001: 34.

6 Dave Van Dyck, "Dye the Kind of Guy Sox GM Wants," *Chicago Tribune*, December 10, 2004: 4-3.

7 Why Is Jermaine Dye Looking for Work?" FoxSports, published February 11, 2010, updated January 8, 2015. https://www.foxnews.com/sports/why-is-jermaine-dye-looking-for-work, accessed May 15, 2024.

8 Why Is Jermaine Dye Looking for Work?"

9 Why Is Jermaine Dye Looking for Work?"

10 Jermaine Dye bio, California Community College Athletic Association, CCCAA (cccaasports.org), accessed May 15, 2024.

11 "Fresh Start Swings into Action, Presenting 8th Annual Celebrity Gold Classic Hosted by Jermaine Dye in Chicago. https://www.freshstart.org/news/fresh-start-swings-into-action-presenting-8th-annual-celebrity-golf-classic-hosted-by-jermaine-dye-in-chicago/, accessed May 15, 2024.

CARL EVERETT

By Joey Elledge

Carl Everett made an impact on and off the baseball field, and not always for positive reasons. Everett, born in Tampa, Florida, was an incredible athlete at Hillsborough High School, where he played three sports, baseball, football, and track. Everett's athletic ability was impressive enough for him to be drafted by the New York Yankees in the first round of the 1990 free-agent draft. While Everett had a bright future, his tumultuous career would span 14 seasons with eight different teams, two All-Star Game appearances, one World Series with the 2005 Chicago White Sox, and plenty of controversy and scandal.

Everett's fiery personality made him a polarizing figure in baseball, as his confrontational nature frequently drew more attention than his undeniable talent. While his skills on the field showcased his athleticism and potential, his temper often disrupted team dynamics and strained relationships with players, coaches, and media members alike. Everett's outbursts and controversial behavior overshadowed his accomplishments, leaving a legacy marked as much by conflict as by his contributions to the game.

Carl Everett　　　2005

Carl Edward Everett was born on June 3, 1971, in Tampa. When he was 7, his parents, Carl Everett and Allie Preston, separated. He grew up in the working-class Belmont Heights neighborhood, where he played in the renowned Belmont Heights Little League program. This league gained fame for competing in five world championships between the early 1970s and early 1980s and for producing future major-league stars like Dwight Gooden and Gary Sheffield.

At Hillsborough High School, Everett excelled as a three-sport athlete, earning statewide recognition for his achievements in football, track, and baseball. As a junior he was part of Hillsborough's state-winning 440-yard relay team and posted an impressive 100-meter time of 10.5 seconds. On the football team in his senior year, he rushed for 948 yards. Everett also formed a significant relationship with his baseball coach, David Pittman, who became a mentor and father figure to him during challenging times.

Although Everett received offers to play football from several Division I colleges, he chose to focus on a baseball career. Known for his blend of power and speed as a switch-hitting outfielder, he was selected by the Yankees as the 10th overall pick in 1990.[1] Earning recognition on *Baseball America's* Top 100 Prospects list, Everett was ranked number 88 prior to the 1991 season, and his stock rose significantly to number 32 before the 1992 season. Everett remained a top prospect heading into 1993, ranked number 69. In 1990 he began in the Gulf Coast League, batting .260 with a .706 OPS. In 1991, with Greensboro in Class A, he improved his production, batting .271 with 96 runs scored and a .376 on-base percentage. Despite some struggles in 1992 with two teams at the high A level, Everett rebounded strongly in 1993, splitting time between high A and Triple A while hitting .296 with 25 doubles, 10 triples, 16 home runs, and a robust .908 OPS. After three seasons in the Yankees' minor-league system, Everett was picked up by the newly created Florida Marlins during the major-league expansion draft in November 1992.

Everett started his major-league journey with the Marlins, where he had limited playing time during his first two seasons. In 1993, his debut year, faced challenges adapting to major-league pitching, finishing with a .105 batting average in 19 at-bats. The next season, he saw a modest increase in playing opportunities, appearing in 16 games and raising his batting average to .216 while hitting the first two home runs of his career. Everett's first major-league home run, on May 22, 1994, against the St. Louis Cardinals' Allen Watson, was a solo shot to center field. His 1994 campaign ended when his Triple-A team, the Edmonton Trappers, suspended him for lack of hustle and insubordination that included a verbal confrontation with his manager, Sal Rende.[2]

Everett's career saw a shift when the Marlins traded him in November 1994 to the New York Mets for Quilvio Veras. With the 1995 Mets, Everett found more opportunities to grow as a player. In his first four games, he made an immediate impact, hitting two home runs – matching the total from his first 70 major-league at-bats – while batting .353. He also showcased his defensive skills, making two remarkable throws, including one that cut down Brian Jordan at the plate on a potential sacrifice fly.

By 1995, Everett began to establish himself as a productive player, hitting .260 with 12 home runs and 54 RBIs in 79 games, contributing a solid 1.9 WAR. He dipped in 1996, despite playing in 101 games, he drove in only 16 runs and hit .240. By 1997, he became a regular starter, appearing in 142 games. He delivered 14 home runs and 57 RBIs, although his .248 batting average continued to reflect some inconsistency at the plate. Over three seasons with the Mets, Everett totaled 27 home runs and 127 RBIs. Despite his on-field contributions, Everett's tenure with the Mets is often remembered more for off-field controversies that ultimately led to his departure.

From the start, Everett's time with the Mets was strained. On his first day at spring training, Everett casually walked to retrieve a ball during batting practice. Mets manager Dallas Green, observing from behind the cage, expressed frustration, muttering, "Now I see why people say the kid's a dog."[3] Green's criticism set the tone for their relationship, and Everett later claimed, "He wanted you to kiss his tail, and I wouldn't."[4] Green, who was fired in 1996, never gave Everett consistent playing time.

In addition to his on-field struggles, Everett faced significant personal and legal challenges. A pivotal moment came when he and his wife, Linda, were investigated for child abuse.[5] The case arose after bruises and welts were found on their 6-year-old daughter, Shawna, prompting the Mets to report the family to child protective services. A judge found the couple guilty of child neglect, citing Linda Everett's use of excessive corporal punishment and Carl's failure to intervene. As a result, the Everetts' 4-year-old son and 5-year-old daughter were placed in foster care.

The case drew widespread media attention, fueled by reports that the couple disciplined their children using a belt. Everett addressed the controversy in an interview with CNN/Sports Illustrated, defending his parenting style in a passionate, meandering statement. "They're trying to say that we beat 'em with our fists," Everett said. "Trying to say that we slapped our kids. I mean, anyone that's my age or older knows you're going to get your spankings, you're going to get discipline. But in this day and age, you have people that don't have any kids trying to tell [other] people how to raise their kids."[6]

Everett also criticized lawmakers, arguing that they lacked the experience to legislate on parenting. "Most of the people that make these laws don't have kids, don't have a relationship. Can't tell you the first meaning of how to change a diaper ... how it is to stay up to 3 or 4 o'clock in the morning with a sick child or a hungry child."[7]

After the 1997 season, Everett was traded to the Houston Astros for pitcher John Hudek. In Houston, Everett found both consistent playing time and personal fulfillment over two seasons, solidifying his reputation as a fierce competitor. His intensity was on full display during one memorable incident when he reacted angrily to being given a day off by manager Larry Dierker. Frustrated, Everett ripped the lineup card off the clubhouse wall, stormed into Dierker's office, tore it into pieces, and threw the scraps onto the manager's desk, demanding that a new one be prepared.[8] Despite the outburst, Dierker stuck to his original lineup.

Everett's performance with the Astros reflected his growth as a player. In 1998 he hit .296 with 15 home runs and 76 RBIs, helping Houston secure a playoff spot. The next season, 1999, Everett reached new heights, delivering a breakout performance. He batted .325 with 25 home runs and 108 RBIs, contributing 5.8 WAR. His .969 OPS and .425 weighted on-base average (wOBA) underscored his elite offensive capabilities.

Despite Everett's success, the Astros faced tough decisions about their roster. With Everett eligible for free agency after the 1999 season, Houston opted to trade him to the Boston Red Sox for infielder Adam Everett and pitcher Greg Miller. Astros general manager Gerry Hunsicker explained the decision: "We chose [second baseman Craig] Biggio and [first baseman Jeff] Bagwell over Everett rather than putting dollars into an outfielder. We had young outfielders, such as Daryle Ward, Lance Berkman, and Richard Hidalgo, who we thought could be impact players."[9] Both Biggio and Bagwell later became Hall of Famers.

Everett's time with the Red Sox was a mix of on-field excellence and off-field controversy. He quickly made his mark. In 2000 he was named an All-Star, hitting .300 with 34 home runs and 108 RBIs – leading the team in the latter two categories by a considerable margin. He posted a .959 OPS and a 4.7 WAR. Despite injuries in 2001, he managed 14 home runs and 58 RBIs in 102 games, finishing his two-year stint in Boston with 48 home runs and 166 RBIs.

In a highlight of his on-the-field production for the Red Sox, Everett, pinch-hitting, broke up Yankees pitcher Mike Mussina's bid for a perfect game in 2001. In the ninth inning, with Mussina one out away from a perfecto, Everett lined a single to left field. Yet, his production as a hitter could not overshadow his actions outside the batter's box.

In a July 2000 Red Sox game against the Mets, Everett argued with umpire Ron Kulpa over batter's box positioning and head-butted Kulpa, drawing a 10-game suspension.[10]

Later that season, during a game against the Mariners, Everett hit a home run but responded to being hit by a pitch from Jamie Moyer by grabbing his crotch and spitting in Moyer's direction, resulting in a fine from Major League Baseball.[11]

Everett had a confrontation with a *Boston Globe* reporter in the clubhouse between games of a doubleheader in 2001.[12] Angered by a story published in the *Globe*, Everett directed a string of expletives at baseball writer Gordon Edes. Even though Edes' name was not attached to the article, the incident followed a report by the *Globe*'s Bob Hohler stating that Everett had missed the team bus from the hotel to Detroit's Comerica Park.

Everett held many unusual beliefs that he openly shared, including the idea that dinosaurs never existed and that the moon landings were staged. These views prompted *Boston Globe* sportswriter Dan Shaughnessy to nickname him "Jurassic Carl."[13]

In response, Everett coined a derogatory nickname for Shaughnessy, calling him the Curly Haired Boyfriend (CHB) of beat writer Edes.[14] The term "CHB" has since become a lasting way for Red Sox fans to refer to Shaughnessy.

Everett's behavior strained his relationship with the Red Sox. He was suspended twice in 2001 – once in spring training for missing a team bus and again in September for being late to a team workout after the 9/11 attacks. His frequent confrontations with manager Jimy Williams and his late arrival to games further isolated him within the organization.

On December 12, 2001, Everett was traded to the Texas Rangers for pitcher Darren Oliver. During his time with the Rangers, Everett provided consistent offensive production. In 2003, he split his season between Texas and the Chicago White Sox, finishing with a strong performance: 28 home runs, 92 RBIs, a .287 batting average, and an .876 OPS.

Everett's tenure with the Rangers was not without controversy. During a game in Arlington, he reported being hit by a cellphone thrown from the stands, stating, "It's just ignorance and alcohol and probably too much of both. That's what causes this." He pressed charges against the person responsible.[15] Everett also accidentally hit an Oakland Athletics employee with a thrown phone while trying to clear debris from the field. The employee was bandaged and returned to work without serious injury.

Another incident occurred when Everett's bat slipped from his hands during an at-bat against the Athletics, striking a 15-year-old girl and a 4-year-old boy in the stands.[16] The game was delayed for medical personnel to attend to the injured fans. While visibly shaken, Everett expressed deep concern for their well-being. Both fans recovered, with the girl receiving hospital treatment and the boy treated at the ballpark.

Despite his offensive capabilities, Everett faced criticism for his defensive play in center field. His performance drew frustration from teammates and management after he failed to catch a routine fly ball and missed a cutoff man, with costly results. Manager Jerry Narron moved Everett to designated-hitter duties, citing dissatisfaction with his defense.

At spring training, Everett confronted *Dallas Observer* columnist John Gonzalez in the clubhouse, questioning his credentials and escalating the encounter into a heated exchange of expletives. When Gonzalez asked Everett a question about professional boxing, Everett responded by saying, "You don't want to talk boxing. You wanna box me? (Turns to me, squares off, puts fists up by his head.) You don't wanna box me.[17]"

Everett was traded to the White Sox on July 1, 2003, for Frank Francisco, Josh Rupe, and minor-leaguer Anthony Webster. He bumped his .274 batting average for the Rangers up to .301 for the White Sox, though in 73 White Sox games he drove in 41 runs as compared to 51 for the Rangers in 74 games.

After signing as a free agent with the Montreal Expos for the 2004 season, Everett was traded back to the White Sox on July 18, 2004, for pitchers Gary Majewski and Jon Rauch.

On August 21, 2004, Everett made headlines when he argued with home-plate umpire Doug Eddings after striking out with the bases loaded during a game against the Red Sox.[18] This fiery demeanor epitomized Everett's competitive intensity throughout his tenure with the White Sox.

In 2005 Everett drew attention for controversial comments to reporters, including remarks on homosexuality, his disdain for Wrigley Field (saying it should be imploded), criticism of baseball fans for not knowing "diddly" about the game, and calling congressional hearings on steroids a waste of time.[19]

Everett became a critical part of the 2005 White Sox, especially after a season-ending injury to Frank Thomas. He delivered 23 home runs, 87 RBIs, and a competitive edge that helped propel the team to the playoffs. Though his batting average dipped to .251, his power hitting and clutch performances were pivotal. In the American League playoffs, Everett returned to Fenway Park, where he faced his former team, the Red Sox, amid heavy boos from the crowd. Everett dismissed any nostalgia for his time in Boston, stating, "It's just another ballpark. There's no special feeling in this ballpark, not even when I played here."[20]

The White Sox swept the Red Sox in the ALDS, and Everett's performance continued to shine during the postseason. In the World Series he batted .444 (4-for-9), with 1 run, 4 hits, and a .889 OPS.

A free agent after the World Series, Everett signed a one-year contract for 2006 with the Seattle Mariners with a club option for the 2007 season. "Today we achieved one of our offseason goals," said Mariners general manager Bill Bavasi in a statement. "Carl Everett is a clutch-hitting run producer with power. As a switch-hitter, he provides our lineup with added versatility. Carl is a winner, most recently as a member of the 2005 World Series Champion Chicago

GRINDERS AND GAMERS

White Sox. His experience and intensity will be welcome additions to our clubhouse."[21]

In his final major-league season, with the Mariners, the 35-year-old Everett struggled at the plate, finishing with a .227 batting average and 11 home runs in 92 games. In the first half of the season, Everett was active in the clubhouse and community but struggled on the field, batting just .159 against left-handers. This prompted manager Mike Hargrove to bench him against left-handed starters and led to the acquisition of Perez as Seattle's DH for such matchups on June 30. Tensions escalated after a July 4 game when Everett and Hargrove had a heated argument over his reduced role. Asked for a comment the next day, Everett responded, "Tell them it's none of their business.[22]" However, on July 26, 2006, The Mariners designated Everett for assignment Wednesday, making Seattle the 35-year-old's eighth former team. The team recalled outfielder Chris Snelling from Triple-A Tacoma to take Everett's roster spot.

Everett played the next four years in the independent Atlantic League, in 2007 and 2008 for the Long Island Ducks and 2009 and 2010 for the Newark Bears, batting over .300 the first three of the four seasons.

Everett's reputation as both a talented player and a polarizing figure has drawn mixed reactions from those who have worked with or competed against him. His confidence is legendary, sometimes bordering on arrogance, as highlighted by pitcher Ryan Dempster: "Carl Everett is the best player in the major leagues. Just ask Carl Everett."[23]

Everett's strong personality often left an impression, both positive and negative. Manager John Boles, who worked with Everett during his time in Florida's player-development system, reflected on the polarizing nature of his character:

"If I didn't know him, I'd say, 'What's his problem?' But I know him, so it doesn't affect me. It's like our catcher, Paul Bako, who played with him in Houston, said: Carl's the kind of guy opponents hate. When you play with him, you appreciate what he brings. Carl shoots from the hip. Sometimes he's accurate. Sometimes he's not."[24]

Despite his fiery demeanor, Everett's talent on the field often overshadowed his outspoken nature. Hall of Fame pitcher Pedro Martinez acknowledged the balance between Everett's brashness and skill: "The guy can yap. But he can back it up. It's a good thing he is this good."[25]

In his post-baseball years, Everett was arrested in Lutz, Florida, a suburb of Tampa, in April 2011 on charges of aggravated assault with a deadly weapon and tampering with a witness.[26] According to police records, Everett pressed a handgun to his wife's head during an argument. Everett's attorney, Clinton Paris, described the situation as a family matter, expressing hope that it could be resolved quickly and efficiently.

The arrest affidavit stated that Everett and his wife of 18 years began arguing when Everett put a handgun against the side of her head. Linda Everett reportedly attempted to call 911 twice, but, according to the affidavit, Everett seized both phones and broke them to prevent her from contacting authorities.

Everett has often claimed that his straightforwardness is misunderstood. Reflecting on how others perceived him, Everett once said: "You might think, 'That butthole,' before you meet me. I don't care. If I'm telling you something, I'm just telling you the truth."[27]

Everett frequently expressed his views with a rigid, absolute perspective, stating that he dealt only in "wins and losses, truths and lies, and what is in the Bible and what is not."[28] While his candor may have resonated with some, others viewed his matter-of-fact tone as confrontational.

As Everett put it, "You heard what Barry Bonds said, 'They don't boo you if you're bad,'" a fitting legacy for Everett, his life, and baseball career.[29]

Since retiring from baseball, Carl Everett has maintained a low profile, staying out of the public eye and refraining from engaging with the media. Attempts to gather more information about his post-baseball life have proven uninformative, leaving little insight into his current activities or whereabouts.

SOURCES

In addition to the sources cited in the Notes, the author consulted Baseball-Reference.com and Retrosheet.org.

NOTES

1   Bryan Hoch, "The Top Yanks Draft Pick from Every Season," MLB.com, July 14, 2024. https://www.mlb.com/news/all-time-yankees-top-draft-picks.

2   Tom Verducci, "Mighty Mouth / A Man of Many Strong Opinions, Boston Centerfielder Carl Everett Speaks Loudly and Carries a Big Stick," *Sports Illustrated*, June 19, 2000. https://vault.si.com/vault/2000/06/19/mighty-mouth-a-man-of-many-strong-opinions-boston-centerfielder-carl-everett-speaks-loudly-and-carries-a-big-stick. See also https://www.espn.com/mlb/news/2001/0917/1251852.html.

3   Verducci.

4   Verducci.

5   Mirta Ojito, "D.A. Still Looking Into Everett Abuse Case," *New York Times*, August 10, 1997, https://www.nytimes.com/1997/08/10/sports/da-still-looking-into-everett-abuse-case.html.

6   Verducci.

7   Verducci.

8   "Carl Everett's Highlights and Lowlights," *Seattle Times*, December 15, 2005, https://archive.seattletimes.com/archive/20051215/everetttimeline15/carl-everetts-highlights-and-lowlights.

9   Verducci.

10   "Everett Head-Butts Umpire," *Tampa Bay Times*, July 16, 2000, https://www.tampabay.com/archive/2000/07/16/everett-head-butts-umpire/.

11   Associated Press, "Everett Fined for Incident with Moyer," ESPN.com, August 17, 2000.

12   "Everett Berates Globe Writers," *Hartford Courant*, September 21, 2000, https://www.courant.com/2000/09/21/everett-berates-globe-writers/.

13   Drew Athans, "Boston Red Sox Most Controversial Figures: Carl Everett," BoSox Injection, https://bosoxinjection.com/2020/05/29/boston-red-sox-controversial-figures-carl-everett/.

14   Athans.

15   John Shea, "A's Ring Up a Win / Rangers Routed, and OF Everett Beaned with a Cell Phone," SFGate, April 20, 2003, https://www.sfgate.com/sports/shea/article/A-s-ring-up-a-win-Rangers-routed-and-OF-2621173.php.

16   Associated Press, "Teenage Girl Taken to Hospital for Observation," ESPN.com, June 25, 2003, https://www.espn.com/mlb/news/2003/0625/1572959.html.

17   John Gonzales, "Sparring with Carl Everett," Deadspin.com, April 8, 2014, https://www.google.com/earch?q=Sparring+With+Carl+Everett&rlz=1C-1VDKB_enUS1069US1069&sourceid=chrome&ie=UTF-8.

18   Travis Landes, "The Curious Case of Carl Everett," 2SeamSports, March 11, 2024, https://2seamsports.com/?p=372.

19   "White Sox's Everett Opines on Gays, Wrigley, Steroids," ESPN.com, June 15, 2005, https://www.espn.com/mlb/news/story?id=2087125.

20   Jeff Horrigan, "Everett Fans Flames," *Milford* (Massachusetts) *Daily News,* October 7, 2005, https://www.milforddailynews.com/story/sports/2005/10/07/everett-fans-flames/41310313007/.

21   "M's Sign Everett," *Seattle Times,* December 14, 2005, https://www.seattletimes.com/sports/ms-sign-everett-for-one-year/.

22   Associated Press, "Mariners designate DH Everett for assignment", July 26,2006, https://www.espn.com/mlb/news/story?id=2530463

23   Verducci, "Mighty Mouth."

24   Verducci.

25   Verducci.

26   Associated Press, "Carl Everett Arrested in Florida," ESPN.com, April 26, 2011, https://www.espn.com/mlb/news/story?id=6430043.

27   Verducci.

28   Verducci.

29   Horrigan, "Everett Fans Flames."

FREDDY GARCIA

By Tony S. Oliver

Mark Langston, Mike Campbell, John Halama, Carlos Guillén, Freddy García, Brad Halsey, Dioner Navarro, Javier Vázquez, Alberto González, Steven Jackson, Ross Ohlendorf, Luis Vizcaíno. These dozen men were traded, in different transactions, for Hall of Famer Randy Johnson. While they share a bond, their major-league careers took different paths. Several would play in the World Series; some in All-Star Games; a few in the Caribbean Series; and others in the World Baseball Classic. Only one – García – would win a game in all four competitions, a feat unmatched as of 2024 by any other player in baseball history.

García was born on October 6, 1976, in Caracas, Venezuela. The year produced four other big- leaguers: Kelvim Escobar, Ramón Hernández, Alex Prieto, and Liu Rodríguez, a bumper crop of talent for the South American nation. Up north, the Cincinnati Reds would win their second consecutive World Series, sweeping the Yankees in their first postseason of the George Steinbrenner era. Fidel Castro's Cuba had been shut down as a baseball factory; Puerto Rico and the Dominican Republic had taken its place. Farther south, agents Peter and Edward Greenberg saw an opening in Venezuela and focused their attention there; at one point, 80 percent of their clients were from the country.[1]

Two days after turning 17, Freddy signed with the Houston Astros. Unlike many of his peers, García began his professional career not back home, but rather in the United States. The Astros assigned him to the Gulf Coast League; he appeared in 11 games and showcased a 6-3 record with a 4.47 ERA. The team featured seven would-be major leaguers, with García and his countryman Guillén the only ones of consequence. The tandem spent the winter with the Navegantes of Magallanes, for whom García appeared in five games; his statistics were far from inspiring: He allowed 21 baserunners in 13⅔ innings.

The Class-A Midwest League was García's home in 1996. Quad Cities won its division, with García providing a sparkling 3.12 ERA in 60⅔ innings, almost a full run better than the 3.94 league average. At 19, he was more than two years younger than his adversaries, but he handled the pressure quite well; however, his winter experience was not quite as successful; he pitched in only three games, all in relief, allowing six baserunners in 2⅔ frames.

Houston was inspired by his prior success and sent García to the Florida State League's Kissimmee club in

the spring of 1997. The Cobras won their division and led the league in ERA; Freddy and future big-leaguer Wade Miller provided a formidable one-two punch with a 20-10 combined record. Perhaps concerned with his youth, the Astros kept him at high A rather than promote him to the more advanced circuits. He tasted his first real success with Magallanes, pitching in 17 games (five starts) and allowing 3.20 runs per game. His control was spotty; he walked 19 while fanning 25. García's "true outcome" (strikeouts, walks, and home runs allowed) performance robbed fielders of two out of three chances, raising his pitch count and prompting questions of his focus.

In 1998 García hurled 133⅔ innings for the Texas League's Jackson team and the Pacific Coast League's New Orleans franchise, striking out almost a batter per inning, but his potential was pitted against Houston's "win-now" mindset. In the Pacific Northwest, the Seattle Mariners were a franchise at a crossroads. From their inception in 1977 until 1994, they had enjoyed only two winning seasons. The 1987 draft brought reason for joy as Seattle chose Ken Griffey Jr.

Freddy Garcia　　　2005

with the first pick; "The Kid," as he would be known, was a blue-chipper; a true "can't-miss prospect," and as of 2024, one of only four top selections enshrined in Cooperstown (Harold Baines, Joe Mauer, and Chipper Jones being the others). In 1995 the Mariners overcame a 13-game deficit on August 2 to tie, and then defeat, the California Angels in a one-game tiebreaker for their first Western Division crown. A young core of Griffey and Alex Rodríguez joined veterans Edgar Martínez and Randy Johnson for another two winning seasons before Johnson demanded a trade in the summer of 1998. Seattle had gambled by looking at the cards on its hand – a two-time MVP in Griffey, a two-time batting champion in Martínez, and the third youngest batting champion in history (Rodríguez), two rubber-armed, inning-eating left-handed veterans – Jamie Moyer and Jeff Fassero – and traded Johnson for three rookies (Guillén, García, and Halama).

The Big Unit was an absolute beast for Houston, winning 10 out of 11 decisions down the stretch as the team crossed the century-win mark for the first time. The fairy tale ended against eventual NL champion San Diego, and Johnson bolted for Arizona in the offseason. García, on the other hand, won three games for Tacoma and earned a spot in the Seattle 1999 rotation. He sought more winter work and appeared in 15 games for the Navegantes but again struggled to keep the opposition off the bases, highlighted by a 1.641 WHIP.

Seattle's future seemed bright, with a brand-new ballpark, Safeco Field (later renamed T-Mobile Park) replacing the monstrous granite monolith known as the Kingdome. *Baseball America* anointed García as the 61st best prospect entering the 1999 season.[2] Manager Lou Piniella entrusted García as the third starter; all García did in return was lead the team in wins (17) and strikeouts (170) and finish second in Rookie of the Year voting and ninth in Cy Young Award balloting. He debuted at home on April 7 against the White Sox in front of 21,050 fans eager to see the centerpiece of the Johnson trade. García did not disappoint; pitching 5⅔ innings, he scattered seven hits, walked two, struck out five, balked once, and allowed two runs, making for a nice assortment of outcomes from his 94 pitches. He struck out his first batter, Ray Durham, but was harmed by his countryman Magglio Ordóñez's double to score Frank Thomas in the first. The Mariners provided Garcia with five runs and García earned the win, pitching a perfect fifth inning and getting two outs in the sixth before being replaced by José Paniagua to the cheers of the Seattle faithful.

On August 7 García earned a hard lesson as the defending (and eventually repeating) Yankees visited Safeco. Although García hurled a complete game, struck out 10, and allowed only three hits, he was bested by Andy Pettitte, Mike Stanton, and Mariano Rivera, none of whose 11 baserunners crossed the plate. Scott Brosius's sacrifice fly to score former Mariner Tino Martínez was the difference in

a 1-0 beauty. Although the team dipped to a 79-83 record, optimism was in the air.

García's April 2000 record (2-1) belied some ugly figures. He gave the team 18 innings but was hit hard; 14 runs were charged to his totals. On April 21 he injured his knee while covering first base and landed on the disabled list; he was far from alone, as the snake-bitten Mariners had previously lost Moyer and Martínez. John Mabry and Mike Cameron would also miss time.[3] After 17 strong rehabilitation frames, García returned to Seattle on July 7, delivering six innings in a 3-2 loss to the Dodgers. He was both durable and valuable the rest of the way, ending 9-5 for the 91-71 club. García opened the first game in the Division Series but the White Sox hammered him for four runs on six hits and three walks. In the type of irony only baseball can sometimes provide, the last batter he faced was Durham, whom he had struck out in his first start. The Mariners, however, won both the game and the series in a 3-0 sweep.

The Yankees had been dominated by García's stuff the prior summer; he was nothing short of spectacular in the Championship Series. In the series opener, he struck out eight and scattered two walks and three hits in 6⅔ innings. His teammates crossed the plate twice, giving him the needed support, as the Mariners took a one games to none lead. The Yankees won the next three games, putting the Mariners on the brink of elimination, but García was once again on the mound on Game Five in Seattle. Pitching five innings, he allowed two runs and seven hits, leaving the game with a 6-2 lead his mates would not relinquish. The Yankees closed the Series two days later, but the baseball world would take notice of Seattle's new ace.

Despite the disappointment of the prior October, the Mariners began 2001 on a roll. The team had lost Rodríguez to free agency but landed Japanese superstar Ichiro Suzuki, who like Madonna, Prince, or Liberace would soon become famous enough to go by one name and win both the Rookie of the Year and Most Valuable Player Awards. The club roared to a modern record 116 wins, with García contributing a career-high 18 wins, 238⅔ innings, and a 3.05 ERA. He finished third in the Cy Young Award voting, and joined teammates Suzuki, Bret Boone, John Olerud, Martínez, Cameron, and Kazuhiro Sasaki in front of the hometown fans for the All-Star Game. Throwing only seven pitches, García retired Chipper Jones, Jeff Kent, and Rich Aurilia in the third inning. The junior circuit scored in the bottom half, giving him the win while Sasaki earned the save in the ninth.

The juggernaut faced the dangerous Indians in the 2001 League Championship Series and García was given the ball in the first contest. Although he struck out eight, he allowed four runs on a string of seven well-placed singles, two doubles, and two walks. His mound opponent, Bartolo Colón, scattered eight baserunners across eight innings, baffling the Mariners with 10 punchouts. The duo had a rematch in Game Four with reversed roles; although both went six-plus innings, it was García who earned the win by allowing one earned run (an additional one unearned) on four hits, one walk, and five strikeouts. Seattle went on to win Game Five and earn a rematch against New York.

Three runs separated the two franchises but ultimately the Yankees prevailed, four games to one. García was a hard-luck loser in Game Two; the second inning was his downfall, as a Brosius double scored Tino Martínez and Jorge Posada; Brosius himself would score later on Chuck Knoblauch's single. The Mariners answered with a pair in the fourth but that was all the scoring the game would see.

In 2002 Oakland and New York won 103 games, Anaheim 99. The Mariners won 93 and stayed home during the postseason. A regression from the mean was to be expected, and García was not an exception. He won 16 games, but his ERA grew to 4.39 though he recorded 181 strikeouts; his record through June (11-5) earned him another All-Star nod. While he did not pick up the win, no one else did either; the 73rd midsummer classic ended as a 7-7 tie when both teams ran out of pitchers. García retired the side in the bottom of the 11th to some boos; he had entered the game in the prior inning and had even picked up an at-bat. Perhaps frazzled from the exercise, he went 5-5 the rest of the year as Seattle was surpassed by both Oakland and Anaheim and missed the postseason.

The next year proved to be disappointing as the Mariners again finished 93-69 but failed to reach the playoffs. García experienced his first losing record in the major leagues, winning 12 games but losing 14. His ERA increased to 4.51 and his control was spotty; he hit 11 batters, unleashed 11 wild pitches, and walked 71. The Mariners were inconsistent in their run support; while they averaged 4.41 runs during his starts, they scored two or fewer in 15 of his games while crossing double-digits in five others. Nevertheless, García's ERA was north of 5.00 for most of the season before he closed September with 27 strong innings (3 runs, 15 hits, 20 strikeouts).

García's hard luck continued in 2004 as he started 15 games for the Mariners. Despite a 3.20 ERA over 107 innings, he was 4-7 before Seattle traded him to the White Sox. He and batterymate Ben Davis went to Chicago for prospects Mike Morse and Jeremy Reed and catcher Miguel Olivo. Although García allowed more runs with the White Sox, he increased his strikeout performance and went 9-4 the rest of the way, for a combined 13-11 season, his fourth consecutive double-digit-win campaign. Chicago was in its first year with Ozzie Guillén as manager and García felt comfortable with his countryman at the helm. The relationship was beneficial in 2005, when the White Sox broke their 88-year drought atop the baseball world, winning the World Series with a dominating 99 regular-season wins and a 13-1 romp over their October rivals.

García pitched to a 3.87 ERA in 33 starts, picking up 14 victories along the way. The team had solid pitching, with Mark Buehrle, García, Jon Garland, and José Contreras

all surpassing 200 innings and 30 starts. Given the team's dominance, García pitched in only one game in each of the postseason series but grew stronger as the leaves fell. He provided five acceptable innings against Boston (three runs), a complete game against the Angels (two runs), and then a masterful seven frames against the Astros (seven strikeouts, four hits, three walks) in the World Series clincher, winning all three games for a storybook October.

If García was on cloud nine after winning a ring, he soon leapt to a 10th one. After years of discussion, a multinational competition modeled after the soccer World Cup was finally a reality. The World Baseball Classic occupied the attention of the sport's fans everywhere, and Venezuela was no exception. Twenty-five of the team's 30 members were current major leaguers; All-Stars were at every position.[4] Placed in Pool D, the country dropped its first game against the powerhouse Dominican Republic, 11-5. As Italy had blanked Australia 10-0, the second contest became a must-win, and manager Luis Sojo called upon García. The pitcher dominated the Europeans (and American-born players representing "the old country" like Mike Piazza and Frank Menechino), allowing one walk and one hit while striking out seven in 3⅓ innings. Under WBC rules, strict pitch counts were in effect, so García picked up the win despite throwing only 61 pitches.[5] Venezuela advanced to the second round with a 2-0 victory over Australia but found itself in a proverbial "group of death" with the Dominicans, the Cubans, and the Puerto Ricans. Once again Venezuela dropped the first game, 7-2 against Cuba, but rebounded with a 6-0 win over host Puerto Rico. García took the mound for the series finale, a loser-goes-home affair against the Dominican Republic. Thousands of fans from both sides were present at the Hiram Bithorn Stadium and they witnessed a beauty as the teams were tied, 1-1, after six innings. The starters, Daniel Cabrera and García, were both lifted after four innings. García had allowed one run in the first frame before the Venezuelans tied it. Kelvim Escobar provided a solid three innings but was charged with a loss as Alberto Castillo scored an unearned run.[6]

The 2006 edition of the White Sox dropped to third place in its division with a solid yet unspectacular 90-72 record. The Twins and Tigers won 96 and 95, respectively, with the latter winning the pennant. García delivered another strong season, leading the team in innings pitched (216⅓) en route to 17 wins and a 4.53 ERA. Controversy surrounded him in early May, as the Venezuelan newspaper *Líder* reported that he had tested positive for marijuana during the WBC.[7] While this merited a two-year ban from the International Baseball Federation, it had no effect on his major-league status and no action was taken. García did not miss a single start, winning his last four, with a masterful performance on September 13. Facing the Angels on the road, he took a perfect game into the eighth inning before allowing a single to Adam Kennedy on his 100th pitch. García did not second-guess himself: "I threw the right pitch," he said, noting that his 8-1 career mark at Angel Stadium gave him confidence.[8] Although he was not as dominant six days later – this time he allowed two walks alongside one hit – his pristine eight innings helped the White Sox defeat the Tigers and pull his club within 4½ games of the wild-card spot; it was the closest they would get before finishing five games off Detroit's pace.

On December 6, 2006, the White Sox surprised their fans by trading García to the Phillies for Gavin Floyd and Gio González. Philadelphia was a team on the rise, with a trio of All-Stars in the infield (Chase Utley, Ryan Howard, and Jimmy Rollins). The team needed pitching, as the rotation was slated to feature now 44-year-old Moyer and hot 23-year-old prospect Cole Hamels. García had earned a reputation as a big-game pitcher during his stay in Chicago to go along with his durability. He had thrown six consecutive 200-inning seasons, each with 30 starts. Though he would enter the season as a 30-year-old with over 1,600 professional innings pitched, the Phillies allegedly relied on Chicago's medical staff reports.[9] They paid dearly for their oversight, as García suffered through a miserable, injury-riddled campaign, starting 11 games and posting an unsightly 5.90 ERA. Though he attempted to play through his ailments, he eventually capitulated and visited pitching savior Dr. James Andrews to repair his labrum.[10] Philadelphia had surrendered two prospects and $10 million for exactly one win.

Since García was set to enter the free-agent market, his arm troubles undoubtedly cost him a fortune. Rehabilitating for most of 2008, he signed a short-term deal with Detroit that showed initial promise: His first game in almost a year yielded five solid innings, facing 18 batters, yielding one run on two hits, striking out three while issuing one walk. Six days later he was rocked by Kansas City, allowing five runs in five innings. A last start against the White Sox was inconclusive; he did not figure in the decision despite hurling five more frames of two-run ball. His season line was 1-1 with a 4.20 ERA on the strength of 206 pitches, and the Tigers declined to bring him back. García sought extra work back home in the 2008-2009 campaign, throwing seven ineffective innings (4 runs, 10 baserunners) for Magallanes.

The New York Mets signed García in early 2009 but released him before the end of April after a disappointing stint with their Triple-A affiliate Buffalo (11 innings, 10 runs). He was at a crossroads but a familiar location would soon beckon him to return. Chicago reached out to García and both sides agreed to a deal. He went back to basics and spent time with Bristol of the Appalachian League, Kannapolis of the South Atlantic League, and Charlotte of the International League before the White Sox recalled him. He appeared in nine games down the stretch, averaging roughly six innings per contest with a respectable 4.34 ERA.

Named the fourth starter, García entered 2010 with certainty for the first time in a few years. He gave the team a solid 157 innings, good for a 12-6 record on a 4.64 ERA. He surpassed 100 pitches five times, including an August 27 matchup against the Yankees (seven innings, one earned run). Little did he know it was far from just a late-season game but rather an unexpected audition. Though the Yankees won 95 games and earned the wild card, their pitching was suspect in the LCS vs. the Texas Rangers. Eager to return to the World Series, the team inked García to a one-year, incentive-laden deal and he proved to be a wise investment for 2011, contributing 12 wins and a 3.62 ERA in 26 games. He was handed the ball in the Division Series, an odd five-game affair that the Yankees dominated batting- and pitchingwise but lost, as Detroit won the close games and New York won the blowouts. García gave up three earned runs in 5⅓ innings but Max Scherzer dominated the Yankees bats to win the second game of the series. This was a different version of García; on the wrong side of 30, he relied on his other pitches rather than attempt to overpower everyone with his fastball. In a 2011 interview, he cited a "new attitude; you have to, 'cause that's your job and you gotta get people out."[11] Earlier in his career, Moyer had prompted him to "take it easy, breathe … you got the stuff" but the bravado of youth (and a strong fastball) had carried him to success.[12] Guile and experience now accompanied García on the mound.

The Yankees brass eagerly brought García back in 2012, but the magic was gone. He pitched his way out of the rotation with a 12.51 April ERA. His next 10 games as a reliever were the opposite; a sparkling 1.56 ERA in 17⅓ innings, but injuries to New York starters returned him to the rotation and he opened 13 games with a 4.67 ERA before wrapping up the year in the bullpen. His emotional apex was a July 24 contest against the Mariners; he shared the mound with the young fireballer Félix Hernández, who wore uniform number 34 in honor of García. In an episode pitting the ghosts of Christmas past and Christmas present, the all-time Venezuelan wins leader (García) was bested by the heir apparent (Hernández) in a 4-2 affair.

As 2013 began, García was looking for employment. A few clubs inquired about his services, and the Padres signed him on January 28. He was released at the end of spring training, but quickly found a suitor in Baltimore. He was ineffective as the Orioles' fifth starter, starting 10 games and allowing 34 earned runs in 53 innings. Atlanta purchased his contract for the stretch run, and his second foray into the National League was much more successful than his first; García allowed five runs in 27⅓ innings for the Braves, helping them to the division title. He was pitted against Clayton Kershaw in the last game of the LDS, with both pitchers throwing six frames of two-run ball. The Dodgers bullpen proved to be stronger, and Los Angeles won the series.

García still had a lot of baseball left in him. In 2014 He joined the Chinese Professional Baseball League in Taiwan, inking with the EDA Rhinos, following in the footsteps of

Manny Ramírez, who had played in 49 contests the prior year.[13] The siren song of his homeland proved irresistible, and he suited for the Tigres of Aragua in the 2014-2015 season, his first appearance in six years. He was on the mound for 27 innings (regular and postseason), allowing eight runs en route to a 2-1 mark.[14]

After a few weeks of rest and eager to prove his value, García signed with the Mexican Baseball League's Olmecas of Tabasco for the 2015 season, catching the eye of the Dodgers brass, who offered him a contract with its Triple-A affiliate. He performed poorly and returned to Tabasco before turning his season around with the Sultanes of Monterrey. Overall in Triple A he threw 76⅓ frames with a 4.38 ERA with an impressive 51/11 strikeout/walk split. Perhaps suffering from fatigue, he struggled with Aragua in eight starts, yielding a 5.17 ERA in the regular season. All was forgotten, though, as the Tigres won the Venezuelan title with García starting one game in the playoffs, giving him the opportunity to perform on a grand stage: the 2016 Caribbean Series.

Former major leaguer Eddie Pérez led the Venezuelan team and put great responsibility on the right-hander's broad shoulders: "Freddy is our guy. To me, he's the right guy at the right time. Freddy has pitched in situations bigger than this, better and in worse."[15] The Dominican Republic hosted and dedicated the event to Hall of Famer Juan Marichal. García announced his retirement at the conclusion of the series; he started game one against Puerto Rico's Cangrejeros of Santurce and pitched six innings while allowing only one run to earn a tough victory.[16] Aragua met Mexico's representatives, the Venados of Mazatlán, in the tournament final but lost a heartbreaker when Jorge Vázquez homered to break a 4-4 tie in the ninth inning. García was named to the all-tournament team for his performance, the eldest statesman of the group.

In 2016 Monterrey requested his return, and García appeared in five games. Although his control was impeccable (7/1 K/BB ratio), he was hit hard with a 5.01 ERA. Nevertheless, he won two games as the club was an offensive juggernaut with a league-leading .464 slugging percentage en route to a 72-39 record and the northern division title. He sat out the winter but made a triumphant return to Aragua in November for 2017. At the ripe age of 41, he announced his intention to retire at season's end and, against all odds, enjoyed his best Venezuelan season. Winning four games with an 11-1 K/BB ratio for Aragua, he earned the Comeback Player of the Year Award.[17] Earlier in the season, the All-Star game was dedicated to him; Edgar Navega, president of the Unique Association of Venezuelan Professional Baseball Players (Asociación Única de Peloteros Profesionales de Venezuela), announced the honor by stating, "Freddy García has been a pitcher who has gifted many great moments to both baseball and Venezuela; for a long time he was the pitcher with most major-league wins."[18]

The Tigres made the postseason but bowed out during the round-robin; the eventual champion Caribes of Anzoategui picked him up as a reinforcement for the finals and García contributed 8⅔ innings in two starts. The triumph afforded García another shot at the Caribbean Series title; the bitter taste of the 2016 defeat still stung: "[I]t would be wonderful. … You know, I tried doing it two years back and we lost in the last inning against México. In short series like these, a team can go on a streak. … A lot of things can happen."[19] The event was bittersweet as its original location, Venezuela, was changed to México due to the unrest in Venezuela. García started game two against the Águilas Cibeañas but struggled early, allowing three runs in 4⅔ innings. He left with the lead and his teammates put on an offensive show, crossing the plate 15 times.

As the seasons changed, Yucatán was impressed and persuaded García to sign with the Leones. Starting five games, he went 2-2. His 5.32 ERA looks lofty, but the league is offense-oriented; the average mark was 5.06 during the 2018 campaign. He followed up his performance with 14⅔ innings in the 2018-2019 Venezuelan season, although his start in the finals was rocky (two innings pitched, four runs allowed, six baserunners). Upon his retirement from the major leagues, García was the career leader among Venezuelans in wins (156), games started (357), and innings pitched (2,264), but he has since been surpassed by Felix Hernández in all three categories.

García has earned his place in the nation's Mount Rushmore of pitchers, alongside Santana (51.08 WAR), Hernández (50.34 WAR), and Carlos Zambrano (38.32 WAR).[20] García's numbers were remarkably consistent: His home ERA, 4.13, was a shade lower than his road mark of 4.18. Batters hit .258 off him during both the first and second halves of his seasons. He was very effective when the bases were loaded, limiting hitters to a .521 OPS and no grand slams. In 181 of his career games – almost half of his tally – hitters were less successful on his 101st and subsequent pitches, with their average dropping to .235. Beyond the success against the Angels, he was dominant in interleague games, going 25-11 with a 2.84 ERA in 43 starts.

With over 3,000 career innings pitched in the major, minor, and winter leagues, García appeared on the 2019 National Baseball Hall of Fame ballot but did not garner a single vote, and was dropped from future consideration by the baseball writers.

ACKNOWLEDGMENTS

JJ Montilla, Venezuelan sportswriter, for sharing the Venezuelan Baseball reference site Pelota Binaria, which includes winter league statistics.

Pete Palmer and Jim Wheeler for detailed disabled-list records.

NOTES

1   Peter J. Schwartz, "Baseball's Best Agents," *Forbes*, June 22, 2007. https://www.forbes.com/2007/06/20/mlb-greenberg-baseball-biz_cz_ps_0622baseballagents.html#11f2825c19fc.

2   http://www.thebaseballcube.com/prospects/byTeam.asp?T=26&Src=BA.

3   "Mariners Overcome Injuries," *Los Angeles Times*, April 22, 2000. https://www.latimes.com/archives/la-xpm-2000-apr-22-sp-22373-story.html.

4   https://www.baseball-reference.com/bullpen/2006_World_Baseball_Classic_(Rosters)#Venezuela.

5   http://mlb.mlb.com/wbc/2009/stats/boxscore.jsp?gid=2006_03_08_itaint_venint_1.

6   http://mlb.mlb.com/wbc/2009/stats/boxscore.jsp?gid=2006_03_14_venint_domint_1.

7   "Sox Downplay Garcia Marijuana Report," *Chicago Tribune*, May 2, 2006. https://www.chicagotribune.com/news/ct-xpm-2006-05-02-0605020277-story.html, May 2, 2006.

8   Mark Gonzales, "García Flirts with Perfection as White Sox Beat Angels," *Chicago Tribune*, September 13, 2006. http://www.chicagotribune.com/sports/cs-060913soxgamer-story.html.

9   "Freddy García: Damaged Goods?" *Seattle Times*, June 19, 2007. https://www.seattletimes.com/sports/freddy-garcia-damaged-goods/.

10   "Shoulder Surgery Ends 2007 Season for Phillies' García," ESPN, August 30, 2007. https://www.espn.com/mlb/news/story?id=2997866.

11   Steve Serby, "Serby's Sunday Q&A with … Freddy García," *New York Post*, May 15, 2011. https://nypost.com/2011/05/15/serbys-sunday-q-a-with-freddy-garcia/.

12   Serby.

13   Jay Jaffee, "Former All-Star Freddy García to Play Professionally in Taiwan," SI.com, April 18, 2014. https://www.si.com/mlb/strike-zone/2014/04/18/freddy-garcia-signs-with-team-in-taiwan.

14   http://www.pelotabinaria.com.ve/beisbol/mostrar.php?ID=garcfre001.

15   "Freddy García Reportedly Will Call It a Career After 15 Major League Seasons," Fox Sports, February 7, 2016. https://www.foxsports.com/mlb/story/freddy-garcia-retiring-after-15-seasons-in-the-majors-020716.

16   https://www.mlb.com/gameday/puerto-rico-vs-venezuela/2016/02/01/459926#game_state=final,game_tab=box,game=459926.

17   http://www.pelotabinaria.com.ve/beisbol/premios.php.

18   "Juego de las estrellas será en homenaje a Freddy García," meridiano.com, November 22, 2017. http://www.meridiano.com.ve/beisbol/beisbol-venezolano/168510/juego-de-las-estrellas-sera-en-homenaje-a-freddy-garcia.html.

19   Rubén Castro, "Freddy García vive su última Serie del Caribe con Venezuela," ESPN Deportes, February 3, 2018. https://espndeportes.espn.com/beisbol/seriedelcaribe2018/nota/_/id/3945916/freddy-garcia-vive-su-ultima-serie-del-caribe-con-venezuela.

20   As of the end of 2020.

JON GARLAND

By Richard O'Connor

Jon Steven Garland was born September 27, 1979, and was raised in Granada Hills, California. He was raised by his mother, Vikki, after she and his father divorced.[1] As a pitcher at Kennedy High School in Granada Hills, he finished his varsity career with a 27-4 record over three seasons. On June 2, 1997, he was drafted in the first round of that year's amateur draft, the 10th overall selection, by the Chicago Cubs, turning down a full scholarship to University of Southern California to sign with the Cubs for $1.325 million. He and reported to the Arizona Fall League on June 27, 1997, and quickly established himself as a top prospect.

With the Cubs' rookie league team, Garland posted a 3-2 record with a 2.70 ERA. However, his performance dipped in the following year, 1998, with Class-A Rockford (4-7, 5.03), and the Cubs, seeking bullpen help, traded the 6-foot-6 righty to the crosstown White Sox in June for major-league right-hander Matt Karchner. The Cubs were looking to bolster the path to closer Rod Beck. Garland said of the trade, "My manager, my pitching coach, and the director of minor league operations pulled me into their office and told me I'd been traded. It was my first full season of baseball it was a big shock."[2]

Assigned to the Single-A Hickory Crawdads, Garland went 1-1 in his first two starts. "I had one good start, and in the other one I threw good pitches, but the breaks just didn't go my way," he said.[3] Despite a mixed start to his tenure with the White Sox, Garland showed glimpses of his potential. With Hickory, he helped contribute to White Sox efforts to rebuild for the future with a high-ceiling rotation that included Aaron Myette and Josh Fogg and future White Sox fan favorite center fielder Aaron Rowand.

The 1999 season saw Garland split time between Double A and Triple A,[4] where he compiled an 8-8 record with a 3.59 ERA. His performance earned him a call-up to the Charlotte Knights for the International League playoffs against the Scranton/Wilkes-Barre Red Barons. In his first minor-league playoff start, with the best-of-five series tied at 1-1, he lasted 5⅓ innings, surrendering 10 hits and four earned runs. Garland left with an 8-3 lead, but his team ultimately fell short in a close 10-9 loss.

After sticking with Charlotte in 2000 and pitching to a 9-2 record with a 2.26 ERA, Garland was given the chance to prove himself. On Independence Day in 2000, Garland was called up to the White Sox, to take the place of Triple-A teammate Kip Wells who had been recently sent down "to get his confidence back" according to manager Jerry Manuel.[5] His first start was against the divisional foe, Kansas City Royals. When he took the mound that day, at 20 years old, he was the youngest player in the major leagues. Garland surrendered eight hits and seven earned runs in three innings pitched. He said of the tough start, "It was a dream come true tonight. It could have gone better, but it happens."[6] He made 13 starts (15 games) and had a 4-8 record with a 6.46 ERA for the 2000 American League Central Division champion White Sox, who ended the season being swept by the Seattle Mariners in the Division Series. He did not pitch in the postseason.

Garland started the 2001 season in Charlotte again and went 0-3 but with a 2.73 ERA, and quickly made it back to the White Sox, making his first start on May 2 against Anaheim. He pitched 2⅔ innings, surrendering six runs (three earned) on six hits and took the loss. Throughout the season he jumped between the bullpen and rotation, pitching in 35 games, starting in 16 of them. He also earned his

Jon Garland   **2005**

only save of his career. Going into the 2002 season, Garland had a spot in the rotation lined up.

From 2002 through the 2004 season, Garland started 98 games and had a record of 36-36 but had become a reliable member of the White Sox staff, averaging 200 innings pitched and 33 starts per season and winning 12 games in each of the three seasons with an average of 12 losses over the three years. Heading into the 2005 season, the White Sox made some wholesale changes including trading slugger Carlos Lee to the Milwaukee Brewers for Scott Podsednik and Luis Vizcaíno and signing right fielder Jermaine Dye, catcher A.J. Pierzynski, and second baseman Tadahito Iguchi.

Garland enjoyed a remarkable start to the 2005 season. He won his first eight decisions, posting a stellar 2.41 ERA. His dominance included two shutouts, showcasing his ability to pitch deep into games. The second half of the season was not quite as impressive as the first. Garland went 5-6 with a 3.65 ERA. But overall, it was his best season in the majors to that point, including logging his most innings, 221.

The 2005 season marked a career milestone for Garland as he made his first All-Star Game appearance, pitching one inning surrendering two bases on balls, but zero hits and zero runs, and finished sixth in the Cy Young Award voting.

Garland's postseason debut in 2005 was memorable for the White Sox. In Game Three of the American League Championship Series against the Los Angeles Angels, Garland took the mound at Anaheim with the series tied at 1-1, the game following the infamous "Pierzynski dropped third strike game." The Angels presented a formidable lineup that included future Hall of Famer Vlad Guerrero.

Garland's teammates presented him with a three-run lead in the top of the first. In the bottom of the inning, he issued a leadoff walk to Chone Figgins, but quickly settled down, striking out Orlando Cabrera – who was in his first season with the Angels and who would be traded for Garland two years later – then inducing a 4-3 double play groundout from Guerrero.

With the White Sox leading 5-0 after five innings, the Angels attempted to stage a comeback in the bottom of the sixth. Garland allowed a two-run home run to Cabrera on a 2-and-2 pitch, following Adam Kennedy's base hit. But he held the Angels off the bases for the remainder of the game, retiring 10 straight batters as the White Sox won, 5-2, on Garland's four-hit complete game. The White Sox went on to win the series, four games to one.

Up two games to none in the World Series, the White Sox looked again to Garland for a Game Three start. He faced off against Houston Astros starter Roy Oswalt, who was coming off his second consecutive 20-win season.

Garland faced adversity out of the gate, surrendering a leadoff double to future Hall of Famer Craig Biggio. Lance Berkman drove Biggio home one batter later.

In the bottom of the third, Biggio drove in shortstop Adam Everett on a single to right and Biggio again was driven home by Berkman, expanding Houston's lead to a 3-0. In the bottom of the fourth, Garland surrendered a leadoff homer to Jason Lane.

The White Sox came back in the top of the fifth, taking a 5-4 lead behind a Joe Crede solo home run, RBI singles from Tadahito Iguchi and Jermaine Dye, and a two-run double by A.J. Pierzynski. During the inning, manager Ozzie Guillén, instead of pinch-hitting for Garland, sent the pitcher up to hit against Astros starter Oswalt. Garland ended up unable to lay down a bunt and striking out.

Garland settled down from the fifth to the seventh, surrendering only a walk to Brad Ausmus. He was pulled after the seventh inning and left with the lead. The Astros tied the score in the eighth inning, but after a 14-inning nailbiter, highlighted by Geoff Blum's home run in the final inning, the White Sox went on to win both the game, 7-5, and the Series.

Amid trade speculation, Garland signed a three-year, $29 million contract to stay in the White Sox rotation.[7] He then spent the 2006 and 2007 seasons with the White Sox going a combined 28-20 with a 4.37 ERA. On May 22, 2006, Garland was the pitcher when Frank Thomas returned to the Chicago as a member of the Oakland Athletics and hit two home runs off Garland: one in the second inning and one in the fifth.

After the 2007 season, White Sox general manager Kenny Williams was attempting to shore up the team's defense in an attempt to make the roster more attractive to free-agent outfielder Torii Hunter. Williams traded Garland to the Angels for slick-fielding shortstop Orlando Cabrera.[8]

Garland went 14-8 with a 4.90 ERA for the Angels in 2008. He fell 3⅓ innings short of pitching 200 innings for the fifth season in a row. Garland was granted free agency after the season.[9] He signed with the Arizona Diamondbacks for 2009.

Garland pitched in 27 games with the Diamondbacks, winning 8 against 11 losses. On August 31 he was traded to the eventual division winner Los Angeles Dodgers for a player to be named later (Tony Abreu). After six starts with his childhood team (he was 3-2, with a 2.72 ERA), Garland did not see any action in the playoffs for the Dodgers. After the season the Dodgers declined the option on Garland and he became a free agent.

Garland stayed in the National League West, signing a one-year, $5.3 million contract with the San Diego Padres, joining former White Sox pitcher Clayton Richard. Garland said, "A place like San Diego was so appealing to me because it's one of the few remaining parks that is a pitcher's park."[10] Garland was saddled with the loss in the season opener, going only four innings and surrendering six runs (two earned). He started 33 games for the second-place Padres, with a record of 14-12 (3.47).

After the season Garland became a free agent again, and he signed again with the Dodgers on another one-year contract for $5 million; the deal included a team option.

His second stint with the Dodgers did not produce similar results as the first. Following nine starts that earned him a 1-5 record and a 4.33 ERA, he was sidelined with shoulder discomfort. On July 5 it was announced that he would undergo surgery to clean his shoulder and would be out for the remainder of the season.

As one might expect, the Dodgers declined the option on Garland, making him a free agent once again. Garland signed a minor-league contract with the Cleveland Indians in early 2012 but he never took the required physical and the deal was canceled.[11]

Garland sat out the 2012 season. He was offered a contract by the Seattle Mariners in February 2013, with an invitation to spring training. Speaking about 2012 season, he said, "Every time I got on the mound, it was getting weaker, and it wasn't recovering well. And I knew right then and there that I had to shut it down and give it the time it needed," After he pitched for Seattle during spring training. Garland exercised his opt-out clause due to the Mariners' inability to commit to providing him with a rotation spot. Mariners general manager Jack Zduriencik said, "We weren't prepared to – at this moment in time – commit a roster spot and one of the starting spots in the rotation to Jon (Garland)."[12]

Garland quickly signed a free-agent contract with the Colorado Rockies. In his first start in the major leagues since 2011, he went six innings on April 6, 2013, and surrendered two earned runs on five hits and earned the 6-3 victory against San Diego. By early June he was 4-6 with a 5.82 ERA, lasting into the seventh inning only once. On June 9, the Rockies designated him for assignment, and he cleared waivers and was released.[13] He ended his career with a record of 136-125, with a 4.37 ERA.

Since leaving baseball, Garland has stayed out of the limelight save for a few instances of 2005 White Sox reunions. As of late 2024, he was dating Lovieanne Jung, a former collegiate softball player.

SOURCES

In addition to the sources cited in the Notes, the author consulted Baseball-Reference.com and Retrosheet.org.

NOTES

1   Steve Henson, "Full Speed Ahead," *Los Angeles Times*, March 5, 1997: 42.

2   Reid Spencer, "He's a Quick-Change Artist." *Charlotte Observer*, August 16, 1998: 282.

3   "He's a Quick-Change Artist."

4   Dan Collins, "Juggler: Terrell Handling Hogs' Changing Roster," *Winston-Salem Journal*, June 14, 1999: 19.

5   Marty Maciaszek, "Manuel hope Wells boosts confidence at Charlotte," *Arlington Heights* (Illinois) *Daily Herald*, July 2, 2000: 3

6   Scott Gregor, "Garland Roughed Up in Major-League Debut," *Arlington Heights* (Illinois) *Daily Herald*, July 5, 2000: 87.

7   Dave Van Dyck, "No Hang-Up with Garland," *Chicago Tribune*, December 29, 2005: 4.

8   Phil Rogers, "Dealing Garland Difficult but Inevitable," *Chicago Tribune*, November 20, 2007: 4-1.

9   Mark Gonzales, "Sox Ship Garland to Angels for Slick-Fielding Cabrera," *Chicago Tribune,* November 20, 2007: 4.

10 Bernie Wilson, "Padres Lock Up Garland with One-Year Deal." *Palm Springs* California) *Desert Sun*, January 27, 2010: C7.

11 Paul Hoynes, "Acta's Old Pal Guzman Gets a Shot on the Infield," *Cleveland Plain Dealer*, February 22, 2012: 3.

12 Ryan Divish, "Mariners Cannot Commit to Garland," *Olympian* (Olympia, Washington), March 23, 2013: B1.

13 Ryan Divish, "Montero Going About His Business as Usual," *Kitsap Sun* (Bremerton, Washington), February 13, 2013: 12.

ROSS GLOAD

By Robert Bionaz

Arguably, the toughest job in baseball belongs to the "utility" or part-time player/pinch-hitter who must come off the bench into a game, often at a critical point in the contest. In the years of the 25-man roster, having players on a club who could deliver as pinch-hitters, or who could provide improved late-inning defense provided a major-league manager with great decision-making flexibility. Today, with enlarged pitching staffs, the multi-position player is an absolute necessity on a big-league roster.

Since all major-league players are exceptional baseball talents, how did one player become a regular, while another settled into the role of part-time utilityman? Historically, sometimes, it was because of a player's defensive deficiencies, with guys like Jerry Lynch or Dusty Rhodes being prime examples. Sometimes a regular player simply got older and settled into a pinch-hitting role, like Smoky Burgess. Occasionally, the player is simply on the wrong team – playing the same position as the team's established star. Charlie Silvera comes to mind as one of those guys. In today's game, the universal designated hitter has diminished

the importance of pinch-hitting or defensive deficiencies, although a player able to play multiple defensive positions is still coveted.

Ross Peter Gload, who performed for 10 seasons in the majors (2000, 2002, 2004-2011), provides an example of a player who played several years with the wrong team. A good hitter (.281 lifetime) and excellent defensive first baseman (.995 lifetime), Gload after two brief stays in 2000 with the Cubs and in 2002 with Colorado, made an Opening Day roster with the Chicago White Sox in 2004. Except for minor-league rehabilitation assignments, he remained in the majors until his retirement in 2011. With the White Sox, he found Paul Konerko blocking his path to full-time play until 2006. Traded to Kansas City for left-handed pitcher Andy Sisco after the 2006 season, he played two years as a semi-regular for the Royals. Days before the 2009 season began, the Royals sent him to the Florida Marlins for a player to be named later (right-handed minor-league pitcher Eric Basurto). He backed up starting first baseman Jorge Cantú in Florida. After one season with the Marlins, he played out his option and signed a free-agent deal with Philadelphia, where for his last two years in the majors he pinch-hit and played occasionally at first, behind Ryan Howard, or in the outfield.

Gload, a 6-foot-2, 210-pound, left-handed-hitting/throwing first baseman, was born on April 5, 1976, in Brooklyn, New York, to Ross P. Gload, a carpenter, and Regina E. (Creegan) Gload. He starred in soccer and basketball at East Hampton High School on Long Island. He was conference all-star in soccer[1] and consistently excelled in basketball.[2] While he performed well in those two sports, he positively dazzled in baseball. He had no opportunity to play baseball during his early childhood in Brooklyn. He remembered, "We didn't even have a backyard." Baseball? "My parents never pushed me into it. I never played."[3] Moving from Brooklyn to Long Island opened up a new world for Gload. He quickly realized that he had considerable ability at the sport and in high school put up spectacular numbers. He began by hitting .368 as a freshman with two home runs. His sophomore year he improved to .492 with 9 home runs, saw his average drop to .338 as a junior, but increased his homer total to 10, then had a ridiculous senior season, hitting .488 with 20 home runs and 61 RBIs in only 26 games. Just to show he was not one-dimensional, he also had a 7-1 record on the mound with a microscopic ERA of 1.16 and

Ross Gload   2005

GRINDERS AND GAMERS

80 strikeouts in 57 innings. That season earned Gload the 1994 (Carl) Yastrzemski Award as the outstanding high-school player in Suffolk County, which encompasses most of Long Island. A number of prior award winners went on to play major-league baseball, including Don DeMola, Tom Veryzer, Neal Heaton, Keith Osik, Jim Mecir, Tony Graffanino, and Bill Koch. Because of his high-school performance, a number of university baseball coaches were very interested in having Gload play for them. Recruited by the University of South Florida, South Alabama, Clemson, North Carolina and West Virginia, Gload chose the South Florida Bulls.[4]

Gload's NCAA debut season drew rave reviews. He hit .352 with 14 home runs and 69 RBIs (regular season).[5] National Amateur Baseball Federation coach Mark Cuseta said, "I've got five former players in the big leagues including (Colorado Rockies) shortstop Walt Weiss and Ross is the best player I've ever coached." Tulane coach Rick Jones chimed in: "He's the best young college hitter I've seen in a long time. And he may be better on defense. My only regret is we'll have to face him three more years."[6] Gload continued his excellent play his sophomore season, hitting .371 with 16 home runs and 68 RBIs (regular season).[7] His junior year provided another spectacular season on the diamond. During the regular season, he hit .417 with 18 home runs and 79 RBIs in 59 games. On the verge of the NCAA tournament, Gload had set South Florida career records with 54 home runs and 240 RBIs (NCAA tournament games in 1995 and 1996 included). He had also compiled the second-best average in school history, .380.[8] In June 1997 the Florida Marlins selected Gload in the 13th round of the amateur draft. Gload signed on June 12 and headed for Class-A Utica in the short-season New York-Pennsylvania League to begin his professional career.

Gload's season at Utica started slowly. Through his first 46 games, he hit only .233, with 3 home runs and 26 RBIs.[9] He improved over his next 22 games, hitting .314, with 17 RBIs, finishing the season with a .261 average, 3 home runs, and 43 RBIs. Surprisingly, the normally smooth-fielding Gload committed 16 errors in 63 games while playing exclusively at first base. Promoted to the Class-A Midwest League for the 1998 season, Gload had a much better year. Playing for the Kane County Cougars, he finished ninth in batting with a .313 average and led the league with 41 doubles. His 92 RBIs were good for third in that category. In 1999, playing for Brevard County in the advanced A Florida State League, Gload had a decent season, a .298 average, with 10 home runs and 74 RBIs. At both Kane County and Brevard County, his fielding improved. Still playing exclusively at first, Gload made 14 errors in 129 games in the Midwest League and improved to 9 errors in 133 games for Brevard County. His .993 fielding percentage placed him second among Florida State first basemen who played more than 100 games at the position. After two solid seasons in Class A, the Marlins promoted him to Portland, Maine, in the Double-A Eastern League.[10]

By the end of July, Gload was hitting .284 and leading Portland with 16 home runs and 65 RBIs. Then on July 31, the Marlins traded Gload to the Chicago Cubs organization for slugging outfielder Henry Rodriguez. His teammates clearly saw Gload's trade as a big loss. Todd Betts said, "We can't let that affect us. ... We have to keep going at it." Chris Norton was even more explicit, saying, "He was carrying us basically. When you lose a good bat like that, it puts more stress on the team as a whole to put up runs."[11] After acquiring Gload, the Cubs promoted him to Iowa of the Triple-A Pacific Coast League.

A new organization was not the only change for Gload in 2000. Portland had begun using him in the outfield as well as at first base, and he played exclusively as an outfielder at Iowa. Gload turned in a schizophrenic performance while playing in Des Moines just over four weeks. He was Ruthian at the plate, hitting .404 with 14 home runs and 39 RBIs in 28 games. For the season, his home-run total placed him in a tie for fourth on the team. But he played the outfield erratically. In 28 games in the outfield for Iowa, Gload made four errors. Nonetheless, his aggregate .309 average, 30 home runs, 104 RBIs, .586 slugging percentage, and .944 OPS, earned him a promotion to the Cubs on August 30.[12]

Called up when the Cubs demoted outfielder Brant Brown to Iowa,[13] Gload debuted at Wrigley Field on August 31, 2000, going 0-for-4 against five San Diego pitchers in an 11-5 loss to the Padres. He flied out to center against Padres right-hander Jay Witasick in his first at-bat. He got his first major-league hit on September 4 at Coors Field in Denver, a solo home run in the fourth inning off Colorado right-hander Brian Rose in a 6-2 Rockies win. Gload played 18 games at the end of the 2000 season, going 6-for-31 (.194). He showed enough potential in his brief late-season trial that one publication claimed that "[h]e has shown enough with the Cubs to be in the mix for a backup role next spring."[14] Apparently the Cubs did not agree; they again assigned him to Iowa for the 2001 season.

Gload spent the next three seasons playing Triple-A ball with three organizations. He had a solid season at Iowa in 2001, .297, with 15 home runs and 93 RBIs. He tied for the league lead in triples with 10 and slugged .501, with an OPS of .845. He again split time between the outfield and first base, making only one error in 50 games at first and only two errors in 72 games in the outfield. The Cubs rewarded Gload by releasing him on waivers on September 8.[15]

Gload signed with the Rockies four days later. They sent him to Colorado Springs in the Pacific Coast League for 2002, his sixth year in the minors. He spent all but two weeks of that season at Colorado Springs and batted .315 in 104 games with 16 home runs and 71 RBIs. On July 1 the Rockies called Gload up to replace Greg Norton, who went on the 15-day disabled list.[16] He was sent back down when

Norton returned on July 18,[17] but returned to the Rockies in September.

Gload did not have long to ponder his future with the Rockies because on January 21, 2003, they sent him to the New York Mets in a deal involving three teams and including 11 players. Five days later, the Mets sold him back to Colorado. Then on March 27, the Rockies traded him to the White Sox for minor-league left-handed pitcher Wade Parrish. The White Sox assigned Gload to Charlotte in the International League, his fourth season in Triple A and his seventh season in the minors. Perhaps Gload had been pigeonholed as a career minor leaguer. While never the best player, he was arguably one of the top 25 players at every level of the minors. Through 2002, he posted a career minor-league average of .302, with 86 home runs and 477 RBIs. His Triple-A statistics were better than his numbers at the lower levels. In the equivalent of two full seasons, he'd hit .315 with an average of 22.5 home runs and 101.5 RBIs a year. He had a .551 slugging percentage and an outstanding OPS of .904. He truly had nothing left to prove in the high minors.

Nonetheless, Gload dutifully reported to Charlotte for the 2003 International League season. Again he had a fine year, hitting .315 with 18 home runs and 70 RBIs, a .524 slugging percentage, and an .873 OPS. (Interestingly, Gload stayed in the minors all year despite the awful season White Sox first baseman Paul Konerko was having. By July 8 Konerko was hitting .183 with 4 home runs, and 18 RBIs. But while Konerko struggled, Gload stayed in North Carolina. Konerko ultimately hit better in the season's second half as the White Sox finished second in the American League's Central Division. At the end of the 2003 season, Gload, 27 years old, likely wondered if he would ever get the chance to spend a season in the big leagues.

Gload's first real chance came in the spring of 2004, and he made the most of it. By mid-March, White Sox manager Ozzie Guillén declared that Gload "right now, in my mind [is] ... on my team. There's no doubt about it."[18] Finally, Gload went to a spring camp with a legitimate shot at making the team, which was "all [I] ever wanted." Discussing his experiences with the Cubs and Rockies, Gload said, "I was never treated unfairly, but just being given a shot here is the thing. I had a good year in Triple A with the Cubs [in 2000], but the next year they knew [coming into camp] there was no way I was going to make that team. ... They knew I was going to be the first guy sent down. From my standpoint that's discouraging." As for his current opportunity, Gload minced no words: "Now it's kind of nice just to be in the running in spring training, where you have a chance and maybe can help the club in April, when it counts."[19]

In 2004 Gload played in 110 games, hitting .321 with 7 home runs and 44 RBIs, with a .479 slugging percentage and an .853 OPS. He started 21 games at first and played as a defensive replacement in 21 more, fielding 1.000 at that

position. He played 39 games in the outfield (25 starts) with somewhat less defensive success (3 errors and .952 fielding percentage) and seven as designated hitter. Gload got off to a slow start; by May 29 he was hitting .241 with 2 home runs and 10 RBIs. By July 21 he was still hitting only .265 with 2 home runs and 20 RBIs. For the remainder of the season, he hit a scorching .372 with 5 homers and 24 RBIs. Arguably the most memorable game during that stretch was his 3-for-5 performance against the Angels on September 11. His three hits included two singles and a home run for four RBIs as the White Sox crushed Anaheim, 13-6. While the club disappointed, finishing a distant second in the division, nine games behind Minnesota, Gload had a thoroughly successful rookie season. At the end of the year, he finished seventh in Rookie of the Year voting.

The 2005 season was a magical year for the club but a lost season for Gload. The team started 15-4, but something was wrong with Gload. By April 24 he had played in only seven of the team's 19 games with 13 at-bats. His left shoulder was inflamed, preventing him from playing in the outfield. On April 30 the club placed him on the disabled list, retroactive to April 25.[20] For the next 2½ months, he tried valiantly to rehabilitate the shoulder. Sent to Charlotte on a rehabilitation assignment, he could play only first base. In mid-June, while the White Sox continued to play well, Gload's balky shoulder kept him in Charlotte. A frustrated Gload, in Chicago for an MRI, told a reporter, "No one likes a setback like this. It's even worse when you see the team's doing so well and you're [not] in the mix. I think a week ago I said, 'Hey, the White Sox won last night,' as opposed to 'We won.'"[21] When the MRI revealed no new damage to his shoulder, Gload returned to Charlotte to continue his rehabilitation. Except for a nine-day period back with the White Sox in late July, he remained in Triple A until September 1. From then until the end of the season on October 2, he played in only 14 games, starting only three, getting 4 hits in 19 at-bats. About the only satisfying moment in a Chicago uniform that season came on September 30, when his two-run double in the 13th inning drove in the winning runs in a 3-2 White Sox victory over Cleveland that clinched home-field advantage for the White Sox in the American League postseason. Ineligible for the postseason, Gload could only watch as the team dominated three postseason series and won its first World Series championship since 1917. As for his performance, while he sizzled at Charlotte with a .366 average, 15 home runs, and 45 RBIs in 59 games, he never found his stroke in Chicago, finishing at .167 with no home runs and 5 RBIs in 28 games. Shortly after his September recall, he summed up his 2005 season this way: "It was disappointing. I didn't want to play this year in Charlotte, it just kind of happened. I don't know what they think of me at this point. I've done everything I could do to get healthy and get back here. I'll just kind of start over again."[22]

Gload did indeed get back, playing another six years in the majors. While his shoulder eventually improved, it likely never really completely healed. For the last six years of his major-league career, he played only 40 games in the outfield. Despite his diminished versatility, in 2006 he turned in a fine season as a utilityman, hitting .327 with 3 home runs and 18 RBIs in 156 at-bats. After that season, the White Sox traded Gload to the Kansas City Royals for Andy Sisco. In Kansas City he got his only chance to play semi-regularly, as he became the club's primary first baseman, playing in 224 games over two seasons, with 200 games at first. He had his only two major-league seasons with more than 300 at-bats. In 320 at-bats in 2007, he hit .288 with 7 home runs and 51 RBIs. In 388 at-bats in 2008, he finished at .273 with 3 home runs and 37 RBIs. Traded from Kansas City to the Florida Marlins on the eve of the 2009 season for a player to be named later, he reacted to the deal philosophically, saying, "It's always shocking. I've been traded. I've been waived. I've been designated. I think (saying goodbye) to the guys is the toughest part. But that's baseball."[23]

In Miami Gload returned to his familiar utility role, while adding significant pinch-hitting duties. He had some experience and some success as a pinch-hitter in his previous major-league stops. For the Cubs, Rockies, and White Sox, he'd come off the bench to hit 89 times, getting 25 hits in 87 at-bats for a .287 average with 2 home runs and 11 RBIs. As Kansas City's nominal starting first baseman, Gload had only 11 pinch-hit at-bats in two years. In Florida, however, he excelled in that role, hitting .318 in 79 games (66 at-bats) and leading all major-league pinch-hitters in runs scored with 14 and hits with 21, while tying Philadelphia's Matt Stairs in RBIs with 15 and total bases with 30. In 2009 Gload displayed a penchant for game-winning hits. On May 24 he singled in the bottom of the 11th to give the Marlins a 5-4 win over Tampa Bay. On July 28 he hit a two-run pinch-hit home run in the bottom of the ninth against Atlanta closer Rafael Soriano as the Marlins came from behind to win 4-3. On September 19 his two-run pinch homer in the eighth off Cincinnati's Bronson Arroyo provided the winning runs in a 3-2 victory. On September 30, another two-run home run, this one against Javier Vázquez, gave the Marlins their winning runs against Atlanta. That season he played the most games in his career, 125. He made only 39 starts and finished the year at .261 with 6 home runs and 30 runs batted in. At the conclusion of the season, he became a free agent, and signed with the Philadelphia Phillies on December 8.

In Gload's final two major-league seasons, he continued to be used almost exclusively as a pinch-hitter, appearing in that role 148 times in the 187 games he played for Philadelphia. In 2010 his pinch-hitting statistics did not equal his 2009 numbers, but he still made 15 hits in 66 at-bats with 3 home runs and 9 RBIs. While not filled

with the dramatics of his 2009 season, 2010 saw Gload enjoy two of his most productive major-league games, a three-hit, four-RBI game against Toronto on June 25 and another three-hit (with two home runs), four-RBI game against the Dodgers on August 10. He finished with a .281 batting average with 6 home runs and 22 RBIs in 94 games. In 2010 Gload participated in his first postseason play as the Phillies won their division by six games over Atlanta. He did not play in Philadelphia's Division Series sweep of Cincinnati but played in all six games of the National League Championship Series against the eventual World Series-winning San Francisco Giants. He went 0-for-5 with a walk as the favored Phillies dropped the Series in six games to the upstart Giants.

Gload played his final season in 2011. He appeared in 93 games, 79 as a pinch hitter, hitting .257 for the season with no home runs and 8 RBIs. The Phillies again won their division by 13 games over Atlanta. Matched against the St. Louis Cardinals in the NLDS, they again disappointed, losing the series three games to two against the eventual World Series winners. Gload made three appearances in the series, all as a pinch-hitter, going 1-for-2. (In his third appearance, he was lifted for another pinch-hitter.) He reached base twice in his two at-bats, hitting a single in the eighth inning of Game Four, and reaching base on Yadier Molina's error in the eighth inning of Game Five. As the 2011 postseason concluded, Gload faced an uncertain future. He had suffered from a degenerative hip problem during the season that was expected to require surgery.[24] On October 30 he again became a free agent. However, no one signed him and he never played again in professional baseball.

Gload finished with a lifetime average of .281, with 470 hits, 34 home runs, and 222 RBIs in 795 major-league games. While managers tended to platoon him, he hit better against left-handers (.293) than against right-handers (.278), but displayed considerably more punch against right-handed pitching, hitting 31 home runs and slugging .415 compared with 3 home runs and a .376 slugging percentage against left-handers. As a pinch-hitting specialist, he finished with a .270 average on 81 hits, with 8 home runs and 43 RBIs. Fewer than 14 percent of Gload's outs came via strikeouts.

Regrettably, the author was unable to contact Gload for an interview. And information on his personal life is scant. However, he apparently remained involved in baseball after the end of his playing career. In 2021, the South Carolina House of Representatives honored Gload as a coach for the Legion Collegiate Academy [High School] baseball team ... winners of the 2021 South Carolina Class AA State Championship.[25] It appears that in 2024 Ross Gload resided in South Carolina with his wife, Elizabeth. They have two teenage children, a son, Greyson, and a daughter, Belle.

SOURCES

In addition to the sources cited in the Notes, the author consulted Baseball-Reference.com and Retrosheet.org. Unless otherwise attributed, all statistics and game accounts come from these sites.

NOTES

1 "Boys Soccer All-Stars, "*Newsday* (Long Island, New York), December 12, 1992: 86.

2 "Another Title for Bay Shore," *Newsday,* February 11, 1994: 187.

3 John Valenti, "No Doubt About It!" *Newsday,* June 16, 1994: 74.

4 Valenti, "No Doubt About It!"

5 "Breeze Takes the Wind out of Jump by UK's Edwards," *Tampa Bay Times* (St. Petersburg, Florida), June 26, 1995: 48.

6 Ron Kaspriske, "USF Discovers Treasure in Long Island Long Shot," *Tampa Bay Times*, April 4, 1995: 40.

7 John C. Cotey, "Had Potential, Has Performed," *Tampa Bay Times*, June 14, 1996: 5C.

8 Scott Purks, "Gload Has One Ring in Mind," *Tampa Bay Times*, May 22, 1997: 1C, 6C.

9 "Minor-League Baseball Statistics," *Tampa Bay Times*, August 9, 1997: 18.

10 Craig Carter and David Sload, eds., *Baseball Guide 2000 Edition* (St. Louis: *The Sporting News*, 2000), 517-18.

11 "Dogs Lose Slugger, Game," *Portland* (Maine) *Press Herald*, August 1, 2000: 1C, 6C.

12 Neil Milbert, "Sosa Says He Expects to Take a Day Off – in October," *Chicago Tribune*, September 1, 2000: 235.

13 "Knoblauch Could Be Out Rest of Season," *Fort Worth Star-Telegram*, August 31, 2000: 53.

14 "Grace Under Pressure as Cubs Look for More Offense," *The Sporting News*, September 18, 2000: 69.

15 Teddy Greenstein, "Fall Play Assigned for Some Prospects, *Chicago Tribune*, September 10, 2001: 42.

16 "Deals," *Reno Gazette-Journal*, July 2, 2002: 11.

17 Associated Press, "Baez Went into Twins' Clubhouse to Confront Hunter, Not Apologize," *Flint* (Michigan) *Journal*, July 19, 2002: 48.

18 John Mullin, "Gload Winning Game of Chance," *Chicago Tribune*, March 17, 2004: 4-4.

19 "Gload Winning Game of Chance."

20 "Thome Leaves Game with Back Spasms," *Hartford Courant*, May 1, 2005: E09.

21 Jeff Carroll, "Thomas: I've Got to Stay Healthy," *Hammond* (Indiana) *Times*, June 15, 2005: 174.

22 George Castle, "Gload Among Three Called Up," *Hammond* (Indiana) *Times*, September 2, 2005: 77.

23 Bob Dutton, "Royals Trade Gload," *Kansas City Star*, April 2, 2009: 33.

24 Mandy Housenick, "The Phillies Have Some Work to Do," *Allentown* (Pennsylvania) *Morning Call*, October 24, 2011: C3.

25 https://www.scstatehouse.gov/sess124_2021-2022/bills/4859.htm. Accessed October 2, 2024.

WILLIE HARRIS

By Michael Marsh

Willie Harris batted only once for the Chicago White Sox in the 2005 World Series. The speedy left-hander used that plate appearance to earn a place in White Sox history.

The White Sox were tied with the Houston Astros 0-0 in the top of the eighth inning of Game Four. White Sox manager Ozzie Guillén sent Harris to pinch-hit for pitcher Freddy García. Harris took Houston reliever Brad Lidge's first pitch for a strike, then fouled off the next pitch. Harris didn't swing at the next two pitches, which were balls. He singled on the fifth pitch. "Lidge, incredulous that Harris hadn't helped him out, didn't want to walk him," sportswriter Phil Rogers wrote. "Instead he threw a fastball that Harris slapped into left field for a leadoff single."[1]

Ten years later, Harris recalled that he persuaded Guillén to let him bat. "I told Ozzie, 'You want to win? Put me in,' Harris said. He put me in and said, 'All right, bring it home.' I was scared as hell. I was sitting on the bench for eight innings. I was nervous. I was facing Brad Lidge. He was one of the best. He was throwing 97 (mph). But I poked a knock to left field and we got it done."[2]

That hit led to the only run of the game and to the championship. Harris advanced to second base on Scott Podsednik's sacrifice. Harris ran to third base when Carl Everett, pinch-hitting for Tadahito Iguchi, grounded out, and scampered home on Jermaine Dye's single up the middle. The White Sox beat the Astros 1-0 to complete a four-game sweep and win their first World Series championship since 1917.

That run highlighted Harris's major-league career. He played parts of 12 seasons between 2001 and 2012. At 5-feet-9 and 195 pounds, Harris used his versatility and speed to play all three outfield positions, second base, shortstop, and third base. In addition to the White Sox, Harris played for the Baltimore Orioles, Boston Red Sox, Atlanta Braves, Washington Nationals, New York Mets, and the Cincinnati Reds. Most often, he played in left field, center field, and second base. Until the end of the 2024 season, Harris served as the third-base coach for the Chicago Cubs.

Willie Charles Harris was born on June 22, 1978, in Cairo, Georgia. Cairo, a small town in southwestern Georgia, earned a reputation as a center for manufacturing syrup. Harris is one of five major leaguers who were born in the city. The most famous is Hall of Famer Jackie Robinson, who integrated major-league baseball when he joined the Brooklyn Dodgers in 1947. Another is Emerson Hancock,

who pitched for the Seattle Mariners during the 2023 and 2024 seasons.[3]

Harris competed in a recreational baseball league as a preteen and participated in a program for troubled youths while he was in the eighth grade. The program paired him with Veon Williams, who mentored him. Harris said the program turned him into a responsible man.[4]

He emerged as a sports star at Cairo High School. He played shortstop for the baseball team and wide receiver and punter for the football team. During his junior year on the football team, he caught 50 passes for 1,010 yards. Then Florida State football coach Bobby Bowden tried to recruit him. Harris's stepfather, Fondren Williams, said: "All these major schools wanted him. I think if he wanted to go to Florida State, he could have gone there easily. I told him, 'You'll get lost in the system.' I knew all the while baseball was the ticket."[5]

During his junior year, Harris had to pick a person to research for Black History Month. The project sparked his interest in Robinson. Harris said later: "Some people took

Willie Harris　　　　2005

Rosa Parks or Martin Luther King. I was into sports big time in high school, and my English teacher said, 'Willie, why don't you do your paper on Jackie Robinson and I'm like, who's that? I had no clue."[6]

His mother, Geraldine Harris, recalled: "To learn about Jackie Robinson he really got on it. he wanted to get deep down, get the full story."[7]

Harris said, "I found out what [Robinson] went through, the way he had to carry himself. He just had to bite his tongue. I found out also he probably wasnt the best player. He wasn't the best African American player, but he was the best fit for that situation. He was fit perfectly for going into the big leagues, and his characteristics and his demeanor were perfect for not fighting back, and keeping his mouth shut, and doing his thing, and letting his bat do the talking and his legs do the running. I learned a ton about him as far as that goes."[8]

During Harris's senior year, the home field of Cairo's baseball team was named Jackie Robinson Field. He told the *Atlanta Journal Constitution*: "It's an honor and a privilege to play on a field named for him."[9]

Harris's family has other successful athletes. One of his uncles is former major leaguer Earnest Riles. Riles played for Middle Georgia Junior College (now Middle Georgia State University) in Macon. He spent nine seasons in the major leagues, playing third base and shortstop from 1985 through 1993 for the Milwaukee Brewers, San Francisco Giants, Oakland Athletics, Houston Astros, and Boston Red Sox. (Guillén, then a shortstop for the White Sox, and Brewers teammate Teddy Higuera finished first and second respectively.) Harris's second cousin, Teresa Edwards, played point guard for the University of Georgia's women's basketball team. She won four Gold Medals as a member of the US Women's basketball team and played in foreign leagues and the Women's National Basketball Association. Harris's stepson, Tre'Vez Johnson, played defensive back and safety for football teams at the University of Florida and the University of Missouri between 2020 and 2024.

During his teen years, Harris played on a local team managed by Riles. "I was the youngest player by far," he recalled. "The talent level was high, lots of people [attended] the games. I played in it from age 15 to my junior year in college."[10]

Harris was drafted by the Pittsburgh Pirates in the 28th round of the amateur draft in 1996 and the Tampa Bay Devil Rays in the 90th round in 1997. He didn't sign with them, opting, like Riles, to attend Middle Georgia Junior College. The baseball team won the NJCAA regional tournament. Harris played second base and earned MVP honors in the regional as MGJC advanced to the NJCAA tournament.[11]

After Middle Georgia, Harris enrolled at Kennesaw State University. There, he became a first-team Peach Belt All-Conference player and a third-team American Baseball Coaches Association All-American in 1999. Harris reached the Division II World Series with the Owls in 1999, in a season where he batted .365, slugged 14 home runs, drove in 49 runs, and stole 40 bases.[12]

In 1999 Harris was drafted by the Baltimore Orioles in the 24th round. During his time in the Orioles organization, he played in the rookie Appalachian League and for low Class-A Delmarva and Double-A Bowie. He earned the nicknames Sparkplug and Hollywood at Delmarva. Teammates gave him the latter for his flashy style of play.[13] He played in nine games for the Orioles in September 2001 and got his first major-league hit, a single to center field, against Oakland pitcher Cory Lidle as the visiting Orioles lost to the Athletics 12-6 on September 5, 2001.

In early 2002 the Orioles traded Harris to the White Sox organization for center fielder Chris Singleton. Assessing the trade, sportswriter Dave Sheinin wrote: "In Harris, a center fielder-second baseman, the Orioles gave up the eighth-ranked prospect in the organization, according to *Baseball America*. Harris, a 5-foot-9 speedster, made an impressive leap from low Class-A Delmarva in 2000 to Class-AA Bowie and eventually a month-long stint in the majors in 2001. However, Harris's path to the majors was blocked at both of his primary positions – in center field by Luis Matos, Keith Reed, and Tim Raines Jr., and at second base by Jerry Hairston [Jr.], Brian Roberts, and Mike Fontenot."[14]

Harris split time with Triple-A Charlotte and the White Sox in 2002 and 2003. He spent the entire 2004 season with the White Sox, playing in 129 games. He often led off and started at second base. In 409 at-bats, he batted .262, drove in 27 runs, scored 68 runs, and had a career-high 19 stolen bases.

After the season, Harris suffered a setback. The White Sox added left fielder and leadoff hitter Scott Podsednik and second baseman Tadahito Iguchi during the offseason.

Harris expressed some frustration after the White Sox signed Iguchi. He said, "I just have to be a man first and then play baseball. If that's their guy and I'm out, then I'm out. It's rough for me because they said they have great expectations, and I felt I would get a real chance to play. But they felt they wanted to get him."[15]

The White Sox used Harris as a bench player in 2005. For the team, he played in 56 games, batting .256 and stealing 10 bases. He spent most of August at Triple-A Charlotte. The White Sox brought him back late that month to provide depth for the end of the season and the postseason run. Besides his World Series at-bat, Harris batted once during the Division Series against the Boston Red Sox and once in the World Series. He finished 2-for-2 with one RBI.

After the White Sox won the World Series, Harris's hometown honored him. The city threw a parade and renamed his childhood street Willie C. Harris Drive. He spoke at a pep rally for Cairo High School's football team.

The festivities pleased Harris. "The way I feel right now, it's almost like being at the World Series," he said. "This is where I grew up at, where I learned how to be an athlete and be a competitor. To hear all these kids and students out here hollering, it just makes me feel good."[16]

After the season, the White Sox did not offer Harris a contract. His departure started a pattern of short stints with several major-league teams. He bounced between the majors and the minors.

Harris signed with the Boston Red Sox in early 2006. He spent time with Triple-A Pawtucket and the Red Sox, for whom he played in 47 games, hitting .156. After the season the Red Sox designated him for assignment and he signed with the Atlanta Braves. He started the 2007 season with the Triple-A Richmond Braves, hitting .362 in 17 games. Atlanta, seeking more offense, called Harris up in late April. The move represented a homecoming for the Georgian and he became the starting left fielder, playing in 117 games and batting .270.

On July 21 against the visiting St. Louis Cardinals, Harris was 6-for-6, with four singles and two triples, driving in six runs, and scoring four. "I like to say I was lucky, just thankful for this day and going to enjoy it," he said. "Days like today don't come around often. You have bad games, you come back the next day and try to fix it. I had no idea I could fix it like that today. I have no words to describe it. I hope my family back home was watching and enjoyed it as much as I did."[17]

Harris made a spectacular defensive play on August 9, 2007. The Braves were leading the New York Mets, 7-6, in the bottom of the ninth at home. Braves pitcher Óscar Villarreal relieved Tyler Yates with one out. The first hitter Villarreal faced, first baseman Carlos Delgado, hit a ball to deep left field. Harris jumped in front of the wall and robbed Delgado of a home run. "We were playing no doubles," Harris said of the outfielders' deep alignment, "because you don't want a guy to hit a ball over your head. So I was already back far enough just in case if he did hit it up toward the wall, I'd have a chance to catch the ball."[18]

Harris had a .342 batting average at the All-Star break. His offense, however, dropped dramatically during the second half of the season. He hit only .214 after the break. The Braves did not offer him a new contract after the season and Harris signed with the Washington Nationals. He played second base, third base, shortstop, and all three outfield positions during the 2008 season. Harris finished the season with a career-high 13 home runs and 140 games. He earned Player of the Week honors for July 14-20. The Nationals rewarded him with a two-year contract worth $3 million after the season. His batting average, however, gradually declined during his time with the Nationals. He batted .251 in 2008, .235 in 2009, and .183 in 2010.

Harris signed as a free agent with the New York Mets after the 2010 season. In 2011 he played in 126 games for the Mets at all three outfield positions as well as second base and third base, and hitting .246.

In 2012 Harris signed as a free agent with the Cincinnati Reds. Batting only .114, with no home runs and 2 RBIs in 44

at-bats, he was sent to Triple-A Louisville in June. Harris retired after the season. He finished his career with a .238 batting average, 1,046 games, 580 hits, 107 stolen bases, 39 home runs, and 212 RBIs.

Harris had lived in Cairo with his family with his wife, Trey, and their two children, Johnson and Arianna Harris, during offseasons. The family eventually moved to Florida. There, he ran a baseball facility and coached youth travel teams.

A trip to Chicago in 2015 started Harris's return to professional baseball. At a 2005 White Sox reunion dinner, club owner Jerry Reinsdorf asked Harris whether he was interested in coaching. Harris said yes.[19] The White Sox hired him to be the hitting coach for the Great Falls Voyagers (rookie Pioneer League) in 2016.

Harris said his experience coaching in Florida helped prepare him for instructing the Voyagers' hitters. "I coached travel ball a few years before I got this opportunity and it helped me to understand that, you know, just because I know how to bunt or I know how to move a runner, it doesn't mean that these guys know how to do it yet."

"It teaches me to be patient with them and share my knowledge with them and just watch

them grow and soon they'll get it and have a little confidence. I have to understand 'Willie,

you've got to have a little patience' and not expect so much from young guys."[20]

Harris was promoted to manager of Class-A Winston-Salem in 2017. In 2018-19 he managed Richmond of the Double-A Eastern League in the San Francisco Giants organization for the 2018 and 2019 seasons.

In 2019, the Reds named Harris their minor-league baserunning and outfield coordinator. Beginning in 2021, the Cubs hired Harris as their major-league third-base coach.

The *Chicago Tribune* said Harris had "a joyful personality and energy that mixes well with 12 years of big-league experience." He demonstrated that energy during the second game of a doubleheader between the host Cubs and the Los Angeles Dodgers on May 4, 2021. Cubs first baseman Anthony Rizzo hit a deep fly ball off Trevor Bauer and ran toward third base. Harris dropped to the ground in foul territory, his body outstretched and his hands tapping the grass. Rizzo heeded Harris's direction, sliding into third safely for a triple. "Harris' visual cue has become a staple of how he directs approaching baserunners. The concept is simple: If Harris is laid out on the ground, it indicates an impending close play so the runner knows he must slide."[21]

Harris told *The Athletic* that Guillén influenced him. "I learned to be myself," he said. "I learned to be authentic. Being around Ozzie and being around that team, I learned the importance of being who you are and not trying to just fit in. I think it's very important to be who you are. Some people are gonna like you, some people aren't. They just have to deal with it. But it's better for you. And it's better for the team that you're being authentic. You know what I'm saying?"[22]

Harris has expressed a desire to manage in the major leagues. He interviewed for the White Sox opening that eventually went to Tony La Russa in 2021.

"I feel like I have the pedigree of knowing my players really well and understanding the game really well," Harris said. "I mean, it'd be a dream come true for me. Hopefully that opportunity presents itself one day down the line."[23]

Harris experienced both professional and personal struggles while he played in the majors. He bounced between the majors and the minors. In addition, he had to take leaves twice during his career. He took bereavement leave in 2005 when the mother of his daughter died after an automobile accident.[24] While he played for the Mets, his wife lost an unborn daughter.[25]

Harris told the *Chicago Tribune* in 2015 that he regarded his run in Game Four of the 2005 World Series as very special. "Right now, that's the highlight of my life," he said. "I will always love Chicago; for me doing that, Chicago will always love me."[26]

ACKNOWLEDGMENTS

The author thanks the Kennesaw State Department of Athletics, the Richmond Flying Spiders, the Great Falls Voyagers, Middle Georgia State University Department of Athletics, the Chicago White Sox, and the Jacksonville Public Library for their assistance.

SOURCES

In addition to the sources cited in the Notes, the author used the Baseball-Reference.com, Baseball-Almanac.com, and Retrosheet.org websites for box-score, player, team, and season pages, pitching and batting game logs, and other material. The author consulted the following periodicals:

"Sox Ship Singleton to Orioles," *DeKalb* (Illinois) *Daily Chronicle*, June 30, 2002: 9

Wittenmyer, Gordon. "Willie Harris on Hometown Pride and Protecting a Dream," NBC Sports Chicago, April 15, 2022, https://www.nbcsportschicago.com/mlb/chicago-cubs/willie-harris-on-hometown-pride-and-protecting-a-dream/323120/

Padilla, Doug. "Harris Learning All He Can," *Chicago Sun-Times*, June 19, 2002: 136

Padilla, Doug. "Oz Good as It Gets: Guillen's Sox Sweep Astros to bring first Series title to Chicago since 1917," *Chicago Sun-Time*s, October 27, 2005, Sox Playoff Extra, A2

Fegan, James. "Q&A with Willie Harris: World Series Hero Turned Minor League Skipper," *The Athletic*, April 18, 2017

Kane, Colleen. "Experience Matters: Mark Grudzielanek, Willie Harris Bring Major Cred to White Sox Farm System," *Chicago Tribune*, May 8, 2017: 3, 8

NOTES

1 Phil Rogers, *Say It's So: The Chicago White Sox's Magical Season* (Chicago: Triumph Books, 2006), 258.

2 Paul Skrbina, "You Can Take It to the Memory Bank," *Chicago Tribune*, July 19, 2015: 3, 4.

3 The other two are Ernie Riles and Herston Waldrep.

4 "Mentor Program Guides Boys from Troubled Lives," *Columbus* (Georgia) *Ledger-Enquirer*, January 12, 1998: 12.

5 Gordon Edes, "History on Harris's Side?" *Boston Globe*, February 27, 2006: D2; Jeff Carroll, "A Tale of One City," *Hammond* (Indiana) *Times*, September 22, 2004: C1, C6.

6 Thomas Stinson, "From Cairo, Proudly," *Atlanta Journal-Constitution*, June 2, 2007: D1, D6.

7 Stinson, D6.

8 Scott Merkin, "Harris Continues Following Jackie's Path: Former White Sox Shares Hometown, Selfless Spirit with Hall of Famer," MLB.com, February 22, 2017. https://www.mlb.com/news/willie-harris-followed-jackie-robinson-s-path-c216768030.

9 Bill Osinski, "Grady County Finally Honors Its Most Valuable Player," *Atlanta Journal-Constitution*, March 12, 1996: C1.

10 Tina Eshleman, "Willie Harris, the Former Major Leaguer and New Richmond Flying Squirrels Manager Answers Our Pressing Questions," *Richmond Magazine*, May 14, 2018.

11 "Colleges: Ole Miss Ponders Change," *Atlanta Journal/Atlanta Constitution*, May 11, 1997: E5.

12 Matteen Zibanejadrad, "Former Owl Joins Chicago Cubs Coaching Staff," Kennesaw State University, December 16, 2020. https://ksuowls.com/news/2020/12/16/baseball-former-owl-joins-chicago-cubs-coaching-staff.

13 Kent Baker, "Harris Makes Most of Second Time Around," *Baltimore Sun*, September 4, 2000: 40.

14 Dave Sheinin, "Orioles Trade for Singleton," *Washington Post*, January 30, 2002.

15 Chris De Luca and Doug Padilla, "Iguchi Deal Frustrates Harris: Infielder Dismayed by Sox' Decision to Replace him," *Chicago Sun-Times*, January 28, 2005, 132.

16 Clint Thompson, "Cairo Honors Local Hero," *Thomasville* (Georgia) *Times-Enterprise*, December 9, 2005.

17 Carroll Rogers, "Harris Erupts: 6 Hits, 6 RBIs," *Atlanta Journal Constitution*, July 22, 2007: E1, E5.

18 David O'Brien, "Save, Harris," *Atlanta Journal Constitution*, August 10, 2007: D1, D6.

19 Meghan Montemurro, "Willie Harris Brings a Joyful Energy to the Chicago Cubs – Along with Unconventional Visual Cues to Baserunners," *Chicago Tribune*, May 11, 2021: 3, 1, 4.

20 Grady Higgins, " Harris a Hit as Voyagers Coach; Billings Tops Great Falls," *Great Falls Tribune*, June 27, 2016.

21 Montemurro.

22 Jon Greenberg, "As the Cubs' Third-Base coach, Willie Harris Is Trying to Be Himself: Just Another Week in Chicago," *The Athletic*, June 30, 2021.

23 Montemurro.

24 Mark Gonzales, "White Sox Bits: Walker's Arrival Makes Deep Bullpen Deeper Still," *Chicago Tribune*, May 10, 2005: 4, 4.

25 "NY Mets to Interview Jim Riggleman for Role as Terry Collins' Bench Coach; Willie Harris Backs Him," *New York Daily News*, October 10, 2011.

26 Skrbina, "You Can Take It to the Memory Bank."

DUSTIN HERMANSON

By Richard Cuicchi

Pitcher Dustin Hermanson routinely switched back and forth between starter and reliever roles throughout his 12-year major-league career. He had moderate success in both roles, saving his best season until the end of his career, when he recorded a career-high 34 saves for the 2005 Chicago White Sox, who won their first World Series since 1917. One of the defining characteristics of his tenure was that he was always willing to fill whatever role his team needed. A recurring back ailment ended his career prematurely at age 34.

Dustin Michael Hermanson was born in Springfield, Ohio, on December 21, 1972, to parents Michael and Jackie (Ruth) Hermanson. His mother and grandmother were part Cherokee and Seminole.[1] Hermanson would become noted for his facial hair. At one point, he shaved his beard in the shape of a peace sign as a tribute to his Native American heritage.[2] His father retired as a police officer and later owned a cleaning service business in Springfield. His mother was a social service worker. He had a sister, Jamie.[3]

One of Hermanson's first brushes with notoriety didn't involve baseball. As a 13-year-old in 1986, he was honored by the local fire department for alerting them to a fire in his neighbor's house, in which no one was at home.[4]

But shortly after that incident, Hermanson was being mentioned in the Springfield newspapers for his participation on the Northridge Babe Ruth team that advanced to the state tournament in three straight seasons.[5]

Hermanson attended Kenton Ridge High School in Springfield. As a sophomore in 1989, the right-handed pitcher helped the team win its first-ever district championship.[6] He was named to the 1990 Central Buckeye Conference All-League team.[7] With one of his personal priorities to attend college, he signed a letter of intent to play for Kent State University before his senior baseball season.[8]

Hermanson led Kenton Ridge into the state playoffs in his senior year in 1991. His team lost in the state semifinal.[9] He was named the Coaches All-Area team and honored as Player of the Year on the strength of his 9-0 record, 0.50 ERA, and 20 hits, 19 walks, and 97 strikeouts in 56 innings. He was also impressive as a batter, hitting .351 with 3 home runs and 24 RBIs.[10] His performance began to attract major-league scouts' attention.

Although he had already committed to Kent State, Hermanson said he was leaning toward signing professionally if he was selected in the June amateur draft. He estimated that his college scholarship was worth between $70,000 and $90,000. "If the money's there, I'm going to sign," he said. "The way I feel is, if I go to college and something happens to my arm, what happens then?" He added, "If I don't get that, then I'll go to Kent State. Either way. I plan to get a college education."[11]

The decision on whether to attend Kent State was made easier since Hermanson wasn't selected until the 39th round by the Pittsburgh Pirates.

Kent State's baseball program had not historically been a strong one in recent years. Their most noteworthy alumni included former major leaguers Gene Michael, Al Oliver, and Thurman Munson from the 1960s. But that would change when Hermanson got there.

On an upper-classmen-dominated team, Hermanson pitched mostly in relief in his freshman season in 1992. Kent State won a school-record 45 wins against only 13 losses. The team was the regular-season champion and winner of the Mid-American Conference tournament in which Hermanson was named the MVP based on a tournament-record three saves.[12] The team made its first NCAA

Dustin Hermanson   2005

Regional since 1964 but was eliminated by losses to Western Carolina and Florida State.[13] Hermanson's season stats included a 2-0 record, 5 saves, and a 1.24 ERA.[14]

In what became a common theme throughout his career, Hermanson was switched to the starting rotation in 1993. Kent State and Central Michigan finished in a tie for the regular-season conference title, with 35-12 records. Hermanson was named to the All-MAC team.[15] Kent State led the nation in ERA, with Hermanson finishing with 1.90 for 11th place. He ranked 22nd in the nation in strikeouts with 10.2 per nine innings.[16] Kent State won its second consecutive MAC tournament with a 4-1 record.[17] The team advanced to the NCAA Regional tournament, where it lost in the semifinals to South Alabama.

Kent State won the regular-season conference title (33-15) in 1994 and was runner-up to Central Michigan in the MAC tournament. Hermanson was an All-MAC selection again. Kent State earned its third straight NCAA tournament bid but lost its first two games to the University of Miami and Minnesota. Hermanson finished with a 5-5 record, including four complete games, and a 3.39 ERA.[18] He was named a 1994 finalist for the Golden Spikes Award, given to the top amateur baseball player in the nation each year. Georgia Tech's Jason Varitek, the future Boston Red Sox All-Star catcher, was the winner.[19]

Even though Hermanson's junior season stats didn't look all that impressive, he was selected by the San Diego Padres as the third overall pick in the first round. He trailed only Florida State's All-American pitcher Paul Wilson and Texas high-school phenom Ben Grieve. Kent State teammate Travis Miller was selected by the Minnesota Twins as a supplemental pick (34th overall) in the first round.

Hermanson received a $960,000 bonus plus $45,000 earmarked for continuing his education. It was the largest signing bonus in Padres history.[20]

San Diego immediately targeted Hermanson as a relief pitcher. Hermanson embraced the role. "I like closing just because there's a lot more pressure on you," he said. "That's the kind of pitcher I am. I want to be in those situations where everybody's relying on what I do. I'm either going to win it or lose it. You're going to get the glory or you're going to be in the doghouse. I like taking those chances."[21]

Hermanson was initially assigned to Double-A Wichita, where he demonstrated that the reliever role might be the right fit. He gave up only one earned run in 21 innings over 16 games, collecting eight saves. His performance earned him a promotion to Triple-A Las Vegas, where his results were not as encouraging (6.14 ERA in seven appearances), albeit a small sample size.

The start of the 1995 major-league season was delayed by a player strike that began in August 1994. With the players union prohibiting major leaguers from participating in spring exhibition games, teams were allowing minor-league players to become replacement players.

In the Padres spring camp, general manager Randy Smith encouraged minor leaguers to play in exhibition games, but also indicated there would be no punishment by the team if they chose not to. Hermanson took the position of not playing. "If there's any replacement players in an exhibition game, you won't see me pitching in one," he said. "I'm not going to go against the union. I've got a long career ahead of me."[22]

The strike came to an official end on April 2, 1995. As the Padres prepared to start the delayed regular season two weeks later, they were looking for a middle reliever who could transition games from the starting rotation to closer Trevor Hoffman.[23] However, Hermanson wasn't deemed to be ready to fill the spot and started the 1995 season with Triple-A Las Vegas. But when the Padres' bullpen began giving up too many runs, he was called up and made his major-league debut on May 8 against the Los Angeles Dodgers. Entering the game with two on base and no outs, the 6-foot-3, 195-pounder pitched a scoreless seventh inning and picked up his first win. He was the first in his draft class to reach the majors.[24]

Over his next five appearances, Hermanson gave up only one run while picking up two more winning decisions. He made his third overall draft selection by the Padres look like a brilliant decision. But then he struggled through a stretch of six games in which he gave up 10 earned runs in only 4⅔ innings, triggering a demotion to Las Vegas to work on his mechanics. He returned to the Padres in mid-August, but his results in 14 games during the remainder of the season (5.95 ERA and 1.63 WHIP) weren't much better.

Hermanson approached the 1996 season with a renewed confidence. Padres pitching guru Dan Warthen, who had spent a week working with him during his 1995 demotion, was the new Padres pitching coach.[25] Hermanson didn't win a roster spot with the Padres coming out of spring training. With Las Vegas again, he began to deliver the type of sustained performance the Padres were expecting. As the primary closer with the Stars, he collected 21 saves in 35 games he finished. He recorded a 3.13 ERA and 10.6 strikeouts per 9 innings pitched in 42 appearances and earned an all-star selection. He was recalled by the Padres on August 1, but his performance for the balance of the season reverted back to his poor showing at the end of 1995. He was left off the Padres' postseason roster after they won the NL West Division championship.

Because of his disappointing results, the Padres made Hermanson available on the trade market, and they ended up dealing him in November to the Florida Marlins for second baseman Quilvio Veras. Hermanson welcomed the change, since he felt the Padres had not given him a fair chance.[26] With two spots open in the Marlins' bullpen, he was initially slated to be a set-up man for closer Robb Nen.[27]

Aided by the addition of a changeup to go along with his fastball, Hermanson wanted a fresh start in his career, and he thought the Marlins offered that opportunity in 1997.

However, Florida traded Hermanson and Joe Orsulak to the Montreal Expos for Cliff Floyd on March 26. Hermanson made the roster and the Expos gave him four middle-relief opportunities during the first dozen games. In his April 16 game against the Houston Astros, he hit a two-run home run off Shane Reynolds in his first major-league at-bat.

When manager Felipe Alou sought to add a fifth man in the starting rotation, he gave Hermanson the opportunity, his first since his college days. He won his first start, against the Chicago Cubs on April 22, and remained in the rotation for the balance of the season. He effectively used his new changeup to go along with his fastball and slider, while enjoying consistency from one start to the next.[28] He pitched his first career shutout on July 15, including nine strikeouts over the Marlins, the team that gave up on him in the spring.

The Expos were obviously pleased with Hermanson's transition to a starter role. Manager Alou was correct in his hunch to put Hermanson into the rotation. He emerged as their second-best starter behind Pedro Martinez, who had a career breakout season that earned him his first Cy Young Award. Hermanson lost his last three decisions to finish with an 8-8 record and a 3.69 ERA.

Meanwhile, in only their fifth season of existence, the Marlins won the World Series, over the Cleveland Indians. It could have been a case of "what might have been" remorse for Hermanson. But years later he had no regrets about having been traded. He said, "The Expos gave me the opportunity of a lifetime to be a starting pitcher and that has changed my career for the better."[29]

Over the winter, Montreal traded Martinez, who was one year away from free agency, to the Boston Red Sox. Montreal received pitching prospects Carl Pavano and Tony Armas Jr. in return. With Martinez gone, Hermanson became the ace of the rotation for the Expos, who won only 65 games in 1998. In 30 starts, he compiled a 14-11 record and lowered his ERA to 3.13. It was the best season of his career as a starter.

A young Expos team had another poor season again in 1999, winning only 68 games. If not for Vladimir Guerrero's offensive production (42 home runs, 131 RBIs, driving in 18 percent of the Expos' runs), Montreal might have lost even more games. Hermanson kept his top-of-the-rotation spot. He was the senior member of the rotation at age 26. He led the team with 34 starts but won only nine games against 14 losses, while his ERA rose to 4.20.

Hermanson continued to demonstrate his durability on the Expos' pitching staff in 2000, as he recorded 30-plus starts for the third consecutive season. He posted a 12-14 record and a 4.77 ERA for the fourth-place team.

Over the winter, Hermanson was traded to the St. Louis Cardinals.[30] He joined their 2001 starting rotation that included top-flight pitchers Darryl Kile and Matt Morris. Hermanson finished behind them in wins and ERA (14-13, 4.45). The Cardinals were in a tight race with Houston for first place in the NL Central Division that went down to

the last day of the season.[31] In the next-to-last game, on October 6 with the teams tied for first, Hermanson was chased early in the game, giving up a Cardinals lead in the fourth. St. Louis ended up winning, 10-6. The Astros won the final game, resulting in a tie for the division title. With a 9-7 head-to-head record against St. Louis, the Astros were awarded the division title and St. Louis the wild card.[32]

The Cardinals faced the Arizona Diamondbacks in the Division Series. Hermanson's only appearance came in Game Four, as he pitched three hitless innings to help the Cardinals even the series. The Diamondbacks ended up winning the championship game, 2-1.

The Cardinals dealt Hermanson to the Boston Red Sox over the winter for three minor-league players. In his first 2002 start, on April 3, he suffered a strained right groin on a wet mound in a rainout game.[33] The injury kept him sidelined until July 20, when he made a relief appearance against the New York Yankees. After his one-inning return, he went on the disabled list again with a staph infection in his left elbow.[34]

Hermanson returned to action with a start on August 20 and recorded his only winning decision of the season. He was relegated to the bullpen for the remainder of the season, as the Red Sox finished 10½ games behind the Yankees. He pitched only 22 innings and finished with a 7.77 ERA for the season. Compared with an average of 190 innings in the previous five seasons, his season was a huge disappointment.

A dejected Hermanson was well aware that the Red Sox had a decision to make about his future with the team. Boston held an option for $7.5 million for 2003. He said, "I'd love to [return next year]. I know it's going to be tough for them to make a decision on me because I've been out so long. I really do understand that but I'd love to make it up."[35]

The Red Sox exercised their option to buy out Hermanson's contract for $1 million, thinking they might be able to re-sign him for fewer dollars.[36] However, in 2003 he went back to the Cardinals, who put him in the bullpen. He had a potential life-threatening moment at his apartment on May 26, when he got light-headed and thought he might be suffering a heart attack. Hermanson was taken by ambulance to a hospital for observation. After undergoing tests, it was determined he had suffered from acute lightheadedness. He was released the next afternoon and was told by doctors to take the night off.

He had been a close friend of Cardinals pitcher Darryl Kile, who died the year before with blockages in his heart. Hermanson said, "I couldn't help but think D.K. When you're fairly young and in good condition, you don't expect something like that to happen. It scares you."[37]

Hermanson made 23 relief appearances with the Cardinals, posting a 1-2 record and a 5.46 ERA. After he declined an assignment to Triple-A Memphis, the Cardinals released him in late June. The San Francisco Giants, who were in first place by five games over Arizona, signed him on July 11 to a minor-league contract. After four starts with Triple-A Fresno, Hermanson was called up to the Giants on August 2.[38] He was reunited with manager Felipe Alou, who had been with him in Montreal. Because the Giants' starters had been significantly impacted by injuries, Hermanson was placed in the rotation.[39] He was effective in six starts and three relief appearances, posting a 2-1 record and a 3.00 ERA.

Despite their pitching woes, the Giants ended up winning their division by 15½ games over the Los Angeles Dodgers. They lost to the Florida Marlins in four games in the Division Series. Hermanson saw relief duty in Game Four.

Hermanson re-signed with the Giants for 2004, for a "bargain basement" price of $800,000.[40] Coming out of spring training, he vied for a spot in the starting rotation and won it. After 18 starts that produced a 4-4 record and a 4.59 ERA, manager Bruce Bochy decided to move Hermanson to the bullpen as the closer in early August. He replaced Matt Herges, who had been ineffective since the All-Star break.[41] Hermanson ended up with 17 saves, yet he failed in his most important outing.

With three games left in the season and the Giants three games behind first-place Los Angeles, San Francisco had an opportunity to finish in a tie, since they played the Dodgers in the final three-game series. The Giants came up short, winning two of the three, with Hermanson taking the loss in the second game. He was called on to get the last out of the eighth and then came back in the bottom of the ninth to protect a 3-0 lead. But he ended up being responsible for four of the Dodgers' seven runs, capped by Steve Finley's walk-off grand slam.

Despite his failure in the final series, Hermanson's versatility had come in handy for the Giants. He finished the season with a 6-9 record and a 4.53 ERA. He started 18 of his 47 appearances while also collecting 17 saves. He was the first Giants pitcher since Scott Garrelts in 1986 to save 10 games and make 10 starts in a season.[42]

Hermanson was not offered arbitration by the Giants and was released. He complained that the Giants had not paid him an incentive worth $200,000 owed to him for being in the starting rotation the entire season. He maintained that when he moved to the closer role, he did it for the good of the team. Hermanson said, "I was surprised [by their decision to withhold the bonus], and it made my decision very easy not to go back to San Francisco."[43]

The Chicago White Sox signed Hermanson to a two-year, $5.5 million contract with a club option for 2007. Well aware of his versatility over the years, they intended to use him initially as a set-up reliever. But he was also their contingency as a closer if incumbent Shingo Takatsu faltered in the role. White Sox GM Ken Williams said, "Dustin was looking for a closing job, but was also looking for a team he could win with."[44]

It was his second stint in the American League. A.J. Pierzynski, who was the Giants' catcher in 2004, also signed with the White Sox after being endorsed by Hermanson. By the first of May, Hermanson replaced Takatsu who had lost confidence in himself.[45] Hermanson said, "I've always considered myself a closer at heart even when I was starting. That's why I got myself into trouble throwing too many pitches because I was out there closing every inning and running myself into the ground."[46] Hermanson embraced his new role. He did not give up an earned run in his first 19 appearances, spanning April and May. By that point he had recorded 11 saves, and the White Sox were in first place by five games over Minnesota.

Hermanson's streak of 21 scoreless innings ended on June 1, when he gave up two earned runs in the ninth inning in a 10-7 loss to the Angels. As of July 14, he had earned 22 saves in 23 opportunities.

Hermanson began to be affected by chronic back problems in mid-July. He was able to avoid going on the disabled list, but his condition caused the White Sox to consider other options for a closer as the trade deadline approached.[47]

Hermanson told manager Ozzie Guillén he was willing to go out and pitch as hard as he could, as long as he could get an occasional break.[48] Hard-throwing rookie pitcher Bobby Jenks, who made his major-league debut on July 6, became an attractive late-inning option. Veteran Cliff Politte and Neal Cotts were other options. But Guillén finally decided to stand pat with the relief staff he had.

Hermanson and Jenks ended up sharing closer duties. Guillén drew criticism for continuing to lean on Hermanson, given his medical condition, during the tight race for a division title. Yet Hermanson didn't have an issue with his utilization, countering that he'd still be pitching even if the team weren't in contention. He said, "I don't think I'd ever shut it down. When you start the season, you want to finish the season unless there's an injury or your arm falls off."[49]

The White Sox ended up winning the AL Central Division by six games over Cleveland. Hermanson racked up 34 saves (ninth in the AL) in 57 appearances, including conversion of 30 of his first 31 save opportunities. His 2.04 ERA was a career best. Hermanson earned a $150,000 bonus for finishing 45 games.[50]

Chicago swept Boston in three games in the Division Series. Jenks performed closer duty. Although Hermanson continued to suffer from occasional back spasms, he made it known to Guillén that he was ready to pitch. But he was not used in the series.

The White Sox defeated the Los Angeles Angels in five games in the Championship Series. Their pitching was the key to their success, as all four White Sox wins came on complete games by the starters. The bullpen was called on only once, when Cotts pitched just two-thirds of an inning in the Game One loss.

Chicago's hot streak in the playoff rounds leading up to the World Series continued against NL champion Houston Astros. Chicago swept the Astros in four games for its first World Series championship since 1917. In his first appearance since September 30, Hermanson pitched only one-third of an inning, in the marathon 14-inning Game Three. He entered the game in the eighth inning in a save opportunity with the White Sox leading, 5-4. With runners on first and second, he gave up a double to Jason Lane that tied the score.

During the offseason, Hermanson participated in a rehabilitation program in Phoenix to address his recurring lower-back problems. With Jenks handling closer duties during the postseason, the White Sox had an option to use Hermanson in a set-up or closer role. Before 2006 spring training, he wasn't sure what his role would be. He said, "I imagine it will be similar to what it was at the start of last season with Shingo. I think I'll probably set up some games and close some games."[51]

But soon after the players reported in mid-February, Guillén announced that Jenks would start the 2006 season as his closer. Hermanson experienced back pains again during spring training. At one point, he considered surgery. He said, "I hope it doesn't come to that. But I can't keep pitching with the pain I had last year. That's why we're resorting to pain management because we are not into the fixing part." Yet he was also hesitant to rely too much on painkilling injections.[52]

Unable to overcome his pain, Hermanson was put on the 15-day disabled list to start the regular season and was assigned to Arizona for rehabilitation.[53] From early July to early September, he did a rehab assignment with Triple-A Charlotte, making 14 appearances. He rejoined the White Sox on September 6 and ended up making six relief appearances, including three as closer.

The White Sox granted Hermanson free agency after the 2006 season, and he ended up signing a minor-league contract with the Cincinnati Reds in March 2007. He wasn't able to return to his 2005 form, and he asked for his release rather than start the season at Triple A.[54]

Hermanson retired after his failed attempt to make the Reds roster. The 34-year-old looked forward to being at home with his wife, Melissa, and young children, Mia and Dreden. In an interview in June 2007, he said, "I have a back problem and I'm told there's a chance I could hurt it worse if I continued to try to pitch." He added, "I thank God for a career that allowed me to be able to raise my kids like this."[55]

Hermanson finished his career with a 73-78 won-lost record and 56 saves in 357 games, which included 180 starts. He posted a 4.21 ERA and a 105 ERA+.

SOURCES

In addition to the sources cited in the Notes, the author consulted Baseball-Reference.com and Retrosheet.org.

NOTES

1 Steve Rosenbloom, "Dustin Hermanson," *Chicago Tribune*, June 8, 2005: 4, 10.

2 David Haugh, "A Cast of Characters," *Chicago Tribune*, October 9, 2005: 17,6.

3 "Anniversaries," *Springfield* (Ohio) *News-Sun*, June 21, 1991: 5B.

4 "Youth Honored for Alertness," *Springfield News-Sun*, March 24, 1986: 13.

5 Andy Woodard, "Third Straight Trip a Rarity," *Springfield News-Sun*, July 21, 1988: 17.

6 Ron Ware, "Cougars Claim District Crown," *Springfield News-Sun*, May 19, 1989: 13.

7 "Prep Teams," *Dayton Daily News*, May 27, 1990: 12-D.

8 Tim Bucey, "Pressure Off KR's Hermanson," *Springfield News-Sun*, November 28, 1990: 7.

9 Ben Begley, "Devils 'Walk' To Win," *Troy* (Ohio) *Daily News*, May 17, 1991: 9.

10 "KR Pitcher, Coach Head All-Area Team," *Springfield News-Sun*, May 26, 1991: 2C.

11 Ron Ware, "Hermanson Leans Toward Signing," *Springfield News-Sun*, June 3, 1991: 5.

12 Jack McDermott, "Flashes Gain NCAA Tourney," *Cleveland Plain Dealer*, May 17, 1992: 5-D.

13 John Wagner, "Tournament Losses End KSU's Dream Season," *Ravenna* (Ohio) *Record-Courier*, May 24, 1992: B1.

14 Ron Ware, "Dustin Answers Padres' Prayers," *Springfield News-Sun*, June 3, 1994: 13.

15 "Kent Nartker Named MAC's Top Pitcher," *Cleveland Plain Dealer*, May 18, 1993: 6-D.

16 "Flashes Maintain Top Spot in National ERA," *Ravenna Record-Courier*, June 10,1993: B-2.

17 "Kent wins MAC Baseball Tournament," *Toledo Blade*, May 23, 1993, D2.

18 Ron Ware, "Dustin Answers Padres' Prayers."

19 Golden Spikes Award Finalists. https://www.usabaseball.com/golden-spikes-award/nominees/finalists. Accessed June 16, 2024.

20 John Schlegel, "Is Dustin Another Hoffman?" *North County Times* (Oceanside, California), February 26, 1995: C1.

21 Schlegel: C5.

22 "Padres GM Disagrees With Union Stance," *The Californian* (Temecula, California), February 22, 1995: B-3.

23 Tom Krasovic, "Strong-Armed Staff Has One Weakness," *San Diego Union Tribune*, April 14, 1995: D4.

24 Bob Nightengale, "Padres Deliver the Goods Against Dodgers," *Los Angeles Times*, May 9, 1995: C4.

25 Shaun O'Neill, "Warthen Delivers Familiar Message," *North County Times*, March 7, 1996: C1.

26 Cheryl Rosenberg, "Hermanson's New Dream Team," *Palm Beach Post* (West Palm Beach, Florida), February 20, 1997: 5C.

27 "Scouting the Marlins," *Miami Herald*, February 20, 1997: 9.

28 Jeff Blair, "A Little Changeup in Hermanson's Routine," *Montreal Gazette*, May 15, 1997: F3.

29 Terry Scott, "Two Sides of Dustin Hermanson," *1998 Expos Magazine*: 64.

30 Montreal traded Hermanson and Steve Kline to the St. Louis Cardinals for Britt Reames and Fernando Tatis on December 14, 2000.

31 The season was extended six days in October to make up games deferred after the 9/11 attacks.

32 "Resolution of Ties in Division Races," https://www.baseball-reference.com/bullpen/Resolution_of_ties_in_division_races. Accessed October 13, 2024.

33 Bob Hohler, "Hermanson's Debut Spoiled by Injury," *Boston Globe*, April 4, 2002: C3.

34 Bob Hohler, "Clubhouse Was a Chat Room," *Boston Globe*, August 21, 2002: F6.

35 Hohler, "Clubhouse Was a Chat Room."

36 Bob Hohler, "Sox Opt to Buy Out Hermanson," *Boston Globe*, November 1, 2002: D2.

37 Joe Strauss, "Hermanson Sits One Out After Fearing Heart Attack," *St. Louis Post-Dispatch*, May 28, 2003: D5.

38 "Giants Steer Clear of Sweep," *San Francisco Examiner*, August 4, 2003: 15.

39 "Correia's Start Another Omen for Giants," *San Francisco Examiner*, August 12, 2003: 14.

40 Larry Krueger, "Too Many Questions," *San Francisco Examiner*, January 9, 2004: 20.

41 John Crowley, "Closer Search Ends," *San Francisco Examiner*, August 4, 2004: 34.

42 Mark Gonzales, "Set Up to Succeed in Any Role," *Chicago Tribune*, March 9, 2005: 4, 4.

43 Mark Gonzales, "Set Up to Succeed in Any Role."

44 "White Sox Sign Hermanson," *San Francisco Examiner*, December 9, 2004: 35.

45 Mark Gonzales, "Door Is Closing on Takamatsu," *Chicago Tribune*, April 21, 2005: Section 4, 3.

46 David Haugh, "Closing: Whole New Ballgame," *Chicago Tribune*, May 20, 2005: Section 4, 5.

47 Dave van Dyck, "Closer on Shopping List," *Chicago Tribune*, July 20, 2005: Section 4, 3.

48 Mark Gonzales, "Hermanson Has Inflamed Disc in Back but Will Pitch," *Chicago Tribune*, July 22, 2005: Section 4, 3.

49 Mark Gonzales, "McCarthy Trying to Pace Self During Stretch," *Chicago Tribune*, September 27, 2005: Section 4, 4.

50 Mark Gonzales, "Uribe Takes Advice, Gets Striking Results," *Chicago Tribune*, October 5, 2005: Section 9, 7.

51 Mark Gonzales, "Closer or Setup Suits Hermanson," *Chicago Tribune*, February 1, 2006: Section 4, 3.

52 Mark Gonzales, "Painful Choices Await Hermanson," *Chicago Tribune*, March 18, 2006: Section 3, 8.

53 Mark Gonzales, "Hermanson's Next Stop? Disabled List," *Chicago Tribune*, March 27, 2006: Section 3, 8.

54 Kyle Nagel, "Red Release KR's Hermanson on Eve of Opening Day," *Springfield News-Sun*, April 2, 2007: D1.

55 Kermit Rowe, "Fatherly Hermanson OK With Retirement," *Springfield Sun-News*, June 17, 2007: B1.

ORLANDO HERNÁNDEZ

By Russ Speiller

The story of baseball pitcher Orlando "El Duque" Hernández might read like a movie script still waiting to be written, yet it could be considered quite a common story for Cuban ballplayers who grew up under the Communist regime of Fidel Castro. Orlando Hernández went from beloved Cuban baseball star to banishment from baseball to becoming a four-time World Series winner in major-league baseball.

Orlando Hernández Pedroso's age has at times been in doubt, but according to his passport, his Havana divorce agreement, and his Cuban baseball card, Orlando was born on October 11, 1965.[1] He was the younger of two children conceived by Maria Julia Pedroso and Arnaldo Hernández Montero, though Arnaldo went on to have additional children with other women, the most notable of whom was Liván Hernández, who had a 17-year career in the majors.

According to an interview with Arnaldo by reporters Steve Fainaru and Ray Sánchez, described in their book *The Duke of Havana*, Arnaldo had named his second son Arnoldo; however, in his youth, the boy rejected this name exclaiming, "Yo soy Orlando! ("I am Orlando!") and thus his parents obliged and called him such.[2]

It was Orlando's father, Arnaldo, while playing for the Pasta Gravy toothpaste company baseball team, who was first given the moniker of El Duque. In the interview with Fainaru and Sánchez, Arnaldo recounted the story of the nickname as follows: "I was a campesino and whenever anyone asked me for anything, I'd say 'Take It.'" One day [my coach] Chico Fuentes said, 'What a noble young man,' and the first name he gave me was El Conde. But it didn't sound right. So then he decided to call me 'El Duque.' I think it also came from (American baseball player) Duke Snider. And from then on my real name disappeared."[3]

In addition to passing on the nickname to his son, Orlando's father also passed along his baseball uniform number, 26. The number represented the date July 26, 1953, when Fidel Castro kicked off the Cuban revolution by launching his attack on the Moncada barracks in Santiago.

Orlando's father and mother met through baseball. Arnaldo had been learning to pitch while playing for the Havana Psychiatric Hospital baseball team. He boarded the bus to go to a baseball game when he caught the attention of Maria Julia, who was working as a lab technician at the hospital.[4]

Though they fell in love, married, and had two boys, the marriage between Maria Julia Pedroso and Arnaldo Hernández Montero did not last more than a few years. Arnaldo was known to drink and play around. Orlando Hernández was just 2 years old when his father left.

In their youth growing up, Orlando and his older brother, Arnaldo Hernández Pedroso, who died at the age of 30 from an aneurysm caused by a cerebral hemorrhage, were extremely close with one another both emotionally and physically. The two boys slept in the same bed until they reached their teens when the bed finally collapsed under their collective growing bodies.[5] Baseball had run in their family's blood, not just with their father but with their uncle, nicknamed Minosito, who was an infielder and the person Orlando credited with teaching him the game.[6] Orlando and his brother lived with their mother and her extended family in adjoining row homes next to a church in the town of Wajay.[7]

Growing up, the family did not have much wealth. Orlando recalled having one pair of pants that he called

S🧦X   **Orlando Hernandez**   **2005**

"the Weeklies" because he wore them every day except Saturdays, when he wore a second pair of pants he called "Big Saturdays" that he dressed in when going to a party.[8]

Orlando grew up in Rancho Boyeros, a district of Havana. As a youth he was coached by Rolando Nuñez, also known as Chavito (Little Chavez).[9] Nuñez described Orlando's baseball ability: "As a boy, he did not distinguish himself as a ballplayer. It was just his perseverance that won out in the end – his dedication. He was in love with the game, it's as simple as that. He loved the game with everything he had. He trained more than any player I've ever seen. He ran for miles and miles and miles and miles. He simply worked harder than anybody else."[10]

By age 16, El Duque had a prodigious curveball, an acceptable fastball, and an ability to concentrate that exceeded his peers leading to his acceptance into a high school for athletes known as the Higher Institute of Athletic Perfection (EPSA).[11]

Orlando was drafted into the army, not to fight but to play baseball. (Army divisions fielded their own teams.) While pitching for the Western Army (Ejercito Occidental) team, he was noticed by Pedro Chavez, the manager of Industriales, who recruited him to play for Industriales. (They were the Cuban equivalent of the New York Yankees.)

El Duque's debut for Industriales in 1986 was a total disaster. Entering as a reliever in the seventh inning with the score tied and the bases loaded against Pinar del Rio, Orlando's assignment was to face Cuban legend Luis Giraldo Casanova. El Duque recalled, "The catcher called for a curve two or three times and I said, 'No, no, no.' I wanted the fastball."[12] Casanova proceeded to hit a grand slam, leaving Orlando feeling as if he was worthless. Yet he also credited that as the moment that made him a pitcher.

After 10 full seasons in Cuban baseball, El Duque had a record of 126 wins and 47 losses. His .728 winning percentage was the best all-time in island league history.[13]

On October 28, 1996, the walls came crashing down on Orlando when the Cuban government banished him and two other Cuban ballplayers from baseball for life. The ban followed a wave of defections by Cuban baseball players, including Orlando's half-brother Liván, who had defected in 1995 to the United States. Angered by the defections, and by individuals who aided and abetted the defectors, the Cuban Sports Ministry decreed the banishment on the basis that Orlando and the other two Cuban ballplayers had consorted with a Cuban American sports agent who had urged them to defect.

As a result of the disgrace, Orlando's wife, whom he married in 1989, Norma Elvira Manzo Ibanez, and with whom he had two daughters, Yahumara Hernández Manzo (born March 15, 1990) and Stheffi Hernández Manzo (born July 15, 1995) proceeded to leave and divorce him.

With his livelihood stripped away and labeled as a traitor to his country, El Duque found himself living in a small, windowless gray cinder-block room, an extension of the home of the parents of his new girlfriend, Noris Bosch.[14] He continued to play baseball in neighborhood leagues situated on cow pastures, acting as a third baseman and manager of his team. Orlando found a job as a rehabilitation therapist at the same psychiatric hospital where his mother had worked. The pay was 207 pesos a month, equivalent to $8.62 in 2024 US dollars.

If El Duque felt defeated, he didn't show it. His attitude was perpetually optimistic. He would run the streets of town every morning shouting his favorite phrase, "Todo bien" (all good), to people he met. A reporter quoted him as saying, "I have to train every day without fail. If I don't, I'm defeated. I'm finished. I keep the arms and the legs strong. My mind is strong. I know I will pitch again."[15]

Orlando's savior came in the form of a 66-year-old great-uncle on his mother's side, Ocilio Cruz, who had arrived in Miami from Cuba after having spent 15 years in a Cuban prison for being part of an anti-Castro group. Having kept tabs on his grandnephew, Cruz, who was known to family and friends as Tio, was determined to free Orlando from Fidel Castro's grasp. He used his connections as a private investigator to deliver $4,000 to El Duque, who then tasked his best friend in Cuba, Osmany Lorenzo, to hire an escape vessel.

Orlando and Noris began their escape on December 25, 1997, during Cuba's first legal Christmas since 1969, when people would likely be traveling around, decreasing the chances that government officials would be out questioning citizens. Their escape vessel was a 30-foot fishing boat powered by a 480-horsepower diesel engine, owned by a fisherman named Juan Carlos Romero. In addition to the $4,000 payment, Juan Carlos was promised that if he secured the boat, then he and his wife would be guaranteed to get into the United States and a job would be waiting for him when they arrived. In addition to El Duque and Noris, as well as Juan Carlos and his wife, Geidy, the passenger list included El Duque's cousin Joel Pedroso and Osmany Lorenzo, as well as Alberto Hernández.[16]

After attending a wedding reception earlier in the day, Orlando and Noris, along with Joel Pedroso and Alberto Hernández, piled into a Chevy and headed off on a five-hour drive to the town of Caibarien, where the escape boat awaited. Along the way they stopped to pick up a man named Lenin Rivero who had made separate arrangements with Juan Carlos to leave Cuba on the boat.

The Cuban defectors arrived at the home of Juan Carlos around 5 A.M. on December 26. After receiving the "all clear" signal from a fisherman friend of Juan Carlos, El Duque and the others proceeded to the launch point, Conuco Cay, and waded into the waters to board the fishing vessel.[17]

El Duque and the other passengers spent the first four hours of the trip staying motionless on the deck while Juan Carlos and his wife maneuvered the boat safely out of Cuban waters to the Bahamian island of Anguilla Cay, where a transfer boat arranged by El Duque's granduncle Tio was to be awaiting to take them to Key Biscayne, Florida. But the transfer boat was not present and Juan Carlos's partners needed to return the fishing boat back to Cuba. El Duque and the other passengers were dropped off at Anguilla Cay, hoping the transfer boat would soon arrive and with very little provisions in hand.

The next morning, the transfer boat had still not arrived. The passengers subsisted on the small amount of canned Spam they brought as well as sugar water and peeled conch shells scavenged from the island rocks. Discovering a rafter's graveyard while wandering the shoreline, they were able to secure tent parts, wood, and a charcoal stove, enabling them to start a fire.

In truth, Tio tried hard to get a transfer boat to his grandnephew. However, each attempt he made failed. One boat launched and quickly took on water. Another attempt involved a volunteer aviator group called Brothers to the Rescue who flew a plane to Anguilla Cay but did not find El Duque and the others because they had been hiding among the island's palmetto trees believing that if they were discovered by the US Coast Guard, they would be sent back to Cuba.[18]

Finally, after three days on the island, a helicopter suddenly appeared. El Duque and the others waved their arms to signal the chopper. Though the pilot acknowledged their waves, the helicopter left, not to be seen again. In the early hours of the next morning, a boat arrived, lowering a raft for the Cuban defectors to board. The boat later transferred the passengers to a Coast Guard boat out of Miami.

El Duque and the others were elated that they were being taken to the United States before noticing the ship had changed direction toward Havana, striking fear in their hearts. El Duque tried to explain to the Coast Guard officers that he was the brother of Florida Marlins pitcher Liván Hernández in hopes that it would aid their cause to get to the United States. However, what really mattered in this incident was the location where El Duque and the others were picked up. Because El Duque's group was discovered on Bahamian soil, they would be transported to the Bahamas.

While the Bahamian authorities weighed the situation, which included the fact that the Bahamas had a repatriation agreement with Cuba, El Duque and the others were placed in a detention center.

Incredibly, the next day a press conference was scheduled at the Bahamas immigration office, attended by the Miami press corps, a camera crew from CNN, and reporters from both the *New York Times* and the *Washington Post*, as well as El Duque's granduncle Tio. Also present was Joe Cubas, the man who had been responsible for aiding and abetting the defection of Orlando's half-brother Livan.

It was Cubas who concocted the idea of the press conference, hoping to cast El Duque and the others as political refugees and shame the Bahamians into releasing the Cuban defectors. Cubas advised the Cubans to keep pressing for political asylum. When the press conference concluded, the Bahamians agreed that no deportations would happen while they considered the case.

El Duque's next move was perhaps his brightest: He made a collect phone call to the Cuban American National Foundation in Miami, where a woman named Ninoska Pérez took the call. Upon hearing the situation, Pérez quickly connected with both the press as well as one of the Foundation's more influential members, Gerardo Capo, a Miami developer who just happened to be vacationing in the Bahamas. Collective media pressure, combined with individual pressures from Capo and Cubas influenced the Bahamians to go against their own repatriation agreement with the Cuban government and stay the deportation.[19]

The Cuban American National Foundation now shifted their rescue efforts to the US government and the mobilization of South Florida politicians. Thanks in large part to the deputy assistant secretary of state for public affairs, Lula Rodriguez, within 24 hours the US government extended humanitarian parole to El Duque, Alberto, and Noris. However, the other five Cuban defectors were left to fend for themselves.

Not wanting to leave his compadres behind, El Duque enlisted Joe Cubas' assistance to secure seven visas from both Nicaragua and Costa Rica, even though it meant having to give up the American visa he had just been granted. In the end, El Duque and the other Cuban refugees left the Bahamas on a flight to Costa Rica.

Within a day, Cubas was able to get Orlando his residency papers in Costa Rica, allowing him to be declared a free agent. Cubas then set up a major-league tryout with invitations sent out to all 30 clubs.

The tryout was held at the Antonio Escarre, a broken-down ballpark in the middle of San José, the Costa Rican capital. Sixty-two scouts showed up along with some media. El Duque's fastballs ranged from 88 to 91 miles per hour. Though many scouts did not appear impressed with his showing, Gordon Blakely, the vice president of international scouting for the New York Yankees, most certainly was. Gordon was entranced by El Duque's accomplishments when he starred for the Cuban National Team. An excerpt from the summary notes of El Duque's tryout performance, written by Blakely and fellow Yankee scout Lin Garrett, went as follows:[20]

Physical Description:
Physical specimen, med-leg frame, muscular yet loose and flexible, proportional, an athlete, phy. mature, strong, Dave Stewart look, reported to be 28 yrs old but may be 32 – body is 25.

Tools and Abilities:
Very easy, loose, and free arm. Sudden violent leg lift (Len Barker) then goes easy with the arm – ball gets in on you (Rivera), fastball 88-92 with sink or bore/sink or riding life or straight. CB (curveball) has occasional hump

but plus rotation – will vary angle, depth and velocity. Mixes pitches well, very confident, poised, athletic and strong, likes being out there, likes the attention, enjoys the game.

Weaknesses:

Saw chg (changeup) only in the pen has turnover life and arm speed but not a good pitch – has a big hump in it and too much "white" showing in the rotation, will have no problem picking up new way to throw the pitch; Saw 2 games for a total of 5 inn's, 2nd outing not as sharp, but has been away from the game for 1 to 2 yrs.

Summation:

3-4th starter on 1st div club now; has a unique presence about him – more than just confidence, like him, high interest.

Returning from the tryout, Blakely and Garrett met with Yankees owner George Steinbrenner and his brain trust and exclaimed that El Duque was a winner. They made it known that while listed as a 28-year-old, El Duque was likely really 32, but that he was a great athlete who could pitch for five or six years.

When the discussion around potential pricetag came up, Blakley told Steinbrenner that an offer of $6 million US or more might be required, to which Steinbrenner replied "Okay, Go get him."[21]

Negotiations between the Yankees and Cubas resulted in a major-league contract worth $6.6 million over four years with a $1 million signing bonus.

Thrilled to be pitching again, the charismatic El Duque arrived at the Yankees' Tampa spring-training facilities in March 1998. He brought with him his distinctive delivery that included an acrobatic leg kick on which his left knee came up, almost brushing his chin, with his cap pulled down and his menacing eyes staring at the batter just above his glove. According to Yankees general manager Brian Cashman, El Duque "just had this presence about him like he was (basketball legend) Michael Jordan."[22]

Hernández started the 1998 season pitching for the Yankees' High-A affiliate Tampa Yankees, pitching in two games before being advanced to the Triple-A Columbus Clippers. Thanks to the actions of a Jack Russell Terrier named Veronica, El Duque made his major-league debut on June 3, 1998, in front of a Yankee Stadium crowd of 27,291. Veronica belonged to the mother of Yankees pitcher David Cone. She bit Cone on his index finger, forcing manager Joe Torre to pencil in a replacement starting pitcher to take Cone's turn in the rotation.[23]

El Duque's debut as a Yankee was spectacular. He struck out the first batter he faced on his way to pitching seven innings against the Tampa Bay Devil Rays, earning the victory, yielding just one earned run, a home run by future Hall of Famer Fred McGriff.[24]

In a postgame interview with the Madison Square Garden television network, El Duque was asked what message he might send to Fidel Castro, to which he replied, "I would not say anything to him because I would not waste my time standing in front of him."[25] Because of El Duque's compelling performance, the Yankees shifted pitcher Ramiro Mendoza to the bullpen, freeing up a regular spot in the rotation for Hernández.

In June of 1998 the Yankees, who went on to win 125 games including the playoffs, were already in top form without El Duque, but he helped make a great team ever greater. Before his arrival, the Yankees' starting pitchers had a collective ERA of 4.14. After his arrival, the ERA dropped to 3.48 across the remaining regular-season and playoff games.

As a pitcher, El Duque was a workhorse because, as he put it, "In Cuba, you don't have a relief pitcher every time out. In Cuba, it's win or die."[26] Here is how Joe Torre described what occurred during El Duque's fifth start when Torre went to the mound to take the ball from him after he had thrown 141 pitches, allowing just one run on two singles to the New York Mets: "I remember I took the ball from him and he didn't let it go. And he just had this confused look on his face. I came to realize that he had never really been taken out of a game before. But he was a master. He could paint the corners with the best of them."[27]

Yankees catcher Jorge Posada, who caught 21 of El Duque's 23 starts, including the playoffs, in 1998, described El Duque in this way: "He was just perfection. He was so … well, perfection is a word, but I'm not sure it's the word I'm looking for. He wasn't nervous. He went through hell and now he's living his childhood dream. He was just saying, 'I'm here. This is the best time of my life and I'm not going to take anything for granted.' Yeah, I guess perfection is the word I wanted to use."[28]

Hernández ended the 1998 season with a record of 12-4 and a 3.13 ERA with 131 strikeouts and a 1.17 WHIP in 141 innings, which earned him a fourth-place showing in the Rookie of the Year vote. Besides his debut, his most memorable moment of the season was his season-saving victory in Game Four of the American League Championship Series over the Cleveland Indians.

A dominant team like the 1998 Yankees would not be remembered in legacy fashion without winning the World Series. This goal was very much in doubt in Game Four of the ALCS with the Yankees trailing the Cleveland Indians two games to one in a seven-game series. According to the book *The 1998 Yankees: The Inside Story of the Greatest Baseball Team Ever* by Jack Curry, the *Record* of Hackensack, New Jersey, reported how Steinbrenner approached El Duque to give him a pep talk about the most critical game of the season. The Boss told El Duque, "If you can't stop them, we're through." The cocksure pitcher waved his hand at the owner and said "Mañana, no problema."[29]

GRINDERS AND GAMERS

Though he hadn't pitched in 15 days, Hernández threw seven scoreless innings in a 4-0 win that enabled the Yankees to breathe a sigh of relief. Part of El Duque's success that day can be credited to David Cone. Cone was known to be a creative pitcher and he marveled at the creativity of his teammate El Duque, who could throw side-arm, three-quarters, and over-the-top – all at different speeds that would tempt and tease batters. Watching Hernández warm up for a game in Oakland, Cone noted the lack of aggressiveness he was showing with his changeup, a pitch that he had not thrown to perfection in games and thus was no longer relying on as a weapon on the mound. Cone marched up to Hernández and said, "Finito. Cambio. Finito." El Duque comprehended the advice which was to "Finish the changeup" by throwing it the same way you throw a fastball.[30]

Having had to leave his mother and two daughters behind in Cuba when he made his great escape, it must have felt like a miracle to El Duque when his agent, Joe Cubas, was able to make the needed connections for Fidel Castro to grant 30-day visas to Orlando's mother, daughters, and first wife to come to New York to visit with El Duque and attend the Yankees' 1998 championship parade.

El Duque continued to be a mainstay in the Yankees' starting rotation from 1999 through 2002, his postseason heroics shining bright yet again in 1999, when he won the ALCS MVP and finished the postseason with a 3-0 record and a 1.20 ERA as the Yankees won back-to-back World Series titles.

With a glut of starting pitchers and a need in the bullpen, the Yankees made a three-team trade in January 2003, sending Hernández to the Chicago White Sox, who then sent him to the Montreal Expos. A rotator cuff injury, however, sidelined El Duque for the entire 2003 season.

In 2004, free-agent Hernández rejoined the Yankees, for whom he started 15 games after recovering from the rotator cuff injury. He completed the season with an 8-2 record and a 3.30 ERA.

The majority of El Duque's postseason appearances came as a starter, but this wasn't the case in 2005 after he signed with the White Sox. He finished the regular season with an unspectacular 5.12 ERA, having started 22 of 24 games in which he appeared, but this didn't matter to White Sox manager Ozzie Guillén, who opted to bring El Duque and his postseason experience into Game Three of the ALCS as a reliever against the Boston Red Sox at Fenway Park.

Reflecting upon the situation years later during an interview with NBC Sports Chicago, White Sox pitching coach Don Cooper said, "There's 45,000 people in the stands with tight a-------," Every fan's got the tight a------. Every coach, every player's got the tight a------. The only a------ that wasn't tight was El Duque's."[31]

In the sixth inning, the bases were loaded with no outs and the White Sox holding a precarious 4-3 lead. The pressure on El Duque was immense and the escape act that ensued was epic, later even immortalized on the 2005 World Series monument sculpture erected at US Cellular Field. Hernández got Red Sox catcher Jason Varitek to pop out, battled the next batter, Tony Graffanino, for 10 pitches before getting him to pop out on a full count, and finished the inning by striking out Johnny Damon on a checked swing. El Duque proceeded to come back out and pitch both the seventh and eighth innings, preserving the one-run lead.

El Duque made just one appearance in the White Sox World Series four-game sweep of the Houston Astros, coming on in relief in the ninth inning of Game Three. He pitched one inning, walking four batters, striking out two, and exiting after facing one batter in the 10th inning without giving up a run.

Not long after the World Series celebration in Chicago ended, the White Sox completed a trade with the Arizona Diamondbacks, sending Hernández, reliever Luis Vizcaíno, and outfield prospect Chris Young for starting pitcher Javier Vázquez.

El Duque's time with the Diamondbacks lasted only two months. In May 2006 he was traded to the New York Mets for reliever Jorge Julio. Hernández made 20 starts for the Mets, finishing with a 9-7 record and a 4.09 ERA. With the Mets winning the National League East Division and El Duque having had a very successful month of September, manager Willie Randolph named him the Game One starter for the National League Division Series. But Hernández experienced right-calf discomfort while running sprints as the Mets tuned up for the series against the Los Angeles Dodgers. The injury was bad enough that he was removed from the postseason roster.[32]

Though El Duque's 2007 season with the Mets included bouts with injuries, he was able to make 24 starts, compiling a record of 9-5 with a 3.72 ERA and 128 strikeouts in 147⅔ innings.

Hernández underwent foot surgery after the 2007 season that required lengthy rehabilitation. He was unable to make any starts for the Mets in 2008. Late in the season, he suffered a toe injury that required season-ending surgery. He became a free agent at the end of the 2008 season.

In 2009 and 2010, El Duque tried to make comebacks, pitching for minor-league teams, initially for the Texas Rangers and then for the Washington Nationals. He never got a major-league call-up by either club, and announced his retirement on August 18, 2011.[33]

Overall, Orlando "El Duque" Hernández spent nine seasons in the big leagues pitching for the Yankees, White Sox, Diamondbacks, and Mets, compiling a record of 90 wins and 65 losses, an ERA of 4.13, and a total of 23.1 WAR.

His career regular-season ERA was in line with the third/fourth starter Yankees scouts had projected him to be, but it was under the bright lights of the postseason where El Duque truly shined as an ace. In 15 postseason series, he went 9-3 with a 2.55 ERA and 107 strikeouts in 106 innings pitched, having contributed to four World Series titles, three with the Yankees and one with the White Sox.[34] In 1999 he was named the ALCS MVP for his performances against the Boston Red Sox.

After retirement, Hernández has spent time as an analyst for ESPN's Spanish-language radio and TV. He has also participated in Yankees' Old Timer's Day events at Yankee Stadium as well as in Yankees' Fantasy Camp.

On Valentine's Day 2000, Orlando Hernández married his girlfriend, dancer Noris Bosch, in Coral Gables, Florida. As of July 2024, their son, also named Orlando Hernández, was a pitcher for the Florida International University Panthers' baseball team.[35] During the 2024 season, Hernández made 13 appearances out of the bullpen, posting a 1.57 ERA, the lowest among FIU relievers. He was named to the Conference USA Second Team All-Conference squad.[36]

SOURCES

In addition to the sources cited in the Notes, the author consulted Baseball-Reference.com.

NOTES

1   Steve Fainaru and Ray Sánchez, *The Duke of Havana* (New York: Villard Books, 2001), xix.

2   Fainaru and Sánchez, 7.

3   Fainaru and Sánchez, 24.

4   Fainaru and Sánchez, 26.

5   Fainaru and Sánchez, 3.

6   Fainaru and Sánchez, 31.

7   Fainaru and Sánchez, 7.

8   Fainaru and Sánchez, 8.

9   Fainaru and Sánchez, 32.

10 Fainaru and Sánchez, 34.

11 Fainaru and Sánchez, 35.

12 Fainaru and Sánchez, 36.

13 Peter C. Bjarkman, "The Hernandez Brothers: Livan and Orlando," https://sabr.org/bioproj/topic/the-hernandez-brothers-livan-and-orlando/, Accessed December 30, 2023.

14 Fainaru and Sánchez, xxi.

15 Fainaru and Sánchez, 165.

16 Fainaru and Sánchez, 192-193.

17 Fainaru and Sánchez, 197-199.

18 Fainaru and Sánchez, 207-208.

19 Fainaru and Sánchez, 215-216.

20 Fainaru and Sánchez, 230-231.

21 Fainaru and Sánchez, 232.

22 Jack Curry, *The 1998 Yankees – The Inside Story of the Greatest Baseball Team Ever* (New York: Twelve, 2023), 76.

23 Curry, 81.

24 Eric Chesterton, "20 years ago, El Duque Made His Major League Debut for the Yankees," Cut 4 by MLB.com, June 3, 2018, https://www.mlb.com/cut4/20-years-ago-el-duque-made-his-debut-for-the-yankees-c279576846, Accessed December 21, 2023.

25 Curry, 82.

26 Curry, 84.

27 Curry, 84.

28 Curry, 85.

29 Curry, 196.

30 Curry, 95.

31 Vinnie Duber, "White Sox 2005 Rewind: 'The Only a--- That Wasn't Tight Was El Duque's,'" NBCSportsChicago.com, May 25, 2020, https://www.nbcsportschicago.com/mlb/chicago-white-sox/white-sox-2005-rewind-the-only-a-that-wasnt-tight-was-el-duques/381281/, Accessed December 21, 2023.

32 Associated Press, "Hernandez's Injury Rocks Mets' Rotation," *Denver Post*, https://www.denverpost.com/2006/10/03/hernandezs-injury-rocks-mets-rotation/, Accessed December 21, 2023.

33 Stowe.

34 Rich Stowe, "Orlando 'El Duque' Hernandez: Former New York Yankees Postseason Hero to Retire," *Bleacher Report.com*, August 17, 2011, https://bleacherreport.com/articles/809071-orlando-el-duque-hernandez-former-new-york-yankees-postseason-hero-to-retire, Accessed December 21, 2023.

35 Mike Depasquale, "Sons of 2 Former MLB Players Aim to Carve Own Path at FIU," WSVN.com, February 6, 2023, https://wsvn.com/sports/sons-of-2-former-mlb-players-aim-to-carve-own-path-at-fiu/, Accessed December 21, 2023.[36] https://fiusports.com/sports/baseball/roster/orlando-hernandez/11303, Accessed July 17, 2024.

TADAHITO IGUCHI

By Bill Staples Jr.

Tadahito Iguchi's favorite motto is the Japanese proverb "The boughs that bear most hang lowest." The literal translation describes how rice stalks, as they ripen and bear more grain, bow down due to the weight. This metaphor for human behavior suggests that the more you achieve in life, the more modest you become as a person.[1]

Grounded by this principle, Iguchi enjoyed a 26-year career (1997-2022) in both Nippon Professional Baseball and the US major leagues, becoming one of the most accomplished and respected figures in the game. His trophy case includes an Olympic Silver Medal (1996 Team Japan), three Japan Series rings (1999, 2003 Daiei Hawks, 2010 Chiba Lotte Marines), and two World Series rings (2005 Chicago White Sox, 2008 Philadelphia Phillies).[2] Iguchi holds the distinction of being the first Japanese player with US major-league experience to compete in and win the World Series. He's the first Japanese player to manage in Nippon Professional Baseball and aspires to become the first Japanese national to manage an MLB team.[3]

Iguchi was born on December 4, 1974, in the Tanashi municipality of Tokyo. His love for the game was nurtured by his parents.[4] His father Mitsuo coached his Little League teams and his mother Shoko accompanied him to all training sessions.[5] He played catcher early on and switched to shortstop in high school, inspired by Cal Ripken Jr., whom he watched play during the 1986 Japan-US All-Star Series. "I was so impressed by his defensive quickness," said Iguchi.[6]

He attended Kokugakuin Kugayama High School in Tokyo, leading his team to the Koshien Tournament in 1991, where they were eliminated on the second day in a heartbreaking 5-4 extra-innings loss.[7] Despite the defeat, Iguchi gained valuable perspective, particularly from watching Seiryo High School star Hideki Matsui. "The power of his swing, the sound of the bat cutting through the air – everything was extraordinary," Iguchi remarked. The "shock of Matsui" convinced him he should play in college, where he could develop in both size and skill level, rather than turn pro immediately.[8]

After graduating in 1992, Iguchi enrolled at Aoyama Gakuin University in Tokyo, helping the varsity baseball team win the All-Japan University Baseball Championship in 1993 and 1996. Inspired by teammate Hiroki Kokubo, Iguchi became serious about weight training.[9] His hard work paid off and in 1994 he became the first Triple Crown winner in the Tohto University Baseball League.[10]

Iguchi earned a spot on the Japanese Collegiate All-Star squad that traveled to the United States in 1995, competing against a Team USA roster that included future major leaguers like R.A. Dickey and Troy Glaus.[11] Team Japan won the first game, 5-3, in Millington, Tennessee, thanks in part to Iguchi's two-run home run. It was the first homer allowed by Team USA pitching in its first five games (152 at-bats).[12] The series moved on to San Antonio, where Team USA went on to win the five-game series over Team Japan, three games to two.[13]

Iguchi's bat stayed hot through his senior year at Aoyama Gakuin University, where he finished his college career with 103 hits, 24 home runs, and a .281 batting average in 101 games.[14]

In 1996 Iguchi played for Team Japan in the Summer Olympics in Atlanta, where they finished with a 4-3 record in the preliminary round. His bat contributed to Japan's 11-2 upset win over Team USA in the semifinals, but they ultimately lost to Cuba in the Gold Medal game. The Olympic experience was transformative for Iguchi. "What made the

Tadahito Iguchi   2005

biggest impression on me was the play of the Cuban national team. Their power and speed were completely different, they were like major leaguers, and I was blown away," he said.[15]

After the Olympics, Iguchi was selected by the Fukuoka Daei Hawks as the top pick in the 1996 NPB draft. He was excited to join the team under legendary player and now manager Sadaharu Oh. He also made his personal goals public: "I want to aim at batting .300, hitting 30 homers and stealing 30 bases."[16] He called this his "Triple Three" and made it his goal for every season.[17]

The Japanese term kōjō means continuous improvement and progress, and best describes both the Hawks' and Iguchi's development between 1997 and 2003.[18] His rookie season in 1997 started strong, with a grand slam in his debut game. However, he struggled with a .203 batting average and 67 strikeouts, underscoring the need for more plate discipline. That offseason, Iguchi joined Hawks teammate Nobuhiko Matsunaka on the West Oahu CaneFires in the Hawaii Winter Baseball League, where he hit 8 home runs, showcasing his potential.[19]

In 1998 Iguchi improved to 21 home runs but still struggled with a low .221 batting average. The Hawks' breakthrough came in 1999, winning the Japan Series with a 78-54 record. His performance improved – 14 home runs and 47 RBIs – and the team celebrated manager Oh's first championship.

Iguchi's hard work culminated in a stellar 2001 season. He batted .261 with 30 home runs, 97 RBIs, 104 runs scored, and 44 stolen bases. The Hawks finished second, narrowly missing the Japan Series. He maintained his form in 2002, hitting .259 with 18 home runs. Inspired by the success of Ichiro and other Japanese players in the United States, he announced he was ready to make the jump to the US major leagues.[20]

All eyes were on Iguchi in 2003, and he rose to the occasion with his best season yet in NPB. In 135 games, he achieved a career-high .340 batting average, 27 home runs, and 109 RBIs. His .438 on-base percentage and .573 slugging percentage resulted in an impressive 1.011 OPS. Iguchi's 112 runs scored and 42 stolen bases highlighted his all-around excellence, establishing him as one of the premier players in NPB. Behind his all-star play, the Hawks soared to first place in 2003 with an 82-55 record, advancing to the Japan Series to take on the Hanshin Tigers.

Iguchi faced adversity in the 2003 postseason. After the Hawks secured the Pacific League pennant, he twisted his right ankle but was later cleared to play. He went hitless in a 6-5 loss in Game One against the Tigers, and then responded in Game Two with two hits, including a home run, in a 5-2 victory. In Game Six he hit another two-run homer, giving the Hawks a 5-1 victory and forcing a Game Seven.[21]

Iguchi connected off Game Seven Hanshin starter Trey Moore with a blast into the right-field stands in the third inning, giving the Hawks a commanding 4-0 lead. "I'm starting to see the ball well, and it couldn't have come at a better time," he said.[22]

The booming bats of the Hawks were too much for the Tigers. Iguchi hit yet another two-run homer and Kenji Johjima added a pair of solo shots as the Hawks defeated the Tigers 6-2 in Game Seven.[23] Daei pitcher Toshiya Sugiuchi, who won Games Two and Six, was named Series MVP.[24]

"We came from behind to win at home despite dropping three on the road. There are no words to express how wonderful I feel now," said manager Oh. "It was a great Series, one that will pop up in my head as the best Series for years to come."[25]

After the Series, Iguchi was named to the Pacific League Best 9 at second base, and more reports of his desire to go to America surfaced in the press. "Even before (joining Daei), I've always wanted to give the majors a shot, and I feel that this is the best chance for me," he told reporters.[26]

Team owner Tadashi Nakauchi was reluctant to lose Iguchi, saying, "I want him to stay. He batted in (more than) 100 runs this season and has played a pivotal role in helping Daei win the championship. I want him to continue playing a leading role for the team."[27]

In early November the New York Mets expressed an interest in Iguchi, but instead opted to sign Seibu Lions all-star second baseman Kazuo Matsui.[28] Weeks later, Iguchi announced that he was putting his US dreams on pause, at least temporarily. The *Japan Times* reported, "Iguchi is set to accept a request from Daei to stay in Fukuoka but has not given up his hopes of a move to the United States in the future."[29]

He was compensated well for his loyalty. Hawks management tripled Iguchi's salary for the 2004 season, increasing it to 240 million yen (roughly $2.4 million).[30] He continued his high level of play that season and was voted in as a starter in the NPB All-Star Game.

Iguchi finished the 2004 season batting .333 with 24 home runs, 18 stolen bases, and 89 RBIs in 124 games. The Hawks finished first with a 77-52 record, earning a spot in the postseason Pacific League playoffs against the Seibu Lions. Despite Iguchi's homers in Games One, Three, and Five, the Lions won the series.

The day after the loss, Iguchi told reporters he was ready for a challenge in the United States. "I don't know if I can move to the majors, but I said talks should be held as quickly as possible," he said, noting that he told Hawks general manager Kenji Sato of his wish to start negotiations.[31]

On November 4, 2004, Iguchi received his unconditional release from Fukuoka. After talks failed through the posting system, he opted for the release to increase his possible choices of selecting an American team.[32] The strategic move paid off and Iguchi's stock began to rise.

The Boston Red Sox and the New York Yankees expressed interest, but the Chicago White Sox looked the most promising. "I hear there have been several offers. The owner of the White Sox said he wants to meet with me," Iguchi told reporters.[33] General manager Ken Williams had never seen Iguchi play in person, but based on the recommendation of international scout Ray Poitevint, the Japanese star made his short list.[34] After watching hours of tape and analyzing the skills and intangibles of Iguchi from afar, Williams was convinced he had found the White Sox' next second baseman.[35]

Chicago offered a two-year, $4 million deal (about 420 million yen, 210 million yen per season). Iguchi's side hoped to at least match his Japanese salary of 240 million yen. Thanks to Poitevint, who helped navigate the international and cultural nuances during negotiations, a compromise was reached.[36] The White Sox offered Iguchi $2.3 million (237 million yen) a year plus incentives in a two-year contract.[37] "Playing in the big leagues has been a longtime dream of mine, and I'm really happy," Iguchi said. "I'm going to give my best and show them everything I've learned in Japan."[38]

On January 27, 2005, Iguchi arrived at U.S. Cellular Field in Chicago for a press conference. Williams, the White Sox general manager, emphasized, "We're not looking for another superstar to come in here. This is about a fit, a piece. I told him earlier today, 'I don't care at the end of the year what your numbers are, just go out and play the game the way you've always played it, and things will take care of themselves.'" Iguchi responded through an interpreter, "I've been doing this style for eight years. There is really no intention to change that."[39]

In early February, Iguchi joined the team for spring training in Arizona. He recorded a hit in his first preseason game, against the Diamondbacks.[40] Throughout the spring he proved to himself and others that he belonged. He finished with a 3-for-4 performance against the Oakland Athletics, improving his Cactus League average to .327.[41]

Iguchi made his regular-season debut on April 4 against Cleveland. He went hitless but contributed to the 1-0 win with his defense. He recorded his first US major-league hit the next day, a double against Kevin Millwood, in a 4-3 victory for Chicago. In the third game of the series, Iguchi recorded his first multihit performance, going 3-for-4 and finishing the series with a .364 batting average.

On May 3 Iguchi had the best game of his early US career. He went 4-for-4 with his first major-league home run (off Brian Anderson) in a 5-4 win over Kansas City. "Of course it will be a memorable day ... but at the same time, I'm glad we got the win." he said.[42]

Iguchi carried a .302 average into June. In the second game of a two-game series against New York, he hit a solo home run to beat the Yankees 2-1. This performance marked the beginning of Iguchi's unique place in history as the hitter with the best career batting average (50 or more at-bats) against the Yankees (.409, 27-for-66).[43]

On September 24 Iguchi recorded his second 4-for-4 game with a double and an RBI in an 8-1 win over Minnesota. Five days later, the White Sox clinched the American League Central Division crown with a 4-2 victory over Detroit.[44] In the next to last game of the regular season, Iguchi hit his 15th home run, a three-run bomb at Jacobs Field that gave the White Sox a 4-3 victory and crushed Cleveland's postseason hopes.

Manager Ozzie Guillén credited his new second baseman as an important ingredient to their winning formula. "One of the biggest reasons we are here is because of Iguchi," said Guillén. "He moves the guy over, he runs for me, he makes the plays, he hits home runs, he runs the bases right. This kid does everything for the team, and that's why I keep on saying he's my MVP."[45]

Iguchi finished the regular season batting .278 with 142 hits in 135 games, with 15 home runs and 15 stolen bases. Of his 71 RBIs, nine were generated through sacrifice bunts (three) and flies (six).

Iguchi's postseason performance in 2005 was instrumental in the White Sox' World Series victory. In the ALDS against Boston, he had a notable Game Two, hitting a crucial home run and driving in three runs. Despite a mixed showing in the ALCS against the Angels, his contributions helped the team advance by winning four games to one.

In the World Series against the Astros, Iguchi's bat cooled. Still, he had key hits, including a two-hit performance in Game Three, and contributed to the team's four-game sweep of Houston. The victory in 2005 ended an 88-year championship drought for the White Sox and brought the third World Series crown to the South Side of Chicago.[46]

The victory also marked an international baseball milestone. Eighty-eight years earlier it was three infielders – Joe Tinker, Johnny Evers, and Frank Chance – who led the Cubs to World Series victory by "turning their opponents' sure hits into double plays." Playing the roles of Tinker, Evers, and Chance in 2005 for the White Sox were Juan Uribe of the Dominican Republic, Iguchi of Japan, and Paul Konerko from the United States. The double-play trio signified that "baseball was transformed and enriched in the last century by globalization and diversity."[47]

While the White Sox were welcomed by President George W. Bush at the White House, Iguchi was celebrated back home in Japan.[48] There he was feted at Prime Minister Junichiro Koizumi's official residence, where the star infielder presented gifts of a White Sox uniform and cap and taught Koizumi proper bunting techniques.[49]

Shortly after the World Series, all eyes shifted attention to the inaugural World Baseball Classic, scheduled for March 2006. "If I have a chance, I want to take part in the tournament, because Mr. (Sadaharu) Oh will coach the national team," said Iguchi.[50]

In December Oh announced his WBC roster for Team Japan, which included several major leaguers: Akinori Otsuka (Padres), Ichiro Suzuki (Mariners), Iguchi (White Sox), and an undecided Hideki Matsui (Yankees).[51]

Shortly after Matsui declined to join the team, Iguchi announced that he too had changed his mind. "Unfortunately,

I've decided to withdraw from the squad. I informed manager Sadaharu Oh of my decision," Iguchi told reporters from his training facility in Okinawa Prefecture.[52] "This is the second year of my two-year contract with the White Sox. The team expects more from me than in the first year, so I would have to be in spring training," he explained.[53]

Iguchi reported a day early to spring training, emphasizing his commitment to the White Sox. "As far as being asked to play in the WBC, I am incredibly happy and incredibly honored," he said. "It just didn't work out this year."[54] Team Japan manager Oh invited Yakult Swallows infielder Shinya Miyamoto to fill the void left by Iguchi.[55]

In his second year with the White Sox, expectations were high for the 31-year-old, who finished fourth in the voting for AL Rookie of the Year honors. Manager Guillén praised his potential, saying, "What I see from (Iguchi) is a great RBI man. I want to get him more home runs."[56] Reflecting on his rookie US season, Iguchi expressed his goals: "I definitely want to build my batting average. I also think I can start running more this year."[57]

Iguchi improved in 2006 with a .281 average, a .352 OBP, 156 hits, 18 home runs, 97 runs, and 234 total bases. Despite these improvements, the White Sox finished third in the AL Central Division behind the Minnesota Twins, led by Justin Morneau and Johan Santana, and the Detroit Tigers, led by rookie Justin Verlander.

The first of several notable highlights from the 2006 season occurred on April 13 when the White Sox faced Verlander at Detroit's Comerica Park. Hitting in the number-two spot, Iguchi drove an 0-and-2 pitch to left-center field. The home-run blast set the stage for Verlander's removal in the third inning and his first loss of the new season. Iguchi ended the day with a 3-for-6 performance and a 13-9 White Sox victory.

On May 20, 2006, at U.S. Cellular Field, Iguchi delivered a standout performance against the Chicago Cubs. Batting third, he went 3-for-3 with 2 runs scored and 6 RBIs. He hit two home runs – a grand slam off Rich Hill in the second inning and a two-run shot in the fifth inning. His contributions were key in the White Sox' 7-0 victory over their crosstown rivals.

On September 30, the next to last game of the season, Iguchi had another notable performance in a 6-3 victory over the Minnesota Twins. He went 3-for-5 with a crucial home run in the seventh inning off Matt Guerrier, finishing the day with 3 RBIs and a stolen base.

In October the major leagues announced the roster of 27 big-league players selected to join manager Bruce Bochy in Japan for a five-game series against the top NPB players. Bochy selected Iguchi and Johjima (with the Mariners), making them the fifth and sixth Japanese players in the past 11 years to return home representing US major leaguers. Hideo Nomo was the first in 1996, followed by Kazuhiro Sasaki in 2000, Ichiro in 2002, and Kazuhisa Ishii in 2004.[58]

"Johjima and I played on the same team in Japan, so it's very exciting to be going back to Japan together," Iguchi said after a workout in Tempe, Arizona. "I don't feel as much pressure as enjoyment. I'm very proud to be selected. These are great players."[59]

Joining Iguchi and Johjima was an all-star lineup including MVP candidates Joe Mauer and Ryan Howard, Atlanta Braves outfielder Andruw Jones, and standout closers Brian Fuentes and Joe Nathan. The infield featured Howard and Lyle Overbay at first base, Iguchi and Chase Utley at second, Rafael Furcal and Jose Reyes at shortstop, and David Wright and Chone Figgins at third.[60]

Bochy, who led the major leaguers to a 5-3 series win in 2004, said he planned to rotate his infielders, giving each a start and then a day off unless needed for pinch-hitting. "There's a lot of pride involved," Bochy said. "We don't want to lose on our watch. … We'll be going all out."[61]

Bochy's team dominated the series, winning five games and tying one. The last time major leaguers went undefeated during a tour of Japan was in 1934 with Babe Ruth, Lou Gehrig, and the rest of the All-Americans going 17-0. "Japan plays with a lot of heart," Bochy said. "But we came over with a real good team and the fans got to see some of the best players in the world during this series."[62]

The games were held in various ballparks, including the Tokyo Dome, Osaka Dome, and Fukuoka Dome. Ryan Howard of the Phillies was named the series MVP. In the second game, Howard and Iguchi led the offensive attack, with Howard hitting a pair of homers and Iguchi driving in two runs with a clutch double, leading the US team to an 8-6 victory.[63]

For Iguchi, the series was his first chance to play in Tokyo since he left for the United States in 2005. Several notable NPB players from this series later joined the US major leagues, including Yu Darvish, Kei Igawa, and Nori Aoki. The 2006 series turned out to be the 10th and final tour of MLB All-Stars in Japan.[64]

In the spring of 2007, Iguchi rejoined the White Sox for spring training. Upon his return to Arizona, he faced questions about his place in the future batting order. "It does not matter where I hit," he said. "I just want to produce in the lineup. … I am just here to play."[65] With a potential lucrative free-agent contract weighing heavily on his mind, Iguchi had a rough start to the season, hitting just .221 in April and May. He improved in June, but on July 27, the White Sox traded him to the Phillies for Single-A pitcher Michael Dubee. Philadelphia was seeking a solid replacement at second base for the injured Chase Utley.[66] Iguchi fit the bill and already had good chemistry with the Phillies all-stars who toured Japan in the offseason.

Iguchi posted a slash line of .304/.361/.442 with Philadelphia, helping them finish first in the NL East. The club wanted to keep him but asked him to make a permanent move to third base. Iguchi respectfully declined, and the Phillies released him in November 2007.[67]

On December 18, 2007, Iguchi signed a one-year deal with the San Diego Padres to continue playing second base. In March 2008, he traveled with the Padres to China, where they played a two-game exhibition series against the Los Angeles Dodgers at Wukesong Baseball Stadium.[68] He hit his first home run as a Padre on April 26, a walk-off homer in the bottom of the 13th inning against the Arizona Diamondbacks at Petco Park.

Iguchi separated his right shoulder on June 5 against the Mets.[69] After eight weeks of rehab, he returned to the Padres on August 2 but struggled, with his .259 batting average dropping to .231. He was released on September 1, 2008. Four days later, he re-signed with the first-place Phillies, who were gearing up for the postseason.[70]

Iguchi's performance with the Phillies in the last month of the season was limited. In his final game, on September 28 against the Washington Nationals, he went 2-for-5 with a double, raising his season average to .232 and contributing to the Phillies' 8-3 victory. Because he was a late-season signing, he was ineligible for postseason play.[71]

The Phillies finished the season with a 92-70 record, first in the NL East. They excelled in the postseason, winning the NLDS 3-1 against the Milwaukee Brewers, the NLCS 4-1 against the Los Angeles Dodgers, and capturing the World Series title by defeating the Tampa Bay Rays in five games. This marked their first World Series championship since 1980. For his contributions to the team during the 2007 and 2008 seasons, the Phillies voted unanimously to award Iguchi a World Series ring.[72]

On November 13, 2008, Iguchi became a free agent again. In early 2009 he signed a three-year contract with the Chiba Lotte Marines worth 540 million yen (roughly $5.14 million), with an additional 20-million-yen bonus. "At the time, I had received an offer to play third base in the majors. But I was really keen to play second base, so I decided to join Lotte, where the conditions suited me," he said.[73]

In his first season with the Marines, Iguchi played 123 games, posting a .281 average with a .391 on-base percentage and a .475 slugging percentage, resulting in an OPS of .866. He hit 19 home runs, drove in 65 runs, and scored 71 runs. His 68 walks contributed to his high OBP, marking a successful return to NPB.

Iguchi's standout season came in 2010 when he played a key role in leading the Chiba Lotte Marines to a Japan Series victory. He appeared in 143 games, achieving a career-high .412 on-base percentage, hitting .294 with 17 home runs and setting a career high with 44 doubles and 103 RBIs. His OPS was .889, making 2010 one of his best seasons.

Iguchi's performance declined in later years, but he remained a consistent presence for the Marines. In 2013, at age 38, he had a strong season, hitting .297 with 23 home runs and 83 RBIs, and reaching 2,000 career hits in NPB and MLB combined. This marked the peak of his later career as he transitioned to first base and DH due to age.[74] His production dropped in 2014, and by 2015 and 2016, his role was reduced, though he still contributed as a veteran presence. In his final season, 2017, Iguchi hit his 250th career home run before announcing his retirement.

On September 24, in his retirement game against the Hokkaido Nippon Ham Fighters, Iguchi had a two-hit performance, including a two-run homer in the bottom of the ninth inning, closing out his career in style just like Red Sox great Ted Williams, who homered in the final at-bat of his career.[75] The Marines won the game with Suzuki Daichi's walk-off hit in the 12th inning.[76]

At 42 years old, his professional baseball career, which spanned 21 years and 2,408 games, had come to an end. During this time, he accumulated 2,254 hits and 295 home runs across both NPB and the US major leagues. By achieving this 2,000/200 milestone, he joined an elite group of eight players who accomplished the same feat.

Table 1. Players with 2,000+ Hits & 200+ HRs in Combined MLB & NPB Careers, by HRs (High to Low)[77]

Player	MLB Hits	NPB Hits	Total Hits	MLB HRs	NPB HRs	Total HRs
Hideki Matsui	1,253	1,390	**2,643**	175	332	**507**
Alex Ramirez	86	2,017	**2,103**	12	380	**392**
Kosuke Fukudome	498	1,952	**2,450**	42	285	**327**
Tadahito Iguchi	494	1,760	**2,254**	44	251	**295**
Ichiro Suzuki	3,089	1,278	**4,367**	117	118	**235**
Kazuo Matsui	615	2,090	**2,705**	32	201	**233**
Warren Cromartie	1,104	951	**2,055**	61	171	**232**
Willie Davis	2,561	237	**2,798**	182	43	**225**

Upon his retirement, Iguchi agreed to become the manager of the Chiba Lotte Marines. On October 14, 2017, he signed a three-year contract, becoming the first former Japanese player with US experience to manage in NPB.[78]

Iguchi had a respectable stint as manager of the Marines. Over five seasons (2018 to 2022), he managed 692 games, securing 324 wins against 338 losses (.489). His most successful season came in 2021, when the team achieved a .540 win percentage (67-57).

In 2022 Iguchi faced controversy when managing young pitching sensation Roki Sasaki. On April 10 Sasaki threw a perfect game, becoming only the 16th player in NPB to achieve this feat. A week later, Sasaki seemed on the verge of a second consecutive perfect game, but Iguchi, prioritizing the pitcher's long-term health, decided to pull him after the eighth inning despite the ongoing perfect game. This decision was based on communication between Sasaki and the coaching staff, acknowledging the young pitcher's growing fatigue and the potential risk to his arm. While some fans were disappointed, Iguchi and the team felt it was the best course of action for Sasaki's future.[79]

Iguchi's tenure as manager of the Marines ended after the 2022 season. Despite progress in building a competitive ballclub, the team finished with 69 wins and ended the season in fifth place, missing the playoffs for the first time in three years. On the morning of the final game, Chiba Lotte leadership informed Iguchi they planned to revise the assistant coaching staff for 2023. Feeling responsible for the team's performance and loyal to his staff, Iguchi decided to resign. His decision was sudden, catching many by surprise. Although Iguchi planned to lead the team until 2025, he left believing he had laid the groundwork for future success, which was later realized when Lotte finished second in the league under new manager Masato Yoshii in 2023.[80]

After stepping away from the game, Iguchi joined NHK Japan as a studio analyst. His role with NHK had him traveling between the two countries he loves. In the spring of 2024, he returned to the Cactus League in Arizona to visit his former White Sox as they battled the Dodgers and new Japanese stars Yoshinobu Yamamoto and Shohei Ohtani.[81]

In August 2024, Iguchi participated in the Suntory Dream Match (an NPB old-timer's game) at the Tokyo Dome attended by 33,079 fans. He helped the Premium Malts defeat the Dream Heroes, 4-3, and was named MVP for his outstanding performance, contributing two hits, two runs, and strong defense.[82]

In early 2024 Iguchi published his autobiography, *Iguchi Vision: The Life Philosophy of Tadahito Iguchi.* In the memoir, he revealed his desire to try coaching and eventually managing in the US major leagues.[83]

He also wants to help Japan become a leader in spreading baseball across Asia. Iguchi believes Japan, having achieved success in the WBC and the 2020 Olympics in Tokyo, is now positioned to promote and develop baseball across Asia. He aims to share Japan's baseball knowledge with emerging baseball nations like China, the Philippines, Thailand, Indonesia, India, and Pakistan, fostering a broader love for baseball and contributing to its global popularity.[84]

In his 2024 autobiography, Iguchi offered this advice for aspiring players: "[C]hallenge the dreams and goals you have set for yourself. You only have one life, and it belongs to you and no one else. … [M]ake choices that you will not regret. However, this is not a world you can take lightly. Don't forget to be prepared to accept the good and the bad, the happy and the sad, as all valuable experiences. You cannot grow as a baseball player, or even as a person, if you are afraid of failure."[85]

SOURCES

In addition to the sources cited in the Notes, the author consulted baseball-reference.com.

NOTES

1 "Yuyu Interview: Tadahito Iguchi," *San Diego Yuyu,* June 16, 2008. https://sandiegoyuyu.com/index.php/features-2/interviews-en/1801-yuyu-interviewtadahito-iguchi.

2 Iguchi joined the Philadelphia Phillies in 2007 as a replacement for the injured second baseman Chase Utley. After a short stint in San Diego, he returned to Philadelphia in late 2008 but was ineligible for the postseason roster because he was signed in September. The Phillies organization still awarded Iguchi a World Series ring after their 2008 victory over the Tampa Bay Rays, as a gesture of gratitude for his contributions to the club during the 2007 and 2008 regular seasons.

3 Pitcher Hideki Irabu received World Series rings as a member of the 1998 and 1999 New York Yankees but did not appear in a game during either Series.

4 In 2001, Tanishi merged with the neighboring Hoya municipality and is known today as Nishi-Tōkyō.

5 Tadahito Iguchi, "Iguchi Vision: Weight Training Brings Out His Striking Ability," *SportsNavi / Yahoo Sports Japan,* April 9, 2024. https://sports.yahoo.co.jp/column/detail/2024040900006-spnavi. The names of Iguchi's parents were shared via email correspondence with his agent, Toru Suzuki, courtesy of Dennis Gilbert, October 30, 2024.

6 "Yuyu Interview: Tadahito Iguchi."

7 Tadahito Iguchi, "Iguchi Vision: The impact of Hideki Matsui at Koshien," *SportsNavi / Yahoo Sports Japan,* April 16, 2024: 1. https://sports.yahoo.co.jp/column/detail/2024040900005-spnavi?p=1.

8 Tadahito Iguchi, "Iguchi Vision: The impact of Hideki Matsui at Koshien."

9 Tadahito Iguchi, "Iguchi Vision: Kokubo's Presence Embodied the Image of a Professional," *SportsNavi / Yahoo Sports Japan.* April 17, 2024 https://sports.yahoo.co.jp/column/detail/2024040900006-spnavi.

10 The Tohto University Baseball League is the intercollegiate baseball league featuring roughly 20 prominent universities in Tokyo.

11 Tony Cooke, "Japan Stymies Team USA," *Memphis Commercial Appeal,* June 23, 1995: 29. https://www.newspapers.com/article/the-commercial-appeal-team-japan-defeats/150627906/.

12 Tony Cooke, "Japan Stymies Team USA," *Memphis Commercial Appeal,* June 23, 1995: 29, 33.

13 "Team USA Baseball Tour," *Reno Gazette-Journal,* June 30, 1995: 51.

14 "Tadahito Iguchi," *namuwiki,* https://bit.ly/namuwiki-iguchi.

15 "Tenma Project: A Challenge to the Future | Pegasus in the Sky," *Challenge Plus,* November 2017. https://www.challenge-plus.jp/tenma/201711/.

16 "Hawks Take Iguchi First Overall in Draft," *Japan Times,* November 22, 1996: 23.

17 Tadahito Iguchi, "Iguchi Vision: A Consistent 'Attitude of Fighting for the Team,'" *SportsNavi / Yahoo Sports Japan,* April 22, 2024: 2. https://sports.yahoo.co.jp/column/detail/2024041000002-spnavi?p=2.

18 Kōjō Life, "Kōjō: □□ Life: A Unique Method for Building Successful Habits and Achieving Your Goals," *Medium,* April 29, 2023. https://medium.com/@kojolife/k%C5%8Dj%C5%8D-%E5%90%91%E4%B8%8A-life-a-unique-method-for-building-successful-habits-and-achieving-your-goals-3056597d482c.

19 Al Chase, "Hawaii Winter Baseball Had Record-Setting Season," *Honolulu Star-Bulletin,* December 25, 1997: 26. https://www.newspapers.com/article/honolulu-star-bulletin-west-oahu-canefir/150636092/.

20 Adam Rubin, "Iguchi Fits Mets' 2nd Options," *New York Daily News,* October 31, 2003: 91.

21 "Hawks Send Series into Game 7," *Japan Times,* October 27, 2003: 20.

22   "Hawks Blast Tigers, Wrap Up Japan Series," *Japan Times*, October 28, 2003: 22.

23   "Hawks Blast Tigers, Wrap Up Japan Series."

24   "Hawks Blast Tigers, Wrap Up Japan Series."

25   "Hawks Blast Tigers, Wrap Up Japan Series."

26   "Iguchi Eyes Majors," *Japan Times*, October 31, 2003: 22.

27   "Second Thoughts," *Japan Times*, November 1, 2003: 18.

28   "Giants Interested in Acquiring Tuffy," *Japan Times*, November 02, 2003: 18.

29   "Lions' Matsui Ready to Jump to Big Leagues," *Japan Times*, November 18, 2003: 20.

30   "Jojima Gets Huge Raise from Hawks," *Japan Times*, December 28, 2003: 20.

31   "Hawks Second Baseman Iguchi Says He's Ready to Fly the Coop," *Japan Times*, October 14, 2004: 21.

32   "Iguchi Released," *Japan Times*, November 4, 2004: 18.

33   "White Sox Keen on Iguchi," *Japan Times*, December 28, 2004: 17.

34   According to White Sox special assistant Dennis Gilbert, international scout Ray Poitevint was friendly with Iguchi's family in Japan and was instrumental in the White Sox signing the Japanese star second baseman. Phone interview with Dennis Gilbert on September 5, 2024.

35   "Tadahito Iguchi," *Chicago Tribune*, October 30, 2005: 17, 13.

36   Mark Gonzales, "Veteran Scout Retains Touch," *Chicago Tribune*, March 10, 2005: 4, 7.

37   "Batista Set for Hawks," *Japan Times*, January 7, 2005: 23. Mark Gonzales, 7.

38   "Chicago-Bound," *Japan Times*, January 27, 2005: 22.

39   "Iguchi Signs Two-Year Deal with White Sox," *Japan Times*, January 29, 2005: 20.

40   Bob MacManaman, "Spring Training," *Arizona Republic* (Phoenix), March 3, 2005: 59. https://www.newspapers.com/article/the-arizona-republic-iguchis-first-cact/154378901/.

41   "Iguchi Has Three Hits in Win over Athletics," *Japan Times*, March 30, 2005: 20.

42   "Iguchi Has Day to Remember; Goes 4-for-4 with Home Run," *Japan Times*, May 5, 2005: 22.

43   "Highest Batting Average vs. the Yankees (All-Time, Minimum 50 At Bats)," *StatMuse*. https://www.statmuse.com/mlb/ask?q=highest+batting+average+vs+the+yankees+all-time+minimum+50+at+bats.

44   "Clinch Runners," *Chicago Tribune*, September 30, 2005: 33, 13.

45   Rick Gano (Associated Press), "BoSox on Brink of Elimination," *Arizona Daily Sun* (Flagstaff), October 6, 2005: 12.

46   Gary Washburn, "White Sox Triumph Gives Mayor a Reason to Cheer," *Chicago Tribune*, October 30, 2005: 2, 2.

47   Newton M. Minow, "Big Year for Sox," *Chicago Tribune*, January 1, 2006: 2, 8.

48   "Guillen's Absence Disappoints Mayor," *Chicago Tribune*, February 10, 2006: 33, 26.

49   "Time Running Out for Matsui to Reach Deal with Yankees," *Japan Times*, November 15, 2005: 22.

50   "Iguchi Released," *Japan Times*, November 4, 2005: 11.

51   Stephen Ellsser, "Matsui Still Missing," *Japan Times*, December 10, 2005.

52   "Report: Iguchi, Buehrle to skip Baseball Classic," *ESPN.com*, January 7, 2006. https://www.espn.com/mlb/news/story?id=2283668.

53   "Report Says White Sox Infielder Iguchi to Skip World Baseball Classic," *Charlottesville* (Virginia) *Daily Progress*, January 8, 2006: 36.

54   "White Sox's Iguchi Passes on World Baseball Classic to Concentrate on His Offense," *Chicago Tribune*, January 1, 2006: 2, 8.

55   "Miyamoto Joins Squad," *Japan Times*, January 13, 2006: 14.

56   "Iguchi Willing to Do What It Takes to Make Himself Better," *Northwest Herald* (Woodstock, Illinois), February 22, 2006, 16. https://www.newspapers.com/article/northwest-herald-iguchi-i-want-to-get-h/159143046/

57   "White Sox's Iguchi Passes on World Baseball Classic to Concentrate on His Offense."

58   Joseph A. Reaves, "Pros Going to Japan." *Arizona Republic*, October 30, 2006: 14.

59   Reaves.

60   Reaves.

61   Reaves.

62   "MLB All-Stars Perfect in Japan," *Kenosha* (Wisconsin) *News,* November 9, 2006: 20.

63   "Howard, Iguchi Lead MLB Stars over Japan," *Passaic* (New Jersey) *Herald-News*, November 5, 2006: D2.

64   "Howard, Iguchi Lead MLB stars over Japan."

65   John Moredich, "Iguchi's Spot in Batting Order Still Not Decided," *Tucson Citizen*, February 23, 2007: 36.

66   Michael Radano, "Phils Acquire Iguchi from the White Sox," *Camden* (New Jersey) *Courier-Post*, July 28, 2007: 47.

67   Todd Zolecki, "Phillies Eye Iguchi Despite Rule Problem," *Philadelphia Inquirer*, December 5, 2007: C09.

68   Dylan Hernandez, "After Hectic 72 Hours, Dodgers Return Home," *Los Angeles Times*, March 17, 2008: D10.

69   "Padres' 2B Iguchi Sidelined," *Springfield* (Ohio) *News-Sun*, June 7, 2008: 19.

70   Scott Lauber, "Iguchi Is Back," *Wilmington* (Delaware) *News Journal*, September 6, 2008: 23.

71   Lauber.

72   Tadahito Iguchi, "Iguchi Vision: New Friends and Inspiration Gained Through Trading." *SportsNavi / Yahoo Sports Japan*, April 23, 2024: 2. https://sports.yahoo.co.jp/column/detail/2024040900008-spnavi?p=2.

73   "Tenma Project: A Challenge to the Future | Pegasus in the Sky," *Challenge Plus*, November 2017. https://www.challenge-plus.jp/tenma/201711/.

74   Tadahito Iguchi, "Iguchi Vision: A Consistent 'Attitude of Fighting for the Team,'" *SportsNavi / Yahoo Sports Japan*, April 22, 2024: 2. https://sports.yahoo.co.jp/column/detail/2024041000002-spnavi?p=2.

75   Ted Williams hit his last home run on September 28, 1960, in his final major-league at-bat. The game was held at Fenway Park, where Williams was playing for the Boston Red Sox against the Baltimore Orioles. In the eighth inning, he hit a solo home run off Orioles pitcher Jack Fisher. This was Williams' 521st career home run, and the iconic moment is celebrated as one of the most memorable in baseball history.

76   Kaz Nagatsuka, "Iguchi Hits Final Home Run to End Career in Style," *Japan Times*, September 25, 2017. https://www.japantimes.co.jp/sports/2017/09/24/baseball/japanese-baseball/iguchi-hits-final-home-run-end-career-style/.

77   As of the end of the 2024 season, Shohei Ohtani is not a member of the 2,000/200 club. He has 273 career home runs (48 NPB + 225 MLB), but with 1,174 career hits (296 NPB + 878 MLB), he's 826 hits short of the 2,000-career-hit milestone. Based on current trends (150 hits per season), he's estimated reach the 2,000-career-hit mark in the 2029 or 2030 season.

78   Jim Allen, "Baseball: Iguchi Looking to Lay Solid Foundation in Chiba." *Kyodo News*, March 3, 2019. https://english.kyodonews.net/news/2019/03/b82e5488d55d-baseball-iguchi-looking-to-lay-solid-foundation-in-chiba.html.

79   Tadahito Iguchi, "Iguchi Vision: Roki Sasaki's Legendary Two Consecutive Perfect Games," *SportsNavi / Yahoo Sports Japan,* April 28, 2024. https://sports.yahoo.co.jp/column/detail/2024041000009-spnavi.

80   "Iguchi Vision: Roki Sasaki's legendary two consecutive perfect games."

81   Scott Merkin, "Brebbia Ditches Walking Boot Ahead of Side Session: Right-Hander Has Been Sidelined by Calf Strain; Iguchi in White Sox Camp to See Yamamoto," MLB.com, March 6, 2024. https://www.mlb.com/news/john-brebbia-to-throw-a-side-session-for-white-sox.

82   "Tadahito Iguchi Named MVP as Premium Malts Win 10th Consecutive Championship," *Sports Hochi,* August 6, 2024. https://hochi.news/articles/20240806-OHT1T51010.html?page=1.

83   Tadahito Iguchi, "Iguchi Vision: I Want to Train as a Coach in America," *SportsNavi / Yahoo Sports Japan*, April 11, 2024: 2. https://sports.yahoo.co.jp/column/detail/2024041100003-spnavi?p=2.

84   Tadahito Iguchi, "Iguchi Vision: The Role That Japan, Now the World Champion, Should Play in Asia," *SportsNavi / Yahoo Sports Japan*, April 11, 2024: 2. https://sports.yahoo.co.jp/column/detail/2024041100002-spnavi?p=2.

85   Tadahito Iguchi, "Iguchi Vision: Advice for Juniors Aiming for the Majors," *SportsNavi / Yahoo Sports Japan*, April 11, 2024: 1. https://sports.yahoo.co.jp/column/detail/2024041100002-spnavi?p=1.

BOBBY JENKS

By Ben Blotner

Over a seven-year big league career, 6-foot-4, 275-pound right-handed reliever Bobby Jenks compiled a 16-20 record with a 3.53 ERA and 173 saves. All of these saves were for the White Sox, putting Jenks second on the team's all-time saves list. He pitched for the White Sox from 2005 to 2010, then spent 2011 with the Boston Red Sox before his career was brought to a premature end by injuries. Jenks was a two-time All-Star and a 2005 World Series champion, and he once tied a major-league record with 41 consecutive batters retired. He overcame significant off-field adversity at both the beginning and end of his unique career, staying in baseball and ultimately moving into his position in 2024 as manager of the Frontier League's Windy City ThunderBolts.

Robert Scott Jenks was born on March 14, 1981, in Mission Hills, California, a Los Angeles neighborhood located in the San Fernando Valley. His family later moved to Idaho, where he attended Lakeland High School. His father, also named Robert, worked in the roofing business while his mother, Carla, worked as a checkout clerk at a store. They lived in a cabin in the woods and often struggled to make ends meet. Jenks played one year of baseball at Lakeland, dominating both on the mound and at the plate during the 1998 season. However, the teenage Jenks had a difficult time academically.

"We knew he struggled in the classroom, and I think he has some learning difficulties and I think he got frustrated," said Ken Busch, his former high-school coach. "As we went through practices, we saw that he could play."[1] Lakeland was eventually split into separate schools, and Jenks was not eligible to play at his new school, Timberlake, due to poor grades. Still, he was able to make a name for himself playing American Legion summer ball, where scouts noticed his electric fastball. Along with this heat came a reputation for wildness, with one account claiming that Jenks' first fastball at a showcase sailed six feet over the catcher's head and nearly struck a scout. After dropping out of Timberlake and transferring to Inglemoor High School in Kenmore, Washington, and graduating, Jenks was selected by the Anaheim Angels in the fifth round of the 2000 free-agent draft.

Jenks began his minor-league career as a starting pitcher. Despite struggling in 2000 with the rookie-league Butte Copper Kings and in 2001 with the Class-A Cedar Rapids Kernels, Jenks was promoted to the Double-A Arkansas

Travelers, where he pitched to a 3.60 ERA over two starts. In 2002 he scuffled again, posting a 4.74 ERA while splitting time between the Travelers and the High-A Rancho Cucamonga Quakes. During this season, he unfortunately gained a reputation as an immature, troubled young man who was squandering his talent, often drinking heavily and getting into trouble. A 2003 *ESPN The Magazine* article took aim at Jenks, calling him "a boy who can throw heat ass and do little else" and "a boy who won't stop drinking, won't stop cussing and won't pay his own bills."[2] Jenks was alleged to have started numerous drunken conflicts with teammates and coaches, referred to his agent using an ethnic slur, and burned his pitching hand with a lighter. In his 2009 memoir *Odd Man Out: A Year on the Mound with a Minor League Misfit,* former Angels minor leaguer Matt McCarthy claimed that Jenks faked an injury and threatened to kill his manager.[3] The credibility of McCarthy's book has been widely challenged, with a *New York Times* article claiming many of its statements to be false.[4] McCarthy spent 2002 with the rookie-league Provo Angels and was

Bobby Jenks   2005

never actually teammates with Jenks, who has vehemently denied the accusations.

"You know what? My friends and family that know me, they know the truth," Jenks told reporters after McCarthy's book was released. "They know none of it is true."[5]

Jenks made up for any off-field distractions during the 2003 minor-league season as a starting pitcher, working to a 7-2 record and a 2.38 ERA as he spent most of the year with the Double-A Arkansas Travelers. However, because of elbow injuries, Jenks pitched in only 17 games. His fortunes worsened in 2004, as he started only five games at three different levels and struggled to a 10.24 ERA before suffering another injury. Jenks underwent season-ending elbow surgery, and the Angels placed him on waivers at the end of the year.

It was the White Sox who decided to give the troubled young pitcher a second chance, claiming Jenks on waivers and putting him in the Double-A Birmingham Barons' bullpen to start 2005. He pitched to a 2.85 ERA and saved 19 games in 21 opportunities with Birmingham. The White Sox called him up on July 5, as Jenks skipped the Triple-A level and finally made his big-league debut. Against the Tampa Bay Devil Rays on July 6, 2005, he pitched a scoreless, hitless ninth inning with two strikeouts to close out a 7-2 Chicago win.

With the White Sox leading the American League Central Division and incumbent closer Dustin Hermanson battling injuries, Jenks began to assume a larger role in the bullpen as his team pushed for the playoffs. He earned his first major-league save on August 25 against the Minnesota Twins and settled into the closer's job, finishing the year with a 1-1 record, 6 saves, and a 2.75 ERA in the majors. After cruising for most of the season but running into a September swoon, the White Sox finished strong and won the AL Central Division comfortably with a 99-63 record, six games ahead of the second-place Cleveland Indians. On to the playoffs they went, facing the defending champion Boston Red Sox in the Division Series.

Jenks saw his first playoff action in Game Two against Boston, throwing two scoreless innings to lock down the save in a 5-4 win. The White Sox went to Boston leading the series two games to none, and with a 5-3 lead in Game Three at Fenway Park, Jenks pitched a scoreless ninth inning for another save. The rookie whose career had been in jeopardy a year before had closed out the defending champs on their home turf, and the White Sox were going to the AL Championship Series.

Surprisingly, Jenks was not needed in the ALCS against his former organization, now called the Los Angeles Angels of Anaheim. For that matter, neither was the majority of the White Sox bullpen. Chicago starters worked all but two-thirds of an inning in the series, as Mark Buehrle, Jon Garland, Freddy Garcia, and José Contreras threw four consecutive complete-game victories in Games Two through Five to win the pennant. As of 2024, they were the only starting staff to accomplish this feat in the postseason since the 1928 New York Yankees.[6] For the first time since 1959, the White Sox went to the World Series, and they faced the National League champion Houston Astros, who were making their first Series appearance in franchise history.

The World Series was Jenks' time to shine. In Game One, at US Cellular Field in Chicago, the White Sox led the Astros 4-3 in the eighth inning, but Houston threatened by putting runners at first and third with no outs. After reliever Neal Cotts struck out Morgan Ensberg and Mike Lamb, Chicago manager Ozzie Guillén went back to his bullpen. As Guillén walked to the mound, he did not make the traditional signal with his right arm to call for Jenks. Instead, he held out his arms high and wide to signal for, as Fox announcer Joe Buck put it, "the wide, tall guy," providing a memorable moment of comic relief.[7] Less than a year after the Angels had unceremoniously released him, Jenks was pitching in a crucial spot in the World Series, facing veteran slugger and future Hall of Famer Jeff Bagwell with the game on the line.

In a six-pitch battle, throwing nothing but fastballs, the rookie blew away the veteran for a huge strikeout, finishing him off with a 99-mph fastball that had wicked lateral movement. The wide, tall guy pumped his arms in celebration as he walked off the mound. After Chicago added a run in the bottom of the eighth to make it 5-3, Jenks returned to the mound for the ninth and set down the Astros in order with two more strikeouts. In the biggest game of his life, Jenks had mowed through four straight batters for a well-deserved save, putting Chicago up 1-0 in the series.

Game Two, however, did not go as smoothly for the big right-hander. Given a clean slate this time with a 6-4 lead to start the ninth inning, Jenks allowed a two-out, two-run single to pinch-hitter José Vizcaino that tied the game, 6-6. Jenks' blown save proved to be inconsequential, however, as it only set his team up for a more dramatic win. In the bottom of the ninth, White Sox outfielder Scott Podsednik – who had not homered for the entire regular season – drilled a fastball from Houston closer Brad Lidge to right-center field for a walk-off blast. It was Podsednik's second homer of the postseason, giving Chicago a 7-6 victory and a 2-0 Series lead.

As the series shifted to Houston, another tight battle followed in Game Three, this time going to extra innings with the score tied, 5-5. Jenks did not pitch until the bottom of the 11th inning, but when he did, he made it count. He bounced back from his Game Two hiccup with two scoreless and hitless innings, walking one, hitting one batter, and striking out three. In the 14th inning, former Astro Geoff Blum, who had entered the game for Jenks as part of a double switch in the prior frame, drilled a two-out, go-ahead home run off Ezequiel Astacio to put his old team in a hole. The White Sox added another run in the inning and won 7-5, taking a 3 games to none stranglehold in the Series.

Game Four was the potential clincher, with 88 years of history on the line for the White Sox, who hadn't won it all since 1917. Starting pitchers Garcia of the White Sox and Brandon Backe of the Astros dueled for seven straight scoreless innings, then a Jermaine Dye RBI single off Lidge gave Chicago a 1-0 lead in the eighth. With the slimmest possible margin, Jenks came out of the bullpen for the bottom of the ninth, looking to nail down the final three outs.

Leading off the inning, Jason Lane blooped a single into center field to put the tying run on base. A sacrifice by Brad Ausmus moved Lane to second, then Chris Burke popped up into foul territory, close to the stands. There didn't seem to be any chance for a White Sox defender to make the play, but shortstop Juan Uribe reached into the crowd and tumbled into the stands, making a spectacular catch for the second out. Up to the plate came pinch-hitter Orlando Palmeiro, Houston's final hope.

Palmeiro hit a high chopper toward the middle of the infield on a 1-and-2 count. Uribe charged in and scooped the ball up, needing to make another fantastic play. His throw nailed Palmeiro at first by an eyelash. For the first time since 1917, the White Sox were World Series champions, and the man being mobbed in the middle of the diamond was 24-year-old Bobby Jenks. While the road he had taken there was already paved with challenges, what he went on to experience after this high would be perhaps the most difficult journey of any of the 2005 White Sox.

In 2006 Jenks continued his success. He was named an AL All-Star in his first full big-league season, finishing 3-4 with a 4.00 ERA and a career-high 41 saves. The White Sox finished with a 90-72 record, but their title defense fell short as they missed the playoffs. Jenks continued to make a name for himself in 2007, saving 40 more games and lowering his ERA to 2.77 as he was again named an All-Star. One historic accomplishment during Jenks' 2007 season particularly stood out. Over a span of 15 appearances from July 17 to August 12, Jenks retired 41 consecutive hitters. When he entered for the ninth inning against the Seattle Mariners on August 12 and retired the side in order to reach 41, he tied Jim Barr of the 1972 San Francisco Giants for the major-league record. In Jenks' next appearance, Joey Gathright of the Kansas City Royals singled to end the streak, denying Jenks a chance to stand alone with the major-league record.[8] However, he still held the AL mark and shared the major-league record until his teammate Buehrle broke both in 2009 with 45 consecutive batters retired.[9]

The 2008 season saw Jenks battle the injury bug for the first time since his minor-league days, being placed on the disabled list in July with left scapula bursitis. Despite this interruption to his season, Jenks put up fine numbers yet again with 30 saves and a career-best 2.63 ERA. After consecutive years of missing the postseason, the White Sox finished 2008 tied with the Minnesota Twins atop the AL Central Division. In the tiebreaker game at US Cellular Field, Chicago held a 1-0 lead entering the ninth inning

and Jenks entered to close it out. After recording the first two outs, he allowed a fly ball to shallow center field off the bat of Alexi Casilla. Chicago's Brian Anderson laid out for a spectacular diving catch to give the White Sox the division title and Jenks the save. Chicago's first playoff appearance since 2005 didn't go as planned, as the ALDS saw them eliminated in four games by the upstart Tampa Bay Rays. Jenks did his part, however, nailing down the save in Chicago's 5-3 Game Three victory, the team's only win of the Series.

Despite a less dominant season in 2009, Jenks continued to hold down Chicago's closer position, finishing with 29 saves and a 3.71 ERA on a sub-.500 team. In 2010 the going became tougher for Jenks. Guillén removed him from the closer role for a time after a number of difficult outings. He was ultimately reinstated, finishing the year with 27 saves and a 4.44 ERA. The White Sox finished with a winning record, but ultimately missed the postseason.

The 2010 season turned out to be Jenks' final year on the South Side of Chicago, as the White Sox did not tender him a contract after the season. On December 21, 2010, Jenks signed a two-year, $12 million contract with the Boston Red Sox, and he exchanged some parting shots with his former manager Guillén on the way out the door. Jenks said he was "looking forward to playing for a manager who knows how to run a bullpen."[10] This led Guillén's son Oney to bash Jenks in a series of social media posts, calling him "ungrateful" and a "punk."[11] Ozzie Guillén himself then spoke out, claiming that Jenks "did a lot of bad things last year" and that the White Sox had "lied for him."[12] Despite his longtime success in Chicago, it appeared a change of scenery would be beneficial for the reliever.

Pitching in a set-up role instead of the closer's spot, Jenks got off to a strong start in Boston with four scoreless appearances, then began to struggle as some shaky outings drove up his ERA. He spent time on the disabled list with a biceps strain, then soon after his return, he suffered a back injury while pitching against the New York Yankees. Jenks later wrote in an article for *The Players' Tribune*, "It's almost like a spoon had been shoved into my back – like someone is trying to dig a hole in me, not with a knife, but with a spoon."[13] He went back on the shelf before returning to make four more appearances, which turned out to be his last games in the major leagues. His final major-league game was on July 7, 2011, when he fittingly pitched a scoreless ninth inning to close out a 10-4 win over the Baltimore Orioles. For the 2011 season, Jenks finished with a 2-2 record, a 6.32 ERA, and no saves in 19 appearances.

While his big-league career may have been over – unbeknownst to him – Jenks' health struggles were just beginning. His back pain was caused by spurs in his spine that had to be removed via surgery. Prior to the operation, Jenks also suffered a pulmonary embolism and colitis, forcing it to be pushed back to December. Upon waking from the surgery, Jenks was told that everything had gone well. A few days later, however, he noticed that there was much more bandaging on his back than he had expected, and he had a much larger scar. Soon after this, his back began leaking large amounts of spinal fluid. After being taken to a hospital and getting emergency surgery, the 30-year-old Jenks was told by a doctor that he was lucky to be alive.

Jenks' original back surgery, performed by Dr. Kirkham Wood at Massachusetts General Hospital in Boston, had been a concurrent surgery with the doctor operating on another patient at the same time as Jenks.[14] During the procedure, Wood decompressed only one of the two levels of Jenks' spine that he was supposed to decompress. In addition, he left a jagged spike in Jenks' back that punctured the membrane around his spinal cord. This caused Jenks to develop an infection that traveled up through his body and nearly reached his brain before the emergency operation saved his life. He reported to 2012 Red Sox spring training in an effort to rehab his back, but at this point his pitching future was very uncertain.

Jenks' problems did not end there. He had become addicted to painkillers, a problem that had initially surfaced before the surgery but was now worse, to the point where he was taking 50 to 60 pills a day. This caused his behavior to become erratic, often without his being aware of it. One day in spring training, an intoxicated Jenks removed all the food from his refrigerator, stabbed his television with a knife, and broke into a stranger's car. He awoke the next day with no recollection of what had happened. On another occasion, he was charged with a DUI after driving recklessly while intoxicated. Jenks was severely depressed, and he fell into a downward spiral so pronounced that his family and counselors had to stage an intervention. Adding insult to injury, his first wife, Adele, filed for divorce. "2012, man ... rough year," Jenks wrote.[15]

Going through intense rehabilitation for both his painkiller problem and his back, Jenks was able to shake the addiction but not the injuries. His spine continued to weaken to the point where he was given two choices: He could continue to go through extremely painful rehab to someday pitch again, or he could have plates and screws added to his spine that would force him into retirement. Having been sober for 11 months and not wanting to relapse on painkillers, Jenks decided to get the operation that would end his playing days.

"I had the game taken away from me because of a botched back surgery in Boston that was supposed to be no big deal – because a level of care and professional expertise that I trusted to be present ... was not there," Jenks wrote.[16]

In his first years of retirement, Jenks spent time with his attorneys researching what had happened with his spine, eventually filing a malpractice lawsuit against the hospital and Dr. Wood. Upon gaining access to hospital records, Jenks discovered that the concurrent surgeries had likely caused the operation to be botched. In 2019 he was awarded a $5.1 million out-of-court settlement in the case. Jenks became an outspoken advocate against concurrent surgeries, looking to raise as much awareness as possible about the unethical practice.

"There are currently efforts in Massachusetts to sign a bill into law prohibiting concurrent surgeries," Jenks wrote. "While these efforts are still in the early stages, it's a start. And ideally Massachusetts can provide an example for those in other states to follow. Maybe you [the reader] can help lead that charge."[17]

After the conclusion of the lawsuit, Jenks was able to find his way back into baseball. He worked as pitching coach of the independent Pioneer League's Grand Junction Rockies in 2021, then was named the team's manager for the 2022 season.[18] Under Jenks, the Rockies rolled to a 62-33 record and took home the league championship. Prior to the 2024 season, Jenks was hired as manager of the Frontier League's Windy City Thunderbolts. He is married to his second wife, Eleni Tzitzivacos, and has five children.

SOURCES

In addition to the sources cited in the Notes, the author consulted Baseball-Reference.com for pertinent game information including box scores and play-by-plays. He also reviewed play-by-play information on ESPN.com.

NOTES

1   J.D. Larson, "Jenks Comes Out Ahead at Last," *Spokane* (Washington) *Spokesman-Review*, October 22, 2005, www.spokesman.com/stories/2005/oct/22/jenks-comes-out-ahead-at-last/.

2   Tom Friend, "Loaded Gun: Great Arm, but Jenks No Angel," *ESPN The Magazine*, June 9, 2003.

3   Matt McCarthy, *Odd Man Out: A Year on the Mound with a Minor League Misfit* (New York: Penguin Group USA, 2010).

4   Benjamin Hill and Alan Schwarz, "Errors Cast Doubt on Matt McCarthy's Baseball Memoir," *New York Times*, March 2, 2009.

5   "Bobby Jenks Overcomes Early Adversity after Attitude, Drinking Problems Surface in 2003 ESPN the Magazine Feature," NESN.Com, New England Sports Network, January 4, 2011, https://nesn.com/2011/01/bobby-jenks-overcomes-early-adversity-after-attitude-drinking-problems-surface-in-2003-espn-the-maga/.

6   Sox on 35th Contributors, "The 2005 White Sox Complete-Game Record Will Be Untouchable for Years," *Sox On 35th*, October 17, 2018, www.soxon35th.com/the-2005-white-sox-complete-game-record-will-be-untouchable-for-years/#google_vignette.

7   "2005 World Series Game 1 Astros @ White Sox," Edited by John Quinn, YouTube.com, May 16, 2020, www.youtube.com/watch?v=ArewsuEIzDk&t=9343s.

8   "Jenks Denied New Record for Retiring Batters," Reuters, August 21, 2007, www.reuters.com/article/idUSB234931/.

9   Associated Press, "Buehrle Sets MLB Mark," ESPN Internet Ventures, July 28, 2009, www.espn.com/mlb/news/story?id=4362558.

10   Aaron Gleeman, "Ozzie Guillen Fires Back at Bobby Jenks: 'He Did a Lot of Bad Things ... We Lied for Him, We Protected Him,'" NBC Sports, February 28, 2011, www.nbcsports.com/mlb/news/ozzie-guillen-fires-back-at-bobby-jenks-he-did-a-lot-of-bad-things-we-lied-for-him-we-protected-him.

11   Jon Bois, "Oney Guillen Flings 400 Words of Twitter Rage at Bobby Jenks," SBNation.com, December 29, 2010, www.sbnation.com/ mlb/2010/12/29/1902175/oney-guillen-twitter-bobby-jenks-rant-ozzie-white-sox.

12   Jon Bois.

13   Bobby Jenks. "Scar Tissue," The Players' Tribune, December 5, 2019, www. theplayerstribune.com/articles/bobby-jenks-baseball-scar-tissue.

14   Craig Calcaterra, "Former Closer Bobby Jenks Wins $5.1 Million Settlement over Botched Back Surgery," NBC Sports, May 9, 2019, www.nbcsports. com/mlb/news/former-closer-bobby-jenks-wins-5-1-million-settlement-over-botched-back-surgery.

15   Bobby Jenks. "Scar Tissue."

16   Bobby Jenks. "Scar Tissue."

17   Bobby Jenks. "Scar Tissue."

18   "Grand Junction Rockies Name Bobby Jenks Manager." MiLB.Com, March 17, 2022, www.milb.com/news/aguilera-makes-history-as-northern-colorado-hailstorm-fc-and-owlz-team-president.

PAUL KONERKO

By Ryan Van Der Karr

Paul Henry Konerko was born on March 5, 1976, in Providence, Rhode Island, to Henry "Hank" and Elena Konerko. Elena, who worked in the medical field, was the first nursing director for Mission of Mercy (MOM), a 501(c)3 nonprofit organization "dedicated to bring healing and wholeness to individuals in need through the practice of medicine."[1] Hank, who served as Paul's agent when he signed his first professional baseball contract, was a business executive who served as CEO of MOM after previously working in the mining industry.[2]

Paul grew up in Connecticut in a hockey household. His father played hockey in high school and a little bit in college. Paul said, "When I moved to Arizona when I was 11, I was a far better hockey player than a baseball player. Out there [Connecticut] you're playing hockey all year and you only get like three months for baseball and half of those games get rained out. When I got out here to Arizona it started to change because you play so much more out here."[3]

"I got to go to spring training things. I didn't have a favorite team, but I could go and my dad would take me.

Paul Konerko   2005

My brother played at a junior college in Arizona where the A's were on the back field, and you could get right up close and see guys."[4]

As a catcher for Chaparral High School in Scottsdale, Konerko hit .556 with 18 doubles, 4 triples, 12 home runs, and 51 RBIs in just 94 at-bats while leading his team to the state championship.[5] He was the 1994 Arizona High School Player of the Year and ranked the number-two high-school player by *Baseball America*.[6] Konerko signed a letter of intent with Arizona State University, but when he was drafted in the first round of the 1994 amateur draft by the Los Angeles Dodgers, he opted to forgo college and turn pro. He signed for $900,000[7] and was assigned to the Class-A short-season Yakima (Washington) Bears. In 67 games with the Bears, he hit .288 with six home runs to lead the team and he had 58 RBIs, which led the Northwest League.[8]

Konerko played for the San Bernardino (California) Spirit in 1995, helping them to their first playoff berth since their inaugural season in 1987.[9] He hit four home runs in nine at-bats during the championship series and led the Spirit to the first-ever California League championship when they swept the San Jose Giants in three games.[10] For the season, he hit .277 with 19 home runs and 77 RBIs. "I think I could have done a lot better," Konerko said. "I didn't really swing the bat that well overall."[11]

The Dodgers moved Konerko to first base at the start of spring training in 1996. "The switch was purely for a medical reason," catching coach Mike Scioscia said. "He showed a lot of problems with his hip flexibility, and we thought that long-range, it might be beneficial to move him to first."[12]

"At first it was kind of a shock," Konerko said. "You put so much time and effort into catching, and you think it's all been wasted. I always loved catching. But if they say it's my best chance of making it, that's what I'll do. They've been around a long time and know more about it than me."[13]

Konerko started the 1996 season at Double-A San Antonio as the youngest player on the team. He got off to a strong start. By the middle of May he had eight home runs while the rest of the team combined for 14.[14] As a result, he was named a starter in the Texas League All-Star game.[15] He was reportedly "considered the best power-hitting prospect in the organization" and "putting on a show that scouts say defies belief."[16] For the season he hit 30 home runs.

Promoted to Triple-A Albuquerque for the 1997 season, Konerko spent time at third base and first base. He had a good first half and was named as a starter at third base for the Triple-A All-Star Game held in Des Moines, Iowa[17] and a participant in the home run derby.[18] In his 130 games at Albuquerque, Konerko hit .323 with 31 doubles, 97 runs, 37 home runs, and 127 RBIs. He was called up to the majors when rosters expanded on September 1. He was sent to the on-deck circle twice and called back twice before he finally pinch-hit in the eighth inning on September 8. He lined an opposite-field single off Dennis Cook of the Florida Marlins for his first hit and was happy that his mother was there to see it.[19]

Konerko was named the Pacific Coast League MVP[20] and the 1997 Minor League Player of the Year by both *Baseball America* and *Baseball Weekly*.[21] He was also named the Dodgers' Minor League Player of the Year for the second consecutive year.[22]

Going into spring training in 1998, Konerko was 21 years old and considered the best hitting prospect in the organization, but he was a man without a position. The Dodgers had played him at first and third base while trying to keep his bat in the lineup, and during spring training they started to play him in the outfield. That spring he was named the number-2 overall prospect by *Baseball America*[23] and the Dodgers decided he would start in the big leagues to bolster the bench that was miserable the previous season.

"Let's face it, he can hit," Dodgers manager Bill Russell said. "We'll try to use him a lot as a pinch-hitter, get him some spot starts and use him as much as we can. If he's just going to sit the bench then he would probably be better off going back down."[24] Konerko was 2-for-4 on Opening Day, but struggled and after 40 games was batting just .198 with three homers as late as June 23.

On July 4 Konerko was traded with Dennys Reyes to the Cincinnati Reds for reliever Jeff Shaw. Interim general manager Tommy Lasorda said the Dodgers had lost too many games because they did not have a quality closer. He said it was tough to trade Konerko, but the Reds insisted that they would not make the trade unless they received the rookie infielder. "I turned down seven teams asking for Konerko," Lasorda said. "The one guy I wanted, I had to give up Konerko to get him."[25]

Konerko had a slow start in Cincinnati and was sent down to Triple-A Indianapolis on July 29. Called back up in September, in 26 games for the Reds, he hit .219. On November 11, he was traded to the White Sox for Mike Cameron.[26]

In 1999 Konerko was the Opening Day designated hitter for the White Sox. He hit a two-run home run in the White Sox win. Konerko recalled that he was very tightly wound up all the time. He had a coach, Joe Nossek, who called him "Slash." He asked, "Coach, why do you call me slash?' Joe said, 'Because you're going to slash your wrists!' He said, 'Listen, I'm going to give you some advice,' and this is probably the best advice with the game of baseball that I ever got, and he said, 'This is a game you cannot play

frustrated, but you can play it angry.' From that point forward I found a reason to be angry every night."[27] One day manager Jerry Manuel came to him and asked him how he was doing. He said he was fine, and Manuel told him to 'relax, you're going to be here all year.' Konerko said, "I was like OK it's not going to be the end of the world if I go 0-for-4 and I started to relax."

That season, Konerko hit his first career grand slam, on June 17 off reliever Jesse Orosco of the Baltimore Orioles, and had his first multi-homer game, against the New York Yankees.[28] He finished the season hitting .294 with 24 home runs (second on the team) and 81 RBIs (third on the team).

In spring training 2000, Konerko was the starting first baseman but spent most of his time at third so they wouldn't lose his bat during interleague games. One of his most memorable moments occurred on April 11 when he hit an inside-the-park home run in Tampa Bay. Upon sliding across home plate he dramatically smacked the plate while lying on the ground.[29] The White Sox upset the Indians that season to win the division and stop Cleveland's streak of five consecutive division titles. Konerko said, "The game is played on the field and not on paper. You can't measure some things. You can't measure how guys will gel or how they will pull for one another. Some things you can't scout, and money has nothing to do with all that."[30] The White Sox were swept by Seattle in the Division Series with Konerko going hitless in all three games.

In 2001 Konerko had a strong season, leading the White Sox in home runs with 32 and finishing second in RBIs with 99. However, with several injuries, including losing Frank Thomas for almost the entire season, the White Sox struggled and ended up in third place.

The next season Konerko had a very good year and made his first All-Star team. He competed in the Home Run Derby, where he fell 7-6 in the semifinals to Jason Giambi. He went 2-for-2 in the game, tying an All-Star Game record with two doubles.[31]

The White Sox finished .500, good enough for second place in the division, but they missed the playoffs again. Konerko again finished the season second on the team (to Magglio Ordóñez) in home runs (27) and RBIs (104, the first of six seasons he drove in 100 or more runs). During the offseason, the White Sox and Konerko agreed to a three-year, $23 million contract extension.

In 2003 spring training began with questions about Konerko's earlier criticism of Frank Thomas and team chemistry. In July 2002, when Thomas was benched because he wasn't supporting his teammates, Konerko said, "It's all about showing up for your teammates, being there whether you're playing or you're not playing, if you're doing good or not doing good. That's the one constant that has to be there every day." He followed up by saying, "He's probably mad at me. But it's no big deal. We'll be fine on Thursday."[32] Konerko was surprised that it was still being discussed. After Thomas sat down for a lengthy meeting with manager Jerry Manuel, it was reported that all of the issues were addressed.[33]

Konerko said that when it came to his career, it really comprised two halves, pre-May 2003 and after. He said he was hitting so poorly to start 2003 that he unfortunately got hitting coach Gary Ward fired. The White Sox then hired Greg Walker. Konerko said Walker looked at him hitting and told him, "I know what you got going on and I can fix it, but you have to 100 percent buy in and it may get worse before it gets better."

Konerko responded, "Let's do it, what do I have to lose?"[34] He ended up batting .234, his worst batting average until his final season with the White Sox, and the team struggled into another second-place finish.

Konerko's hitting improved in 2004. His batting average went up over 40 points to .277 and he finished tied for second in the league in home runs (41) and sixth in RBIs (a team-leading 117). He won *The Sporting News*' Comeback Player of the Year, and received MVP votes for the first time in his career. The White Sox ended the season four games over .500, finished in second place, and missed the playoffs again.

The 2005 season started out strong with timely hitting and good pitching, leading the team to its best start since the 1959 "Go-Go" White Sox. The strong start was fueled by the other pieces of the team as both Konerko and Jermaine Dye were hitting under .200 and Frank Thomas missed the start of the season with an ankle injury. By mid-May, Dye and Konerko were hitting well and Thomas returned to the lineup. Konerko told reporters he liked hitting behind Thomas in the lineup – "no matter how he's going – good or bad – the other team focuses on him a lot. Sometimes I get a good pitch to hit because it seems so much energy is (devoted) to him."[35] He was named a reserve to the All-Star team and with teammate Scott Podsednik winning the extra-man vote and pitchers Mark Buehrle and Jon Garland selected, the White Sox sent four to the All-Star Game for the first time since 1975.

In mid-August, Konerko had to sit out with a strained lower back. His first game back, he hit a home run off Randy Johnson. On September 24 the Cleveland Indians closed within 1½ games of the White Sox, who had led the division all season but had struggled lately. During the next day's game, the crowd at US Cellular Field roared when the scoreboard posted that the Indians had lost their game. The White Sox responded by winning and clinched the division title four days later. The team finished the regular season with a 35-19 record in one-run games. Konerko hit 40 homers and drove in 100 runs, leading the White Sox with 13 more RBIs than the second-best Carl Everett.

In an interview in 2022, Konerko reflected on that year: "The team really came together as an eclectic group of characters. I just love that team from the standpoint of I was a power hitter but my mind is that of small ball really the historic, classic way to play the game. Moving guys over, hit-and-runs, bunts, I really dig that stuff, and that team was really good defensively and it always felt like any game [that was close] we felt like we were going to win that game."[36]

The White Sox swept the defending champion Red Sox in the Division Series. They lost the first game of the Championship Series, 3-2, but bounced back to win the series four games to one over the Angels. Konerko hit two home runs, had seven RBIs, and was named the ALCS MVP. He said that with the great pitching they'd had, "really you can split that thing five ways. Those guys were unbelievable."[37]

In Game Two of the World Series, Konerko had his signature moment as a player. With the White Sox trailing the Astros, 4-2, in the bottom of the seventh inning, he came to the plate with the bases loaded and two outs. He hit the first pitch from Chad Qualls over the left-field fence for a grand slam. "It's the second-best feeling I had all week. I had a baby born Tuesday night. That's first for the week," Konerko said. "[The grand slam] is second. I wasn't thinking home run. I was thinking base hit to drive in two runs. [Qualls is] nasty. I hadn't taken a swing all night. I took one swing, and it was on that pitch."[38]

When Orlando Palmiero hit a grounder to shortstop Juan Uribe and first baseman Konerko caught the throw in the ninth inning of Game Four, the White Sox won their first World Series since 1917. At the subsequent victory parade and rally in downtown Chicago, Konerko proudly declared, "Chicago, Second City no more," and then he presented the ball from the final out to owner Jerry Reinsdorf.[39]

In multiple interviews, Konerko has stated, "I think about the World Series every day. It comes into my mind at some point every day, whether I bump into somebody on the golf course, or a song comes on the radio and it's a big deal. It's a life changing event."[40] "I felt like I was on my way to having a good career, but I don't even know if I'm with the White Sox after [the season if there's no Series win] and then if I finish out the same career statistically speaking, it never would have been the whole package if there was no World Series."[41] Tom Verducci of *Sports Illustrated* named Konerko his choice for Sportsman of the Year, noting that he was "a grinder who plays every game as if he's still trying to prove himself in the big leagues."[42]

At the conclusion of the season, Konerko was a free agent. He was reportedly offered more money by both the Orioles and the Angels, but after the White Sox added a fifth year, he re-signed for $60 million. "He had a hard time turning down the chance to go back and try to win another championship in Chicago," said his agent, Craig Landis. "He has loyalty to his teammates and to the fans there and feels very wanted, not just by the White Sox organization but by the whole city of Chicago. He felt that that could not be matched by other cities."[43]

Konerko was named team captain in 2006 and had a strong start to the season. He was again named a reserve on the All-Star team and went 2-for-2 in the game before he was lifted for a pinch-runner. At the break, the White Sox were 26 games over .500 but still trailed Detroit by two games for the division lead. Konerko continued his strong performance in the second half and had a memorable game on August 8 when he hit a home run off closer Mariano Rivera to lead a comeback over the Yankees. The White Sox slumped in September and were passed by Minnesota for the wild card. On the final day of the season, the White Sox lost to Minnesota, which secured the division title. The White Sox finished 90-72 but ended up third in the division and missed the playoffs. Konerko finished the season with 35 home runs, 113 RBIs, and a career-best .313 batting average. In November the *Arlington Heights Daily Herald* of suburban Chicago said that he had struggled with back pain throughout the season and was focusing on new workouts during the offseason to try to help.[44]

Konerko had a slow start to 2007 although he picked it up in June. The White Sox struggled all season and finished in fourth place. Konerko finished hitting .259 with 31 home runs and 90 RBIs. During an interview in 2008 spring training, he said the 2007 team was the first truly bad team he had been on with the White Sox. However, with the off-season additions, he felt that the 2008 team was "solid and veteran like. We're built right and we have the right people in the right spots."[45]

Konerko battled with injuries throughout 2008, playing in his fewest games with the White Sox before his final season. A sore right hand kept him out of the lineup on May 1 and he struggled with it the entire season. It eventually got so sore that it was treated with a cortisone shot.[46] On June 4 he hit a walk-off home run against the Royals in the 15th inning and said he felt like a rookie again, but on June 15 he strained a rib muscle during batting practice and had to go to the disabled list for the first time in his career. Teammate Nick Swisher said, "Losing him is a big hole for us to fill. Not only all the things that he's capable of doing on the field, but all the things he brings to us in the locker room. He's the king. He's our leader. But I know regardless of whether he's on the field, he's going to help lead as best as he can."[47]

After a rehab stint in early July, Konerko was reactivated on July 8. He was part of the record-tying back-to-back-to-back-to-back home runs in a game on August 14 with Jim Thome, Alexei Ramirez, and Juan Uribe. However, he again missed time after he injured his knee on September 9. He came back a week later and got two hits in a win over the Yankees.

Despite Konerko's struggles with injuries and .240 batting average, the White Sox finished the season tied for the division lead. In a one-game tiebreaker to decide the Central Division winner, they beat the Twins 1-0 and faced Tampa Bay in the Division Series. Konerko hit two solo home runs in the series against the Tampa Bay Rays but the White Sox lost three games to one.

The 2009 season was one of several milestones. On April 13 Konerko and Jermaine Dye hit back-to-back home runs. They were the 300th career home runs for both Dye and Konerko, the first time two players reached that milestone in the same game. On July 7 against the Indians, Konerko hit three home runs, including a grand slam, in a 10-6 win. He became only the 12th White Sox player with a three-home-run game.[48] Then on August 19, he doubled in a run in the first inning and joined Frank Thomas and Luke Appling as the only White Sox with 1,000 RBIs. The team struggled during the season and at the end of August traded one of its best hitters, Jim Thome, and pitcher José Contreras, leaving Konerko as part of a rebuilding effort. The White Sox finished third. Konerko led the team with 28 home runs and 88 RBIs.

Konerko started 2010 strong and was leading the American League in home runs in May, but the team started slow and was in fourth place. He had to sit out a couple of games in early May because of his sore back. By June the team had climbed to third place but was almost 10 games back. On June 9 the White Sox started a run of 15 wins in 16 games. In a June 25 interview Konerko said, "A few weeks ago … it just wasn't very fun around here. We've got smiles on our faces now. It's fun again which is nice. The longer you can keep baseball from becoming a job, the better."[49] He was named to his fourth All-Star team.

On September 12 Konerko hit two home runs against Kansas City, giving him 362 for his career and moving him ahead of Joe DiMaggio. On the 16th, in the bottom of the first inning, he was hit in the face by Carl Pavano of the Twins. He refused to leave the game and in his next at-bat, in the third inning, he hit a home run – his third home run off Pavano in a two-month span. The White Sox missed the playoffs again, ending in second place, six games behind Minnesota. Konerko hit .312 with 39 home runs (second in the American League) and was sixth with 111 RBIs.

During the offseason Konerko heard that the White Sox had signed Adam Dunn and thought that they might not be re-signing him, but he received a three-year, $37 million extension. He expressed an optimistic outlook for 2011: "We certainly have what we need in every area, starters, bullpen, lineup […] It's just a matter of coming together as a team and executing."[50] He had another good start to the season but the White Sox were struggling in fourth place. He made his fifth All-Star team and at the break had moved to the top four in the American League in batting average, home runs, and RBIs while the White Sox moved up to third place. After the break, Konerko struggled with floating bone fragments in his wrist and a knee injury after Andrew Miller hit him in the knee with a pitch at the end of July. The White Sox struggled without their captain and finished in third place.

On October 22, 2011, Konerko became the 27th member, and first local product, of the Arizona Fall League Hall of Fame and the number that he wore for the 1996 Sun City

Solar Sox was retired. He said, "I'm probably also the first member of the Hall of Fame that came to games here as a kid."[51]

After offseason wrist surgery, 2012 proved to be another very good year for Konerko. "The Chicago White Sox first baseman is in a hitting 'zone,'" a newspaper commented."[52] In early June he was leading the American League with a .371 batting average. He was named to his sixth All-Star team; he had one at-bat and was hit by a pitch. After the break, he again had to deal with injuries and returned to the disabled list for the second time in his career. The White Sox played well that season and spent most of the year in first place although never more than 3½ games ahead. A late-season slump in which they lost 11 of their last 15 games put them in second place and they missed the playoffs again. Konerko finished with a .298 average.

In 2022 Konerko said, "The thing I'm probably most proud of in my career is 2010-2012. [The 2004 season] may have been my best year in terms of just being dangerous the whole year, I was right in the middle of my prime so you should be, but those last years – 2010-12 – I was an older player [....} I take most pride in those years because it was complete mental control. When you start waking up and you can't get out of bed and your back aches you have to be mentally superior."[53]

In 2013 Konerko struggled with a nagging back injury and ended up on the disabled list for the third time. In 2022 he said, "I got really good there in my mid-30s and had a resurgence for a while and it's like shoot, am I one of those guys who plays until he's 42 because it was becoming easier to me to play the game at 35-36 than 26 because I was better at what I was doing and I understood it better, but then right there in 2013 it just kind of hit a wall and then you just try to make do and do the best you can."[54]

Konerko considered retiring after the season (his 15th with the White Sox) but decided to come back for one final season, knowing that he would have a limited role with José Abreu and Adam Dunn on the roster. He signed a one-year contract and told his teammates it would be his last. "In the arc of your career, if you want to be a great big leaguer, it includes a lot of things, like how to conduct yourself, after you're there for a few years, how do you treat the young guys?" he said in 2022. "There are all these boxes along the way that the guys who do it right have to check off and one of those things is at the end, you have to let it go. You know that the whole time I was there the position of first base for the White Sox was just on loan to me, you know it wasn't mine, I was just keeping it warm for the next guy."[55]

Konerko ended up playing 81 games in that final season. On his last visit to each ballpark, that team would present him with a retirement gift. During the final homestand in Chicago, the White Sox unveiled a statue depicting his celebration after hitting the grand slam in the World Series. On his final day, there was a retirement ceremony on the field before the game started, and after the game he walked around the entire field waving and shaking hands with the fans who were still gathered to celebrate his career. Konerko finished with a career average of .279, 439 home runs, and 1,412 RBIs. After the season he was named the 2014 Roberto Clemente Award winner, recognizing his charitable work.

After retiring, Konerko went home to Arizona, where as of 2025 he lived with his wife, Jennifer, and three children, Nicholas, Owen, and Amelia. He became the assistant coach for his son's baseball team where his friend and former teammate, JJ Putz, is the head coach.[56]

In 2015 the White Sox retired Konerko's number 14. He said, "I always just wanted to be a good producing baseball player. I was not out after all the other stuff that came with it. It probably never even crossed my mind until the second half of the last year that, you know, I could get my number retired. I was always thinking that what I was doing was not enough."[57]

In 2020 Konerko was on the ballot for the National Baseball Hall of Fame for the first time. "I was a big fan of the game growing up in terms of being a fan of the players and living on the East Coast, a Yankees fan and you just don't think you're in that group no matter what the numbers say." He only received 2.5 percent of the vote and fell off the ballot after the first year. His former teammate Sean Casey summed it up after having Konerko on his podcast: "We talk to players who are friends and in the same community as him and everyone said [Konerko] thinks about baseball differently and at an advanced level. The word they used was he's an artist in the batter's box and in the batting cage. Paulie is probably the second-best hitter in White Sox history and 2.5 percent of the vote is a shame. The Veterans Committee needs to be calling."[58]

SOURCES

In addition to the sources cited in the Notes, the author consulted Baseball-Reference.com. Thanks to Jeff Findley for helping shepherd this biography along.

NOTES

1   https://www.amissionofmercy.org/about-us/#history, accessed December 24, 2024.

2   "Big Bear Mining Corp Announces the Addition of New Board Member, Hank Konerko, and the Addition of New CFO, Mike Schifsky," https://www.prnewswire.com/news-releases/big-bear-mining-corp-announces-the-addition-of-new-board-member-hank-konerko-and-the-addition-of-new-cfo-mike-schifsky-112243529.html, accessed December 24, 2024.

3   Sean Casey and Rich Ciancimino, "Episode 53 Paul Konerko How I See the Game," *The Mayor's Office with Sean Casey* [Video Podcast]. February 2022.

4   Casey and Ciancimino.

5   Ken Daley, "Dodgers Draft Potential Power Hitter with Catcher," *Los Angeles Daily News*, June 3, 1994.

6   James Curran, "Spirit's Konerko Keeping Spirit Up Despite Slow Start," *San Bernardino County* (California) *Sun*, April 19, 1995.

7   Ken Daley, "Myers Gives Dodgers Reason to Regret Their Choice in '92," *Los Angeles Daily News*, June 12, 1994.

8   Doug Padilla, "S.B. Will See Club's Top Prospects," *San Bernardino County Sun*, September 23, 1994. Curran, "Spirit's Konerko Keeping Spirit Up Despite Slow Start."

9   Lisa Renfro, "Konerko Can't See His No. 1 Season," *San Bernardino County Sun*, September 13, 1995.

10 James Curran, "Spirit Sweeps San Jose to Win Title," *San Bernardino County Sun*, September 16, 1995.

11 Renfro.

12 Steve Dilbeck, "Dodgers' Konerko Can Get to 1st Base," *San Bernardino County Sun*, February 24, 1996.

13 Dilbeck, "Dodgers' Konerko Can Get to 1st Base."

14 Steve Dilbeck, "Alou Is the Glue That Binds Expos," *San Bernardino County Sun*, May 16, 1996.

15 Danny Summers, "Stampede routed, faces elimination," *San Bernardino County Sun*, June 13, 1996.

16 Bob Nightengale, "Piazza Works with Scioscia on Delivery," *Los Angeles Times*, July 14, 1976: 14.

17 "Record Book, Minor Leagues," *Greenville* (Ohio) *Daily Advocate*, June 28, 1997.

18 "Helton Wins Triple-A Homer Contest," *Logansport* (Indiana) *Pharos Tribune*, July 9, 1997.

19 Andrew Baggarly, "Dodgers Pull Switcheroo on Marlins," *San Bernardino County Sun*, September 9, 1997.

20 Jason Reid, "Konerko Ready for Rah-Rah Deal," *Los Angeles Times*, September 5, 1997: 11.

21 Steve Springer, "Konerko to Wait, but Not Patiently," *Los Angeles Times*, September 13, 1997: 9.

22 Steve Dilbeck, "Next Up, Konerko," *San Bernardino County Sun*, March 10, 1998.

23 Cary Osborne, "The Dodgers' History in Baseball America's Top 100 Prospects List," dodgers.mlblogs.com, February 21, 2015. https://dodgers.mlblogs.com/the-dodgers-history-in-baseball-america-s-top-100-prospects-list-6b34026d3a21.

24 Steve Dilbeck, "Konerko Gets His Shot," *San Bernardino County Sun*, March 7, 1998.

25 "Dodgers Get Closer Shaw," *Annapolis Capital*, July 5, 1998.

26 Teddy Greenstein, "Sox Ship Cameron to Reds; Konerko, 22, to Get Shot at First Base Job," *Chicago Tribune*, November 12, 1988: 1.

27 Casey and Ciancimino, "Episode 53 Paul Konerko How I See the Game."

28 David Ginsburg (Associated Press), "Morgan Makes 400th Start Memorable," *Tyrone* (Pennsylvania) *Daily Herald*, July 30, 1999.

29 Associated Press, "Tigers Christen New Park with 5-2 Win," *Santa Cruz* (California) *Sentinel*, April 12, 2000.

30 Associated Press, "October Calling: Who Will Answer?" *Greenwood* (South Carolina) *Index Journal* October 3, 2000.

31 "Baseball Today Stars," *Hays* (Kansas) *Daily News*, July 10, 2002. Because the game ended in a tie, no MVP was named. See Fred Mitchell, "Konerko the Almost MVP," *Chicago Tribune*, July10, 2002: 5.

32 Fred Mitchell, "Konerko Fires Away at Thomas," *Chicago Tribune*, July 9, 2002.

33 Associated Press. "Thomas Hurting Opponents Again, Slugs Two More Homers," *Tyrone Daily Herald*, March 12, 2003.

34 Casey and Ciancimino.

35 "White Sox Outlast the Royals," *Iola* (Kansas) *Register*, June 21, 2005.

36 Casey and Ciancimino.

37 Rick Gano (Associated Press), "White Sox Armed for Success," *Indiana* (Pennsylvania) *Gazette*, October 17, 2005.

38 Rick Gano, "Konerko's Slam Sparks Chicago," *Indiana Gazette*, October 24, 2005.

39 Tara Burghart, "Second City No More: Chicago Hails Sox," *Salina* (Kansas) *Journal*, October 29, 2005.

40 Jenna Duddleston (host), "Episode 105 "White Sox Legend Paul Konerko," *Bar Talk with Jenna* [Video Podcast], November 2022.

41 Jason Benetti and Len Kasper (hosts), "Season 2 Episode 2 Paul Konerko," *Sox Degrees* [video podcast], April 2022.

42 Tom Verducci, "Konerko True Team Player," *Chicago Tribune*, November 9, 2005:10.

43 Rick Gano (Associated Press), "Konerko Stays with White Sox," *Indiana Gazette*, December 1, 2005.

44 Scot Gregor, "Sox Trainer Schneider Having Busy Off-Season Healing Players for 2007," *Arlington Heights Daily Herald* (Chicago), November 10, 2006.

45 Scot Gregor, "Konerko on 2007: Not Good, Not Fun," *Arlington Heights Daily Herald*, March 6, 2008.

46 Scot Gregor, "A First for Konerko: Trip to Disabled List," *Arlington Heights Daily Herald*, June 18, 2008.

47 Scot Gregor, "Sox (19 hits) Take Big Bite Out of Pirates' Pitching," *Arlington Heights Daily Herald*, June 18, 2008.

48 Harold Baines accomplished this twice.

49 Associated Press, "Konerko HR Lifts White Sox to Series Sweep over N.L. East-Leading Braves," *Greenwood Index Journal*, June 25, 2010.

50 Associated Press. "Red or White? Pair of Sox Seem Set to Go," *Iola* (Kansas) *Daily American Republic*, March 30, 2011.

51 "First Basemen Ryan Howard & Paul Konerko Elected to Arizona Fall League Hall of Fame," Arizona Fall League News Release, August 12, 2011. https://www.oursportscentral.com/services/releases/first-basemen-ryan-howard-&-paul-konerko-elected-to-arizona-fall-league-hall-of-fame/n-4273401.

52 Gus Goodsport, "Supersport: Paul Konerko," *Greenwood Index Journal*, July 9, 2012.

53 Casey and Ciancimino, "Episode 53 Paul Konerko How I See the Game."

54 Duddleston, "Episode 105 "White Sox Legend Paul Konerko."

55 Duddleston.

56 Daryl Van Schouwen, "Little League Dad Konerko Loving Life after White Sox," *Chicago Sun-Times*, March 4, 2018. https://chicago.suntimes.com/2018/3/4/18367957/little-league-dad-konerko-loving-life-after-white-sox.

57 Duddleston.

58 Casey and Ciancimino.

PEDRO LÓPEZ

By J.P. Garrett

Discovered in the Dominican Republic by Chicago White Sox scout Denny Gonzalez, 16-year-old infielder Pedro Michel López signed as an amateur free agent in 2000. He was born in Moca, Dominican Republic, on April 28, 1984, and attended high school there. A prospect touted for his defensive prowess, he played in the major leagues for only 16 games, never quite reaching his potential but finding his place in the game as a manager.

After signing with the White Sox, López was assigned to the Arizona League White Sox in 2001. The team was managed by Jerry Hairston Sr., who spent all but 51 games of his 14-year major-league career with Chicago's Southside team.

López appeared in 50 games in 2001, splitting time between third base, second base, and shortstop. He finished his first rookie-league season at .312/.359/.412 with one home run and 19 RBIs, and for 2002 was assigned to his second rookie-league team, the Bristol White Sox of the Appalachian League.

In Bristol, he played in 63 games; a few at shortstop. He batted a consistent .319/.370/.362, nearly doubled his

Pedro Lopez   2005

RBI tally from the previous year with 35, and ranked third in the Appalachian League in hits. He stole 22 bases in 30 attempts and finished the season as the number-19 prospect in the White Sox system. López received his first invitation to major-league spring training in 2003, and he continued to rise through the White Sox system that year with another promotion, this time to the Kannapolis Intimidators of the Low-A South Atlantic League.

In Kannapolis, López played more than 100 games in a season for the first time, again primarily at second base, with time at shortstop and third. While his batting numbers were down (.264/.314/.323 with 33 RBIs), he did lead the team in doubles (23), stolen bases (24), and sacrifice hits (16). Near the end of the season, López was promoted again, to the High-A Winston-Salem Warthogs of the Carolina League. He spent four games there and began the 2004 season with the Warthogs.

López spent most of the season in Winston-Salem, penciled into 104 games at shortstop. With a slash line of .288/.328/.347 with 35 RBIs and 4 home runs (his first since the Arizona Rookie League), he finished out the year with the Birmingham Barons of the Double-A Southern League. At that time, *Baseball America* rated López as the best defensive infielder in the White Sox organization. White Sox manager Ozzie Guillén agreed: "From the first day I saw Pedro catching the ball, to me, he was the best in the organization defensively."[1]

López's stay in Birmingham was brief. He made the White Sox' 40-man roster in 2005 and began the season with Chicago's Triple-A team, the Charlotte Knights, again splitting time between shortstop and second base. After only a month in Charlotte, López was called up to the White Sox. He debuted at age 21 on May 1, 2005, at US Cellular Field in Chicago to fill in for shortstop Willie Harris, who was on bereavement leave. López had four at-bats and got his first major-league hit in the sixth inning. He singled to left field off Wil Ledezma and drove in Chris Widger. Later in the inning he was driven in by Carl Everett, contributing to an 8-0 victory over the Detroit Tigers. In his second game for the White Sox on May 8, he played second base; his one hit turned out to drive in the game-winning RBI in a 5-4 victory over the Blue Jays in Toronto.

Less than two months into the season, the White Sox were 24-7, tying the record for their best 31-game start since the Black Sox season of 1919. "I don't want to say it's good, but they're playing good baseball," Guillén said. "They stick up for each other and carry each other. They have good pitching and play the way you're supposed to play, [so] you get good results. Tying a record doesn't mean anything. It's nice to be part of it, but I don't look at that. I look forward to the next game."[2]

Despite his contributions in the May 8 game, López was sent back to Triple A when Harris returned. He struggled in Charlotte (.198/.226/.278) and after about a month, was sent back down to Double-A Birmingham, where he hit .238/.287/.314 in 68 games. He was not selected for the playoff roster as the White Sox began their journey to winning the 2005 World Series.

While not on the World Series team, López did receive a championship ring. Some, including López himself, questioned whether he should have, even though he was on the 40-man roster.

"Why shouldn't he have gotten one?" Guillén later said. "We have secretaries who never played one inning that have one. That one or two games he helped us win could have been the difference between us being in the playoffs or not. Pedro was a good player to be around. He didn't say much. He was like a lot of guys on that team who did little things to make it easy for me."[3]

At the end of the 2005 season, López was selected to play for the Peoria Saguaros of the Arizona Fall League, where in six games he hit .375/.400/.500. That performance enabled him to start the 2006 season back in Charlotte (.274/.320/.404 with 5 home runs and 24 RBIs), though he also spent about half of the season in Birmingham (.322/.358/.454 with another 5 home runs and 34 RBIs).

That winter López honed his skills with Estrellas Orientales of the Dominican Winter League, then headed back to Triple-A Charlotte to start the 2007 season. Having already been dropped from Chicago's 40-man roster, on May 20 he was released by the White Sox. The next day he was picked up off waivers by the Cincinnati Reds and sent to the Triple-A Louisville Bats.

After 34 games in Louisville, batting an impressive .339/.396/.427, López made his Reds debut on July 14. In a 2-1 loss to the New York Mets at Shea Stadium, he started at shortstop and went 0-for-3 against future Hall of Famer Tom Glavine. On July 25 against the Milwaukee Brewers in Cincinnati, López suffered a broken jaw when he was hit by a pitch from Matt Wise. He was able to return to the team on September 21 as a pinch-runner against the San Francisco Giants at AT&T Park and rejoined the starting lineup on September 27 at home against the Houston Astros.

López played in 14 games for Cincinnati, including a game against the Atlanta Braves on July 18 in which he went 3-for-6, including a double, off another future Hall of Famer, John Smoltz. His 1-for-4 appearance on September 30, 2007, at Great American Ball Park in Cincinnati was his last game played in the major leagues. With a season slash line of .178/.213/.222, no home runs, and no RBIs, he was

released by the Reds. On October 26 he was selected off waivers by the Toronto Blue Jays.

Still only 23 years old, López spent another offseason with Estrellas of the Dominican Winter League, finishing at .271/.350/.295 with 18 RBIs. He did not make the Blue Jays' major-league roster coming out of spring training in 2008; he spent the entire year with the Triple-A Syracuse Chiefs, finishing at .236/.306/.295 with 2 home runs and 27 RBIs. At the end of the season, López was granted free agency, and after spending another winter with Estrellas (.286/.432/.321), he signed a minor-league deal with the Pittsburgh Pirates on January 7, 2009.

The 2009 season was another one spent in the minors for López, with 42 games for the Triple-A Indianapolis Indians (.275/.316/.310), and 53 games with the Double-A Altoona Curve (.263/.311/.337). After another winter season with Estrellas, López signed with the Washington Nationals on January 13, 2010. After another season (.216/.293/.304 in 58 games) at Triple-A Syracuse (which had switched its affiliation from Toronto to Washington), and 24 games with the Double-A Harrisburg Senators (.174/.206/.203), López was granted free agency for the final time in November 2010.

He then spent the next two winters with Leones del Escogido of the Dominican Winter League (.206/.277/.260 in 2010-2011, and .160/.276/.240 in 2011-2012). In 2012 López joined the Bridgeport Bluefish of the Independent Atlantic League, batting .272/.404/.296 in 41 games. He played part-time for Escogido the next three winters, appearing in 29 games over three seasons.

In 2015 López ventured north of the border, playing 85 games for Aigles de Trois-Rivières of the Canadian-American Association. There he put up some of the better numbers of his career at .314/.388/.345 with one home run and 39 RBIs. He returned to Escogido in 2015-2016 and played with the team in the Caribbean Series in February 2016. The Dominican team finished fifth out of five teams in the series with zero wins, while López had four hits in the series.

The 2016 season found López in the Mexican League, playing for Olmecas de Tabasco and again batting over .300 (.307/.372/.349 with 18 RBIs). His last two seasons of professional baseball were spent with the Escogido team, for whom he played 40 games in 2016-2017 and 24 games in 2017-2018. At age 33, his playing career had come to an end. Overall, he had 52 at-bats with a .192 average, no home runs, and 2 RBIs in the majors.

One thing that remained from López's career, besides his memories, was his 2005 World Series ring. A decade after López got it, a reporter asked the retired player about it. "It's a secret where I keep it stored – I'm serious," López told the reporter. "I don't want anybody to know so I tell nobody. People in the Dominican can get crazy. They might try to steal it. I've never worn my ring out anywhere." López had been surprised to receive the ring, given that he played in only two games for the White Sox that season. He was grateful, however. "Everybody believed in me and always told me, 'You can play,' López said. "I remember everything about it. It was a dream. It was unbelievable. I love you, Chicago, and what you did for me."[4]

A year later, however, López sold the ring for $19,550 at an auction featuring items from the estate of White Sox legend Minnie Miñoso. The 14-carat-gold ring with 95 diamonds was the highest-selling item in the auction, with a portion of the proceeds going to Chicago White Sox Charities.[5]

With López's playing career over, he turned his attention to managing. In the 2017-18 Dominican Classic, he won Manager of the Year when he led Gigantes del Cibao to a first-place finish and a 29-21 record. The next year, he was bench coach for the Estrellas Orientales team that won the 2018-19 championship.

López then joined the Dominican team as a strategist, helping lead them to a slot in the 2019 Pan American Games in a qualifying event in Brazil. "We will go for something big, we are working to reach a good place," López said. "I know that this event is of greater magnitude than in Brazil, but we will strive to be among the first positions on the podium."[6]

While the Dominican Republic did not medal in baseball in the PanAm Games, the team finished fifth out of eight, bettering their performance in the Caribbean Series. For the 2019-20 season, he was named manager of Tigres del Licey, leading them to a 27-23 record.

In 2022 López he came back to Leones del Escogido as manager. "I love baseball in the Dominican Republic," López told Dominican Today. "It is the reason why I keep coming because I really tell you, from my heart, of all the years that I have been in baseball, I have been around 30-odd years, and I tell you with all honesty, this has been the best baseball that I have been part of and I enjoy it, with the ups and downs."[7]

SOURCES

In addition to the sources cited in the Notes, the author consulted Baseball-Almanac.com, Baseball-Reference.com, milb.com, NBCsports.com, and StatsCrew.com

NOTES

1 Jim Margalus, "Terrerobytes: A 2005 White Sox Story Seldom Told," southsidesox.com, July 20, 2015, accessed November 23, 2024. https://www.southsidesox.com/2015/7/20/9002149/terrerobytes-a-2005-white-sox-story-seldom-told.

2 Mark Gonzales, "Somber Streak," ChicagoTribune.com, May 9, 2005, accessed November 23, 2024. https://www.chicagotribune.com/2005/05/09/somber-streak/.

3 Margalus.

4 David Haugh, "Forgotten 2005 Champion Grateful for Ringing Endorsement from White Sox," ChicagoTribune.com, July 18, 2015, accessed November 23, 2024. https://www.chicagotribune.com/2015/07/18/forgotten-2005-champion-grateful-for-ringing-endorsement-from-white-sox/.

5 Danny Ecker, "Sox 2005 World Series Ring Sells for Nearly $20K," ChicagoBusiness.com, September 19, 2016, accessed November 23, 2024. https://www.chicagobusiness.com/article/20160919/BLOGS04/160919846/white-sox-2005-world-series-ring-sells-for-nearly-20k.

6 "Dominican Baseball Will Go to Panama with a Lot of Talent," DominicanToday.com, July 20, 2019, accessed November 23, 2024. https://dominicantoday.com/dr/sports/2019/07/20/dominican-baseball-will-go-to-panama-with-a-lot-of-talent/

7 "Pedro López: I Keep Coming Back to the DR Because This Is the Best Baseball," DominicanToday.com, October 7, 2022, accessed November 23, 2024. https://dominicantoday.com/dr/local/2022/10/07/pedro-lopez-i-keep-coming-back-to-the-dr-because-this-is-the-best-baseball/.

DAMASO MARTÉ

By Carter Cromwell

Dámaso Marté had good moments during his 11-year major league career, but two shone particularly brightly because they occurred on the big stage of the playoffs and World Series, and also because both were unexpected. The first was with the Chicago White Sox in 2005, as they won their first World Series in 88 years. The second came with the New York Yankees in 2009, when they won their only World Series in the twenty-first century.

Marté had established himself in a relief role with solid seasons for Chicago from 2002 to 2004, and he continued to be effective through much of the 2005 season. In late May, his earned-run average was 1.86.

But by the end of the regular season, his ERA stood at 3.77 and his WHIP at an unsightly 1.72.

In his last 14 appearances, Marté allowed nine hits, walked six, and gave up seven earned runs in 6⅔ innings. For the season, he walked 33 batters in 45⅓ innings, a bloated rate of 6.6 per 9 innings. His employers were not pleased.

Toward the end of the 2005 season, White Sox manager Ozzie Guillén said, "Seeing what [stuff] he has and what he can do and seeing how much we lean to him to win, that makes you angry. I don't like when Marte goes [out] there and doesn't want to attack people. That's all that bothers me."[1]

Pitching coach Don Cooper added, "The way I've seen him approach things [lately] isn't the way he or any of us would want. Just give us the same [bleeping] fastball and breaking balls you have for the first three years of your career and we'll go from there. But the way he's thrown the last two nights, we can't ... anticipate that he's going to be our late (-game) lefty. He's got to go out and earn things again."[2]

Marté was sent home by Guillén for arriving late for a September game, and he also reported issues with a sore neck and a muscle strain in his upper back, though Guillén said, "[The team doctor] said Marté is fine. He's 100 percent to go. It makes you wonder if the injury was mental or physical. If the injury was mental, it's a shame because that kid has better stuff than a lot of people in this game. If Marte's not ready to help this team, he can have a nice trip [home] to the Dominican Republic by himself."[3]

Marté did not inspire confidence in his first playoff appearance, in Game Three of the Division Series against Boston on October 7, allowing all three hitters he faced to reach base. He didn't pitch again until Game Three of the

World Series against Houston on October 25, but he came through then.

In a game that went 14 innings – at the time tied with Game Two of the 1916 Series as the longest by innings in World Series history – Marté entered at the beginning of the 13th inning, the eighth of nine White Sox pitchers that night. Joe Buck, the play-by-play announcer on the Fox Sports telecast of the game, noted that Marté's ERA in his previous nine games had been 12.27 and his opponents' batting average was .421.

"Marté, who for a while was in the doghouse with the White Sox ... has great stuff, but sometimes they wonder about the effort and the concentration. And here he is ... if you can't concentrate in a game like this ..."[4]

But he pitched a hitless, scoreless 1⅔ innings that night to get credit for the win in the 7-5 White Sox victory. All of which was a departure from his performance in the season's late stages.

"I'd had a good career with the White Sox, but all athletes have ups and downs," Marté said in Spanish through

Damaso Marte   2005

a translator long after his career had finished. "At the time, I was very down, but the team needed me, so I kept at it. I gave it my all and had a great outing in Game Three of the Series."[5]

Those comments could also have applied in 2009.

The Yankees had acquired Marté and Xavier Nady from Pittsburgh in July 2008 for José Tábata, Ross Ohlendorf, Jeff Karstens, and Daniel McCutchen. He did not particularly stand out the rest of that season, though his statistics are somewhat misleading. He had a 5.40 ERA in 25 appearances, but eight of the 11 earned runs he allowed as a Yankee came in just three outings. The Yankees declined his $6 million option for 2009, paid him a $250,000 buyout, and then re-signed him to a three-year, $12 million contract.

The deal did not seem a good one at first, as Marté experienced shoulder inflammation after pitching two shutout innings for the Dominican Republic in the 2009 World Baseball Classic and began the season by giving up nine earned runs over 5⅓ innings in his first seven outings. Again, those figures were distorted because six of the earned runs came in a single appearance. Nonetheless, he wasn't sharp, went on the disabled list in early May, and spent rehab time at the rookie league and Triple-A levels before returning to the Yankees in late August. From that point, he gave up five earned runs in eight innings the rest of the way, though four came in one game.

One report speculated that Marté got a spot on the postseason roster because of his success against left-handed hitters – a .120/.214/.280 slash line – and lefties Joe Mauer and Jason Kubel were in the middle of Minnesota's lineup for the American League Division Series.[6] In fact, for his career, he limited left-handed batters to a .195 batting average and .575 OPS over 898 plate appearances.

As in 2005, the playoffs did not begin auspiciously for Marté; he allowed hits to both batters he faced in Game Two of the ALDS against the Twins. But then he hit his stride. In his last seven playoff outings – three against the Los Angeles Angels in the ALCS and four in the World Series against the Philadelphia Phillies – he did not give up a hit, walk, or run, and was particularly effective against left-handed hitters as the Yankees won the title.

Philadelphia's Matt Stairs said after Game Six that "[Marté has] surprised us a little bit. He's pitching us really well. We've been able to get to [set-up relievers Phil] Hughes and [Joba] Chamberlain, but Marte has done the job for them."[7]

"When we think about the 2009 World Series, we think of Hideki Matsui, who was [voted] the MVP," then-Yankee manager Joe Girardi said. "But, to me, the MVP in that World Series was Damaso Marté.

"The Phillies [had] really good left-handed hitters [such as Ryan Howard and Chase Utley]. In the top of the eighth inning of Game One, the first two batters get on and I bring in Damaso and he strikes out Utley and I go, 'Uh, oh!' Then Game Three in Philly, he strikes out Howard [and] he strikes out Jayson Werth. ... I've got a super weapon here. Then Game Six. There's two on in the top of the seventh, [and he strikes out Utley]."

"Damaso Marte was the unsung hero of that World Series, and I'll never forget it."[8]

Marté later said that "it was tough to get used to that city – the fans, the journalists. Every time you pitched badly, you'd hear it from the fans. There was a time leading up to that World Series in which I lost confidence, but, thank God, I was able to come through when the team needed me."

That was perhaps the highest point of his professional career, the road to which had begun on February 14, 1975, when Dámaso Savinon Marté was born in Santo Domingo, the capital city of the Dominican Republic. He said his mother, Ramona Savinon, was 16 at the time, and that he didn't know his father until later in life. She didn't say anything to her parents when she discovered she was pregnant, instead leaving the city and not returning until after the birth. He was raised by one of his mother's nieces, whom he calls his second mom.[9]

Marté began playing baseball at the age of 12, hanging around Estadio La Normal, the oldest ballpark in the Dominican Republic, where young players try to get noticed.

"My mom – the one who raised me – sold tea in the streets to make ends meet," he said. "It was very tough growing up. We sometimes had no food and sometimes had to sleep in the streets. There were times I went to the field without shoes."

Eventually, his efforts paid off. After going to tryouts with several major-league teams – Cleveland, Baltimore, Oakland, the Chicago White Sox – he was finally signed at 17 by Seattle Mariners scout Dintacora de los Santos on October 28, 1992.[10] His first contract was for $2,500.[11]

Marté spent the next two seasons playing with Santo Domingo in the Dominican Summer League, a developmental set-up for very young players. In his second season, he was 7-0 with a 3.86 ERA in 17 games (13 starts). In 1995 he began in the U.S. minor leagues with the Mariners' Low-A Everett (Washington) affiliate in 1995. There he was 2-2 with a 2.21 earned-run mark in 11 games (five starts) and held opposing batters to a .195 average.

Marté spent the 1996 season at Appleton, Wisconsin, in the Class-A Midwest League, making 26 starts and posting an 8-6 record with a 4.49 ERA and 1.47 WHIP. A year later, he advanced to High A with Lancaster in the California League, where he went 8-8 in 25 starts with a 4.13 ERA and was named pitcher of the week on August 16 after allowing just one earned run in two starts covering 16 innings. He moved to Double-A Orlando in 1998 and was 7-6 with a 5.27 earned-run mark in 22 games, 20 of them starts.

The next season, Marté began at Triple-A Tacoma and began relieving more. After starting 76 of 84 games in his first four minor-league seasons, he started just 11 of 31 in 1999.

"[The Mariners] wanted me to switch to relieving," Marté said. "I was OK with it. I'd done that some in the minors and felt it was easier for me to be a reliever."

Marté was called up by the Mariners and made his major-league debut on June 30, 1999, in a 14-5 loss to the Oakland Athletics. He pitched the eighth inning and gave up three runs on two hits. The first batter, John Jaha, greeted Marté with a solo home run. Then, after a walk to Jason Giambi, Ramón Hernández hit a two-run shot.

"I was very nervous, and it was an exciting moment," Marté said of his debut, "but also a very tough moment because I gave up the runs."

He made four other relief appearances for Seattle, the last against Arizona on July 20, when he pitched the final four innings and allowed 10 hits and all six runs in a 6-0 defeat. With an 0-1 mark and 9.35 ERA in 8⅔ innings, the Mariners returned Marté to Tacoma.

Marté's 1999 Triple-A numbers included a 3-3 mark, a 5.13 ERA, and a high 1.62 WHIP. Much of the latter was due to his tendency to walk batters. He averaged 2.5 walks per nine innings at Everett, 4.7 at Wisconsin, 4.0 at Lancaster, 3.5 at Orlando, and 4.9 at Tacoma. In his brief stay with the Mariners, he walked six in 8⅔ innings.

Marté saw only brief action in 2000 because of a left elbow strain that kept him on the disabled list from April 7 until August 22. After returning to action, he got two starts with Seattle's rookie-league team in Arizona and four relief appearances with Double-A New Haven (Connecticut). Overall, he was 0-0 with an 0.84 earned-run average and a 0.844 WHIP.

Marté was released by Seattle on October 16, 2000, and signed with the Yankees on November 18. "They released me after elbow surgery, and the only team interested was the Yankees. I signed a contract with a clause that [said] I would stay in the big leagues if I could make the team, but, unfortunately, I couldn't do it and was sent to the minors."[12]

Marté began the 2001 season with Norwich in the Double-A Eastern League, making 23 relief appearances and posting a 3-1 mark, a 3.50 ERA, and an excellent 1.00 WHIP before being traded to Pittsburgh on June 13, 2001. for infielder Enrique Wilson. Marté then made four relief appearances for the Pirates' Triple-A affiliate in Nashville before making his Pittsburgh debut on June 24 when he hurled three innings of one-hit ball against the Montreal Expos.

"This time, I was a little older and less nervous," he said. "I was more confident about what I could do."

Marté had 22 more outings that season, finishing with an 0-1 record and a 4.71 ERA. However, he was on the move again the following spring, this time to the White Sox with infielder Ruddy Yan in a trade for minor-league pitcher Matt Guerrier on March 27, 2002. Marté was said to have been fighting for the final bullpen spot on the Pirates roster and was out of minor-league options, so the trade gave him a new lease on his baseball life.[13] It also set him up for the most successful period of his MLB career.

"I was happy with the trade," Marté said. "I was already in the major leagues, but the White Sox really opened a door for me, and I took advantage of it."

He pitched in 68 games in 2002, finishing with a 1-1 mark, a 2.83 ERA, 10 saves, and the best WHIP of his career, 1.028. His walk rate, 2.7 per 9 innings, was also the lowest of his career and was the only time in his 11 major-league seasons that his walk rate was lower than 3.0/9. He got his first major-league victory and save vs. Cleveland on April 16 and July 6, respectively. He held left-handed hitters to a .149 average, the lowest mark in the American League.

The next season was even better in some ways when Marté set career highs in saves (11), innings pitched 79⅔), and strikeouts (87). He was 4-2 with a 1.58 ERA and a 1.05 WHIP. He was again effective in 2004, with a 6-5 won-lost record, a 3.42 ERA, a 1.22 WHIP, and six saves, although his walk rate climbed to 4.2 per 9 innings and he had a 6.30 ERA over his final 12 games. He had a 2.45 ERA before the All-Star break and a 4.59 mark afterward.

Then came the up-and-down 2005 campaign, the first of a three-year contract. Though it finished on a high note for Marté and the White Sox, he was traded back to Pittsburgh on November 8 for outfielder Rob Mackowiak. In early 2006 he pitched for the Dominican Republic team in the World Baseball Classic, making three relief appearances.

Marté's first season back with the Pirates was spotty. He was limited to one game in spring training while battling left-shoulder irritation and a stiff neck.[14] Establishing a career high in appearances (75), he was 1-7 with a 3.70 earned-run mark and held left-handed hitters to a .225 average, but he continued his trend of pairing good strikeout rates (9.7/9) with high walk rates (4.8/9).

Nonetheless, Marté, then 31, got a two-year contract for $4.7 million in November that extended through the 2008 season.

"We think Marte is a valuable guy in our bullpen," Pirates general manager Dave Littlefield said. "It is another asset to give [Pirates manager] Jim Tracy from the left side a little earlier in the game. He has had some very good years in the past," Littlefield said. "We think he'll do a good job for us and continue to give us strong depth in the bullpen."[15]

And he did in 2007, posting a 2.38 ERA, a 1.10 WHIP, and improved strikeout and walk rates. He held left-handed batters to a minuscule .094 average. A year later, he was 4-0 with a 3.47 ERA through 47 outings before the July 2008 trade to the Yankees.

"It was hard to give up the players we did. I like those players," Yankees general manager Brian Cashman said. "[But] the players we got back – Marte and Nady – both will hopefully contribute to the 2008 season, and we have them for '09."

"I think it's a very good move for us," manager Joe Girardi added. "Xavier is having a very good year. ...

And then we get Marté, who has been very good against left-handed hitters – and right-handers, too."[16]

But Marté was inconsistent the rest of that season and then was limited by the shoulder issues during the 2009 regular season. When he went on the disabled list on May 3, his ERA was 15.19 and opponents were batting .360 against him.[17] He did not pitch again until August 21, after which he remained inconsistent.

But Marté then had his resurgence in the 2009 World Series, and in the wake of that, his outlook for 2010 was hopeful. With Phil Coke having been traded to Detroit, Marté was envisioned as a set-up reliever and perhaps the Yankees' designated left-handed-one-out-guy – that, of course, before the current rule requiring that a reliever face at least three batters.

One report predicted that "[n]o matter how the bullpen shapes up, Damaso Marté will be a part of it. Given the team's other options for the remaining five spots, he also figures to be the only lefty in the pen. ... He's not a guy you bring into a game with three righties due up, but he can certainly handle the righty residing between two lefties."[18]

But it didn't work out as had been hoped. Marté continued to have issues with his shoulder and delivered mixed results. He made 30 appearances, posting a 4.08 ERA. Though he allowed only 10 hits in 17⅔ innings and held opponents to a .161 batting average, he walked 11 batters. His final outing was a clean inning against Oakland on July 7. He was placed on the 15-day disabled list on July 17 with left-shoulder inflammation and then was transferred to the 60-day list on September 1, missing the remainder of the season.

Marté had surgery for a torn labrum on October 22, 2010. The surgery was performed in Cincinnati by the Reds medical director, Dr. Timothy Kremchek. Marté, 35 at the time, said he had been told that he should be able to begin a throwing program after the 2011 All-Star break.[19]

At the time, Marté said, "I thought maybe I wouldn't throw anymore. It was a lot of pain. Right now I feel comfortable because my doctor, he gave me a good idea with my arm and he told me it's getting better."[20]

However, he made just one rehab appearance, for the Yankees' entry in the Gulf Coast League on August 25, and gave up six hits and six earned runs in two-thirds of an inning. On October 19, 2011, the Yankees declined their $4 million option for the 2012 season and paid Marté a $250,000 buyout, making him a free agent, after which he went unsigned. He was 2-6 with no saves and a 6.02 ERA in 76 games as a Yankee.[21]

Marté said he wanted to keep playing, but his shoulder and back issues prevented it.[22] He did not get any offers and retired with a career record of 23-27, a 3.48 earned-run average, a 1.26 WHIP, 36 saves, and strikeout and walk rates of 9.5/9 and 4.1/9, respectively.

After leaving the game, Marté was able to spend more time with his family. He and his wife, Flerida Marilori Marté, have three children, Angelica, Anyelina, and Dámaso Israel. At the time of the July 2024 interview, Dámaso Israel was just 12, but a second baseman with "good potential," according to his father. He also had two children with his first wife, Rosa Dianelis – Anyelis and Dámaso Jr.[23]

Dámaso Jr., at age 16 signed a one-year contract with the Los Angeles Dodgers in July 2015 for $300,000. A shortstop, he was assigned to the Dodgers team in the Arizona rookie league in June 2016. The Dodgers released him in February 2017.

In addition, the elder Marté also established a foundation called "Fundamas," the goal of which is to support children in various ways – food, money, school supplies, and more. The foundation also includes a church, of which Marté is the "shepherd," or minister. "We've helped several hundred kids over the years, and it's been great to be able to do that," he said.

Of his family, his "second mom" died about a year after he signed his first professional contract, but he said he stayed in contact with his father, Francisco, and biological mother, Ramona.

"My mother and I get along well," he said. "I didn't have any contact with my father while I was growing up, but I was always interested in knowing him, so I talked with my mom and she put me in touch. We get along well, and he even comes to our church."

SOURCES

In addition to the sources cited in the Notes, the author consulted Baseball-Reference.com, MLB.com, and a number of other sources.

Francisco Castillo served as translator for the July 2024 telephone interview.

NOTES

1   "White Sox Expecting More Fire from Marte," *Chicago Tribune*, September 9, 2005: https://www.chicagotribune.com/2005/09/09/white-sox-expecting-more-fire-from-marte/.

2   "White Sox Expecting More Fire from Marte."

3   Associated Press, "White Sox Manager Guillen Questions Injury," ESPN.com, September 14, 2005: https://www.espn.com/mlb/news/story?id=2162055.

4   For a video of the entire game, see "2005 World Series Game 3 White Sox @ Astros," on YouTube:https://www.youtube.com/watch?v=KHYwcwtzdkk'.

5   Author interview with Damaso Marté, July 8, 2024. Unless otherwise attributed, all direct quotations from the player come from this interview.

6   Mike [no last name provided], "The Rise of Damaso Marté," November 2, 2009: http://riveraveblues.com/2009/11/the-rise-of-damaso-marte-19360/.

7   Mira Wassef, "World Series: Marte Is Right Medicine for Sickly Bullpen," *Middletown* (New York) *Times Herald- Record*, November 5, 2009: https://www.recordonline.com/story/sports/mlb/2009/11/05/world-series-marte-is-right/51811212007/.

8   "Joe Girardi Looks Back on His Secret Weapon in the 2009 World Series," October 6, 2019. https://twitter.com/MLBNetwork/status/1184636141536010240?ref_src=twsrc%5Etfw%7Ctwcamp%5Etweetembed%7Ctwterm%5E1184636141536010240%7Ctwgr%5E775852e39b5662c0343bd5aa94be1f-

9818c9728e%7Ctwcon%5Es1_&ref_url=https%3A%2F%2Fyanksgoyard. com%2F2020%2F04%2F30%2Fnew-york-yankees-ten-unsung-heroes-2000s%2F. Accessed July 10, 2024.

9   Marté telephone interview.

10   https://www.baseball-almanac.com/players/trades.php?p=marteda01.

11   Marté telephone interview.

12   Telephone call with Damaso Marté, September 23, 2024.

13   Paul Sullivan, "Deal Brings Lefty Reliever," *Chicago Tribune*, March 28, 2002: https://web.archive.org/web/20140728103354/http:/articles. chicagotribune.com/2002-03-28/sports/0203280271_1_sox-bullpen-jerry-manuel-damaso-marte.

14   https://www.mlb.com/player/damaso-marte-150122.

15   "Reliever Damaso Marte Stays Put with Pirates," CBC Sports, November 27, 2006: https://www.cbc.ca/sports/baseball/reliever-damaso-marte-stays-put-with-pirates-1.629772.

16   Associated Press, "Yankees Add Nady, Marte in Trade with Pirates," ESPN. com, July 25, 2008: https://www.espn.com/mlb/news/story?id=3505686.

17   Anthony McCarron, "Yankees Place Struggling Reliever Damaso Marte on Disabled List," *New York Daily News*, May 3, 2009: https://www. nydailynews.com/2009/05/03/yankees-place-struggling-reliever-damaso-marte-on-disabled-list/.

18   Joe Pawlikoski, "Damaso Marte: Setup Man or LOOGY," riveraveblues.com, February 22, 2010: https://riveraveblues.com/2010/02/damaso-marte-setup-man-or-loogy-24222/.

19   "Yankees Reliever Damaso Marte Has Shoulder Surgery," foxsports.com, October 24, 2010: https://www.foxsports.com/stories/mlb/yankees-reliever-damaso-marte-has-shoulder-surgery.

20   Connor Orr, "Yankees' Damaso Marte Expected to Start Throwing after 2011 All-Star Break," nj.com, October 24, 2010: https://www.nj.com/yankees/2010/10/damaso_marte_expected_to_start.html.

21   "Yankees Decline Damaso Marte's $4M Option," cbsnews.com, October 19, 2011: https://www.cbsnews.com/newyork/news/yankees-decline-damaso-martes-4m-option/.

22   Marte telephone interview.

23   Marte telephone interview.

BRANDON MCCARTHY

by John Bauer

Brandon McCarthy entered professional baseball with great promise. His minor-league performances fast-tracked him to the major leagues, but that promise was undermined by a series of injuries that often paused his career. In spite of injuries, McCarthy had a big-league career spanning 13 seasons in which he played a significant role on several contending teams and even took the mound in a World Series game.

Brandon Patrick McCarthy was born in Glendale, California, on July 7, 1983. He grew to become a 6-foot-8, 225-pound right-hander, graduating from Cheyenne Mountain High School in Colorado Springs. He would become the second major-league product from Cheyenne Mountain, joining 1990s journeyman pitcher Dave Mlicki with that distinction.

After a season at Lamar Community College in Lamar, Colorado, McCarthy had the choice of either upgrading his experience to college baseball powerhouse Louisiana State University or the Chicago White Sox organization. The White Sox drafted McCarthy in the 17th round of the June

Brandon McCarthy   2005

2002 amateur draft, following a season in which he set the wins record (12-0) for national junior college semifinalist Lamar. McCarthy opted to turn pro. McCarthy later said, "I was all set to go to LSU. But certain things happened and I decided to give pro ball a shot."[1] The White Sox assigned McCarthy to their Arizona Rookie team and he went 4-4 with a 2.76 ERA over 14 starts through the remainder of the 2002 season.

Pioneer League baseball awaited McCarthy in 2003 with the White Sox' Rookie-level farm team in Great Falls, Montana. Manager Chris Cron said of McCarthy, "He's gonna be a good kid for us. The bottom line is that at this level we want guys to throw strikes, and it looks like he's going to be able to do that."[2] McCarthy described his pitching style: "I'll throw fastball, curveball, changeup. I won't really dominate anyone with my fastball – I'd rather place it around you than throw it by you."[3] He won the Jim Brewer Award as Great Falls' best pitcher, with a 9-4 record, a 3.65 ERA, and 125 strikeouts in 101 innings.

Cron served as McCarthy's manager when both were promoted to Kannapolis of the Low-A South Atlantic League for the 2004 season. After going 8-5 with a 3.64 ERA over the first half, McCarthy was named to the Northern Division staff for the Sally All-Star Game and was also rewarded with a promotion to Winston-Salem of the High-A Carolina League. Manager Nick Leyva observed, "I think he's one of the top young pitchers in our organization."[4] On July 31, McCarthy struck out 16 Myrtle Beach batters. Over eight starts at High-A, he sported a 6-0 record, a 2.08 ERA, and an astonishing 60/3 strikeout/walk ratio. On August 12, the White Sox promoted McCarthy again, to Birmingham of the Double-A Southern League.

McCarthy was clearly marked for the fast track. *Chicago Tribune* sportswriter Phil Rogers labeled him a starter candidate for 2006 and a workhorse in the mold of Jack McDowell.[5] McCarthy's tall, lean frame alone begged the comparison. Rogers noted, "McCarthy isn't a fireballer. He has command of a low-90s fastball, a hard curveball and an improved change-up. … He looks like the real thing."[6] Pitching for three teams in three leagues in 2004, McCarthy compiled a 17-6 record with a 3.14 ERA in 27 starts and led the minors in strikeouts (202 in 172 innings).

McCarthy continued his upward trajectory at the White Sox' 2005 spring training. Chicago manager Ozzie Guillén dubbed him "the best pitcher we have in camp –no doubt about it."[7] The issue was finding a place for McCarthy given the already stacked White Sox rotation. The White Sox assigned McCarthy to Charlotte of the Triple-A International League, and he opened the season with a 10-strikeout performance against Columbus. Throughout the opening weeks, there was ample speculation about the timing of McCarthy's promotion. On May 21, the call arrived.

The day after his recall, McCarthy was thrown into the deep end, starting in his first big-league game against the crosstown Cubs at Wrigley Field while facing Mark Prior. He enjoyed a successful debut by striking out six in 5⅓ innings and giving up four hits and two runs in a no-decision. Afterward, McCarthy said, "I felt a little more comfortable than I thought I would as far as nerves and jitters."[8] McCarthy had arrived just in time for some rookie hazing as the White Sox departed for a road trip, with an orange blouse and blue culottes his prescribed attire.[9]

After his next start, in which McCarthy allowed four home runs in a loss to Texas, he was returned to Charlotte so the White Sox could activate Frank Thomas from a rehabilitation stint. The Sox recalled McCarthy weeks later when pitcher Orlando Hernández was placed on the disabled list. McCarthy struggled upon his return, seeing his ERA balloon over 8.00 before being optioned to Charlotte in July. By late August, he was back in Chicago to provide rotation relief for the White Sox stretch run. On August 30 he earned his first major-league win with 7⅔ shutout innings in an 8-0 victory against Texas, and followed up that performance with a seven-inning, seven-strikeout winning performance opposite Boston's Curt Schilling.

McCarthy's September performances created a dilemma for Guillén relative to the playoff roster. Hernández struggled down the stretch as McCarthy excelled. Guillén observed, "I don't think anybody has any doubts this kid can pitch."[10] Despite McCarthy's winning the final regular season game at Cleveland, Guillén opted for the veteran Hernández over the rookie. McCarthy seemed to take the news in stride: "It sounds cheesy but it's an honor to be passed up for El Duque."[11] Although he joined the team as part of their traveling party, McCarthy did not pitch during Chicago's 2005 postseason run.

McCarthy became a fixture on the White Sox pitching staff in 2006 as a late-inning reliever with the possibility of starting should a spot open up. Remaining a big leaguer was his objective. "This year I just want to be part of the team," he said. "I think I can learn more by staying at this level."[12] The season started well enough as McCarthy threw three scoreless innings and earned the win against Cleveland in the season opener. By early May, McCarthy was struggling in the new role. He suggested his mechanics were off, saying, "I'm still trying to learn how to keep my mechanics from day to day."[13] After a run of clean appearances in June, Guillén declared McCarthy the primary set-up man. For McCarthy, the new role had its challenges. He said, "I've been taken out of that comfort level where you have to

learn a different way to pitch."[14] His season numbers reflected those challenges: In 84⅔ innings over 53 appearances, McCarthy had a 4.68 ERA.

When White Sox general manager Ken Williams traded Freddy García to Philadelphia on December 6, 2006, it seemed that a rotation spot might open. Two weeks later, however, the White Sox packaged McCarthy with minor leaguer David Paisano to obtain pitchers John Danks and Nick Masset and minor leaguer Jake Rasner, from Texas. For the Rangers, there was no question about McCarthy's pitching role as he projected as their number-three starter for the 2007 season. McCarthy's eagerness impressed the Rangers brass. GM Jon Daniels observed, "We've almost had to slow him down a little bit ... because he wants to come out and prove himself."[15]

McCarthy's Texas career got off to a rough start. At the end of April, his record stood at 1-4 with a 9.90 ERA. He recovered to win three of his next four starts before blisters and control problems prematurely ended a May 25 outing against Boston. Rangers manager Ron Washington observed, "I think he was just trying to prove the trade was worth it. His back was against the wall, and he came back fighting."[16]

The blisters sent McCarthy to the disabled list, where he mostly remained until early July. McCarthy had a promising summer return but earned only a single win in eight starts. He expected better results, saying, "I don't want to be the guy who tries real hard, gives a bulldog effort and loses. I want to be the bulldog who wins."[17] On August 16 McCarthy returned to the DL because of a stress fracture in his right shoulder blade – something that would become a recurring source of DL stints. He returned on September 11, but forearm tenderness ended his season after his second start back. McCarthy's 2007 record was 5-10 with a 4.87 ERA in 101⅔ innings.

Despite the challenges of 2007, McCarthy expressed optimism about the new season, but his season never got off the ground. As spring training wrapped up, a right forearm inflammation sent him to the 60-day DL. His layoff was extended when he aggravated the same muscle. After rehab assignments in Arizona and with Triple-A Oklahoma, McCarthy finally appeared on a big-league mound on August 23 against Cleveland. He pitched a creditable four innings, leaving with a 7-1 lead that the bullpen turned into an 8-7 loss. On September 15 his day and season ended early when a strained flexor tendon in his right middle finger sent him to the showers after five pitches. McCarthy's 2008 account closed with only five starts with a 1-1 record and a 4.09 ERA.

By now a theme was emerging about McCarthy: When he's healthy, he's good, but he seemed to spend a lot of time on the DL. Sportswriter Jeff Wilson called McCarthy a "sports medicine marvel and a headache for the Texas Rangers because he can't avoid freakish baseball injuries," while observing that McCarthy "showed the form that would have made him as effective as any other Rangers pitcher this season."[18] And with John Danks enjoying success in Chicago, comparisons between their relative fortunes could not be avoided. McCarthy observed, "If I buckle down and show what I'm supposed to and stay healthy, I know I'm good enough."[19]

McCarthy arrived at spring training in 2009 with an additional 20 pounds of weight on his frame. Although he missed a spring-training start with shoulder stiffness, he was ready for the start of the season. He won his first start, lasting five innings against Cleveland and striking out seven in the Rangers' 12-8 win. On May 24 he achieved his first complete game – a shutout – throwing 124 pitches, scattering nine hits, and striking out six in a 5-0 victory at Houston. He lasted only two more starts before an MRI revealed a stress fracture in his right shoulder blade.

After spending most of August rehabbing at Oklahoma City, McCarthy returned to the Rangers for the second game of a doubleheader against Toronto on September 1. He allowed one run in 6⅓ innings for the win. McCarthy said, "I'm going to pitch as much as I can, as many innings as I can eat up in September for everybody. I owe that back to the guys around me."[20] He closed out the season 7-4 with a 4.62 ERA in 17 starts, but his late-season return equated to 2-2 with a 4.05 ERA.

McCarthy entered 2010 spring training as one of several pitchers competing for rotation spots and he worked on his sinker and cutter to claim a starting role.[21] Circumstances again conspired against McCarthy. He struggled through the spring and was assigned to Oklahoma City. After a handful of starts, a stress fracture in his troublesome right shoulder blade sent him to the DL once again. He shuttled between the DL and Oklahoma City throughout 2010, never playing a part in what became a pennant-winning campaign for Texas. The year was not a complete bust: On December 10 McCarthy married Amanda Nelson, a model and a Cheyenne Mountain graduate with whom he had reconnected while in Texas.[22]

A free agent after the 2010 season, McCarthy signed with Oakland. He claimed the fourth spot in the Athletics 2011 rotation and after nine starts, was 1-4 but with a 3.39 ERA that included two complete-game losses. After spending June on the DL, McCarthy managed 6⅔ innings and a no-decision in a 2-1 loss to Seattle on July 4. He seemed to find his groove through the summer. On August 29 he achieved a career-high 10 strikeouts in a 2-1 complete-game loss at Cleveland and equaled that career high in a three-hit shutout against Seattle in his next start, on September 3. McCarthy's potential seemed to reveal itself, as he ended the season by shattering his prior marks for big-league production with 170⅔ innings pitched in 25 starts, which resulted in a 9-9 record, a 3.32 ERA, and a 123/25 strikeout/walk ratio.

McCarthy received the nod to pitch the Athletics' 2012 season opener at the Tokyo Dome against Seattle. The Athletics lost 3-1, but McCarthy permitted only one run while scattering six hits over seven innings. In another sign of his increased prominence, he and Amanda featured on the March cover of *ESPN: The Magazine*. Outside of baseball's competitive landscape, McCarthy and Amanda were also developing social media followings on Twitter. By mid-May of 2012 he had a 3-3 record and a 2.95 ERA. Shoulder soreness, however, caught up with McCarthy and he spent a couple of weeks on the DL. He returned in early June and won three starts during the month before a recurrence of shoulder soreness put him out of action for several more weeks before an August return.

McCarthy's September 5 start proved his final appearance of the season, but not because of recurrences of old injuries. Rather, a line drive off the bat of Angels infielder Erick Aybar struck McCarthy in the back of the head just below his right ear. McCarthy collapsed in front of the mound and, while he walked off the field without assistance, the injury was quite severe. A CT scan revealed an epidural hemorrhage, a brain contusion, and a skull fracture. He had emergency surgery and would not step on a ball field again in 2012. His season ended with an 8-6 record and a 3.24 ERA in 111 innings. There appeared some possibility that he might re-sign with Oakland, but it was Arizona that offered a two-year, $15.5 million contract.

The Diamondbacks were excited with their addition. GM Kevin Towers declared, "We're able to acquire what we feel is a frontline pitcher without having to give up any of our pitching depth."[23] McCarthy did not enjoy instant success in Phoenix, however. He was knocked around throughout April, not achieving a quality start until May 7 at Dodger Stadium. The outing in Los Angeles portended good things, as McCarthy threw eight scoreless innings against Philadelphia before a complete-game shutout at Miami on May 18. After rough early footing, McCarthy's ERA finally dropped below 5.00.

After the Rangers hammered McCarthy on May 30, chasing him from the game in the third inning, McCarthy suffered another right-shoulder breakdown. After a two-month DL stint, he returned and closed the year with a 5-11 record and a 4.53 ERA in 135 innings pitched.

Before the 2014 season, McCarthy conceded that he spent the prior season dealing with the aftereffects of the brain injury and surgery that ended his 2012 campaign. "I spent last year basically as a shell of myself and what I wanted to be," he said.[24] McCarthy had spent time working with isoBlox and Major League Baseball on pitching headgear intended to prevent injuries like his. McCarthy suggested, "It should be strong enough that literally if I got hit by the same exact ball I would have been able to keep pitching in that game."[25] The resulting product proved too bulky for on-field use, and even McCarthy declined to wear it.

After the Diamondbacks returned from a season-opening series in Australia, McCarthy pitched the home opener against San Francisco. He was not getting the results, however. Arizona lost McCarthy's first six starts, which included a new career high of 12 strikeouts in a 2-0 loss to Philadelphia on April 27. He was 1-10 with a 5.38 ERA in late June. After he beat San Diego and Pittsburgh in consecutive starts, the Diamondbacks and New York Yankees agreed a deal on July 6 that sent Vidal Nuño III to Arizona in the exchange for McCarthy and $2 million to cover half of his remaining salary.

The deal's timing worked well for the Yankees. New York placed pitcher Masahiro Tanaka on the DL just as McCarthy arrived, and manager Joe Girardi saw the benefit of McCarthy's arrival. Girardi commented, "McCarthy is an experienced starter that we expect to pitch well for guys and give us distance."[26] McCarthy found a synergy with the Yankees that was lacking in Arizona. The Yankees' approach to analytics suited McCarthy, who later said of New York, "They gave me, basically, a dossier of myself."[27] To another sportswriter he said, "It just so happened that the trade happened right when I was feeling that I was right back where I wanted to be."[28] McCarthy wound up with his most complete season yet: 10-15, 4.05 ERA, 200 innings pitched, with 175 strikeouts and only 33 walks. Moreover, his numbers in New York told a better story when separated from his first half with Arizona: 7-5 with a 2.89 ERA.

McCarthy's tenure with New York set him up to take advantage of free agency. The Los Angeles Dodgers engaged in offseason payroll restructuring to create the flexibility to commit $48 million over four seasons to McCarthy. He was being paid to be a major factor in LA's 2015 rotation. McCarthy's first four starts had mixed results, however; he won three and struck out 29, but his ERA was 5.87 and he served up nine homers. Small sample sizes may even out, but McCarthy would not have that opportunity. After he left his April 25 start against San Diego with a tight right elbow, an MRI revealed a torn elbow ligament. On April 30 the Dodgers announced that McCarthy would undergo Tommy John surgery.

McCarthy did not return to the Dodger Stadium mound until July 3, 2016, against Colorado. He lasted five scoreless frames, allowing two hits and fanning eight, in the Dodgers' 4-1 victory. It seemed vintage McCarthy. He said, "I felt surprisingly normal. ... I just sort of settled in out there."[29] After several starts, it became apparent that all was not "normal." McCarthy struggled with his command, allowing an uncharacteristically high number of walks. By mid-August he was back on the DL, not to return to action until September 25. That game proved to be the NL West Division clincher in Vin Scully's final home contest as a Dodgers broadcaster. McCarthy lasted into the sixth inning against the Rockies, striking out six, in a 4-3 extra-innings win. He was pitching for a spot on the Dodgers postseason roster, but a disastrous relief outing the following week in San Francisco decided the question. McCarthy proved

unable to retire any of the six batters he faced, allowing six earned runs on five hits and a walk.

Despite two years remaining on his contract, McCarthy's career seemed on the line heading into 2017 spring training. He said, "I'm going to give everything I can."[30] By then, McCarthy had become a resident of Phoenix and, engaging with a sport he played into his teens, he became a minority owner of Phoenix Rising FC. While the foray into soccer ownership may have suggested a post-baseball future, McCarthy beat out Alex Wood for the final spot in the Dodgers rotation.

After five starts, McCarthy sported a 3-0 record with a 3.10 ERA but a weight-room mishap that resulted in a dislocated left (nonthrowing) shoulder placed him on the disabled list. He returned to the mound on May 15, enjoying a run of starts that improved his mark to 6-3 with a 2.87 ERA in late June. Facing Colorado on June 25, McCarthy exited after three innings and he knew something was off. He explained, "It certainly wasn't the usual feeling. Something was going on there with my cutter and four-seamer."[31] He headed to the DL with knee tendinitis, returning July 8 to make three starts before blisters sent him back. McCarthy did not pitch again until September 23, when he made the first of three bullpen appearances to prove his postseason readiness.

The Dodgers did not select McCarthy for the NL Division Series or League Championship Series, but activated him for the team's first World Series since 1988. McCarthy received the bullpen call against Houston in Game Two, taking the mound in the 11th inning of a 5-5 game. He allowed a single to Cameron Maybin before George Springer blasted the ball into the right-field pavilion to give the Astros a 7-5 lead. McCarthy recovered to retire Alex Bregman, Jose Altuve, and Carlos Correa. The Dodgers clawed back a run in the bottom of the inning, but lost the game as McCarthy took the loss. His first postseason appearance proved to be his last. He did not appear again as the Dodgers lost the Series in seven games.

In December McCarthy was swept into a trade that had more to do with resetting the Dodgers' luxury-tax threshold than it did with positioning the club for 2018. They sent McCarthy, Charlie Culberson, Adrián González, Scott Kazmir, and cash (partly to cover McCarthy's salary) to Atlanta in return for Matt Kemp. The Braves were in a rebuilding cycle at the time of the deal, but it was believed that McCarthy's experience would assist the Braves' young arms. McCarthy had a record of 4-0 with a 3.09 ERA at the end of April, surviving starting the second-coldest game in major-league history (at 27 degrees) in Denver on April 6[32] and dodging the DL following a partial shoulder dislocation covering first base in an April 11 game against Washington. McCarthy was hammered in consecutive May outings against San Francisco and Miami, and by June he was missing starts. The Braves, however, were off to a great start and it appeared the rebuild might be ahead of schedule.

Atlanta defeated Baltimore, 7-3, on June 24, to take a 2½ game lead over Philadelphia. McCarthy earned that victory with five strikeouts in five innings of work in what was the 69th and final win of his major-league career.

On June 28 right knee tendinitis sent McCarthy to the DL. By August, he announced the 2018 season would be his last. McCarthy said, "I'm done after this. This is it."[33] McCarthy appeared in three games with Triple-A Gwinnett, but never made it back to a major-league mound. Injuries had caught up to him. In announcing after the season that he would join the Texas Rangers as a special assistant to the general manager, McCarthy said, "Everything hurts. Sitting through a four-hour meeting seemed easier than a one-hour workout. I wanted to go out on my own terms rather than being spit out by the baseball washing machine."[34]

After three seasons with the Rangers front office, McCarthy's interest had diverted to soccer. The interest was rewarded when Phoenix Rising FC won the 2023 playoffs for the United Soccer League championship, the second tier of US professional soccer. (As of January 2025, he remains a board member and Sporting Director of the club.)

McCarthy's career encompassed 13 major-league seasons, with a 69-75 record in 255 appearances (197 of them starts), a 4.20 ERA, and 908 strikeouts.

SOURCES

In addition to the sources cited in the Notes, the author consulted BASE-BALL-REFERENCE.COM.

NOTES

1   Scott Mansch, "Opening-Day Starter Poses Imposing Figure," *Great Falls* (Montana) *Tribune*, June 14, 2003: 1S.

2   "Opening-Day Starter."

3   Scott Mansch, " Opening-Day Starter."

4   Dan Collins, "Hogs, Indians Split," *Winston-Salem Journal*, July 6, 2004: 1C, 5C.

5   Phil Rogers, "Sox Prospect Can Deal," *Chicago Tribune*, September 5, 2004: 3-4.

6   "Sox Prospect."

7   Mark Gonzales, "Podsednik Doesn't Demand Center Stage," *Chicago Tribune*, March 16, 2005: 4-4.

8   David Haugh, "Mr. Unflappable," *Chicago Tribune*, May 23, 2005: 3-6.

9   "Mr. Unflappable."

10   Dave van Dyck, "Rotation Situation Looming," *Chicago Tribune*, September 12, 2005: 3-3.

11   Mike Downey, "Fun Should Factor In," *Chicago Tribune*, October 11, 2005: 7-2.

12   Phil Rogers, "McCarthy Will Take Whatever He Can Get," *Chicago Tribune*, April 3, 2006: 7-3.

13   Dave van Dyck, "Retooling His Mechanics," *Chicago Tribune*, May 4, 2006: 4-4.

14   Mark Gonzales, "McCarthy's Learning Curve Has Been Steep," *Chicago Tribune*, September 20, 2006: 4-3.

15   Jan Hubbard, "Daniels Hoping Rotation Blossoms During Spring," *Fort Worth Star-Telegram*, February 13, 2007: D1, D5.

16   Gil LeBreton, "Don't Put McCarthy in the Same Category," *Fort Worth Star-Telegram*, June 13, 2007: D1.

17   Jennifer Floyd Engel, "On Second Thought, It Was a Good Deal," *Fort Worth Star-Telegram*: July 22, 2007: 2C.

18   Jeff Wilson, "Pitcher Hurt, but Not Broken," *Fort Worth Star-Telegram*, September 19, 2008: A5.

19   Jeff Wilson, "McCarthy Ready for a Fresh Start and Healthier Results," *Fort Worth Star-Telegram*, February 28, 2009: 49.

20   Jeff Wilson, "Spotlight: Brandon McCarthy," *Fort Worth Star-Telegram*, September 8, 2009: 3D.

21   Jeff Wilson, "McCarthy Hoping Refined Mechanics Keep Him off DL," *Fort Worth Star-Telegram*, March 7, 2010: 1C.

22   Paul Cardoso, "Who Is Brandon McCarthy's Wife? His Contract, Injury and Other Facts," *Naija News* (Nigeria), March 30, 2022, accessed at https://www.naijanews.com/buzz/people/who-is-brandon-mccarthys-wife-his-contract-injury-and-other-facts/.

23   Nick Piecoro, "D-Backs Bolster Staff, *Arizona Republic* (Phoenix), December 8, 2012: C1.

24   Nick Piecoro, "No Longer Playing Catch-Up, Mccarthy Feels 'a Lot Stronger,'" *Arizona Republic*, March 31, 2014: C1.

25   Nick Piecoro, "Grace to Stay in Organization," *Arizona Republic*, December 21, 2013: C2.

26   Pat Borzi, "Yankees Make Pitching and Hitting Moves Before Dispatching Twins," *New York Times*, July 6, 2014: https://www.nytimes.com/2014/07/07/sports/baseball/Yankees-Alfonso-Soriano-Brandon-McCarthy-Vidal-Nuno-Diamondbacks.html.

27   Dylan Hernandez, "In Final Analysis, Numbers Added Up to a Turnaround," *Los Angeles Times*, March 9, 2015: D5.

28   David Waldstein, "Arsenal Refilled, a New Yankee Throws a Gem," *New York Times*, July 19, 2014: https://www.nytimes.com/2014/07/20/sports/baseball/for-new-yankee-stadium-wasn8217t-a-nice-place-to-visit.html.

29   Mike DiGiovanna, "Back From Long Layoff," *Los Angeles Times*, July 4, 2016: D1.

30   Bill Shaikin, "Thrown Off Tracks by 'yips,'" *Los Angeles Times*, March 4, 2017: D4.

31   Mike DiGiovanna, "McCarthy Temporarily Loses Control," *Los Angeles Times*, June 26, 2017: D3.

32   Danny Summers, "From the Sidelines: Little-Known Facts About Brandon Mccarthy's Career in the Majors," *Colorado Springs Gazette*, July 23, 2019, accessed at https://gazette.com/cheyenneedition/from-the-sidelines-little-known-facts-about-brandon-mccarthys-career-in-the-majors/article_082fe3a2-a980-11e9-b6bf-772df31f2a4f.html.

33   Mark Bowman, "McCarthy to Retire after 2018 Season," mlb.com, August 14, 2018 https://www.mlb.com/news/brandon-mccarthy-will-retire-after-2018-season-c290323362#:~:text=McCarthy%20to%20retire%20after%202018%20season,-Dealing%20with%20knee&text=%22I'm%20done%20after%20this,the%20rest%20of%20my%20life.

34   T.R. Sullivan, "Texas Lands Wisdom, Deals Robinson to Cards," December 11, 2018, mlb.com *https://www.mlb.com/rangers/news/rangers-acquire-patrick-wisdom-from-cardinals-c301726512*.

PABLO OZUNA

By Jim Margalus

Pablo Ozuna was born on August 25, 1974, in Santo Domingo, Dominican Republic. Until 2002 Ozuna was believed to have been born on August 25, 1978, and this had a dramatic impact on the way he was viewed in his first several seasons in professional baseball.

The son of Sotero Ozuna, who was employed at a sugar mill and also worked as a fisherman and barber, and Carmen Roque, a homemaker, Ozuna grew up in Santo Domingo as the youngest of eight children. Multiple Ozuna siblings tried out for major-league teams, and the second-youngest child, Pedro, signed with the Yankees in 1994, and played a year with the Gulf Coast Yankees in 1996. [1]

That same year, Pablo Ozuna signed with the St. Louis Cardinals at the perceived age of 16. He experienced immediate success. He batted .323 in his first 56 games as a pro with Johnson City of the Appalachian League in 1997, then followed it up by hitting .357/.400/.494 with 62 stolen bases in his first full season, with Peoria in the Class-A Midwest League.

This production, all of it coming at shortstop, and most of it before Ozuna turned his listed age of 20, put him on the map. He was named the Most Valuable Player of the Midwest League, and the Cardinals named him their Minor League Player of the Year for 1998, although his time in the organization was limited. On December 14, 1998, the Cardinals traded Ozuna, Braden Looper, and Armando Almanza to the Florida Marlins for Edgar Renteria. After making the trade, St. Louis general manager Walt Jocketty said Ozuna "was the toughest one to give up."[2]

Heading into the 1999 season, Ozuna was considered a top-10 prospect by *Baseball America*.[3] His first go-around at Double A, with the Eastern League's Portland Sea Dogs, posed his first professional challenge. He hit .281/.315/.400 in 117 games. Besides losing 76 points in batting average, he also saw sizable decreases in both walks (from 29 to 13) and stolen bases (from 62 to 31).

However, Ozuna's production rebounded well enough in 2000 to earn him a couple of auditions with the Marlins. They called him up in April as a temporary replacement for Luis Castillo, who headed to the disabled list with a back injury. Ozuna made his major-league debut on April 23 against the Phillies – at second base, as the Marlins had moved him from shortstop after the 1999 season – and went 1-for-4. His first hit was an infield single off Robert Person. He appeared in four more games before the Marlins optioned him back to Portland, but after hitting .308/.368/.433 with better plate discipline, the team brought him back to Miami as a September call-up.

Ozuna mostly appeared as a pinch-runner, scoring his first run in that capacity on September 17 against the Phillies, but he made his final start of the season on September 30 and went 3-for-4 with his first double to finish the year batting an even .333 (8-for-24).

By the next time Ozuna reached the majors, it was as a utility player just trying to get by.

Ozuna broke his left wrist when he was hit by a pitch in winter ball after the 2000 season, then had it broken again by another HBP in 2001 spring training. He underwent surgery to repair torn cartilage and missed the entire 2001 season.[4] When he returned to action in spring training in 2002, he had effectively aged four years.

As a ramification from changes in national security measures after the terrorist attacks on September 11, 2001, anybody applying for a work visa in the United States had to show a birth certificate.[5] This had had unintended effects

Pablo Ozuna　　2005

in baseball, because as foreign-born players reported to their teams in the spring of 2002, nearly 300 of them had new birthdays assigned to them.[6]

The majority of the players hailed from the Dominican Republic, because the US Embassy in Santo Domingo had become increasingly aware of false birthdates and required additional verification.[7] Ozuna was among them, and his birthdate was revised to August 25, 1974. Suddenly, the 23-year-old Ozuna was 27.

"I had tried out a few times with the Cardinals and wasn't signed, so I'd grown disenchanted. I'd even left baseball for a year or so," Ozuna said. "I played in an amateur league and Robert (Bobby) Díaz was told about how well I was hitting. He thought they were talking about my brother, until someone said 'no, not Pedro...Pablo, the youngest one.' Iván Díaz, Bobby's son, gave me his glove and told me to go to third base, then left field. (Cardinals coach) José Oquendo saw me hustling and running and said, "We like this guy.'"

"Four years were shaved off, but I wasn't affected when it was revealed. When you're hungry and overlooked, you'd do it a hundred times if need be to reach your goal."[8]

While Ozuna reached the majors, his prospect performances wouldn't have resonated as much as they did if teams and evaluators knew that he was posting those impressive numbers against younger competition, rather than older players. The Marlins certainly wouldn't have considered him a potential replacement for Renteria, given that Renteria turned out to be two years younger than Ozuna the whole time.

The recontextualization of his record, along with lingering effects from the wrist injury, put Ozuna on the journeyman course from that point forward. He made the Marlins' Opening Day roster in 2022, but only as a temporary roster-filler for the first week of the season, and that set the tone for the rest of the season. The Marlins called Ozuna up from the minors four times, and his first 18 appearances came off the bench, including a pinch-hitting appearance against the Mets on July 4 that resulted in a two-run triple for his first major-league runs batted in. He wasn't penciled into a starting lineup until the second game of a doubleheader on September 3.

Ozuna thrived at Triple-A Calgary (Pacific Coast League) around all the major-league cameos, hitting .326/.371/.475 in 77 games, but it didn't move the needle with the Marlins. Instead, on November 16, 2002, Florida traded him to Colorado in a six-player deal. This time, he was an undercard in the package, as the Marlins bundled him with Preston Wilson, Charles Johnson, and Vic Darensbourg in exchange for Mike Hampton, Juan Pierre, and cash to offset Hampton's considerable salary. (The Marlins then flipped Hampton with cash to the Braves in a salary dump.)

With Colorado, Ozuna bounced between levels and positions. He spent most of the year at Triple-A Colorado Springs, dividing his playing time between third, second, shortstop, and center field. He resurfaced in the majors for the final month and a half, hitting .200/.273/.225 in 17 games and 45 plate appearances. The Rockies released him after the season, and while he signed on as a nonroster spring-training invitee with the Detroit Tigers on January 9, 2004, he spent the entire season in the Phillies organization after Philadelphia acquired him for cash before Opening Day.[9] He fared well for Triple-A Scranton/Wilkes-Barre, hitting .307/.344/.415 in 126 games, but whenever the Phillies needed to call up an infielder from their Triple-A roster, they called on Chase Utley, then in his second season as a major leaguer.

After the 2004 season, Ozuna was once again a free agent, and his career was at a crossroads.

"The Phillies wanted me to re-sign for 2005, but they hadn't called me up despite my numbers," Ozuna said. "I had an offer to play in Japan for a million dollars, but my friend Felix José told me [White Sox manager] Ozzie Guillén was interested in me since he'd seen me play in the DR. I asked my mother for her advice, and she suggested I try one more year in the US."[10]

On January 19, 2005, he signed a minor-league deal with the White Sox with an invitation to spring training. Now 30 years old, Ozuna arrived at camp in Tucson to compete for a utility infield spot behind the set lineup of Joe Crede at third, Juan Uribe at shortstop, and Tadahito Iguchi at second base. Wilson Valdez had the inside track for the spot, since he was already on the 40-man roster and had played in 19 games the previous September, but Ozuna won over White Sox coaches by hitting during the entirety of spring training.

"Ozuna came to spring training with a mission – to make the team," said manager Ozzie Guillén two weeks before Opening Day.[11]

And thanks to a record-setting spring, Ozuna accomplished the mission. His .527 batting average was the highest by any White Sox player with more than 40 at-bats in spring training.[12] As the start of the season neared, the White Sox placed Valdez on waivers and purchased Ozuna's contract.

"At the time, I had long hair, and Ozzie told me, 'The team owner said that if you cut your hair, you'll make the team.' I told him I'd do it right away," Ozuna said. "That was his way of telling me I'd made the team."[13]

In Chicago, Ozuna found stability due to his willingness to play irregularly. Along with 10 plate appearances as a pinch-hitter and seven pinch-running opportunities, he logged playing time at every position save pitcher, catcher, and center field. A minor injury to Scott Podsednik pressed Ozuna into a left-field rotation in mid-April, and he further showcased his adaptability in an April 24 game against the Kansas City Royals when he came off the bench to deliver a go-ahead RBI double with two outs in the eighth inning, then finished the game playing first base for the first time in his professional career, even making a diving stop on a grounder by Mike Sweeney in the ninth.

"I felt OK, because I'm an infielder," Ozuna said after the game. "I'm ready for everything. That's my job."[14]

Ozuna logged 217 plate appearances in this fashion over the course of the season, with his only regular work coming at third base in late August when Crede suffered a hairline fracture of his middle finger. Ozuna made 11 starts over the course of 14 games, all at third base, but when Crede returned from the injured list, Ozuna returned to the jack-of-all-trades lifestyle.

Ozuna hit a respectable .276 in 70 games in 2005, albeit with little power or patience. He finished the year still in search of his first major-league homer, collecting just nine extra-base hits and seven walks. His ability to fill in at nearly any position on short notice proved valuable to the division-winning club over the long season, but when the postseason arrived with every White Sox infielder in full working order, Ozuna's October opportunities were limited to just two pinch-running appearances in the American League Championship Series.

That said, one of them turned out to be critical to the White Sox' eventual championship.

Ozuna came off the bench in Game One to run for Carl Everett after Everett reached on an error to start the ninth, but he was forced out at second on an unsuccessful sacrifice attempt by Aaron Rowand.

The next night, Ozuna again came off the bench as a pinch-runner in the ninth, but under far more dramatic circumstances. A.J. Pierzynski had just extended the inning by reaching on a controversial dropped third-strike call, sprinting toward first base as Los Angeles catcher Josh Paul rolled the ball to the mound and headed to the dugout along with the rest of the team. When play resumed after minutes of argument from Angels manager Mike Scioscia, Ozuna stood in Pierzynski's place at first base with Crede at the plate. This time Ozuna made it to second with a stolen base on an 0-and-1 pitch. One pitch later, Crede doubled off the base of the left-field wall. Ozuna scored the game-winning run in a 2-1 White Sox victory. Ozuna did not appear in another postseason game that year.

In fact, Ozuna was the only nonpitcher Guillén didn't use in the 14-inning Game Three of the World Series, but he initially wrote Ozuna's name on the lineup card for a double switch in the bottom of the 13th. Guillén changed his mind and opted for the switch-hitting Geoff Blum, who then hit the game-winning homer off right-handed Ezequiel Astacio in the 14th.[15]

Every other player on the 24-man roster made at least one appearance in the World Series, but Ozuna earned his World Series ring regardless. After the season, he earned another reward when he signed a one-year, $500,000 contract.[16] It was his first major-league contract, and although it contained a provision that reduced his salary to $330,000 if

he was sent to the minors, Ozuna never spent a day in Triple A during his White Sox years.

He secured his spot on Guillén's roster with a career year in 2006, hitting .328/.365/.444 in 203 plate appearances. After 145 major-league games spanning five seasons, Ozuna hit his first homer, and in dramatic fashion. On May 3 against Seattle's Eddie Guardado at US Cellular Field, he came off the bench with two outs in the ninth and hit Guardado's first pitch into the left-field seats to tie the game at 5-5. With the same score two innings later, Ozuna turned a two-out grounder through the middle into a hustle double, then scored on Uribe's single to win the game.[17] On May 22 the White Sox beat the Oakland Athletics, 5-4, in 10 innings on a two-out Ozuna squeeze bunt.[18]

Ozuna summoned his 2005 spring-training form during the first half of 2006, hitting .413 in 100 plate appearances dispersed over 42 games. While Guillén joked that he would use his powers as the American League's manager in the All-Star Game to put Ozuna on the roster,[19] he said that Ozuna's torrid half wouldn't persuade him to carve out a spot in the starting lineup.

"I don't think Ozuna can play every day," Guillén told reporters. "That's my opinion. … The way we used him … we're better off using him the same way."[20]

Ozuna regressed immediately after the All-Star break, opening the second half 3-for-36. He righted the ship afterward to hit .344 over his final 66 plate appearances of 2006, but whether Ozuna ran hot or cold, all of his ups and downs were contained to sporadic playing time in the utility role to which he was accustomed.

After reaching the peak of the sport with the World Series champion White Sox in 2005 and putting together a career year in 2006, Ozuna was rewarded with additional security when the White Sox in December agreed to an $800,000 contract for 2007,[21] then agreed to an additional $1.25 million extension that covered the 2008 season before Opening Day.[22]

But Ozuna got off to a quiet start in 2007, and did not get the opportunity to hit through it. His season ended on May 27 when he fractured his right leg and tore an ankle ligament rounding first base in the first inning of a game against the Tampa Bay Rays.[23]

Ozuna returned to the field for Opening Day in 2008, and while he returned to his usual levels of production by hitting .281/.313/.328, it was over increasingly sporadic playing time. He started just 16 games over the first half of the season, drew just two walks, and was unsuccessful on his only two stolen-base attempts.

Still, Ozuna was playing well enough that it caught the White Sox clubhouse by surprise when the team designated him for assignment on July 8. With Uribe still capable of playing all around the infield, and with journeyman outfielder Dewayne Wise providing surprising production, Ozuna's versatility wasn't as much needed.

Guillén took no pleasure in the decision.

"To me, it was one of the hardest things I ever did because Ozuna is doing something that isn't his fault," Guillén said. "This is the part of the game I don't like to do, especially with Ozuna. If it was somebody else, (bleep) it. I'll get him out of here as soon as possible."[24]

Paul Konerko, whose return from the injured list necessitated the roster move that resulted in Ozuna's DFA, said, "Pablo was one of the most, if not the most, well-liked guys. In the years he was here, I never saw him not go about his business the right way."[25]

Ozuna didn't spend long on the open market, signing with the Los Angeles Dodgers for the remainder of the 2008 season.[26] A return to the National League meant more pinch-running and defensive-replacement duties and fewer plate appearances. He played in 36 games for the Dodgers, but came to the plate only 33 times, hitting .219/.242/.375, although he did manage to hit his third and final major-league homer on September 19 against the Giants, accounting for the only run scored off Barry Zito in a 7-1 loss to San Francisco.

The Dodgers won the NL West championship with an 84-78 record and swept the Chicago Cubs in the Division Series before losing to the Phillies in five games in the NL Championship Series. Ozuna made his only postseason appearance in the Dodgers' final game, bunting into a groundout as a pinch-hitter for pitcher Chan Ho Park in the third inning.

That turned out to be Ozuna's final appearance in a major-league game. The Dodgers declined his club option after the season, and although he returned to the Phillies on a minor-league contract in January 2009, he didn't make the team out of spring training. Instead, he reported to Triple-A Lehigh Valley, where he played 51 games before he was handed a 50-game suspension in June for violating baseball's minor-league drug program due to an elevated ratio of testosterone to epitestosterone.[27] The Phillies released him two months later.[28]

Ozuna continued his playing career outside the purview of Major League Baseball, playing with the Newark Bears of the independent Atlantic League in 2010, and three seasons in the Dominican Winter League afterward. He last played 14 games for the Tigres del Licey during the 2012-13 season, briefly overlapping with his 21-year-old cousin and future major-league star Marcell Ozuna, who played for Gigantes del Cibao.

After retiring from baseball, Ozuna turned his attention to real estate in the Santo Domingo area. He said he began investing during his playing days with the Marlins, and his portfolio includes homes, apartments, commercial lots, and a gym.[29]

SOURCES

In addition to the sources cited in the Notes, the author consulted Baseball-Reference.com and Baseball America's prospect coverage, and SABR member Tony Oliver Diaz conducted a Spanish-language interview with Pablo Ozuna on January 15, 2025.

NOTES

1   Tony Oliver Diaz, interview with Pablo Ozuna, January 15, 2025. Hereafter noted as Ozuna interview.

2   "Pitchers Are Likely to Hit 8th Again," *St. Louis Post Dispatch*, December 16, 1998: D1.

3   "1999 Top 100 Prospects," BaseballAmerica.com. https://web.archive.org/web/19991012195112/http:/baseballamerica.com/features/top100/2-20.html.

4   "Millar Puts His Mark on Bats, Territory," *South Florida Sun-Sentinel*, February 23, 2002: 4C.

5   Michele Orecklin, "Keeping Score," Time.com, March 4, 2002. https://time.com/archive/6665899/people-mar-4-2002/.

6   "Dawn of a New Age," BaseballAmerica.com, July 8, 2002. https://www.baseballamerica.com/today/features/agechart.html

7   Murray Chass, "Inside Baseball: Changing Birthdates: An Ancient Practice," *New York Times*, February 24, 2002.

8   Ozuna interview.

9   Todd Zolecki, "Team Pleased as All Phillies in Place in Lineup," *Philadelphia Inquirer*, March 29, 2004: E-5.

10 Ozuna interview.

11 Mark Gonzales, "No Stretch to Say Buehrle Is Perfect," *Chicago Tribune*, March 20, 2005: A6.

12 Mark Gonzales, "It's Official: Ozuna, Widger on Roster," *Chicago Tribune*, April 3, 2005: 3-7.

13 Ozuna interview.

14 Scot Gregor, "White Sox 'Work Out' Another Victory," *Arlington Heights* (Illinois) *Daily Herald*, April 25, 2005: 1.

15 John Harper, "Blum Fitting Hero for Unlikely Sox," *New York Daily News*, October 27, 2005: 74.

16 Associated Press, "Ozuna Re-Ups with ChiSox," ESPN.com, November 18, 2005.

17 Dave van Dyck, "Ozuna or Later," *Chicago Tribune*, May 4, 2006: 4-1.

18 Dave van Dyke, "Squeezy Does It," *Chicago Tribune*, May 23, 2006: 4-1.

19 Mark Gonzales, "Guillen Partial to Sox as All-Stars," *Chicago Tribune*, May 11, 2006: 4-4.

20 Mark Gonzales, "Ozuna Hot but Won't Be a Regular," *Chicago Tribune*, June 17, 2006: 3-3.

21 Associated Press, "White Sox Agree to Terms with Ozuna," ESPN.com, December 5, 2006.

22 Associated Press, "Thornton, Ozuna Agree to Contracts with White Sox," ESPN.com, April 1, 2007.

23 Dave van Dyck, "Versatile Ozuna Out for 2 Months," *Chicago Tribune*, May 28, 2007: 4-6.

24 Scot Gregor. "Ozuna's Departure Unpleasant for Guillen," *Arlington Heights Daily Herald*, July 9, 2008: 3.

25 "Ozuna's Departure Unpleasant for Guillen."

26 "Dodgers Sign Utility Man Ozuna," *Hermosa Beach* (California) *Daily Breeze*, July 21, 2008.

27 Associated Press, "Phillies' Ozuna Suspended 50 Games," ESPN.com, June 11, 2009.

28 Associated Press, "Phillies Release Ozuna," ESPN.com, August 8, 2009.

29 Ozuna interview.

TIMO PÉREZ

By Alan Cohen

*"An indispensable playoff weapon
here on pocket change."*
– Sportswriter Mike Lopresti commenting on
Timo Pérez, October 17, 2000.[1]

*"I'm still very new at this; I don't
know everything that entails fame. I love
the fans. All game long, they're yelling
at me and having fun with me."*
– Timo Pérez, October 16, 2000[2]

Timoniel "Timo" Pérez was born on April 8, 1975, in Bani in the Dominican Republic, and remained there through his high-school years. Little more is known of his childhood experiences.

Pérez's first professional playing experience came in Japan. He spent four seasons (1996-1999) with Hiroshima of the Japan Central League. When he asked to be released from his contract with Hiroshima in 1999, he was assigned to the Japan minor league, becoming a free agent under Japanese baseball rules.[3]

On March 27, 2000, it was announced that the 5-foot-9, 180-pound lefty had signed a minor-league contract with the New York Mets organization. He was first assigned to Class-A St. Lucie (Florida State League), where he played in eight games and batted .355. He was quickly promoted to Triple-A Norfolk of the International League, where he batted .357 in 72 games.

Pérez was called up to the Mets at the end of August, and he made his debut with New York on September 1. In a tight game in St. Louis, he was called upon to pinch-hit with two out in the ninth inning. He singled off Dave Veres, but was thrown out trying to steal second base; the Cardinals scored in the bottom of the ninth and won the game, 6-5.

The Mets, who had entered September leading their division, got off to a horrific start in September. They lost seven of their first eight games, including a game in Cincinnati when Pérez, batting in the first spot in the lineup, had two doubles. But the Mets righted their ship, and Pérez played a significant role down the stretch, batting .286 with six extra-base hits in 24 games as New York tracked down a wild-card berth.

In the first playoff game against San Francisco, on October 4, Mets right fielder Derek Bell was injured in the bottom of the third inning and left the game. Pérez entered the game as a pinch-hitter in the seventh inning and moved to right field in a double-switch. He was inserted in the lineup the next day as the starting right fielder. Now, there have been other right fielders who took center stage in New York in October, but for the next fortnight Timo Pérez was Señor Octobre.

In nine games against the Giants and Cardinals, Pérez provided a career's worth of highlights. He went 5-for-15 in the three wins against the Giants and 6-for-19 in the four wins against the Cardinals.

On October 5, in the second game of the Division Series against the Giants at San Francisco, Pérez had his coming-out party. The Mets, who had lost the first game of the series, needed the win to avoid going two games down in the best-of-five series. After striking out to lead off the game, Pérez came to bat in the second inning with the bases loaded. The Mets had loaded the bases without the benefit of a hit, and there were two men out. Pérez singled up the middle off Shawn Estes, and Jay Payton and Mike Bordick scored to give the Mets a 2-0 lead.

Timo Perez   2005

The Giants picked up a run in the bottom of the inning, and the Mets clung to a scant one-run lead going into the ninth. Félix Rodríguez was on to pitch for the Giants and registered two quick outs. Pérez came to the plate and singled to left field. Edgardo Alfonzo then homered to give the Mets a 4-1 lead. Three outs away from winning the game, the Mets pitching staff squandered the lead. Barry Bonds doubled, chasing starter Al Leiter from the game. An infield hit by Jeff Kent and a homer by J.T. Snow off Armando Benitez knotted the score and forced extra innings. The Mets pushed across a run in the 10th inning to even the series.

The series resumed at Shea Stadium two days later and once again extra innings were needed. Pérez had only one hit in the game, but it brought in the Mets' first run. In the bottom of the sixth inning, with the Mets trailing 2-0, Pérez singled home Bordick. The Mets tied the game in the eighth and won, 3-2, on Benny Agbayani's 13th-inning homer.

The Mets clinched the series the next day and although it was Bobby Jones who deservedly got the headlines, Pérez singled and scored with Jones on a double by Alfonso to extend the Mets' lead to 4-0 as they advanced to the NLCS for a second consecutive year.

Timo wasted no time against St. Louis. He doubled in the first inning and scored the game's first run on Mike Piazza's double. The Mets won the opener, 6-2. Game Two went into the late innings with the score tied 3-3. In the top of the eighth, with two out, Pérez singled and when Alfonso singled to short center field, Pérez, taking off on the 3-and-2 pitch, ran all the way home and the Mets had the lead.[4] Although the Cardinals tied the game once again, the Mets scored a run in the ninth to give them a 6-5 win.

In Game Three, at the Mets' Shea Stadium, Pérez singled and scored in the first, but the Mets were already behind and fell to Andy Benes, 8-2.

In Game Four the Mets were down once again in the first inning, but the results would be far different. Pérez doubled leading off against Darryl Kile to ignite a four-run rally, fueled by five doubles, and the Mets added another three runs in the second to take a commanding lead. During the three-run rally, Pérez singled and stole second base. That commanding lead proved to be not so commanding, and the Cardinals cut the margin to two runs in the fifth inning, knocking out Mets starter Bobby Jones. Pérez reached base on an error by third baseman Fernando Tatis in the sixth and came around to score as the Mets widened the gap to four runs and went on to win, 10-6.

With one more win, the Mets would be on their way to the World Series. Pérez, for the fourth time in five games, led things off with a base hit. He stole second and scored on Alfonso's single, giving the Mets the lead. It was the only run they would need as they won 7-0 to advance to New York's first Subway Series since 1956. But the Pérez magic did not continue. He had only two base hits in the World Series and the Yankees won in five games.

Game One was scoreless as the Mets came to bat in the sixth inning at Yankee Stadium. Pérez, leading off, singled. With the single, he had hit safely in nine consecutive postseason games. Two outs later, he was still at first base. Todd Zeile doubled to left, high off the wall, and Pérez tried to score from first base, only to be gunned down at home. He had not been hustling on the play, thinking that the ball could be a home run. By the time he got things in gear, David Justice had flawlessly grabbed the ball off the wall and unleashed a throw that was relayed by shortstop Derek Jeter to catcher Jorge Posada.[5] The game remained scoreless, and the Yankees won in 12 innings.

"I was confused by the ball. I saw the fans put their hands up, and I thought it was a home run. I slowed up a little. If I would've run all the way through, I would've scored. I have no excuses about it."
– Timo Pérez, October 21, 2000.[6]

Pérez returned to the Mets in 2001 and could not replicate his 2000 playoff heroics. A trip to the disabled list in April with a pulled groin did not help matters and Pérez's productivity was not as expected. On July 17 he was sent back to the minors and spent 48 games with the Norfolk Tides, regaining his hitting eye. He batted .359 at Triple A and rejoined the Mets in September. His last 18 games with the Mets in 2001 were essentially a mirror of his first 67. He batted .244 down the stretch to bring his season's average to .247. The Mets finished two games over .500.

After the season, Pérez played for Licey in the Dominican Winter League and suffered a broken hand. He had surgery on the hamate bone in his right wrist and was a bit late reporting in the spring as it was discovered that he had shaved a couple of years off his age when completing a form to play in Japan back in 1996. Once everything was sorted out, Pérez returned to the field.

Pérez posted the best numbers of his career in 2002. His batting average was over .300 for most of the season. Playing in a career-high 136 games (starting 107), he finished at .295, the highest in his career. In August, the Mets had seen any chance for a postseason berth vanish when they lost 12 straight games to slip to 58-69, putting them in fifth place, 23 games behind the division leaders.

On August 24 Pérez entered the game at Colorado in the fifth inning and regained some of the magic from 2000. In the ninth inning, with two outs and the Mets trailing the Rockies 2-1, Mets shortstop Joe McEwing prolonged the inning with a single, bringing Pérez to the plate. Pérez homered off Jose Jimenez to give the Mets a 3-2 lead, and they tacked on a pair of insurance runs for a 5-2 win. It was Pérez's seventh home run of the season. The following night proved interesting. Pérez's exuberance in celebrating his homer had not been well received by the Rockies, and Timo's head was targeted not once, but twice in the next game. Denny Neagle threw behind him in the first inning.

GRINDERS AND GAMERS

In the ninth inning, Kent Mercker threw above Pérez's head and was ejected along with manager Clint Hurdle.[7]

Pérez was in a Mets uniform for the fourth consecutive year in 2003 and batted .269 in 127 games. The Mets were in decline and finished the season with a 66-95 record, in last place in the NL East Division. As the season advanced to September, the Mets were reduced to a spoiler role. They hosted Atlanta for three games and swept the front-runners. In the third game of the series, on September 3, Pérez, hitting in the number three slot, contributed to a 9-3 win with two RBIs. In the first inning, his sacrifice fly brought in Roger Cedeño with the game's first run. In the bottom of the fifth, Pérez stretched the Mets' advantage to 6-1 with a home run off the right-field scoreboard. It was his fourth homer of the season and his last as a Met.

On March 27, 2004, as spring training wound down, Pérez was traded to the Chicago White Sox for relief pitcher Matt Ginter. The White Sox opened the season in New York against the Yankees and Pérez showed some of his old flair in his second game of the season. It was his first start for his new team and, with Chicago trailing 1-0 he singled leading off the top of the fifth. He stole second base, took third on a wild pitch, and scored the tying run on a sacrifice fly by Willie Harris. An inning later, Pérez walked and scored as the White Sox tallied five times and assumed a 9-1 lead. The Yankees scored two late runs to make the final score 9-3. Pérez finished the season with a .246 batting average and 5 homers in 103 games (70 starts) as the White Sox finished with an 83-79 record and a second-place finish in the AL Central Division.

The next season, 2005, the White Sox climbed to the top of baseball. Pérez got into only 70 games and batted .218. There were some highlights. On April 9 at Minnesota, with the score tied, 3-3, Pérez led off the seventh inning with a home run, giving the White Sox a lead they would not relinquish. Chicago scored four runs in the inning and prevailed, 8-5. Pérez's next big game came on May 1 against the Tigers at Chicago's US Cellular Field (previously Comiskey Park). In the bottom of the third, he batted with the bases loaded and two out. His bunt single gave the White Sox a 2-0 lead. The lead was 6-0 when Pérez came to bat in the seventh inning with a runner on base. His two-run homer ended the scoring in the 8-0 Chicago win, which took their record to 18-7.

The White Sox won the AL Central Division by six games. In the Division Series against the Boston Red Sox, Pérez made only one appearance, flying out as a pinch-hitter in the first game, as the White Sox swept Boston in three games. He did not play in the ALCS as Chicago defeated the Angels in five games. In the World Series against the Astros, Timo was sent up as a pinch-hitter in the 11th inning of Game Three with two outs and runners on first and second. He grounded out to end the threat. The White Sox won the series in four games.

Pérez became a free agent after the season and signed with the Cincinnati Reds in February 2006. The Reds, in turn, sold Pérez to the St. Louis Cardinals, for whom he played in 2006. He played in only 23 games (four starts) and batted .194. (He spent much of the season at Triple-A Memphis.)

Pérez signed with Detroit for the 2007 season and spent most of the season with Toledo of the International League. He was batting .314 through his first 77 games with Toledo. He was called up to the Tigers in July when Marcus Thames went on the disabled list.[8] Pérez's stay with the Tigers was brief. After appearing in three games, he was optioned back to Toledo, where he spent the rest of the minor-league season, batting .309 with 13 homers and 69 RBIs for the year in 122 games. At the end of August, he rejoined the Tigers when Gary Sheffield was placed on the disabled list.

Pérez started paying dividends early with the Tigers this time around. On August 30 against the Kansas City Royals, he went 2-for-4 with a fifth-inning RBI double as the Tigers won 6-1. On September 1 he had three hits in a 6-1 win over Oakland. On September 5 he broke up a tie game in the 11th inning with a run-scoring single off the right-field wall. But the Tigers remained seven games out of first place.[9] In 26 games during August and September, Pérez had 11 multihit games, and he batted .410. But the team was unable to move up in the standings and settled for second place in the AL Central with an 88-74 record.

Pérez did not figure in the Tigers' plans, and on September 29, he played his last major-league game. He was designated for assignment after the season. In parts of eight big-league seasons, Pérez had batted .269, with 26 home runs and 185 RBIs.

But Pérez was ever the optimist. He went to spring training with the Tigers in 2008 as a nonroster player and batted .400 in 17 games. He spent the 2008 season with Toledo, batting .302, but there would be no late season call-up. Pérez was not ready to give up and spent the next three years playing in the Dominican Republic, Mexico, and Triple A. He was back in Toledo in 2011 and batted .304.

After the 2011 season, Pérez was given a 50-game suspension for testing positive for Ritalinic Acid and Methylphenidate. At that point, he left Organized Baseball. He played a season with the Long Island Ducks of the independent Atlantic League and finished his career with two seasons with Licey in the Dominican Winter League.

At that point, there were the memories, the greatest being of three short weeks in 2000 when Timo Pérez made a big difference for the New York Mets.

SOURCES

In addition to the sources shown in the Notes, the author used Retrosheet.org and Baseball-Reference.com, and the following:

Amore, Dom. "Wild Ride! Vizcaino's Single Wins It in 12th," *Hartford Courant*, October 22, 2000: E1, E14.

NOTES

1   Mike Lopresti, "Mets Enjoy a Revelation," *Binghamton* (New York) *Press and Sun Bulletin*, October 17, 2000: 1C.

2   Lopresti.

3   T.J. Quinn, "World of Difference," *New York Daily News*, October 7, 2000: 31.

4   David Heuschkel, "Payton Drives in Winner in Ninth," *Hartford Courant*, October 13, 2000: C-4.

5   Greg Gutes, "Mets Hurt Themselves on Bases," *Newsday* (Long Island, New York), October 22, 2000: 3.

6   Peter Botte, "Mets Blunder on Basepaths," *New York Daily News*, October 22, 2000: 21.

7   Quinn, "Timo a Target Once Too Often," *New York Daily News*, August 26, 2002: 72.

8   John Lowe, "With Thames Out, Pérez Summoned," *Detroit Free Press*, July 20, 2007: 6D.

9   John Lowe, "Timo-Ment," *Detroit Free Press*, September 6, 2007: C1.

A.J. PIERZYNSKI

By Ann S. Johnson

White Sox manager, Ozzie Guillén once said of A.J. Pierzynski: "If you play against him, you hate him. If you play with him, you hate him a little less."[1] Pierzynski was a fierce competitor with a strong desire to win. This desire at times could rub teammates the wrong way and many times would get under his opponents' skin. Despite being a magnet for controversies, Pierzynski amassed a 19-year career across seven major-league teams. Through the 2024 season, he was ninth on the all-time games played as a catcher with 1,936.

Anthony John "A.J." Pierzynski was born on December 30, 1976, in Bridgehampton, New York, to Ed and Mary Jane Pierzynski and was an only child. Catching was in the family bloodline. A.J.'s grandfather, whom he is named after, was a catcher in the minor leagues before World War II.[2] Ed and Mary later divorced and Mary remarried, to Jack Harrelson, whom she met at one of A.J.'s Little League games in Orlando, Florida, where they lived.[3] Jack was there watching his own son umpire and later went on to coach A.J. in Little League.[4] Mary was an administrative assistant at the Clermont (Florida) Chamber of Commerce and said her son's love for baseball was evident from an early age.[5]

Even as a child, controversies seemed to find the youngster, Danny Allie, Pierzynski's high-school baseball coach, remembered that after he hit a walk-off home run in the 1992 prep World Series game for Dr. Phillips High School in Orlando, Florida, Pierzynski offended the opposing coach by flipping his bat as he admired his shot.[6] Future major leaguer Johnny Damon was a teammate at Dr. Phillips and they both later made the 2002 American League All-Star team.[7]

In 1994, as a senior, Pierzynski was drafted out of high school by the Minnesota Twins in the third round. He also signed a letter of intent to play baseball for the University of Tennessee but chose to go straight to the pros at age 17. He was asked why he chose baseball. His words reflected on his enduring passion for the game, starting at the age of 4: "I loved baseball when I was a child. Tried other things – was always the thing I went back to. Never really thought about anything else – fortunate to make it a career."[8]

Pierzynski worked his way through the Twins' minor-league system starting with the rookie Gulf Coast League Twins team, then on to the Elizabethton Twins of the Appalachian League, the Fort Wayne Wizards of the Class-A Midwest League, the Fort Myers Miracle of the Florida State League, the New Britain Rock Cats of the Double-A Eastern League, and finally the Triple-A Salt Lake Buzz of the Pacific Coast League through the late 1990s.

Pierzynski's quick ascension through the minors at a demanding position demonstrated his ability to handle the rigorous demands of professional baseball. In 1998 he spent time with the Rock Cats and the Buzz when he was only 21 years old. He was over 5½ years younger than the average age of the competition at Triple A.[9] In January of 1998, Scott Muhlhan, a lifelong friend and baseball teammate at Dr. Phillips High, died at the age of 23 from cancer. Muhlhan was often on Pierzynski's mind as he progressed in his career. However, some good came out of this: A.J. reconnected with their former classmate Lisa whom he married a year later. "It was sad, but it brought us together."[10]

Pierzynski made his major-league debut in a brief call-up to the Twins visiting the Anaheim Angels on September 9, 1998, replacing Terry Steinbach in the bottom of the fifth.

A. J. Pierzynski   2005

He got his first major-league hit on September 12 at home vs. the Oakland A's, pinch-hitting in the bottom of the ninth for Denny Hocking. It was a groundball between third base and shortstop off Billy Taylor. Reflected on his first at-bat, he said his goal simply was "don't strike out." He viewed grounding out to second as a success because he "was able to make contact in the big leagues."[11]

Pierzynski spent most of the 1999 season with the Salt Lake Buzz, playing 63 games at catcher with a .984 fielding percentage and hitting .259/.307/.316 before another late-season call-up. This time he played in just nine games for the Twins but expanded his experience to catching four full games. At the plate in 24 plate appearances, he batted .273/.333/.364 before once again starting the following season in Triple A.

In his final season with Salt Lake, at age 23, Pierzynski had a slash line of .336/.345/.516 with 4 home runs and 25 RBIs in 41 games. His consistent performance earned him recognition as one of the top catching prospects in the Twins organization. Minnesota had a solid young core, and Pierzynski looked to be part of the long-term solution.[12] He joined the Twins on August 13 and stayed for the reminder of the 2000 season after fellow catcher Chad Moeller injured his right knee.[13] His performance showed promise as he continued to develop his abilities both behind the plate and at bat. In 33 games, he hit .307/.354/.455 with eight extra-base hits. He hit his first home on September 8 off the Mariners' Paul Abbott.

Pierzynski developed a reputation for his defensive skills and game-calling abilities during his early years with the Twins. He worked closely with the Twins pitching staff, helping to guide young pitchers such as Johan Santana and Brad Radke. Pierzynski's leadership on the field was instrumental in the Twins' success, and his contributions were recognized by both his teammates and coaches. "He's got power. He's got arm strength and he's got a good feel on how to call a game," Twins general manager Terry Ryan said. "He's calm, but he has some fire out there, too. There are still pieces of his game that need to come together before you can consider him a complete everyday catcher."[14]

Then in 2001, Pierzynski began to establish himself as a regular, playing in 114 games. His efforts helped solidify his position as the Twins' primary catcher, demonstrating both offensive and defensive skills (.289/.322/.441, .985 fielding average).

The 2002 season was Pierzynski's breakout campaign. Playing in 130 games and hitting .300 with 6 home runs and 49 RBIs, he earned his first All-Star selection with teammates Torii Hunter and Eddie Guardado. His performance helped the Twins secure a spot in the playoffs, and he helped push the Twins past the Oakland A's with a two-run home run in the top of the ninth off closer Billy Koch in the deciding Game Five of the Division Series. Postgame, Koch called Pierzynski a "jackass." Earlier in the series, he stood on home plate without the ball which required Oakland's

Eric Chavez to push him out of the way. Pierzynski said he talked to himself during games, which many took as trash talk; all little things that can rub the opposing team the wrong way. Manager Rod Gardenhire commented, "A.J.'s one of those guys. We like the way he plays. If he gets under other players' skins, then they're not concentrating on their games."[15]

After defeating Oakland, the Twins lost the American League Championship Series in five games to the eventual World Series winner, the Anaheim Angels, in five games.

Playing in 137 games in 2003, Pierzynski batted .312 and led the team in WAR at 4.5. The Twins were AL Central Division champions for the second year in a row but were eliminated by the New York Yankees in the Division Series in four games.

After the season Pierzynski was traded to the San Francisco Giants for Boof Bonser, Francisco Liriano, and Joe Nathan. It would seem crazy to trade a young catcher but the Twins had another young catcher waiting in the wings whom they wanted to make playing time for, future Hall of Famer Joe Mauer. Pierzynski's trade value would never be higher, so he was dealt.

Pierzynski's time with the Giants was short and followed the familiar pattern of either you love him, or you hate him. In 131 games, he batted .272 with 11 home runs and 77 RBIs. Those stats were not enough to overcome clubhouse controversy. In April several Giants pitchers anonymously ripped Pierzynski in a newspaper story calling him a clubhouse "cancer."[16] Some of the complaints also focused on his pregame preparation with the pitchers, or lack thereof.[17] It would later be revealed that pitcher Brett Tomko was the chief source of the complaints.[18] In December Pierzynski was released, a free agent for the first time in his career.

White Sox general manager Kenny Williams took a risk bringing someone with that public reputation to the team, but Williams felt those issues were a thing of the past and Pierzynski acknowledged the mistakes he made in San Francisco. "Who among us hasn't had a second, and in some cases third, chance?" Williams said. "A.J. is a fierce competitor. Often times that comes out in an abrasive way."[19]

Pierzynski started the 2005 season on the right foot. Arriving at spring training, he immediately met with pitching coach Don Cooper. "We've had some enjoyable conversation about everything and everybody," Cooper said. "He's a veteran guy, and he's showing me he wants to do the job he needs to do. He wants to learn the pitchers, he wants specifics about the guys. He wants to be on the same page."[20]

Pierzynski played a crucial role in the White Sox' 2005 championship run. In the playoffs he was at his best with his pitching core of Mark Buehrle, Jon Garland, Freddy Garcia, and José Contreras. All four pitched complete games in the ALCS in Games Two through Five to eliminate the Los Angeles Angels of Anaheim.

Controversy once again found Pierzynski, though, in the ALCS. Known as a hitter and for his defense, he was not as well known for his baserunning. At 6-feet-3 and 250 pounds, he was not the fastest runner on the basepaths, but he was one of the smartest and had an intimate understanding of the baseball rules and how to make the most of any situation.

The White Sox dropped Game One at home, 3-2. In Game Two, with the score tied 1-1 in the bottom of the ninth, controversy arose. On an apparent third strike, Pierzynski looked back at plate umpire Doug Eddings. He did not witness a strike call while the catcher, Josh Paul, tossed the ball toward the mound and began to leave the field, assuming that was the third out.

Pierzynski then took off for first base and was safe due to the dropped third-strike rule. He did not stay on the field long enough to witness the end of Mike Scioscia's pleadings with the umpires, bounding into the dugout with Pablo Ozuna taking his place as a pinch-runner. Ozuna stole second and scored the winning run on Joe Crede's double. After the game Pierzynski said, "I didn't fake them out. I was off-balance. I took one step to the dugout and realized he didn't tag me so I ran. There's no faking. ... It just happened, and I always seem to be in the middle of it."[21]

It's this type of heads-up and hard-nosed baseball that gained Pierzynski the respect of his fellow teammates. After the game, Carl Everett – who himself was no stranger to controversy – said, "A.J. is A.J. People love to hate him. They don't realize he plays hard."[22] "There are a lot of people who give A.J. a bad rap for the way he goes about the game," reliever Cliff Politte said. "But he plays hard, and he's doing the little things right and always is thinking ahead."[23]

Pierzynski's play restarted the White Sox offense and they went on to win the ALCS, and the World Series. Nearly 20 years later, he recalled the exact moment he knew they had won the World Series. "Holy (expletive), we did it. I can't believe we did it. Disbelief we did it." He went out to discuss how in that era the Yankees and Red Sox were dominating the AL, and he was concerned he would need to play for one of those teams to achieve the ultimate prize. Pierzynski said that after hugging everyone he could find, he took a moment to reflect on all the people who contributed to this achievement – family, coaches, friends, fellow players. Both his passion for the game and his love of the people in his life was demonstrated by the gratitude he expressed.[24]

In 2006 Pierzynski played in 140 games with slash line of .295/.333/.436 and 16 home runs. Controversy once again found him. One of his most infamous moments as a White Sox occurred at home on May 20 during a crosstown game against the Chicago Cubs. In the bottom of the second inning, Brian Anderson hit a fly ball to left fielder Matt Murton. Pierzynski tagged at third and crashed into Cubs catcher Michael Barrett as he scored. He emphatically slapped home plate and on his way back to the dugout he bumped into Barrett, who held Pierzynski with his left arm and punched him in the face with his right hand. Chaos ensued. Both benches cleared and Anderson tackled Cubs player John Mabry.[25] Barrett, Mabry, Pierzynski, and Anderson were ejected. Barrett was suspended for 10 games, Anderson for five, and Pierzynski was fined an undisclosed amount. Afterward, the White Sox' Mark Buehrle jokingly said, "Once Barrett hit him, I think the whole league wanted to give Barrett a pat on the back."[26] That year Pierzynski made his second All-Star team, voted by the fans thanks to the "Punch A.J." popular voting campaign.[27]

Reflecting on the fight 10 years later, Pierzynski said, "What's happened now is most people don't remember what really happened. They just know Barrett and I got into a fight. Most people actually think that I hit him. People (say to me) 'Remember that time you punched Barrett and knocked him down?' So, it's kind of funny how it's kind of changed over the years."[28]

In July 2006 Pierzynski became a further irritant to the Cubs and their fans by hitting a go-ahead three-run home run in the top of the ninth at Wrigley Field off Cubs closer Ryan Dempster. The White Sox won the game, 8-6, and took the series, further enduring Pierzynski to the team's fans.

Pierzynski also got to play the role of the villain in the wrestling ring. White Sox strength and conditioning coach Dale Torborg was also a professional wrestler, best known for portraying the Kiss-themed character The Demon in the World Championship Wrestling. Torborg and Pierzynski would talk professional wrestling all the time. Pierzynski got to play the role of the manager of Torborg, Sonja Dutt, and Chris Sabin at the 2005:BaseBrawl.[29] Pierzynski and Torborg would team up as heels in a future event against fellow wrestling fan David Eckstein, who had just been named World Series MVP in 2006.[30]

The rest of Pierzynski's time with the White Sox was one of consistency behind the plate – catching between 128 and 136 games a season while being a leader of the team and handling the pitching staff. This included catching Buehrle's no-hitter on April 18, 2007, against the Texas Rangers and Phil Humber's perfect game on April 21, 2012, against the Seattle Mariners. That 2012 campaign was his final season with the White Sox and one of his best offensively; he received the Silver Slugger award with a .278/.326/.501 slash line to go with 27 home runs and 77 RBIs.

As the White Sox focused on rebuilding with a younger team, rookie GM Rick Hahn let Pierzynski leave as a free agent, turning the day-to-day catching duties over to Tyler Flowers. Pierzynski signed a one-year deal with the Texas Rangers with a team president who also hadn't made a lot of friends in his playing days, Hall of Famer Nolan Ryan. Ryan loved how Pierzynski reacted in the 2005 ALCS hustling to first base: "That was a heads-up play. If somebody's in the game mentally like that, I want him on my team."[31]

Pierzynski still had the talent and skills to contribute to major-league teams, even as he was older in his career and was still hated by opponents. (In a July 2012 *Men's Journal* survey of 100 anonymous major leaguers, Pierzynski was named "Most Hated Player" on 34 of the votes. No other player had 10.[32])

Pierzynski split the 2014 season between the Boston Red Sox and the St. Louis Cardinals, appearing in a total of 102 games. No official explanation was provided by the Red Sox, but speculation in multiple publications blamed Pierzynski's lack of offensive production. Young players would ask his advice during games, Pierzynski said, and he was thrilled to see the difference he could sometimes make with them.[33]

The 2015 and 2016 seasons were the culmination of Pierzynski's career, and he signed with the Atlanta Braves, playing in 113 games in 2015 and 81 in 2016. Despite the Braves' struggles, Pierzynski's performance was a bright spot, as he provided stability and leadership. He retired as a player at the end of the 2016 season.

In 2024 Pierzynski, reflecting on his feelings as he contemplated retirement, said he had been losing his mental edge – it was not a physical issue. He felt he could continue to play physically, but "[i]t was harder and harder to prepare." He was also looking toward his family: His children were 10 and 9 years old, and he was approaching 40. "What am I missing at home" was part of his retirement decision. "I wasn't excited to take the field. I wasn't excited for the grind. Nineteen years was enough."[34]

During the 2005 pennant season, Pierzynski set an American League record for errorless innings for a catcher. From April 19 through October 2, he caught 117 consecutive games without an error. When the 2006 season started, he continued his streak, handling 962 consecutive errorless chances and breaking Yogi Berra's record of 950, set in 1959.

Pierzynski is also tied with Berra for sixth on the all-time catcher hitting list with 2,043 career hits. He had a career slash line of .280/.319/.420 with 188 home runs.

Of his records and career, he said, "The World Series is far and away my number-one achievement, but the 2,000 hits as a catcher is a big deal – and that I've played no other position than catch."[35] Of his 2,059 games played, 1,936 were as a catcher; the others were as a designated hitter (32) or pinch-hitter.

After his playing career, Pierzynski became a baseball commentator for Fox Sports. He was close to longtime White Sox broadcaster Ken Harrelson, and once said that Harrelson was part of the reason he joined the 2005 White Sox.[36] He said he had been in high school with Harrelson's children and that his wife was a roommate of Harrelson's daughter at Florida State. That relationship played a role in his decision to join the White Sox.[37]

"When I call a game, the best 15 minutes of the day is when we talk to the managers," Pierzynski said. "You learn so much. Most of these guys are really good, and they open up to you."[38] The announcing role also offered Pierzynski more time to spend with this family. "It's been awesome" is how he describes his current broadcaster role. "I am in baseball legit every day. Every Saturday during the season I go to a game. I talk about baseball two hours every day. I was blessed to walk into a job to keep doing baseball every day. The first games I did sucked, but I live and learn." Pierzynski said he was grateful for the introduction by Harrelson to continue pursuing a sport that he called "the best game in the world."[39]

As a player, a father, a husband, and now an announcer with a large social media following, A.J. Pierzynski is one of the biggest personalities, most knowledgeable players, and best catchers to ever grace the major leagues. His passion is unparalleled.

SOURCES

In addition to the sources cited in the Notes, the author consulted Baseball-Reference.com.

NOTES

1   Tim Keown, "White Noise," ESPN, August 28, 2006. https://www.espn.com/espnmag/story?id=3657165.

2   Larry Paladino, "A.J.'s Edgy Rep Muted by Stellar Career," National Polish-American Sports Hall of Fame, 2021, https://www.polishsportshof.com/portfolio_page/aj-pierzynski/.

3   Josh Robbins, "Orlando's All-Stars; Perseverance propels Dr. Phillips Graduates To 1st Berths," *Orlando Sentinel*, July 8, 2002: D1.

4   David Haugh, "Man in the Middle; Trouble Seems to Follow A.J. Pierzynski. But the Sox and Their Fans Have Grown to Love Him," *Chicago Tribune*, October 21, 2005: 1.1.

5   Thomas E Lowe, "Baseball Is Year-Round for Pierzynski; The Love for the Game Began for Twins Catcher A.J. Pierzynski When He Was Just 4 Years Old," *Orlando Sentinel*, January 13 2002: 14.

6   Haugh, "Man in the Middle."

7   Neal E. La Velle III, "Pierzynski Takes in the Moment; Twins Catcher Relishes 'Fun Ride and Long Road,'" *Minneapolis Star Tribune*, July 9, 2002: 4C.

8   AJ Pierzynski, telephone interview with author, November 8, 2024. Hereafter, Pierzynski interview.

9   Cody Christie, "Former Twins Cooperstown Case: AJ Pierzynski," *Twins Daily*, December 8, 2021. https://twinsdaily.com/news-rumors/minnesota-twins/former-twins-cooperstown-case-aj-pierzynski-r11620/.

10   Haugh, "Man in the Middle."

11   Pierzynski interview.

12   Christie, "Former Twins Cooperstown Case."

13   Neal E. La Velle III, "Twins Notebook Hall of Famers Are Announced," *Minneapolis Star Tribune*, August 13, 2000: 11C.

14   Neal E. La Velle III, "Clear Signs of Catching On; Twins Catcher A.J. Pierzynski Says He Has Learned From His Mistake and Never Again Will Take His Starting Position for Granted," *Minneapolis Star Tribune*, February 22, 2002: 08C.

15 Jim Souhan, "Playoff Insider; Lighting Rod for Conflict; Pierzynski's Hard-Nosed Play Gets Misunderstood," *Minneapolis Star Tribune*, October 10, 2002: 3S.

16 Bob Foltman and Jessie Rogers, "A.J. Has Sox Appeal; Pierzynski Draws Contract Offer," *Chicago Tribune*, December 31, 2004: 4.1.

17 Foltman and Rogers

18 Mark Gonzales, "A Wanted Man; White Sox Ignored Talk About His Past and Gave Pierzynski a Place to Call Home," *Chicago Tribune*, March 12, 2006: 3.1.

19 Foltman and Rogers.

20 Mark Gonzales, "Goal for '05? Catch Less Flak; Pierzynski Striving to Mend Bad Reputation in New Gig With Sox," *Chicago Tribune*, March 6, 2005: 3.11.

21 Mark Gonzales, "Sox Respect Hard-Nosed Pierzynski," *Chicago Tribune*, October 14, 2005: 4.1.

22 Gonzales, "Sox Respect Hard-Nosed Pierzynski."

23 Gonzales, "Sox Respect Hard-Nosed Pierzynski."

24 Pierzynski interview.

25 Mike Kiley, "Mabry Injured after Brawl with Anderson," *Chicago Sun-Times*, May 21, 2006: A97.

26 Keown, "White Noise."

27 Keown, "White Noise." "Punch A.J." refers to a hypothetical All-Star voter punching Pierzynski's name on the ballot.

28 Chuck Garfien, "Ten Years Later, A.J. Pierzynski Recalls Michael Barrett Encounter in Crosstown Classic," NBC Sports, July 25, 2016. Accessed on July 18, 2024, https://www.nbcsports.com/chicago/white-sox/white-sox-talk-podcast-10th-anniversary-mark-buehrles-perfect-game.

29 Scott Merkin, "Pierzynski: WS Champ, AS ... Pro Wrestler?" MLB, February 11, 2021. https://www.mlb.com/news/a-j-pierzynski-professional-wrestling-career.

30 Scott Maxwell, "For Celebrity Couple, Life's Still Sweet – Like a Bowl of Cereal," *Orlando Sentinel*, January 9, 2007: B2.

31 Phil Rogers, "Grate Deal: Ryan Admires A.J.'S Grit: Rangers President and Hall of Famer Loves Pierzynski's Will to Win, Durability," *Chicago Tribune*, February 26, 2013: 3.3.

32 Tyler Kepner, "A.J. Pierzynski, the Man They Love to Hate, Is Still Behind the Plate," *New York Times*, February 22, 2016. https://www.nytimes.com/2016/02/23/sports/baseball/a-j-pierzynski-atlanta-braves-catcher-hate.html.

33 Kepner.

34 Pierzynski interview.

35 Paladino, "A.J.'s Edgy Rep Muted by Stellar Career."

36 Ed Sherman, "In My Words: Pierzynski on Life in the Booth," MLB.com, August 28, 2018. https://www.mlb.com/news/a-j-pierzynski-in-my-words-c292298062.

37 A.J. Pierzynski, Teddy Greenstein interview, June 6, 2018. https://www.youtube.com/watch?v=NvV3I1SHWuU.

38 Ed Sherman

39 Pierzynski interview.

SCOTT PODSEDNIK

By Doug Barker

Scott Podsednik made his money stealing bases, distracting defenses, and putting pitchers off their game, but it's his unlikely and now legendary walk-off home run to win Game Two of the 2005 World Series that he's most remembered for and that will forever endear him to White Sox fans.

The Chicago White Sox had gone ahead of the Houston Astros in the seventh inning on another legendary homer, a grand slam by Paul Konerko. But the Astros took the air out of the home crowd by tying it in the top of the ninth. In the bottom of the inning, Podsednik – a speedy lead-off hitter who hadn't hit a single home run in the regular season and was 0-for-4 that night – came up facing Brad Lidge, then one of the dominant closers in baseball. With his mind on a single and a plan to steal second on the first pitch, Podsednik instead hit a blast into the first few rows of seats in right-center. It set off delirium at what was then US Cellular Field and fueled momentum for a White Sox sweep that brought a World Series championship to the South Side of Chicago for the first time since 1917.

Scott Podsednik   2005

Podsednik, a lefty-batting, lefty-throwing outfielder, had an 11-season major-league career. He hit .281 lifetime, led the majors in steals and finished second in Rookie of the Year voting in 2003, and was an American League All-Star in 2005. But it was the improbable homer on a damp and cold Chicago night that gives him a place among the most storied White Sox moments of all time. An MLB.com story rating the top 10 moments at US Cellular Field rated Podsednik's walk-off at the top.[1] Next was Konerko's grand slam.

In 2007, when a seat-replacement project was completed at the ballpark, two of the light blue originals were left where they were to mark the spots where Podsednik's and Konerko's homers landed. The walk-off bat went to the Hall of Fame. "To have a bat of mine going to the Hall of Fame, that's pretty special," said Podsednik, who wasn't known for his power. "If that doesn't define irony, I don't know what does."[2]

Scott Eric Podsednik (pronounced Puh-sed-nick, despite various nicknames that pronounce the first syllable as pod) was born on March 18, 1976, to Duane and Amy Podsednik in West, Texas. This was not West Texas as in the sprawling region home to more than 2 million Texans in 70 counties, but West, Texas, a town of fewer than 3,000 people about two hours' drive south of Dallas. It's known for kolaches, a sweet Czech pastry that immigrant settlers brought with them. There are knowing travelers who wouldn't think of passing by on I-35 without pulling off for kolaches.

The Podsedniks are part of West's large Czech community. Scott's father worked at a glass plant in Waco, which is about an hour away, and his mother worked for the school district. His sister, Shana, his only sibling, married Kevin Mench, who played eight seasons in the major leagues, mainly for the Texas Rangers.

In 2008 Podsednik married Lisa Dergan, a well-known sports television personality and model in the 2000s. The couple divorced in 2017. They have two children, a daughter, Peytra, and a son, Nixon.

Podsednik played 19 seasons of professional baseball, including nine persistent, often injury-affected seasons in the minor leagues for three different organizations before breaking into the majors with the Seattle Mariners. He had a handful of appearances with Seattle in 2001 and 2002. His first major-league appearance was July 6, 2001, as a pinch-runner for Ichiro Suzuki, but his official major-league rookie year wasn't until 2003 with the Milwaukee Brewers.

His 11 seasons in the majors came with seven teams – the Mariners, Brewers, White Sox, Colorado Rockies, Kansas City Royals, Los Angeles Dodgers, and the Boston Red Sox.

Podsednik was a speedster at every level of his athletic career. He played baseball and basketball and ran track at West High School, graduating in 1994. In his junior year he finished second in the 300-meter hurdles in the Texas 2A classification.

He turned down college track scholarships when the Rangers picked him out of high school in the third round of the June 1994 amateur draft. Just 18 years old, he began his professional baseball career in Port Charlotte, Florida, with the Rangers' team in the rookie Gulf Coast League.

In several interviews, Podsednik described himself as a "deer in the headlights" that first summer and a few after it. "I went to a really small high school and was somewhat sheltered there," he told interviewer Chuck Garfien on an episode of the *White Sox Talk* podcast. "I was a good athlete, I could run, I had good hands, but using all of that out on the baseball field, I didn't know how to do yet."[3]

In Podsednik's first four years in the minors, his numbers improved every year, but he didn't progress past Class A. That first year in Florida he hit .228 and stole 18 bases. The next year, with Hudson Valley in the Class-A New York-Pennsylvania League, his average edged up to .266 and he swiped 20 bases, but Texas traded him to the Florida Marlins after the season.

After the 1997 season, the Rangers reacquired Podsednik through the Rule 5 draft. He got some time at Double-A Tulsa in 1998 but spent most of the year in long-season Class A. Injuries held him back the next two seasons. Still in the Rangers farm system, in 1999, he appeared in just 42 games, and in 2000, just 49.

"I was doing so bad I was considering shutting it down, (but coaches) were like, 'You can play, you are talented.' So from that point forward, I started asking why," he said. "'Why am I rolling over this pitch? Why am I getting injured? Why is my footwork bad?' … I wanted to play big-league baseball. I grew up wanting to do that. I started asking why and then it became an obsession."[4]

Podsednik's speed continued to get him chances. When Texas released him after the 2000 season, he signed with the Mariners and was invited to his first big-league spring training. The questions and introspection began to help him define his playing style, he told Garfien. "In 2001, which was my first big league spring training – with Seattle – I had a pretty good year … and started gaining some confidence. I had no confidence in the minor leagues."[5]

Podsednik spent most of 2001 with the Mariners' Triple-A team in Tacoma. That was Seattle's 116-win season, tough to break through for a roster spot. He was called up for about two weeks in July, playing mostly as a defensive substitute, and his first major-league at-bat was the stuff of dreams, literally. Manager Lou Piniella called on him to pinch-hit for Ed Sprague with the bases loaded in the seventh inning against Erik Sabel of the Arizona Diamondbacks. He sliced a triple into the left-center-field gap, clearing the bases.

Although Podsednik played in only five games with the Mariners during their historic 2001 season, he just missed making history on his own, and it cost him money. An unbylined notes column on TribLive.com a week after the triple reported that "even though outfielder Steve Finley bobbled the ball, Podsednik hit the brakes when third-base coach Dave Myers held up the stop sign. It was a prudent decision. But it cost Podsednik a chance to become the first player in major-league history to hit an inside-the-park grand slam in his first big-league at-bat. So Podsednik and Myers were fined when the Mariners' kangaroo court met later in the clubhouse. 'The kid's got to go down in the book (of fines),' said catcher Tom Lampkin, one of the veterans who runs the court. 'We're talking about history here. You've got to send him.'"[6]

The triple also showed Podsednik what it's like to get a big-league crowd on its feet. He stayed in the game after the pinch hit and when he went out to left field the next inning, he got a standing ovation. "I had electricity flowing through me. With 50,000 people hollering and screaming, I can't describe it. It's something I've been dreaming about since I was a young kid," he said.[7]

As if the cake needed any more icing, the game was on ESPN's *Sunday Night Baseball* telecast. Jon Miller and Joe Morgan were calling it and did right by Podsednik's moment:

"You never forget your first major-league hit," said Morgan, who noted his surprise that with two out, Podsednik got the stop sign at third. "You'll fall asleep thinking about it the next 30 or 40 years."

"*I'll never forget it*" Miller replied.[8]

Podsednik had solid seasons with Tacoma both years in the Mariners organization but didn't make much of the slim opportunities he did get with the big club. In 2001 the nearly historic triple was his only hit in five games and six at-bats. In 2002 he hit .200 while up for 14 games in September. He had only 20 at-bats, but one resulted in a homer.

The 2002 season was Podsednik's last extended stint in the minors. He hit .279 in 125 games with Tacoma and stole 35 bases. He was also caught stealing 13 times, but that, too, was a part of the process that would eventually serve him in the majors. He was 26 years old that season and learning what it meant to be a leadoff hitter and a base thief.

"I'm a pretty introverted, shy guy and I did not play with swagger," Podsednik told Garfien on the White Sox Talk podcast. "… I had to come out of my shell and change my personality to be the leadoff hitter I needed to be. The leadoff is a guy who provides energy, provides spark, gets things cranked up. I looked in the mirror and thought, 'Well, you're just this introverted, shy guy. That's not going to cut it.'

"I remember, Greg Walker (longtime White Sox first baseman and later the hitting coach when Podsednik played in Chicago), he would always talk about swagger. He knew me and he could always tell when I was playing careful. … And to be a basestealer, you have to play the game with no fear. You have to take a risk; you have to get out there and fly by the seat of your pants. … And that started happening around (those) 2001, 2002 years. I had a full season and had a full year of at-bats and I started gaining some traction and gaining some confidence.

"That word was big for me: 'swagger.' (You have to) take the field like you're the best player in the ballpark. You might rub some people the wrong way, the opposition is going to hate you, but I had to do that to be my best and reach my potential as a player."[9]

After the 2002 season, Podsednik was claimed off waivers by the Brewers. He played winter ball in Puerto Rico and hit .467. When the 2003 season started, he was 27 and on the cusp of a breakout year.

Podsednik started the season on the Brewers' bench but got his shot early on. "I showed up to the park and found out I was in the lineup. I thought it was odd because we were facing Shawn Estes, who's a lefty, so I thought, 'Something is up here,'" Podsednik explained. During stretching, he heard from a teammate that the Brewers were considering making a change from their everyday center fielder, Álex Sánchez. "'They are going to run you out there for a few days.' I immediately (thought), 'This is it.' I'd spent a long time in professional baseball and I knew the window of opportunity is a small one. I knew this was my shot. I went 0-for-4 that night. … The next night I think I hit a home run in like the seventh that tied the game." Soon after that, the Brewers traded Sánchez to the Tigers to open the center-field spot. "And that's how it happened."[10]

Podsednik went on to hit .314 that season, steal 43 bases, score 100 runs, and run up an OPS value of .822. He finished second in the Rookie of the Year voting in the National League, losing out to pitcher Dontrelle Willis, who won 14 games for the Marlins.

Podsednik gave former Brewers first-base coach Dave Nelson a lot of credit for making him think and act like a basestealer, melding fearlessness, attention to technique, and the study of pitchers.

"I got to Milwaukee in '03, and Dave was like, 'Hey, you got to get out there and run. If you run well enough to impact the game with your legs, you can't be scared.' Dave really helped me a lot. He taught me about getting leads, some footwork and some technical aspects. … He really impacted my career. … Playing with that swagger and fearlessness, I played well and stole a lot of bases (and realized) this is what I'm here to do and I can impact ballgames."[11]

In 2004, his second full season in the majors, Podsednik took a step back at the plate, with a 70-point drop in batting average to .244, but he led the major leagues in steals with 70, a full 25 more than National League runner-up Juan Pierre, and 11 more than Tampa Bay's Carl Crawford, who led the American League with 59.

Meantime, in Chicago second-year manager Ozzie Guillén was remaking his club to be faster and more athletic and was willing to give up power to do it. That winter the White Sox traded slugging outfielder Carlos Lee to the Brewers for Podsednik and reliever Luis Vizcaíno. As it turned out, both Lee and Podsednik were All-Stars in their leagues that year.

In the 2005 championship season, Podsednik hit .290 in the leadoff spot and was often the guy who got things going. Guillén called him the "igniter." He was on his way to leading the majors in steals again but was slowed in the second half by a groin injury and time on the disabled list. He finished second in the American League to Chone Figgins, who stole 62 bases for the Angels and led the majors. At the All-Star break, Podsednik already had 44 and ended the season with 59.

When Podsednik was healthy and liberally using the green light Guillén had given him (Podsednik also led the league in caught-stealing that year and the next), it could change the character of the game. "Once Scott gets on, the defense is moving all around, holes are opening up all over the place, guys are cheating to the bag, catchers are edgy, moving around behind the dish, not really giving the umpire a chance to see pitches. He changes the whole outlook of the game," said Tim Raines, the White Sox' first-base coach.[12] Raines stole 808 bases in his career, ranking him fifth all-time.

In a *New York Times* profile on Podsednik that summer, Piniella, his first major-league manager at Seattle, talked about the challenge of facing speed. Then managing the Tampa Bay Rays, Piniella said of Podsednik, "Oh, he's disruptive. He makes the pitcher really concentrate, and he takes attention away from the hitter. And then, because of fear of him stealing, the rest of the batting order sees more fastballs than breaking balls. And then the infield has to shift a little differently, open wider holes in the defense. That's what speed can do for you. And a good leadoff batter – and Podsednik is one of the few really good ones in baseball – is the catalyst for any team. I tell my pitchers: 'Just don't let him get on base. Make sure you don't walk him. He's going to have to hit his way on if he's going to get on.'"[13]

The 2005 season was the only time Podsednik appeared in the postseason and he put up strong numbers, hitting .286 with three triples, two home runs, and six RBIs. He stole six bases in nine attempts and compiled a .948 OPS. He already had good looks to go with his polite charm, Texas accent, and mad dashes on the basepaths, but the Game Two walk-off raised his profile considerably. When the White Sox made a team appearance on the *Oprah Winfrey Show* the same day as their downtown Series victory parade,

Podsednik was one of the players Winfrey spoke to individually. "Is this your wildest dream?" she asked.

"Comin' on the Oprah Show, or winning the World Series?" Podsednik replied wryly as the studio audience broke up and Winfrey beamed.[14]

Soon after that, Podsednik had a speaking part on *Saturday Night Live*, being interviewed by former Chicagoans Tina Fey and Amy Poehler for the Weekend Update segment. The gag was for Podsednik to out the former North Siders as bandwagon White Sox fans. Later, when he was breaking into television as a studio analyst, he told interviewer and historian George Castle of the Chicago Baseball Museum that those appearances, and the added media attention after the Series, helped him have the confidence to try being a television analyst after he was done playing, despite his shy nature.

The next several seasons after the World Series, Podsednik established a hard-won journeyman label. The groin injury in the second half of the championship season followed him the next two seasons as well. In 2006 he played in just 139 games for the Sox. His average fell to .261 but he managed to steal 40 bases. Then 2007 was worse. Still bothered by groin problems, he played in just 62 games for the White Sox, hit .243, and stole 12 bases. The White Sox released him after that.

Reflecting on the role of injuries on his career, Podsednik has said he worked hard in the offseasons but not effectively for what his body needed in order to stand up to what he put it through. "I wasn't doing the right things. I was not doing the things that my body needed specifically. ... So I kept getting injured." The 2006 and 2007 seasons were the worst of his career, Podsednik said. "I was injured and not in any type of shape to play whatsoever," he told Garfien. After that he sought out the help of specialists to develop training that fit him specifically, he said. "I was in my mid-30s and needed some counsel." He said one person he worked with told him he had a "Ferrari engine, but a Honda Civic frame. You have horsepower, but you weren't strong in the right areas to withstand the horsepower."[15]

Defensively, Podsednik never won a Gold Glove and is often referred to as an average outfielder. As of 2024, Baseball Reference noted that he ranked 69th (tied with four others) among all outfielders since 1953 in the category of Total Zone Runs, a formula that uses four other metrics to determine what the Baseball Reference glossary describes as the "number of runs above or below average the player was worth based on the number of plays made." He led the National League in the category in 2004. He also had high numbers for range in several years and led the National League in putouts in 2004. But he also led American League left fielders in errors (8) in 2006.

Before the 2008 season, Podsednik signed a minor-league contract with the Colorado Rockies, which included an invitation to spring training. He made the Opening Day roster and appeared in 93 games for Colorado,

hitting. 253. He played sparingly in left field, where Matt Holliday was the regular, and platooned some in center. Nearly half his appearances involved pinch-hitting (57 at-bats) or pinch-running.

Podsednik was a free agent for 2009 and signed again with the Rockies but was released just before Opening Day. He wasn't idle for long. The White Sox signed him to a minor-league contract two weeks later and he began the year at Triple-A Charlotte. He was called up on April 30.

The Chicago homecoming was good for the White Sox and for Podsednik, who batted leadoff much of the season and went on to hit .304 and steal 30 bases in 132 games. Injuries to outfielders Brian Anderson and Carlos Quentin increased his playing time. Then 33 and a free agent, he had extended negotiations with the White Sox after that season, but they didn't result in a deal, and in January he signed with the Kansas City Royals. He put together another solid offensive year in 2010, splitting time between the Royals and the Dodgers. He was hitting .310 with 30 stolen bases in late July when the Royals traded him to the Dodgers. The Royals weren't contending for a playoff spot and the Dodgers were within striking distance in the National League West Division. He played left field and some center for the Dodgers but was slowed by a painful plantar fasciitis condition in his left foot. He played in just 39 games for the Dodgers and missed most of the last month of the season with his foot problem.

The 2011 season was essentially a lost year, at least in part because of ongoing foot problems. The Dodgers had exercised a $2 million option to secure Podsednik for 2011, but he passed on it in favor of free agency. He didn't attract the interest he might have expected and eventually signed a minor-league deal with the Toronto Blue Jays but continued to deal with plantar fasciitis and was released in May. He signed another minor-league deal, this time with the Philadelphia Phillies, but played in just 17 minor-league games in the farm system. All told, he appeared in only 34 minor-league games that season, dealing with injury and shuttling between four Toronto and Philadelphia farm clubs.

Podsednik's last season as a player was 2012, spent mostly with the Boston Red Sox. He began the year with Lehigh Valley, Philadelphia's team in the Triple-A International League, but in mid-May the Phils sold his contract to the Red Sox, who had five injured outfielders early in the year, including Carl Crawford and Jacoby Ellsbury. In July the Red Sox traded him to Arizona. He had yet to appear in a game for the Diamondbacks when in late July they elected to send him to Triple A. Podsednik declined the assignment and became a free agent.

He was idle only a week or so before the Red Sox brought him back for his second stint of 2012. After a slow start, he got hot and ended the year hitting .302 in 63 games. He stole eight bases. Podsednik played his last major-league game on October 3 at the age of 36. There was no formal retirement announcement, but he didn't play in the majors again.

Podsednik hasn't gotten too far from baseball. From 2017 through the 2024 season, he was a pregame and post-game studio analyst, part of NBC Sports Chicago's studio team that included Garfien as host and ex-Sox notables Guillén, Frank Thomas, and Gordon Beckham. After the 2024 season, NBC Sports Chicago ceased broadcasting and was sold to another group. The new ownership did not immediately announce broadcast plans.

In a 2017 interview, Podsednik said he still thought of himself as shy and introverted and never considered broadcasting as a second career until it was proposed to him. Perhaps he saw a second career in broadcasting in the same way he saw his shot with the Brewers his rookie season: "I thought to myself there's no way I would pass up this opportunity. Obviously, they had enough confidence in me going in. I felt I had nothing to lose, let's go see what this is about, talk some baseball and see if I enjoy doing it."[16]

He still heard about the walk-off all the time, he said. "When I'm in Chicago, probably not a day goes by where I'm not talking about it with someone, which is fine. That is obviously the highlight of my career. It doesn't get old. It gives me goose bumps to talk about it no matter what.

"I catch myself looking up (at photos from the World Series that hang in his office) and saying, 'How in the world did I run into that ball?' I only hit 42 homers in my career and none in the regular season (that year). How in the world did you weasel your way into hitting one in the World Series?'

"It was not supposed to come off my bat. Thinking back to it, I wasn't thinking home run, I wasn't looking to hit a home run. I was ahead in the count 2-and-1, and I was looking to put a good swing on the ball. Fortunately, I got a perfect pitch right out over the plate. I put as good a swing as I could on it and didn't miss it."[17]

SOURCES

In addition to the sources cited in the Notes, the author consulted Baseball-Reference.com, MLB.com, Retrosheet.org, and the following:

Machann, Clinton. "Czech Immigrants," https://www.tshaonline.org/handbook/entries/czechs#:~:text=By%20the%20twentieth%20century%20approximately,%2C%20Burleson%2C%20and%20Brazos%20counties.

Merkin, Scott. "Guaranteed Rate Field's Top 10 Moments," https://www.mlb.com/news/guaranteed-rate-field-best-moments, accessed November 14, 2024.

Visale, Joe. "Catching Up: Q&A with Scott Podsednik," https://www.milb.com/news/catching-up-q-a-with-scott-podsednik, accessed November 14, 2024.

Illinois Sports Facilities Authority. https://www.isfauthority.com/facilities/guaranteed-rate-field-renovations/, accessed November 14, 2024.

NOTES

1 Scott Merkin, "Guaranteed Rate Field's Top 10 Moments," MLB.com. December 1, 2021. https://www.mlb.com/news/guaranteed-rate-field-best-moments. Accessed November 14, 2024.

2 Mark Gonzales, "Suddenly a Hall of a Hitter," *Chicago Tribune*, October 25, 2005. https://www.chicagotribune.com/2005/10/25/suddenly-a-hall-of-a-hitter/.

3 Chuck Garfien, "Podsednik Advice for White Sox Prospects Hoping for a Major League Career," Sox Talk Podcast (NBC Sports Chicago) May 9, 2024. https://podcasts.apple.com/us/podcast/scott-podsedniks-advice-for-white-sox-prospects-hoping/id1162163703?i=1000655038437.

4 Garfien interview.

5 Garfien interview.

6 https://triblive.com/search/?search=rookie+just+following+orders.

7 Jim Moore, "Rookie Makes Impression in First At Bat," *Seattle Post-Intelligencer*, July 15, 2001. https://www.seattlepi.com/sports/baseball/article/rookie-makes-impression-in-first-at-bat-1059930.php.

8 "Diamondbacks vs. Mariners 7-15-01< From YouTube channel *This Is Where You Find Baseball*, https://www.bing.com/videos/riverview/relatedvideo?q=mariners+game+notes+july+15%2c+2001&mid=69390C-F0AD757BDDCA9269390CF0AD757BDDCA92&FORM=VIRE.

9 Garfien interview.

10 Garfien interview.

11 Garfien interview.

12 Daniel Habib, "Stealing the Show," *Sports Illustrated*, October 31, 2005. https://vault.si.com/vault/2005/08/15/stealing-the-show. Ira Berkow, "The Art of the Steal: Podsednik Keeps Pitchers on Edge," *New York Times*, July 11, 2005, https://www.nytimes.com/2005/07/11/sports/baseball/the-art-of-the-steal-podsednik-keeps-pitchers-on-edge.html.

14 https://www.oprah.com/oprahshow/chicago-celebrates/all.

15 Garfien interview.

16 George Castle, "Podsednik Shakes Off Shyness to Analyze Sox with Garfien, Melton on CSN Chicago," Chicago Baseball Museum, May 18, 2017, https://chicagobaseballmuseum.org/wp-content/uploads/CBM-Scott-Podsednik-20170518.pdf.

17 Castle interview.

CLIFF POLITTE

By Tom Alesia

Chicago White Sox relief pitcher Cliff Politte, practically floating on adrenaline, jogged off the mound after the eighth inning of Game Two in the 2005 World Series. He faced the Houston Astros' top hitters – two-three-four in the lineup – and got each of them out, holding the White Sox' slim lead. Nearing the dugout, Politte jerked back as a baseball slowly looped in front of his face. "Someone tossed it underhand," Politte said. It was first baseman Paul Konerko, whose grand slam gave the White Sox a 6-4 lead in the seventh inning. Konerko also caught the third out in Politte's appearance.

"What the hell are you doing?" Politte asked.

Konerko said, "Pick it up and put it in your pocket."[1]

Politte then understood: Konerko made certain that Politte's first World Series game experience would include a cherished souvenir. "And I still have it," said Politte, who created a wood box with memorable baseballs from an almost 10-year major-league career, featuring the World Series one that Konerko delivered, in his St. Louis-area home.

It's all part of Politte's dramatic career, which wasn't quite a roller-coaster ride – because the heights were too steep and the downfalls too sudden.

His start was unusual. Politte was born on February 27, 1974, in St. Louis to Clifford E. Politte, a former minor-league pitcher and a salesman, and Lorraine J. (McKay) Politte. Growing up, he played baseball and soccer, preferring the latter. He did not play baseball during his freshman year at Vianney High School in Kirkwood, a St. Louis suburb. As a sophomore, he joined the baseball team because his friends played. By his senior year, Politte was co-captain of the school's 1992 undefeated soccer team, which the USA Today newspaper called the mythical national champion.[2] College baseball coaches noted his hitting skills, but he admitted about his teens, "I hardly remember baseball, but I remember everything about soccer."

Politte played baseball at Memphis State University, but it was not a good match. He had about 50 at-bats in the spring of 1994, but his pitching was limited to one inning of a blowout game. While playing in a Missouri collegiate summer league that summer, Politte wanted to become an active two-way player. Jefferson College, a Hillsboro, Missouri, junior college, offered him that opportunity, so he transferred there.[3] The move worked extremely well: Politte starred as a right-handed pitcher and center fielder.

In a doubleheader, he threw a no-hitter in game one, then returned to the mound to earn the save in game two. He went 3-for-3 in each contest.[4] That helped lead to Politte's spot on the NJCAA first-team All-American team. Despite having a stunning second college season, the 5-foot-9, 185-pound Politte gave little thought to the 1995 major-league draft, which he assumed lasted two days. It lasted three days – and on the third day he was a 54th-round pick (the 1,439th overall) by the St. Louis Cardinals and their scout Tom McCormick.

Politte initially declined the Cardinals' offer. "I wasn't playing baseball to get drafted," he said. "I didn't know much about it. I played baseball because I was having fun and I did well at it." Politte was wanted by the Cardinals as a pitcher after he impressed them at collegiate league games in Cape Girardeau, Missouri. Politte relented and agreed to play minor-league baseball, although before 1996 spring training he hesitated because he expected to be a 22-year-old player in a rookie league with 18- and 19-year-old teammates.

Cliff Politte   2005

Politte's father played seven seasons (1959-1965) as a pitcher in the Cardinals' minor-league system, peaking in Double A with the Tulsa Oilers in 1964.[5] "When I was second-guessing everything and didn't want to start in a rookie league, my dad said, 'Maybe you can go to spring training and change that.'"

And at spring training in 1996, Politte did that. He pitched well enough to start the 1996 season with the Cardinals' Class-A Peoria (Illinois) Chiefs, then began a swift and remarkable climb to big-league starter on April 2, 1998. Used exclusively as a starting pitcher in the minor leagues, he earned a 14-6 record for Peoria in 1996. The next year, Politte was selected as the Carolina League Pitcher of the Year after going 11-1 with the Prince William Cannons of high Class A. To finish the 1997 season, he won four starts and lost one with the Double-A Arkansas Travelers – and that earned him the top minor-league pitcher nod in the Cardinals' system.[6]

"In Peoria, my goal was never, 'I have to get to the big leagues,'" Politte said. "I wanted to get there, but I thought, 'I want to be the best at whatever level I was at and compete with everybody.'" Still, Politte's arc to the big leagues progressed like that of a big-bonus newcomer, not someone a Kansas City Royals scout dismissed to his father as an "undersized" pitcher. (Politte said he was 5-feet-9½ "with cleats on.")

Politte learned on the radio that he would be in the Cardinals' 1998 spring-training camp.[7] He made the major-league team and slightly more than a month after his 24th birthday, he was the starting pitcher in the Cardinals second game of the season, on April 2, 1998, against the visiting Los Angeles Dodgers. Cardinals President Mark Lamping, who graduated from the same high school as Politte, donated tickets to Vianney students. Hundreds of students and staff attended Politte's debut "looking on from the upper deck at old Busch Stadium as the former (Vianney player) lived the dream of many a young St. Louis ballplayer."[8] Politte allowed one run and two hits in five innings. Because the game went to extra innings, with Mark McGwire hitting a walk-off homer for an 8-5 win in 12 innings, Politte didn't figure in the decision.

By May, Politte was sent down to Triple A with a 2-3 record and a 6.32 ERA. Pitching at a young age with high expectations from many hometown fans put excessive pressure on him. "My initial reaction was I was letting everyone down," he said.[9] That began a career of huge highs and low lows. He was 1-4 with the Triple-A Memphis Redbirds, then finished the season with the Double-A Arkansas Travelers. By mid-November 1998, he was traded to the Philadelphia Phillies as part of a five-player deal, and the Phillies shifted him from starter to reliever. For three seasons and part of a fourth, he bounced between minor-league time and the big leagues with Philadelphia.

Politte's father – a 6-foot-2 lefty who threw curveballs and who died in 2021 – encouraged him during minor-league stints. "He was more of a supporter from the mental side," Cliff said. "I struggled in Triple A and Double A. He drove to a game in Ohio when I was down and I pitched well. He said, 'That's all you needed was your dad here.'"

In the book *Major League Dads*, Politte described his father's influence: "I would not have been a big-leaguer without some of the stuff he taught me. … I used to call my dad after every game I pitched. Good or bad, we talked. If it was bad, I knew I had someone I could complain to or help me get it off my shoulders. We talked about pitches and how I could do better next time. I remember struggling one time and I couldn't figure it out, so I called my dad. He said I was mixing my pitches well, but it was all about location. I went back to the tapes, and he was right. I had to remember each time he did that, that it wasn't his first rodeo, he had done it all before."[10]

On May 26, 2002, the Phillies traded Politte to the Toronto Blue Jays for 40-year-old pitcher Dan Plesac.[11] "I was blindsided," he said, "but I was happy." He threw 57⅓ innings for the Blue Jays in 2002 before becoming the team's closer in 2003. At one point, Politte earned nine saves in 11 appearances. "My agent told me, 'Keep this up and I can get you *a lot* of money,'" he said. "I went downhill after that. I didn't get another save the rest of the year." Four days before Christmas in 2003, he was cut.

That set the stage for Politte's arrival in Chicago as a White Sox reliever during the 2004 season. "I couldn't establish a role in the bullpen, but I was throwing the hardest of my career: 95 to 97 miles per hour." In early September, his season ended early when he had his appendix removed.[12] "It was close to bursting," he said. "My son was only one year old, but he sat on my stomach and I almost went through the roof. The next day, I went to the doctor. I thought it was gas pains. Before I knew it, I was on the operating table."

Politte's finest season happened during the White Sox' World Series championship in 2005. As that season began, he felt that "[e]verybody that was ahead of us was just as good as they were the year before. We had no clue what would happen." Politte enjoyed a blazing first half of the season, with a 1.02 ERA, just behind Mariano Rivera's 1.01.[13] Still, Politte failed to make the All-Star team, a snub that bothered him almost 20 years later. Thirteen pitchers were picked for the American League roster.

On ESPN, Politte heard Joe Torre, who managed five All-Star Games – but not the one in 2005 – say Politte was deserving of an All-Star spot. But Torre added that relievers who were not closers faced hurdles to make the All-Star roster. Politte also found encouragement from White Sox pitching coach Don Cooper. "He was the most supportive pitching coach that I had. He said that I should have been an All-Star," Politte noted, then gave a short laugh. "He still says it."

Politte finished the 2005 regular season with a record of 7-1 and a 2.00 ERA. He had worked in 68 games, closing 14 of them, striking out 57 batters in 67⅓ innings.

Politte entered the White Sox' first Division Series game against the Boston Red Sox in the top of the ninth with the White Sox leading 14-2. He finished the game with a scoreless inning, but he was rattled. "I could feel my glove shaking," he said. "I didn't want to blow it." In the remaining Division Series games and the American League Championship Series, Politte never pitched, largely because the team's starters carried the load.

He entered the World Series, though, in Game Two after 19 days without pitching. It didn't matter. Politte thrived in one inning, retiring the three Astros he faced in the top of the eighth and holding a two-run lead. He entered with a one-run lead in Game Three. He got two outs in the bottom of the eighth inning. The second out was a strikeout of Houston slugger Lance Berkman after a full count. "I always struggled with the changeup and didn't throw it for effect until 2005," Politte said. "With a 3-and-2 count on Berkman, A.J. (Pierzynski) calls for changeup. I wasn't going to shake him off. A.J. had called the game well for me all year. I threw it and struck him out." Then he walked Morgan Ensberg on another full count. Politte was taken out. His pitching mates walked the next batter, then Jason Lane hit an RBI double to tie the game, 5-5. (The White Sox won in 14 innings.)

In the Series-ending Game Four, Politte entered in the bottom of the eighth inning with a 1-0 lead and got future Hall of Famer Craig Biggio to ground out and – after hitting Willy Taveras and walking Berkman intentionally – got Ensberg to fly out. Neal Cotts took over and got the third out. Bobby Jenks worked the bottom of the ninth and secured the victory. That score held – and the celebration began. "To jump on a pile of teammates that you've been through thick and thin with and finish it off was an amazing experience," he said.

In 2006 the euphoria ended quickly for Politte. Before the season and during spring training, he pitched through shoulder pain and then went on the disabled list. He returned in July but wasn't ready. "I could have thrown a marble to batters with blindfolds and they would have hit me," he said. "I couldn't get anyone out." The White Sox released him on July 20, 2006. The Cleveland Indians signed him for the 2007 season, but he pitched only eight innings for the Double-A Akron Aeros and Cleveland gave up on him.[14] In 2008 the Cardinals offered another opportunity. "I went to big-league camp. Tony (La Russa) said, 'Go to Triple A, get some innings there and you'll be one of the first guys up.' I was optimistic." This time, after surgery on a torn rotator cuff, Politte lasted only 9⅓ innings of work.[15] "I blew out (my shoulder) again," he said. "It was a fairly clear time to retire."

Adjusting to life after baseball took time. And nagging injuries did not go away. He had hip replacement surgery in 2009, stemming from a minor-league injury when he dived back into second base in 1998, and two more hip surgeries in 2011 and 2013. He considered coaching, but when Cleveland offered a minor-league job, he and his wife, Jennifer, had three young boys, so he picked family. He invested in a promotional supplies business and coached his sons' travel baseball teams. In 2021 he began working as a project manager at American Fire, a St. Louis company producing interior sprinkler systems.

In 2017 Politte's family and in-laws watched when 2005 World Series games were rerun on TV. "I watched with a big smile on my face," he said. Then he stepped into another room and became tearful. "Once you get to the majors, you want to stay there. Then you win the World Series, you want to keep doing that. Then it was over. I was happy and emotional at the same time."

SOURCES

In addition to the sources cited in the Notes, the author consulted Baseball-Reference.com, TheBaseballCube.com, and baseball-almanac.com.

NOTES

1 Author interview with Cliff Politte on August 22, 2024. Unless otherwise indicated, all direct quotations attributed to Politte come from this interview.

2 Missouri Sports Hall of Fame, St. John Vianney High School Boys Soccer Program, https://mosportshalloffame.com/inductees/st-john-vianney-high-school-boys-soccer-program/.

3 Mark Buehrle had played at Jefferson three years earlier.

4 "Cliff Politte," NJCAA Region 16 Hall of Fame, https://njcaaregion16.org/hall_of_fame/Cliff_Politte.

5 "Clifford Edward Politte" (Cliff's father), https://www.statscrew.com/minorbaseball/stats/p-49ddccb4.

6 "Baseball Prospectus 1998," https://www.baseballprospectus.com/player/1006/cliff-politte.

7 Politte interview.

8 Scott Fitzgerald, "Former MLB Pitcher Politte Has Come Full Circle Since Vianney Days," *St. Louis Today*, October 26, 2011. https://www.stltoday.com/sports/high-school/baseball/former-mlb-pitcher-politte-has-come-full-circle-since-vianney-days/article_e5966dd4-ffeb-11e0-adcf-0019bb30f31a.html.

9 Fitzgerald.

10 Kevin Neary and Leigh A. Tobin, *Major League Dads: Baseball's Best Players Reflect on the Fathers Who Inspired Them to Love the Game* (Philadelphia: Running Press, 2012), 173.

11 Building a Champion: Cliff Politte, SB Nation, South Side Sox, https://www.southsidesox.com/2005/11/9/173034/181.

12 Chris Kamka, "Remember That Guy: White Sox Reliever Cliff Politte," NBC Sports Chicago, March 31, 2020, online link no longer exists.

13 Kamka.

14 "Cliff Politte," St. Louis College Baseball Hall of Fame alumni, https://stlcollegebaseball.com/hall-of-fame-alumni/33-cliff-politte.

15 Fitzgerald.

AARON ROWAND

By Carter Cromwell

More than once, Aaron Rowand's style of play has been described as hard-nosed. The world saw why on May 11, 2006.

Rowand was in his first season with the Philadelphia Phillies after five years with the Chicago White Sox, and his team was hosting the New York Mets, who had loaded the bases with two out in the top of the first inning. Xavier Nady worked the count to 3-and-2, jumped on a belt-high fastball from Phillies right-hander Gavin Floyd, and drove the ball to deep center field at Citizens Bank Park.

Running at full speed and with his back to home plate, Rowand reached above his head to make the catch and almost simultaneously crashed into the fence, his nose colliding with the bar on top of the fence.[1] His knee dented the "M" in the W.B. Mason ad on the fence.[2] He suffered a broken nose and facial fractures around one eye that put him on the disabled list.

"What a great, great – perhaps game-saving – catch by Rowand!" legendary Phillies broadcaster Harry Kalas exclaimed on the telecast.[3] Kalas was right. The play saved three runs in a game Philadelphia won by 2-0.

Aaron Rowand   2005

"The effort, the determination, the want-to," Phillies manager Charlie Manuel said afterward. "The way he caught the ball. He knew he was going to hit the fence."[4] Mets manager Willie Randolph said "You see great catches all the time, but to see a guy sacrifice his body like that made it even greater."[5] But no one was surprised. As Kalas said, "[He] would run into a brick wall to help his team win."[6]

Recalling the play years later, Rowand said, "I remember thinking that if I catch this ball, we're going to win the game."[7] In fact, he nearly ran into the wall in a game not long after returning from the lineup and said simply, "My job is to catch balls hit in my direction."[8]

It wasn't the first time Rowand had made contact with an outfield wall. In August 2001, he temporarily preserved White Sox pitcher Dan Wright's no-hit bid with a spectacular seventh-inning catch followed by a crash into the wall.[9] Nick Capra, the director of player development for the White Sox, said in 2015 that "fans [in Chicago] have always reserved a special place for Aaron because of his all-out style of play and love for the game."[10]

Rowand showed that later in his career with the San Francisco Giants, a classic example coming on July 10, 2009. With one out in the ninth inning, San Diego's Edgar Gonzalez hit a rocket that Rowand tracked down to preserve an eventual no-hitter by the Giants' Jonathan Sanchez. Rowand made a leaping grab and then smacked back-first into the center-field wall.[11] "I played hard," Rowand said. "My coaches and my father taught me to play like that."[12] I played baseball with a football mentality."[13]

Aaron Ryan Rowand was born on August 29, 1977, in Portland, Oregon. His father, Bob, owned an air-conditioning business, and his mother, Connie, was a registered nurse in a neo-natal intensive care unit. He had a brother, Don, and a sister, Christie.[14]

When he was 10 years old, Aaron often played slow-pitch softball with his father in an adult league when the team was short on players. "He played better than a lot of the grownups," Bob recalled. "So he worked on his skills."[15]

After later moving to Southern California, Rowand graduated from Glendora High School. After that, Rowand narrowed his college choices to Southern Cal and Cal State-Fullerton. Fullerton Coach George Horton was at Rowand's home to sign him when USC coach Mike Gillespie called. Rowand told him that he was about to sign with Fullerton, "and he told me, 'It's my fault. We didn't get there soon enough.'"[16]

Soon after, Rowand had another decision to make, as the Mets had drafted him in the 40th round of the 1995 amateur free-agent draft. Rowand said he weighed his options as to where he'd be drafted and how much money he'd be offered, compared with the benefits of getting an education. "I thought I would be a top-three-round pick, but the scouts realized I kind of wanted to go to college, so I fell to late in the draft. After summer ball, they offered a lot more money, but it still wasn't enough to keep me from going to college."[17]

He was named an All-American after his final season in 1998, in which the Titans won the South Division of the Big West Conference, and finished with a career batting mark of .345.[18] He played in the summers of 1996 and 1997 with the Brewster Whitecaps of the prestigious Cape Cod League.[19]

Rowand acknowledged how much he learned in both places. "When I was in high school, I thought I had the game figured out," he said, "but then I went to Fullerton and felt dumb. There was so much stuff that I didn't have a grasp of. Fullerton is where I learned to play the game the right way. The same with my two years in the CCBL – Bill Mosiello was one of the toughest coaches I ever played for, and he was tougher on me than the other guys. He saw something in me that I didn't see in myself. It was there that I learned more how to hit with my hands instead of with my body."[20]

Rowand's decision to reject the Mets after high school and attend college paid off, as his stock rose dramatically in the ensuing three years. He improved from a 40th-round pick in 1995 to a supplemental first-round selection – the 35th player chosen – by the White Sox in 1998 and received a bonus of $575,000.[21]

"It was his dream come true," Bob Rowand said. "He made us all cry and we were all excited. We couldn't wait for the next step in his life. He competed well in high school and in college and stuff, and now it was on to the Minor Leagues."[22]

Duane Shaffer, then the White Sox scouting director, said, "I was extremely happy to get a kid like him. I knew the physical tools, but it was the mental side for him. He was going to make himself a big-leaguer – no matter what. This kid had tremendous determination. When he was there for the taking as the supplemental pick, we were extremely happy – because we knew we were getting a gamer, one of those guys that loved to put the uniform on and do whatever he could do to help a ballclub win. I just had a really good feeling about him … the way he went about his business. … You look at him, and you know this guy is a big-leaguer."[23]

As Bob Rowand said, "He just has the desire and energy about him that doesn't stop. He'd be the first one to practice and the last one to leave all the time. There were times even during high school; we would go back after practice at 8 p.m. to the batting cages."[24]

Reportedly, the evaluation was that Rowand had good power and good arm strength, but some wondered about his strike-zone judgment and ability to make firm contact.[25] In the long term, Rowand largely overcame those concerns, at least when based simply on strikeouts and walks as percentages of plate appearances. He struck out 16 percent of the time in the minor leagues and in 19 percent of his major-league plate appearances. In 2023 major-league players struck out an average of 22.7 percent. On the other hand, Rowand's walk rate was never high. He walked about 6.4 percent of the time in the minors and 5.4 percent of the time in the majors. Major leaguers' average walk rate in 2023 was 8.6 percent.[26]

Regardless, Rowand made an impact at the beginning of his professional career, averaging .342 with a .410 on-base percentage and .906 OPS for Hickory (North Carolina) in the Class-A South Atlantic League. The next season, he moved up to High-A ball with Winston-Salem in the Carolina League, finishing with a .279 batting average and an .840 OPS, along with 24 home runs and 88 RBIs, and earning a spot on the league all-star team. His on-base percentage, though, fell to .336, as his strikeout rate increased and his walk rate decreased.

After that second season, on November 27, 1999, Rowand married the former Marianne Griffen on November 27, 1999. They have two children, daughter Tatum and son McKay.

In 2000 Rowand stepped up to Birmingham of the Double-A Southern League and got all-star recognition, though his numbers again dropped from the previous season to a .258 batting average, .321 on-base percentage, and .759 OPS. He again showed some power by hitting 20 home runs and having 37 percent of his hits go for extra bases.

That performance earned Rowand a shot at Triple A with Charlotte of the International League, where he batted .295, posted an .879 OPS and hit 16 home runs in 82 games before getting called up to the White Sox in June.

"I was about halfway home from a game when I got a call from our manager, Nick Leyva," Rowand recalled, "so I turned around and went back to the field. I was wondering what I'd done wrong, and then he told me I was going to the big leagues."[27]

Joining the White Sox in St. Louis, he got to Busch Stadium extra early that first day and simply sat in the dugout for an hour or so – "Just in awe of the surroundings. Later, I watched [Cardinal slugger] Mark McGwire take batting practice and thought that if everyone hit the ball that far, I wasn't going to be there long."[28]

"I'd called a couple of guys I'd played with earlier, and they took me to the field and told me some of the unwritten rules," he added. "A funny thing – to get to our workout facility, we had to go the Cardinals' side of the stadium. They told me where the gym was, but when I opened the door it turned out to be the Cardinals' training room and

McGwire was sitting there. He just smiled and said, 'Next door down.'"

Rowand's first action was in an 8-3 loss to St. Louis on June 16 when he pinch-hit in the ninth inning. He acknowledged that he was both excited and nervous. "We were losing, and our manager, Jerry Manuel, said to grab a bat and hit third. They brought their closer, Dave Veres, in to get some work. With two out, the entire crowd was standing, clapping and cheering, and I think everyone could see my legs shaking. I popped out to the pitcher on a 1-and-1 count, but at least I didn't punch out in my first at-bat."[29]

Rowand got his first hit three days later – a seventh-inning single on a 1-and-1 pitch from Tony Cogan of the Kansas City Royals. "I'd faced Tony in college and in the Cape Cod League, so I was comfortable against him," he recalled. "I ended up getting a single down the right-field line. I thought about trying to stretch it into a double, but I didn't want to get thrown out after getting my first hit."[30]

Rowand, a cousin of former major-league pitcher James Shields, got his first major-league home run off Pittsburgh's Jason Schmidt on July 7. Overall, he had 123 at-bats for the White Sox and averaged .293. He then spent the entire 2002 season with the White Sox, batting .258 in 126 games. After beginning his White Sox career as a reserve, he became the regular center fielder when the team traded Kenny Lofton to San Francisco on July 28. Rowand had batted just .204 until the trade, but averaged .291 the rest of the way.

After the season, however, he broke a rib and his left shoulder blade in a dirt-bike accident. "I did something really stupid," Rowand admitted. "I had to call [general manager] Kenny Williams to tell him, and he hung up on me."

"I had surgery on November 13 [2002]. [Afterward] I was in the gym eight hours a day, six days a week to get ready for [spring training]. I started swinging the bat a month and a half before I was supposed to. I wasn't at 100 percent when camp started, but I made it through and started Opening Day. Still, I got off to a slow start."[31] He hit just .133 in 23 games and was sent to the minors for 32 games before being recalled.

"I started questioning myself – was I ever going to be the same as I had been before the accident? I started trying not to fail instead of trying to succeed. But I felt better in Charlotte, where it was warmer. When I came back up, I hit a home run in my first game and took off after that."[32]

The 2004 season was Rowand's best from some statistical standpoints – a .310 batting average, .905 OPS, 17 stolen bases, and a 5.7 WAR – and his 24 home runs represented his second-highest season total.

Rowand's offensive statistics the next season fell off – a .270 average, .736 OPS, and 13 home runs – but he was an important factor in the White Sox' drive to their first World Series championship since 1917. Defensively in the regular season, Rowand averaged 15 defensive runs saved (DRS) above average and had an Ultimate Zone Rating (UZR) of

17.4.[33] His DRS figure tied for second in the major leagues. His UZR was best among American League center fielders and second in both leagues only to that of Andruw Jones (26.2) of the Atlanta Braves.[34]

Chicago won the AL Central Division title with a 99-63 mark and then dispatched Boston, the Los Angeles Angels, and Houston in the playoffs. The White Sox barreled through the playoffs, losing only the first game of the American League Championship Series to the Angels. Rowand batted .400 against the Red Sox in the Division Series, .167 in the ALCS, and .294 against the Astros in the World Series. For the 12 games, he averaged .267 with a .733 OPS.

Rowand said the club had begun "seeing our capabilities toward the end of spring training. We had upgraded our defense, had more speed on the basepaths, and the pitching staff was solid. Another big moment was when our closer, Dustin Hermanson, got hurt and they brought up Bobby Jenks and he stepped in and did a great job."[35] Jenks came up in July, earned six saves, and then got four saves in the playoffs, including in the clinching Game Four of the World Series.

"The media picked us to finish fourth in our division, and that pissed a lot of people off," Rowand said, "so we played with a chip on our shoulders. We won so many one-run games that year [a 35-19 mark in those] that we were used to pressure-filled at bats, so the playoffs didn't feel any different."[36]

He added that "the ALCS was amazing. We won in five games, and the bullpen guys only pitched two-thirds of an inning [in Game One]. We got four straight complete games after that. I don't think you'll see that again."[37]

For him, though, things were different soon after. On November 25, 2005, less than a month after the World Series, Rowand was traded to Philadelphia with minor-league pitchers Gio González and Daniel Haigwood for eventual Hall of Famer Jim Thome.

"I was heart-broken," Rowand said. "Ironically, not long before that, I'd been in Chicago for the unveiling of a DVD about the World Series. I was talking with reporters beforehand and said I wanted to wear [the White Sox] uniform the rest of my career. The next day I was in a taxi going to the airport, heard on the radio a rumor that I was going to be traded for Thome, and thought that was the stupidest thing I'd ever heard. [But] then I got the call from Kenny (Williams) a couple of weeks later."[38]

The 2006 season was difficult one, as Rowand missed time after crashing into the wall against the Mets and, later, after breaking an ankle on August 21 in a collision with second baseman Chase Utley. Rowand batted .301 through June 5, but only .236 afterward and finished with a .262 mark and a .745 OPS.

The next season was better, though. The Phillies won the National League East Division title, and Rowand had perhaps his best year, averaging .309 with 189 hits, 27 home runs, and 89 RBIs. He won a Gold Glove Award, made the All-Star team, finished fifth in the league with 11 outfield assists, and topped National League outfielders with a .995 fielding percentage. "Making the All-Star team was a dream come true, and so was winning a Gold Glove," he said. "I've always prided myself on defense."[39]

Rowand called 2007 a breakout year, and it came at a perfect time since he was a free agent at the end of that season. He parlayed his success into a five-year, $60 million contract with the San Francisco Giants. "Aaron is an all-around player who is coming into his prime and helps us check off two boxes – an extremely talented defensive center fielder and a middle-of-the-order presence," Giants general manager Brian Sabean said. "His ability in center field definitely plays to our ballpark and will help provide more stability to our pitching staff."[40]

However, Rowand did not do as well as expected, batting .253 with a .704 OPS over four seasons. In 2008 he batted .271, a 38-point drop from the year before, and his OPS fell to .749. The next season he posted a slash line of .261/.319/.419.

In 2010 the Giants won their first World Series title since 1954, but Rowand's batting average dropped to .230 and his OPS to .659. He played in just 105 games, his fewest since 2003, when he spent part of the year in the minor leagues. The next season, he struggled even more, batting just .233 with a career-low .621 OPS. With a year remaining on his contract, he was designated for assignment on August 31, 2011, and released on September 8.

On December 12, 2011, Rowand signed a minor-league contract with the Miami Marlins that included an invitation to spring training, but he hit just .128 that spring and was released on March 29, 2012. He finished his career with a .273/.330/.435 slash line, along with 136 home runs, 536 RBIs, and 1,193 hits.

Aside from his hell-for-leather approach to the game, Rowand is remembered for his unusual batting stance.[41] One writer said it could "most simply be compared to someone with a really straight back sitting on an invisible stool (or some other thing one might sit on) with their feet pointed out."[42] Another described it this way: "First, as he settles, bowlegged, in the batter's box, he does some sort of retro homage to Elvis the Pelvis ... as he bends his knees and seems to slowly gyrate his hips. Then he holds his bat outward, at groin level, parallel to the ground. And then he wags the bat, slowly, while continuing to stand bowlegged and undulate his hips. And this goes on for ... well, a beat too long to avoid an NC-17 rating if it were a movie."[43]

After retiring, Rowand occasionally filled in on the White Sox' radio or television broadcasts. He also was a guest instructor in spring training of 2015, worked for few years as the White Sox' minor-league outfield and baserunning coach, and managed the Glendale team in the Arizona Fall League in 2016.

He says he stopped coaching in 2018 when his son, Tatum, began high school – "I wanted to be able to see him play," Rowand said. His son now is in college, though no longer playing baseball, while his daughter graduated from college in 2023 and plans to work in physical therapy. He and his wife divorced in 2017, and he is engaged to Lisa Dinubilo.[44]

With a permanent home in San Clemente, California, he spends much of his time golfing and fishing.[45]

He had something left as a player, too, participating four years at the annual Hall of Fame Classic exhibition game at Cooperstown, New York, and winning the MVP award twice. In 2017 he also won the pregame home-run derby.[46]

It was just one more example of Rowand giving it all. As he said when looking back on his catch against the Mets, "When I'm through playing, if that's the one thing I'm remembered for, I'll gladly take that. ... It means that I played the game hard. I played the game right. As a player, I don't think you could ask for anything more."[47]

NOTES

1   "Aaron Rowand breaks his nose going for a catch and holds on" (2006), Video on Reddit: https://www.reddit.com/r/baseball/comments/opc1zk/aaron_rowand_breaks_his_nose_going_for_a_catch/, accessed January 10, 2024.

2   Dan McQuade, "10 Years Ago Today, Aaron Rowand Ran Into a Wall in South Philly," *Philadelphia Magazine*, May 11, 2016, https://www.phillymag.com/news/2016/05/11/aaron-rowand-phillies-wall-broken-nose/, accessed December 14, 2023.

3   Video of play on Reddit.

4   McQuade.

5   McQuade.

6   Video of play on Reddit.

7   Tommy Canale, "Aaron Rowand – 2005 WS Champion w/Chicago White Sox," *Before The Lights Podcast*, April 30, 2020, https://www.beforethelightspod.com/beforethelights-episodes/aaron-rowand-2005-ws-champion-w-chicago-white-sox, accessed January 13, 2024.

8   McQuade.

9   YouTube Video, https://www.youtube.com/watch?v=dpaBmWmsjPc, accessed January. 10, 2024.

10   Scott Merkin, "White Sox Tab Rowand as Minors Instructor," MLB.com, November 23, 2015, *https://www.mlb.com/whitesox/news/aaron-rowand-hired-as-white-sox-instructor/c-157978288*, accessed January 16, 2024.

11   E.A., "A Real Twist of Fate: Jonathan Sanchez Throws a No-Hitter," *Bleacher Report*, July 11, 2009, https://bleacherreport.com/articles/216274-a-real-twist-of-fate-jonathan-sanchez-throws-a-nohitter#:~:text=In%20what%20was%20perhaps%20the,outs%20in%20the%20ninth%20inning, accessed January 11, 2024. See also YouTube video: https://www.youtube.com/watch?v=H2-uBVoEOn0, accessed January 11, 2024.

12   McQuade.

13   Canale.

14   Aaron Rowand telephone interview, July 17, 2024.

15   Brittany Ghiroli, "Path of the Pros: Aaron Rowand," mlb.com, November 2, 2009: https://web.archive.org/web/20091108104256/http://sanfrancisco.giants.mlb.com/news/article.jsp?ymd=20091102&content_id=7602048&vkey=news_sf&fext=.jsp&c_id=sf.

16 Matt Brown, "Aaron Rowand Chats about Baseball and Life," Video on YouTube, HTTPS://WWW.YOUTUBE.COM/WATCH?V=AUPXV0ZF9IG, accessed January 13, 2024.

17 Canale.

18 Cal State-Fullerton baseball website, https://fullertontitans.com/sports/2023/8/3/sports-m-basebl-archives-index.aspx#1996, accessed January 16, 2024.

19 Taylor Viles, "All-Time Roster Breakdowns: East Division," Cape Cod Baseball League website, November 5, 2020, https://www.capecodbaseball.org/news/index.html?article_id=2816, accessed January 16, 2024.

20 Canale.

21 https://www.thebaseballcube.com/content/player/1440/salaries/, accessed January 9, 2024.

22 Ghiroli.

23 Chuck Wasserstrom, "Inside the Draft Room: The 1998 White Sox," mlb.traderumors.com, April 3, 2017, https://www.mlbtraderumors.com/players/aaron-rowand, accessed January 9, 2024.

24 Ghiroli.

25 John Sickles, "Career Profile: Aaron Rowand," MinorLeagueBall, May 22, 2011, *https://www.minorleagueball.com/2011/5/22/2182112/career-profile-aaron-rowand-san-francisco-giants*, accessed January 11, 2024.

26 FanGraphs.com, https://www.fangraphs.com/leaders/major-league?pos=all&stats=bat&lg=all&qual=0&type=1&season=2023&season1=2023&ind=0&rost=0&age=0&filter=&players=0&team=0%2Css.

27 Canale.

28 Brown.

29 Canale.

30 Canale.

31 Canale.

32 Canale.

33 Joshua Finkelstein, "The 2005 Chicago White Sox Team Was Phenomenal, but Never Would Have Been So Great Without the Help of One Man's Defense," *Southside Showdown,* May 17, 2020, *https://southsideshowdown.com/2020/05/17/chicago-white-sox-aaron-rowand-defense/*, accessed January 15, 2024.

34 FanGraphs.com, https://www.fangraphs.com/leaders/major-league?lg=al%2Cnl&qual=0&ind=0&rost=0&age=0&filter=&players=0&season1=2005&season=2005&stats=fld&pos=cf&team=0&sortcol=13&sortdir=default.

35 Aaron Rowand telephone interview, July 17, 2024.

36 Canale.

37 Aaron Rowand telephone interview, July 17, 2024.

38 Canale.

39 Canale.

40 Associated Press, "Aaron Rowand Agrees to $60 Million, 5-Year Deal with Giants," *San Mateo* (California) *Daily Journal*, December 12, 2007, https://www.smdailyjournal.com/news/bay_area/aaron-rowand-agrees-to-60-million-5-year-deal-with-giants/article_ea5b093b-490b-51c4-8bff-d01905c89e8c.html, accessed January 15, 2024.

41 https://www.youtube.com/watch?v=XDWQOiTtVic.

42 Jacob Shafer, "Ranking the 10 Most Unique Batting Stances in Recent MLB History," *Bleacher Report,* May 12, 2020, *https://static-assets.bleacherreport.com/articles/2891152-ranking-the-10-most-unique-batting-stances-in-recent-mlb-history*, accessed January 15, 2024.

43 Robert Rubino, "Giants Outfielder Has Lewdest Batting Stance in Baseball," *Santa Rosa* (California) *Press Democrat*, July 16, 2011, https://www.pressdemocrat.com/article/news/giants-outfielder-has-lewdest-batting-stance-in-baseball-2/, accessed January 15, 2024.

44 Aaron Rowand, telephone interview, July 17, 2024.

45 Aaron Rowand, telephone interview, July 17, 2024

46 Bill Francis, "Rowand Stars, Legends Shine at Hall of Fame Classic," BaseballHall.org, May 28, 2017, https://baseballhall.org/HOFClassic/rowand-stars-legends-shine-at-hof-classic, accessed January 15, 2024.

47 YouTube Video, "Aaron Rowand's Catch 2006," undated, www.youtube.com/watch?v=MS5GCKXO7D0, accessed January 12, 2024.

DAVID SANDERS

By Kenneth Huang

There is a dream of baseball that most Americans know. A small-town boy from a working-class family making it to the major leagues and pitching. Few realize their dream. David Sanders did. He progressed from being an all-state player for his high school in rural Kansas to contending for pitching records at the collegiate level to making appearances at the highest levels of professional baseball with the Chicago White Sox in 2003 and then pitching in two games for the World Series championship team in 2005. Though his time at the professional level was cut short by injury, he lived out a childhood dream shared by millions of Americans.

David Andrew Sanders was born in Oklahoma City, Oklahoma, on August 29, 1979, to Don and Debbie Sanders. His father, who owned a home remodeling company, introduced David to a variety of sports, including baseball and football. David's mother was an elementary-school principal. When he was 9, his family moved two hours away to the quiet town of Derby in Kansas. He attended Derby Middle School and kept pursuing his childhood sports, mainly baseball and a year of wrestling.[1] "My parents had discouraged football at a young age, but said I could play if I wanted to when I got to high school," he told the author. "I had looked forward to playing it, but decided I would be better off focusing on baseball."[2] "My dad is a baseball guy and he recognized how much of a blessing it was to be left-handed. When I got to high school, he told me, 'If you're still excited about football, by all means, go for it.' I had started doing so well on baseball that I continued that focus."[3]

Sanders played baseball throughout high school and kept honing his craft. He excelled academically and in baseball, being placed on his school's honor roll for all four years, while also being named an All-League Player in his sophomore year and an All-State Utility Player in his senior year.[4] His backyard fence became riddled with circular indents from his constant practice and training.[5] Sanders' pitching prowess caught the attention of numerous Division I scouts. Not wanting to miss varsity play in his freshman year, he decided instead to commit to a junior college, Barton Community College in Great Bend, Kansas. He graduated from high school in 1997 and set off to Barton, two hours away from Derby.[6]

At Barton Community College, in a sleepy area that captured the idyllic Kansas environment and atmosphere,

Sanders excelled in pitching. He posted an ERA of 3.34 with 82 strikeouts in 52⅓ innings in his sophomore year.[7] His performance earned him recognition as an all-conference pitcher and secured him the third spot in the school's single-season strikeout record at the time.[8] Sanders began to catch the attention of major-league baseball scouts, particularly that of White Sox scouts Ken Stauffer and John Kazanas.[9] In the 1999 amateur draft, Sanders was the White Sox' sixth-round choice and signed a contract.[10]

The White Sox envisioned the 6-foot-tall 200-pounder as a strong reliever. He made his rookie-league debut for the White Sox' team in the Arizona League.[11] In seven appearances he posted an ERA of 1.10 with 26 strikeouts in 16⅓ innings.[12] For 2000 he was promoted to the Advanced-A Winston-Salem Warthogs (CarolinaLeague).[13]

At the Advanced-A level, larger crowds, better competition, and more investment by the organization combine to create a semblance of what the majors are like. Manager Brian Dayett was determined to make his players understand the rigors of professional baseball and to turn them

David Sanders   2005

into true professional players.[14] He told a writer, "We're trying to instill the work ethic into these kids. We try to tell them, you get past this level to Double A, you've made the most important step in pro ball. ..."[15]

Sanders joined the ranks alongside future major leaguers such as future Olympic gold medalist Jon Rauch, future Team USA pitcher Gary Majewski, and others.[16] He pitched in a team-high 51 games. He accrued a 3-2 won-lost record and a 5.21 ERA with 50 strikeouts in 48⅓ innings.[17] For the 2001 season he was promoted to the Double-A Birmingham Barons (Southern League).

Sanders spent two seasons with the Barons. In 2001 he was 3-0 with a 2.65 ERA in 36 games out of the bullpen.[18] In his second year, Sanders posted a 1.84 ERA in 47 appearances. In his last 30⅔ innings, he gave up only three runs, for a 0.88 ERA.[19] Thirty-five of his 47 appearances were scoreless and 16 were hitless; he averaged 8.6 strikeouts per nine innings pitched.[20] His performance led him to be rated the number-13 prospect in the White Sox organization and he was promoted to the Triple-A Charlotte Knights (International League) and invited to the White Sox' 2003 spring training.[21]

After pitching in five games for Charlotte, Sanders was called up by the White Sox.[22] The White Sox sent down catcher Josh Paul to make room for Sanders. White Sox manager Jerry Manuel said, "For the most part, we know we'll need a pitcher before we need a catcher. [Sanders is] a guy that has pitches that can get a righty out and can get a left-handed hitter out. There was no doubt he was the guy."[23]

On April 23, 2003, Sanders made his major-league debut against the Baltimore Orioles at Camden Yards, relieving Tom Gordon in the bottom of the eighth with the White Sox trailing 7-1.[24] He recorded his first big-league out by forcing Jay Gibbons of the Orioles to pop up to the first baseman, then he recorded his first strikeout by freezing José León, and finally striking out Geronimo Gil swinging to end the inning and his first outing.[25]

Speaking of his debut, Sanders said, "That first appearance is unlike any other. It just becomes baseball again with the rest of them, but the first one for a reliever is such a strange feeling. ... I got to the mound, started taking it all in and I had 'that moment' where you realize why you sacrificed so much to be there in that moment."[26]

Outside of the game, in his time in the majors, Sanders attended media events and participated with the rest of the team, one notable event being when the White Sox visited the University of Chicago Children's Hospital during its opening year.[27]

Perhaps his best moment of the season came in Cleveland on July 13. The Indians had just scored three runs off Jon Garland in the fifth and tied the game, 4-4, with runners on second and third and two outs. Sanders walked Ben Broussard, loading the bases, then struck out Travis Hafner. Two weeks later, on July 25, he was optioned to Charlotte, having made a total of 20 appearances for Chicago. He

worked 22 innings in relief, facing 102 batters, opponents batting .281 against him. His ERA was 6.14.[28]

With Charlotte, he worked 19 games in relief, closing 10, with a 3.68 ERA.

Sanders spent all of 2004 with Charlotte, with 40 appearances, 18 as the closer, and averaging 7.8 strikeouts per nine innings pitched.[29] He finished 2-2 with a 6.06 ERA. His 2005 season saw markedly better results, Sanders appearing in 56 games (closing 18) and having a 3.08 ERA and a record of 4-2. When major-league rosters expanded, he was a September 1 call-up.[30]

Sanders returned to the White Sox against the Detroit Tigers on September 2 at US Cellular Field.[31] He relieved starter Freddy Garcia, who departed after seven innings with a 9-1 lead. Pitching the top of the eighth, Sanders faced four batters, allowing a double to Curtis Granderson before finishing the inning. Bobby Jenks worked the ninth.

Sanders made his final professional baseball appearance against the Los Angeles Angels on September 10 in Chicago. Starter Jon Garland had been hit hard and departed after six innings with the White Sox losing, 7-2. Sanders was hit hard, as well. giving up a first-pitch home run to Chone Figgins and a total of three runs on a walk, two hits, and a sacrifice fly. Jeff Bajenaru worked the eighth and ninth of the 10-5 loss. This was Sanders' last professional baseball game. Following a shoulder injury, Sanders retired shortly after with a career ERA of 6.75 in his 22 major-league games.[32]

Returning to Kansas, Sanders integrated himself into a nonbaseball life. He worked for different companies in Kansas and in 2025 was the director of strategic partnerships for Towerstone Inc., an insurance broker. He kept baseball in his life as well, being inducted into the Derby Hall of Fame for his baseball career, becoming a coach for a local summer baseball team, and opening a baseball school, D3 Training.[33] He and his wife, Kilee, have three children. Seeking to instill the same passion for sports that his father did for him, he takes his children to Kansas City Royals and Chiefs games.

NOTES

1   Adam Suderman, "Sanders Set to Join the Derby Hall of Fame," *Derby* (Kansas) *Informer*, August 4, 2020. https://www.derbyinformer.com/sports/sanders-set-to-join-the-derby-hall-of-fame/article_9bb2bb9e-d67b-11ea-87c2-3300aa3323ab.html.

2   Email from Dave Sanders on January 16, 2025.

3   Suderman.

4   "David Sanders," MLB.com, https://www.mlb.com/player/david-sanders-425553, accessed October 3,2024.

5   Suderman.

6   Suderman.

7   Suderman.

8   Individual single-season records provided by the Barton Community College Athletics Department, https://d2o2figo6dddog.cloudfront.net/o/x/oe3umkkajoc1jo/IndividualSingleSeasonRecords.pdf.

9   "David Sanders," MLB.com.

10   "David Sanders," MLB.com.

11   "David Sanders," MiLB.com, https://www.milb.com/player/david-sanders-425553?stats=career-r-pitching-minors&year=2024. Accessed October 2, 2024.

12   "David Sanders," MiLB.com.

13   "2000 Winston-Salem Warthogs Statistics," StatsCrew.com, https://www.statscrew.com/minorbaseball/stats/t-ww15442/y-2000. Accessed October 7, 2024.

14   Pete Zanardi, "Dayett Back Managing in White Sox System," *Connecticut Insider,* July 11, 2000. https://www.ctinsider.com/news/article/Dayett-back-managing-in-White-Sox-system-16953524.php.

15   Zanardi.

16   "2000 Winston-Salem Warthogs Statistics."

17   "2000 Winston-Salem Warthogs Statistics."

18   "David Sanders," StatsCrew.com.https://www.statscrew.com/minorbaseball/stats/p-16c5c6fe. Accessed October 8, 2024.

19   "Sanders Called Up to White Sox; Pitches Against Baltimore," *Barton Sports*, April 24, 2003, https://www.bartonsports.com/sports/bsb/2002-03/releases/20140710z9gkb0.

20   "Sanders Called Up to White Sox; Pitches Against Baltimore,"

21   Suderman.

22   Suderman.

23   "Sanders Called Up to White Sox; Pitches Against Baltimore."

24   "Sanders Called Up to White Sox; Pitches Against Baltimore."

25   "Sanders Called Up to White Sox; Pitches Against Baltimore."

26   "Sanders Set to Join the Derby Hall of Fame."

27   "David Sanders," MLB.com.

28   "David Sanders," MLB.com.

29   "David Sanders," MLB.com.

30   "David Sanders," MLB.com.

31   "Detroit Tigers vs. Chicago White Sox – September 2, 2005," Baseball-Almanac.com, https://www.baseball-almanac.com/box-scores/boxscore.php?boxid=200509020CHA, accessed October 12, 2024.

32   He had surgery to successfully repair the injury, but not enough to play again at the professional level. Sanders email January 16, 2025.

33   Suderman. Kelly Breckunitch, "Training Businesses Partner to Expand Local Opportunities," *Derby Informer*, January 20, 2023, https://www.derbyinformer.com/news/business/training-businesses-partner-to-expand-local-opportunities/article_21041b40-990b-11ed-bdc4-c3aafbfad706.html.

SHINGO TAKATSU

By Will MacLean

Shingo "Mr. Zero" Takatsu: His nickname sounds like a superhero. He earned it by giving up zero runs while pitching in 11 Nippon Series championship games for a 0.00 ERA. His key pitch, "The Frisbee," sounds like a superpower. It was a side-arm sinker averaging around 68 mph, so slow that Brooks Boyer, the White Sox' senior vice president of sales and marketing, described it as "like Bugs Bunny coming in. People get to swing at it two or three times when they miss it."[1]

When Takatsu entered the game, a gong rang out through the ballpark, thrilling the fans. Takatsu was a right-handed side-arm pitcher listed at 6 feet tall and 180 pounds, who was beloved by White Sox fans during his brilliant but brief time on the White Sox. As of 2023, he is the first and only pitcher to record saves in all four top-level leagues in four countries – Japan, the US major leagues, Korea Professional Baseball, and the Chinese Professional Baseball League (Taiwan).[2] He is like a gunslinger with the card: "Have gun, will travel." There is so much more to his Japanese Baseball Hall of Fame career.

Shingo Takatsu   2005

He was born on November 25, 1968, in Hiroshima, Japan. His father, Toshiaki Takatsu,[3] was a self-employed plasterer and business owner, with a hired crew to help him lay tiles, bricks, and paint, while his mother, Mitsue Takatsu,[4] cared for the household.[5] From birth to elementary school, his family lived in a one-story house in Danbara-cho, Hiroshima City. Takatsu remembered, "It was an old wooden house with impressive glass doors … at the foot of a mountain [Hijiyama], right behind where the atomic bomb was dropped. There must have been some damage, but thanks to the mountains, this area survived without burning."[6]

They later moved into a four-bedroom high-rise apartment in front of Mount Hijiyama. From his bedroom, Takatsu had an excellent view of Hiroshima Municipal Stadium, the home ballpark of the local team, the Hiroshima Toyo Carp.[7]

"Of course, I was a huge Carp fan," said Takatsu. "For a year, I went to [Hiroshima] Municipal Stadium, with my dad and [riding bicycles] with my friends. Back then, fans would rush down to the field after the game. … As [kids], we would always race to see who could get over the fence and reach second base first. … When I returned, I was unable to climb the fence. … I had to have the security guard push [me] up."[8]

The Takatsu family would go to a fugu restaurant owned by his aunt, where young Takatsu once saw one of his Carp heroes, closer Yutaka Enatsu. Takatsu thought, "Enatsu is cool" when he watched him pitch – he always liked the closer.[9]

He was too shy to approach the player, but his aunt said to Enatsu, "My nephew plays baseball and is a big Carp fan. Would you like to [meet him]?"[10]

When Enatsu agreed, young Takatsu said to his hero, "I play baseball, too."[11] Takatsu had started playing baseball with the local team, the Danbara Red Eagles, at age 9.

Enatsu replied, "Do your best."[12]

Relating the story 30 years after, Takatsu said, "I didn't [ask] anything. else … I was so nervous … [the] intimidating feeling … aura … and power remain clear after many years. It's burned into my memory."[13]

Takatsu went to Hiroshima City Danbara Junior High School, then transferred to Hiroshima Technical High School. There, he went to the Japanese national high-school tournament: the "Koshien."[14] But his dream was to play in a Carp uniform. Takatsu said, "My dream stadium is Hiroshima Municipal Stadium. If I was offered a match at either Koshien or Municipal Stadium, I would choose Municipal Stadium without hesitation."[15]

Takatsu wasn't a star in high school. "There were other super aces and I couldn't compete with the same pitching style," he said.[16] One was his childhood friend Shunji Ueda. "I wondered how I, who was mediocre in everything, could become an asset to the team."[17] He wasn't as strong as Ueda, but he searched and found his own way – pitching underhand.[18]

In his first two years of high school, Takatsu did not make the first team. But his manager, Narumi Ogawa, believed in him, saying "[You] are a late bloomer. ... Someday, [you] will become something" – words that Takatsu later remembered as "a precious treasure."[19] Working on his underhand delivery, he became the second starter in his third season, 1986. "Ueda was the absolute ace ... and I was a distant second," he acknowledged.[20]

In the semifinals of the Hiroshima prefectural tournament, Ueda was out with appendicitis,[21] and Takatsu started in four games, threw two shutouts, and pitched a complete-game victory over Onomichi Higashi High School to help his team advance to Koshien.[22]

But at the Koshien, Ueda returned, and Takatsu struggled – instead of pitching, he played infield, with no hits in seven at-bats. Takatsu felt a little overshadowed by Ueda, saying, "Ace Ueda was said to be the number-one pitcher in the tournament at Koshien ... and I didn't get any attention. ... It's all Ueda, Ueda, Ueda. Ueda's presence was too big."[23] Even with his struggles, the upbeat Takatsu said, "I was very happy to be able to play in ... Koshien."[24]

This drove him to improve in college at Asia University. Takatsu compared the dormitory to a "prison sentence" – a former hospital where, he said, "[The] construction was questionable ... [and] the dining room was a former operating room."[25] Rooms were cramped, practices grueling, and some players ran away.

At Asia University, Takatsu again found himself in the role of second starter behind southpaw Hideki Koike, soon to be drafted by eight NPB teams. As Takatsu put it, "Seriously, there's a monster pitcher everywhere I go."[26]

To adjust, Takatsu said, "I look at [the] Ace ... and figure out what I'm lacking."[27] So he lifted his delivery to side-arm and learned the slider, which would become his superpower. He explained: "When I entered college, I couldn't throw the speed or breaking ball to match that level, so I changed myself to survive ... raising [my] arm a little to increase the speed of the ball."[28] Through four years of college, Takatsu pitched in 40 games and had 11 wins and 15 losses.[29]

With his side-arm delivery, Takatsu was drafted by the Yakult Swallows in the third round of the Japanese 1991 draft. For his first couple of seasons in the NPB, Takatsu bounced between starter and reliever. In his first season,

1991, he started two of 13 appearances with a 1-2 record and a 4.23 ERA.

During 1992 fall training, manager Katsuya Nomura told Takatsu to focus on the sinker.[30] At that time, the velocity of his sinker was about 74 mph[31] and they wanted to slow it down.[32]

Takatsu experimented with the sinker that season. "I thought of various ways to avoid speeding up by waving my arms. The way you grip, the way you use your arms, the way you pull your elbows out ... then I created my own original grips and ways to use them that suited me."[33]

Takatsu described his sinker: "Hook the outside of your middle finger into the seam and pull it out between your middle and ring fingers ... gripping deeply and applying spin ... with my sinker, it spins and drops ... more ... a changeup than a fork."[34] Echoes of Boyer's Bugs Bunny joke: "The timing goes awry when it suddenly rises ... you ... think a slow ball was coming and go to swing, only to find out it was even slower."[35] With this new grip, Takatsu would shine.

In 1992, he appeared in 23 games, started in 11, went 5-3 with a 4.68 ERA, and helped the Swallows win the NPB Central League pennant, the second in franchise history. The Swallows lost to the Seibu Lions of the Pacific League in the Nippon Series.

On May 2, 1992, Takatsu earned his first save, against the Yomiuri Giants, and became a closer.[36] In his third season, 1993, he started only one game and pitched in a career high 56 games. He ended the season with a record of 6-4, 20 saves, 72 strikeouts, and a 2.30 ERA. That postseason, the Swallows again faced the Lions in the Nippon Series, and this time they won, beating the Lions four games to three, with Takatsu notching three saves in the series and closing game seven to clinch the championship. Summarizing his first three seasons, Takatsu said, "The first year or two was tough ... in my third year, I became a closer, and I felt the thrills and excitement. ... Once I learned how to hold back batters, I started to really enjoy baseball."[37]

In 1994 Takatsu continued this success, with eight wins, four losses, 19 saves, a 2.30 ERA, and his first NPB All-Star Game.

In 1995 Takatsu again helped his team win the Central League pennant with 28 saves. The Swallows went on to win their third Nippon Series championship, 4-1 over the Orix Blue Wave, featuring Ichiro Suzuki. Takatsu was the winning pitcher in Game Three and saved Games One and Five – again on the mound to clinch the championship.

He had 21 saves in 1996, finishing 36 of his 39 games, and made his second NPB All-Star Game.

The Swallows won the 1997 Nippon Series championship over the Lions – a rematch of 1993, featuring shortstop Kazuo Matsui. The Swallows beat the Lions 4-1, with Takatsu winning Game Three and earning a save in Game Five. He struggled as a closer that season and bounced between middle relief and spot starter, recording seven wins and four losses, with a 2.04 ERA.

In 1997, Takatsu married his wife, Maki. Next year, she was pregnant[38] with their first of two sons, Daishi and Shota.[39] His struggles continued in 1998, with only three saves and a 5.56 ERA. But he became an elite closer the next two seasons. That year, Takatsu made a brief appearance in the first scene of Hideo Nakata's horror movie *Ringu*, via actual game footage on the spooky TV. *Ringu* was later remade in the U.S. as *The Ring* (2002).

In 1999 he had 30 saves with a 2.18 ERA. and in 2000, 29 saves with a 2.08 ERA. He made the All-Star Game both years.

In 2001 the Yakult Swallows won their fourth Nippon Series championship with Takatsu as closer, 4-1 over the Osaka Kintetsu Buffaloes, who featured US import Tuffy Rhodes. Again, Takatsu clinched the winning game. That season, he had 37 saves and a 2.61 ERA.

In 2002 Takatsu continued his dominance as a closer, with 32 saves in 44 games. That year Takatsu's teammate for four championships, pitcher Kazuhisa Ishii, signed with the Los Angeles Dodgers as a free agent.[40] Takatsu thought of joining Ishii in moving to US baseball, but he was so close to the NPB all-time saves record that friend advised, "Why don't you break the Japanese record and then think again?"[41] He stayed another season.

In 2003 Takatsu continued dominating, with 34 saves, and made his fifth NPB All-Star Game. After setting a new NPB all-time saves record with 260, Takatsu declared his free agency. He held an open workout in Los Angeles, and the White Sox signed him for the 2004 season. He was the first Asian player signed by the team. He was 34 years old.

Baseball America listed Takatsu as the number-eight prospect in the White Sox organization that preseason.[42] During spring training the White Sox kept Takatsu's secret weapon, the sinker, under wraps. According to manager Ozzie Guillen: "He kept shaking off. ... He wanted to throw it. We explained to him why we didn't want [him] to throw it: We didn't want anybody to see it."[43]

Takatsu began the season as a set-up man. He made his first US major league appearance on April 9, 2004, at Yankee Stadium, where he first introduced his secret weapon, the sinker known as "The Frisbee," to MLB hitters. The first batter he faced was Hideki Matsui, who having hit his first NPB home run off Takatsu back in Japan, already knew the pitch. Matsui doubled. But Derek Derek Jeter had never seen it before, and became Takatsu's first US strikeout victim.[44] Takatsu soon hit his stride, compiling 26⅔ scoreless innings pitched, from April 23 to June 30. He moved into the closer role during that streak and earned his first save against Atlanta on June 12.

The *Chicago Tribune* wrote, "Takatsu has become something of a phenomenon at U.S. Cellular Field. ... When he enters the game, the crowd gives him a standing ovation and a gong sound is played over the loudspeaker."[45]

Takatsu's entrances into a home game were announced with the ring of a Japanese gong through the ballpark loudspeaker and a video montage on the Jumbotron, like a Shogun warrior, and the fans would stand and cheer. Takatsu said through translator Hiroshi Abei, "The fans give [me] the energy to pitch good."[46] "When my name was called and the bell rang, it felt like the whole stand came forward at that moment ... a feeling I had never experienced before in Japan."[47] Out of respect for Takatsu's heritage, Boyer, the marketing executive, did his research, asking Takatsu for his approval.[48]

It was a wonderful time for Takatsu and Chicago. He said: "Honestly, I wasn't expecting all that. I didn't know how successful I would be coming over to the major leagues in my first year. The team just went out of their way, and you know they created all of that kind of ... the gong and the video. The fans, I wasn't expecting the fans to have that reaction. It did catch me by surprise, but I loved every moment of it."[49]

In 2004 Takatsu had 19 saves and a 2.31 ERA, and finished second in the AL Rookie of the Year voting, behind shortstop Bobby Crosby of the Oakland A's. White Sox pitching coach Don Cooper said, "I'd hate to think where we'd be without him. He's jumped over all the hurdles. Now we can see what made him a good closer in Japan. He's calm, but he's got a fire and enthusiasm."[50]

By 2005, the American League had figured out The Frisbee. He saved the season opener for Mark Buehrle, a 1-0 win over Cleveland. But on April 7 with the Sox up over the Indians 5-2, Takatsu came out in the top of the ninth to close. Instead, he gave up home runs to Casey Blake, Coco Crisp, and Ronnie Belliard to tie the game in what turned into an 11-5 loss. From around April 10 to May 10 the team went to closer-by-committee and Takatsu recorded another six saves and two losses in that month. Some solid performances by Dustin Hermanson, with five saves for the Sox over that stretch, plus 17 saves for the San Francisco Giants in 2004, earned him the closer role, and Takatsu became expendable. Takatsu was released on August 1.

Despite his struggles, Takatsu contributed eight saves to the White Sox' 2005 championship season, earning a ring for his fifth championship between the United States and Japan.

He signed with the New York Mets, pitching well briefly for the minor-league Norfolk Tides, and was called up for his National League debut on September 3, pitching 1⅓ innings of scoreless relief against the Florida Marlins. With the Mets, he was reunited with his Swallows teammate Kazuhisa Ishii and Lions rival Kazuo Matsui. He pitched well the rest of the season, with a 1-0 record, a 2.35 ERA. The Mets did not re-sign him for 2006.

Takatsu returned to the Swallows for a couple more seasons. He pitched well in 2006, with a 2.74 ERA. But 2007 was rough, ending with a 6.17 ERA, but making his sixth NPB All-Star Game. It was his final season in NPB. He compiled 286 saves, since surpassed by Hitoki Iwase.[51]

Takatsu signed a minor-league deal with the Chicago Cubs in 2008 but was let go.

Then he signed with the Woori Heroes of the KBO League in South Korea.[52] He made his debut on June 24 vs. the Doosan Bears. His first KBO save came on June 29, against the LG Twins. He pitched brilliantly the rest of the season, with a 0.86 ERA and eight saves. In Korea, Takatsu said, "I realized the joy I feel when I win is the same no matter where I am."[53]

About the level of play in Korea, Takatsu said, "I think top-class players can do reasonably well in the first team in Japan. …"[54] Comparing its batters to the United States and Japan, he said, "Korean batters didn't make too many tricks. Like in America, everyone from number one to number nine seemed to take big swings."[55]

Takatsu signed a minor-league contract with the San Francisco Giants in 2009.[56] Showing his determination to compete, he said, "I'm prepared for it to be difficult, but I don't want to give up easily."[57] He pitched for Triple-A Fresno but struggled. He never returned to the US major leagues.

In 2010 Takatsu received an offer to play for the Sinon Bulls of the Chinese Professional Baseball League in Taiwan. He said, "I really didn't know anything about Taiwanese baseball. I knew there was a professional baseball game, but I had no knowledge of the level of baseball or the players."[58] But he was happy for the offer and signed. His final season as a player was good: 26 saves and a 1.88 ERA.

On March 31, 2010, Takatsu saved his first game for the Bulls, becoming the first player to get a save in the United States, Japan, South Korea, and Taiwan.[59] He has 347 total saves between all four leagues.

About the Chinese league, Takatsu recalled his little league days. "There's no dugout, no lockers. A tree. I changed my clothes in the shade of a tree, [like when I] started playing baseball … so I didn't mind."[60] He relished the chance, saying, "I'll be able to experience this again this year … happiness … I love closing out matches … I can't believe I'm playing baseball again!"[61]

Comparing baseball from all four countries, Takatsu said, "Japan is without a doubt the biggest disadvantage for pitchers. The strike zone is narrow, the ball flies, and the stadiums are small. When it comes to strike zones, America, South Korea, Taiwan, all of them are wide."[62] And on travel between the leagues, "All travel in Korea and Taiwan was by bus. … It used to take many hours to travel from Seoul to Busan in South Korea or from Taipei to Kaohsiung in Taiwan. … In America, traveling on the team's chartered plane seemed like a dream."[63]

In 2014 Takatsu rejoined the Tokyo Yakult Swallows as a coach, and in 2015 helped them to win another pennant, the seventh in franchise history, and his sixth with the team.

He coached there until 2019, when he left to manage their Eastern League farm team.[64]

The Swallows tapped Takatsu as manager for 2020. They finished last for the second year in a row, maybe in part because, according to the *Kyodo News*, they lost home field advantage "having to play home games away from Tokyo's Jingu Stadium, which was closed for much of the summer due to its proximity to the National Stadium, the centerpiece of the Tokyo Olympics and Paralympics."[65]

Finishing last in 2019 and 2020, the Swallows were the "perennial underdogs fac[ing] the prospect of another long season at or near the bottom."[66] Later in 2020, Takatsu ran into his former manager Nomura. Just a couple weeks after their last meeting, Takatsu would recall his mentor's sage advice that day, in a eulogy for Nomura's passing: "Use your head. If you use your head, you can win."[67]

With this advice, two Gold Medal Olympians in sluggers Tetsuto Yamada and Munetaka Murakami, and a return to their home ballpark, Takatsu led the Swallows to the Central League pennant in 2021 and they won the Japan championship, for their sixth overall Japan Series win, and the fifth with Takatsu on the team.

It was a high point for the team. Takatsu said: "It was really a hard season, coming off back-to-back last-place finishes, so the joy right now is off the charts. We wanted to represent the Central League with pride, but the Buffaloes were extremely difficult opponents, so this was no easy task."[68] The Swallows led the Central League again in 2022, the ninth league championship in franchise history.[69] They lost the Japan Series that year.

In 2021 Takatsu was awarded the Matsutaro Shoriki Award, an honor reserved for those who have made great contributions to professional baseball. In 2022 he was elected to the Japanese Baseball Hall of Fame, listed on 311 ballots, well over the 271 (75 percent) needed for election.[70] With managerial success, he has authored several books about managing.[71]

Despite Takatsu's seriousness on the field, he has a great sense of humor. To help keep the team loose at spring training, he would don a wig and do a funny impersonation of Monsieur Yoshizaki, the lead singer of the Japanese rock band Crystal King, singing their hit, "Daitokai (Big City),"[72] once performing the act on TV.[73]

Of his time with the White Sox, Takatsu said, "After all was said and done, I really, really enjoyed my time with the White Sox, and I really love the city of Chicago and their fans."[74]

ACKNOWLEDGMENTS

Thanks to Yuichi Ando, Heather Kerrigan, Dr. Taku Hayashi, and Kanya Honoki for research assistance.

Articles in Japanese were translated with Google Translate. Where possible, quotes from English articles were preferred, as in at least some of those cases, it is clear both Takatsu and a translator were present at that time, and the translation therefore closer to the direct source.

SOURCES

In addition to the sources cited in the Notes, the author consulted Baseball-Reference.com, www.baseball-almanac.com, and MLB.com.

NOTES

1 Scott Merkin, "The Gong Tolls Reminder of Takatsu's Reign," mlb.com, December 24, 2019, https://www.mlb.com/news/shingo-takatsu-white-sox-cult-hero.

2 As of 2023, 23 players have played in all four leagues: MLB, NPB, KBO, and CPBL. Nineteen of them are pitchers. Three have recorded saves in three leagues (Mike Johnson, José Núñez, and Ben Rivera). Three have recorded saves in two leagues (Alfredo Figaro, Radhames Liz, and José Parra). Three have recorded saves in one league (Ariel Miranda, Ken Ray, and Bryan Corey).

3 "Former Professional Baseball Pitcher Shingo Takatsu's Father Passes Away," *Sponichi*, August 6, 2013, https://www.sponichi.co.jp/baseball/news/2013/08/06/kiji/K20130806006367260.html.

4 "All-Star team Yakult Coach Takatsu Takes Charge in His Hometown," *Sanspo*, July 20, 2023, https://www.sanspo.com/article/20230720-5PXI5RXWNVIEBDQXQBFKTVHCFY/?outputType=theme_swallows.

5 "Shin Ie no Rirekisho. Takatsu Shingo," [New Resume of Family: Shingo Takatsu"], *Shūkanbunshun* [*Weekly Bunshun*], March 3, 2011: 96.

6 "New Resume of Family: Shingo Takatsu," 96.

7 "New Resume of Family: Shingo Takatsu," 96.

8 "New Resume of Family: Shingo Takatsu," 96.

9 "Takatsu Shingo chō rongu intabyu" [Shingo Takatsu Long Interview], *Yakyū Kozō* [*Baseball Boy*], February 2011: 19.

10 "Shingo Takatsu Long Interview": 19.

11 "Shingo Takatsu Long Interview": 18-19.

12 "Shingo Takatsu Long Interview": 19.

13 "Shingo Takatsu Long Interview": 19.

14 *Chicago White Sox 2004 Media Guide*, 122-123.

15 Yasutaka Nakamizo, "The Origins of the Greatest Closers of All Time: The Unknown Era of Kazuhiro Sasaki and Shingo Takatsu,'" *Sports Graphic Number Web*, June 27, 2017, https://number.bunshun.jp/articles/-/828338?page=1.

16 "Mr. Shingo Takatsu, the Original Magic Ball That Nomu-San Devised After Being Told to Do," *Shizuoka*, July 2, 2023, https://www.at-s.com/sp/news/article/national/1269827.html.

17 Nakamizo.

18 "Mr. Shingo Takatsu, the Original Magic Ball That Nomu-San Devised After Being Told to Do."

19 "Shingo Takatsu Long Interview": 20.

20 Nakamizo.

21 "New Resume of Family: Shingo Takatsu," 97.

22 "Shingo Takatsu Long Interview," 20.

23 Namakizo.

24 "New Resume of Family: Shingo Takatsu," 97.

25 "New Resume of Family: Shingo Takatsu," 97-98.

26 Namakizo.

27 Namakizo.

28 "Mr. Shingo Takatsu, the Original Magic Ball."

29 "New Resume of Family: Shingo Takatsu," 96.

30 "Mr. Shingo Takatsu, the Original Magic Ball."

31 "Shingo Takatsu Long Interview": 22.

32 "New Resume of Family: Shingo Takatsu," 98.

33 "Mr. Shingo Takatsu, the Original Magic Ball."

34 "Mr. Shingo Takatsu, the Original Magic Ball."

35 "Mr. Shingo Takatsu, the Original Magic Ball."

36 "Shingo Takatsu Long Interview": 20.

37 "Shingo Takatsu Long Interview": 23.

38 "New Resume of Family: Shingo Takatsu," 99.

39 Chris Kuc, "What Baseball Fathers Know: Advice from Cubs and White Sox Dads," *Hartford Courant*, June 19, 2016, https://www.courant.com/2016/06/19/what-baseball-fathers-know-advice-from-cubs-and-white-sox-dads/.

40 Associated Press, "Dodgers, Ishii Beat Deadline with $12.3M Deal," ESPN.com, February 8, 2002, http://www.espn.com/mlb/news/2002/0207/1324786.html.

41 "Shingo Takatsu Long Interview": 23.

42 *Baseball America*, https://www.baseballamerica.com/rankings/2004-top-100-prospects/.

43 Kyodo, "Masahiro Yamamoto and Shingo Takatsu Elected to Japan's Baseball Hall of Fame," *Japan Times*, January 14, 2022, https://www.japantimes.co.jp/sports/2022/01/14/baseball/japanese-baseball/yamamoto-takatsu-hall/.

44 Merkin.

45 Chris Chamska, "Remember That Guy: White Sox Reliever Shingo Takatsu," NBC Sports Chicago, March 25, 2020, https://www.nbcsportschicago.com/mlb/chicago-white-sox/remember-that-guy-white-sox-reliever-shingo-takatsu/320081/.

46 Dave Van Dyck, "Bang That Gong: Cell Fans Fire Up Takatsu," *Chicago Tribune*, July 7, 2004, https://www.chicagotribune.com/news/ct-xpm-2004-07-12-0407120100-story.html.

47 "Shingo Takatsu Long Interview": 26.

48 Merkin.

49 Merkin.

50 Van Dyck.

51 Kyodo, "Iwase Records 287th Save to Surpass Takatsu," *Japan Times*, June 17, 2011, https://www.japantimes.co.jp/sports/2011/06/17/baseball/japanese-baseball/iwase-records-287th-save-to-surpass-takatsu/.

52 Patrick, "Shingo Takatsu on His Way to Korea," *NPB Tracker*, June 15, 2008, http://www.npbtracker.com/2008/06/shingo-takatsu-on-his-way-to-korea/#content.

53 "New Resume of Family: Shingo Takatsu," 99.

54 "Shingo Takatsu Long Interview": 30.

55 "Shingo Takatsu Long Interview": 29.

56 "40-Year-Old Takatsu Tries Again as Giants Minor Player," Nikkan Sports, June 16, 2009, https://www.nikkansports.com/baseball/mlb/news/p-bb-tp2-20090616-506979.html.

57 "40-Year-Old Takatsu Tries Again as Giants Minor Player."

58 "Shingo Takatsu Long Interview": 31-32.

59 "Shingo Takatsu: From BR Bullpen," baseball-reference.com, https://www.baseball-reference.com/bullpen/Shingo_Takatsu.

60 "Shingo Takatsu Long Interview": 32.

61   "Shingo Takatsu Long Interview": 32.

62   "Shingo Takatsu Long Interview ": 34.

63   "Shingo Takatsu Long Interview": 34.

64   Kyodo, "Former Star Closer Shingo Takatsu to Manage Swallows, Source Says," *Japan Times*, September 27, 2019, https://www.japantimes.co.jp/sports/2019/09/27/baseball/japanese-baseball/former-star-closer-shingo-takatsu-manage-swallows-source-says/.

65   Kyodo, "Baseball: Swallows Capture 8th Central League Pennant," *Kyodo News*, October 26, 2021. https://english.kyodonews.net/news/2021/10/19a5ef30d93b-baseball-swallows-capture-8th-central-league-pennant.html.

66   Jim Armstrong, "Birds of Prey: Unsung Swallows Upstage Giants, Tigers in Central League," *Japan Forward*, October 2, 2021, https://japan-forward.com/baseball-birds-of-prey-unsung-swallows-upstage-giants-tigers-in-central-league/.

67   Tamura, Ayumi, "Katsuya Nomura's 'Another Testament' and One Suggestion That He Wants to Convey to Shingo Takatsu, Who Is Getting Thinner," note.com, July 2, 2023, https://note.com/avocado5037/n/ne038005b5cf8.

68   Kyodo, "Baseball: Shingo Kawabata Pinch-Hit Drives Swallows to Japan Series Title," *Kyodo News*, November 27, 2021, https://english.kyodonews. net/news/2021/11/ae31be57e4c3-baseball-kawabata-pinch-hit-drives-swallows-to-japan-series-title.html.

69   Kyodo, "Baseball: Yakult Wins 2nd Straight Central League Pennant in Walk-Off," *Kyodo News*, September 25, 2022, https://english.kyodonews.net/news/2022/09/1a12347287f7-urgent-baseball-yakult-swallows-win-central-league-title.html.

70   Kyodo, "Masahiro Yamamoto and Shingo Takatsu Elected to Japan's Baseball Hall of Fame," *Japan Times*, January 14, 2022, https://www.japantimes.co.jp/sports/2022/01/14/baseball/japanese-baseball/yamamoto-takatsu-hall/.

71   Shingo Takatsu, *Ideal Workplace Management - The Work of a First Team Manager* (Tokyo: Kobunsha, 2023).

72   "A Fan for 32 years. Editor Yohei Kumagai Talks About the Appeal of the Strong and Weak Swallows," *Niew Media*, September 25, 2023, https://niewmedia.com/en/specials/022071/.

73   "Shingo Takatsu's Big City," https://www.youtube.com/watch?v=7oCFCXOK_fA.

74   Merkin.

FRANK THOMAS

By Eric Conrad and Mark Morowczynski

Being enshrined in the National Baseball Hall of Fame in Cooperstown puts a player in an elite class among their peers. Achieving the required 75 percent of votes in their first year of eligibility is something only 60 players have done. Frank Thomas was one of those 60; he also did things in his career that nobody else has accomplished.

Thomas was a contact hitter trapped inside a slugger's body.[1] He is the only player to have seven consecutive seasons with at least a .300 batting average, 100 runs batted in, 100 runs scored, 100 base on balls, and 20 home runs. He achieved this feat from 1991 to 1997, in the heart of Baseball's steroid era.

In the now famous 2007 Mitchell Report, former US Senator George Mitchell was tasked by the commissioner's office to investigate the illegal use of steroids and other performance-enhancing substances. Mitchell wrote to five major leaguers who had spoken publicly about performance enhancers, seeking their cooperation.[2] Frank Thomas was the only active player willing to meet. "It was weird," Thomas said. "The whole reason I did it was because I

Frank Thomas   1994

couldn't believe the other guys weren't talking to him. I had nothing to hide."[3]

Thomas's career stats are even more impressive when viewed through the lens of a clean player during a dirty time of the game. He achieved a .301 lifetime batting average, 521 home runs, 1,704 runs batted in, 1,494 runs, and 1,667 bases on balls to go with 2,468 hits. He is the all-time White Sox leader in home runs, doubles, runs batted in, runs, bases on balls, on-base percentage, and slugging percentage. Thomas achieved all this through persistence, hard work, and never taking anything for granted: lessons he learned early in his life.

Frank Edward Thomas was born on May 27, 1968, in Columbus, Georgia, to his mother Charlie Mae and his father Frank Sr., the original "Big Frank." Charlie Mae worked at the Fieldcrest Milling filling orders.[4] Frank Sr. worked as a bondsman, an animal catcher, a delivery-truck driver for a liquor distributor.[5] Frank Sr. was also a deacon at the Nazareth Baptist Church, where he preached his gospel: Place God, family, and education at the top of the order; see the ball and swing at strikes; and clean your plate.[6] Young Frank grew up with three older sisters – Gloria, Mary, Sharon – and one older brother Michael, all from Charlie Mae's previous marriage.[7]

While most kids dream of reaching the majors by imitating their heroes in the backyard, the young Thomas set his mind at the age of 9 to becoming "a great pro baseball player." His motivation was fueled by profound loss.[8] Tragedy stuck the Thomas family on Thanksgiving Day 1977 when the youngest of the Thomas family, Pamela, lost her battle with leukemia at the age of 2.[9] "It inspired me, it definitely inspired me," Thomas said. "From that point on, I thought something was wrong with me [too]. I thought I had to get everything I can out of life, and I did. From that point forward, she has stuck with me every day of my life."[10]

Frank participated in many future charity endeavors that focused on leukemia. He charged $1 for his autograph, donated to the Leukemia Society of America which Thomas matched dollar for dollar.[11] He also donated the proceeds from the special gold edition of his Leaf baseball card to the Leukemia Society.[12] Rod Carew's daughter Michelle also battled with leukemia and Thomas donated $45,000 to the Leukemia Society of America and the Michelle Carew fund when Carew's Angels visited the White Sox in 1997.[13]

GRINDERS AND GAMERS

The Thomas family were a close group, and the youngest, Frank, was spoiled by his siblings and was close with his father. Frank excelled at all sports, but baseball was where he stood out. In Little League at age 9, when most kids struggled to hit the ball out of the infield, the ball zoomed off Frank's bat to all fields.[14]

Thomas established his discipline at the plate early. "From the time he was in Little League he had a good eye," his father said. "I always told him, 'Don't swing at bad pitches. Watch the ball all the way from the pitcher's hand to the plate.' It started at home and continued through Little League, high school and college. He had good teachers along the way, and he stuck with them."[15]

Young Frank grew into what became his towering 6-foot-5, 275-pound frame. His siblings chipped in for shoes for his growing feet. He wore a size 14 shoe as a 14-year-old.[16]

Frank played varsity baseball, basketball, and football at Columbus High School.[17] The baseball team won the 1984 state championship and Frank was named the Georgia player of the year.[18] He displayed tremendous power even as a sophomore. His high-school coach, Bobby Howard, recalled Glenn Davis and a few minor leaguers from the area working out and Thomas showing up in high-top tennis shoes and connecting just as much as they did. "They couldn't believe it," Howard said. "They all said to me, 'Who is that big boomer you got out here in tennis shoes?' Everyone called him the 'big boomer' before he became the 'Big Hurt.'"[19]

Many high-school pitchers did not give Thomas much to hit. He became frustrated and swung at bad pitches. Coach Howard had a fix for that: "After the game he'd count how many bad pitches I swung at and I'd have to run that many sprints. Discipline came really quick because I didn't like running sprints like that. They weren't easy sprints. Some days it was like puking out there," Thomas recalled.[20] Howard said, "He was a natural, but I stayed on him to make sure he didn't stray too much. Frank was so passionate about hitting he would hit before basketball game days in the offseason. Frank just wanted to hit."[21]

As Thomas finished high school, he faced two career paths. The most obvious: be drafted by a major-league team and start his professional baseball career. However, to the surprise to many, he entered Auburn University on a football scholarship in 1986 to play tight end.[22] Football coach Pat Dye exempted Thomas from spring practice, allowing him to play on the Auburn baseball team.[23]

Many organizations assumed drafting Thomas would be a waste of a draft pick due to this scholarship. Baseball coach Hal Baird thought the opposite. "When Frank was in high school, I was convinced he was going to sign with the baseball club that drafted him. I thought he would not come to Auburn," Baird said.[24] Lucky for Baird he did.

"When he first came out, we figured he'd see some playing time as a freshman, said Baird. "Then he hit the first pitch he saw at practice. It was a bullet of a line drive at short. We knew then he'd play every day as a freshman."[25] He did more than play: He set records. Freshman Thomas led the team in RBIs, walks, total bases, slugging percentage, and homers at age 19. He was named to all-Southeast Conference team.[26] Thomas made Team USA for the 1987 Pan Am Games.[27] (The Americans ended up losing to Cuba in the baseball finals.)

Thomas played one season of football for Auburn, which had more impact on his future than he knew at the time. He made the team as a redshirt freshman and caught three passes for 45 yards. Coach Dye said Thomas had the potential to become the greatest tight end in Auburn history.[28] It wasn't meant to be. Thomas suffered a minor knee problem during practice, leading him to quit football and focus solely on baseball.[29] However, his time on the football team helped propel him to the professional player he would become. "I worked hard on the weights during my time on the football team," he said. "… [A]ll that work made me stronger, and it made a difference. Without it, I don't think I would have been a first-round draft pick."[30]

During Thomas's sophomore season, Coach Dye asked Coach Baird how good a baseball player Thomas was, and whether he could make a living playing baseball. Baird assured him that Thomas could. "Good, we will keep him on a football scholarship and let him just play baseball," Dye said.[31]

SEC pitchers wanted no part of Thomas during his sophomore season. "He was so refined and sophisticated when he got here. He knew the strike zone better than five or six guys I had played with in the pros," Baird said.[32] Thomas hit only 9 home runs but led the SEC in batting average (.385) and walks and had an on-base percentage of .509.[33] His lack of power led to his being left off the 1988 US Olympic team. This snub was the first of several that would leave Thomas feeling he was not respected.

Between his sophomore and junior seasons, Thomas played in the Cape Cod League, where collegians play a minor-league-like schedule.[34] The 1988 season produced 40 major leaguers including players such as Jeff Kent, Jeff Bagwell, Chuck Knoblauch, and Mo Vaughn. In a home-run derby at the Orleans ballpark, Thomas defeated Vaughn, taking advantage of the 300-foot distance down the left-field line.[35]

Thomas continued to show that he had little left to prove at the college level during his junior year. He won the SEC batting title for the second straight year, finished third in home runs with 19, set the school record once again for RBIs at 83, and was named an All-American. He was also named to the SEC All-Tournament team and made the NCAA Atlantic Regional All-Star team. He set 14 records at Auburn, including both season and career marks in home runs, extra-base hits, total bases, walks, and on-base percentage.[36] The 1989 draft class produced four future Hall of Famers.[37] Thomas was selected by the White Sox in the first round.

He started his minor-league career at the Gulf Coast League. It provided little challenge for him; after just 66 plate appearances with a batting average of .365, he was promoted to the High-A Sarasota White Sox. In 55 games for Sarasota, Thomas batted .277 with 4 home runs and 30 RBIs. This earned him an invitation to the White Sox' 1990 spring-training camp.

Thomas had about as good a spring training as anyone could ask for. In seven games, he was 9-for-17 (.529) with 2 home runs and 7 RBIs.[38] One of the home runs, off Nolan Ryan, cleared the left-field scoreboard at the Texas Rangers' ballpark in Port Charlotte, Florida. "I didn't measure it, but it was a blast. It looked like 500 feet," said White Sox manager Jeff Torborg.[39]

Despite his impressive showing, Thomas's destination fate had been decided by White Sox general manager Larry Himes before spring training: He needed more seasoning, especially focusing on his defense. Torborg didn't agree and thought Thomas was ready for the big leagues but was overruled. Thomas would start his 1990 season in Double-A Birmingham.[40]

During this time, Thomas found his personal hitting guru in Walt Hriniak, the new White Sox hitting coach. Hriniak held this position until 1995 but stayed in contact with Thomas long past that. In 2000 Hriniak said, "People ask me who was the greatest hitter I ever saw, and I said if you need a base hit, Wade Boggs, but as far as the best all-around hitter, it was Frank Thomas, hands down. He would win a game with a single down the right-field line or a home run to left."[41]

At Birmingham, Thomas batted .323 in 109 games with 18 home runs, and 71 RBIs, and was leading the Southern League in slugging percentage, on-base percentage, and runs scored when he was called up.[42] On August 2, 1990, he made his major-league debut against Teddy Higuera and the Milwaukee Brewers. He went hitless in his first game but got his first major-league hit the next day, a two-run triple off the Brewers' Mark Knudson. The drive launched a seven-game hitting streak. Thomas hit his first home run on August 28, off Twins pitcher Gary Wayne. Thomas was the White Sox' regular first baseman the rest of the season, batting .330 with 7 home runs, 31 RBIs, and a .983 OPS.

The start of the 1991 season was a new page for the White Sox and Thomas. The White Sox debuted a new logo and color scheme for their home uniforms. Out were the blue, red, and white colors with the batterman logo the team had used since 1976. In was the white, silver, and black with an Old English logo of the Sox. Off the field, the new logo was adopted by many West Coast rappers such as Ice Cube, Dr. Dre and Eazy-E, with Dr. Dre wearing the new hat and logo in the popular "Nuthin' Like a G Thang" music video. In 1990 New Era made 9,000 White Sox hats; in 1991 they made 544,000.[43]

Thomas wore this new color scheme and struck fear in opposing pitchers with his 34-ounce bat.[44] Teammate Steve

Lyons said, "Frank is too big to be a man and too small to be a horse."[45] Thomas swung something unusual in the on-deck circle to prepare for battle at the plate: a three-foot-long piece of rebar that weighed about four pounds. "I like swinging something heavy so when I get to the plate my bat will feel light. That way you don't have to over-swing to catch up to stuff. You feel natural," Thomas said.[46]

Thomas was compared to fellow White Sox and Auburn alum Bo Jackson. Though they never overlapped on the football field at Auburn, to Thomas it wasn't a comparison worth making. "You can't compare me with Bo Jackson. That's just the bottom line. Bo Jackson was probably the best athlete there's ever been. You can't compare me with that guy."[47]

What separated Thomas from Jackson and others was his command of the strike zone. Even at the early age of 23 it stood out immediately. "What he's got going for him is he's got a pretty good idea of his strike zone at the plate. That's going to be a benefit for him. Most big hitters don't have that good sort of patience of the kind of discipline at the plate he seems to have." Carlton Fisk said.[48] Mainly a designated hitter in '91, Thomas finished third in the AL MVP voting behind Cal Ripken Jr. and Cecil Fielder, but took home his first Silver Slugger award at DH.

At the start of the 1992 season the 23-year-old Thomas was compared to many of the greatest hitters past and present. *Washington Post* columnist Thomas Boswell said that if there was ever another Ted Williams, a perfect blend of hitter and slugger, Thomas might be it.[49]

With those big expectations came a new contract: three years and $4.3 million – a relative steal that later led to animosity between Thomas and the White Sox. White Sox broadcaster Ken "Hawk" Harrelson coined a term that that both summarized Thomas's size and what he was capable of doing to opposing teams and the baseball: "The Big Hurt."[50]

Thomas met some of the sky-high expectations as he started to become a superstar during the 1993 season. He made his first All-Star Game appearance and signed a shoe deal with Reebok. Reebok had Thomas star in a commercial based on his new shoe – "the Preseason" – and introduced Thomas to a wider audience.[51]

Thomas led the 1993 White Sox to the AL West Division championship with a 94-68 record, their first postseason appearance in 10 years, despite a late season injury to his left triceps.[52] The White Sox fell to the Toronto Blue Jays in six games in the AL Championship Series. Thomas was named the AL MVP, receiving all of the first-place votes, beating out Blue Jays Paul Molitor and John Olerud.

Thomas was the third White Sox player to win the award after Nellie Fox in 1959 and Dick Allen in 1972. "I was very nervous. I thought there would be four or five guys splitting the first-place votes," he said.[53] He also won his second Silver Slugger award. The White Sox extended Thomas's contract to cover the 1995-1998 seasons with club options in 1999 and 2000 for a total of $43 million, second only to Barry Bonds.[54] The contract included other performance-based incentives such as bonus for league, playoff, and World Series MVP awards. Thomas would meet one of those in the following 1994 season.

The 1994 season will always be known as a "what could have been" season for many players and teams as the players strike cut the season short on August 12. In the National League, the Montreal Expos had the best record in the majors at 74-40. Matt Williams of the Giants had 43 home runs as he was pursing Roger Maris's single-season record of 61 and Tony Gwynn was chasing Ted Williams's .400 average milestone, with a .394 average with 45 games remaining.

Frank Thomas was also having a career year that he did not have a chance to finish. "Walt [Hriniak] and I busted our butts so I wouldn't have my normal slow start," Thomas said.[55] In 23 games in April, he batted .295, with 8 home runs and 20 RBIs. It paid off and Thomas, whose teammates called him Stat King, checked the stats daily for motivation.[56] "Pete Rose was exactly the same way," Hriniak noted. "That's the way he stayed motivated. Frank ain't trying to fool anybody. He ain't trying to hide it. He's right out in the open with it, so I respect him for that. Pete Rose knew what he was hitting, and he always knew what everybody else was hitting. He always wanted to get more hits than anybody who ever lived. That drive, that determination, that's a motivating factor in improving."[57]

Thomas made the All-Star team, led all first basemen in votes, and participated in the Home Run Derby which was won by Ken Griffey Jr.[58] In 113 games Thomas batted .353, hit 38 home runs, drove in 101 runs, and led the league with 106 runs and 109 walks as well as several other hitting categories. He was named the MVP once again, becoming the 11th major leaguer to win consecutive awards.[59] When the season was called off, the White Sox were leading the AL Central Division with a 67-46 record.

The unexpected time off let Thomas focus on spending time with his family – his wife, Elise, and their two children, Sloan (7 months) and Sterling (2 years). "Now, it's like being a normal father," Thomas said. "I'm at home, I wake up with the kids, I go to sleep with the kids. It's been fun."[60] Thomas also had time to set up Big Hurt Enterprise, which handled his marketing, fan mail, and fundraising opportunities.[61]

On March 28, 1995, the strike was officially over with a shortened 144-game season ahead. Thomas picked up where he had left off and was once again an All-Star. At the All-Star Game he participated in the Home Run Derby, winning this time, beating future teammate Albert Belle. Thomas also drove in the only two runs for the American League with a home run in the bottom of the fourth inning, the first time a White Sox player hit a home run in an All-Star Game.[62] The White Sox fell short of making the postseason, finishing third in the AL Central Division.

The rest of the late 1990s followed a similar pattern for the White Sox. Fans dying for a World Series were frustrated by second-place finishes in the 1996, 1997, 1998, and 1999 seasons. Thomas, despite making the All-Star team in 1996 and 1997, bore the wrath of the fan base and the media for years to come. To many he was portrayed as what was wrong with the modern athlete, focused on one's self over the team. Thomas left the 1995 All-Star Game early with permission of MLB to make it back to Chicago for the game the next day. Combined with his focus on his own stats and his personal branding opportunities,[63] he would become a favorite target of *Chicago Sun-Times* journalist Jay Mariotti, who referred to him with nicknames like The Big Killjoy[64] and, when injuries were suspect, The Big Skirt.[65]

Also not helping how fans viewed Thomas was a new contract signed at the end of the 1997 season that on its face appeared to be for $80 million over nine years.[66] However, this contract was heavily incentive-laden and much of the money deferred. It also included a diminished-skills clause that the team could invoke, altering his pay and making him a free agent. This clause proved the ultimate wedge between Thomas and the White Sox.

The 1999 season was one of the most difficult years of Thomas's life, both professionally and personally. He continued to play with a bone spur in his foot, but his normal power production was not there. He ended the season with just 15 home runs (but a .305 batting average). He had surgery after the season to have the bone spur removed. Normal bone spurs are the size of a dime; the one removed from Thomas's foot was the size of a chicken wing.[67]

Thomas's personal life was just as bad: He was going through a divorce with Elise. His friend Derrick Thomas of the Kansas City Chiefs died of a heart attack. His agent, Robert Fraley, died in the plane crash that also took the life of golfer Payne Stewart. His father was on a dialysis machine three times a week for kidney failure and already had a weak heart. "I was at rock bottom," Thomas said a year later.[68]

During the offseason, Thomas worked with his hitting guru Hriniak in the cage to regain his swing. "He had me fixed in 30 minutes," Thomas said.[69] Fixed indeed, Thomas ended the 2000 season more like his old self, hitting 43 home runs and winning another Silver Slugger Award. He finished second in the MVP voting to the Oakland Athletics' Jason Giambi. The White Sox finished first in their division but were quickly swept by the Seattle Mariners, in the Division Series. The White Sox didn't make the playoffs again until 2005.

The 2001 season was a season of loss once again professionally and personally for Thomas. After only 20 games, on April 27, Thomas dove for a ball hit by Ichiro Suzuki and suffered a torn right triceps that required surgery. He missed the rest of the season.[70] The same week that he was injured, his father died. "This is the worst week of my life," Thomas said.[71]

The diminished-skills clause in Thomas's contract became a point of contention and further added to the stress between him and the White Sox. He asked for a new contract in 2001 before his injury and was assured by team owner Jerry Reinsdorf that the White Sox would not leverage this clause.[72] The White Sox suffered another lackluster year, finishing second in the division. Tempers flared all season between manager Jerry Manuel and Thomas, leading to Thomas's being benched for being late to a game.[73]

Thomas received a standing ovation from the crowd at the last home game of the season, possibly his last at-bat in a White Sox uniform. Rumors had swirled for months that the diminished-skills clause would be used at the end of the season. "I expect to be back fully. I've built a legacy here and I'm not going to throw it away," Thomas said.[74]

On October 6, 2002, the White Sox notified Thomas they were invoking the diminished-skills clause. He tested the free-agent waters but ended up back with the White Sox with a new contract through the 2006 season.[75] He was back in his old form in 2003, hitting his 400th career home run on July 25 off Tampa Bay Devil Rays pitcher Jorge Sosa. The White Sox once again finished second in the AL Central Division.

The 2004 season started with a fresh outlook. The White Sox had a new manager, Ozzie Guillén. The two had been teammates for eight years. Thomas specifically avoided all media during the offseason, moved to Las Vegas, and reported to camp on time. It seemed things were finally getting off on the right foot. "A lot of people expected him to show up here moody and with a negative attitude and complaining and stuff. But this is the happiest I've seen him," Guillén said. "He showed up in shape and with enthusiasm. He's involved in every drill. I can't be more pleased."[76] The season didn't turn out differently for the White Sox; they finished second again. Thomas once again voiced displeasure with his current contract.[77] Then his season ended when he suffered a left-ankle stress fracture in early July.[78]

At age 37, the 2005 season became Thomas's last with the White Sox. He returned in late May after recovering from offseason surgery on his left ankle, but refractured it on July 21, limiting him to just 34 games. He still managed 12 home runs in 105 at-bats. He missed the historic playoff and World Series run he had worked his entire career with the White Sox to attain.[79] "It means everything to me personally," he said of the team's postseason success. "It's like I told the guys earlier, whatever I do forward from here, it's all gravy now. I always wanted to do what I did right here, and that's a world championship."[80]

The final breakup with the White Sox left a bad taste in Thomas's mouth. The White Sox bought out the remaining part of his contract in early November. Aaron Rowand was traded for Jim Thome on November 25 and Paul Konerko re-signed on November 30. There was no room for Thomas on the roster. Kenny Williams left a voice mail for Thomas after the Konerko signing, which Thomas

found disrespectful; he felt that the organization owed him more than that. "If they had just called and said, 'Thanks for the ride, we're going in a different direction,' I could have handled that.[81]

Despite Jerry Reinsdorf saying it would kill him to see Thomas in another uniform,[82] it happened. Thomas signed a one-year contract with the Oakland A's that included incentives based on plate appearances and staying off the disabled list.[83] Thomas started the season slowly, with a .178 batting average heading into his return to Chicago on May 22. He was greeted with a video tribute and a three-minute standing ovation by the crowd. Thomas homered in his first at-bat and again later in the game. "I left on bad terms there, and I was really just going through the motions until I got back to say goodbye to the fans," he said. "It was a good feeling. The season seemed to take off right after that point."[84] He batted .270, hit 39 home runs, finished fourth in the MVP voting at age 38 and once again entered free agency.

Thomas signed a two-year contract for $18 million with the Toronto Blue Jays to take over their DH spot and chase the 500-home-run mark. He started the season needing 13 homers to reach the magic number.[85] That day came on June 28, 2007, in Minnesota in the top of the first inning off Carlos Silva, when Thomas became the 21st player to join the 500-homer club.

The next season, 2008, was his last. The Blue Jays released him in late April and Thomas re-signed with the A's on April 24. He hit his final home run (number 521) on August 9 at Detroit off Armando Galarraga, tying for 18th on the all-time record with Willie McCovey and Ted Williams. He played his final game later that month on the 29th, going 2-for-4 with a run and a strikeout against the Minnesota Twins. A Hall of Fame-worthy career had come to an end.

Time eventually heals all wounds, and in 2009 Thomas rejoined the White Sox as a broadcaster for Comcast SportsNet.[86] (In 2019 he began broadcasting as an analyst for Fox Sports.[87]) Thomas joined the White Sox as an ambassador in 2010[88] and his number was retired on August 29, 2010, in a ceremony that brought him to tears.[89] It was also announced that day that Thomas would receive a statue on the outfield concourse in 2011[90] beside White Sox greats Luis Aparicio, Harold Baines, Charles Comiskey, Carlton Fisk, Nellie Fox, Minnie Miñoso, and Billy Pierce. (Paul Konerko joined the group in 2014.)

On January 8, 2014, Thomas, along with Braves pitchers Greg Maddux and Tom Glavine, was elected to the National Baseball Hall of Fame. This was the second time that three first-ballot Hall of Famers were elected; the previous time was the first class inducted in 1936.[91] Joining the trio in the 2014 class were managers Bobby Cox, Joe Torre, and Tony La Russa.

The outpouring of support and congratulations from friends, family, and fans was overwhelming. President Barack Obama, a noted White Sox fan, called to congratulate

Thomas.[92] The family that supported Frank Thomas at the start was there to support him at the end in Cooperstown when he gave his speech as the first player inducted with most of his games being played at DH. Thomas's speech thanked family, friends, coaches, teammates, members of various organizations, doctors, and the cities he played in. He closed his speech with what was instilled in him early in life. "To all you kids out there, just remember one thing from today. There are no shortcuts to success. Hard work, dedication, commitment, stay true to who you are."[93] Pamela would have been proud of what her big brother accomplished.

SOURCES

In addition to the sources cited in the Notes, the authors consulted Baseball-Reference.com.

ACKNOWLEDGMENTS

Thank you to Joe Wancho for providing a fantastic base of research and to Bobby Howard for agreeing to the interview.

NOTES

1   David Haugh, "Hitting Guru Recalls Thomas' Prowess," *Chicago Tribune*, February 12, 2000.

2   Jack Curry, "One Player Who Spoke With Mitchell Wonders Why So Few Others Did," *New York Times*, December 15, 2007.

3   "One Player Who Spoke With Mitchell Wonders Why So Few Others Did."

4   Alva James-Johnson, "Frank Thomas' Family Looks Forward to Hall of Fame Ceremony," *Columbus* (Georgia) *Ledger-Enquirer*, July 17, 2014. Accessed September 3, 2024, https://www.ledger-enquirer.com/news/local/article29337022.html.

5   "Frank Thomas' Family Looks Forward to Hall of Fame Ceremony."

6   Paul Ladewski, "Big Hurt," *Inside Sports*, no 14 (1992), 46-49.

7   "Frank Thomas' Family Looks Forward to Hall of Fame Ceremony."

8   Phil Rogers, "Big Hurt Never Took Anything for Granted," MLB.com, January 8, 2014. Accessed September 7, 2024, https://www.mlb.com/news/hall-of-famer-thomas-never-took-anything-for-granted/c-66417646.

9   "Big Hurt Never Took Anything for Granted."

10 "Big Hurt Never Took Anything for Granted."

11 Rick Reilly, "The Big Heart," *Sports Illustrated*, August 8, 1994.

12 "The Big Heart."

13 Carrie Muskat, "Big Heart," *USA Today Baseball Weekly*, August 20-26, 1997.

14 Paul Ladewski, "Big Hurt."

15 Paul Ladewski, "Big Hurt."

16 Alva James-Johnson, "Frank Thomas' Family Looks Forward to Hall of Fame Ceremony."

17 Chuck Williams, "From Junior to Big Hurt: How Frank Thomas Went from Columbus to the Hall of Fame."

18 Paul Ladewski, "Big Hurt."

19 Bobby Howard, telephone interview, September 21, 2024.

20 Phil Rogers, "Big Hurt Never Took Anything for Granted."

21 Bobby Howard, telephone interview, September 21, 2024.

22 Paul Ladewski, "Big Hurt."

23 Chuck Williams, "From Junior to Big Hurt: How Frank Thomas Went from Columbus to the Hall of Fame."

24 Williams.

25 Dave Platta, "Proving the Doubting Thomases Wrong Mr. Cub Predicts White Sox Slugger Has Great Career Ahead," *Sports Collectors Digest*, April 26, 1991.

26 Platta.

27 Platta.

28 Platta.

29 Platta.

30 Platta.

31 Williams.

32 Williams.

33 Platta.

34 Williams.

35 Bill Whelan, "Frank Thomas: From Cape Cod to Cooperstown," *Wareham Week*, January 21, 2014. Accessed September 8, 2024, https://wareham.theweektoday.com/article/frank-thomas-cape-cod-cooperstown/12807.

36 Platta.

37 The other three were Jeff Bagwell, Trevor Hoffman, and Jim Thome.

38 Paul Sullivan, "Thomas Having a Walk in the Park," *Chicago Tribune*, July 21, 1998.

39 Jerome Holtzman, "No Rookie Problems for Sox's Thomas," *Chicago Tribune*, August 12, 1990.

40 Platta.

41 David Haugh, "Hitting Guru Recalls Thomas' Prowess," *Chicago Tribune*, February 12, 2000.

42 Holtzman.

43 Matthew Ritchie, "How an MLB Rebrand Shook Up the Hip-Hop World," September 26, 2023. Accessed September 14 2024, https://www.mlb.com/news/white-sox-1990-rebrand-instilled-a-sense-of-pride-in-fans

44 Ladewski.

45 Nicholas Dawidoff, "The Not-Really Rookies," *Sports Illustrated*, April 1, 1991.

46 Daniel Brown, "Raising the Bar," *San Jose Mercury News*, August 11, 2006.

47 Dan Kitkowski, "Frank Thomas," *Baseball Card News*, August 19, 1991.

48 Kitkowski.

49 Thomas Boswell, "Thomas Is Polite, Patient and Pow!" *Washington Post*, March 19, 1992. The Baseball Writers Association of America will present its Career Excellent Award in ceremonies at the 2025 Hall of Fame induction weekend at Cooperstown, New York. https://www.mlb.com/news/thomas-boswell-wins-bbwaa-career-excellence-award.

50 Jack Bourboushian, "Frank Thomas Puts the Hurt on Reebok," *Courthouse News Service*, March 21, 2014. Accessed September 21, 2014, https://www.courthousenews.com/frank-thomas-putsthe-hurt-on-reebok/.

51 Milton Kent, "Thomas Gets Starring Role," *Baltimore Sun*, July 11, 1993.

52 George Kimball, "Thomas Has No Doubts About MVP," *New York Post*, October 5, 1993.

53 Chuck Johnson, "Thomas: Award an Honor, but There's More Work to Do," *USA Today*, November 12, 1993.

54   Mel Antonen, "Thomas Attacks Defense," *USA Today*, October 22, 1993.

55   Murray Chass, "Thomas Is Changing Name of the Game," *New York Times*, May 31, 1994.

56   Tom Keegan, "The Big Hurt," *Sport*, May 1994.

57   Keegan.

58   Rick Reilly, "The Big Heart," *Sports Illustrated*, August 8, 1994.

59   Joel Sherman, "Big Hurt Racks Up Back-to-Back MVPs," *New York Post*, October 27, 1994.

60   Carrie Muskat, "Good Works, Family Fill Thomas Time," *USA Today*, October 18, 1994.

61   "Good Works, Family Fill Thomas Time," *USA Today*, October 18, 1994.

62   Bill Francis, "All-Star Game Bats Land at HOF," *Freeman's Journal* (Cooperstown, New York), July 16, 1995.

63   Tom Keegan, "Image Hinders Big Hurt," *New York Post*, July 12, 1995.

64   Jay Mariotti, "Talk About Cutting Remarks," *Chicago Sun-Times*, February 24, 2003.

65   Jay Mariotti, "Big Frank Won't Get Big Finish He Deserves," *Chicago Sun-Times*, July 30, 2005.

66   "Red Sox' Martinez Has Competition," *Syracuse* (New York) *Herald American*, December 14, 1997.

67   Bob Nightengale, "At Last, Big Hurt Feeling No Pain," *USA Today Baseball Weekly*, September 6-12, 2000.

68   Nightengale.

69   Nightengale.

70   Peter Gammons, "Thomas Has Something to Prove," ESPN.com, November 18, 2002.

71   "Chicago's Big Hurt," *Jet*, May 28, 2001.

72   "Thomas Won't Lose Pay," *Albany* (New York) *Times Union*, June 10, 2001.

73   Paul Sullivan, "Benched Star's Tardiness Elicits Teammates' Barbs," *Chicago Tribune*, July 8, 2002.

74   Paul Sullivan, "'I Expect to Be Back'/Thomas Counting On Wearing Sox Uniform Next Year," *Chicago Tribune*, September 26, 2002.

75   Paul Sullivan, "Thomas Starts From Scratch," *Chicago Tribune*, December 7, 2002.

76   Chuck Johnson, "Frank Expectation Set for White Sox's Thomas," *USA Today*, March 23, 2004.

77   Joe Cowley, "Frank to Sox: It's Time to Talk," *Daily Southtown* (Chicago), April 16, 2004.

78   Dave van Dyck, "It's Doubtful Thomas Will Play Much More in 2004," *Chicago Tribune*, July 9, 2004.

79   Scott Merkin, "White Sox Buy Out Thomas' Option," MLB.com, November 4, 2005.

80   Scott Merkin, "Thomas' Legacy Includes Championship," MLB.com, October 27, 2005.

81   Phil Arvia, "Southtown Exclusive: Bitter batter?" *Daily Southtown*, February 26, 2006.

82   Nathaniel Whale, "Reinsdorf Would Like to See Thomas Finish Here," *Daily Southtown*, October 6, 2005.

83   Andrew Baggarly, "A's Hope to Put 'Big Hurt' on Rivals," *Inside Bay Area*, January 26, 2006.

84   Jorge L. Ortiz, "'Big Hurt' Finds Healing," *USA Today*, September 26, 2006.

85   "Blue Jays Sign Thomas for Two Years, $18 million," ESPN, November 17, 2006.

86   Carol Slezak, "Time Healing the Hurt for Frank Thomas, White Sox," *Chicago Sun Times*, June 12, 2009.

87   Charles Oduamp (Associated Press), "Thomas Headed to 'Big Leagues' as Baseball Analyst," *Sports Illustrated*, February 22, 2019.

88   Chris De Luca, "Feud Is in the Past as Frank Thomas Rejoins White Sox," *Chicago Sun Times*, July 28, 2010.

89   Rick Morrissey, "A Hurt-Warming Event," *Chicago Sun Times*, August 30, 2010.

90   Doug Padilla, "More Thomas Honors to Come in 2011," ESPN, August 29, 2010, https://www.espn.com/blog/chicago/white-sox/post/_/id/1766/more-thomas-honors-to-come-in-2011.

91   "BBWAA Elects Greg Maddux, Tom Glavine and Frank Thomas," BBWAA, January 8, 2013. https://bbwaa.com/14-hof/.

92   Associated Press, "Former Chisox Star Frank Thomas Tours Hall of Fame," *Boston Herald*, March 3, 2014.

93   "Transcript: Frank Thomas Hall of Fame Speech," *Chicago Tribune*, July 27, 2014.

JUAN URIBE

By Bill Pruden

Inspired in part by his older cousin José Uribe, who returned every winter to the Dominican Republic with tales of his life in major-league baseball, Juan Uribe from an early age aspired to play in the big leagues. That dream ultimately became a reality as Uribe crafted a 16-season major-league career that saw him playing an important role on two World Series champions, the 2005 Chicago White Sox and the 2010 San Francisco Giants.

Juan Cespedes Uribe Tena was born on March 22, 1979, in Palenque, San Cristobal, Dominican Republic. He attended high school at Abel Uribe, Juan Baron in the Dominican Republic, but did not attend college, signing with the Colorado Rockies in 1997. He had been identified as a prospect by Jorge Posada Sr., the father of the veteran New York Yankees catcher, and was signed by Posada and Rodolfo Rosario on January 15, 1997, as an undrafted free agent. Uribe began his professional career that summer playing on the Rockies team in the Dominican Summer League.

In 1998, the 19-year-old Uribe appeared in 40 games for the Rockies' Arizona Rookie League club, which won the league championship. He hit .277, scored 25 runs, drove in 17, and stole eight bases in nine attempts. In the field the six-foot shortstop posted a .927 fielding average, committing 14 errors while turning 25 double plays.

The next season, Uribe was promoted to the Asheville Tourists of the low Class-A South Atlantic League. Appearing in 125 games he hit .267 while scoring 57 runs and driving in 46. He also showed more power than previously, hitting nine home runs. He improved his fielding average to .938.

The 2000 season saw Uribe continue his climb toward the majors as he appeared in 134 games for the Rockies' high-A Carolina League entry, the Salem (Virginia) Avalanche. He hit .256 with 124 hits, 64 runs scored, and 65 RBIs with 13 home runs. The young shortstop continued to show improvement in the field, raising his fielding average to .961, handling 667 chances with only 26 errors.

The 2001 season was something of a yo-yo or roller-coaster ride for Uribe. While the season included a three-game stint with the Carolina Mudcats of the Double-A Southern League, for the most part he went back and forth between the Rockies and the Triple-A Colorado Springs Sky Sox (Pacific Coast League). There he ended up playing a total of 74 games, hitting a then career-best .310, with 40

runs scored and 48 RBIs. But more importantly, he played in 72 games with the Rockies.

Making his major-league debut on April 8, 2001, in the bottom of the ninth with the Rockies trailing 11-3 against the San Diego Padres, Uribe led off the inning, pinch-hitting for Mike Myers. Facing Jay Witasick, he grounded out to second. He made his first start the next day, going hitless, before collecting his first major-league hit – a line-drive single to center – on April 11 in St. Louis off Cardinals right-hander Matt Morris. Uribe was sent back to Colorado Springs on April 23. Called up again on May 19, he was sent back down on the 23rd.

Uribe was called back up for good on July 25 after the Rockies traded Neifi Pérez to Kansas City. Taking advantage of the opportunity, he started 59 of the Rockies' final 61 games and put together a performance that made clear he was major-league-ready. Indeed, Uribe's totals for his time with Rockies included a .300 batting average, with 82 hits, 32 runs scored, and 53 runs batted in. He posted a .983 fielding average with only five errors. Paired with

Juan Uribe   2005

second baseman Jose Ortiz, Uribe was seen as being part of a "promising double play combination."[1] In addition, his 11 triples in 72 games placed him tied for second in the National League and tied the Rockies team record. Also, while he did not have enough plate appearance to qualify for the batting title, only Albert Pujols ranked ahead of him of those who did qualify. He also ranked fourth among NL rookies in RBIs, extra-base hits, and total bases. It was, by any measure, an auspicious start to his major-league career.

It also undoubtedly contributed to Uribe's earning the nod as the team's starting shortstop when the 2002 season began. In his first full season in the major leagues, Uribe played 150 games at shortstop for the Rockies, while appearing in a total of 155 contests. He started off strong, hitting .373 for the month of April, and while he slumped in midseason, at one point he put together a 17-game hitting streak and ranked third on the team with 38 multihit games. At the same time, he also struck out 120 times, the fourth most in team history. Uribe hit a strong .314 in September to finish on a high note. While his .240 overall batting average was certainly not what he wanted, his play at shortstop made him a valuable asset. He led all shortstops with 261 putouts, 792 total chances, and 118 double plays and he was second with an average of 3.45 assists per nine innings.

Uribe's hopes of building upon his solid rookie campaign were derailed by injury issues that left him able to play in only 87 games in 2003. He opened the season on the 60-day disabled list after fracturing a bone in his right foot on March 1 while running the bases in a spring-training game. Undergoing surgery in the first week of March, he began his rehabilitation assignment the last week in May and joined the Rockies on June 3. He returned in fine style that night, going 2-for-5 with two home runs and four RBIs, leading the Rockies to a 7-3 win over the visiting Cleveland Indians. Overall, Uribe hit .253 while playing 74 games at shortstop and 11 at second base. Anxious to make up for the time he had lost, he played 21 games in the Dominican Winter League.

Everything changed for Uribe on December 2, 2003, when the Rockies traded him to the Chicago White Sox for infielder Aaron Miles, who had played only eight games in the majors.

Joining a White Sox team in the midst of a major overhaul and with a new manager, Ozzie Guillén, Uribe in 2004 recorded career bests in pretty much every offensive category, starting with a batting average of .283. He hit 23 home runs while driving in 74 runs.

The following year brought Uribe his first taste of postseason baseball, and while he was not able to match his 2004 offensive efforts, he was still a critical cog in the 2005 White Sox team that took the baseball world by storm. After winning 99 games in the regular season, the team dominated in the postseason, winning 11 of 12 contests, culminating with a sweep of the Houston Astros in the World Series to win their first title since 1917.

While Uribe had been moved around a bit in 2004, spending time at shortstop, second, and third, in 2005, he was the team's shortstop from day one. Starting 143 of the team's regular-season games and all the postseason ones, he contributed in countless ways at bat and in the field. Uribe hit .252, with 16 home runs, and 71 RBIs while also tying for second in the American League with 10 sacrifice flies. His fielding average of .977 ranked third among American League shortstops. In the postseason he reached base safely in 11 of the 12 games and was at the center of the final two outs of the World Series, first making an "acrobatic leap into the stands" in shallow left field for the next to last out, an effort immortalized in the Championship Monuments statue outside the ballpark, and then making a "slick, off-balance assist" on Orlando Palmeiro's "slow roller up the middle" to seal the win and the championship.[2]

As the White Sox sought to repeat in 2006, Uribe turned in a performance comparable to his efforts in their championship season. While his batting average dropped to .235, his 21 home runs – in 14 fewer games – represented an increase over the 16 he hit in 2005, and he matched his RBI total of 71.

Uribe's offseason was marred by charges of a reported shooting incident. The shortstop was accused of shooting a farmer in the Dominican Republic in October of 2006, a charge he denied. An attempted-murder investigation commenced but the case was settled when Uribe paid a reported $25,500, after which all charges were dropped, with Uribe's lawyer saying it was recognized that Uribe was not in fact involved in the incident.[3] While the whole episode was unsettling, Uribe arrived at spring training only two days late. The 2007 season itself was very similar to the previous campaign, although he played in 150 games. His 20 home runs placed him third among American League shortstops as did his .976 fielding average.

Uribe's 2008 performance was mixed. Injuries, especially hamstring issues, reduced his playing time and he ended up playing in only 110 games, his fewest since the injury-plagued 2003 season. But he continued to show his versatility, being the only American Leaguer to play in more than 50 games at both second and third, and he raised his batting average to .247, even if the reduced game total lowered his home run and RBI totals.

After the 2008 season, Uribe was granted free agency, and he signed a one-year deal with the San Francisco Giants at the end of January 2009. The 2009 season made clear Uribe's versatility as he started 34 games at second base, 34 at third, and 35 at shortstop, committing only nine errors total in 123 games and 600 chances. He had one of his best seasons at bat, hitting .289 with 16 home runs and 55 RBIs. After again signing a one-year deal with the Giants, Uribe played in 148 games in 2010, primarily playing shortstop. While his batting average dropped to .248, he achieved career highs with 24 home runs and 85 RBIs.

In the postseason, Uribe's clutch Game Six, eighth-inning home run broke a 2-2 tie and propelled the Giants to their pennant-clinching win over the Phillies, and he finished second on the team in postseason RBIs with nine, five of which came in the World Series as Uribe earned his second championship ring.

While Uribe's time with the Giants was brief, he had endeared himself to Giants fans and teammates alike. As *Sports Illustrated* writer Ann Killion wrote at the end of the season, just after the Giants had won the World Series, "Juan Uribe is the Giants' sometime shortstop, sometime third baseman, all the time clutch hitter. He is a clubhouse leader, a playful presence, a World Series winner."[4] She added that "he's one of the characters that have given the Giants so much personality."[5]

With a second World Series ring in hand, Uribe again tested the free-agency market and ended up signing a three-year contract with the Los Angeles Dodgers. The security of the contract proved valuable for Uribe when the 2011 season proved to be a colossal disappointment: A left hip flexor muscle caused him to miss time in May and June, before a left hip strain, followed by season-ending sports hernia surgery in July, ended his season after he had played in only 77 games. The 2012 season was little better as nagging injuries, especially a wrist injury, kept him on the disabled list while also limiting his ability to compete for playing time. After hitting .204 in his limited playing time in 2011, Uribe dropped to .191 in the injury-shortened 2012 season.

But after the two disappointing seasons, and in the final year of his contract, Uribe bounced back in 2013. Starting the season as a utility infielder, by June he had made third base his own. He ultimately appeared in 132 games, including 123 at third base, where his play earned him the Dodgers' Wilson Defensive Player of the Year Award. He was also a finalist for the Gold Glove Award. Meanwhile, the 34-year-old Uribe hit .278, with 12 home runs and 50 RBIs as the Dodgers reached the postseason and they lost to the Cardinals in the NL Championship Series. While the season ended on a disappointing note, Uribe's performance earned the free agent a new contract with the Dodgers.

While hamstring strains twice landed Uribe on the disabled list and resulted in his playing in only 103 games in 2014, when he was in the lineup he turned in a performance that was one of his best ever. He posted a career-high batting average of .311, hit 9 home runs, and drove in 54 runs, his most since 2010. His fielding average at third base was tops among National Leaguers and he earned the Wilson Defensive Player of the Year Award as the major leagues' top-fielding third basemen. And in a nod to the respect accorded him by the team, manager Don Mattingly allowed Uribe to manage the team's regular-season finale, aided by Clayton Kershaw serving as pitching coach.[6]

A healthy, but 36-year-old Uribe opened the 2015 season for the Dodgers at third base, but after appearing in 29 games and hitting .247, on May 27 he was traded to the Atlanta Braves along with Chris Withrow for Alberto Callaspo, Juan Jaime, Eric Stults, and Ian Thomas. Despite the trade but reflective of the respect accorded Uribe, the Dodgers still held their Juan Uribe Bobblehead night as scheduled for July 11.[7] Two weeks later, his stint in Atlanta was over. After hitting .285 over 46 games, 38 of which he started, he was traded to the New York Mets on July 24 along with Kelly Johnson for John Gant and Rob Whalen. Uribe played in 44 games with the Mets, starting 29, and hitting .219 as the team advanced to the World Series, where they lost in five games to the Kansas City Royals. While a chest contusion prevented Uribe from playing in either of the first two rounds of the postseason as the Mets won the National League pennant, he made his mark in the third game of the World Series. Pinch-hitting for pitcher Noah Syndergaard in the bottom of the sixth, he stroked a line-drive single to right, sparking a four-run outburst that secured the Mets' 9-3 win, their only victory in the Series.

The winter after the 2015 season again saw Uribe a free agent and in late February he signed with the Cleveland Indians, agreeing to a one-year, $4 million contract. Even though he was 37, as word of his impending signing got out, the value of his "dynamic clubhouse presence" to an Indians team that featured a strong young core was recognized by local media.[8] Manager Terry Francona, who said the team had been trying to get Uribe all winter, installed the veteran as the starting third baseman.[9] While clearly nearing the end of his career, his value to the team was evident. As Francona observed, "We got a kid in here that has played on winners and is a really good guy in the clubhouse, especially with the younger Latin kids. But it doesn't just have to be Latin."[10]

Uribe was in the team's Opening Day lineup at third base and he held the position until June 12, when, after being hit in the groin by a 106 mph groundball off the bat of Mike Trout, he had to be carted off the field. The injury was diagnosed as a testicular contusion with the injury being made worse by the fact that he was not wearing a cup.[11] Uribe was replaced by the rising young star José Ramírez, who had been playing other positions in order to keep his bat in the lineup while Uribe held down the hot corner but who slid smoothly into his preferred position when the veteran was hurt. The injury signaled the end of Uribe's career. He was designated for assignment by the Indians on August 1 and released on August 5.

Over the course of his 16 seasons and over 1,800 major-league games, Uribe put together a solid record. While playing on two World Series champions with the White Sox and Giants as well as the National League pennant-winning Mets, Uribe posted a career batting average of .255 with 1,568 hits, 199 home runs, and 816 RBIs. A star shortstop early in his career, his later shift to third not only enhanced his reputation for versatility but earned him formal recognition. And beyond the statistics, his consistent performance, coupled with his infectious spirit and enthusiasm earned

Uribe a reputation as a tough, versatile ballplayer, one who could contribute at bat, in the field, and in the clubhouse, where he was "extremely popular with his teammates and appreciated for his sunny disposition."[12]

While playing for seven different teams in both leagues, Uribe was recognized as a player who added much to his team. His White Sox manager Ozzie Guillén called him "the most beloved guy" on the team, adding that he was the "funniest man, great player … played hard every day."[13] White Sox general manager Kenny Williams said that Uribe "remains one of my favorite guys to ever put on a White Sox uniform. He's a prince of a guy and if you get to know him, he's one of the funniest guys you'll ever know."[14] His White Sox teammate Aaron Rowand recalled how Uribe "walk[ed] into the clubhouse every day like a little kid. ... He never changes."[15] And his Giants teammate Aubrey Huff joked that he didn't "really know how he is as a teammate because he doesn't speak English very well," but added, "We love him as a teammate. He's got a lot of energy. And he's a fun guy. If you can understand him."[16] As *Sports Illustrated*'s Ann Killion wrote after the 2010 World Series win, "Uribe is beloved, always happy, consistently upbeat."[17]

Before his retirement had been made official, baseball observers noted that Uribe was the kind of player whose value could be partly quantified, but who had an additional human-based value that resulted in important but often unrecognized contributions to a team's success. He was, as one writer put it, the embodiment of the "glue-guy," the type of player whose value "can never be measured but should 'always be respected.'"[18] The writer also noted that the effort and value of such players was a reminder of the fact that "baseball is still a human game in an era dominated by a growth of admiration for statistics."[19] But in the end, the most important statistic in baseball is wins and as that same writer observed, "[O]ver 16 years, having Uribe in the clubhouse has translated to quite a bit of team wins."[20]

In retirement Uribe, who has four children with his wife, Anna, returned to the Dominican Republic, where he established a baseball academy, Uribe Academy, in Nizao, Peravia. In developing the Academy, Uribe has assumed the role of a supportive father, commenting, "In my academy we are like a family. All these kids are like my kids. I go there with them, I play with them, I eat with them. ... We do all the same stuff, all together."[21] The academy serves as their school while also helping them develop as ballplayers. Befitting his reputation as an invaluable dugout presence during his playing days, Uribe noted, "They do everything they need to do there. ... I take a lot of pride in that because we are like a family. I like to be inclusive with all of them. I like to be part of their routines."[22]

One of the first players to be trained at the Academy before going on to play professional baseball was Uribe's son, Juan Uribe Jr., who signed with the White Sox during the January 2023 international signing period. Juan Sr. commented, "You want your son to be in a good place, the right place. I'm proud of the player he is and the player he is going to become and how he is going to represent the Chicago White Sox."[23] Juan Jr. and the Academy are fitting legacies of the career Juan Uribe crafted, one that reminds us all that even in an era of ever-increasing, if not encroaching, analytics, "baseball is still a human game."[24]

SOURCES

In addition to the sources cited in the Notes, the author consulted MLB.com, baseball-almanac.com, and Baseball-Reference.com.

NOTES

1   "Bumpy Ride Finally Ends for Rockies," (Grand Junction, Colorado) *Daily Sentinel*, October 9, 2001; https://www.newspapers.com/image/539309829/?terms=%22juan%20uribe%22%20.

2   Art Berke, "White Sox A-Z: Uribe," *Inside the White Sox*, August 20, 2020; https://whitesoxpride.mlblogs.com/white-sox-a-z-uribe-2b6c7175f963; Scott Merkin, "Chicago-Born Uribe Jr. Follows Dad to White Sox," MLB.com, January 16, 2023; https://www.mlb.com/news/juan-uribe-jr-signs-with-white-sox.

3   Associated Press "Farmer Accepts Settlement, Drops Charges against Uribe," ESPN, June 11, 2007; https://www.espn.com/mlb/news/story?id=2901210.

4   Ann Killion, "Giants, Fans Embracing Do-It-All Infielder 'Ooooh! ... Ree-Bay!'" *Sports Illustrated*, October 29, 2010; https://www.si.com/more-sports/2010/10/29/uribe.

5   Killion.

6   Dan Arritt, "Dodgers Shake Up Coaching Staff," ESPN.com, September 27, 2014; https://www.espn.com/los-angeles/mlb/story/_/id/11602043/juan-uribe-manage-los-angeles-dodgers-regular-season-finale-vs-colorado-rockies.

7   Jon Weisman, "Juan Uribe Bobblehead Night Still Set for July 11," *Dodger Insider*, May 27, 2015; https://dodgers.mlblogs.com/juan-uribe-bobblehead-night-still-set-for-july-11-5b2f206c4cc5.

8   Jeff Todd, "Indians to Sign Juan Uribe," MLB Trade Rumors, February 18, 2016; https://www.mlbtraderumors.com/2016/02/indians-to-sign-juan-uribe.html.

9   Zack Meisel, "Juan Uribe Relieved to Finally Be in Camp: Cleveland Indians Morning Briefing," cleveland.com, February 29, 2026; https://www.cleveland.com/tribe/2016/02/cleveland_indians_morning_brie_6.html.

10   Jesse Sanchez, "Uribe Could Be Force in Tribe Clubhouse," MLB.com, March 11, 2016; https://www.mlb.com/news/juan-uribe-will-be-force-in-indians-clubhouse-c167098910.

11   Matt Lyons, "Juan Uribe Took a 106-MPH Shot to the Groin," SB Nation: Covering the Corner, June 12, 2016; https://www.coveringthecorner.com/2016/6/12/11916200/juan-uribe-took-a-106-mph-shot-to-the-groin.

12   Art Berke, "White Sox A-Z: Uribe."

13   Berke.

14   Berke.

15   Ann Killion, "Giants, Fans Embracing Do-It-All Infielder 'Ooooh! ... Ree-Bay!'"

16   Killion.

17   Killion.

18   Will Templin, "Is This the End of Juan Uribe?" Off Base Baseball, February 7, 2017; https://offbasebaseball.com/2017/02/07/is-this-the-end-of-juan-uribe/.

19   Templin.

20   Templin.

21   Scott Merkin, "Chicago-Born Uribe Jr. Follows Dad to White Sox."

22   Merkin.

23   Merkin.

24   Templin.

LUIS VIZCAÍNO

By Bob LeMoine

"Vizcaíno did an unheralded role that in some ways can be not recognizable, but valuable nevertheless."
– Don Cooper, Vizcaíno's pitching coach, on his role on the 2005 World Series Champion Chicago White Sox.[1]

Luis Vizcaíno pitched 11 seasons as a reliever in the major leagues with eight teams, including the 2005 World Series champion Chicago White Sox. A workhorse, Vizcaíno achieved six straight seasons of at least 65 appearances and 62 innings pitched. He was a hard-throwing righty who depended on his fastball and slider. He is also one of just a handful of pitchers in baseball history (minimum 500 innings pitched) to have a perfect 1.000 fielding percentage in his career. Vizcaíno was primary a seventh- and eighth-inning set-up reliever, holding batters to a .234 batting average over that time, and more than doubling his strikeout-to-walk totals in those innings (380/189).

Vizcaíno was born on August 6, 1974, in Baní, Peravia, Dominican Republic, to Juanita Vizcaíno. While information on his father was not found, Luis was the fourth of eight children. Vizcaíno played on the Bali Little League team with future major leaguers Mario Encarnación and Miguel Tejada, the future MVP and six-time All-Star.[2] Baní is described as "a long trip over bumpy roads to the major leagues" by Mark Saxon of the *Oakland Tribune*, yet the out-of-the-way spot has yielded a bumper crop of major-league talent. In addition to Vizcaíno's Little League teammates, José Bautista, Manny Aybar, and Timo Pérez (his teammate on the '05 White Sox) are three notable major leaguers from Baní.[3]

Vizcaíno, Tejada, and Encarnación were three skinny kids who made the journey from Little League to the Oakland A's Dominican summer league. "Vizcaíno was the skinniest of all," A's director of player development Keith Lieppman said, "just almost like a pencil." Luis signed as a nondrafted free agent on December 9, 1994, through Oakland scout Santiago Villalona.[4]

Vizcaíno spent 1995 in the Dominican League, going 10-2 with a 2.27 ERA. He pitched in 1996 in the Arizona Rookie League, going 6-3 with a 4.07 ERA. In 1997 he went 1-6 with a 7.93 ERA for Southern Oregon in the short-season Northwest League and finished with Modesto in the

California League (Advanced A ball), where he was 0-3 with a 13.19 ERA. Vizcaíno began the 1998 season with Modesto (6-3, 2.74 ERA) and finished with seven games at Huntsville in the Double-A Southern League (3-2, 4.66 ERA). Vizcaíno started 59 games in his minor-league career, using his hero as inspiration "I've always looked up to Pedro Martinez," Vizcaíno said of his role model. "He is always consistent when he pitches. I like his toughness, too. He's always going after the hitters. The way he pitches motivates me when I go out to pitch."[5] He would never start a game in the major leagues.

Familysearch.com records list Vizcaíno marrying Zoila Esmeralda Pimentel Alvarez in December of 1998.[6]

Vizcaíno began the 1999 season with Midland in the Double-A Texas League (8-7 with a 5.85 ERA in 25 games) and was the pitcher of the week in July with 12 scoreless innings with nine strikeouts in two starts.[7] He did not have long to savor it, however, as he was promoted to Oakland to make his major-league debut. The A's had traded starting pitcher Kenny Rogers and needed another arm in the

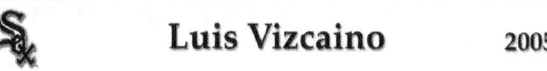

Luis Vizcaino　　2005

bullpen. "I was a little nervous," he admitted. "The ambience was very different, incredible."[8]

On July 23 the Royals scorched the visiting Athletics for 10 runs in the first four innings and Vizcaíno entered in the bottom of the fifth with the bases loaded and the A's trailing, 10-6. He retired Carlos Beltrán on a grounder to second to get out of the jam. He finished the game, allowing two runs in 3⅓ innings, including a home run to Johnny Damon. "Not nervous," Vizcaíno affirmed.[9] It was his only big-league appearance of the year.

Vizcaino finished the season with seven games at Vancouver of the Triple-A Pacific Coast League. Over the winter, A's GM Billy Beane considered Vizcaíno "un-trade able," along with pitchers Mark Mulder and Barry Zito. Beane unsuccessfully sought Angels center fielder Jim Edmonds because Beane refused to part with Vizcaíno. His arm was "electric," in the opinion of manager Art Howe. "This guy throws bullets," catcher A.J. Hinch said.[10]

In 2000 Vizcaíno joined the A's spring training in Arizona and showed promise. At the same time, wrote Howard Bryant in the *San Jose Mercury News*, "Vizcaíno says life is lonely as all of his family (including his wife, Esmeralda) resides in Santo Domingo, Dominican Republic, but seeing himself in the major leagues eases his troubles. 'I'm close,' he said of his prospects. 'I have more confidence in my control, and confidence is everything.'"[11]

Vizcaíno's confidence paid off and he won a job in the A's bullpen with a shiny spring 2.03 ERA.[12] He threw 8⅓ innings with 9 strikeouts and 4 walks before being optioned to Sacramento.[13] He was recalled in early May but was not as effective, allowing nine earned runs in 10 innings. He made just two more appearances for Oakland in June and finished the season in Sacramento (6-2 for the River Cats in 33 games, 5.03 ERA with five saves). Vizcaíno finished 0-1 in 12 appearances with a 7.45 ERA in his rookie season with the A's.

Vizcaíno dominated in spring training 2001 (a scoreless streak of 10⅔ innings) but began the season in Sacramento.[14] He was recalled in mid-April and threw six innings of relief with a 6.00 ERA. He returned to Sacramento as the A's called up submarine specialist Chad Bradford.[15] Vizcaíno served as the closer for the River Cats, compiling seven saves and a 2.14 ERA.

He returned to Oakland on July 15 and was thrust into an immediate closer situation when Jason Isringhausen needed a day off. With the A's leading Colorado, 6-3, in the top of the ninth and a runner at first, Vizcaíno retired the side, with two strikeouts to earn his first save.[16] He had a stellar month of August, allowing only two earned runs in 11⅓ innings (ERA 1.59, WHIP 0.706) with opponents batting just .135 against him. Vizcaíno celebrated his first major-league victory on August 6 in Detroit. He entered a pressure-cooked eighth inning with runners on second and third and the game tied, 3-3. He struck out Shane Halter to end the threat and the A's went on to victory. "I think it's a very important

thing for me, because it shows they have confidence going to me," Vizcaíno said.[17] He faltered down the stretch, allowing nine runs and 19 hits in 8⅔ innings with a 9.35 ERA as opponents batted .432 against him. He finished 2-1 with a high 4.66 ERA. Oakland (102-60) won the wild card but lost to the Yankees in the AL Division Series.

The A's young right-hander was not *as* young as they thought. Vizcaíno revealed he was 26, not 24 as reported in their media guide. Stricter rules on providing birth certificates for international players, a post-9/11 immigration enforcement, was responsible for the revelation. It mattered little to the A's. "It doesn't change the fact he throws 96 MPH," A's assistant GM Paul DePodesta said.[18]

The A's were more concerned with Vizcaíno's inconsistent arm than the candles on his birthday cake. In 59⅓ innings in his Oakland career, his ERA was 5.61 with a very high 1.55 WHIP. Vizcaíno was out of minor-league options, so in March, he was traded to Texas for pitcher Justin Duchscherer.[19] "Luis has an outstanding arm," Beane said, "but it doesn't do us any good if he's not going to make our club. If we had exposed him to waivers, somebody would have taken him."[20] Vizcaíno's chances with the Rangers were just as precarious, so they traded him to Milwaukee for reliever Jesús Peña.

Vizcaíno became a reliable reliever for the Brewers right from the start, often serving as Mike DeJean's set-up man. Through May 10, he had struck out 21 batters in 22⅔ innings, was 2-1 with one save, four holds, a 2.38 ERA, and a .188 batting average against him. He had 10 scoreless appearances between April 17 and May 4. Pitching coach Dave Stewart was credited with adjusting Vizcaíno's grip on his slider, making him more effective.[21] Vizcaíno struck out the side four different times that season and was unscored upon in 11 July appearances (0.750 WHIP). After a strong August (2.45 ERA in 11 appearances), he ran out of gas, likely due to tying with Ray King for most appearances (76). While his overall numbers were impressive (2.99 ERA, 1.045 WHIP, opponents batting .192), Vizcaíno was *most* impressive in the clutch. With runners in scoring position and two outs, opponents batted a paltry .087 against him (4-for-46). The solid effort was lost in the Brewers' franchise-worst 56-106 record (excluding strike and pandemic-shortened seasons).

Vizcaíno's 2003 season went in the opposite direction right from the start. He allowed eight earned runs in his first 2⅔ innings. Through May 9, he was 0-2 in 12 innings with three blown saves and a 12.00 ERA with opponents batting .364. Maybe it was all the innings in 2002, his arm slot angle, or various other theories that were offered. There were no answers.[22] Vizcaino recovered to have respectable numbers in August-September (3.00 ERA). "I try to look at each day as a new day," he said optimistically.[23] He surrendered 16 home runs in 62 innings compared with six in 81⅓ in 2002. He finished with a 6.39 ERA but still led the team with 75 appearances. The Brewers set a franchise record for home runs allowed with 219 (surpassed in 2019).

GRINDERS AND GAMERS

The Brewers re-signed him to a one-year contract for $550,000.[24]

Vizcaíno found his groove again as the primary set-up man for closer Danny Kolb, lowering his ERA to 3.75 with opponents batting .228. He again led the Brewers in appearances (73) and dominated June and September, allowing just five earned runs in 23⅔ innings combined. Vizcaíno was highly effective vs. lefties, who batted a lowly .163 against him (21-for-129).

The Brewers floundered again at 67-94 with an offense ranked last in batting average. During the winter meetings, they acquired power hitter Carlos Lee from the Chicago White Sox for Vizcaíno, outfielder Scott Podsednik (major leagues' stolen-base leader), and a player to be named later (Travis Hinton) in a deal White Sox beat reporter Scott Merkin would later call the best winter meetings deal in White Sox history.[25] The White Sox avoided arbitration with Vizcaíno and signed him to a one-year contract for $1.3 million.[26]

Vizcaíno stumbled out of the gate, producing gaudy numbers of 17 earned runs, 29 hits, and 11 walks in his first 23⅔ innings through the end of May (6.46 ERA). Numbers can be deceiving, however. In his second appearance of the season, Vizcaíno "took one for the team" in a blowout loss to Cleveland. White Sox pitching coach Don Cooper later called Vizcaíno an "unsung hero" for throwing 60 pitches while surrendering six runs in an 11-5 loss in 11 innings. "We had nobody else left to use one day," recalled Cooper. "This guy had a role that he picked up all of the loose innings, and he picked it up well. He pitched if we were up by a lot, down by a lot or had to finish out a game. He did not [complain] or moan at all. He kept everything, in my mind, in order to where we would have our better guys always available."[27] These are moments worth remembering, particularly on a championship team.

Vizcaíno's early struggles didn't do great harm to the White Sox, who had built a five-game lead in the AL Central Division. That lead would grow to 10½ games at the end of June as Vizcaíno started to find his role in the White Sox bullpen. He had six consecutive scoreless appearances from May 27 to June 13, then again June 24 to July 8. In July he allowed just two earned runs in 15 innings with a 1.20 ERA. "I've been pitching more," Vizcaíno said. "I'd like to pitch every day. I've never had a sore arm. More pitching means more concentration. I'm pitching more inside now. Lots of fastballs. Not as many sliders."[28]

Vizcaíno had solid months of August and September (3.12 ERA in 17⅓ innings) while holding batters to a .230 BA. The White Sox slumped and their once 15-game lead in the Central Division dwindled to 1½ on September 24. They held off a pesky Cleveland club, however, by six games and secured their first playoff berth in five years. Vizcaíno filled many roles in a crowded White Sox bullpen. His 65 appearances (3.73 ERA) were surrounded by a formidable pen of Neal Cotts (69 appearances, 1.94 ERA), Cliff Politte

(68, 2.00), and Damaso Marte (66, 3.77) supporting closer Dustin Hermanson (34 saves, 2.04). Rookie Bobby Jenks (2.75 ERA) eventually became the team's closer. Vizcaíno threw 48 innings 7 through 9 and 13 innings 4 through 6, showing his flexibility. Manager Ozzie Guillén's staff tied for first in the AL in ERA (3.61), complete games (9), and saves (54).

The offense was not spectacular, but gritty, led by Podsednik's 59 steals, .351 on-base percentage, and solid defensive play in left field which earned him an All-Star selection and MVP votes. They swept the Red Sox in the Division Series and won their first pennant since 1959 with a League Championship Series win in five games over the Angels. The White Sox swept the Astros for their first World Series championship since 1917. Vizcaíno threw a scoreless 10th inning in Game Three of the World Series, which Chicago won in the 14th inning. This was his only postseason appearance for the White Sox. But Cooper remembered Vizcaíno for "an unheralded role that in some ways can be not recognizable, but valuable nevertheless."[29] He will forever be a significant piece of Chicago White Sox history.

Vizcaíno moved on to his fourth team in eight years when, on December 20, the White Sox dealt him, pitcher Orlando Hernández, and outfielder Chris Young to Arizona for pitcher Javier Vázquez. The Diamondbacks gave Vizcaíno a one-year contract for $1.77 million, avoiding arbitration.[30]

Vizcaíno had another solid year in the bullpen. Through the end of May, his ERA was 2.73 and he limited batters to a .213 batting average. In July and August he held batters to a minuscule .164 BA with a 2.11 ERA. He held lefties to .164 (17-for-104) and led his team in appearances (70). His strikeout percentage (26.5) was the highest of his career and he limited all batters to a meager .215 average. Vizcaíno finished 4-6 with a 3.58 ERA and 1.224 WHIP with 72 strikeouts against 29 walks for the fourth-place Diamondbacks (76-86).

Vizcaíno was on the move again as the Diamondbacks reacquired future Hall of Fame pitcher Randy Johnson from the Yankees on January 9, 2007. Going to New York with Vizcaíno were infielder Alberto González and pitchers Steven Jackson and Ross Ohlendorf. He would be in the mix of set-up men for Mariano Rivera. Vizcaíno struggled, carrying a 7.27 ERA through the end of May with an astounding 20 walks to 13 strikeouts. He was seen taking out his frustrations on a water cooler after a bad night. The suspicion was his arm angle was again the culprit as his slider was flat. "We all expect more from him," manager Joe Torre said, "and he expects more from himself. That's where the frustration comes in. We'll keep working on it until we get it."[31]

Vizcaíno became more efficient in June, July, and August, with a 1.31 ERA over 41⅓ innings, going 6-1 with nine holds and a .182 batting average. He had a string of 12 consecutive scoreless appearances in June and 11 in July.

September was a different story. Vizcaíno was up to 68 appearances at that point. He was pounded for nine earned runs in eight innings with a 10.13 ERA, opponents batting .417 off him. Vizcaíno simply said, "I pitched too much."[32]

Nevertheless, Vizcaíno was on the Yankees' postseason roster and made one appearance in the Division Series against Cleveland. He entered Game Two in the 11th inning of a 1-1 tie. This is the infamous game at Jacobs Field in which earlier Yankees reliever Joba Chamberlain was seemingly attacked by the flying insects known as midges. Luis walked Kenny Lofton and allowed a single to Franklin Gutierrez. Casey Blake sacrificed the runners to second and third which prompted an intentional walk to Grady Sizemore. Vizcaíno forced Asdrúbal Cabrera on a popout, but Travis Hafner singled to right to give Cleveland the win and a 2-0 lead in the Series. Cleveland went on to win the series, three games to one. "I want to throw my best pitch," Vizcaíno said, "and he was able to get a hit. It's tough."[33]

Vizcaíno, a free agent, signed a two-year contract in December with the NL champion Colorado Rockies for $7.5 million, the largest contract for a reliever in Rockies history at the time. "There's no pressure," he said about the deal. "It's just baseball."[34] But baseball was rough for him in the 2008 season. In his first appearance, on April 2 at St. Louis, Vizcaíno entered the game in the bottom of the eighth, the Rockies trailing 4-3. He lasted one-third of an inning, allowing four hits, two walks, and four earned runs. After just two appearances, he was on the disabled list with a shoulder issue and didn't return until early June. He had decent numbers in July and August (3.54 ERA while holding opponents to a .200 BA) but was lit up in September and finished the season 1-2 with a 5.28 ERA. Lefties batted a hefty .372 against him. Vizcaíno was displeased at losing the main bullpen set-up role as manager Clint Hurdle used him in mop-up roles. "I didn't pitch enough," he concluded. "That was hard. I like pitching every day. I don't like going into games that are 10-1 or 11-1. I want to be out there for the close games."[35] To make matters worse, Vizcaíno was arrested for drunk driving in the offseason and his time with the Rockies was over.[36] In January 2009 he was traded to the Cubs for pitcher Jason Marquis.

After four scoreless appearances with the Cubs, Vizcaíno was designated for assignment, released, and signed a one-year contract with Cleveland. His first appearance was a disaster on the road in Tampa on May 15. The Indians built a 7-0 lead only to watch the Rays rally and tie the score. He faced just one batter, B.J. Upton, who slammed a walk-off home run for the 8-7 victory. "Vizcaíno threw a fastball that screamed 'hit me!' as it arrived down the middle and up at 89 mph," wrote Dennis Manoloff of the *Cleveland Plain Dealer*.[37] What are the odds such a thing would happen yet again? Yet, it did, in Vizcaíno's last appearance in a major-league game, on June 19. The Indians again built a 7-0 lead at Wrigley Field, only to see the Cubs rally and tie the game in the eighth inning, 7-7. Vizcaíno pitched the 10th, retiring the first two batters. He walked Alfonso Soriano, who stole second. Ryan Theriot hit a weak grounder that took a weird hop over Victor Martinez at first and Soriano scampered home with the 8-7 win. Vizcaíno suffered losses in both his first and last appearances for Cleveland in come-from-behind 8-7 walk-off losses in which they blew 7-0 leads. He walked off a major-league mound for the final time, finishing 1-3 with a 5.40 ERA for Cleveland.

Over a year later, Vizcaíno signed a minor-league contract with the Yankees in December 2010. However, the contract was voided after Vizcaíno was suspended by Major League Baseball for testing positive for metabolites of Stanozolol, a banned performance-enhancing substance. The 50-game suspension would take effect if Vizcaíno was on a major-league team's roster, but this never happened.[38] In 2014 he signed a minor-league contract with Baltimore but was soon released. Between 2010 and 2015, Vizcaíno pitched for seven teams in the Dominican Winter League, in Mexico, China, and Venezuela.

The author and others tried but were unable to get details about Vizcaíno, his family, early life, and post-retirement – even with the help of the Juan Marichal SABR Chapter in Santo Domingo and FENAPEPRO (National Federation of Professional Baseball Players), we were unable to get more details.

SOURCES

In addition to the sources cited in the Notes, the author consulted:

Baseball-reference.com

"Luis Vizcaíno," Fangraphs. Retrieved March 2, 2024. fangraphs.com/players/luis-vizcaino/714/stats?position=P

Luis Vizcaíno file, provided by the A. Bartlett Giamatti Research Center, National Baseball Hall of Fame.

Retrosheet.org

Saxon, Mark. "A's Will Spare No Expense to Keep Reliever Vizcaíno," *Oakland Tribune*, April 10, 2000: S-5.

NOTES

1   Scott Merkin, "Cooper: Luis Vizcaíno Was '05 Unsung Hero," MLB.com, May 28, 2020. Retrieved February 29, 2024. mlb.com/news/luis-vizcaino-white-sox-unsung-hero.

2   Jim Van Vliet, "Long Has an Eye for Ball Now That He Dons Glasses," *Sacramento Bee*, April 21, 2000: E5.

3   Mark Saxon, "From Bani to the Big Leagues," *Oakland Tribune*, March 19, 2000: 6-S.

4   *Oakland Athletics 2000 Information Guide*, 62.

5   Alex Valdez, "A Few Minutes with Luis Vizcaíno," *Modesto Bee*, June 28, 1998: C5.

6   "República Dominicana, Registro Civil, 1801-2010," *FamilySearch* (https://www.familysearch.org/ark:/61903/1:1:6RGQ-VMB9 : Sun Mar 10 13:19:29 UTC 2024). Entry for Luis Vizcaino and Juanita Vizcaino, December 19, 1998.

7   John Erfort, "Rockhounds Take Advantage of Jackson Miscues for Come-From-Behind Victory," *Odessa* (Texas) *American*, July 20, 1999: 3C.

8   Howard Bryant, "Vizcaíno Shows Mound of Talent," *San Jose Mercury News*, February 29, 2000: 6D.

9   John Hickey, "Stein to Take Starting Role Again for A's," *Oakland Tribune*, July 24, 1999: S-6.

10   Bryant, "Vizcaíno Shows Mound of Talent,"

11   Bryant, "Vizcaíno Shows Mound of Talent,"

12   Mark Saxon, "Valdez Wants to Prove His Big League Worth," *Oakland Tribune*, February 24, 2001: S-4.

13   Mark Saxon, "Vizcaíno's Optioning Back to Triple-A Proves Bittersweet," *Oakland Tribune*, April 19, 2000: S-6.

14   Mark Saxon, "10-Run Inning Stuns Mulder," *Oakland Tribune*, March 23, 2001: S-6.

15   Mark Saxon, "Oakland Welcomes Bradford," *Oakland Tribune*, April 25, 2001: S-3.

16   Mark Saxon, "Vizcaíno's Save: First of Many?" *Oakland Tribune*, July 16, 2001: S-6.

17   Mark Saxon, "Vizcaíno Gets 1 Out, First Victory," *Oakland Tribune*, August 7, 2001: S-5.

18   Mark Saxon, "Vizcaíno's True Age: 26, not 24," *Oakland Tribune*, February 22, 2002: S-8.

19   Mark Saxon, "A's Remain Uncertain on Dye's Availability," *Oakland Tribune*, March 19, 2002: S-4.

20   T.R. Sullivan, "Rangers Deal for Oakland Reliever," *Fort Worth Star-Telegram*, March 19, 2002: 7D.

21   Michael Cunningham, "Vizcaíno Earns His Keep," *Milwaukee Journal Sentinel*, May 15, 2002: 5C.

22   Tom Haudricourt, "Vizcaíno a Changed Man," *Sunday Journal Sentinel*, May 11, 2003: 7C.

23   Drew Olson, "Vizcaíno's Back Up to Speed," *Milwaukee Journal Sentinel*, August 18, 2003: 5C.

24   Tom Haudricourt, "Brewers Re-sign Vizcaíno, Pass on Durocher" *Sunday Journal Sentinel*, December 21, 2003: 10C.

25   Scott Merkin, "White Sox Top 5 Winter Meetings Deals," MLB.com, December 7, 2020. Retrieved March 1, 2024. mlb.com/news/white-sox-biggest-winter-meetings-moves.

26   "Vizcaíno Gets $1.3 Million from Sox," *Chicago Tribune*, January 19, 2005: 4: 5.

27   Merkin, "Cooper: Luis Vizcaíno Was '05 Unsung Hero."

28   Bill Jauss, "Relief to Vizcaíno? More Work," *Chicago Tribune*, August 3, 2005: 4:3.

29   Merkin, "Cooper: Luis Vizcaíno Was '05 Unsung Hero."

30   Associated Press, "Top Pitcher Agrees to 4-year, $19.5 Million Deal," *Tucson Citizen*, January 14, 2006: 5C.

31   Anthony Rieber, "Giambi's Bat Foot: Let's Go to the Tape," *Newsday* (Long Island, New York), May 11, 2007: A77; "Damon Back in as DH; Jason Returns Today," *New York Daily News*, May 12, 2007: 45.

32   Troy E. Renck, "Vizcaíno Brings Punch(outs) – Veteran Relief," *Denver Post*, February 18, 2008: B-01.

33   Kat O'Brien, "Joba Thrown Off by Bugaboo," *Newsday*, October 6, 2007: A38.

34   Renck, "Vizcaíno Brings Punch(outs)."

35   Troy E. Renck, "Trends Show Vizcaíno Will Rebound in '09," *Denver Post*, October 3, 2008: CC-04.

36   Patrick Saunders, "Rockies – Vizcaíno Arrested for Drunken Driving," *Denver Post*, October 28, 2008: C-06.

37   Dennis Manoloff, "Comic Relief," *Plain Dealer*, May 19, 2009: D1.

38   Associated Press, "Luis Vizcaíno Suspended by MLB," ESPN, June 29, 2011. Retrieved June 25, 2024. espn.com/mlb/news/story?id=6717591.

KEVIN WALKER

By Jason Scheller

*"I've loved baseball ever
since I can remember."*
– Kevin Walker[1]

A relief pitcher most of his career, Kevin Walker played for his only World Series championship team when he appeared in nine regular-season games with the Chicago White Sox in 2005. Standing 6-feet-4-inches tall and weighing 190 pounds, the fiery southpaw was an imposing presence on the mound. Being a relief pitcher is unlike any other position in the sport, according to Walker. "You're on an island out there. That island is just so different from any position in sports. In basketball you have four other guys out there to help you. In baseball, it is you against that batter, and how you pitch makes all the difference in that moment." In 14 seasons of professional baseball, Walker spent time with many storied franchises, including the San Diego Padres, San Francisco Giants, Chicago White Sox, Texas Rangers, Houston Astros, and the Colorado Rockies.

Kevin Walker   2005

Kevin Michael Walker was born on September 20, 1976, in Irving, Texas to Wesley and Judy Walker.[2] Wesley was a truck driver for Yellow Freight who worked the midnight-to-8 shift and then coached Kevin and his older brother Doug's baseball teams all the way up to high school. His mother, Judy, was a homemaker. Both brothers and Kevin's older sister, Audria, were involved in sports from an early age, and their mother made sure they made it to their practices on time all while managing the household. Kevin seemed destined to be a baseball player. "In school you would get those assignments to write a paper about what you wanted to be and for me it was always a baseball player," Walker said.[3] From the age of 5, he played baseball and wiffleball on the weekends with his older brother and his friends. "My dad was the coach, so me and my brother basically grew up at the ballfield," Walker said. "Ever since I can remember I was always at the field and baseball was what I wanted to do."[4] Growing up, Kevin was a Texas Rangers fan but wasn't drawn to them by the typical players you might think. "Pete O'Brien was a first baseman for the Texas Rangers, and I loved watching him play. Of course everyone loved Nolan Ryan, but I was also a fan of Rafael Palmeiro and Juan González," Walker said.

At Grand Prairie High School, Kevin got to play with his brother for one year when Kevin was a freshman, and his brother Doug was a senior. As a member of the Gophers pitching staff, he played alongside teammate Kerry Wood. "I threw about 86 miles per hour, so I wasn't really lighting up radar guns. But Kerry was a number one pick in those days so, if we played a doubleheader, scouts would come to see him and then stay and watch me," Walker said. With Grand Prairie in 1995, he performed well in the playoffs, pitching a no-hitter and hitting a grand slam in the regional quarterfinals. Walker was the pitcher of record in the 4-1 state semifinal loss to the Lubbock Coronado Mustangs.

Walker received multiple college offers his senior year to play baseball. He had already signed to play baseball with the Texas Christian University Horned Frogs. As luck would have it, the majors came calling before he ever got the chance to play college baseball.

Walker was drafted by the San Diego Padres in the sixth round of the 1995 amateur draft. He was signed by the team on June 13, 1995. Reflecting on his choice to go pro as opposed to staying in college, Walker said, "I thought that I would do everything I could to get there. I didn't go to college then, but I don't regret the decision I made." He spent his first season with the rookie-level Arizona League Padres. He made 12 starts in 13 games, finishing with a record of 5-5 and a 3.01 ERA.

In 1996 Walker combined to go 5-6 with a 4.61 ERA in 14 games between the Pioneer League (Rookie) Idaho Falls Braves and the Clinton LumberKings of the Class-A Midwest League. With the Braves he started one game before being moved up to the LumberKings.

In 1997 Walker continued to pitch for the LumberKings. He pitched 110⅔ innings while making 19 starts. He finished the season with a 6-10 record and a 4.88 ERA.

In 1998 Walker went a combined 13-7 over 136 innings pitched and started 24 games between the LumberKings and the high Class-A Rancho Cucamonga Quakes of the California League. Walker won six consecutive starts between June 14 and July 12, finishing second in the San Diego organization in victories with an ERA of 3.84.

Walker spent 1999 with Rancho Cucamonga Quakes, working out of the bullpen for much of the season and earning four saves. In 2000 he moved up to the Mobile Bay Bears of the Double-A Southern League. Before the season, he was ranked as the number-14 prospect in the Padres' minor-league system by *Baseball America*. Walker was called up by the Padres on April 13 after pitching in four games for Mobile.

Walker made his major-league debut on April 14, 2000, at home against the Houston Astros. He entered the game in the sixth inning, relieving Will Cunnane after the Astros had scored two runs. Walker walked a batter, then gave up a grand slam to Jeff Bagwell. "My parents had flown in, and I was nervous. It's a packed Qualcomm Stadium, and I'm not throwing anything else but fastballs, and I gave up a grand slam," Walker said in the 2024 interview. "I remember distinctly getting booed off the field. I felt terrible, but that is where I give a lot of credit to (Padres manager) Bruce Bochy. He could tell it was eating at me and he put me back in two games later and I had a one-two-three inning in relief. That took a lot of the pressure off me." Calling Bochy the best manager he has ever played for, Walker said. "He treated everyone really well and made them feel like a valuable part of the team. He cared about who you were and wanted to see you maximize your potential as a ballplayer." Walker took Bochy's philosophy to heart. He finished the season with a 7-1 record and a 4.19 ERA. His 70 game appearances ranked second behind the Chicago White Sox' Kelly Wunsch (83) and were the second most in Padres' history for a rookie with no prior major-league experience since Larry Hardy accomplished the feat in 1974 with 76. Walker also recorded a career-high four strikeouts on August 29, 2000, against the Chicago Cubs in Wrigley Field.

In his second season with the Padres, Walker was limited to 16 games in 2001 because of problems with his left elbow. He underwent Tommy John surgery at Anaheim Memorial Hospital performed by Dr. Lewis Yocum and Dr. Jan Fronek. In the 16 games he appeared in, Walker retired 12 of the first 17 batters he faced, stranded five of six inherited runners, and did not allow a run in 14 of the 16 appearances. In 2001 Walker met his future wife, Aimee, who was a ball girl for the Padres while playing softball at Point Loma Nazarene University. "She would play catch with players, and she was a babysitter for Phil Nevin, who was a player for San Diego and a friend of mine," Walker said. They were married in January of 2003.

After the successful surgery, Walker was reactivated by the San Diego Padres on August 8, 2002. On August 9 he worked the sixth inning of a game against the Cincinnati Reds. After allowing a double to Todd Walker, he settled in, striking out Aaron Boone and Ken Griffey Jr. before allowing Todd Walker to score on a wild pitch and giving up a double to Adam Dunn, who scored on Austin Kearns' single.[5] It was his first appearance in the major leagues since May 21, 2001. Walker pitched only two games before being placed on the disabled list with tendinitis in his left elbow, and didn't return until September 1, after rehab stints with the Pacific Coast League Portland Beavers and the Lake Elsinore Storm of the California League.

Walker missed most of the 2003 season recovering from a strained left elbow, pitching in only 11 games. He was placed on the 15-day disabled list, then the 60-day disabled list,[6] was optioned to Portland on June 9, and was recalled on August 29.

A week before the 2004 season opened, Walker was claimed off waivers by the San Francisco Giants. After making five relief appearances for the Giants, he was optioned to the Fresno Grizzlies of the Pacific Coast League. Walker pitched in 48 games for the Grizzlies, earning one save. He was released by the Giants after the season.

Walker signed with the White Sox on November 23, 2004. He spent much of the 2005 season with the Charlotte Knights of the International League. He had two stints with the White Sox – from May 9 to June 1 and from June 30 to July 10. His final appearance for the White Sox was on July 9, against the Oakland A's at US Cellular Field. Walker replaced Shingo Takatsu in the top of the ninth inning with Bobby Crosby on first and no outs. Walker gave up a home run to the first batter he faced, Eric Chávez, increasing the Athletics' lead to 10-1. Walker settled down after the home run to coax Bobby Kielty into a groundout before striking out Eric Byrnes and getting Nick Swisher to ground out to end the inning.

Walker attributed much of the success of the 2005 White Sox to their pitching staff, both starters and bullpen. "When you can get seven-plus innings and 15 or more wins out of everyone in that rotation, it is truly incredible. There is just nowhere in that rotation that you could find a weakness," he said. "The use of analytics and information in today's game has killed the (complete-game) pitcher. 2005 might have been teetering on the edge of the last of those long-term, complete-game pitchers."

Walker remains one of a unique club of players who were part of the team but did not play in the division series, championship series, or World Series and still got a ring. Reflecting on that unique status, he said, "I only played a couple of months for the White Sox, and did not make the postseason roster." He added, "I believe the rings were designed by owner Jerry Reinsdorf's wife. They were incredibly beautiful, and I was fortunate enough to get one. Jerry Reinsdorf wanted every player who had been part of the team to get one, since it had been 88 years since the White Sox had won a World Series." When asked if he ever wore it, he said, "No, but I still have the ring in a safe at home."

Walker was released by the White Sox on October 3, the day after the regular season ended. He signed a minor-league contract with the Texas Rangers on November 6. He attended 2006 spring training as a nonroster invitee, then spent the season with the Oklahoma City RedHawks of the Pacific Coast League. He pitched in 46 games, starting five, earned two saves, and finished with a 4.63 ERA and a record of 6-5.

After the 2006 season, Walker became a free agent once more and was signed by the Houston Astros to a minor-league contract on January 4, 2007,[7] but was released on April 3. Walker began the 2007 season with the Camden River Sharks of the independent Atlantic League, going 4-1 with a 1.74 ERA before signing with the Colorado Rockies on June 14.[8] Walker spent the rest of the season with the Colorado Springs Sky Sox of the Pacific Coast League. (4-6, 5.31). Released after the season, he pitched in three games in the winter of 2007-2008 for the Guasave Algodoneros (Cotton Growers) of the Mexican Pacific Winter League.

For the 2008 season, Walker re-signed with the Camden River Sharks. This proved to be his last season as a player in professional baseball. Walker appeared in 14 games for the River Sharks, finishing the season with a 2-2 record and a 6.37 ERA.

Over the course of his 14-year career, Walker appeared in 122 major-league games over six seasons, compiling a 7-3 record with a 4.76 ERA. He finished his career with 102 innings pitched, gave up 84 hits and walked 63 while striking out 95 batters. Asked to reflect on his career, Walker said, "I am super grateful for the time I got. This is something I thought about since I was a kid writing papers about what I wanted to be when I grew up. Through my career as a pitcher, I was able to achieve my dream of playing professional baseball."

After the 2008 season, Walker became a pitching coach in the Boston Red Sox farm system. He began with the short-season Class-A Lowell Spinners in 2009. That season's Spinners pitchers led the New York-Penn League with 638 strikeouts and ranked second in the league with a franchise-best 2.96 ERA.[9] Walker continued to work his way through the Red Sox farm system as a pitching coach for the Class-A Greenville Drive (2010), Class-A Salem Red Sox (2011-2014), Double-A Portland Sea Dogs (2015-2017), and the Triple-A Pawtucket Red Sox (2018-2019). Coaching with kids and schedules to juggle can be difficult. Fortunately for Walker, his wife, Aimee, told him, "You go coach, and I'll do the rest."

Walker has fond memories of his time in the Red Sox minor-league system. "My wife had gotten her teaching credentials, and we were able to travel while I coached, and she homeschooled our kids. I hope that my kids, Kamryn and Brady, will look back on that time and be thankful for the experience that they had," he said. It certainly appears as though his daughter Kamryn has fond memories. "She tells people that she got to field grounders with Mookie Betts and Xander Bogaerts or play catch with Christian Vázquez. People think she is joking, but they forget that those guys came up through that system," Walker said.

On October 31, 2019, Walker was named the assistant pitching coach for the Red Sox. On November 20, 2020, he was promoted to bullpen coach, where he remained through the 2024 season.

Walker's favorite memory as a Red Sox bullpen coach was the 2021 one-game wild-card playoff between the Red Sox and the New York Yankees in Fenway Park on October 5, 2021. Before a sellout crowd of 38,324, the Red Sox sailed to victory on a Xander Bogaerts home-run blast that traveled 427 feet over the center-field fence in the first inning. Bogaerts continued that magic in the field after gunning down Aaron Judge at home plate to block a Yankees comeback attempt in the sixth inning. Nathan Eovaldi pitched strong into the sixth inning, giving up four hits while striking out eight. After Garrett Whitlock coaxed Gleyber Torres to pop up and end the game, the Red Sox bench and bullpen emptied as the speakers played "Dirty Water" and the players made their way to the pitcher's mound to celebrate the 6-2 win.[10] "Gerrit Cole vs. Nate Eovaldi. It was the loudest, most electric game I had ever been a part of," recalled Walker. "When we play the Yankees it's a different level. That '21 game was unbelievable. The fans never sat down for one pitch, and Eovaldi was an incredible big-game pitcher."

Because baseball was a part of Kevin Walker's life from the beginning, it should come as no surprise that sports have been a significant part of their family life since he and Aimee were married in 2003. Both Kamryn and Brady have been involved in sports from a very early age. "I wouldn't know how to raise the kids without sports being a part of it," Walker said.[11]

After the Red Sox missed the postseason for the third straight year and finished third in the AL East with a record of 81-81, the team parted ways with Walker and five other coaches in October of 2024.[12]

As of November 2024, Walker was looking for his next post in baseball. "I've been in contact with some clubs, but I've also thought about building my own program in college. I'm not sure what the future holds, but I am open to all opportunities," he said.

GRINDERS AND GAMERS

SOURCES

In addition to the sources cited in the Notes, the author consulted Ancestry.com, Baseball-Reference, Retrosheet, Baseball Almanac, Stats Crew, and the Kevin Walker player file at the National Baseball Hall of Fame.

ACKNOWLEDGMENTS

Thanks to Kevin Walker for taking the time for an interview. Thanks to the Boston Red Sox organization and Sarah Coffin, Rachel Wells at the National Baseball Hall of Fame, as well as Pat Scheller and Holly Scheller. In memory of Greg Fowler.

NOTES

1   Kevin Walker, interview with author, November 25, 2024. Unless indicated, all unattributed quotations from Kevin Walker come from this interview.

2   "Howe Sports Data Questionnaire," February 12, 1996, Ancestry.com, https://www.ancestry.com/discoveryui-content/view/60006403:61599, accessed May 31, 2024.

3   Eddie Merino Jr., "Dodger Dawgs Podcast: Episode 4: From World Champion MLB Pitcher to Red Sox Bullpen Coach, Kevin Walker," Youtube.com, https://www.youtube.com/watch?v=vfWLVEzYnLg, accessed May 31, 2024.

4   Murray Anderson, "Big League Family: Walkers Make Athletics a Family Affair, *Holtville Tribune* (El Centro, California), https://holtvilletribune.com/2021/12/22/big-league-family-walkers-make -athletics-a-family-affair/, accessed May 31, 2024.

5   Joe Kay, "Boone Blasts Reds Past San Diego 12-10," *Greenville* (Ohio) *Daily Advocate,* August 10, 2002: 7.

6   "Transactions," *Ukiah* (California) *Daily Journal,* May 17, 2003: 8.

7   "Transactions," *Huntingdon* (Pennsylvania) *Daily News,* January 5, 2007: 6.

8   "Riversharks Pitcher Kevin Walker Signed by Colorado Rockies," OurSportsCentral.com, June 13,2007. https://www.oursportscentral.com/services/releases/riversharks-pitcher-kevin-walker-signed-by-colorado-rockies/n-3487019, accessed May 31, 2024.

9   *Boston Red Sox Media Guide*, 2018, 426. https://www.sportsarchive.net/documents/702#page/n5/mode/2up, accessed May 31, 2024.

10   "Boston Red Sox Oust New York Yankees, Ready for 'Huge Challenge' against Tampa Bay Rays in ALDS," ESPN.com, https://www.espn.com/mlb/story/_/id/32346019/boston-red-sox-oust-new-york-yankees-win-wild-card-advance-alds, accessed May 31, 2024.

11   Murray Anderson, "Big League Family: Walkers Make Athletics a Family Affair, *Holtville Tribune*, https://holtvilletribune.com/2021/12/22/big-league-family-walkers-make -athletics-a-family-affair/, accessed October 2, 2024.

12   Jen McCaffrey, "Red Sox Fire 6 Coaches, Including First Base Coach Andy Fox, Bullpen Coach Kevin Walker," *The Athletic*, https://www.nytimes.com/athletic/5832486/2024/10/09/red-sox-coaches-fired-andy-fox-kevin-walker/, accessed October 10, 2024.

CHRIS WIDGER

By Mark S. Sternman

One of the last full-time catchers in the truncated history of the Montreal Expos and a backup backstop for the World Series champion 2005 Chicago White Sox, Chris Widger parlayed below-average production into a 10-year major-league career with four teams and later successfully managed in the minors.

Widger came from an athletic family as "his uncle, Mike, played with the Montreal Alouettes and the Ottawa Rough Riders of the Canadian Football League from 1970-78."[1] His father, Bill, worked for more than three decades for DuPont as a mechanic and along with his wife, Doris, raised Chris and his sister, Toni.[2]

Having attended Pennsville Memorial High School in New Jersey and George Mason University in Virginia, Widger was picked in the third round of the 1992 amateur draft by Seattle. Considered a candidate for the 1992 Olympic team,[3] Widger lost out to Charles Johnson and Jason Varitek.

At George Mason, Widger as of 2021 ranked among school leaders in batting (18th at .334), hits (22nd with 200),

 Chris Widger 2005

doubles (tied for ninth with 52), triples (tied for 24th with 6), homers (7th with 32), runs (15th with 142), RBIs (7th with 149), total bases (13th with 360), walks (20th with 82), slugging (tied for 11th at .602), on-base percentage (19th at .418), and putouts (11th with 758).[4] Only five other George Mason players besides Widger have made the majors.

"From my first day, I was lucky to start as a freshman," Widger said. "I was allowed to make my own mistakes. I was allowed to call my own game (as a catcher). I think I was more prepared for pro ball."[5]

Widger showed steady improvement as a professional, progressing from the Bellingham Mariners of the Northwest League in 1992 to the Riverside Pilots of the California League in 1993 to the Jacksonville Suns of the Southern League in 1994 to the Tacoma Rainiers of the Pacific Coast League in 1995. His OPS went up each year except in 1993, ranging from .731 to .817. Widger debuted with Seattle on June 23, 1995. In his third game, he got his first hit, off Kevin Gross, "a solid single to right-center field."[6]

Widger appeared in 23 games and batted .200 in 49 plate appearances. He drove in two runs, scored twice, and had one home run. He handled 65 fielding chances – primarily as a catcher – without an error.

He spent most of 1996 with Triple-A Tacoma, where he hit .304 in 97 games, with a .988 fielding percentage, and got into eight games with Seattle, going 2-for-11.

After having a bone spur removed from his elbow[7] in the offseason, Widger spent most of 1996 with Tacoma although he did play in eight games for Seattle. Along with two other players, Widger reportedly would have gone to Baltimore for lefty hurler David Wells[8] before the Orioles killed the deal.[9] This move represented a stay of execution as Widger soon left the Mariners for another southpaw pitcher in a momentous personal and professional offseason.

On October 29, 1996, Seattle traded Widger, Trey Moore, and Matt Wagner to Montreal for Jeff Fassero and Alex Pacheco. *The Sporting News* characterized the inclusion of Widger as "the key in the deal."[10]

Widger married Theresa Kidwell on December 27, 1996.[11] They had two children together, a boy named C.J. and a daughter named Ashlynn. The marriage ended in divorce. Chris later married Whitney, and they had a son named Skylar.

The trade to Montreal brought Widger to the city where his uncle had played and, after his CFL career had ended, was a part-owner of the Longest Yard, a downtown Montreal bar.[12]

Widger played more games at catcher than any of his teammates for each of his four seasons with the Expos. He got off to a hot start with the bat in Montreal with an .830 OPS after his first 20 games. On May 16, 1997, the Expos beat the Giants 14-13; Widger went 4-for-5 with a double, triple, and 5 RBIs. "He's always been able to handle the fastball in. What he's starting to do now is use his strength to go to the other field," said hitting instructor Tommy Harper.[13]

Widger ended 1997 with a .693 OPS and threw out just 23 of 139 would-be basestealers. "I know a lot of people keep mentioning that part of the problem is a lot of our pitchers are slow to the plate, but it still comes down on me," he said. "A lot of … errors were just me messing up my mechanics and throwing the ball wildly."[14]

Widger turned 27 in 1998, and proving the Bill James analysis asserting that that age represents the peak for players, set career highs in games (125), plate appearances (448), at-bats (417), homers (15), and stolen bases (6). He managed to attain these milestones despite suffering from various ailments[15] that culminated in a sprained ligament in his left thumb[16] that ended his season on September 9. While Widger's caught-stealing percentage more than doubled from 17 percent in 1997 to a career-best 36 percent in 1998, he led the National League with 14 passed balls in the latter campaign. He drove in 53 runs, ranking fifth on the Expos. Manager Felipe Alou called Widger "the team's most improved player."[17]

In an ominous sign for the future of the Montreal franchise, the Expos played two games in Washington before the 1999 season. Having spent his college years near DC, Widger spoke enthusiastically in evaluating the exhibition experience: "It's nice to play in an area that has the type of baseball fans that we have here. I've been to Redskins games … and the atmosphere is outstanding. If something happens to Montreal, I hope we'd come here."[18]

Widger's final full season with the Expos represented the pinnacle of his offensive prowess "because of longer stretches of rest when [Michael] Barrett sees action behind the plate."[19] He set personal bests in hits (101), doubles (24), and RBIs (56). Widger's slash line marks (.264/.325/.441) also represented peaks as did his OPS+ (94). With a younger and cheaper player poised to play every day, Montreal would move on from Widger less than five years before the franchise moved on to Washington: In June 1999, Stephanie Myles, a beat writer covering the Expos, observed, "It seems fairly obvious … Barrett will be the team's everyday catcher for years to come."[20] Her analysis began to come true via an August 2000 trade.

On July 18, 1999, David Cone threw a perfect game in Yankee Stadium against Montreal, with Widger batting seventh. Cone "was amazing, He had a great fastball and his slider just kept getting better," Widger said after striking out twice.[21]

Widger had surgery on his left knee after the 1999 season,[22] but that did not deter teams from trying to trade for him. The Yankees sought his services as a backup to Jorge Posada.[23] The Expos on August 8, 2000, instead traded him back to the Mariners for players to be named later (eventually Sean Spencer and Terrmel Sledge). Having played just 31 games over his first two Seattle seasons, Widger appeared in just 10 games in his second stint, with only one hit – a solo homer. Widger made his biggest impact in a simulated game. Turning around to hit lefty for the first time since high school, he smacked a shot that broke the kneecap of Jamie Moyer,[24] ensuring that the 13-game winner would not pitch in the playoffs.

After shoulder surgery, Widger played in only a handful of minor-league games for Seattle in 2001 before the still-interested Yankees signed him as a free agent in 2002. "It's been a long road to get back here," he said, "and now that it's over it was worth it because this was where I wanted to be."[25]

Accordingly, Widger expressed no bitterness about the end of his second Seattle tenure: "I kind of expected it. They had an option they could have used on me, but that's a lot of money for a guy coming off having his shoulder reconstructed twice. Plus, they probably wanted to have a left-handed bat there (as the second catcher), so there was no reason to have me and Danny (Wilson)."[26]

Widger played in 21 games for New York in 2002, debuting with the team on July 4. Prior to the call-up, he had purchased a house big enough for his wife, two children, brother-in-law, and five nieces because he still had family in New Jersey. His sister Toni, a nurse, had died in 2001 at the age of 36.

In limited action, Widger produced for New York. In 25 plate appearances in July, he hit .304 with 5 RBIs. In 26 plate appearances in August, he hit .385 and slugged .500. But, wrote a New York sportswriter, "playing sparingly does have its drawbacks and Widger experienced them in the Yankees' 6-2 loss to the Rangers [on August 25] at the Stadium. 'This was the first time I caught Andy [Pettitte] in a regular season game,' said Widger. … 'I thought we worked well together … but the results weren't there.'"[27]

Widger did not play in the 2002 postseason, and the Yankees again signed him as a free agent due to his "decent bat and – quite important – … placid demeanor and excellent work ethic."[28] Widger's mood decidedly soured after New York brought in John Flaherty to compete with him. "It's like a slap in the face," he said. "… What the hell did I do to lose the job I had last year?"[29]

Electing to go with Flaherty, New York released Widger on April 7, 2003. The Cardinals brought him back to the National League five days later. Widger played 44 games for St. Louis in 2003 with a poor .235/.279/.324 slash line and then lost his roster spot in 2004 to Cody McKay, the son of Dave McKay, who served as the first-base coach of the Cardinals from 1996 to 2011. Again, Widger seemed hardly sanguine about the switch in words that echoed those he uttered after wearing pinstripes: Tony La Russa, the St. Louis manager, "called me into his office and made it clear that the job was up for grabs. How that happened I don't know. Nothing changed from last year. They told me how happy they were with how I ran the pitching staff. I don't understand."[30]

Widger had seemingly developed a sense of entitlement and had failed to appreciate that a team would not hesitate to jettison a backup catcher past the prime of a less-than-stellar career for reasons both fair (Flaherty was a better player) and unfair (McKay's relationships likely played a role in the release of Widger).

In 2004 Widger played independent ball for the Camden Riversharks of the Atlantic League, a spot that returned him close to his family during its time of need. At the age of 33, Widger faced long odds in returning to the majors after his unhappy endings in both New York and St. Louis.

He went to 2005 spring training as a nonroster invitee of the White Sox. Backing up A.J. Pierzynski, Widger had an unexpected revival. He enjoyed playing for manager Ozzie Guillén. "What you see is what you get," said Widger. "… He let his backup guys play a lot. If I was up in the seventh inning of a tie game, I didn't have to look over my shoulder for a pinch-hitter."[31]

After failing to homer in the majors from 2001 to 2004, Widger hit four in 2005. After last appearing in the play-offs a decade earlier during the 1995 American League Championship Series, Widger sat out the first 10 games of the 2005 playoffs before unexpectedly playing in the third game of the World Series via a double switch in the bottom of the ninth inning that inserted him for former Expo Dustin Hermanson in the ninth spot of the batting order.

Widger struck out swinging against Houston closer Brad Lidge in the top of the 10th and drew a walk from Chad Qualls in the top of the 13th before a double play took him off the bases. In the top of the 14th, Geoff Blum, another ex-Montrealer, homered off Ezequiel Astacio with two outs to give the White Sox a 6-5 lead. The score stayed the same when Widger came up with the bases loaded. He took five pitches[32] to earn an RBI on the bases-loaded walk that put Chicago up 7-5. Widger caught the final six innings of the game, which ended 7-5, with the White Sox completing a sweep the next evening. The transformation of Widger from a past-his-prime player trying to hang on in an independent league to a contributor to a World Series champion was complete as well.

Singling out the team's "guys in there that nobody wanted," and others who were "fringe players," Widger said, "Here we are, sweeping the World Series with … castaways, misfits. It makes it that much sweeter. We didn't have the best talent. We had the best team."[33]

Widger started 2006 with Chicago and hit the last of his 55 career homers on May 15 off Scott Baker in a 7-3 win in Minnesota. He had homered off four pitchers who won a Cy Young Award: Chris Carpenter, Tom Glavine, Barry Zito and [Randy] Johnson.[34] The White Sox released him in July, and Widger joined the Orioles in August. In his first game with Baltimore, Widger faced the Yankees. His old team beat his new one, 6-1, but the losing pitcher praised his new backstop. "Pretty good," Rodrigo López said of working with Widger, "I like him a lot. He had a lot of good ideas, the way I like to pitch. We worked on the same page."[35]

Widger played in his last major-league game on September 15 and had just two hits in 17 at-bats for the Orioles. He returned to Camden, at first serving as pitching coach for 2013 and 2014 as well as having two hitless at-bats at the age of 43 for the Riversharks. In 2015 he became the team's manager. "I am excited to be managing the Riversharks, a home team for me, but more importantly a team who gave me a chance to resurrect my career at a time when I was nearly out of baseball," Widger said.[36]

Camden went 56-83 under Widger and moved in 2016 to New Britain. Staying with the team seemed less attractive once it left New Jersey, so Widger contacted another former George Mason player in the Kansas City organization to secure a part-time coaching slot with Wilmington in the Carolina League.

Widger did far better in his second stint as manager, leading the Burlington Royals of the Appalachian League to a 39-29 record and a second-place finish in 2019. In 2021 *Baseball America* named him as Minor League Manager of the Year for skippering the Quad City River Bandits to the championship of the High-A Central League. Alec Zumwalt, Kansas City's director of hitting performance/player development, said of Widger, "His players love playing for him and … he creates a winning environment in the clubhouse that plays out on the field."[37]

The Rangers drafted Chris's son C.J. in the 10th round in 2021. "I'm happy he did it on his own, did it his way," said Widger. "I'm a little excited that he's not with Kansas City so that he could be on another team and do his thing. … He's always loved baseball, but I never pushed him into it."[38] The younger Widger advanced to the Rangers of the Arizona Complex League at the Rookie classification in 2023. A 24-year-old lefty reliever, he went 1-0 with a save in seven games. In 2024, he received a promotion to Modesto of the Class-A California League.

Chris Widger made the jump to Double-A ball in 2022, managing the Northwest Arkansas Naturals of the Texas League. The team went 58-79, which ended his tenure with the Kansas City organization. "Probably I wasn't analytical enough or was maybe too, quote, unquote, old school," Widger said.[39] He returned to New Jersey in 2023 to manage the Sussex County Miners of Augusta in the Frontier League to a 55-40 record.

GRINDERS AND GAMERS

NOTES

1 *Guide 1997* [Montreal Expos media guide], 232.

2 Melissa Isacson, "A Rock in Role at Home," *Chicago Tribune*, October 16, 2005.

3 Frank Hughes, "Patriots Jostle Virginia Tech, 10-1," *Washington Post*, April 8, 1992: F2.

4 "George Mason University Career Baseball Records," s3.us-east-2.amazonaws.com/sidearm.nextgen.sites/georgemason.sidearmsports.com/documents/2022/2/16/Base_2022_Career_Baseball_Records_Updated_Dec_12_2019_.pdf (accessed December 6, 2023).

5 David Driver, "Chris Widger Adds to the Mason-to-Royals Pipeline," gomason.com/news/2016/5/12/210948491, May 12, 2016 (last accessed December 15, 2023).

6 Jim Street, "Seattle Mariners," *The Sporting News*, July 10, 1995: 38.

7 Jim Street, "Seattle Mariners," *The Sporting News*, December 4, 1995: 53.

8 Mark Maske, "Sooner or Later, Bonilla or Wells Are Likely to Be Dealt by Orioles," *Washington Post*, July 29, 1996: C2.

9 Bob Nightengale, "With Lasorda Out, Job Is Russell's to Win or Lose," *The Sporting News*, August 12, 1996: 18.

10 Jeff Blair, "Montreal Expos," *The Sporting News*, November 11, 1996: 37.

11 *Guide 1999* [Montreal Expos media guide], 246.

12 "Former Als Star Mike Widger, 67, Lived as Hard Off the Field as He Played on It," Canadian Football League Alumni Association website, www.cflaa.ca/former-als-star-mike-widger-67-lived-as-hard-off-the-field-as-he-played-on-it/ (accessed December 6, 2023).

13 Jeff Blair, "Montreal Expos," *The Sporting News*, May 26, 1997: 36.

14 Jeff Blair, "Montreal Expos," *The Sporting News*, January 26, 1998: 42.

15 Widger had "asthma, migraines, and a bad back," according to Stephanie Myles, "Montreal Expos," *The Sporting News*, July 20, 1998: 27. Shortly after this report appeared, Widger "strained his neck in a bench-clearing incident," according to Myles, "Montreal Expos," *The Sporting News*, July 27, 1998: 34.

16 Stephanie Myles, "Montreal Expos," *The Sporting News*, September 28, 1998: 74.

17 Stephanie Myles, "Montreal Expos," *The Sporting News*, November 23, 1998: 57.

18 Camille Powell, "Expos-ing Their Wishes for the Future," *Washington Post*, April 4, 1999: D9.

19 Stephanie Myles, "Montreal Expos," *The Sporting News*, August 30, 1999: 29.

20 Stephanie Myles, "Montreal Expos," *The Sporting News*, June 21, 1999: 31.

21 Dan Martin, "'spos Are in Awe of Dazzling David," *New York Post*, July 19, 1999.

22 *Guide 2000* [Montreal Expos media guide], 255.

23 George A. King III, "Bombers Eyeing Deal with Expos for Widger," *New York Post*, April 25, 2000.

24 Larry LaRue, "Seattle Mariners," *The Sporting News*, October 23, 2000: 59.

25 Sam Carchidi, "Pride of Pennsville Puts It in Perspective," *Philadelphia Inquirer*, July 9, 2002: D4.

26 "A Moment with … Chris Widger, Former Mariners Catcher," *Seattle-Post Intelligencer*, March 4, 2002.

27 Dan Martin, "Widger Catching On; Spot Starts Work for Backup Backstop," *New York Post*, August 26, 2002.

28 Ken Davidoff, "New York Yankees," *The Sporting News*, December 16, 2002: 60.

29 Vic Ziegel, "Widger Can't Mask Feelings About Role," *New York Daily News*, March 11, 2003.

30 Joe Strauss, "Widger: La Russa 'Didn't Want Me,'" *St. Louis Post-Dispatch*, April 4, 2004.

31 Carl Barbati, "Widger Named as New Manager," sussexcountyminers.com/widger-named-new-manager/ November 1, 2022 (last accessed December 15, 2023).

32 2005 World Series Game 3 White Sox @ Astros, www.youtube.com/watch?v=KHYwcwtzdkk (accessed December 15, 2023).

33 Jon Paul Morosi, "ChiSox Won with Misfits and Castaways," *Seattle-Post Intelligencer*, October 27, 2005.

34 Chris Kamka, "Remember That Guy? Chris Widger," www.nbcsportschicago.com/mlb/chicago-white-sox/remember-that-guy-chris-widger/320042/, October 18, 2019 (last accessed December 15, 2023).

35 Adam Kilgore, "Yankees Hit 4 Homers To Sink Lopez, Top O's," *Washington Post*, August 7, 2006: E8.

36 "'Sharks Name Widger New Manager," ism3.infinityprosports.com/ismdata/2014100700/std-sitebuilder/sites/201401/www/en/team/news/index.html?article_id=8&content_type=printable&plugin_id=news.front.system&block_id=5001, December 5, 2014 (last accessed December 15, 2023).

37 Bill Mitchell, "Chris Widger Named 2021 Minor League Baseball Manager Of The Year," *Baseball America*, November 30, 2021.

38 Kevin Minnick, "The journey to pro baseball has been long, but Widger thrilled to see career continue," NJ.com, July 13, 2021, www.nj.com/highschoolsports/2021/07/the-journey-to-pro-baseball-has-been-long-but-widger-thrilled-to-see-career-continue.html (accessed December 22, 2023).

39 Mark Singelais, "Widger, '05 World Series Champ, leads Miners against ValleyCats," [Albany] *Times Union*, August 19, 2023.

OZZIE GUILLÉN

By Gerard Kwilecki

Ozzie Guillén was born to compete. The competition and motivation to win were the forces that drove the 5-foot-11 shortstop and future manager to put on the uniform every day. The fiery and combative personality was on display every game. He often vocalized his opinions; making controversial statements to the press became his trademark, much to the dismay of management. Often Guillén's comments would make it on the internet and in newspapers. Victims included former players, like future Hall of Famer Frank Thomas and White Sox general manager Ken Williams. Even the local press in Chicago was not immune from outbursts. His Gold Glove, clutch hitting, and work ethic helped him enjoy a 16-year major-league career. His aggressive nature and knowledge of baseball led him to a World Series title as the manager. But he was unable to manage his mouth and temper his comments. That inability eventually drove him out of baseball.

Oswaldo José Guillén Guillen Barrios was born on January 20, 1964, in Ocumare del Tuy, in northern Venezuela. Guillén's mother, Violeta, was a school

Ozzie Guillen   2005

principal. Ocumare del Tuy is known for its warm and clear climate. The average temperature is 64 to 83, with 60 days of rainfall annually: ideal conditions for playing baseball. Ozzie's childhood was not easy. He witnessed criminal activity in many forms. His formal education lasted until the seventh or eighth grade. The only outlet was baseball. The weather was perfect and it was his ticket out of poverty. Ozzie was determined to prove the doubters and naysayers wrong, by making it to the major leagues in the United States. The drive to prove people wrong was what propelled him to keep striving for the next step.

The person who had the most profound influence on Guillén's young life was Ernesto Aparicio, a longtime youth baseball coach and the uncle of Hall of Fame shortstop Luis Aparicio. Ernesto saw Guillén play and wanted to instruct him. Aparicio was the only teacher who could reach Ozzie. Guillén was not a great student, he only wanted to play baseball. All of his teachers reported to his mother about his lack of coursework. His teachers flunked him, and he turned to the prospect of playing professional baseball. Guillén had something that could not be taught and it made a huge impression on Aparicio: his love of the game.

Ozzie was signed by the San Diego Padres on December 17, 1980, a month shy of his 17th birthday. He was assigned to the Padres Gulf Coast League rookie team for the 1981 season, one of several teenagers on the team. He played in 55 games, finishing the season with a .259 batting average in 189 at-bats. Each year he moved up the Padres minor-league system, and played the entire 1984 season for the Padres' Triple-A affiliate, the Las Vegas Stars. The next step was breaking camp with the big-league club in spring training 1985. Before that could happen, Guillen's career took a different path.

The Padres were coming off a 92-win season and a trip to the World Series in 1984. Even though they lost to the Detroit Tigers in five games, the plan was to add pieces to win it all in 1985. They had future Hall of Famer players Tony Gwynn and Goose Gossage, along with a veteran-laden team. They felt they needed one more ace to get them over the hump to win the first championship for San Diego. The Padres wanted a proven starting pitcher while the White Sox wanted a young player to take over at shortstop. The clubs hooked up for a seven-player trade on December 6, 1984. The Padres acquired starting pitcher LaMarr Hoyt and two minor leaguers, and the White Sox received two pitchers, a utility player, and one young shortstop who had yet to play a major-league game: 20-year-old Ozzie Guillén.

The Chicago White Sox were coming off a disappointing fifth-place finish in 1984, going 74-88 and finishing 10 games out of first place. They were managed by future Hall of Fame manager Tony La Russa. The shortstop for the 1984 team was Scott Fletcher. The White Sox wanted an upgrade at the position, and also wanted to dump salary. Owner Jerry Krause had roots as a baseball scout and he had watched Guillénplay at Las Vegas. Krause[1] said, "He's as smart a young player as I have ever seen."[2] He liked what he saw. He liked his hustle and the way he played the game.

Guillén married Ibis Cardenas in 1983. They had three sons. Ozzie Jr. was born in 1985, followed by Oney in 1986 and Ozney in 1992. Ozzie Jr. earned his MBA and went to work for Cisco Systems. Oney was drafted in the 36th round by the White Sox in the 2007 amateur free-agent draft. He played two seasons of minor-league baseball before he retired and became a scout. Ozney was drafted by the White Sox in 2010, but retired as a player after five seasons of independent-league baseball. He managed the Houston Astros' short-season affiliate in the New York-Penn League in 2019.

Ozzie Guillén made the 1985 White Sox in spring training. He joined three future Hall of Fame players – Carlton Fisk, Harold Baines, and Tom Seaver. Guillén's style of play earned him comparisons to two Venezuelan shortstops who had storied major-league careers, Luis Aparicio and Dave Concepción. Guillén idolized both; he chose the number 13 in honor of Concepción. Guillén was in the starting lineup on Opening Day, April 9, 1985, leading off and playing shortstop. The White Sox were playing at Milwaukee. He got his first major-league hit in the top of the ninth off Brewers pitcher Ray Searage, a bunt single to first base. His first professional hit defined Guillén's hustling style of play. He finished the game 1-for-5 at the plate, while making two putouts and getting three assists at shortstop in a 4-2 win over the Brewers in front of 53,027 fans.

The White Sox finished the 1985 season in third place in the American League West Division, six games behind the eventual World Series champions Kansas City Royals. Their 85-77 record was an 11-win improvement over the previous season. Guillén won the Rookie of the Year voting, receiving 72 percent of the first-place vote. He finished with a .273 batting average, one home run, 33 RBIs, and 134 hits in 150 games.

While Guillén was fast becoming a Chicago fan favorite, he was also gaining a reputation for being a talker. His teammate and future White Sox manager Robin Ventura said Guillén was "nonstop, never shuts up. He's talking to me, he's talking to umps, he's talking to fans, he's talking to the base runners."[3] The talker reputation would follow Guillén for the rest of his career, as both a player and a manager.

Guillén was considered a free swinger at the plate. In his rookie season he struck out 36 times and drew only 12 walks. The next season, in 547 at-bats, he struck out 52 times and again drew only 12 walks. Jim Fregosi, who managed Guillén for the White Sox from 1986 to 1988, considered him the "best defensive player I've ever seen," adding, "Nobody reads a groundball like Ozzie."[4] However, Fregosi wished his star shortstop would be more "disciplined and not swing at every pitch."[5] Guillén finished his 16-year career with 511 strikeouts and only 239 walks. However, in a testament to the way he played the game, his 511 whiffs constituted less than 8 percent of his at-bats.

Guillén spent 13 seasons with the White Sox, from 1985 to 1997. He suffered torn ligaments in his right knee in a collision with teammate Tim Raines in the 13th game of the 1992 season. A pop fly in short left field by the Yankees' Mel Hall in the top of the ninth inning sent Guillén back and Raines racing forward. They collided, allowing Hall to reach second base. Guillén left the game with his knee in tatters. Guillén's season was over. Before the 1992 season he had made the All-Star team three times (1988, 1990, and 1991). He earned a Gold Glove in 1990. His career can be defined by two halves, one before the injury and one after the injury.

Guillén's playing career with the White Sox ended after the 1997 season. His contract called for an automatic club option for $4 million for 1998 if he reached 550 plate appearances, with a $500,000 buyout. At age 34, he finished the season with 527 plate appearances, batting .245 with 120 hits, 4 home runs, and 52 runs batted in. He still maintained his excellence in the field, committing only 15 errors in 570 chances, for a .974 fielding percentage. The White Sox chose the buyout. Guillén signed with the Baltimore Orioles on January 29, 1998. He appeared in 12 games for the Orioles, playing shortstop and third base. He went 1-for-18 and was released on May 1. Guillén signed with the Atlanta Braves on May 6. The Braves were looking for a utility player, one who could come off the bench.

Guillén spent the rest of the 1998 season and all of 1999 with the Braves. He provided veteran leadership while playing all of the infield positions. He made his first World Series appearance in 1999 for the Braves versus the New York Yankees, going 0-for-5 in three games in the Yankees' sweep. The Braves released Guillén after 2000 spring training, and he immediately signed a free agent contract with the Tampa Bay Rays. He played in 63 games for the Rays, mostly at shortstop. He signed with the Rays for the 2001 season, but decided to retire to begin his coaching/managing career.

Guillén finished his 16-year playing career with 1,764 hits, 28 home runs, 619 runs batted in, and a .264 batting average. His calling card, his glove, defined his career. He made only 222 errors in 8,468 chances for a .974 fielding percentage, while playing one of the busiest positions on the field.

THE 2005 WORLD CHAMPION CHICAGO WHITE SOX

The next chapter of Guillén's career started in Montreal. He became a coach for the Expos in 2001, then the next season joined Jack McKeon's Florida Marlins, and was their third-base coach in 2002-03. The 2003 team won the World Series over the New York Yankees.

Guillén was ready to take his next step: managing. While the Marlins shocked the baseball world by beating the 101-win Yankees team, the Chicago White Sox finished second in the AL Central Division with an 86-76 record under six-year manager, Jerry Manuel. The White Sox made the playoffs only once under Manuel. They finished first in 2000, but lost to the Seattle Mariners in the Division Series. Manuel was voted Manager of the Year in 2000 but the team missed the playoffs he next three seasons. Ken Williams, Guillén's former teammate and now the club's general manager, was looking to breathe some new life into a White Sox team that had not been to the World Series since losing to the Los Angeles Dodgers in 1959.

Guillén had an interview set with Williams for the end of October 2003. He was in the middle of the World Series as the third-base coach of the Marlins, so some in the press thought his chances were not good to get the White Sox job. Others were being considered for the job – former Blue Jays manager Cito Gaston and other former managers Wally Backman, Buddy Bell, and Terry Francona. Guillén learned that Kenny Williams was leaning toward hiring Cito Gaston and became irate and wondered if "he was wasting his time if Williams' mind was already made up."[6] Gaston was the manager of the Toronto Blue Jays, winning back-to-back World Series titles in 1992-93. Guillén and Williams had a heated exchange discussing the managerial opening and Williams's leanings toward Gaston. Guillén's fiery personality changed Williams's mind. Williams felt his personality was just what the White Sox needed. Guillén was named the White Sox manager on November 3. Guillén became the first Venezuelan manager in the major leagues.

It did not take long for Guillén to raise eyebrows. His first game as manager was Monday, April 5, 2004, versus the Kansas City Royals. It was Opening Day game at Kansas City in front of 41,575 fans. The White Sox built a 7-3 lead going to the bottom of the ninth. The bullpen could not hold the lead, surrendering six runs in the bottom of the ninth and giving the Royals a 9-7 win. Guillén addressed his team, and told them to "go out and get drunk, do whatever … forget about this game."[7] He thought it was an innocent comment, but it was picked up by the press. Guillén did not apologize for the comment, saying he just wanted his players to forget about the game and be ready to play the next day. The comment may have worked, for the White Sox won the next game. The White Sox finished the 2004 season with an 83-79 record, earning a second-place finish in AL Central, nine games behind the Minnesota Twins. However, no one expected the season that lay ahead. The 2005 White Sox were ready to make history and Ozzie Guillén was ready to take his team to the next level.

The main theme for the 2005 White Sox was respect. Guillén felt the team needed to go earn it on the field. He always felt he and his teams were not getting the respect they deserved. Guillén first wanted the team to pick up his 2006 option before the 2005 season started. The team eventually did so in late May. Ken Williams made some trades and moves, setting the pieces in play for a historic 2005 run. The team had let longtime outfielder Magglio Ordóñez walk in free agency at the end of the 2004 season. He and Guillén did not get along. Guillén and Ordóñez had an exchange of words in the early part of 2005, which garnered a lot of front-page press. Ordóñez felt Guillén was behind the White Sox decision not to re-sign him. He called Guillén his "enemy."[8] The White Sox traded outfielder Carlos Lee to the Milwaukee Brewers for another outfielder, Scott Podsednik. Guillén also had an exchange of words in the press with Carlos Lee. This was be a pattern in Guillén's life. He would lash out in the harshest way if he felt a player was not hustling, not giving everything, and was not loyal.

The 2005 White Sox finished first in the AL Central Division with a record of 99-63. It was a dramatic turnaround from the previous season. All the pieces were in place and everything clicked. Guillén's White Sox swept the defending World Series champion Boston Red Sox in the Division Series, then defeated the Anaheim Angels four games to one in the Championship Series. They squared off against the Houston Astros in the World Series. The surprising Astros were led by future Hall of Fame sluggers Craig Biggio and Jeff Bagwell. They also had six-time All-Star Lance Berkman filling in for an injured Bagwell. The Astros pitching staff was led by All-Stars Roy Oswalt, Andy Pettitte, and Roger Clemens, and closer Brad Lidge. The White Sox swept the Astros in four games with Joe Crede, Jermaine Dye, and Paul Konerko providing the offense. The pitching staff was led by Mark Buehrle, José Contreras, and closer Bobby Jenks. The White Sox had finally reached the top of the mountain with their scrappy manager. But a quick rise to the top could only mean a quicker fall.

Guillén was named the American League Manager of the Year by *The Sporting News*. He was the fifth White Sox manager to win the award. There was some discord, though: Guillén skipped the team's visit to the White House. Chicago Mayor Richard Daley felt Guillén should go to the White House. However, Guillen said he had already set his Venezuelan vacation for the same time as the White House visit. White Sox Chairman Jerry Reinsdorf defended Guillén, saying he had done everything asked of him after the World Series.

The next offseason story was Frank Thomas. Thomas was declared a free agent on November 8, 2005. He and general manager Williams did not get along, especially since his last contract with the White Sox contained a "diminished skills" clause. As the controversy unfolded in the press, Guillén took Williams's side.

Over the offseason the White Sox made several additions and had several departures. In addition to Frank Thomas, they traded Aaron Rowand to the Phillies and added future Hall of Fame designated hitter Jim Thome. They finished the 2006 season in third place in the Central Division with a record of 90-72, six games behind the division champion Minnesota Twins. The 2007 season was a disappointment: The White Sox plummeted to a record of 72-90. They rebounded in 2008 with a first-place division finish but lost to the Tampa Bay Rays in the Division Series. The 2009 season ended in another losing record (79-83) and a third-place finish. The 2010 team improved to 88-74 and a second-place finish. But Guillen was nearing an end to his time with the White Sox. The only question was how ugly it would get.

There had been tensions brewing between Guillén and Williams. They included many squabbles and disagreements. Guillén wanted a contract extension and raise. However, Reinsdorf was unwilling to give one given the sub-.500 season they were about to conclude. (The team finished 78-82.) Even Guillén's son, Oney, made comments on social media criticizing the front office. They cost Oney his job in the White Sox scouting department. The Miami Marlins were about to finish the 2011 season in fifth place in the National League East with a 72-90 record. They had gone through three managers during the season. They were looking for a new voice in the clubhouse, and contacted the White Sox about Guillén's availability. The Marlins and White Sox agreed on a trade in late September 2011 as the season neared an end. The Marlins sent two minor-league players to the White Sox for Guillén. Guillén became the manager of the Marlins for the 2012 season.

Guillén was introduced as manager of the Miami Marlins on September 28, 2011. He signed a four-year, $10 million contract. Guillén inherited a team composed mostly of veterans with a few young players. He persuaded veteran pitcher Mark Buehrle to join the Marlins from the White Sox. Veterans Carlos Lee, Hanley Ramirez, Carlos Zambrano, and Aníbal Sánchez anchored the team along with young stars Giancarlo Stanton, Nathan Eovaldi, and Logan Morrison. Guillén was the third-base coach when the Marlins won the 2003 World Series. It was hoped that he would find happiness, stability, and peace with the Marlins, having been given a long-term contract he so desperately craved. However, the honeymoon with the Marlins would be short and he quickly began to wear out his welcome.

Guillén sat down with *Time* magazine during spring training. The magazine's article was published on April 9, five days after Opening Day. Guillén covered a wide range of topics, from baseball to bullfighting to politics. Most of his comments did not raise any concern. However, it was his comments on Fidel Castro that gained headlines. "I love Fidel Castro … I respect Fidel Castro. … You know why? A lot of people wanted to kill Fidel Castro for the last 60 years, but that (expletive) is still here."[9] This comment created a firestorm and many called for Guillén's resignation. The outrage was especially high in the Miami Cuban community, many of whom had risked their lives to escape the communist regime. The Marlins suspended Guillén for five games. Guillén apologized for his comments, asking for forgiveness. The apology was not enough to stop the protests at the Marlins ballpark and calls for the Marlins to fire him. This was just the beginning of a trying year for Guillén and the Marlins.

The Marlins brought in a number of free agents to bolster the team. They also opened a brand new $634 million ballpark. The Marlins were 41-44 at the All-Star break, in fourth place and nine games out of first place. The season did not get better. The Marlins finished with their worst record in 13 years, in last place in the National League East with a 69-93 record, 29 games behind the first-place Washington Nationals. Players were making negative comments in the press about their opinionated managers. The final nail in Guillén's job as manager came when he criticized Marlins owner Jeffrey Loria. Guillén said, "If Jeffrey doesn't think I'm doing the job I should do … it's not the first time he's fired a manager. Look yourself in the mirror and ask why so many (expletive) managers come through here."[10] Needless to say, the comments were not taken favorably. Guillén was fired on October 23, after just one season on the job. The Marlins still owed him $7.5 million on his contract. The disappointing season along with his comments earlier in the season about Castro made for an easy decision for the Marlins at the end of 2012.

Ozzie Guillén will be remembered as player who hustled, played the game the right way, and played like an underdog with a chip on his shoulder. He loved the game of baseball. Playing baseball was all he ever wanted to do. He was able to carve out a 16-year major-league career. He wanted to transition to coaching, hoping one day to manage. He got his big break, taking the reins of the White Sox. He led them to their first World Series championship since 1917. He was opinionated and everyone knew his style. However, it was his opinions and brash attitude that prompted his downfall and cost him his jobs as manager. Only time will tell if this is how is he is remembered.

Guillén has said he wants to get back into baseball. He has granted some interviews and has shown a level of maturity and contrition. He has done some television work and coaching in the Venezuelan Baseball League. He has made some appearances at the annual SoxFest festivities. His son, Ozney, has been working in baseball, most recently with the Astros.

SOURCES

In addition to the sources cited in the Notes, the author consulted Baseball-Reference.com and the following:

Greenstein, Teddy. "Reinsdorf Bored with Issue, Says Guillen's Done 'Everything' Thus Far," *Chicago Tribune*, February 10, 2006.

Price, S. L. "War of the Words," *Sports Illustrated*, March 20, 2006: 74-81.

Rogers, Phil. "Guillen Won't Sell Himself Short," *Chicago Tribune*, March 2, 1997.

NOTES

1   Krause would go on to fame as the owner of the Chicago Bulls and the architect of their championship run in the 1990s.

2   Brett Ballantini, *The Wit and Wisdom of Ozzie Guillen* (Chicago: Triumph Books, 2006), 18.

3   Richard Hoffer, "Heeeere's Ozzie," *Sports Illustrated*, April 6, 1992: 93-95.

4   Hoffer.

5   Hoffer.

6   Ballantini, 25-26.

7   Scot Gregor, "Guillen Not Apologizing for 'Drunk' Comment," *Chicago Daily Herald*, April 8, 2004.

8   Ballantini, 52.

9   Ken Rosenthal, "This Time Guillen Has Gone Too Far," foxsports.com, April 9, 2012. https://www.foxsports.com/mlb/story/ozzie-guillen-should-be-suspended-by-miami-marlins-for-fidel-castro-comments-040912.

10   Sport Xchange. "Guillen's Comments Anger Marlins Owner," *Chicago Tribune*, September24, 2012. https://www.chicagotribune.com/sports/whitesox/ct-xpm-2012-09-24-chi-guillens-comments-anger-marlins-owner-20120924-story.html.

HAROLD BAINES

By Malcolm Allen and Tim Deale

Harold Baines played 22 years in the majors (1980-2001), mostly with the Chicago White Sox. In 2019, following years of brisk and at times vociferous debate, Baines was enshrined in the National Baseball Hall of Fame. Though he led the league just once in any offensive category, he was a major threat at the plate. After suffering a knee injury during his prime, the lefty-hitting outfielder persevered and established himself as a premier designated hitter. As his plaque in Cooperstown also attests, Baines was respected, clutch, professional, humble, consistent, and reliable.

Harold Douglas Baines was born to Linwood Baines Jr. and Gloria Baines on March 15, 1959, in Easton, Maryland. He grew up in nearby St. Michaels, on the state's Eastern Shore, with four siblings: Linwood III was a year older; the late Irving and Curtis were his younger brothers, with sister Bertha arriving in between. Their father was a mason. "He worked from dawn to dusk. By the time I saw him it was night," Harold recalled.[1] "He showed me what was important in life. We didn't have those extra things, but we had what we needed."[2]

Linwood Baines had played baseball for the Eastern Shore Negro League's St. Michaels Red Sox.[3] "He was my hero," Harold said.[4] "Not from a baseball aspect, it was just from the way he raised his kids." Nevertheless, the sport helped form a strong bond between father and son. "Harold's glove was bigger than he was, but he'd be dragging me down to the diamond," the elder Baines recalled.[5] "I think I played the game professionally for my dad, because he couldn't," Harold reflected.[6]

By the time Harold was a 12-year-old Little Leaguer, his hitting ability was undeniable. Former major-league owner Bill Veeck, who owned a home in the area, went to see him play at the suggestion of a friend, Bob Boinski.[7] "[Baines] was hitting the ball 400 feet," Veeck recalled.[8] "You didn't forget a bat that quick or a swing that compact and powerful. I didn't."[9]

Baines starred in three sports at St. Michaels High School, including soccer during his senior season. "He scored 15 goals and took us to the state final," said coach Denver Leach.[10] Baines captained the basketball squad and considered hoops his best sport. "I played forward, center and guard. I could dunk the ball and I averaged 22 points a game," he said. "Nobody called with any scholarship offers, so I started turning my thoughts to baseball."[11]

By his sophomore year, big-league scouts knew about the promising first baseman-outfielder (who also occasionally pitched). The field at St. Michaels wasn't fenced, so right field ended when the ground sloped into a drainage ditch after about 390 feet. A running track sat atop a hill another 100 feet away. One day, after the scouts' plans to observe Harold were frustrated by an opponent's intentional walks, they asked the teen to take postgame batting practice. "He took eight or 10 swings and hit three balls over the ditch," recalled Coach Leach. "A couple of them bounced up onto the track."[12] They had seen enough.

Veeck, meanwhile, had repurchased the White Sox in 1975 and moved to Chicago. He continued to receive reports from Eastern Shore sources and a scout who'd seen Baines play in an American Legion tournament.[13] Following a last-place finish in 1976, the White Sox held the first pick in the 1977 amateur draft, just as Baines was completing his senior season with a .532 batting average.[14] Veeck had seen him only a few times, so he sent Chicago's most trusted scouts to crosscheck: Walt Widmayer, Bennie Huffman, and Paul

Harold Baines   2005

Richards.[15] "Bill wanted to be sure we were doing the right thing," explained Roland Hemond, then the White Sox' vice president.[16]

"Harold wasn't exactly playing in what you'd call a 'class' league," Richards explained. "His swing was a natural, but there's no way you could measure that against the pro pitchers until he actually hit against them."[17] Though Chicago's need for pitching was more acute, and Bill Gullickson from nearby Joliet Catholic Academy was a local favorite, the White Sox made Baines the number-one overall pick in the country.

Veeck and Hemond traveled to Maryland the night before the draft and signed Baines minutes after the pick became official. "I doubt he'd ever been off the Eastern Shore much until the day he signed with us," Veeck recalled. "They were a century behind there in race relations during the time Harold grew up. It was like growing up in the Deep South."[18]

When the White Sox played in Baltimore that weekend, Baines took batting practice with them but didn't show his ability. Veeck told Hemond that the new draftee was nervous but promised, "Don't worry, he'll be OK."[19]

Baines debuted with the Appleton (Wisconsin) Foxes, batting .261 with 5 home runs in 69 games for the worst club in the Class-A Midwest League. Promoted to Double A in 1978, he got off to a miserable start with a sub-.200 batting average into June.[20] He raised it to .275 by season's end as the Knoxville Sox won the Southern League title. Next, in the Florida Instructional League he hit .333 with 38 RBIs in his first 32 games to help the White Sox clinch their division.[21]

When Baines struggled early again after advancing to the Triple-A Iowa Oaks of the American Association in 1979, teammate Rusty Kuntz recalled that the media was hard on the number-one pick. "They subjected him to a lot of abuse: 'What are they doing sending us a 20-year-old who can't hit?'"[22]

Unfazed, Baines kept improving and finished the year batting .298 with 22 homers and 87 RBIs. Two of the four-baggers came in the same inning on August 4, and he hit two more round-trippers two nights later.[23] "I'll give my best effort every day," he said. "The only way to do that is by eliminating the negatives and concentrating on being myself."[24]

"Each time I thought I was pushing him beyond what he was capable of doing the last two years, he has responded," remarked Tony La Russa, Baines's manager at both Knoxville and Iowa.[25] "From day one, he's always been his own man," said a sportswriter. "Nobody can lead him astray."[26]

La Russa took over as the White Sox skipper that summer, and many believed Baines could join him in 1980. Orlando Cepeda likened the 21-year-old's swing to that of Billy Williams. Jimmy Piersall compared him to Al Kaline. After working with Baines in spring training,

Piersall gushed, "Give him the bat and ball and see you in 15 years. He's not only got all the tools, but he's got instinct. When you talk to him about baseball, you don't have to tell him what base to throw to. He KNOWS that."[27] "This kid is going straight into the starting lineup and then straight to Cooperstown," insisted Richards.[28] Yet as Baines himself observed looking back in 2019, "I inherited athletic ability but you have to put in the work."[29]

At the time, however, he recognized that he was still just a prospect. "How can people be calling me a superstar when I haven't even made the team?" he protested.[30] He worked his way into Chicago's Opening Day lineup at Comiskey Park, batting sixth and playing right field. He went hitless against Baltimore's Jim Palmer. "The first game I ever played in the big leagues stands out in my mind the most because my father was there to see it," he said.[31]

Baines started 0-for-19 before ripping an RBI double against the Yankees' Jim Kaat on April 17 for his first hit. Two nights later in Baltimore, he went deep against Palmer. One week after his sudden-death homer beat the Rangers' Ferguson Jenkins on July 26, Baines was in Cooperstown … albeit for the Hall of Fame exhibition contest against the Pirates. He stroked three extra-base hits including a home run.[32] In the games that counted, he homered 13 times as a rookie and batted .255.

In 1981 Baines rarely played against left-handers after hitting only .159 against southpaws in his first year. Yet he hit .320 against them, which helped raise his average to .286 overall. After the season, he added 16 pounds of muscle to his 6-foot-2, 175-pound frame through a diet of 3,300 calories a day and a regimen of free weights.[33] The White Sox hired renowned batting coach Charlie Lau, who spent two years with the team before succumbing to cancer. "Charlie taught me what pitches to look for on the particular ball-strike count," Baines said. "I turned my stats around immensely after that."[34] Describing his approach to hitting in 2019, he cited one thing above all: "Concentration." He added, "I would give the pitcher a part of the zone but the other part of the zone was mine."[35]

Playing every day in 1982, Baines become the youngest player in franchise history to drive in 100 runs.[36] In July he homered six times – including two grand slams – and drove in 15 runs in a six-game span. "He's going to be the kind you'll pay to see in a few years," La Russa predicted. The White Sox signed him to a new contract guaranteeing $3.25 million over four seasons.[37] "He's the most unchanged player by success I've ever known," marveled Veeck the following summer.[38]

The 1983 White Sox won 99 games – one shy of the franchise record. Baines was in the middle of a career-best 19-game hitting streak when his game-ending sacrifice fly clinched the club's first postseason appearance in 24 years. The RBI set off a raucous celebration at Comiskey Park in which fans flooded the field to celebrate with the players. But Chicago fell to the Orioles in the ALCS.

Baines married the former Marla Henry that fall, months after she earned her bachelor of education degree from Bowie State University. When they had met in high school, she'd been the scorekeeper for some of his teams.[39] Their first child, daughter Toni, arrived in 1984, followed by sisters Britni and Courtney, with brother Harold Jr. in between, over the next six years. They decided to raise their family in St. Michaels, a place Baines described as "the kind of place where you can have peace of mind."[40]

In 1984 one of Baines' bats went straight to the Hall of Fame. On May 9 he homered to end the longest game in American League history, a 25-inning marathon that took 8 hours and 6 minutes. The hit also generated one of his signature moments. When a reporter tried to elicit a comment by noting that he'd gotten all of the ball, the taciturn Baines simply replied, "Evidently." He became "Mr. Evidently" to his teammates and, in 2019, the White Sox gave away Baines bobbleheads that played a recording of the single word.

But Baines had been in the worst slump of his career at the time. The historic blast was his first homer in a month, and his batting average didn't get over .200 until Memorial Day weekend. In 81 games from May 29 through the end of August, however, he batted .364 and slugged .655, including eight four-hit contests. "The way he's going now, he could hit a golf ball," said teammate Rudy Law. "He had flaws when he was rushed to the majors, but he corrected them all," Hemond observed.[41] Baines insisted that he was just being more selective.

Baines finished the season as a .300 hitter for the first time, with personal bests in triples (10), homers (29), and a league-leading .541 slugging percentage. "To do what Harold does, his fire has got to be burning very brightly, whether anyone can see it or not," said La Russa.[42]

In 1985 only nine of Baines's 22 homers came before the end of July. "I have to go to left field. I have to take what they give me," he explained.[43] Nevertheless, he played in his first All-Star Game, raised his batting average to .309, and drove in a career-high 113 runs. He impressed Tom Seaver, his teammate that season. "He's in the lineup every day and always has the same mental approach, whether he was 0-for-4 the previous day, or 4-for-4," said Seaver. "Mental discipline is tough, but he shows it every day."[44]

Chicago's incoming GM, Ken Harrelson, remarked, "There are some teams out there that I wouldn't take straight up for Harold."[45] The White Sox endured a disappointing 1986 that cost La Russa his job, but Baines returned to the All-Star Game, and became the first player in franchise history with at least 20 homers in five consecutive years.[46] His season ended early, however, because of a right-knee injury sustained on the next-to-last weekend. "A pitcher covering first base had his foot on the bag the same time I reached the base, and I stepped on his ankle," Baines explained.[47]

Looking back in 2019, Baines said, "I had eight knee surgeries during my career starting from that injury."[48]

He missed half of spring training in 1987 while rehabbing from an arthroscopic procedure. Yet he was in the lineup on Opening Day and banged out two hits from his customary third spot in the batting order. He left the contest early for a pinch-runner, however, and underwent another operation. In July he became the White Sox' all-time home-run leader. As of 2024, he ranked fourth behind Frank Thomas, Paul Konerko, and José Abreu, but ahead of Carlton Fisk, who temporarily passed him in 1990.[49]

Throughout his career, Baines had been considered just above average as a right fielder with a strong arm. But in 1987 his knees forced him into the DH role. From then until the end of his career, he played in just 81 games in the field, and never more than 25 in any single season.

After a third operation on his right knee that winter, Baines arrived at spring training early each morning and split his days between swimming and physical therapy.[50] He struggled early in 1988, but the White Sox still extended his contract that summer and made him the club's first player with a $1 million annual salary.[51] He earned a second straight Outstanding Designated Hitter award.[52] "The first thing I thought about when I realized that I physically couldn't play defense in the outfield on a regular basis was what I could do to help the team," he explained. He studied pitchers and catchers intently, searching for clues. "I put all that concentration on offense."[53]

After a down year statistically in 1988, Baines ran all winter to strengthen his knees.[54] He also worked with incoming hitting coach Walt Hriniak.[55] "[Hriniak] refreshed my memory of what Charlie Lau taught," he said.[56] Though Baines' return to right field mostly ended after April, the notorious slow starter was the AL's leading hitter into late May. For the fourth time in five seasons, he returned to the All-Star Game, which allowed designated hitters for the first time in 1989. He started for the American League and became the first DH to hit safely in an All-Star Game with an RBI single off the Cubs' Rick Sutcliffe.

Less than three weeks later, however, Baines was traded to the Texas Rangers. The last-place White Sox acquired future All-Stars Sammy Sosa and Wilson Álvarez in the five-player deal, but many of Chicago's fans and players were upset. "Baines comes as close to anyone as being Mr. White Sox," acknowledged GM Larry Himes.[57] "As a person, it will not be possible to replace him," remarked club owner Jerry Reinsdorf.[58]

"After being in place for 10 years, you thought you could stay here your whole career, but it didn't work out," Baines said. "I wasn't happy with the way [Himes] was doing things, but I was never mad at the fans or the organization itself."[59] When the Rangers visited Comiskey Park three weeks later, he received two standing ovations and went 3-for-3.[60] The White Sox surprised him by retiring his uniform number 3 before the series finale.

The trade proved disappointing for both the Rangers and their new DH. The team never climbed above fourth place, and his 16 RBIs in 50 games were fewer than those tallied by Fred Manrique, the utility infielder Texas also received in the deal.

In 1990 Baines was batting .290 with 13 homers in late August, but he was sitting more frequently against left-handers. "I just wasn't happy," he admitted. "I didn't feel I was being utilized the right way."[61] On August 29 Texas traded him to Oakland for two pitchers who combined to win three big-league games. The Athletics were on their way to a third straight American League pennant led by La Russa, the ex-White Sox skipper.

In Game Three of the World Series, La Russa gave Baines his first start against a southpaw in almost eight weeks. He responded with a two-run homer off Tom Browning of the Reds, but Cincinnati upset the Athletics in a four-game sweep.

Baines remained with Oakland for the next two seasons. In 1991 he walked more than he struck out for the first time in his career, batted .295, and drove in 90 runs. Seven of the RBIs came in a three-homer performance against the Orioles on May 7 in which he set an Oakland record with 14 total bases.[62] On May 18, 1992, in Baltimore, his father was on hand to witness his 1,000th RBI.[63] Baines hit just .253 that season, but batted .440 in Oakland's ALCS loss to Toronto, including a game-winning ninth-inning homer off Jack Morris in Game One.

On January 9, 1993, St. Michael's celebrated Harold Baines Day, which grew into an annual event with a golf tournament to raise scholarship money for dozens of local high schoolers to attend college or trade schools.[64] Five days later he was traded to the Orioles for two young pitchers shortly after he'd re-signed with Oakland. The arrangement allowed Roland Hemond, who'd become Baltimore's GM, to avoid losing a draft pick. Veeck had died in 1986 but Bob Boinski, who'd recommended Baines to him, remarked, "I guess Bill's smiling now that Roland got him back."[65]

Baines had reason to smile, too. All four of his children would still be under age 10 on Opening Day and playing in Baltimore meant he could commute from St. Michael's, just a 90-minute drive away. "Not too many guys get a chance to play in their home state, so playing with the Orioles meant a lot to me," he said. "I enjoyed every minute of it."[66]

In 1993 Baines reached base in 13 straight plate appearances (eight hits and five walks) to tie a Baltimore record.[67] He notched his 2,000th hit in August and finished the season batting a career-high .313. "When I left Texas, they assumed I was done. When I left Oakland, they assumed I was done," he said. "That has been my motivation."[68]

Baines underwent another operation after the 1993 season – this time on his left knee – but had two more strong years for the Orioles.[69] By the end of 1995, he'd become the first big-leaguer in history to appear in at least 1,000 games at both a *single* defensive position and as a DH.[70]

Baines had to find a new team in 1996 after Pat Gillick replaced Hemond as Baltimore's GM. He signed with the White Sox as a free agent, rejoining the club that displayed his retired number at the ballpark. "I'm taking it down," he said. "A retired number means you're supposed to be dead and done already."[71] At 37, he was the oldest Chicago player on the roster for the entire season, but he enjoyed an excellent year, batting .311 with 22 homers and 95 RBIs. "I can't run, but I can still see," he quipped.[72]

"Harold's amazing," raved teammate Frank Thomas. "He hits with authority and he takes care of himself."[73]

The articular cartilage in both of Baines' knees was so worn down that bone ground against bone in spots. He spent time each day with trainer Herm Schneider, who believed the way he planted his front foot after lifting it before swinging exacerbated the stress on his knees. "I give myself a lot of credit for staying in there and fighting all the obstacles I've had," Baines said. "I've had to work to get on the field."[74]

In June 1997 Baines played what proved to be his final two innings of defense. On July 11, he homered in Kansas City for his 2,500th hit. Three weeks later, he was batting .305 when the sub-.500 White Sox traded him back to the Orioles. He hit .364 in two rounds of playoffs as Baltimore advanced to the ALCS, but the club fell two wins short of reaching the World Series.

Baines hit .300 again in 1998 but missed nearly a month with a strained hamstring. At age 40, however, he still commanded respect. *The Scouting Notebook 1999* said, "Baines remains a productive hitter with outstanding plate coverage."[75] That year, a red-hot first half gave him a .355 batting average with 21 homers in 234 at-bats by mid-July. One memorable blow came against the White Sox on May 4 – a game-ending homer (his 10th) that was also a grand slam (his 13th).[76]

On July 16, 1999, Baines passed Hal McRae as the all-time hit leader among designated hitters with a four-hit performance. The next day, he homered to move ahead of Don Baylor atop the position's home-run leaderboard.[77] Though David Ortiz surpassed both marks in 2013, Baines' teammate Cal Ripken noted, "Harold helped define the DH in baseball. It's a position now. That was a discovery to a lot of people."[78]

"Nobody wants to be a DH," Baines said. "I loved playing the outfield. But with my knees, I've known for a long time the way I can help a baseball team is with my offense, not my defense. … I'm lucky there's still a DH in the American League. If there wasn't, I would have been done."[79]

Hopelessly out of contention, the Orioles traded Baines to the first-place Indians on August 27, 1999. With Cleveland, he surpassed the 100-RBI mark for the first time since 1985. His .533 slugging percentage shattered Stan Musial's 1962 mark for 40-year-olds.[80] He batted .357 with a homer in the Division Series, but the Indians fell to the Red Sox.

Baines re-signed with the Orioles for 2000, even though it wasn't clear exactly how much he'd be utilized. "From what I know about baseball, if you're hitting, you'll play. If you're not hitting, you won't play," he said.[81] He platooned at DH again but struggled through a poor first half for a losing club. At the end of July, he was traded for the third time in four seasons, back to the White Sox, who were leading the AL Central Division. On a visit to Baltimore on August 15, he hit his 384th and final homer. In Chicago's ALDS loss, he went 1-for-4 to complete his postseason career with a .324 batting average in 31 games.

The 2001 season was Baines' 22nd in the majors. When he lined a single off Cincinnati's Jim Brower for his 2,686th career hit in an interleague game on June 14, his average was an awful .133. Even worse, he severely pulled a hip flexor on a checked swing.[82] He returned for his 2,830th and final game on September 27 in Chicago but struck out looking in his only at-bat.

Baines tried to keep playing in 2002, but he couldn't find any takers. "I didn't know it [2001] was going to be my last season," he said in 2019, "but the reality is at age 42 you don't expect the phone to ring."[83]

Baines finished his career with a .289 batting average, 384 home runs and 1,628 RBIs. Only Al Kaline, with 399, hit more homers among players without a single 30-homer season. When he retired, only two dozen major leaguers in history had driven in more runs.[84]

A word often associated with Baines is "clutch" – he had a rep for coming up big in tough situations. Yet according to one analysis, "Baines's numbers at crucial moments were about the same as in all other situations."[85] This underscores that he was quite simply a very consistent and reliable hitter.

After his playing days ended, Baines became a roving minor-league hitting instructor for the White Sox. When coach Joe Nossek retired during spring training 2004, Chicago skipper Ozzie Guillén asked his former teammate to become his bench coach, and Baines agreed. He led the club for four games when Guillén was suspended, just long enough to confirm to himself that he didn't want to manage.

Baines finally earned a World Series ring when the 2005 White Sox became the first Chicago team in 88 years to win the fall classic. It meant a lot to him to accomplish a longstanding goal and to be there every day working with the players.[86] He remained in uniform for another decade, as the first-base coach and later the assistant hitting instructor.

In 1984 a 25-year-old Baines had said, "I want to be remembered as somebody they enjoyed watching at the ballpark, but it doesn't have to be a superstar or anything like that."[87] Nevertheless, in 2008, the White Sox unveiled a bronze statue of him outside US Cellular Field. He was inducted into the Orioles Hall of Fame the following year. As for his chances to make it to Cooperstown, he remarked in 1997, "The only thing I can control is when I'm at the plate. Other people vote for stuff. If it happens, great. If not, I've had a very good career."[88]

Baines was considered on the National Baseball Hall of Fame ballot for five consecutive years beginning in 2007. His candidacy received support from the likes of Cal Ripken, who'd entered the Hall himself in 2007.[89] Yet he never received more than 6.1 percent of the votes from members of the Baseball Writers Association of America – far short of the 75 percent required for induction. After receiving less than 5 percent support in 2011, he dropped off the writers' ballot entirely. The numbers he'd compiled were deemed closer to good than great, lacking the milestone totals or league-leading figures usually achieved by the game's immortals. To some, the fact that he'd been a platoon player for a significant part of his career neutralized the benefits of his 22-season longevity. The stigma of being primarily a DH after suffering a career-altering injury at age 27 certainly factored in as well.

After the 2015 season, Baines retired from coaching. Late in 2018 he learned that he would finally receive a plaque in Cooperstown. The Today's Game Era Committee – including his longtime supporters Tony La Russa and Jerry Reinsdorf – gave him the 12 votes he needed out of 16 required to earn induction. Even La Russa admitted, "There were some very candid discussions" during the voting process.[90] Baines himself was widely quoted as being "shocked." It was a secret ballot and nobody else besides Reinsdorf or La Russa has gone on the record. But it's noteworthy that eight other members of the committee besides La Russa were also members of the Hall.

When the news broke, the other most prominent and vocal defender of Baines and his worthiness was former White Sox teammate Paul Konerko, who cited mental strength and leadership by example along with performance.

The election of Baines remains as controversial – one especially heated exchange featuring La Russa took place on MLB Network[91] – as it is irreversible. Yet in his quiet and humble way, Baines expressed his gratitude to the voters and for the existence of the Today's Game Era Committee.[92]

Baines became the third player picked number-one overall in the June amateur draft to enter the Hall, after Ken Griffey Jr. and Chipper Jones – even though he was drafted a decade ahead of Griffey and 13 years ahead of Jones.

Baines's father had died in 2014, prompting the remark, "The only thing missing when it comes to being elected to the Hall of Fame is my dad's not here to see it."[93] On July 21, 2019, he took his place among the game's all-time greats, closing his uncharacteristic 9 minute and 54 second speech with a lesson that his father taught him when they played catch: "Words are easy, deeds are hard. Words can be empty. Deeds speak the loudest, and sometimes they echo forever."[94]

In May 2021 Baines had heart replacement surgery, followed by a kidney transplant the next day.[95] After recuperating, he returned to Chicago in 2022 to throw out the ceremonial first ball before the White Sox' home opener.[96] As of 2024, Baines still lived in St. Michaels and worked for the White Sox as a community relations representative.

THE 2005 WORLD CHAMPION CHICAGO WHITE SOX

ACKNOWLEDGMENTS

Special thanks to Harold Baines, who graciously granted several telephone interviews to Tim Deale, including one on his 60th birthday in 2019.

This biography was reviewed by Rory Costello and Norman Macht, fact-checked by Chris Rainey, and copy-edited by Len Levin.

SOURCES

In addition to the sources cited in the Notes, the authors consulted www.baseball-reference.com, www.retrosheet.org, and www.tcdb.com.

NOTES

1   Jerome Holtzman, "Low-keyed Baines Still Doing Talking with His Bat," *Chicago Tribune*, June 22, 1995: E3.

2   Mike Kiley, "Baines Appears Set to Make Some Noise – on the Field," *Chicago Tribune*, April 7, 1985: C1.

3   "Harold Baines," https://libapps.salisbury.edu/nabb-online/exhibits/show/friends-rivals-baseball-delmar/national-baseball-hall-of-fame/harold-baines (last accessed November 13, 2020).

4   Bert Lehman, "For Harold Baines, Chicago Was Always His Kind of Town," https://sportscollectorsdigest.com/news/harold-baines-chicago-town (last accessed November 13, 2020).

5   Peter Schmuck, "Baines' Happy Landing," *Baltimore Sun*, January 29, 1993: 1C.

6   Lehman, "For Harold Baines, Chicago Was Always His Kind of Town."

7   Bill Veeck, "Maryland, My Maryland," *Chicago Tribune*, October 4, 1983: C3.

8   Mike Kiley, "The Big RBI Goes to Baines," *Chicago Tribune*, September 18, 1983: B3.

9   Veeck, "Maryland, My Maryland."

10   Schmuck, "Baines' Happy Landing."

11   Dave Nightingale, "Naturally, Baines Is a Success," *Chicago Tribune*, April 27, 1980: C1.

12   Schmuck, "Baines' Happy Landing."

13   Veeck, "Maryland, My Maryland."

14   Harold Baines, 1981 Topps Baseball Card.

15   Veeck, "Maryland, My Maryland."

16   Kiley, "The Big RBI Goes to Baines."

17   Nightingale, "Naturally, Baines Is a Success."

18   Kiley, "The Big RBI Goes to Baines."

19   Ken Rosenthal, "The Beginning for Baines Was Humble One," *Baltimore Sun*, October 10, 1990.

20   Bob Verdi, "Sox's Baines Dazzles All – Except Baines," *Chicago Tribune*, March 18, 1980: D1.

21   Richard Dozer, "Sox Notes," *The Sporting News*, December 9, 1978: 42.

22   Nightingale, "Naturally, Baines Is a Success."

23   "Baines' Blasts," *The Sporting News*, August 25, 1979: 40.

24   Bob Logan, "Can't Miss Baines Becomes Sox Hit," *Chicago Tribune*, May 6, 1983: D2.

25   Richard Dozer, "Bleak Outlook for Claudell," *The Sporting News*, February 9, 1980: 40.

26   Jerome Holtzman, "Shell Still Perfect Fit for Baines," *Chicago Tribune*, February 24, 1983: B5.

27   Verdi, "Sox's Baines Dazzles All – Except Baines."

28   Nightingale, "Naturally, Baines Is a Success."

29   Harold Baines, telephone interview with Tim Deale, March 15, 2019 (hereafter Baines-Deale interview).

30   Verdi, "Sox's Baines Dazzles All – Except Baines."

31   Lehman, "For Harold Baines, Chicago Was Always His Kind of Town."

32   Harold Baines, 1982 Topps Baseball Card.

33   "Cubs Rough Up Gaylord," *The Sporting News*, April 3, 1982: 38.

34   Kiley, "Baines Appears Set to Make Some Noise – on the Field."

35   Baines-Deale interview.

36   Another 23-year-old, Frank Thomas, was 10 weeks younger than Baines when he drove in 100 runs for Chicago in 1991.

37   Murray Chass, "55 Players Rate 'Super Rich' Tag," *The Sporting News*, February 14, 1983: 39.

38   Kiley, "The Big RBI Goes to Baines."

39   Veeck, "Maryland, My Maryland."

40   Schmuck, "Baines' Happy Landing."

41   Joe Goddard, "Patience at Plate Pays Off for Baines," *The Sporting News*, July 2, 1984: 19.

42   Dave Van Dyck, "Baines Critics Out of Ammo," *The Sporting News*, August 27, 1984: 32.

43   Dave Van Dyck, "Over the Long Run, Baines' Stats Better," *The Sporting News*, May 20, 1985: 17.

44   Kiley, "Baines Appears Set to Make Some Noise – on the Field."

45   Joe Goddard, "Sox Seek to Make Baines a 'Lifer,'" *The Sporting News*, March 31, 1986: 37.

46   "A.L. West," *The Sporting News*, September 15, 1986: 16.

47   Baines-Deale interview.

48   Baines-Deale interview.

49   In 1990, Fisk passed Baines to become the White Sox' all-time home-run leader. By the time Baines moved back in front of Fisk in 1997, Frank Thomas had surpassed both players.

50   "White Sox," *The Sporting News*, January 25, 1988: 48.

51   "White Sox," *The Sporting News*, July 4, 1988: 21.

52   Since 2004, it's been called the Edgar Martinez Award.

53   Lehman, "For Harold Baines, Chicago Was Always His Kind of Town."

54   "White Sox," *The Sporting News*, January 16, 1989: 44.

55   "White Sox," *The Sporting News*, January 2, 1989: 64.

56   "A.L. West," *The Sporting News*, August 14, 1989: 23.

57   Joe Goddard, "'Mr. White Sox' Goes to Texas," *The Sporting News*, August 7, 1989: 23.

58   Goddard, "'Mr. White Sox' Goes to Texas."

59   Joe Goddard, "Chicago White Sox," *The Sporting News*, August 19, 1996: 27.

60   "Rangers," *The Sporting News*, August 28, 1989: 22.

61   "Gonzalez's Progress Means Bye-Bye Baines," *The Sporting News*, September 10, 1990: 14.

62 Kit Stier, "Oakland Athletics," *The Sporting News*, May 20, 1991: 17. In 1932 Jimmie Foxx had a 16-total-bases game for the Philadelphia Athletics.

63 Harold Baines, 1993 Topps Baseball card.

64 Schmuck, "Baines' Happy Landing."

65 Schmuck, "Baines' Happy Landing."

66 Lehman, "For Harold Baines, Chicago Was Always His Kind of Town."

67 *2000 Baltimore Orioles Media Guide,* 51.

68 Phil Rogers, "Baines Tips Cap to Trainer," *Chicago Tribune*, March 9, 1997: 3

69 Peter Schmuck, "Baines Hurting but Should Return," *The Sporting News*, October 18, 1993: 22.

70 Harold Baines, 1996 Collector's Choice Baseball Card. Baines played 1,042 games in right field. While both Paul Molitor and Chili Davis exceeded 1,000 games played on defense, neither player saw action in 1,000 games at any single defensive position.

71 Dave Van Dyck, "Back to Future," *The Sporting News*, February 19, 1996: 27.

72 Joe Goddard, "Chicago White Sox," *The Sporting News*, June 3, 1996: 32.

73 Joe Goddard, "Chicago White Sox," *The Sporting News*, August 19, 1996: 27.

74 Rogers, "Baines Tips Cap to Trainer."

75 John Dewan, Don Zminda, and Jim Callis, eds., *The Scouting Notebook 1999* (Chicago: STATS Inc., 1999), 47.

76 Chris Bodig, "Harold Baines Hall of Fame Moments," Cooperstown Cred, July 21, 2019 (https://www.cooperstowncred.com/harold-baines-hall-of-fame-moments/).

77 *2000 Baltimore Orioles Media Guide*, 50.

78 Bonnie DeSimone, "Pursuit of the Ring, Forget Sentiment," *Chicago Tribune*, September 30, 1997: 4, 1:4.

79 Rogers, "Baines Tips Cap to Trainer."

80 *2000 Baltimore Orioles Media Guide*, 50.

81 Dave Buscema, "Baines Home, Again," *York* (Pennsylvania) *Daily Record*, December 10, 1999: B01.

82 Scot Gregor, "Hip Injury Sidelines Baines and Might End His Career," *The Sporting News*, June 25, 2001: 33.

83 Baines-Deale interview.

84 Harold Baines, 2005 Donruss Classics Stars of Summer Baseball Card.

85 Bill Deane, *Baseball Myths* (Lanham, Maryland: Scarecrow Press, 2012), 145.

86 Baines-Deale interview.

87 Phil Hersh, "Baines Is a Star Lost in the Shadows," *Chicago Tribune*, September 9, 1984: C1.

88 Bonnie DeSimone, "Pursuit of the Ring, Forget Sentiment," *Chicago Tribune*, September 30, 1997: 4.

89 Mike Klingaman, "A Classy Guy Who Could Hit," *Baltimore Sun*, August 28, 2009.

90 David Schoenfeld, "Harold Baines Wasn't 'Sitting Around Thinking About' Hall of Fame Nod," ESPN.com, December 10, 2018.

91 For further discussion, see the biography of Al Oliver on the SABR BioProject.

92 Baines-Deale interview.

93 Lehman, "For Harold Baines, Chicago Was Always His Kind of Town."

94 "National Baseball Hall of Fame Weekend," http://www.asapsports.com/show_interview.php?id=152264 (last accessed November 18, 2020).

95 Scott Merkin, "Baines Thankful for Second Chance with New Heart, Kidney," MLB.com, April 11, 2022, https://www.mlb.com/news/harold-baines-heart-kidney-transplant (last accessed January 30, 2024).

96 Jasmine Smith, "MLB Legend Harold Baines Receives Second Chance with New Heart," *BlackDoctor.org*, April 19, 2022, https://blackdoctor.org/mlb-legend-harold-baines-recieves-second-chance-with-new-heart/3/ (last accessed January 30, 2024).

DON COOPER

By Phil Angelo

Don Cooper, the pitching coach of the 2005 World Series champion White Sox, had exactly one win as a major-league pitcher.

His sole victory came September 2, 1981, in his rookie season with the Minnesota Twins. Over the course of four years in the big leagues, Cooper would win one, lose six, and put in 44 major-league appearances with the Twins, Toronto Blue Jays, and New York Yankees. He had three starts, all with the Twins. His lifetime ERA was 5.27.

Cooper's sole triumph came against the Yankees at now-gone Metropolitan Stadium in the Twin Cities. He got the last five outs in relief and became a winner when the Twins scored two in the bottom of the eighth. The Twins won 4-3. Cooper struck out Reggie Jackson looking to end the game.

While his major-league playing career may have been short, Cooper's coaching career was long and distinguished. His one win as a pitcher was dwarfed by 1,441 major-league victories as the White Sox pitching coach. Cooper took the job July 22, 2002, under manager Jerry Manuel. The team was 46-54 then. It went 35-27 the rest of the way to finish

Don Cooper   2005

at exactly .500. Cooper served the next year under Manuel and then all of the Ozzie Guillén, Robin Ventura, and Rich Renteria years, through 2020.[1]

Coaches tend to be overlooked in baseball history. The *Total White Sox Encyclopedia* has entries for players, managers, front-office personnel, and even broadcasters, but no list of coaches.

Patrick Comiskey of *Sportsnet* wrote that "[f]or one assistant to survive four different managers is something out of a science fiction novel."[2] Paul Sullivan of the *Chicago Tribune* commented that the average tenure of a pitching coach is akin to the "life span of a fruit fly."[3]

And while there are lists of "best" this and "best" that by position in the game, lists of best pitching coaches seem to be few. *Bleacher Report* has a 2012 vintage list of best pitching coaches.[4]

Cooper was ranked 40th best on the list. It's a list that includes some ex-catchers, like Dave Duncan; some former stars, like Johnny Sain; and a whole lot of folks like Don Cooper. Those players were pitchers like Cooper who had to use every ounce of guile and training to learn their craft to make, to remain and even to come near the big leagues. A more modern list of pitching coaches would include a fourth category – the numbers experts who know what pitch works at what spin to what batter at what moment.

"When I started (as pitching coach) my goal was to help the team win a world championship," Cooper said. "That was always my goal. The first part of that goal is to make the playoffs each year. I was named pitching coach in 2002 and can remember driving around, thinking to myself that this would be a hell of a place to win the World Series. The fans were hungry for it, and that was always my goal. You have to get to the playoffs for it to happen, though."[5]

Cooper called Sammy Ellis his mentor. Ellis won 63 games in the '60s for the Reds, Angels, and White Sox. He was an All-Star in his best season, 1965. After his playing days ended, Ellis was a pitching coach for a dozen years, serving the Yankees, White Sox, Cubs, Mariners, Red Sox, and Orioles. In 1989 Ellis was the minor-league pitching coordinator for the White Sox.[6] When Cooper listened to Ellis speaking Spanish to Hispanic pitchers, he went out and learned Spanish.[7]

Cooper says that Ellis was the best "delivery and mechanics guy I've ever been around."[8] Ellis died of cancer in 2016.

Cooper also cited Pat Dobson, Hoyt Wilhelm, and Johnny Podres as coaches he learned from, along with tips picked up in discussions with Dave Righetti, Roger McDowell, and Leo Mazzone.

Cooper, naturally, learned his pitching craft in the minor leagues, where he appeared in 289 games. He had stops in Oneonta, Fort Lauderdale, West Haven, Columbus, Nashville, Toledo, Syracuse, and Rochester. He tried both starting and relieving. In 1982 he was in 28 games for the Toledo Mud Hens, all starts. The next year, 1983, he was the International League reliever of the year, saving 22 games for the Syracuse Chiefs. In all, Cooper won 65 games in the minors, including a no-hitter for Class-A Fort Lauderdale in 1978.[9] In coaching, though, he consciously wanted his pitchers to have a better career than he had.[10]

As he came up, Cooper was the type of player who absorbed coaching. "I would say, 'Give me help.'"[11]

Cooper's coaching work showed the same propensity to work and learn. Hired on October 11, 1987, by the White Sox as the pitching coach for Class-A South Bend, he steadily climbed the ladder with stints at Sarasota, Birmingham, and Nashville, as well as being a roving instructor and the minor-league pitching coordinator at times. In 2000 the White Sox gave him an award for player development. He also served as pitching coach and manager for Caribes de Oriente in the Venezuelan Winter League. He had an interim assignment as pitching coach for the major-league White Sox in 1995. Overall, though, it took 15 years of work to earn the permanent big-league job.[12]

Major-league coaches can come and go quickly. Cooper rapidly became "the longest-tenured member on the White Sox coaching staff."[13]

Communication, Cooper said, is a key. He tried to listen to the pitchers because they needed to listen to him.

In *What It Means to Be a White Sox*, Cooper said, "I enjoyed the whole 2005 season, the beginning, middle and end. I enjoyed all of it."

"It was a wonderful season," he said, "and it's one that we will always be trying to duplicate," That didn't happen again during Cooper's tenure, but the White Sox did make postseason appearances during his time in 2008, when they lost in the Division Series, and in 2020 when they lost in the wild card.

He remembered the 2008 season fondly. That team, he said, had to fight 163 games to make the playoffs. "We maxed out everything we could get out of our guys and pitching staff."[14]

The 2005 season was even better.

Phil Rogers of NBC Chicago, giving a retrospective of Cooper's career, said, "There's no way the Sox win the 2005 World Series without Cooper, who did a yeoman's work handling a patchwork pitching staff for Ozzie Guillén."[15]

Pitching is important for any champion, but the 2005 White Sox cobbled together an amazing staff under Cooper. The group combined for an ERA of 3.61 and 54 saves. They were even better in the postseason, dropping their ERA to 2.55.

"Our pitching staff exceeded my expectations," Cooper said, and "I don't know if anyone has higher expectations than me."[16]

Dustin Hermanson arrived as a free agent and saved 34 games before a late-season back injury. Hard-throwing, wide-bodied Bobby Jenks, claimed off waivers, took his place. Jenks went on to save 173 games for the White Sox in his career. Jenks closed out a clinching World Series game, a real feat for a rookie (but one that was duplicated the very next year by Adam Wainwright of the Cardinals).

Cliff Politte, 7-1, with the best season of his career, was the right-handed set-up man. Neal Cotts, 4-0, set up from the left side.

Orlando "El Duque" Hernández had just enough left in the tank at age 39.[17] In the Division Series against the defending champion Red Sox, El Duque was called on in a bases-loaded nobody-out relief appearance. He got two popups and struck out Johnny Damon to help preserve the clinching game in a 3-0 sweep.[18]

"He's a New York legend," Cooper said of El Duque. "Now he's going to be a legend in Chicago."[19]

The big four of Mark Buehrle, Jon Garland, Freddie García, and José Contreras was 63-33. In the American League Championship Series, they fired four complete-game victories in a row, a feat unlikely to be repeated in the modern era of pitch counts.

"It did cross my mind that it wouldn't stink to get to four," Cooper said of the complete-game streak.[20]

Cooper had links to many of his pitchers. He had helped develop Buehrle and Garland as they came up. Originally number 34, Cooper switched to 21 so García could have his Seattle number when he joined the White Sox.[21] García, Cooper said, was a big-game pitcher.[22] When the fourth game of the World Series rolled around, a García start, Cooper assured manager Ozzie Guillén that García had great stuff that day. The White Sox won the clincher, 1-0.

Cooper, having become a Spanish speaker, would wind up having close ties with José Contreras and El Duque, both pitchers from Cuba. "I'd say El Duque has 500 different pitches from 500 different places," he said.[23]

Cooper recalled Buehrle volunteering to put on his spikes and be ready to pitch in relief in World Series Game Three if needed. Cooper told him that if the game went 12, 13, 14 innings, they might need him. Buehrle, the White Sox' ninth pitcher of the night in the extra-inning game, wound up getting the last out in the bottom of the 14th for the save.

Extraordinary times, Cooper said, require "extraordinary decisions and extraordinary men."[24]

The next game, the final game, was closed out by Bobby Jenks. Cooper called Jenks "the manchild, the monster, the biggest monster of the Midway."[25]

"The last out in 2005 was the moment I will always cherish," Cooper continued. "I can still see Bobby Jenks jumping to try and get that groundball, and you couldn't slide a slice of American cheese under his feet. Juan Uribe came out of nowhere and threw the batter out at first base."[26]

Cooper described the fans of Chicago as very special. For him the World Series title was "humbling." He did not go out on the town after the last victory. He went back to his room with his family and thought about what a championship meant.

"The next day when I woke up, I had to think to myself whether that really happened, and the answer was 'Yes.' We did it and it was an unbelievable sense of accomplishment."[27]

Born on January 15, 1956, in New York City, Cooper played his high-school ball at Monsignor McClancy High School, run by the Brothers of the Sacred Heart in East Elmhurst, part of the Borough of Queens.

A member of the Class of '74, Cooper helped lead the Crusaders to three straight City Championship appearances. He was All-City in his senior year.

That earned him a scholarship to play basketball and baseball at the New York Institute of Technology. The Yankees drafted him after his junior year, but he stayed in school for his senior season and signed with the Yankees in 1978.[28] Cooper is a member of the athletic halls of fame at both Monsignor McClancy and the New York Institute of Technology. In 1978, while at the New York Institute, he was the East Coast Athletic Conference Player of the Year. In 2006 his collegiate alma mater awarded him an honorary doctorate in humane letters. The White Sox Media Guide credits Cooper with passing the time with crossword puzzles and *Jeopardy*.

By 2020, as he returned for what would be his last season, his 19th, he was the longest-tenured pitching coach in the big leagues. *Athlon Sports* simply said, "Coop is forever."[29]

Cooper never had a Cy Young Award winner. "Black Jack" McDowell in 1993 was the last White Sox winner, though Esteban Loaiza once finished second and Chris Sale once finished third under Cooper.

Cooper's tenure saw 11 different White Sox pitchers become All-Stars: Esteban Loaiza, Jon Garland, José Contreras, Bobby Jenks, Mark Buehrle, Matt Thornton, Jake Peavy, Jesse Crain, José Quintana, Chris Sale, and Lucas Giolito. Sale was selected five times as a member of the White Sox under Cooper, Buehrle three times, and Jenks and Loaiza twice apiece.

Phil Rogers cited Cooper for having a rich legacy of reclamation projects.[30] One of his best was one of his first. Esteban Loaiza was an early positive surprise. Signed to a minor-league contract for 2003, he proceeded to lead the league in strikeouts with 207 and had a record of 21-9. He was the last White Sox pitcher to win 20.

The Cooper years saw four White Sox no-hitters: two by Buehrle (in 2007 and 2009); one by Philip Humber in 2012, and one by Lucas Giolito in 2020. Humber's game and Buehrle's second no-hitter were perfect games.

One might think that given his long stint with the team, perhaps the game changed and Cooper didn't. Not so. Billy Ripken interviewed Cooper in his 42nd spring training before what would be his last season with the White Sox.[31]

Cooper said the club was now gathering data on spin rates and the vertical rise of pitches and sharing the information with players. Cooper considered himself a "teacher" and told Ripken that there were three ways of learning something: listening, watching, and doing.

Of course, it wasn't always success. Pitcher Carson Fulmer was picked in the first round but never fulfilled his early promise. The White Sox traded for Jeff Samardzija only to see him lead the league in home runs given up in 2015.

Near the end of Cooper's time with the White Sox, Lucas Giolito turned to Ethan Katz, his former high-school coach, to help improve his mechanics. Katz wound up succeeding Cooper as pitching coach.

Yet in firing Cooper, White Sox general manager Rick Hahn thanked him for his years and his contributions, citing his work with Mark Buehrle, Jon Garland, and Chris Sale. Cooper thanked the White Sox back, but also said, "The bottom line is it hurts. When you're no longer part of something it hurts. But I'm over the hurt and trust me, I've moved on."[32]

When he departed at the end of the 2020 season, Cooper was the last link in uniform (player or coach) to the 2005 World Series champions.

Cooper even served two games as the White Sox manager in 2011 following the late-season departure of Ozzie Guillén and bench coach Joey Cora. The White Sox broke even in the two games.

On September 27, 2011, they beat the Blue Jays, 2-1. Mark Buehrle was the winner. It was his last victory in a White Sox uniform. The next day they lost, 3-2, to the Blue Jays. Chris Sale blew the save in the ninth, yielding a double, a single, and three walks, one of them intentional. It was one of Sale's last appearances as a reliever. By 2012 he would be in the White Sox rotation, start 29 games and be an All-Star.

SOURCES

In addition to the sources cited in the Notes, the author consulted Baseball-Reference.com.

NOTES

1 The team won 30 games while he was the interim pitching coach from June 2 to August 11, 1995; 35 after taking over July 22, 2002, to the end of the season; 86 in 2003; 678 under Ozzie Guillén; 375 under Robin Ventura; 236 under Rich Renteria; and 1 as manager himself.

2 Patrick Comiskey, "Former Pitching Coach Don Cooper Has Choice Words for White Sox," *On Tap Sports Net*, March 12, 2021. https://ontapsportsnet.com/white-sox/former-pitching-coach-don-cooper-has-choice-words-for-white-sox.

3   Paul Sullivan, "Don Cooper's Departure from the Chicago White Sox after 32 years – 18 as Pitching Coach – Marks the End of an Era," *Chicago Tribune*, October 12, 2020.

4   Doug Mead, *Bleacherreport.com*, February 1, 2012.

5   Bob Vorwald, *What It Means to Be a White Sox* (Chicago: Triumph Books, 2010), 284. The Cooper chapter, written in the first person, is on pages 284-287.

6   Richard Goldstein, "Sammy Ellis, All-Star Starter Who Later Made Dave Righetti a Reliever, Dies at 75," *New York Times*, May 17, 2016: A17; Associated Press, "Former Big-League Pitcher Sammy Ellis Dies at 75," May 15, 2016. https://apnews.com/article/98b6cb0255d142b49a6065f9a9006abc.

7   Vorwald, 284-85. Cooper would later learn that Ellis's actual Spanish vocabulary was pretty short.

8   Vorwald, 284.

9   *Chicago White Sox 2006 Media Guide*, 26-27. The same profile was repeated many times in White Sox media guides.

10 Vorwald, 285.

11 Vorwald, 284.

12 *Chicago White Sox 2006 Media Guide*, 26-27.

13 *2008 Chicago White Sox Division Series Special Postseason Edition*, 40.

14 Vorwald, 286.

15 Phil Rogers, "Chicago White Six Are Counting On Bond Between Lucas Giolito and New Coach Ethan Katz," *Forbes*, November 12, 2020. https://www.forbes.com/sites/philrogers/2020/11/12/chicago-white-sox-count-on-bond-between-ethan-katz-lucas-giolito/.

16 *Sox Pride: The Story of the 2005 World Champion Chicago White Sox*, Comcast SportsNet DVD. Cooper speaks directly on camera. He speaks on 10 different occasions, far more often than any other coach.

17 Baseball-Reference.com lists El Duque's age as 39 that year, though some other sources give it as 36.

18 *Believe It! The Story of Chicago's World Champions: A Chicago Tribune keepsake book* (2005), 64. The chapter on the Division Series was written by Dan McGrath.

19 *World 05 Series*, Major League Baseball Productions Presents DVD. Cooper speaks directly on camera. Like in *Sox Pride*, Cooper is the coach most frequently seen and speaking.

20 *Sox Pride: The Story of the 2005 World Champion Chicago White Sox*.

21 Phil Rogers, *Say It's So: The Chicago White Sox's Magical Season* (Chicago: Triumph Books, 2006), 55.

22 *Sox Pride: The Story of the 2005 World Champion Chicago White Sox*

23 Phil Rogers, *Say It's So: The Chicago White Sox's Magical Season*, 61.

24 *World 05 Series*.

25 *Sox Pride: The Story of the 2005 World Champion Chicago White Sox*.

26 Vorwald, 286-7.

27 *What It Means To Be a White Sox*, 287.

28 "Monsignor McClancy Athletic Hall of Fame citation," https://msgrmcclancy.org/athletic/hall-of-fame. Additional information from White Sox media guides.

29 "2020 MLB Preview," *Athlon Sports*: 86. This was Cooper's final year.

30 Phil Rogers, "Chicago White Sox Are Counting On Bond Between Lucas Giolito And New Coach Ethan Katz," *Forbes* November 12, 2020. https://www.forbes.com/sites/philrogers/2020/11/12/chicago-white-sox-count-on-bond-between-ethan-katz-lucas-giolito/

31 "Talking Pitching: Bill Ripken & Don Cooper," MLB Network, YouTube, February 27, 2020. https://www.youtube.com/watch?v=HhkUZ1d_764

32 Steve Greenberg and Daryl van Schouwen, "Ex-White Sox pitching coach Don Cooper on firing: 'The bottom line is it hurt'," *Chicago Sun-Times*, March 11, 2021. https://chicago.suntimes.com/white-sox/2021/3/11/22326416/don-cooper-white-sox-fired-pitching-coach-am-670

JOEY CORA

By Alan Cohen

*"El problema de'ser un bien deportista,
es que hay que perder para probarlo"
(The problem with being a good sportsman
is you must lose to prove it)*
From a sign on 22-year-old Joey Cora's room
posted by his sister Iris in 1988.[1]

*"He was everything to me. As far as
baseball and discipline and being a man,
he was the one who taught me."*
Joey Cora speaking of his father, José, in April
1990.[2]

*"He was the first infielder I ever saw
who practiced diving for balls. He was one
of those guys who got to the park very early
and worked his tail off to stay ready for any
situation. He went all out, all day and had a
lot of fun doing it. He gave us a lot of laughs
and was tight with Ozzie Guillen. It was great
to see them win a World Series together."*
- Matt Merullo, 2017.[3]

Joey Cora was the second child and first of two sons born to José Cora and his wife, Iris, in Caguas, Puerto Rico. José Manuel Cora Amaro was born on May 14, 1965, in Caguas, Puerto Rico. Brother Alex Cora came along 10 years later. Their older sister became a medical technologist. Their younger sister, Iris, was born in 1968. When his father took a position with Gillette, the family moved to New York not long after Joey was born. However, they were in New York for only a short time before returning to Puerto Rico, where his father started and served as president of the local Little League. Joey first made his mark in Little League at age 7, playing with and against much older youngsters. His father took a position with the Sports Recreation Department of Puerto Rico and went on to become a scout for the Texas Rangers. Once José Jr. (Joey) joined the Padres, José Sr. did as well.

At 16, Joey graduated from Baptist College of Caguas (a high school) and was courted by the Yankees, Phillies, and Brewers. But his family had other ideas and Joey took his track-and-field skills and 3.97 grade-point average to the University of Puerto Rico. "The only reason I didn't get the 4.0 is because of the 'B' I got in Christian Education, and the reason I got the 'B' was we had to go to chapel every Thursday and I didn't go."[4]

American Legion ball became Joey's ticket to a career. While playing at a tournament in Ohio, he was scouted by Vanderbilt coach Roy Mewbourne and offered a scholarship to play baseball. Not versed in English, Joey headed to Vanderbilt with an English dictionary. A scholar in any language, Joey quickly learned English and compiled a 3.50 grade-point average in his first semester. He elected to major in math.

While at Vanderbilt, Cora was named to the American Baseball Coaches Association All-South Region Team as a shortstop in 1984. He was only a sophomore at the time. That summer he ventured north to play for Chatham in the Cape Cod League; he was a league all-star selection at second base. He also was selected as the league's MVP, after finishing second in the league in batting.[5]

In 1985, during his junior year at Vanderbilt, Cora led the Southeast Conference in triples with six, and was named to the All-SEC team at shortstop. His efforts in the classroom

Joey Cora   **2005**

were recognized when he was named to the SEC's Athletic All-Scholastic Team. He batted .403 and stole 51 bases. By that point, Cora had broken 10 school records for hits and stolen bases. He was named to the second team Converse All-American team. (Only Barry Larkin was better at the shortstop position.) In the draft that June, Cora was the first-round pick (23rd overall) of the defending National League champion San Diego Padres.

In the rookie Northwest League, Cora batted .324 with 3 homers and 26 RBIs with Spokane. His career seemed to be on the fast track and a promotion was on the horizon when his season was interrupted after a collision at second base. An oncoming runner decided that Cora's knee was a better target than the base and Cora required surgery that ruined his hopes of an early promotion. After playing for Leones in the Puerto Rican Winter League, he joined the Beaumont Golden Gators of the Double-A Texas League for the 1986 season.

An incident that season almost finished off Cora's career before it had begun. In early June Joey's father was battling colon cancer and had surgery. Joey left his Beaumont teammates to be with his father and family. A week later, he returned to his team, and his head admittedly was not in the game. After a game in which he went hitless at San Antonio on June 21, Cora and teammate Sandy Alomar Jr. were accosted while waiting for the team bus in the parking lot. Under normal circumstances, Cora would have just walked away, but these were not normal circumstances. Words were exchanged, a fight broke out, and Cora's teammate Eric Hardgrave was knocked to the ground. The leader of the gang of outsiders, Jose Puente, stabbed Cora twice. Joey was seriously injured and was tended to by team trainer Ray Suarez. Cora had to have part of his small intestine removed.

Hospitalized, he missed most of the balance of the season, returning to Beaumont in mid-August.[6] In the 81 games he played, he batted .305 with 24 stolen bases. Both father and son emerged from the ordeal, with Joey having learned a life lesson. "It affected me that, in a way, off the field I had to be more careful with where I was and what I was doing. As far as playing the game, no, it didn't affect me, but off the field, it definitely changed me. Because I took a lot of what was happening on the field and in the game, and I was taking it off the field wherever I was. It changed me a lot, actually."[7]

Cora made his debut with the Padres the next season. Before the season, scout Dick Hager, reflecting on the adversity of Cora's first two professional seasons, said, "I don't recall just how many knife wounds he received, but for a while he was in serious condition. The kid is a real gamer. He can play. We don't know whether he is ready to play in the majors, but Larry Bowa (the Padres manager) plans to find out."[8] Unfortunately for Cora, the chemical reaction of the no-longer-combative player and

the ever-combustible manager Bowa would be such as to ultimately prolong Cora's apprenticeship.

On Opening Day, April 6, 1987, Cora was at second base, batting eighth for the Padres. In his first at-bat, facing Mike Krukow, he lined out to shortstop. In the top of the eighth inning, in his third at-bat, he singled with one out, stole second base, and scored on a single by Marvell Wynne. Tied, 3-3, the game went into extra innings. Cora's bunt single in the top of the 12th inning put him at first base with one out, but he was caught stealing and the Giants won the game in their half of the inning. Cora played in each of the Padres' first 54 games, but was batting only .234 when he was sent down to the minors on June 4. His fielding and immaturity caused more problems than his tired bat. He had committed nine errors, including two in the same game on a pair of occasions. He also was perceived as being uncooperative by the coaches. His reaction was to say, "I'm listening. Sometimes they tell you things that you don't feel comfortable doing. You're not confident because you have not done it their way before. And I've got to practice it before I go out and use it in a game. Like bunting. They're trying to teach me a new way, but I think too much. It doesn't come natural to me. If I go to the minors, I've got to practice, practice until it becomes natural."[9] So, to the minors he went. He played his next 81 games at Triple-A Las Vegas, batting .276, before returning to the Padres in September. For the Padres, he batted .237 with 13 RBIs and 15 stolen bases.

Cora had arthroscopic knee surgery during the offseason and the following spring was assigned back to Las Vegas to get "more playing time." Manager Bowa and the local media had been highly critical of Cora's defense while he was with the club in 1987. Cora accepted the demotion, saying, "It's all right, I guess. I just have to play when I get a chance. I like it like this. I don't have to talk a lot. I can be by myself and be myself. I'm ready for Triple-A."[10]

The experience with Bowa in 1987 had been traumatic. "It was terrible," he told a sportswriter in 1989. "Larry said so much, all the time. I did not want to come to the ballpark. And when I got there, I didn't want to be there. I got so down and lonely. I went home every night and tried to cook, to help me forget."[11] Cora remained in Las Vegas for the 1988 season, as well as most of 1989. After batting .296 with 21 extra-base hits and 31 stolen bases in 1988, he batted .310 in 1989 with 29 extra-base hits and 40 stolen bases. In 1989, he put together a 37-game hitting streak, and at the end of the season he was named to the Pacific Coast League All-Star team. In September Cora got his second bite of the big-league apple, playing for new manager Jack McKeon. He batted .316 in 12 late-season games. In the offseason, there was bad news on the home front as his father died from hepatitis on October 5, 1989.

Playing for Ponce in the Puerto Rican Winter League, Cora batted .293 with 15 thefts. Ponce was managed by Padres third-base coach Sandy Alomar,[12] and the Padres were impressed enough to keep Cora in "The Show." But the 1990 season was one of frustration. After playing in only 31 of his team's first 77 games, he was once again sent back to Las Vegas, where in 51 games he batted .351 with 22 extra-base hits and 15 stolen bases. During his time with the Padres, he showed himself to be the ultimate team player, going behind the plate for the final two innings of the game on June 14 after each of the Padres catchers went down with injuries. Listed generously at 5-feet-7 and 150 pounds, Cora was not a catcher out of Central Casting, but he played an errorless two innings while setting up the target for pitcher Mark Grant. In the offseason between 1990 and 1991, while playing winter ball, Cora fractured his ankle in a collision while chasing a pop fly. The Padres were unsure of his status for 1991, and eventually, after a good spring training, he was traded along with Kevin Garner and Warren Newson to the Chicago White Sox for pitchers Adam Peterson and Steve Rosenberg. Cora reacted to the trade by saying, "This is the team I've always been with, since '85 when I was drafted. They made my family happy and everything. They gave me a shot in the big leagues. I've been through a lot with these guys. I love them very much, but life goes on and you have to do what you have to do."[13]

Cora spent the entire 1991 season with the White Sox. After spending the early part of the season backing up Scott Fletcher at second base, he was inserted into the lineup, getting his first start and first multi-hit game on May 17. It took some time for him to find a consistent stroke, but manager Jeff Torborg saw Cora as a player who "seems to be able to make things happen." Those things included a spectacular fielding play to end a game on June 10. In the bottom of the 13th inning at Texas, with two outs and the White Sox clinging to a 3-2 lead, Cora, going to his left, grabbed a groundball that had deflected off the glove of first baseman Dan Pasqua and threw a strike to catcher Matt Merullo to nip pinch-runner Mario Diaz and end the game. Joey said, "I look at it as a job I have to do. Whatever they ask me to do, I'll do."[14]

From June 8 through June 21, Cora batted .395 over a 13-game stretch to raise his average from .229 to .321. But once again injury interrupted his season. He sprained his right knee sliding into third base in the ninth inning of a game against the Texas Rangers. Subsequently, the White Sox filled the bases, and Cora came home with the tying run on a walk to Robin Ventura. After the game, he was placed on the 15-day disabled list.[15] After his return from the DL, Cora was unable to match his performance prior to the injury. He finished the season with a .241 batting average.

In 1992 Cora only got into 68 games with the White Sox. In the offseason, Chicago had acquired Steve Sax and his $3.5 million salary from the Yankees. Cora, in his limited appearances, batted .246. "I am not a superstar or anything," Cora said. "I'm the just the kind of player who's going to be there doing what I did last season (1991) – be a backup, work hard. They call you, go and do the job. That'll be my role. I really enjoy it. I'm that type of guy – a kamikaze type of guy. Wherever they put me, I'll go after it hard. Whatever they ask me to do, I'll be ready."[16]

And ready he became. As Sax only batted .236, and was second on the team with 20 errors, he and his big contract would wind up on the bench the following spring. An injury to heir-apparent Craig Grebeck during the last weekend of spring training gave Cora an opportunity that he did not waste. For Cora, 1993 was a breakout season. He played in 153 games and batted .268. The smallish Cora hit his first two career homers and had 51 RBIs. He stole a career-high 20 bases and had a career-high 13 triples. He led the league in sacrifices with 19. Paired with Ozzie Guillen, Cora improved his fielding, and through the first 29 games he was involved in 22 double plays.

On April 20, 1993, Cora was at his acrobatic best. This time, the folks in Baltimore witnessed the unfathomable. In the fourth inning, the Orioles had loaded the bases with two out. The Sox tried to pick off the runner at second base, but the ball bounced off Guillen's glove. Cora pounced on the ball and his side-arm throw to Ron Karkovice nailed Chris Hoiles trying to score from third base. The game remained tied, 1-1, and the Sox went on to win 2-1 in 14 innings with Cora, after walking, scoring the winning run.[17]

But Cora's main contribution to the team had nothing to do with the type of statistics that fly off the page. Batting in front of Frank Thomas, he was adept at working deep into counts. From the on-deck circle, Thomas thus got a good look at a pitcher's repertoire and was ready when he made it to the plate.[18] Ready enough to win the first of two MVP awards. He also had many chances to drive in Cora who, via hit or walk or hit by pitch, reached base 231 times during the season. Cora still led the league with errors by a second baseman with 19. The White Sox won the AL West and Joey advanced to the postseason for the first time. His bat grew cold in the playoffs; he batted only .136 as Chicago was eliminated by Toronto in the American League Championship Series.

In the strike-shortened 1994 season, Cora played in 90 of his team's 113 games and batted .276. Other than a trip to the DL in early July, he never had more than one day off between starts. His injury, as usual, came at the worst possible time. He had been on a tear, going 27-for-74 (.365) during June to raise his average for the season to .287. The injury occurred in a game against Kansas City on June 29. Leaping for a line drive, he pulled a muscle in his rib cage.[19] At the time of the strike in August, the White Sox led the AL West by one game, a lead that was wiped out along with the season.

Before the 1995 season the White Sox let Cora go to free agency and he signed with the Seattle Mariners. He was with Seattle for four seasons, during which his salary increased from $425,000 to $1.7 million. In Seattle, he became known not only for his dedication on the field but for his work with the Joey Cora Children's Foundation.

GRINDERS AND GAMERS

With Seattle in 1995, Cora raised his batting average to .297 and was once again in the postseason. In August, he batted .392 with 10 extra-base hits and 10 RBIs in 23 games, and the Mariners took a 7½-game lead into September. They would need every bit of that as the fight for the division championship went down to the last weekend with Seattle winding up tied with the California Angels. In a one-game playoff for the division championship, Cora had three productive at-bats as the Mariners won, 9-1, behind Randy Johnson. He singled during a rally in the fifth inning that plated Seattle's first run, was hit by a pitch and scored during a four-run outburst in the seventh, and drove in a run with a sacrifice fly in the eighth inning.

Seattle lost the first two games of the Division Series against the wild-card Yankees in the Bronx. In Seattle, the Mariners won Game Three, 7-4, and Game Four, 11-8, with Cora going 2-for-4 and scoring two runs. With Seattle trailing 5-0, Cora led off the third inning with a bunt single and scored on an Edgar Martinez homer as the Mariners erupted for four runs. In the decisive eighth inning, Cora again reached on a bunt and again came home on an Edgar Martinez homer. This one was a grand slam. In Game Five Cora gave Seattle a 1-0 lead with a third-inning home run off David Cone. The game went into extra innings and New York took a 5-4 lead in the top of the 11th. Cora led off the bottom of the inning with his third bunt single in two games. After a single by Ken Griffey Jr., Edgar Martinez doubled both runners home and Seattle advanced to the League Championship Series.

In the LCS, the Mariners lost to Cleveland in six games. Although Cora had only four hits in the series, he had a key hit in Seattle's Game Three win. The game went into extra innings and, in the 11th Cora led off with a single. He scored on a three-run homer by Jay Buhner, giving Seattle a 2-1 edge in the Series. But Seattle would not win another game in 1995.

In 1996 Seattle slipped to second but Cora had another good year, batting .291. His 37 doubles were the best in his career to that point, as were his six home runs. He had 43 multiple-hit games. The Mariners were nine games out of the league lead on September 11, when they launched a 10-game winning streak to make things tight. During that stretch, Cora had two homers and three RBIs in seven games. But although the Mariners pulled to within one game of the division lead, they were unable to close the deal, losing six of their last eight games.

In 1997 Seattle won its division for the second time in three years, but lost the best-of-five Division Series to Baltimore in four games. For Cora, it was a banner year. He had career highs in batting average (.300), doubles (40), home runs (11), and RBIs (54). Most impressive was his setting a franchise record by hitting in 24 consecutive games. The streak lasted from May 2 through May 29. Cora batted .475 during the streak, raising his average for the season from .247 to .374. In the 24th game, he kept the streak alive with an infield hit with two outs in the ninth inning. Once the streak concluded, he proceeded to reach base in another dozen games, making his on-base consecutive streak 36 games. His hit streak stood as the record for switch-hitters in the American League until 1998. The franchise record stood for 10 years until Ichiro Suzuki hit in 25 straight games in 2007. (Ichiro set the current Seattle standard by hitting in 27 consecutive games in 2009.)

In 1997 Cora was named to the All-Star team for the only time in his career. He was one of eight players born or raised in Puerto Rico to be chosen for the 1997 game. He entered the game as a pinch-runner in the fifth inning and replaced Roberto Alomar at second base. He had a fielding gem in the sixth inning when he dived to grab a grounder and rob Tony Gwynn of a base hit. In his only at-bat, Cora hit a fly ball to left field in the seventh inning. Cora's teammates praised his selection for the squad. Ken Griffey Jr. said, "Before he was chosen, we were all asked if Joey Cora was an All-Star, and we all said he deserves to go. He's worked hard at this sport. He's a quiet player, but he's a spark plug. It is fun just to watch him every day, diving for balls, hustling."[20] Cora himself relished being honored as an All-Star. "I get excited when I play a regular season game, but an All-Star Game, this is it," he said. "Until you're here, you don't understand. There's no way I would trade this for anything."[21]

In the 1997 Division Series loss to Baltmore, Cora went 3-for-17. The following season would be his last as a player. He was batting .283 with 6 homers, 26 RBIs, and 13 stolen bases when the soon-to-be free agent was traded to Cleveland on August 31 for infielder David Bell. Despite their high-powered offense, the Mariners had fallen on hard times. At the time of the trade they were 11 games below .500 and trailed the first-place Angels by 12½ games. In 24 games with Cleveland, Cora batted .229. Cleveland won the Central Division and went as far as the LCS in the postseason, losing to the Yankees in six games. Cora's postseason performance was disappointing. He played in six games and went 1-for-17.

In the offseason, Cora signed with Toronto as a free agent, but after faring poorly in the field in six exhibition games, the 33-year-old on March 11 decided to retire.

After his playing days, Cora stayed in baseball in a variety of positions. He coached at Daytona, the Cubs affiliate in the Florida State League, in 2000. He joined the Mets organization in 2001 and managed at Kingsport, Tennessee, in 2001 and 2002. In 2003, he managed Montreal's Class-A affiliate in Savannah. In 2004 friend and former double-play partner Ozzie Guillen hired Cora as the third-base coach with the White Sox. He stayed with the White Sox through 2011 and received his first World Series ring in 2005 after the White Sox swept the Houston Astros. He became the bench coach in 2007 and served in that capacity until Guillen was fired toward the end of the 2011 season. In

2012, when Guillen took over as manager of the Marlins, Cora became the bench coach in Miami.

After the 2012 season, Guillen was fired by the Marlins, and Cora spent the next three seasons out of professional baseball. In 2013, he worked as an analyst with MLB, and in the following two seasons, he stayed at home with his family.

In 2015, the Mariners invited Cora back to Seattle to throw out the first pitch on Opening Day.

In 2016, at the invitation of Larry Broadway, the Pirates' farm chief, Cora joined the Pittsburgh organization, managing their Double-A affiliate in Altoona, Pennsylvania. He was named the Pirates' third-base coach for the 2017 season. In 2003 Broadway had played for Cora at Savannah. Thirteen years later, Broadway reached out to his old mentor.[22] During his time in Pittsburgh, his younger brother, Alex, had been tabbed to manage the Boston Red Sox, Alex, in 2018, led Boston to the World Series championship.

Joey Cora remained with the Pirates through the 2021 season. In 2022, he joined the staff of the New York Mets.[23] He served as an infield coach and coached at third base for the Mets. At the end of the 2023 season, he left the Mets and moved on to the Detroit Tigers, working with the middle infielders and coaching at third base.

Cora has had a lifelong dream. "My dream wasn't to be a major-league baseball player. My dream always, when I was little, was to be a big-league manager."[24] Maybe that dream will come true.

SOURCES

In addition to the sources cited in the Notes, the author used Baseball-Reference.com and the Joey Cora player file at the National Baseball Hall of Fame Library.

NOTES

1   Barry Bloom, "Coras Hang Tough During Rough Times," *San Diego Union Tribune*, April 4, 1988: Baseball-4.

2   James Posner, "Cora Making Most of Second Chance," *San Diego Union Tribune*, April 26, 1990: E-1.

3   Matt Merullo email to author, March 10, 2017.

4   Chris Jenkins, "The Drive to Excel: At 21, Cora Won't Rest in His Quest for perfection," *San Diego Union-Tribune*, April 26, 1987: H-1.

5   *Boston Herald*, August 19, 1984: 72.

6   Chris Jenkins.

7   Doug Padilla, "Tragic Incident Becomes Life Lesson for Cora," *Chicago Sun-Times*, October 19, 2005.

8   *New Orleans Times Picayune*, March 29, 1987: C-20.

9   Tom Friend, "Is Joey Cora Stubborn, or Is He Scared? Only He Knows for Sure," *Los Angeles Times*, May 22, 1987: 1.

10   Bill Plaschke, "Padre Notebook Joey Cora: "The Forgotten Man' Knows He's Heading Down," *Los Angeles Times*, March 16, 1988: 3.

11   Bill Plaschke, "No Fist in His Glove: Joey Cora Doesn't Want to Fight, He Just Wants a Chance," *Los Angeles Times*, March 9, 1989: 1.

12   Phil Collier, "Angels Stockpile Pitchers in Bid for Hitter," *San Diego Union Tribune*, January 14, 1990: H-15.

13   Barry Bloom, *San Diego Union Tribune*, April 2, 1991: C-3.

14   Alan Solomon, "Cora Not 'Starter' Yet, but Boss Is Impressed," *Chicago Tribune*, June 12, 1991: B-9.

15   John Mulka, "Cora's a Bright Spot for Gloomy Sox," *Northwest Indiana Post-Tribune*, June 23, 1991: C7.

16   Alan Solomon, "On 2nd Thought ... Cora, Grebeck Adjust," *Chicago Tribune*, March 15, 1992: B6.

17   Joey Reaves, "Cora Play Gives Sox a Huge Lift: Arm, Legs Trip Orioles in 14," *Chicago Tribune*, April 21, 1993: B3.

18   Bill Jauss, "Cora Takes a Long Look at His Contributions," *Chicago Tribune*, August 26, 1993: B12.

19   Dan Binkley, "Cora Goes on DL – Grebeck Returns," *Chicago Sun-Times*, July 1, 1994.

20   Claire Smith, "Worthy of the Honor, Based on Enthusiasm Alone," *New York Times*, July 9, 1997.

21   Smith.

22   Alan Saunders, "New Coach Joey Cora Embraces Mental Approach – Pirates," *Allegheny Times* (Beaver, Pennsylvania), November 16, 2016: B-1.

23   Matthew Roberson, "Meet Mets' Candidate Joey Cora," *New York Daily News*, January 6, 2022: 41.

24   Kevin Thomas. "On Baseball: Joey Cora Has a Big-League Resume and a Minor League Job," *Portland* (Maine) *Press-Herald*, August 18, 2016.

KEVIN HICKEY

By Alex P. Blair

Kevin Hickey had one of the most unlikely careers in the history of baseball. Then he had another one.

In the span of a few years, he transformed himself from 16-inch softball ringer into a big-league reliever deployed against some of the best left-handed hitters of his era. When he found himself at rock bottom, the White Sox welcomed him home.

Kevin John Hickey was born in the Brighton Park neighborhood on the South Side of Chicago on February 25, 1956.[1] He was the second of five children born to Donald and Kathleen Hickey.[2] Kathleen was a native of England, and met and married Donald when he was stationed in Surrey with the US Air Force.[3] They moved back to Donald's hometown of Chicago and he went to work for the phone company.[4] The Hickey family's roots ran deep in the neighborhood: Just down the alley from Donald and Kathleen's home was the Burroughs Park playground, where Donald and his brothers had played as children.[5]

All the Hickey children were Burroughs Park regulars, but it was Kevin who became a neighborhood legend. His best sport may have been ice hockey, which he would play when the locals converted the playground into a rink in wintertime.[6]

"Our neighborhood was filled with kids," Kevin's brother Tom Hickey recalled.[7] "It was very blue collar, and all we did was play sports." Kevin "was so good it was beyond. He was playing with kids in the neighborhood four years older than him. … He was just a natural athlete."

Kevin earned a scholarship to the prestigious local private school St. Rita's to play basketball. He proved to be a poor student, to put it mildly, and lost his scholarship when he cut class to run numbers for a bookie.[8] He finished his education at the local public school, Kelly High. He never played baseball in high school.[9]

Hickey married young, had two daughters in quick succession, and started working at Ryerson Steel.[10] The marriage didn't last and neither did his career as a steelworker. Hickey later described himself as a "dead end kid," divorced and living back at home with his parents, not even 20 years old.[11] To earn extra cash, he turned to where he was still a legend: the playgrounds of Chicago.

It is hard to explain the degree to which 16-inch softball captured the attention of the twentieth-century Chicago sports fan. It is a version of the game almost unique to Chicago and the Midwest, and distinct from the more widely known 12-inch version of slow-pitch. A 16-inch softball is truly "soft," and generally played without gloves. The 16-inch game proved especially popular in Chicago because it could be played in the city's small parks and schoolyards.[12] At one point, 16-inch softball games were broadcast from Thillens Stadium on the North Side on WGN-TV, with the games called by broadcaster Jack Brickhouse, the voice of the Cubs.[13] The 1975 16-inch Softball World Series was played at Soldier Field, home of the NFL's Chicago Bears.[14]

"You could bet hundreds or thousands of dollars on a game," said Tom Hickey.[15]

The local 16-inch softball circuit was an easy way for a talented young athlete to earn some money under the table. Hickey was the star center fielder and a power bat for one of the best-known softball teams in the city, the Bobcats, and helped them win the 1976 World Series.[16] Hickey could

Courtesy of Karen Puccinell

Kevin Hickey

catch the massive 16-inch ball one-handed and "run like a deer."[17] He once hit four home runs off legendary Chicago newspaperman Mike Royko.[18] Thousands of people would watch Hickey and the Bobcats play at Kelly Park.[19] When Hickey was short on funds, he had his younger brother Tom call the Bobcats to report he was sick and unable to play. An envelope of cash would find its way to the Hickey household, and Kevin would make a miraculous recovery before game time.[20]

Hickey also demonstrated his all-around athleticism and competitiveness in the city's basketball scene. In one game, for a church league no less, he threw a chair at a referee.[21] That referee happened to be White Sox scout Joe Begani. When Hickey, a lefty, later threw two no-hitters with a local semipro baseball team, Begani was in the stands and remembered the talented hothead who narrowly missed him with the folding chair.[22]

Impressed, Begani invited Hickey to try out for the White Sox at Comiskey Park. Hickey thought it was a private tryout[23] and was surprised when he showed up to the ballpark to find himself participating in an annual promotional scheme invented by White Sox owner Bill Veeck.[24]

"There were 250 guys there, some wearing bellbottom pants and using Kmart gloves," Hickey later recalled to the *Chicago Sun-Times*.[25] Begani stopped Hickey from turning around and leaving, and got him to throw second. His first pitch caught the catcher unawares and spun his mask around.[26] It was a fastball clocked at 95 mph.[27] The scouts watching asked Hickey to throw some breaking pitches, but he didn't know any. After some on-the-spot instruction, he was able to snap off a hard slider.[28] Here was a diamond dug out of the Chicago sandlots.

Begani came to Hickey's parents' house the next day, signed him to a $500 pro contract, and he was off to Paintsville, Kentucky, for rookie ball in the Appalachian League. Hickey earned an invitation to spring training with the big-league team in 1980.

Hickey "wouldn't be coming to spring training if we didn't think he could make it," Veeck told the *Sun-Times*.[29]

Although he didn't make the team that season, Hickey continued to improve as a professional: In 1980 he recorded a winning record for the White Sox' Double-A affiliate Glens Falls and won a Silver Glove as the best fielding pitcher in the minor leagues after making no errors in 169 innings pitched.[30] In Hickey's neighborhood watering hole, his fielding prowess as a pitcher was later attributed to his softball career: Hickey came off the mound with both hands up, ready to field like a softball pitcher.[31] In 1981 Hickey earned another invitation to spring training. He performed spectacularly, throwing 22 scoreless innings.[32] He was going back to Chicago as a member of the White Sox.

"I called my mom collect," Hickey told the *Sun-Times*.[33] "I came out of the booth like Superman. That's how I felt."

Hickey made his first big-league appearance at the White Sox home opener against the Milwaukee Brewers on April 14, 1981. With the White Sox ahead comfortably, 9-1, entering the top of the ninth, the Brewers started the inning with a double and a home run. With much of Hickey's friends and family from Brighton Park in the bleachers, White Sox manager Tony La Russa made a call to the bullpen.[34] Hickey sprinted to the mound to the roars from the bleachers, which were full of Kelly High classmates and Brighton Park neighbors. He induced two groundouts, then got future Hall of Famer Paul Molitor to pop up to second for the final out of the game.[35]

Hickey's rookie year was interrupted by the 1981 players strike. During the midseason labor stoppage, Hickey and fellow pitcher Ed Farmer would toss in the alley behind Hickey's parents' house. Neighborhood children would line up to watch them, and Hickey would sign every autograph.[36]

Hickey was loved by his teammates for his relentlessly positive attitude. La Russa once called him "the personal pet of everybody on this team because when he puts on that uniform, he is pure joy."[37] One spring training he gave up a home run against a team of student-athletes from Eckerd College.[38]

"So from now on," Hickey reportedly said, "we should play Walgreen's instead of Eckerd's."[39]

He recorded his first career win on Easter Sunday 1982, Opening Day at Yankee Stadium. His jubilant teammates retrieved the game ball and painted it like an Easter egg.[40] Hickey was still devoted to his neighborhood, occasionally venturing back to Brighton Park and jumping into a pickup game of softball or to watch his brothers and friends play.[41]

Over the course of his big-league career, Hickey proved himself to be a valuable middle reliever and was often used against the opposing team's best left-handed hitter. Kevin Hickey is the only pitcher George Brett faced at least 15 times and failed to get a hit. Wade Boggs faced him 12 times, got one hit, never walked, and struck out five times. Left-handed batters hit only .218 against him vs. a .270 average for right-handed batters. In 1982 Hickey had the lowest ERA of all White Sox pitchers that season, 3.00 in 78 innings pitched. He was second in appearances, second in saves, and third in WHIP. But 1982 was his only season with the White Sox not curtailed by labor strife or injury.

During the 1983 season, Hickey threw a warm-up pitch to batterymate Carlton Fisk. The veteran catcher caught the ball, walked to the mound and asked "What are you doing? I told you to throw a fastball." Hickey replied: "That was my fastball."[42] His shoulder was shot. He did not appear in a game for the White Sox after July, and watched from the dugout as the team went on to win 99 games and the AL West Division championship before falling to the eventual World Series champion Baltimore Orioles in the ALCS. Hickey was not part of the playoff roster and was cut the following season.[43]

"It was like someone sticking a knife in me," Hickey told the *Sun-Times*.[44]

From 1984 to 1987, Hickey bounced around the minor leagues in the White Sox, Giants, Yankees, and Phillies organizations, unwilling to surrender his improbable baseball career.

"I'm not going to give up," Hickey told the *Albany Times Union* after being released from the Yankees' Double-A team despite posting a 2.92 ERA in 11 games.[45] "My goal is to get back to the big leagues. I know I can go out there and do the job."

The 1987 season was perhaps the low point of Hickey's exile to the minors: He found himself playing for the Hawaii Islanders in a deserted Aloha Stadium during the last year of the team's existence.[46] But Hickey would get one more chance. At the end of that year, former White Sox GM Roland Hemond offered Hickey a minor-league contract with the Orioles.[47] After one more season in the minors, Hickey went to spring training in 1989 and slept on a cot in the trainer's room.[48] Although he was told that the big-league club had no plans for him, injuries to two other left-handed pitchers in Baltimore's spring camp created an opportunity.[49] He didn't allow a run all spring, and when camp broke, Kevin Hickey was on his way to Baltimore and back in the big leagues.[50]

Statisticians have long debated how to quantify the contributions of middle relievers like Hickey, but the Orioles recognized his value. Hickey told the *Baltimore Sun* that his job was to get "half-saves."[51] In the 1989 and 1990 seasons, he entered the game in a save situation a combined 23 times and never blew a save, recording 16 holds.

"If he comes in and gets one man out and that's all he's asked to do, then he's done his job," manager Frank Robinson told the *Sun*. "He doesn't need to put up big numbers."[52] Hickey told the paper that he was just "happy to be here and helping the club win."[53]

Hickey made many friends during his three seasons in Baltimore, including one friend in the highest possible place. He was on a first-name basis with sitting President George H.W. Bush, and when Hickey's mother came to Maryland to see him, she was picked up via limousine sent from the White House.[54] He stayed in Baltimore during the offseason, playing ice hockey in a local league and working out at Cal Ripken's house to stay in shape.[55]

By 1991 Hickey was 35 and did not have much left. He had hung on to his professional baseball career for 13 seasons, but Baltimore released him in July after he logged a 9.00 ERA in 19 appearances. Desperate to stay around the game, he became a greeter at Camden Yards.[56] It was while working for the team he used to pitch for that he befriended the casting director for *Major League II*.[57] He became friends with the actor Charlie Sheen, and landed a speaking part in the movie as "Schoup."[58] In the film, Hickey's character is a starting pitcher who pitches a shutout against the White Sox in Game One of the ALCS.[59] Schoup also leaves the mound in the bottom of the ninth of Game Seven in line for the win after issuing an untimely walk to put two men

on with two outs in a 6-5 ballgame.[60] After handing the ball to the manager for Sheen's closer to earn the save, Hickey's character mutters, "Can't believe I walked that Punch-and-Judy hitter."[61] Desperate for cash, Hickey sold Sheen two minor-league championship rings from his career. At the end of filming, Sheen gave them back for free.[62]

Hickey made one final attempt to get back into the big leagues during the 1994-1995 players strike when he crossed the picket lines and reported to the New York Mets spring training as a replacement player at age 38.[63] Hickey felt that the 1981 strike cost him part of his major-league career when he was making only $32,500 per year, and that the current generation of players owed him for his sacrifice.[64] Hickey's participation in spring training prompted an angry phone call from a family friend who was a higher-up with the Chicago Fire Fighters Union.[65]

"I'm not taking anybody's job away," Hickey told the *New York Daily News*. "They can have their jobs back any time they want. But if they're saying they're trying to make the game better for upcoming players, I feel I made the game better for these guys now. And I should reap the benefits of that."[66]

But he never made it back to professional baseball. Hickey finished his major-league career with a 9-14 record, a 3.91 ERA, and 17 saves in 231 games.[67]

Hickey got divorced again, was diagnosed with diabetes, and moved into the basement of his ex-in-laws' house in Ohio.[68] He sold used cars to try to make ends meet. Times were dark when his brothers showed up to move him back home to Chicago. All of Hickey's worldly possessions fit inside a couple of duffel bags.[69] At a 2003 golf tournament honoring the 1983 team, Hickey confided in former teammate and White Sox hitting coach Greg Walker that he was unemployed with no health insurance.[70] A courtesy invite to spring training as a White Sox alumnus led to Hickey hitting it off with manager Ozzie Guillén and the players.[71] By the time the White Sox left Glendale, Hickey was employed as an extra batting-practice pitcher at $30,000 per year.[72]

"He brought energy every day," Walker told the *Sun-Times*. "You never had to worry about the bench being dead."[73]

Guillén told the *Chicago Tribune* that carrying a full-time lefty as a batting-practice pitcher benefited his team from seeing a left-handed arm angle.[74] Hickey was always eager to throw whenever a player asked him to, staying long after a game and tossing bucket after bucket of balls, never complaining.[75] The only time he missed work was when third baseman Joe Crede bounced a line drive off the back of his head.[76] Jim Thome was particularly fond of using Hickey, and credited Hickey with his success against left-handed pitchers.[77] It helped that Hickey's pitches could still zip.

"You have to throw strikes with something on it," Hickey said. "You can't throw a carnival fastball or a Bugs Bunny curveball."[78]

Hickey still believed in his ability, and bragged that he had better stuff than anyone "from 40 feet."[79] He might have been right: Tom Hickey told how in 2011, newly acquired White Sox slugger Adam Dunn showed up to spring training, grabbed his bat, and tried to go into the batting cage where Hickey was tossing. Guillén stopped him and told him Dunn wasn't ready to face Hickey: He didn't want Hickey to destroy Dunn's confidence.[80]

"He's a luxury," Walker told the *Chicago Tribune* about having Hickey on the team. "He's got some gas in the tank and can still whip it up nicely."[81]

After the White Sox' 2005 World Series victory, the players voted for Hickey to receive a full share of the player proceeds from the playoff gate receipts.[82] Hickey cried when he heard the news.[83] It amounted to $390,000.[84] The money afforded Hickey a level of financial security he had never had. He was even able to afford a small condo in Wisconsin where he enjoyed hosting family and listening to music.[85] After scratching out a life in baseball against all odds, he was finally at peace.

Hickey continued to throw for White Sox hitters through the 2011 season and the following spring. On April 5, 2012, the White Sox were in Arlington, Texas, for their season opener against the Rangers the next day. Hickey was found unresponsive in his hotel room, the result of a seizure that cut off oxygen to his brain.[86] He was flown home to Chicago, but never woke up. The White Sox' Paul Konerko and A.J. Pierzynski visited him in his hospital room, which had a view of the White Sox ballpark, then called US Cellular Field.[87]

"Ask anyone in our clubhouse, every person here appreciated what Kevin did to help the White Sox win baseball games," Konerko told the *Sun-Times*. "No one wanted to win more, no one was more optimistic, no one cared more and no one took more pride in his job. He made all of us better."[88]

Kevin Hickey died on May 16, 2012, at the age of 56, survived by his siblings, his mother, five daughters, and three grandchildren.[89] The entire White Sox team served as honorary pallbearers at his funeral at Old St. Patrick's Church in Chicago.[90]

"There was only supposed to be four people from the White Sox attending, then the whole team pulled up in a bus," said Tom Hickey. "It's something I can't ever forget."[91]

That season, the White Sox wore a black diamond patch on their right sleeve embroidered with Hickey's nickname.[92] On September 3, 2012, the team honored Hickey in a pregame ceremony. It was announced that the ballpark batting cages would be renamed the Kevin Hickey Batting Cages, with the placement of a special commemorative plaque honoring his career and contributions to the White Sox.[93]

Kevin Hickey had made it back to the big leagues for good.

SOURCES

In addition to the sources cited in the Notes, the author consulted Baseball-reference.com and Stathead.com.

ACKNOWLEDGMENT

The author would like to thank Thomas and Karen Hickey for sharing memories of their brother. He would also like to thank the SABR BioProject committee, his wife, and two children for their patience during this article's too-long germination. Finally, as a Houston native he feels compelled to note for this volume that Orlando Palmeiro was safe.

NOTES

1   Mark Konkol, "Kevin Hickey, a Long Shot Who Fulfilled a Neighborhood Dream, Dies at 56," *Chicago Sun-Times*, May 16, 2012.

2   Judy Shoemaker, "The Hickeys of Brighton Park: Mother and Son," *Bill Gleason's Chicago Sports*, May 1983: 20-22.

3   Judy Shoemaker, "The Hickeys of Brighton Park."

4   Konkol, "Kevin Hickey."

5   Konkol, "Kevin Hickey."

6   Karen Hickey, in-person interview, February 23, 2024.

7   Thomas Hickey, in-person interview, July 27, 2023.

8   Konkol, "Kevin Hickey."

9   Thomas Hickey, in-person interview.

10   Konkol, "Kevin Hickey."

11   Konkol, "Kevin Hickey."

12   "Our History," 16inchsoftballhof.com. Accessed October 22, 2024, https://16inchsoftballhof.com/our-history/. A brick-and-mortar hall of fame for 16-inch softball resides in the Chicago suburb of Franklin Park, a sign of the enduring passion for the game in the city.

13   Larry Mayer, "Thillens Stadium: A Field of Memories Is Still Going Strong," *Chicago Tribune*, August 31, 1991. Accessed October 24, 2024, https://www.chicagotribune.com/1991/08/31/thillens-stadium-a-field-of-memories-is-still-going-strong/.

14   "Our History," 16inchsoftballhof.com.

15   Thomas Hickey, in-person interview.

16   Konkol, "Kevin Hickey"; Bill Gleason, "Hickey's Real Claim to Fame: He Was A Bobcat," *Chicago Sun-Times*, April 20, 1981.

17   Thomas Hickey, in-person interview.

18   Konkol, "Kevin Hickey."

19   Thomas Hickey, in-person interview.

20   Thomas Hickey, in-person interview.

21   Thomas Hickey, in-person interview.

22   Konkol, "Kevin Hickey."

23   Thomas Hickey, in-person interview.

24   "Why 'Schoup' was the ultimate character for Major League," JohnPielli.com, January 18, 2022. Accessed October 22, 2024. https://www.johnpielli.com/bases-empty-blog/why-schoup-was-the-ultimate-character-for-major-league.

25   "What's Up With … Kevin Hickey: Former Lefty Reliever Still Living Baseball Dream," *Chicago Sun-Times*, September 28, 2003: 90A.

26   Thomas Hickey, in-person interview.

27   Joe Goddard, "Lefty-Laden Chisox to Try Another," *Chicago Sun-Times*, February 23, 1980.

28   "What's Up With … Kevin Hickey."

29   Goddard, "Lefty-Laden Chisox to Try Another."

30   Judy Shoemaker, "The Hickeys of Brighton Park."

31   Bill Gleason, "Kevin Hickey's Place in Chicago Is Secure," *Chicago Sun-Times*, August 27, 1981. Hickey made only one error in 232⅔ big-league innings.

32   Konkol, "Kevin Hickey."

33   Konkol, "Kevin Hickey."

34   Thomas Hickey, in-person interview.

35   "Milwaukee Brewers vs Chicago White Sox Box Score: April 14, 1981," Baseball-Reference.com. Accessed October 22, 2024, https://www.baseball-reference.com/boxes/CHA/CHA198104140.shtml.

36   Thomas Hickey, in-person interview.

37   "Sox's Hickey Frets Only About the Hawks," *Chicago Tribune*. Date unknown, sourced from Hickey family scrapbook.

38   Frank Deford, "Some Like It Hot," *Sports Illustrated*, August 22, 1983. Accessed November 7, 2024, https://vault.si.com/vault/1983/08/22/some-like-it-hot.

39   Deford, "Some Like It Hot."

40   Deford, "Some Like It Hot."

41   Thomas Hickey, in-person interview.

42   Thomas Hickey, in-person interview.

43   Konkol, "Kevin Hickey."

44   Konkol, "Kevin Hickey."

45   Paul Schwartz, "Yanks Couldn't afford Hickey?" *Albany Times-Union*, May 24, 1985.

46   Attendance for the over the final two seasons of the Hawaii Islanders was under 100,000. Stacy Kaneshiro, "Islanders a Fan Hit During 27-Year Run," *Honolulu Advertiser*, July 4, 2009. Accessed October 22, 2024, https://the.honoluluadvertiser.com/article/2009/Jul/04/sp/hawaii907040333.html.

47   Konkol, "Kevin Hickey."

48   Thomas Hickey, in-person interview.

49   Konkol, "Kevin Hickey."

50   Jim Henneman, "Orioles' Hickey Happy to Help With 'Half-Saves,'" *Baltimore Sun*, July 3, 1989.

51   Jim Henneman, "Orioles' Hickey Happy to Help With 'Half-Saves.'"

52   Jim Henneman, "Orioles' Hickey Happy to Help With 'Half-Saves'"

53   Jim Henneman, "Orioles' Hickey Happy to Help With 'Half-Saves.'"

54   Thomas Hickey, in-person interview. Hickey met President Bush on a visit the president made to Baltimore's Memorial Stadium. One of the Bush grandchildren somehow became a fan of Hickey's, and during a meeting with his fan the gregarious lefty hit it off with the president. Bush also threw left-handed despite batting righty. On April 3, 1989, the 41st president threw out the first pitch on Opening Day in Baltimore. "President Bush Throws Out First Pitch," YouTube.com. Accessed October 26, 2024, https://www.youtube.com/watch?v=Gt_bQ_hveRo.

55   Ken Rosenthal, "'Immaculate' Hickey Is Looking to Clean Up on Mound, Too," *Baltimore Sun*, March 8, 1991. Accessed November 7, 2024. https://www.baltimoresun.com/1991/03/08/immaculate-hickey-is-looking-to-clean-up-on-mound-too/.

56   Thomas Hickey, in-person interview.

57   Konkol, "Kevin Hickey."

58   Major League II: Full Cast & Crew," Imdb.com. Accessed October 22, 2024, https://www.imdb.com/title/tt0110442/fullcredits/?ref_=tt_cl_sm.

59   *Major League II*, 1994, 1:10:17.

60   *Major League II*, 1:31:05.

61   *Major League II*, 1:31:22.

62   Konkol, "Kevin Hickey."

63   John Giannone, "Hickey: I Paid My Dues," *New York Daily News*, February 20, 1995.

64   Giannone, "Hickey: I Paid My Dues." The author also relied on his in-person interview with Thomas Hickey on July 27, 2023, regarding Kevin Hickey's sentiments about the 1981 and 1995 labor stoppages.

65   Thomas Hickey, in-person interview.

66   Giannone, "Hickey: I Paid My Dues."

67   "Kevin Hickey, 56; Orioles, White Sox Pitcher and Coach," *Boston Globe*, May 17, 2012: B12.

68   Konkol, "Kevin Hickey"; Thomas Hickey, in-person interview, July 27, 2023.

69   Thomas Hickey, in-person interview.

70   Konkol, "Kevin Hickey."

71   Thomas Hickey, in-person interview.

72   Konkol, "Kevin Hickey."

73   Konkol, "Kevin Hickey."

74   Dave van Dyck, "Sox Have What the Cubs Are Missing," *Chicago Tribune*, May 8, 2006. Accessed October 22, 2024, https://www.chicagotribune.com/2006/05/08/sox-have-what-the-cubs-are-missing/.

75   Thomas Hickey, in-person interview.

76   Konkol, "Kevin Hickey."

77   Scot Gregor, "Crede, Quentin escape to N.Y.," *Arlington Heights* (Illinois) Daily Herald, July 13, 2008. Accessed October 22, 2024, https://www.dailyherald.com/20080713/other-sports/crede-quentin-escape-to-n-y/. In 22 big-league seasons, Jim Thome posted a career .766 OPS against left-handed pitching. In 2008 he was in his age 37 season with the White Sox, and had an .858 OPS against lefties, the fourth-best mark of his career.

78   Dave van Dyck, "Sox Have What the Cubs Are Missing."

79   Konkol, "Kevin Hickey."

80   Thomas Hickey, in-person interview.

81   Mark Honzales, "Alternatives Left and Right for Guillen," *Chicago Tribune*, February 27, 2007, Section 4, 3.

82   Konkol, "Kevin Hickey."

83   Konkol, "Kevin Hickey."

84   Thomas Hickey, in-person interview.

85   Karen Hickey, in-person interview.

86   Konkol, "Kevin Hickey."

87   Konkol, "Kevin Hickey"; Judy Shoemaker, "The Hickeys of Brighton Park."

88   Konkol, "Kevin Hickey."

89   "White Sox Pregame Instructor Kevin Hickey Passes Away," MLB.com, May 16, 2012. Accessed October 22, 2024, https://www.mlb.com/news/white-sox-pre-game-instructor-kevin-hickey-passes-away/c-31426096.

90   Thomas Hickey, in-person interview, July 27, 2023.

91   Thomas Hickey, in-person interview, July 27, 2023.

92   "Dressed to the Nines: A History of the Baseball Uniform," National Baseball Hall of Fame and Museum online exhibit accessed November 7, 2024, http://exhibits.baseballhalloffame.org/dressed_to_the_nines/patches.htm.

93   "White Sox Honor Kevin Hickey," MLB.com, September 3, 2012. Accessed October 22, 2024, https://www.mlb.com/news/white-sox-honor-kevin-hickey/c-37843000.

ART KUSNYER

By Robert Bionaz

As a young and hopeful Art Kusnyer (pronounced KUSH-ner) started his professional baseball career in 1966, he made a contingency plan: "If I didn't make it in baseball, I wanted to be a highway patrolman," he told the author.[1] He never got to work for the highway patrol. Instead, the solidly built 6-foot-2, 197-pound Kusnyer, possessor of a powerful right-handed swing and a strong right arm, forged a 57-year career in professional baseball – 14 years as an active player, including parts of six seasons as a major-league catcher, 26 years as an active big-league coach, a year each as a rookie-league manager and advance scout, and 15 more years as a minor-league bullpen instructor and special assistant to the major-league staff with the Chicago White Sox.[2]

Born on December 19, 1945, in Akron, Ohio, to Ernest J. and Irene (Szalay) Kusnyer, Arthur William "Cave" Kusnyer,[3] the oldest of the family's four children, displayed athletic ability early. His father, Ernest, the owner of Ohio Speedometer Company in Akron, "took me out to play catch, and started me in a pee wee league when I was about five." Art's diamond exploits were being covered in the

Art Kusnyer   2005

local press by the time he was 10. On May 22, 1956, the local paper reported that he had hit a three-run home run for his Little League team in a 10-4 victory.[4] He continued to excel as he matured, pitching a no-hitter at 13 in 1959.[5] By 1962, he starred in both baseball and basketball at Buchtel High School, swinging a "merciless bat,"[6] and displaying "an eagerness for board work,"[7] as the starting center on the varsity basketball team. Competition for the best athlete was fierce in the Kusnyer family. By the time he graduated from Buchtel in 1964, Kusnyer had made a name for himself in and around Akron as a two-sport star:

> Art was not the only Kusnyer who excelled at sports. His father had been a force as a high school third baseman in Akron, eventually achieving induction into the Greater Akron Baseball Hall of Fame.[8] Irene, a bookkeeper in her husband's company, raised the children and fully participated in the family basketball games, where, her husband said, 'We'll knock [her] around a bit, but she can take it.'[9] Brother Jim, who Art said 'could jump out of the building,' starred in basketball as did Ernie and Andy. All four Kusnyer brothers eventually played college basketball, with Art averaging 10.5 points and four rebounds a game for Kent State in 1965-66, and Ernie starting for three years at Kansas State, averaging 12.7 points and 7.5 rebounds a game from 1971 to 1973.[10] It is little wonder that the Kusnyers were dubbed Akron's 'current No. 1 sports family,' and eventually, 'Akron's Athletic Family of the 20th Century.'[11]

After his high-school graduation in 1964, Art enrolled at Kent State University, where he played baseball and basketball. On June 7, 1966, the White Sox selected him in the 37th round of the amateur draft. White Sox scout Fred Schaffer signed Kusnyer contract on July 25,[12] and Kusnyer played for the White Sox' entry in the Gulf Coast League that summer. He moved to the Appleton Foxes in the low Class-A Midwest League in 1967. Playing primarily in the outfield on the league's best team, Kusnyer held his own, hitting .250 in 81 games with 7 home runs and 37 RBIs. He remained at Appleton in 1968, becoming a full-time catcher. He spent 1969 at Lynchburg in the high Class-A Carolina League, then moved up to Mobile in the Double-A Southern

League for 1970. On September 3, the White Sox recalled him from Mobile and he debuted in the second game of a Sunday doubleheader against the Kansas City Royals on September 21, 1970. He caught the entire game, going 0-for-4 at the plate against left-hander Bill Butler and right-hander Jim York. The last-place White Sox lost the game 8-2, loss number 97 in a wretched season that ended with the club posting a 56-106 record, the most losses in franchise history through 2023. Kusnyer played three more games that season, getting his first major-league hit on September 30, a single against California's Dave LaRoche. After the season the White Sox traded him to the Angels for right-handed pitcher Steve Kealey and catcher Dave Adlesh. Kusnyer spent most of the 1971 season at Triple-A Salt Lake City, again joining the major-league team in September. Finally, Kusnyer made the Opening Day roster of the 1972 Angels, spending the entire season in the majors. He hit .207 with 2 home runs and 13 RBIs in 64 games that season.

Ultimately, Kusnyer's major-league career fell short of what he wanted it to be. Looking back on his career in 1982, he said his intensity made things on the field more difficult than they might have been. "I worried so much that I'd press. It was like, if I didn't get four hits, I thought I'd failed."[13] Certainly his performance in Triple-A play did not presage his major-league hitting problems. Between 1971 and 1976, Kusnyer hit .280 in 445 games, with 63 home runs and 259 RBIs. In 1971 he hit .316, with 10 home runs and 75 RBIs for Salt Lake City in the Pacific Coast League. However, this minor-league record got him no consistent playing time in the big leagues. Part of a three-man catching tandem in his only full season, he started only 54 games. He later remembered, "I always wished I could've caught for two months straight. The most at-bats I ever got in a row was 16. ... Hitting was my downfall."[14]

Kusnyer played in only 41 games in 1973, none after July 31, as the Angels sent him to the minors in August, recalled him but did not play him in September, then traded him to the Milwaukee Brewers in a nine-player deal after the season.[15]

One of Kusnyer's final starts for California put him in august company: catching the 186th no-hitter in major-league history.[16] On July 15, 1973, at Detroit's Tiger Stadium, the Angels' Nolan Ryan pitched his second no-hitter of the season, beating Billy Martin's Tigers 6-0. Kusnyer, who had caught several of Ryan's starts in 1972 and 1973, scored the only run Ryan needed in the third inning when he singled, took third on a single by Sandy Alomar, and scored on a sacrifice fly by Vada Pinson.

Reminiscing about that day, Kusnyer remarked that Ryan, whose sometimes erratic control "could really beat you up behind the plate," had superb command, throwing his blazing fastball and sharp-breaking curve "almost always where he wanted to" on the way to 17 strikeouts in a dominant performance. Kusnyer knew in the first inning that Ryan had exceptional stuff, as he overheard Duke Sims

at the end of the first inning asking Norm Cash, "What's he throwing?" Cash, who had struck out to end the inning, told Sims, "Don't go up there." Cash came to the plate with two outs in the ninth holding a table leg as a bat. Told by umpire Ron Luciano that he couldn't use the piece of furniture, Cash replied, "Why not, I won't hit him anyway."[17] Cash then popped out to end the game. Four days later in Anaheim, Kusnyer caught Ryan again as the Angel right-hander took another no-hitter into the eighth. With consecutive no-hitters only six outs away, Ryan allowed a single to light-hitting Orioles shortstop Mark Belanger. Ryan went on to lose the game 3-1 in 11 innings.

Just over two weeks after he celebrated Ryan's no-hit achievement, the Angels optioned Kusnyer to Salt Lake City. Obviously disappointed, Kusnyer nevertheless went to the minors with his own slice of major-league immortality.

After 1973, Kusnyer got only another 47 at-bats in the major leagues, getting seven hits, dropping his final lifetime average to .176. He continued to have productive Triple-A seasons, but apparently no big-league team could use him, even as a backup. Despite his scant time on a major-league roster in his last two seasons, they were not without highlights: He had a single and a three-run double to key Milwaukee's 6-2 win over the Red Sox at County Stadium on July 3, 1976. Eighteen days later, he got his only major-league stolen base, a theft of second in Milwaukee's 5-0 win over the Kansas City Royals and his old Appleton teammate, right-hander Al Fitzmorris. When asked about the steal in 2024, he explained, "I got the steal sign and just hauled ass." In his final major-league season, playing for the Kansas City Royals, he hit his last major-league home run, against Frank Tanana of the Angels on June 26, 1978. Then on the final day of the 1978 season, in his final game as a major leaguer, Kusnyer drive in the only run of the game with a single against Twins left-hander Geoff Zahn.

The next season Kusnyer was back in the minors, playing for the Iowa Oaks in the Triple-A American Association. Kusnyer's manager in Des Moines was Tony La Russa, who liked his work with the team and wanted to make him a player-coach. As La Russa described it, "Art has an attitude about him, a play-hard, no-nonsense, winning-is-everything attitude that I like around a ballclub. ... Art works his butt off."[18] Although at first hesitant, Kusnyer eventually accepted La Russa's offer.

Most important, that position opened the possibility of getting back to the majors, as La Russa promised Kusnyer, "If I get a big-league job, I want you as a coach. I like the way you're working."[19] Kusnyer soon got his chance. On August 2, 1979, Don Kessinger resigned as Chicago's player-manager and was replaced by La Russa.[20] On November 14 La Russa kept his promise, hiring Kusnyer as the first-ever bullpen coach for the White Sox. Back in the majors, he stayed for more than 40 years.

In 1980 Kusnyer began an active coaching career that lasted 26 seasons, more than half of them working under

La Russa, "the best manager I ever worked for." Imbued with a solid work ethic provided by his father, along with a fierce competitiveness, Kusnyer tempered his intensity by developing a practical approach to dealing with professional players of varied backgrounds, temperaments, and abilities. He summed it up succinctly: "I let the guys have their fun as long as they took care of their business." That said, Kusnyer, renowned as a bullpen storyteller, always made taking care of business the priority. As he said, "To stay as long as I did, I had to be doing something right." The components of that something included game preparation in the La Russa mode, hours spent analyzing the opposition, potential strategies, potential personnel matchups, and ways to put the players he coached in the best possible situations.

Working with La Russa and the team's pitching coaches, Ron Schueler until 1982 and Dave Duncan from 1983 on, Kusnyer proved adept at creating a reasonably successful bullpen out of disparate pieces. During the 1980s the White Sox had no pitcher who filled the closer role for multiple seasons. Kusnyer's search for a reliable finisher depended upon identifying the guys "who wanted the ball, who had no fear," rather than using "the guys who talked a lot." In the 1980s, the White Sox never found that guy. In succession they used as the main closer Ed Farmer, rookie; Salomé Barojas, who inherited the closer role in 1982; a 1983 bullpen by committee – Barojas, Dennis Lamp, and Dick Tidrow. In 1984, no reliever posted more than 12 saves. In 1985 Bob James saved 32 games. Injured the next season, James dropped to 14 saves. Despite the club's lack of a reliable closer during the period from 1980 through 1986, Kusnyer's bullpen provided above-average production. Bettering the league bullpen ERA of 3.77, the White Sox posted a 3.58 ERA for the years 1980-86 and saved 263 games, an average of 37.6 saves a season, fourth in the American League. Although the White Sox often struggled during that era, Kusnyer's bullpen performed more than adequately.

Kusnyer's first stint as the White Sox bullpen coach ended after 1986. La Russa had been fired in midseason and at the beginning of 1987, first-base coach Ed Brinkman had health problems. At the request of new manager Jim Fregosi, Kusnyer assumed Brinkman's duties at first. The next year, 1988, the White Sox offered Kusnyer a managing job with the White Sox team in the Gulf Coast Rookie League. After managing the team to the third best record in the league, Kusnyer decided that he would prefer to remain a coach in the majors. "I liked what I was doing, I liked coaching," he said. He again got to do what he liked to do: On December 1, 1988, La Russa brought him to Oakland.

In Oakland Kusnyer inherited a far more stable bullpen than the one he had coached in Chicago. During each of his years with the Athletics, Dennis Eckersley worked as the club's closer. For five of his six years, left-hander Rick Honeycutt performed as one of the late inning set-up men for Eckersley. Complementing Honeycutt was right-hander

Gene Nelson. Kusnyer expressed great respect for both those players, noting that although they had their bullpen roles, they were always willing to pitch "whenever we needed them; if we need a lefty to pitch to left-handed hitters in the seventh, Honeycutt wanted the ball. Same with Nelson for the righties."

During Kusnyer's time as Oakland's bullpen coach, the Athletics won three division titles, two pennants, and one World Series – the 1989 "Earthquake Series," a 4-0 Athletics sweep, with play halted for 12 days by the devastating Loma Prieta quake on October 17.[21] With the A's victory in the Series, Kusnyer had achieved the ultimate goal for a major leaguer, winning a World Series ring.

Another American League pennant came in 1990, followed by a down year in 1991, then a rebound to a division championship in 1992. However, after 1992, the pitching staff deteriorated – veteran starters saw their performances decline, and young pitchers failed to pitch effectively. Although Eckersley continued as the closer, his ERA climbed above 4.00 as he got fewer save opportunities. With the Athletics committed to a youth movement and lots of losses in the near future, their manager chose to take another job. In late October, La Russa parted ways with the Athletics, signing a contract to manage the St. Louis Cardinals. He took Kusnyer with him, this time as an advance scout.

Kusnyer's time as a scout did not prove agreeable. He said, "I didn't like scouting, I wanted to be back on the field." Kusnyer succeeded in getting back on the field in 1997 as the White Sox hired him on the last day of October 1996, to again be their bullpen coach. His coaching career had come full circle. It proved to be his last major-league stop.

Now a veteran big-league coach, Kusnyer again handled the bullpen, as well as helping White Sox catchers with their defensive mechanics. Although the 1997 White Sox had an established closer in Roberto Hernández, his trade to San Francisco created uncertainty for Chicago's relievers. Matt Karchner took over the closer's role after Hernández left, followed in successive years by Bill Simas, Bob Howry, Keith Foulke, two seasons of closer by committee, then an emergent Shingo Takatsu in 2004. As for the team's performance, except for the surprise division title in 2000, it had been mediocre since 1994. In 2004 the White Sox finished a distant second after leading the division in July. However, during the 2004 season, general manager Ken Williams began remaking the club. The 2004 team had tied with the Yankees for the most home runs in the majors, but the 2005 squad would feature better speed and stronger pitching.

The formula worked as the 2005 White Sox, won their division by six games over the Cleveland Indians. The team then went 11-1 in the postseason, sweeping the Red Sox in the Division Series, beating the Angels in five games in the American League Championship Series, then sweeping the Houston Astros in the World Series – a dominant regular-season and postseason performance.

In truth, there was nothing easy about the 2005 White Sox season, particularly for Kusnyer and his bullpen. In the bullpen, Dámaso Marté, Cliff Politte, and Luis Vizcaíno were pitching effectively early in the season, soon to be joined by Neal Cotts, but Takatsu was having problems. After saving his eighth and final game on May 5, his ERA stood at 6.23. At that point, manager Ozzie Guillén, pitching coach Don Cooper, and Kusnyer, installed veteran Dustin Hermanson as the team's closer. Hermanson did the job, saving 30 games from May 6 to September 7. However, Hermanson's effectiveness began to be degraded by a back problem. With less than three weeks left in the season, the White Sox had to come up with someone who could close games. They decided to go with rookie Bobby Jenks. Kusnyer said the White Sox "had good reports on his pitching, and he could throw 100 miles an hour." Jenks saved six games for the White Sox down the stretch.

Kusnyer described that White Sox team, particularly the pitchers, as guys "who went out there every day knowing they were going to win." In the third game of the Division Series, Orlando Hernández demonstrated that unshakable belief. He was summoned to face the Red Sox in the sixth inning with Chicago leading 4-3 and the bases loaded with no outs. Someone in the bullpen mentioned pressure. Kusnyer heard Hernández reply, "Let me tell you what pressure is. Castro tried to kill me for five years." Hernández then calmly walked to the mound and retired the side without a run scoring. He pitched two more scoreless innings as the White Sox completed the sweep with a 5-3 win. Hernandez's effort typified the Chicago bullpen's performance that postseason. In 21 innings the bullpen allowed only three runs and nine hits and struck out 22.

Not to be outdone, after losing Game One of the ALCS, Chicago starters pitched four consecutive complete games – by Mark Buehrle, Jon Garland, Freddy Garcia, and José Contreras – to win the pennant. In the World Series sweep over Houston, Jenks pitched in all four games, saving two. Overall in the postseason, he made six appearances, allowing only two runs in eight innings, while saving four games. When he got pinch-hitter Orlando Palmeiro to ground out to shortstop Juan Uribe for the final out in the 1-0 title-clinching game, the White Sox celebrated their first World Series championship in 88 years.

After winning his second World Series ring, Kusnyer remained as bullpen coach in 2006 and 2007, finally relinquishing his coaching duties after his vision deteriorated due to detached retinas, for which multiple surgeries and other treatments proved unsuccessful.

After 42 years as an active player and coach in major-league baseball, how can Kusnyer's performance be evaluated? We have his playing record, but there are no parameters to gauge a coach's effectiveness. Nonetheless, it is possible to glean some insight into this question by listening to what his contemporaries said about him – managers and players especially. For Kusnyer, the record is decidedly not silent. In 1991, Tony La Russa said: "He was an excellent catcher. Kush knows a lot about setting up hitters. He's very important in the bullpen. ... There's no better work coach in baseball."[22] Rick Honeycutt emphasized Kusnyer's light but firm touch: "What Cave does, he's pretty much the kind of guy who keeps everybody loose down there ... but at the same time he takes control, too."[23]

The 2006 White Sox bullpen crew echoed La Russa and Honeycutt. Bobby Jenks mentioned the importance of bullpen humor because "we're allowed to be kids." He said Kusnyer had T-shirts made that said "Cave's Crew" on the front and featured Kusnyer's "top 10 sayings on the back."[24] David Riske found Kusnyer's unending store of tales therapeutic After a bad day, he said, "all you have to do is go out there the next day and listen to Cave."[25]

While they had fun in the bullpen, Kusnyer's crew knew that the time would come during a game "to stop laughing and start listening." After Kusnyer left the coaching ranks, Matt Thornton and Bobby Jenks summed up what he meant to them, to the team. Thornton described baseball as "his life, his passion," and noted that "he loved his guys."[26] Jenks credited Kusnyer with helping him "grow" into the closer's role, saying, "He'll always let you be yourself," while affirming his professionalism: "No matter what the situation was, he was able to get [each player] ready for that situation."[27]

Not surprisingly, after his eye problems precluded a return to coaching, Kusnyer continued his affiliation with the team another 15 years, going to spring training as a uniformed member of the club, traveling with the team during the season, and contributing wherever he could. Finally, after the 2022 season, he actually retired.[28]

In 1968 Kusnyer wrote that his ambition in baseball was "to play in the majors." He did that and much more, as during his major-league playing and coaching career, he earned the admiration and respect of both his managers and his players. His career spanned nearly 60 years, beginning in the pitching-rich era of the 1960s and 1970s, and ending in the high-scoring, home-run-happy 2000s. He experienced the end of the reserve clause, the drug scandals of the 1980s, and the steroid era of the late 1990s and early 2000s. All that time, he was able to adapt to the game's changes and get the most out of the men who played for him.

As of 2024, Kusnyer lived in Florida with his wife, Judy. They have been married since 1967, and have a son, Ryan. The highway patrol? It turned out Art Kusnyer never had to apply.

THE 2005 WORLD CHAMPION CHICAGO WHITE SOX

SOURCES

In addition to the sources credited in the Notes, the author consulted Baseball-Reference.com and Retrosheet.org for background information on players, teams, and seasons.

The author thanks Art Kusnyer for his indispensable contributions to this biography.

NOTES

1   Unless otherwise attributed, all direct quotations from Art Kusnyer come from interviews with the author on May 24, June 11, and June 13, 2024.

2   Scott Gregor, "With His Future in Doubt Because of Injury, Kreuter Is Released," *Arlington Heights* (Illinois) *Daily Herald,* November 1, 1996: 27.

3   According to Kusnyer, in 1976 Lenn Sakata was responsible for the nickname Cave, which is short for Caveman. Mike Berardino, "q&a with Art Kusnyer," *South Florida Sun-Sentinel* (Fort Lauderdale), July 23, 2007: 42.

4   "Little League Openers Feature 2 No-Hitters," *Akron Beacon Journal,* May 22, 1956: 34.

5   "Anop Wins Homerun Duel," *Akron Beacon Journal,* July 17, 1959: 34.

6   "Hoban Ready for ICC Final," *Akron Beacon Journal,* May 15, 1962: 14.

7   John Flynn, "Pressure Is on Garfield, Buchtel," *Akron Beacon Journal,* May 5, 1962: 20.

8   Ernie Kusnyer Sr., Greater Akron Baseball Hall of Fame. Ernie Sr. was a decorated Marine, serving during World War II in the Pacific; he was wounded in the 1944 invasion of Guam. "The Big Parade," *Akron Beacon Journal,* October 19, 1944: 8.

9   John Flynn, "Even Mom Plays for Kusnyers," *Akron Beacon Journal,* February 4, 1968: 39.

10 SRCBB (college basketball), https://www.sports-reference.com/cbb/, accessed May 25, 2024.

11 Bill Lilley, "First Family of Akron Athletics," *Akron Beacon Journal,* January 2, 2000: 47, 52.

12 LA84 Foundation, "The Sporting News Baseball Players Contract Card Collection," https://digital.la84.org/digital/collection/p17103coll3, accessed June 11, 2024.

13 Bob Nold, "Kusnyer Story Has a Happy Ending," *Akron Beacon Journal,* August 5, 1982: 17.

14 Nold.

15 "Kusnyer Goes to Brewers," *Akron Beacon Journal,* October 23, 1973: 17. From California, Kusnyer, left-handed pitchers Clyde Wright and Steve Barber, and outfielder Ken Berry went to the Brewers for catcher Ellie Rodriguez, outfielders Ollie Brown and Joe Lahoud, and right-handed pitchers Skip Lockwood and Gary Ryerson.

16 No-Hitters.com, https://www.nonohitters.com/no-hitters/, accessed June 11, 2024.

17 Gregory H. Wolf, "July 15, 1973: Nolan Ryan tosses second no-hitter of season for Angels," in Scott Ferkovich, ed., *Tigers by the Tail: Great Games at Michigan And Trumbull* (Phoenix: SABR, 2016); https://sabr.org/gamesproj/game/july-15-1973-nolan-ryan-tosses-second-no-hitter-of-season-for-angels/, accessed June 11, 2024.

18 Nold, "Kusnyer Story Has a Happy Ending."

19 Nold.

20 "Kessinger Calls It Quits with Chicago," *San Francisco Examiner,* August 2, 1979: 67.

21 John Hillyer, "Game 3 Put on Hold," *San Francisco Examiner,* October 18, 1989: 14.

22 Casey Tefertiller, "Unknowns Who Craft Bay Clubs," *San Francisco Examiner,* April 7, 1991: 34.

23 Tefertiller.

24 David Haugh, "Secret of Sox Relievers' Success? Hijinks, Till It's Time to Buckle Down," *Chicago Tribune,* August 13, 2006: 3-12.

25 Haugh.

26 Mark Gonzales, "Sox Look Forward To Kusnyer Reunion," *Chicago Tribune,* April 18, 2008: 4-4.

27 Gonzales.

28 2022 *Chicago White Sox Media Guide,* 49.

TIM RAINES

By Norm King

When fans watched the Montreal Expos in the early 1980s, it was sometimes hard for them to determine if they were at a baseball game or a track meet. Players like Rodney Scott, Andre Dawson, and Jerry White ran roughshod over National League catchers. But no Expos player turned the tools of ignorance into tools of frustration more than Tim "Rock" Raines. He stole 70 or more bases six times and as of 2024 was fifth in career steals with 808, behind Rickey Henderson (1,406), Lou Brock (938), Billy Hamilton (914), and Ty Cobb (897), all of whom are in the Hall of Fame.

Raines was elected to the National Baseball Hall of Fame in 2017. The Hall notes, "Raines finished his big-league career with the best stolen base percentage (84.7) of any player with 400-plus steals (since caught stealing became an official statistic in 1951)."[1]

Timothy Raines was born on September 16, 1959, in Sanford, Florida, to Ned and Florence Raines. Ned was a semipro player in the Sanford area and Raines grew up in an athletic and competitive household of six children. (A seventh died at the age of 4 when she was hit by a car.) "We'd race against Pop as kids until somebody beat him," said Tim. "I was the first to do it. I was 15."[2]

Raines was one of five boys, and in one local all-star game, the entire infield for one team consisted of Raines brothers: Levi at first, Sam at second, Ned III at the hot corner, and Tim at shortstop. Raines recalled, "In one all-star game of my childhood, my brothers and I formed the entire infield. It may have been one of the games that my father volunteered to umpire, though he refused to call balls and strikes in any games we played in. The local newspaper took note of our family ties, publishing stories about our exploits with headlines like When It Raines, It Pours."[3]

In fact, Ned thought that his namesake would make the majors before Tim did. Ned III played in the San Francisco Giants' system, but never made the major leagues. "When we were in the minors, my dad thought he was the better player," said Raines with a mischievous grin. "Ned is just as good as I am, he just wasn't as lucky as I am."[4]

Raines was a multisport athlete at Seminole High School. In addition to playing baseball, he ran track, and in football scored 18 touchdowns and averaged 10.5 yards per carry as a running back. Despite his impressive gridiron statistics, Raines chose baseball as a career and signed with the Expos after he graduated from high school when they chose him in the fifth round of the 1977 amateur draft.

Raines said, "Back then, the draft wasn't televised, so I had no option other than to wait for our home phone to ring. And when it finally did, it wasn't someone from the Dodgers on the other end. The call came from the Montreal Expos, who despite never making their interest in me known, had caught enough of a glimpse of me to pick me with the second pick of the fifth round. (Seeing as I was the first nonpitcher drafted by the Expos that year, I've jokingly referred to myself over the years as a number 1 pick)."[5]

Still not old enough to drink or vote, the 17-year-old Raines reported to the Expos' Gulf Coast League rookie-level team, where he batted a respectable .280 with a noteworthy .381 on-base percentage in 49 games (he walked 27 times), stole 29 bases, and, more significantly, was caught only twice. He played 27 games at second base and six games each at third base and the outfield.

Raines really gave the Expos an idea of what they had when he moved up to the West Palm Beach Expos of the Class-A Florida State League in 1978. Despite missing 30 games because of injury, he hit a respectable .287 and, with

Tim Raines   2005

64 walks, had an excellent .400 on-base percentage. But what set him apart was his 57 stolen bases, which broke the team record of 48 set the previous season by Lonnie Harris, and placed him third in the league behind Tito Landrum (68) and Dennis Webb (61).

Any doubts the Expos had about their budding star disappeared in 1979 when Raines moved up to Memphis of the Double-A Southern League. Although still a teenager, Raines hit a solid .290, whacked his first five home runs as a professional, stole 59 bases (second in the league), led the league with 104 runs scored, and had a .390 on-base percentage. This led to his first taste of life in "The Show," during which he appeared in six games for the Expos as a pinch-runner and stole two bases without getting thrown out.

Raines also married his high-school sweetheart, Virginia Hilton, in 1979. Their first child, Tim Raines Jr., was also born that year.

The great numbers notwithstanding, the Expos felt that Raines still needed some seasoning, so they sent him to the Denver Bears of the Triple-A American Association for 1980. This club is listed at number 37 in the milb.com list of greatest minor-league teams of all time.[6] The Bears roared to a 92-44 record and won their division by 21½ games, with Raines a major factor in the team's success. He won the league batting title with a .3543 batting average, .0002 points ahead of Orlando Gonzales of the Oklahoma City 89ers. Raines tied for the league lead in triples and set a league record for stolen bases with 77. He won the American Association Rookie of the Year award and was *The Sporting News'* 1980 Minor League Player of the Year.

Raines also got into 15 games that year with the Expos and managed only a single in 20 at-bats. He played a few games in left field, a position he had never played in the minors (he had been almost exclusively a middle infielder) but where he became an All-Star seven times in the majors. Raines also stole five bases, again without being caught stealing.

Raines launched his major-league career with the Expos in 1981. And launched is the appropriate word because, unlike the Energizer Bunny, opposing batteries couldn't stop him from going and going; he stole 20 bases in his first 19 games before finally getting thrown out in a game against the Dodgers on May 2. As Jim Kaplan wrote in *Sports Illustrated:*

"There was rejoicing in the National League last Saturday. Baseball's Raines of Terror had ended. After stealing 27 consecutive bases over three seasons, just 11 short of the major league record, Montreal's Tim Raines was thrown out by Los Angeles Catcher Mike Scioscia trying to steal third at Olympic Stadium. From New York to San Diego pitchers and catchers embraced, second basemen and shortstops cried for joy and managers began to breathe again, albeit nervously."[7]

It was also when he became a full-fledged Expo that Raines earned his nickname, Rock, because he had only 7.8 percent body fat. For good measure, Tim Jr. was called Little Rock.[8]

The fast start was no fluke. In 88 games during that strike-shortened season, Raines hit .304, scored 61 runs, and led the league with 71 stolen bases. He made the All-Star team and finished second in the Rookie of the Year vote behind Fernando Valenzuela.

Raines had a decent second year, but the sad part about any sophomore jinx he may have had was the fact that it was self-inflicted. He was an All-Star again and led the league in stolen bases for the second year in a row, with 78. He also had 179 hits, good enough for eighth in the National League. However, his average dropped to .277, and he hit four home runs, one less than 1981, despite having more than twice as many at-bats. He also got caught off base numerous times, and often appeared lost in the outfield. The Expos even moved him back to his original position of second base to get him on track.

"We moved him to second base for a while and there were times he held the ball without making a play," said former team President John McHale.[9]

At the time, Raines blamed his diminished play on personal difficulties, including a miscarriage by his wife and the death of a favorite uncle. But in truth, the early 1980s were an era of extensive drug use among major-league players. In order to fit in, Raines began experimenting with cocaine and eventually got hooked.

"Once I got into the big leagues, you just sort of want to fit in," Raines told a sportswriter. "I felt it was an experiment. I tried and I got hooked. You can't just turn it on and off that easily. I just got in with the wrong people."[10]

Fortunately for Raines, he made the right decisions and got in with the right person after the 1982 season ended. He went into drug rehabilitation and forged a strong relationship with teammate Andre Dawson. Their friendship grew so strong that Raines named his second son after his mentor. Raines later said, "When Virginia gave birth to our second son in July 1983, we had an easy time selecting a name: Andre. We wanted to honor my friend and all he had done to help get me on the straight and narrow. My second son even took on a miniature version of his godfather's nickname: Little Hawk."[11]

The drug rehabilitation worked as Raines rebounded to have an excellent 1983 season and, more importantly, he stayed off drugs. He led the league in steals again, with a career-high 90, as well as in runs scored, with 133. His batting average improved to .298, and he was fourth in the league with a .393 on-base percentage. He drove in 71 runs, making him the first player in the National League to drive in 70 runs and steal 70 bases in the same season.[12] He also made his third straight All-Star team.

The 1984 season was a tough one for the Expos; their 78-83 record marked the first time they played below .500

GRINDERS AND GAMERS

since 1978. Nonetheless, Raines had another excellent season. He hit over .300 (.309) for the first time over a full season (160 games). He made it 4-for-4 in both All-Star Game appearances and stolen-base crowns (75 steals) and led the league in doubles, with 38.

Raines' 1985 season was a winner before he even set foot on a diamond when he was awarded $1.2 million in his pay arbitration case, a record at the time. (The Expos had offered $1 million even.) On the field it was more excellent numbers. Raines made his fifth All-Star Game appearance, his 70 steals were second in the league to Vince Coleman's 110, and he was third in the league in both batting (.320) and on-base percentage (.405).

Excellent numbers aside, Raines' past peccadillos were again brought to public attention when he was one of more than 11 players who testified at a grand jury hearing that led to the indictment of seven men on 165 drug counts in Pittsburgh. He did not testify at the trial.

Raines' next two seasons were perhaps the finest of his career, even though he didn't win the stolen-base crown either season. He won his only batting title in 1986 with a .334 average and led the league with a .413 on-base percentage. He was an All-Star again and won the Silver Slugger award for his position. He stole 70 bases – the sixth season in a row in which he had 70 or more steals – good for third in the league.

Ordinarily, a free agent would have difficulty keeping track of all the offers coming his way after a season like that, but this was the infamous era of collusion among major-league owners, so for Raines the overtures from other teams were few and far between. Raines recalled, "The owners' unwillingness to pay the best players in the game what we deserved left a bad taste in my mouth. Baseball fans should have been talking about my accomplishments on the field, not my contract situation. All I wanted was to play ball. But I also felt I deserved fair compensation for my services. It didn't seem right that a bunch of rich owners could get together and collude to drive salaries down. It became a matter of principle."[13]

"Raines, given no opportunity to counter take-it-or-leave-it offers from the San Diego Padres, Houston Astros and Atlanta Braves, has reportedly agreed to return to the Montreal Expos at the same terms he initially rejected: Three years for $4.8 million, with another $200,000 a year thrown in to counter Canadian taxes," wrote Ross Newhan in the *Los Angeles Times*.[14]

Under the rules at the time, Raines couldn't sign with the team until May 1. He made his return on May 2, 1987, when the Expos played the World Series champion New York Mets at Shea Stadium. His belated season debut went down in Expo lore as one of the great days in team history. Without having the benefit of spring training, Raines was spectacular in his first game back: 4-for-5, a triple (off the first pitch he saw that season), a stolen base, and a 10th-inning grand slam that was the difference in an 11-7 Expos

win. Raines said, "That game remains one of the most memorable of my career. In addition to solidifying my role as a team leader, it served as a great national showcase for the Expos. I think it also showed that teams had made a mistake by not bidding for my services."[15]

Raines' return sparked the Expos as well. Nobody expected much from the team that season. *Sports Illustrated* predicted they would lose 98 games, and that number looked optimistic when the Expos lost their first five games of the season. They were 8-13 the day Raines' name first appeared on manager Buck Rodgers' lineup card, but they went 83-58 the rest of the way and were in the race up until the last week of the season, finishing in third place, four games out, with a 91-71 record. For the year, Raines led the league in runs scored, with 123, hit .330, achieved a career high in home runs with 18, and had a .429 on-base percentage.

As well, Raines was not only an All-Star, but he was also voted All-Star Game MVP on the strength of three hits, a stolen base, and a two-run triple that broke up a scoreless tie in the 13th inning. The irony of that performance was that it was his last appearance in an All-Star Game.

As good as 1987 was for Raines, the rest of the decade was eminently forgettable. Injuries limited him to 109 games in 1988. His average plummeted 60 points to .270 and his stolen-base total dropped to 33. He bounced back in 1989 with a .286 average, and while the days of 70-plus steals were only a memory, he still swiped 41. Also, his .395 on-base percentage was good enough for fifth in the league. Injuries again limited Raines' playing time to 130 games in 1990. He hit .287 and scored only 65 runs, but he stole 49 bases, sixth in the league.

By the end of the 1990 season, the Expos looked at their options regarding Raines and arrived at the following conclusions:

- His production had declined in the past few years.
- He was 30 years old.
- They had younger, promising outfielders, including Larry Walker, Marquis Grissom, and Dave Martinez.

Consequently, the Expos traded Raines to the Chicago White Sox on December 23, 1990, along with pitcher Jeff Carter and a player to be named later (minor-league pitcher Mario Brito) for outfielder Iván Calderón and pitcher Barry Jones.

The trade worked out well for Raines. In 1991, he played in more than 150 games (155) for the first time since 1986. Statistically, he had the lowest batting average of his career up to that point (.268), but was third in the league in stolen bases with 51, and his 102 runs scored were ninth in the league. He crossed American League home plates 102 times in 1992, sixth in the league this time, as his batting average shot back up to a more Raines-like .294.

The White Sox were an up-and-coming team when Raines joined them. They hadn't reached the playoffs since 1983, and despite some good records early in the 1990s, they had the misfortune of being in the same division as some strong Oakland and Minnesota clubs. They finally won another division crown in 1993, with a significant contribution from Raines, even though he missed six weeks early in the season with a thumb injury. The 33-year-old Raines was slowing down, as he stole only 21 bases in 115 games, less than half his total the previous season. Nonetheless, he hit .306 and had 16 home runs to go along with a .401 on-base percentage. That last total would have put Raines in the league's top 10 if he had had enough plate appearances to qualify.

The White Sox lost the American League Championship Series to the Toronto Blue Jays in six games. Raines had an excellent series, with 12 hits in 27 at-bats (.444) and a .483 on-base percentage in a losing cause.

Had there been a playoff in 1994, the White Sox would have been there again; they were leading the American League Central Division when the season-ending strike began. Raines hit .266 in 101 games and his stolen-base totals continued to decline as he stole only 13. Injuries continued to dog him in 1995; he played in 133 games. Despite a .285 batting average and 12 home runs, Raines again reached only 13 in the stolen-base department. The team itself was also in decline, finishing with a 68-76 record (.472) after being a contender every year since 1990. Those 13 steals were the result, Raines said, of hitting in front of Frank Thomas.

"[Raines] says part of the reason he stole just 13 bases was that the White Sox, particularly cleanup hitter Frank Thomas, didn't want him running," wrote Jon Heyman in *The Sporting News*. "'I don't feel like I've slowed. I feel like I was slowed down by them not wanting me to run,' Raines says."[16]

The White Sox obviously disagreed with Raines' self-assessment, because they traded him to the New York Yankees in December 1995 for a minor-league pitcher named Blaise Kozeniewski, whose career ended after 1995. In essence, the White Sox gave Raines away.

If timing is everything, then Raines had everything when he joined the Yankees. The Bombers were just beginning their late-'90s era of dominance when Raines joined the roster. Injuries plagued him in his three years with the team (1996-98) and limited him to an average of 81 games per season, but he finally got to play in a World Series (1996) and he won two World Series rings (1996, 1998). Despite the limited playing time, an analysis of Raines' numbers shows that he was quite productive when he did play. His cumulative batting average for the three seasons was .299 with a .395 on-base percentage, but he stole only 12 bases. He scored a total of 154 runs, which would have averaged out to 104 runs over a 162-game season.

Raines became a free agent after the 1998 season, and he signed on with the Oakland A's for $600,000, less than half of his $1.3 million salary of the previous season. Money matters became of secondary importance, however, on July 16, 1999, as Raines ran to the outfield for a game against the Giants. After what had been a routine jog to his position, he suddenly felt exhausted, and went to the hospital that day with swollen ankles and knees. He underwent a series of tests, including a kidney biopsy.

"The tests showed Raines had lupus, a chronic auto-immune disease that causes the immune system to attack normal tissue," wrote Jeff Pearlman in *Sports Illustrated*. "It is incurable but treatable. In Raines's case the lupus attacked his kidneys, causing excessive water retention."[17]

The subsequent eight months were difficult for Raines as he underwent treatment that included radiation and medication. His weight fell to 170 pounds.

"My jeans would hang off my body, like the kids today wear them," he told Pearlman. "But it wasn't on purpose."[18]

Raines' health improved as spring training for the 2000 season rolled around. He attended the Yankees' training camp but didn't make the team. Yankees general manager Bob Watson, who co-chaired the US Olympic baseball team selection committee, invited him to try out for the squad, but he didn't make that roster, either.

Not all the news was bad for Raines in 2000. He was inducted into the Expos Hall of Fame that year, and while he was in Montreal, he told team owner Jeffrey Loria in all sincerity that he wanted a shot at returning to the Expos in 2001.

Raines was invited to the 2001 Expos training camp and he made the team on the strength of a .414 spring-training average. He served as a fifth outfielder and unofficial coach for the team's young outfielders. He played in 47 games, hit .308 with a .433 on-base percentage, and stole the 808th and final base of his career on September 25 against the Mets at Olympic Stadium.

Nine days later, the Expos sold Raines to the Orioles, which gave him an opportunity to do some father-son bonding in a way that had been done only once before in the major leagues, by Ken Griffey Sr. and Ken Griffey Jr. with Seattle in 1990. The Raineses duplicated the feat on October 3, 2001, when Tim Sr. pinch-hit in a game in which Tim Jr. was playing center field. Raines recalled, "We stood next to each other during the national anthem that night. I'm not a guy who sheds many tears, but after everything I had experienced the previous couple of years, not to mention what the country was going through at the time, I couldn't help but get emotional. With Tim Jr. batting leadoff and playing center field that night, manager Mike Hargrove inserted me into the game as a pinch-hitter in the seventh inning."[19] The following night, the two played the full game together. In all, father and son appeared in the same box score four times.[20]

Raines' playing career finally came to an end in 2002. The Marlins signed him as a free agent during spring training, and in 98 games during the season, the 42-year-old hit only .191, after which he retired. And so ended a career in which he batted .298 with 2,605 hits, a .385 on-base percentage and 1,571 runs scored. He was one of a few players to play in four different decades and one of only four to steal a base in four decades. (The other three are Ted Williams, Rickey Henderson, and Omar Vizquel.)

After retiring as a player, Raines stayed in baseball. He managed in the Expos' minor-league system, and the team retired his number 30 in 2004, its last year in Montreal. He was a coach with the White Sox in 2005, the year they broke the Curse of the Black Sox and won the World Series. Raines said, "The combination of power, speed, and pitching took the White Sox to new places, and it was a joy to be along for the ride. After winning 99 games and the division title, we ripped through the competition in the postseason, losing only one game, in the American League Championship Series, en route to the White Sox's first title since 1917. I'm not sure that winning a World Series as a coach is the same as winning one as a participant, but as someone who had two rings as a player, I found special meaning in getting another as a coach. I was equally excited for my onetime teammate Frank Thomas, who, after 16 years with the White Sox, finally got to play on a championship team in his last season in Chicago. Unfortunately, Frank didn't participate in the postseason due to injury, but he got a tremendous ovation when he threw out the first pitch of Game 1 of the ALDS."[21]

Raines has managed in the independent Atlantic League, and was back in Organized Baseball in 2013 with the Toronto Blue Jays as a minor-league baserunning and outfield instructor.

Also in 2013, Raines was inducted into the Canadian Baseball Hall of Fame in St. Mary's, Ontario. The occasion gave him an opportunity to reflect on how he felt playing for the Expos.

"I loved the fans in Montreal," Raines said during his acceptance speech. "I loved the noise they made at the Big Owe. The more they cheered the more I wanted to do for them."[22]

Tim Raines was elected to the National Baseball Hall of Fame in 2017, voted in by 86 percent of those who cast ballots.

In June 2017 Triumph Books published Tim Raines' autobiography, *Rock Solid: My Life in Baseball's Fast Lane*, written with Alan Maimon.

SOURCES

In addition to the sources cited in the Notes, the author consulted Baseball-Reference.com and numerous other sources.

This biography of Tim Raines was updated in 2024 by Eric Conrad.

NOTES

1 https://baseballhall.org/hall-of-famers/rainestim#:~:text=Raines%20 finished%20his%20big%20league%20career%20with%20the%20best%20 stolen,Hall%20of%20Fame%20in%202017.

2 Ron Fimrite, "Don't Knock the Rock," *Sports Illustrated*, June 25, 1984.

3 Tim Raines and Alan Maimon, *Rock Solid: My Life in Baseball's Fast Lane* (Chicago: Triumph Books, 2017), 21.

4 Associated Press, "Ned Raines missed guessing who's best," *Tuscaloosa News*, April 4, 1982.

5 Raines and Maimon, 30-31.

6 100 Best Minor League Baseball Teams https://web.archive.org/ web/20221112223244/https://secure.milb.com/milb/history/top100.jsp.

7 Jim Kaplan, "Raines Really Pours It On," *Sports Illustrated*, May 11, 1981.

8 Kaplan.

9 Murray Chass, "Cocaine Confessions: Players, Teams Lose Out," *Palm Beach Post* (reprinted from the *New York Times*), August 20, 1985.

10 Chass.

11 Raines and Maimon, 75.

12 Ian MacDonald, "Montreal Rehashes Carter Signing," *The Sporting News*, October 12, 1983.

13 Raines and Maimon, 98.

14 Ross Newhan, "Collusion, or a New Coercion?: Baseball Is Paying Under New Rules," *Los Angeles Times*, April 4, 1987.

15 Raines and Maimon, 100-101.

16 Jon Heyman, "Raines Thrilled," *The Sporting News*, January 8, 1996.

17 Jeff Pearlman, "Like a Rock," *Sports Illustrated*, April 16, 2001.

18 Pearlman.

19 Raines and Maimon, 233.

20 That's where any comparison between Ken Griffey Jr. and Tim Raines Jr. ends. Raines played only 75 major-league games over three seasons.

21 Raines and Maimon, 238.

22 Bill Young, "Tim Raines Says Thank You Montreal," *Montreal Gazette*, July 24, 2013.

GREG WALKER

By Kirk Weber

Greg Lee Walker was born in the south-central Georgia town of Douglas on October 6, 1959. He was the youngest of three children. His father Billy was a feed salesman and then a vocational agriculture teacher. During his free time he was a well-known local softball player. Greg credits inheriting his work ethic from his father who told him, "You go to work every day no matter how you feel and you give it your best shot and take the results."[1] Greg was a multi-sport athlete at Coffee High School where he won the Trojan Award given to the best athlete at the high school. In baseball he started off as a catcher, but switched over to first base after separating his shoulder while playing quarterback for the football team. He was described by his principal as "a serious student," adding "You would never notice him in a group of people because he was always listening."[2]

After graduating from Coffee High, he was selected as the 511th pick in the 20th round of the June 1977 amateur draft by the Philadelphia Phillies, where he was scheduled to report to their Class-A short-season club in Auburn, New York. He played in 33 games for the Auburn Phillies that

Greg Walker   2005

season, with 114 plate appearances, batting a .255 batting average, with two home runs and eight RBIs. He continued to play in the Phillies farm system for three seasons, all in Class-A ball – including 1978 Spartanburg of the Western Carolina League, and in 1979 Peninsula of the Carolina League. It was during the 1979 season that Walker attracted the attention of White Sox special assignment scout, and future general manager of the six-time NBA champion Chicago Bulls, Jerry Krause. Specifically, what impressed Krause was Walker's swing. "You look for swings. Walker has a short swing for a big man. Guys with short strokes leave less room for error."[3]

Walker stood 6-foot-3 and is listed at 205 pounds. He batted left-handed but threw right-handed. When Walker was left unprotected by the Phillies after the 1979 season, Jerry Krause put in a call to White Sox general manager Roland Hemond. "He can hit." Krause told him. "He's 20, the same age as a college junior. If he'd been in college, he'd have been a high draft choice."[4]   So the White Sox claimed him. From there Walker began to steadily move up the White Sox farm system. advancing from Single-A Appleton to Double-A Gens Falls, to Triple-A Edmonton.

In September of 1982, after 560 total games in the minor leagues, Walker was called up to the White Sox due to both Tom Paciorek and Mike Squires suffering injuries. Joining the club on September 15, he collected his first base hit in his first time up, on September 18th a pinch-hit single to right field off the Oakland Athletics' Brian Kingman. He finished the season playing in 11 games and getting seven hits in 19 plate appearances, hitting for a .412 batting average. Walker's major-league career was just getting started.

1983 was quite the eventful year on the south side of Chicago. Comiskey Park hosted the 50th All-Star Game, won by the American League 13-3 with Fred Lynn of the California Angels getting the game MVP award. That year the White Sox did something no Chicago baseball team had done since 1959. They made the postseason. Walker said, "We knew we had a good team coming off of the year before, I was just happy to be in the big leagues. We knew we had great pitching but we didn't get off to a great start. We made the comeback and the starting pitching was just phenomenal in the second half."[5] "Winning Ugly" was what they called their style of baseball on the south side of Chicago that summer, and win they did. The Sox won the American League West title by 20 games over the Royals with a record of 99-63, a regular-season record they would match again in 2005. In his first full season, Greg Walker played in 118 games and had a batting average of .270 with 10 home runs and 55 RBIs. In the field he had a .985 fielding percentage at first base.

The White Sox played the Baltimore Orioles in the American League Championship Series, winning the first game 2-1, but the Orioles took control after that, winning the series three games to one. Greg Walker played in two games, getting one hit in three at-bats, a leadoff single in the bottom of the seventh of Game Four.

Walker continued producing in his quiet way as his career continued.   In 1984, he hit .294 for the season .308 after the All-Star break, and .381 in the month of September earning him the American League Player of the Month Award. "I'm not really worried about what numbers I have or am going to have.   At this point, I just want to put consistent years together."[6]

In 1985, Walker hit .258 with 24 home runs and 92 RBIs while he appeared in 163 games – the 163rd game being a tie game that was called due to rain in the seventh inning on July 31 against the Red Sox. This tied him for the team record for most games played in a season. Looked at as a solid team leader and a consistent player. The 1986 season he only played in 78 games due to wrist injuries, but batted .277 with 13 home runs and 51 RBIs. Then came July of 1988. The summer of 1988 in Chicago was one of the hottest on record up to that time, with 47 days of 90-plus degrees and seven days in the triple digits.[7] July 30 was hot and muggy as the White Sox prepared for their game at Comiskey Park against the California Angels. Walker was fielding grounders at first base when he suddenly went down on one knee. As Walker tells it, "It felt like something stabbed me in my hip. I knew it was bad. The first thing it thought of was, I'm having a heart attack and I'm dead."[8]

Walker collapsed and went into convulsions. Right there on the infield Herm Schneider, the White Sox trainer – with the assistance of the Angels trainer – used a pair of tape-cutting scissors to pull Walker's tongue from his throat. "It was a life threatening situation," Schneider said. "He was struggling to stay alive. He turned blue."[9] He was rushed to a nearby suburban hospital.   The next day in the hospital with his six-months-pregnant wife Carman in the room, he suffered another seizure.

During his hospitalization Walker went through a battery of tests, and it was determined that the seizures were caused by cerebral vasculitis, inflamed blood vessels of the walls in the brain, a condition that is serious but treatable with medication. On August 15, Walker had an allergic reaction to Dilantin, the medication he was prescribed for his seizures. He had to be placed on drugs that kept him heavily sedated. "For the next two months I just walked around in a daze.[10]

Once home from the hospital, teammate Bobby Thigpen lived with Walker and his family and helped him adjust to life and preparing to play baseball again with the

medication, along with being an occasional babysitter for their daughters. The White Sox looked for Walker's leadership both on and off the field again in the 1989 season.

Then 30, Walker began experiencing problems with his throwing shoulder caused by his old high-school football injury. He hit .210 in 77 games and 263 plate appearances. He ended up having surgery after the season. Walker started off the 1990 season, but played sparingly. After the White Sox attempted, but were unable to trade him, he was released at the end of April. He was picked up by the Baltimore Orioles who immediately sent him to Triple-A Rochester, where he played in 22 games before being called back up to Baltimore. He played with the Orioles for 14 games before they released him on July 3.

His playing career done, Walker went home to Douglas, Georgia with his wife and three daughters. He stayed busy getting involved in different businesses as well as outdoor activities he enjoyed like golf and fishing, but other people had thoughts about his future. "Sox Chairman Jerry Reinsdorf tried to inspire his comeback by mentioning Charlie Lau, Walker's old hitting coach for the Sox. "Each year I would come up for a charity golf tournament or whatever, and Jerry would ask me, is this the year?" Walker recalled. "He thought I would love it."[11]   2002 finally became the year, and Walker came on board as the hitting coach for the Triple-A team, the Charlotte Knights, where Walker was able to work with some of the White Sox top prospects. In 2003, when White Sox batters got off to a slow start hitting just .249 – and .232 with runners in scoring position – coach Gary Ward was fired, and Walker was brought up to Chicago to replace him.

In 2004, the White Sox hit 242 home runs, tied with the Yankees for the most home runs hit in the American League team that season, continuing with 200 home runs and 713 RBIs in the World Series Championship year of 2005. White Sox hitters gave Greg Walker much credit for their success at the plate. Paul Konerko said, "Walker will always be my guy... I trust him with every inch of my swing. He doesn't get the credit he deserves. Catcher A.J. Pierzynski said, "I've known him for seven years. He taught me more than I ever knew about hitting."[12] Konerko also said about Walker, "He knows everybody has their own style and he doesn't try to change you or try to mold you into his way. He tries to take what you do and go with it. He's a different hitting coach for every guy on this team."[13] While the White Sox team hitting continued to be solid, over time turmoil began to take over the clubhouse. Due to disagreements with manager Ozzie Guillén, and general manager Kenny Williams, Walker let owner Jerry Reinsdorf know that 2011 would be his last season as hitting coach with the White Sox. He had no plans for his near future at that point, but then his home state Atlanta Braves called.

On October 21, 2011, the Braves hired Greg Walker to be their next hitting coach. His experience and his ability to communicate with the players were credited for his hire. He served as the hitting coach for the Braves for three seasons, working with both their young stars, as well as their established players. Freddie Freeman said of Walker, "The main focus is us. He's always there for us. He's always there in the cage. He's always wanting to do something extra.   He always has time for you. That's what you want in a hitting coach."[14] Dan Uggla said, "I think our mentality as a team, which Greg helped us with, is being aggressive, but having controlled aggressiveness. If you are just aggressive and up there hacking at the first pitch, you're going out of your zone and putting yourself in a hole. But if you're aggressive on your pitch. it lets you see the ball better."[15] After the 2014 season, with the Braves struggling offensively, Walker stepped down as hitting coach.

In February of 2015, Greg Walker and Fred McGriff were hired as special assistants for the Braves. Walker's focus was to work with the minor-league hitters.

As of 2024, Walker is still employed with the Braves, he and his wife Carman live in their home town of Douglas, Georgia. They have three daughters and multiple grandchildren. The youth baseball complex in Douglas was named for him.

SOURCES

In addition to the sources cited in the Notes, the author consulted Baseball-Reference.com and Retrosheet.org.

NOTES

1   Melissa Isaacson, "Not Picture Perfect," https://chicagosports.com, October 3, 2005. /sports/baseball/whitesox/cs-051003soxwalker.1.194651.story?coll=cs-whitesoxheadlines

2   Jim Kaplan, "A Pair of Young Sox With Sock," *Sports Illustrated*, March 21, 1983. https://vaultsi.com/vault/1983/03/21/a-pair-of-young-sox-with-sock

3   Kaplan.

4   Kaplan.

5   Paul Banks, "Remembering the 1983 White Sox With Greg Walker," https://Thesportsbank.net, July 14, 2010. thesportsbank.net/mlb/remembering-the-1983-white-sox-with-greg-walker/

6   Mike Fish, "Walker Ready to Build on his Late Performance of '84," *Kansas City Star*, April 7, 1985.: 14.

7   Tom Skilling, "Ask Tom," WGNTV.com, June 13,2017. https://www.wgntv.com>weather>weatherblog>ask-tom-why>chicago-hot-summer-of-1988

8   "A Long Road Back For Walker," *Chicago Tribune*, May 23, 2003. https://www.chicagotribune.com/2003/05/23/a-long-road-back-for-walker/

9   Dave Van Dyck, "Walking Back From Zombie Land," *The Sporting News*, March 6, 1989: 32.

10   Bruce Newman, "Just Happy To Be Here," *Sports Illustrated*, April 17, 1989. https://vaultsi.com/vault/1989/04/17/just-happy-to-be-here-opening-day-was-special-for-white-sox-first-baseman-greg-walker-eight-months-ago-he-thought-he-hed-died

11   "Long Road Back For Walker."

12   Daryl Van Schouwen, "Hitting Coach Greg Walker Leaves White Sox on His Terms," *Chicago Sun-Times*, September 29, 2011. http://www.suntimes.com/sports/baseball/whitesox/7933144-574/hitting-coach-greg-walker

13   Isaacson.

14   Jeff Schultz, "Braves Bats Come Alive-Is it All About Greg Walker?," AJC.com, April 19, 2012. http://blogs.ajc.com/jeff-schultz-blog

15   Schultz.

KENNY WILLIAMS

By Bill Pruden

Over the course of a professional baseball career more than four decades long, Kenny Williams has done pretty much everything a person can do. After having navigated the grind of over a decade as a player, he made a smooth transition into the front office, where he came to be recognized as an astute baseball man. His career was capped by 22½ years as general manager and head of baseball operations with the Chicago White Sox, during which he led the 2005 team to its first World Series victory since 1917, ending the longest drought in American League history at 88 years.

Kenneth Royal Williams was born on April 6, 1964, in Berkeley, California. He was the only child of Jerry and Ethel Williams.[1] His father, desiring to be a firefighter, sued to win the right to serve on the San Jose Fire Department, a legal fight he ultimately won, but which engendered no small amount of resentment among the other firefighters, not to mention the public at large.[2] In fact, the legal challenge and the trial, which the young Williams attended, led to death threats and not long afterward, Williams recalled, his father gave him a .22 caliber handgun and taught him how to use it, if only to protect the family.[3] Growing up in the Berkeley/Oakland area at that time, he could not help but be affected by the issue of race. His father's willingness to go to court to secure his rights was not an isolated event. Williams's biological mother was an early Black Panther and his godfather is the iconic sprinter John Carlos, whose raised-fist podium salute along with Tommie Smith in the 1968 Olympics was a defining moment in sports history.[4] His father's example, as well as those other strong and proud figures, provided the young Kenny with role models and experiences that arguably prepared him for the ups and downs he would experience during his baseball career.

Williams attended Mount Pleasant High School in East San Jose. There he shined in both football and baseball, and after the right-handed-hitting outfielder was drafted by the White Sox in the third round of the 1982 draft, he began his climb up the baseball ladder. After signing with the White Sox, he was assigned to the team's Rookie League affiliate, the Gulf Coast White Sox. He hit .298 in 31 games there, scoring 19 runs while driving in 11.

At season's end, Williams headed off to Stanford University, where he distinguished himself as a kick returner on the football team. He said he regrets having left Stanford early and regularly advises young prospects to remain in school and complete their degrees.[5]

Returning to professional baseball in the spring, Williams spent the 1983 season with the Appleton Foxes of the Class-A Midwest League. He hit .231 in 124 games, scoring 60 runs, driving in 53, and stealing 27 bases. He returned to Appleton at the start of 1984, and after hitting .286 with 23 runs scored and 26 RBIs in his first 38 games, he earned a promotion to Glens Falls of the Double-A Eastern League. In 97 games, he batted .246, with 35 runs scored, 47 RBIs, and 16 stolen bases.

In 1985, Williams spent a full season with Glens Falls. In 133 games he batted .250, with 87 runs scored, 66 RBIs, and 27 stolen bases.

The 1986 season saw Williams moving among three teams. He started the season with Birmingham in the Double-A Southern League, where he batted .331 in 68 games. While he struggled after being promoted to the Triple-A Buffalo Bisons, batting only .212 in 50 games, he nevertheless got an end-of-season call-up to the White

Kenny Williams

Sox. Williams made his major-league debut on September 2 when he started in right field against the Kansas City Royals at Kansas City.

After popping out to first base in the top of the third, in the fifth Williams got his first big-league hit on a groundball single to third off left-hander Danny Jackson. He finished the day 1-for-4. For the White Sox, Williams batted .129 in 15 games, eight of which he started as he put in time in each of the outfield positions.

While he started the 1987 season back in Triple A, this time with the Hawaii Islanders of the Pacific Coast League, Williams was soon back in Chicago, where he enjoyed what proved to be his most successful major-league season. Playing in 116 games, he hit .281 with 11 home runs, 50 RBIs, and 21 stolen bases for a White Sox team that finished in fifth place in the American League West Division.

The 1988 season saw Williams again back in the minors, but not until after he had started the season playing third base with the White Sox. The experiment ended when he was sent down to the Triple-A Vancouver Canadians. After playing in 16 games with Vancouver, he was brought back up to the White Sox. For the season he hit just .159 in 220 at-bats. During 1989 spring training, Williams was sent to the Detroit Tigers for pitcher Eric King. He started the season with the Triple-A Toledo Mud Hens, but was recalled after playing in 14 games. In 94 games for the Tigers, he batted .205. The 1990 season was no better. In 57 games he hit .133 before the Toronto Blue Jays picked him up off waivers in mid-June. Things were little better in Toronto, where he hit .194 over the remainder of the season.

Williams began the 1991 season with the Syracuse Chiefs, the Blue Jays' Triple-A team, but went to the Montreal Expos on waivers after only 15 games. After a short stint with Triple-A Indianapolis, he was promoted to the Expos, and while he hit .271 in 34 games, offering some evidence of why teams had perhaps continued to give him a chance, the Expos released Williams after the season. He made one final effort in 1992, playing in 36 games with the Denver Zephyrs, the Milwaukee Brewers' Triple-A affiliate, but despite hitting .291, it was not enough to earn another shot in the major leagues and Williams's playing career came to a close at the end of the 1992 season. He was 28.

Overall, Williams played in parts of 10 minor-league seasons. He appeared in 675 games, finishing with a batting average of .262, with 72 home runs, 330 RBIs, and 142 stolen bases. In 451 games over six major-league seasons, Williams batted .218 with 27 home runs, 119 RBIs, and 49 stolen bases.

Williams rejoined the White Sox organization as a scout in 1992, the first of a number of positions that exposed him to different aspects of team operations.[6] In 1994 Williams was named a special assistant to White Sox Chairman Jerry Reinsdorf. He spent time in 1995 as a studio analyst for White Sox games on SportsChannel Chicago.[7] Then in 1997 Williams was named vice president of player development,

a job he held until October 2000, when he was named general manager of the White Sox, becoming at 36 the second youngest GM in the major leagues. (Only the Yankees' Brian Cashman was younger.[8])

The team Williams took over had a record of 95-67 in 2000 and finished first in the AL Central Division. After they were swept by the Seattle Mariners in the Division Series, general manager Ron Schueler stepped down. Reinsdorf named Williams to replace him. Williams immediately negotiated an extension with manager Jerry Manuel. (Together they became the first African American GM/manager duo.) Williams also began looking to strengthen the roster.[9]

By the time spring training arrived, Williams had signed free-agent catcher Sandy Alomar, traded for shortstop Royce Clayton, and traded for left-hander David Wells from Toronto. He then had to hold the line when Toronto attempted to rescind the deal after they discovered that Mike Sirotka, part of the deal, had an injured shoulder.[10] Despite these and other less dramatic moves, the 2001 White Sox were unable to match the 2000 team's performance. After a slow start, they were three games under .500 at the All-Star break and ultimately finished in third place in the Central Division at 83-79, a 12-game decline from the previous year.

During the next offseason, continuing to try to bolster the pitching staff, Williams traded for Pittsburgh Pirates starter Todd Ritchie, a workhorse who had started 33 games in 2001 and had won 35 games over the previous three years for the Pirates. But at 5-15 with an ERA of 6.06, the trade was a bust and none of the other lesser deals that Williams made had any great impact. Suddenly, just two seasons after winning the division and 95 games, the White Sox were a .500 team, finishing the 2002 season with a record of 81-81, although that was good enough for second place in a weak Central Division. Seeking to get the team back to where it had been when he started Williams again went looking for pitching, this time trading for Bartolo Colon, who won 15 games with an ERA of 3.87 in 2003, good enough to get him a new contract from the Angels as a free agent the following year. However, Colon did lead a stronger starting rotation as home-grown Mark Buehrle continued to develop, winning 14 games, while Esteban Loaiza, signed as a free agent, proved a big surprise, winning 21 games while posting a 2.90 ERA. Efforts to shore up the bullpen were unsuccessful, and the team improved to only 86-76, with the second consecutive second-place finish not enough to save Manuel's job.

Having made no substantive progress in his first three years at the helm, Williams decided to go in a new direction. He hired his former teammate Ozzie Guillén as manager. Guillén, who had retired as a player after the 2000 season, immediately went into coaching, serving two years with the Montreal Expos before helping the Florida Marlins win the 2003 World Series. While hoping the fiery Guillén could help change the culture of the team, Williams continued his efforts to strengthen the team, especially the pitching staff.

While his first three years had not yielded success, the trades and free-agent signings Williams had made left little doubt that he was willing to pursue change in an aggressive manner. Also, his years as vice president in charge of player development had given him an in-depth familiarity with the White Sox' and other teams' prospect pools, and from the start he showed himself willing to trade young prospects for established players. That continued even into the season when in June 2004, in the continuing effort to bolster the pitching staff, he traded for starter Freddy García after having signed free-agent reliever Shingo Takatsu, who provided valuable bullpen help, in January. He also traded Aaron Miles for Juan Uribe in December 2003.

After the White Sox finished 83-79 in Guillén's first year, Williams put together the final pieces of what would prove to be the 2005 World Series champions. In December 2004 he claimed Anaheim relief pitcher Bobby Jenks, who would emerge as the team's postseason closer, off waivers. Seeking additional depth in the starting rotation, he signed free agent Orlando Hernández, who been traded away as part of the deal to get Colon back in 2003. Williams also made some important acquisitions to upgrade the offense. He signed free-agent outfielder Jermaine Dye and traded for outfielder Scott Podsednik, although his trade of Carlos Lee was not universally well received. And he signed free-agent catcher A.J. Pierzynski and second baseman Tadahito Iguchi in January. The additions of the last two years, coupled with holdovers Joe Crede, Paul Konerko, and Aaron Rowand, left the White Sox ready to make a run.

The team that broke camp in 2005 was markedly different from the one Williams had been handed when Reinsdorf promoted him to general manager in October 2000. Of the position players on the 2000 team, only first baseman Paul Konerko retained his place in the everyday lineup, while none of the starting pitchers were the same and only two – Mark Buehrle and Jon Garland – remained on the roster. Williams had engineered a massive overhaul, and from the beginning, the effort paid dividends. The 2005 White Sox got off to a strong start, going 17-7 in April, 18-10 in May, and 18-7 in June, and at the All-Star break they were 57-29, in first place in the AL Central Division, nine games ahead of the second-place Minnesota Twins. While they cooled off a bit in the second half, going 42-34 after the All-Star break, they ended the season winning eight of their final 10 games to finish at 99-63, the best record in the American League and only a single victory less than the St. Louis Cardinals.

In the postseason, the White Sox made quick work of their opponents, sweeping the defending World Series champion Boston Red Sox in three games before taking the best-of-seven League Championship Series vs. the Los Angeles Angels of Anaheim in five games to win the American League pennant for the first time since 1959. Then they swept the Houston Astros to claim their first World Series championship since 1917.

While the glow of the World Series victory would last well into the spring, the offseason did not allow Williams to rest. In December he released longtime White Sox star Frank Thomas. Although injuries had limited the future Hall of Famer to barely 100 games over the past two seasons, the parting was acrimonious as Thomas felt he was due the courtesy of a call from Reinsdorf as well as an effort to trade him. Meanwhile, in an effort to replace the big bat Thomas had wielded prior to his injuries, Williams had already traded Aaron Rowand and two other players for Indians slugger Jim Thome.

There were other lesser transactions as the team sought to stay on top, but it quickly became clear that as defending champions, the 2006 White Sox were in a different, unfamiliar, and uncomfortable position. Looking back in October, once the unsuccessful title defense was over, Williams talked about what the team had experienced, explaining, "You have the trophy and you have the rings, and people tend to look at you a little bit differently. They are a little bit more focused when they come out and play you."[11] But in fact, the White Sox title defense actually got off to a good start. While their Opening Day victory was followed by four straight losses, the team bounced back to win 22 of its next 27 games, and the White Sox entered the All-Star break with a record of 57-31, the second-best record in baseball, bested only by the Detroit Tigers (59-29). But the magic did not last. With a record of 33-41 after the break, the White Sox finished third in their division, six games behind the Minnesota Twins, who came on strong to finish first, one game ahead of the Tigers, who got the wild-card spot.

As the years went by and the memories of the 2005 championship season progressively faded, the White Sox struggled to replicate that accomplishment. During the seven seasons after the World Series win, with Williams as general manager, only the 2008 team made the postseason. But after winning the Central Division crown they lost to Tampa Bay Rays in the Division Series.

The years also included a number of unsettling incidents, most prominently the acrimonious departure of Ozzie Guillén in September of 2011 (a rift that was ultimately repaired[12]), and the later controversial decision by Williams to limit the access of players' children in the locker room, a decision that led to the premature retirement of Adam LaRoche before it almost led to a player rebellion.[13] None of this enhanced Williams's public image or standing in the community, especially as things on the field only got worse. Nor did the October 2012 promotion of Williams to the position of executive vice president. Titles notwithstanding, he continued as head of baseball operations, while his former assistant general manager Rick Hahn assumed the role of GM.

The 2013 season saw the White Sox finish in the Central Division cellar, and while they quickly escaped last place, finishing fourth in 2014, that was the first of five fourth-place finishes in a row. They finished third in 2019 before returning to the postseason in the COVID-shortened 2020 campaign, securing the wild-card bid, but losing to the Oakland Athletics two games to one in the best-of-three series. The 2021 season saw the White Sox win 93 games, their highest total since the 2005 championship season, to win the Central Division, but they were defeated by the Astros in the AL Division series three games to one. In 2022 the team took a major step backward, finishing 81-81. Then in 2023, the bottom fell out: The White Sox were 38-54 at the All-Star break. On August 22, 2023, with the White Sox sitting at 49-77, owner Reinsdorf, in what he said "was one of the most difficult decisions of (my) life," fired Williams and Hahn.[14]

In the eyes of many observers, it was a move long overdue. Over the course of Williams's 22½ seasons at the helm, beyond the 2005 World Series title the White Sox claimed only three Central Division crowns, and a single wild-card bid in 2020. They finished second six times, third six times, fourth seven times, and fifth once, and not only did the 2023 team finish in fourth place with a 61-101 record, but the 2024 team set a modern-day record for losses at 121, eclipsing the 1962 New York Mets.[15] It was not a sterling record, but one that left many wondering why Williams had not been fired sooner. But for a team whose last previous World Series championship had come in 1917, the 2005 crown loomed large. Years later, one baseball blogger called the 2005 White Sox "the greatest team no one remembers."[16] But the lack of recognition aside, in the eyes of Williams's critics the increasingly distant championship season was all that kept him employed, especially when, as the years went by and the team proved unable to match it – or even come close, the calls for change had increased, with many observers and the members of the Chicago press believing that Reinsdorf's "well-known loyalty was ... the only thing saving" Williams's and Hahn's jobs.[17]

In response to the decision, Williams issued a statement that was professional and appreciative. He said, "I'm not really a 'Statement' kind of guy and had no intention of releasing one. That said, the volume of messages I have received in the wake of the news compels me to say something. First, I never knew so many people had my number." He then went on to thank the fans, the players and staff, and everyone in the White Sox organization with whom he had worked, and especially Reinsdorf, for the opportunity to lead the team. He expressed both his pride in their championship and his disappointment that they had not been able to do more, and then closed with a personal note, saying, "I know that not everyone has warm and fuzzy feelings about me, but I tried to be honest and fair with everyone at every turn. At times, admittedly, maybe a little too direct. Sometimes I hit the mark and sometimes I missed the mark on my messaging, but there wasn't a player who walked through our doors I didn't care about or wished the best in his baseball career and family life."[18]

Whatever criticism people might have had about Williams, there was no denying that he had spearheaded the effort that after almost 90 years, brought a World Series championship back to the south side of Chicago. It had not been easy, but he had done it, representing the team and the city in a professional, if often passionate, manner, while handling the critics and second-guessers who are an inevitable part of the job. While proud of the 2005 team and its accomplishment, like the fans he too had wanted more. In the end, he acknowledged mistakes, he took responsibility, but cherished what they had accomplished and the people he had accomplished it with.

One of the things that was not prominently mentioned at the end of Williams's tenure but which can't be ignored is the fact that in addition to the obvious pressures that were central to his job as head of the team's baseball operations, Williams had to contend with another reality of the game, one that applied only to him. He was a Black man in a White man's world. And whether his White Sox teams won or lost, that did not change. When Williams was named GM, he was the only Black GM in the majors, and only the third all-time, following Bill Lucas of the Atlanta Braves (1976-79) and Bob Watson (1995-98). The Yankees' World Series win in 1996 made Watson the first and until Williams the only African American GM to win a World Series title. Williams never harped on any of this, but the challenges were real.

During an interview with a Chicago TV station in the summer of 2020, Williams shared a story of a conversation with a "very close white friend of his, an older man," who asked Williams "What is it like to be Black?" Williams recalled that he responded, "It's exhausting. And at times it has been more exhausting than others. At times you want to give up and you don't see hope or a vision for a better future."[19] It was an unavoidable part of his life – a reality that was made all too clear soon after his appointment as GM when he returned home to "find a vulgar racial slur on the side of his house stating that no African American should run the White Sox, with the word White in all caps."[20] And it was no less an issue in his professional life. During his almost quarter-century in charge of White Sox baseball operations, he had witnessed many changes in the game, but one that had not occurred was a substantive change in the number of people like him – non-White males – who headed their team's baseball operations. It was an issue to which MLB had increasingly paid lip service, especially the previous year in the midst of the George Floyd murder and the Black Lives Matter movement, but as Williams made clear in an unexpected set of remarks at the 2021 GM meeting, it was one that had long frustrated him.

Some of his colleagues were struck by the incident at the 2021 winter general managers meeting where Williams, having reached a "boiling point," expressed the frustration that had been building up over two decades.[21] He asked his peers to imagine if the situation he had lived with had been reversed, if for the past two-plus decades a White person at the meeting had walked into a room filled with Blacks, after having been promised annually that the racial makeup of the group would change, only to see the promises prove false. And then he asked forcefully, but plaintively, "Would you feel included? Would you feel as though you belonged?"[22] Observers said that his comments made some feel uncomfortable, but Williams had felt he had to say his piece. He acknowledged later that over the 25 years that he had been attending the meetings there had been times when things were better, "[b]ut the last X number of years it feels like I'm on an island."[23]

The unanticipated comments by Williams made an impact on many of his peers. Chris Antonetti, head of baseball operations for the Cleveland Guardians, called Williams's comments "incredibly powerful," adding that "[i]f someone was in that room and they weren't moved by it and didn't feel that it was a call to action for us to be better, than that would be alarming to me."[24] And Giants president of baseball operations Farhan Zaidi said that Williams's comments "really struck a chord with me, his frustration and disappointment. Beyond calling the industry to task, which was totally appropriate, I just really felt for him as a person, knowing what he has seen and what he hoped things would look like 25 years ago, fast-forwarding it into the future."[25]

Unfortunately for Williams, while his message may have been heard, he had little time left to try to achieve the changes he so desperately sought. But it was not a cause he would abandon. Instead, in the aftermath of his departure from the White Sox, Williams has found another venue in which to pursue and foster the opportunities that had for so long been denied people like him. Acknowledging that the move was "born out of frustration fatigue, and angst," Williams became active in the world of diversity, equity, and inclusion, in an effort to "help open doors for minorities in business."[26] He is executive chairman and co-founder for the DEI Network and CLARA. CLARA is a tool to "mitigate bias in the hiring process, level the playing field for candidates, and help organizations find untapped talent."[27] The company says its mission is "to create access to opportunities and help people take advantage of those opportunities."[28] His work with CLARA represents Williams's clear commitment to addressing some of the problems he spotlighted. Meanwhile he has not ruled out becoming involved in major-league baseball again. In an interview he gave in the summer of 2024, Williams indicated that if he "gets a call from a team he believes he can help win, he'll listen," but as he also told the reporter, "If I don't get the call, then you can write about life after baseball."[29]

Williams was divorced from his first wife, Jessica (Estrada) Williams, in April 2012. In July 2014, he was married to a CNN morning host, Zoraida Sambolin. With five children from his first marriage and with Sambolin having one son, Williams is deeply aware of the challenges young people face and so in his life after the White Sox he is working hard at CLARA to open up new opportunities for the next generation of Black leadership, in whatever field they may occupy. It is no small challenge. But he has taken on that kind before.

SOURCES

In addition to the sources cited in the Notes, the author consulted baseball-almanac.com and Baseball-Reference.com.

NOTES

1   Ken Rosenthal, "White Sox G.M. Brings with Him a Legacy of Courage," *The Sporting News*, November 20, 2000.

2   Rosenthal.

3   Scott Merkin, "Ken Williams on Facing Racism, Hope for Future," MLB.com, June 15, 2020: https://www.mlb.com/news/ken-williams-on-how-racism-impacted-his-career.

4   Merkin.

5   Gary Libman, "Now He Swings Deals," *Stanford Magazine*, July/August 2001: https://stanfordmag.org/contents/now-he-swings-deals.

6   Libman.

7   Ryan Taylor, "Guillen Shares Kenny Williams Story after Winning in '05," NBC Sports Chicago, July 20, 2022: https://www.nbcsportschicago.com/mlb/chicago-white-sox/guillen-shares-kenny-williams-story-after-winning-in-05/328773/.

8   Libman.

9   Libman.

10 Libman.

11 Scott Merkin, "2006 Chicago White Sox Schedule," Baseball Almanac: https://www.baseball-almanac.com/teamstats/schedule.php?y=2006&t=CHA.

12 Doug Padilla, "Kenny Williams Ozzie Guillen: It's Complicated," ESPN.com, April 11, 2015: https://www.espn.com/blog/chicago/white-sox/post/_/id/23644/kenny-williams-ozzie-guillen-its-complicated.

13 Matt Bonesteel, "White Sox Almost Boycotted Spring Training Game Over Adam LaRoche," *Washington Post*, March 17, 2016: https://www.washingtonpost.com/news/early-lead/wp/2016/03/17/white-sox-reportedly-almost-boycotted-spring-training-game-over-adam-laroche/.

14 "White Sox Fire President Kenny Williams, General Manager Rick Hahn," SportsNet, August 22, 2023: https://www.sportsnet.ca/mlb/article/white-sox-fire-president-kenny-williams-general-manager-rick-hahn/.

15 The 1962 Mets, in the first year of the franchise, lost 120 games. The 2024 White Sox had a winning percentage of .253, however, compared with the Mets' .250.

16 Adam Kaplan, "10 Years Later: A Look Back on the 2005 Chicago White Sox, the Greatest Team No One Remembers," The Cover 3, March 14, 2015: http://www.thecover3.com/2015/03/10-years-later-look-back-on-2005-white-sox-greatest-team-nobody-remembers.html.

17 "White Sox to Look for Single Voice on Baseball Side After Firing of Williams, Hahn," *Street & Smith's Sports Business Journal*, August 8, 2023: https://www.sportsbusinessjournal.com/Articles/2023/08/23/chicago-white-sox-jerry-reinsdorf-fires-rick-hahn-ken-williams#:~:text=White%20Sox%20Assistant%20GM%20Chris,franchise's%20%E2%80%9Cawful%20performance%20on%20the.

18   Joe Binder, "Kenny Williams, Rick Hahn Release Statements After Firing," Sox on 35th, August 24, 2023: https://www.soxon35th.com/kenny-williams-rick-hahn-release-statements-after-firing/.

19   Merkin, "Ken Williams on Facing Racism."

20   "Ken Williams on Facing Racism."

21   Ken Rosenthal, "At GM Meetings, White Sox's Ken Williams Expresses Frustration, Disappointment with MLB's Lack of Progress in Front Office Diversity," *The Athletic*, November 15, 2021: https://www.nytimes.com/athletic/2956711/2021/11/15/at-gm-meetings-white-soxs-ken-williams-expresses-frustration-disappointment-with-mlbs-lack-of-progress-in-front-office-diversity/.

22   Rosenthal.

23   Rosenthal.

24   Rosenthal.

25   Rosenthal.

26   Ryan Taylor, "Here's What Former White Sox VP Kenny Williams Is Up To after South Side," NBC Sports Chicago, May 7, 2024: https://sports.yahoo.com/heres-former-white-sox-vp-024226932.html?guccounter=1&guce_referrer=aHR0cHM6Ly93d3cuZ29vZ2xlLmNvbS88&guce_referrer_sig=AQAAABtHqzVWVq_LJImGIzfqlRf-g11Tfvk KF4OGkloFDAlhg1p5UQessmS2RckBzV9sNXbBl2LVbq9dXCODjIjrh vveVww7WiqgcN5uveN1jU7mvv#:~:text=After%20his%20playing%20career%2C%20which,position%20he%20held%20until%202023.

27   CLARA Facebook page, https://www.getclara.io/people/kenny-williams.

28   "About Us," CLARA Facebook page; https://www.getclara.io/about-us.

29   Daryl Van Schouwen, "Exclusive: Ex-White Sox VP Ken Williams Wants Another Title, Open to Return to Baseball," *Chicago Sun-Times*, July 3, 2024: https://chicago.suntimes.com/white-sox/2024/07/03/former-white-sox-vp-ken-williams-wants-another-title-open-to-returning-to-baseball.

JERRY REINSDORF

By Phil Angelo

January 29, 1981, was one of the most impactful days in White Sox history.

That was the day Jerry Reinsdorf assumed control of the club, getting a 14-to-0 vote from American League owners at the O'Hare Hilton. Reinsdorf would go on to become the longest-tenured owner in the major leagues. At age 88 in 2024, he was also the oldest owner.

The White Sox have two owners in the Hall of Fame. Charles Comiskey (Commie, The Old Roman) ran the club from 1900 until his death on October 26, 1931. Bill Veeck, whose Hall of Fame plaque identifies him as "A Champion of the Little Guy," had two stints owning the club. Veeck ran the team for the 1959, 1960, and part of the 1961 seasons. Then he owned the White Sox from 1976 through 1980 before selling to Reinsdorf's group. Reinsdorf's tenure now exceeds that of both Hall of Famers – put together.

In retrospect, the White Sox sale of $20 million in 1981 appears to be a bargain. The Philadelphia Phillies sold later in the same year for $30 million.[1] The Twins went for $44 million in 1984.[2]

To be clear, Reinsdorf is not the sole owner. The *White Sox Media Guide* phrases it a particular way. He heads a limited partnership and is the "controlling" owner.[3]

While details are not public, *Forbes* has reported that Reinsdorf owns 19 percent of the White Sox.[4]

A Phil Rosenthal story says there were as many as "25 to 30" limited partners at the start, but the key executives were Reinsdorf and Eddie Einhorn.[5] Einhorn and Reinsdorf had met in law school. Einhorn was a successful broadcasting pioneer. Reinsdorf was a successful tax attorney. Einhorn died on February 24, 2016.

Reinsdorf had long dreamed of becoming a major-league owner. He had been a passionate childhood fan of the Brooklyn Dodgers since age 9. His favorite player was Pee Wee Reese, with a soft spot also for Duke Snider, who once lived on his block. Reinsdorf had attended, he said, the first game where Jackie Robinson suited up as a Dodger in Brooklyn.

As an adult, Reinsdorf answered an ad in the *Wall Street Journal* looking for potential baseball investors, and he was part of a group trying to buy first the San Francisco Giants, then the Cleveland Indians and finally the New York Mets.

Then it came to him. He would become an active leader of an ownership group.

He reckoned his chances of achieving that dream as "Infinity to 1."[6]

"I've always looked at the ownership of a baseball franchise as a public trust, maybe even a charitable thing," Reinsdorf said. "I'm serious about that. I never did forgive Walter O'Malley for moving the Dodgers from Brooklyn to Los Angeles."[7] Reinsdorf once said he rooted against the transplanted Dodgers. Yet calling himself a practical businessman, Reinsdorf has the White Sox share a spring-training facility with the Los Angeles Dodgers at Camelback Ranch in Glendale, Arizona.

Born February 25, 1936, Reinsdorf is the son of Max and Marion Reinsdorf. His father was a sewing machine mechanic and salesman. Jerry grew up in a middle-class Brooklyn family, which lived in an apartment. He slept on a rollaway cot in the hallway.

Jerry Reinsdorf

He was educated at George Washington University and earned his law degree at Northwestern. Northwestern changed him from a New Yorker to a Chicagoan. He worked as a lawyer for the Internal Revenue Service and also became a certified public accountant, a registered mortgage underwriter, a certified review appraiser, and a real estate securities specialist.[8]

Reinsdorf was a co-founder of one of the nation's first businesses that specialized in real estate partnerships. He sold the firm to American Express for $102 million, leaving the firm in 1987.

The success of the Reinsdorf-led bid to buy the club was not a given. There were other suitors, notably Edward J. DeBartolo Sr. DeBartolo was the early front-runner, but there were concerns. As an Ohioan, he would have been an absentee owner. There was also a worry about his links to horse racing, which by 2024 seemed completely out of date given baseball's on-air promotion about betting parlays. So the Reinsdorf group prevailed.

The Reinsdorf era started dramatically and well. Reinsdorf and Einhorn said they were not interested in building a team with free agents.[9] But in March 1981 the White Sox added free-agent catcher and future Hall of Famer Carlton Fisk and purchased slugger Greg Luzinski from the Phillies. But Reinsdorf also expanded the farm system.[10]

In 1979 the White Sox had a meager three farm teams, in Des Moines, Knoxville, and Appleton. By 1982 the minor-league roster had expanded to include the Triple-A Edmonton Trappers, Double-A Glens Falls White Sox, the Single-A Niagara Falls Sox, and the Rookie-level Gulf Coast Sox. Management continued to build the farm system for the next decade. By 1995 Chicago had seven minor-league affiliates: Triple-A Nashville; Double-A Birmingham; Advanced-A Prince William; Single-A Hickory and South Bend; Rookie League teams in the Gulf Coast and Appalachian leagues; and a Foreign Rookie team shared with the Baltimore Orioles in the Dominican Summer League.

For immediate help, "Carlton Fisk just fell into our laps," Reinsdorf said. "Boston lost him on a technicality, and we thought we had a great opportunity to get a great player. The White Sox hadn't had a great player in a long time."[11]

But while the team was about to turn north, its media presence headed south. The year 1982 marked the beginning of SportsVision, an Eddie Einhorn project.

Under the slogan of "Chicago's Winners on Cable," the games of the White Sox, Bulls, Blackhawks, and Chicago Sting soccer team would be beamed to your television screen if you purchased a $50 converter box. Almost immediately, cheaper knock-off boxes appeared. The goal was 50,000 customers. Promoters never came close to that.

The choice between free televised Cubs and White Sox games that required a special price and effort was not a good one for the South Siders. Broadcaster Harry Caray described the White Sox on television as a "best kept secret."

SportsVision was dead before the end of the decade, but not before it had widened the public gap in baseball interests between the North and the South Sides.[12]

In 1983 White Sox pitchers LaMarr Hoyt (24-10, Cy Young Award winner) and Richard Dotson (22-7) both had the best years of their careers. Ron Kittle was Rookie of the Year with 35 homers and 100 RBIs. The White Sox were 59-26 in the second half and won the Western Division title by 20 games. Texas Rangers manager Doug Rader accused the White Sox of "Winning Ugly." The name stuck. To this day, the 1983 season evokes nostalgia among fans and those throwback uniforms remain popular.

Reinsdorf would later say that while the 2005 World Series championship was the most satisfying thing, 1983 was "the most fun I ever had.[13]

Starting a pattern, the White Sox fell short in the postseason, losing to the Baltimore Orioles in the AL Championship Series. The year also proved to be a single high peak, followed by a valley. Reinsdorf called the balance of the 1980s "the outhouse."[14]

A crisis came in 1986, broadcaster Ken Harrelson, who had been openly critical on the air of general manager Roland Hemond, was elevated from microphone to management. Harrelson fired future Hall of Fame manager Tony La Russa. He himself stepped down with a week to go in the season. Reinsdorf called the dismissal of La Russa "the dumbest mistake of my life."[15]

That year Reinsdorf announced plans to build a new ballpark in the suburbs. Before the 1998 arrival of the expansion Devil Rays, Tampa was ready to host the White Sox.

"It was very hard to get our new ballpark built, but it had to be done because the old ballpark was going to fall down." Reinsdorf said.[16] "It was truly at the end of its useful life, and it was well beyond the end of its economic life, because with the salaries escalating the way they had, you had to have new sources of revenue from a ballpark and you couldn't find them in the old Comiskey Park. Also physically it wasn't going to last much longer."

On June 30, 1988, time stood still as the Illinois legislature raced a deadline to approve the funding for a new White Sox stadium, which was first named Comiskey, then US Cellular, and later Guaranteed Rate Field.

"Now we stay. This thing was dead and one man did it," Reinsdorf said of the stadium vote.[17] He meant Illinois Governor James Thompson, who lobbied hard on behalf of the White Sox. In 2022 the team installed a bust of Thompson outside Gate 4.

Much of the lease agreement held the Illinois Sports Facility Authority to a strict deadline to get the new ballpark open and then specified responsibility for repairs. Clearly, the deterioration that occurred in Old Comiskey would not be repeated. Today, the ballpark is no longer "new," but it appears well maintained.

The White Sox are tenants. They do not own the ballpark.

The Authority gets a share of ticket sales. Since 2001 the Sports Facility Authority begins getting paid once home attendance hits 1.5 million. The White Sox have hit that number every year since, with the exception of the Covid year in 2020 (when there was no attendance) and the dismal 2024 season. Increased attendance not only benefits the White Sox, but also the Authority.

The Authority is responsible for all property taxes. The lease makes that clear. The White Sox get the revenue and have control of all concessions and souvenirs. The team also has control of and revenue from all signs. The Authority gets 35 percent of all "Media Fees" above $10 million.

It was a detailed lease, setting aside specific tickets and a suite for the Authority's use and even specifying the material for the infield tarp used when it rains.[18]

The team returned to relevance in the early 1990s. Old Comiskey closed. The new ballpark opened in 1991. Three straight years above .500 were followed by a Western Division title in 1993. It was the birth of "Good Guys Wear Black," which started as an advertising promotional slogan.

The 1993 team was fueled by home-grown players signed and developed by the White Sox: Frank Thomas (MVP, 41 homers, 128 RBIs); Robin Ventura (22, 94); Jack McDowell (Cy Young Award, 22 wins) and Alex Fernandez (18 wins). As in 1983, the White Sox exited the playoffs in the first round, this time losing to the Blue Jays.

Reinsdorf bought the NBA's Chicago Bulls in 1985 and hired Jerry Krause as general manager. Krause inherited Michael Jordan, but built the team of Scottie Pippen, Bill Cartwright, and Horace Grant around him. It was the first of two three-peats for the Bulls in the NBA. In 2016, Reinsdorf was elected to the Naismith Memorial Basketball Hall of Fame as a contributor.

When Jordan temporarily retired in the middle of these title runs, Reinsdorf accommodated his wish to try the sport of baseball.

August 11, 1994, was another watershed day in the history of the White Sox, in all of major-league baseball and in the way Jerry Reinsdorf would be regarded.

That was the last day major-league baseball was played that year after players went on strike. When the schedule stopped, the White Sox were in first place in the new American League Central Division by a game. The short season wasted what was the best year in Frank Thomas's career: his top season for batting average (.353) and slugging (.729), with 38 homers and 101 RBIs. Thomas was a near-unanimous MVP, getting 24 of 28 first-place votes. It was his second straight MVP, an achievement ironically celebrated with a bobblehead during the disastrous 2024 season.

Major-league baseball teams had drawn an average of 30,965 fans a game in 1993. That dropped by more than 5,000 per game in 1995 after the strike. It would take until 2006 to reach the pre-strike per-game average. Overall attendance was juiced by the addition of Arizona and Tampa Bay in 1998. Some fans stayed away – for years.

If the fans were losers, so was Reinsdorf. The media portrayed him as "the influential anti-union hardliner."[19] Steve Wulf called him "the hardest of the hard-line owners warring with the players' union."[20] Reinsdorf said he was a "dove" on the issue until the strike began, then he became a "hawk."[21]

While Reinsdorf was described as a "back-room puppeteer" powerbroker, *Sports Business Journal* said that more often Reinsdorf zigged while the other owners zagged.[22]

During the strike, Reinsdorf advocated that the owners introduce their own labor rules. The counter-argument was to wait and use the threat as a warning. Reinsdorf's proposal lost in committee, 18 to 1.

"I had it right, but nobody went along with me. So we had to fold our tent," Reinsdorf said. "I know that I got blamed for the strike, but the only one to blame for the strike, in my opinion, was Don Fehr. He's the guy who called the strike."[23]

Forgotten by many fans today, Donald Fehr was the executive director of the Major League Baseball Players Association from 1983 to 2009. For Fehr and the players, the key issue was avoiding a salary cap, but the new contract would establish a "luxury tax," which the highest-spending teams would have to pay.[24]

Back on the field, in the late '90s through 2000, the White Sox added thump. Ray Durham joined in 1995 (106 homers with the White Sox, career of 192). Magglio Ordóñez came in 1997 (187 homers with White Sox in a career total of 294). Former Dodger and Red Paul Konerko started with Chicago in the same year (439 homers lifetime, all but seven with the White Sox). Carlos Lee arrived in 1999 (152 home runs with the White Sox, career of 358). José Valentin started in 2000 (136 with the White Sox in a career of 249).

The most controversial add was Albert Belle, he of the corked bat, "batgate." Reinsdorf signed Belle for an estimated $52.5 million for five years, making the oft-suspended hitter the highest paid player in the major leagues.[25] Reinsdorf had often preached fiscal responsibility to other owners, but now seemed to have not listened to himself.

"Any owner who breaks the market like this with the industry in trouble, it makes you scratch your head," said John Hart, the general manager of the Cleveland Indians.

Reinsdorf countered. "In the current climate, you have to pay to win. Look at the World Series: the No. 1 payroll vs. the No. 2."

Reinsdorf declared that if the Chicago fans could accept Dennis Rodman, "the fellow with the pink hair," they would accept Belle.[26]

Belle had two good seasons for the White Sox, setting a team record with 49 homers and 152 RBIs in 1998. But a clause in his contract allowed him to try to renegotiate if he was not among the three-highest paid players in the game. Reinsdorf said no. Belle's stay was short.

A breakthrough came in 2000. The White Sox had six players with 17 home runs or more en route to a team record of 216. They won the Central Division, but had another quick playoff exit, swept in three games by the Seattle Mariners. Once more, it was one and done.

By 2005 the White Sox had a new manager in Ozzie Guillén, a new fight song in Journey's "Don't Stop Believin'" and a new philosophy, discarding power for speed, defense, and pitching. Every acquisition seemed to work.

Orlando "El Duque" Hernandez, A.J. Pierzinski, Jermaine Dye, and Tadahito Iguchi would arrive as free agents. The White Sox traded for Scott Podsednik and Freddy García. Bobby Jenks was plucked off the waiver pile. All would play vital roles in a 99-victory regular season and an 11-1 roll through the postseason.

The acquisition of Podsednik was a clear signal of a changing team. Essentially, the White Sox swapped outfielders with the Brewers. Gone was Carlos Lee, who would hit 32 homers for the Brewers in 2005. Podsednik would steal 59 bases in 2005. Power out, speed in. Podsednik did not hit a home run in the 2005 regular season, but did win a World Series game with a walk-off homer.

But there were two other aspects of the trade. Pitcher Luis Vizcaino joined Chicago. He went 6-5 for the season, making 65 appearances. There was a significant cash benefit for Chicago, too. Lee's leaving took a $6.5 million contract off the books, while Podsednik was making $700,000.

The new team speed and the ability to play for one run when needed were key factors in a world championship.

"It was only afterward that I realized the impact that winning the World Series had on our community. You could have gone to any cemetery in the Chicago area and found graves decorated in White Sox paraphernalia," Reinsdorf said.[27]

At the victory celebration, Reinsdorf was "stunned" when first baseman Paul Konerko handed him the ball that was the last out of the World Series.[28] The year before, the Red Sox ended up with a lawsuit to recover their last ball from their first baseman.

"When Paul handed me that ball, it just choked me up. It was a tremendous feeling," Reinsdorf said.[29] It even got Jerry in a bit of trouble with his wife when he said it was most emotional moment of his life. Wife Martyl reminded him of their marriage and the birth of their children.

The 2006 season marked a familiar regression. Broadcaster Harrelson kept telling the audience that the team would win 90 games and be fine. The White Sox did indeed win 90, but that was only good for third place. The top of the mountain was again followed by a valley.

There was a rebound in 2008. A coin flip gave the White Sox the home field in a one-game tiebreaker against the Twins for the Central Division title. Jim Thome won the

"blackout" game (so named because the fans were encouraged to wear black shirts) in dramatic fashion with a solo shot for the game's only run. The playoff series against the Rays, though, was another quick exit.

It took another dozen years for the White Sox to get back to the postseason. Bopper Adam Dunn arrived in 2011 for four years that would see 106 homers and 720 strikeouts. All or nothing. From 2013 to 2019, there were seven straight years when the team finished under .500.

Mired in the middle, Reinsdorf gave the signal to team architects Kenny Williams and Rick Hahn to rebuild the team. That meant trading some quality veterans for prospects.

"We always say we want to win multiple titles," Reinsdorf said. "The real plan is we want to be competitive year after year. It's very hard to win one title, let alone multiple titles. I just want us to be playing meaningful games every October. … (Deciding to rebuild) was an easy decision, because (if) we didn't make that decision, we were going to be caught in mediocrity, and that's no fun."[30]

There were three key trades. Star pitcher Chris Sale was sent to the Red Sox for Yoan Moncada and Michael Kopech. Pitcher Jose Quintana was dealt to the Cubs for Eloy Jiménez and Dylan Cease. Outfielder Adam Eaton traveled to the Nationals in return for Lucas Giolito, Reynaldo López, and Dane Dunning.

At first it seemed to work. The 2020 season was abridged by covid, but José Abreu was an RBI machine, knocking in 60 runs in 60 games and winning the MVP Award. Yet while it was back to the playoffs, it was another fast exit, courtesy of Oakland.

That was followed by the speedy exit of manager Rich Renteria, who seemed to have performed his designated role of teaching the team's younger players. Renteria's departure prompted a stunner – the return of Tony La Russa. There were two immediate media and fan reactions, both negative.

La Russa had last actively managed in the 2012 All Star Game after winning the 2011 World Series with the Cardinals. He had been out of baseball for three years, then successively served as chief baseball officer for the Diamondbacks, adviser for the Diamondbacks, and assistant to the general manager for the Red Sox.

The change seemed to cement the idea that Reinsdorf was still actively running the team. And La Russa was seen as out of touch with today's players, out of touch with the modern rules, and out of touch with baseball analytics.

Reinsdorf was having none of it.

"As everyone in baseball is well aware, I have always respected Tony and am proud to have maintained a great friendship with him over the decades in the game. But his hiring is not based on friendship or on what happened years ago, but on the fact that we have the opportunity to have one of the greatest managers in the game's history in our dugout as a time when we believe our team is poised for great accomplishments."[31]

At 76, La Russa was the oldest manager in baseball. He already had a plaque in Cooperstown. Yet it did seem to work: The White Sox won 93 games in 2021 and won the Central Division by 13 games – the first time they had back-to-back postseason teams. But once again, the White Sox were out in the first round, losing to Houston in four games.

In 2021 the White Sox won the nationally televised Field of Dreams game in Dyersville, Iowa, with a sensational bottom-of-the-ninth homer from Tim Anderson. The bat-flipping Anderson was the inspiration for another memorable slogan, "Change the Game."

The next year, 2022, started a steep decline. The playoffs were expanded, but the team slumped to 81-81 and missed them entirely. On the advice of his cardiologist, La Russa stepped down as August ended.

Pedro Grifol was hired as the manager for 2023. The team did not respond well. Losing 101 games, the White Sox had their worst season since 1970, when they lost 106. Toward the end of the season, Reinsdorf fired both Kenny Williams and Rick Hahn, the two men responsible for the roster. It wasn't an easy decision for Reinsdorf.

"One alternative was to do nothing. Another was to keep Kenny and let Rick go, and another was to keep Rick and let Kenny go. And I came to the conclusion that it'd be better to let them both go and have a fresh start," Reinsdorf said. "A change killed me because it wouldn't have been any harder for me to fire my son, Michael, than it was to fire Kenny because Kenny was my son and is still my son."[32]

While the firings were generally expected, the replacement was a disappointment to many fans and the media because Reinsdorf simply elevated Chris Getz, the White Sox assistant general manager in charge of minor-league operations. Criticism ran along two lines. Should a more thorough search have been done? Had the White Sox minor league operation been all that great anyway?

Speed, Reinsdorf said, was of the essence. He wanted a quick turnaround. There was no widespread job search, there were no interviews of anyone outside the organization.

"It became clear to me that (Getz) would be one of the major candidates, alongside these other candidates. And then I started thinking of the speed I owe the fans, I realized that if you bring in somebody from the outside, it's gonna take him a year, he's gonna have to evaluate everybody in the organization. So you'll lose a year."[33]

The hiring of Getz from inside the organization was the latest in a long-term trend of loyalty, for better or worse, for current and former employees. Hawk Harrelson is in the broadcast booth, gets promoted to run the team and fails there. He returns to telecasts. Ozzie Guillén departs as a player, returns as a manager, departs again, and returns again as a television analyst. Frank Thomas leaves as a player and returns as an analyst, too. Robin Ventura also leaves Chicago and comes back as a manager.

Institutional loyalty is a White Sox value for Reinsdorf. "Peter Gammons once said to me, 'Is there anybody here who answers the telephone who hasn't been here for 20 years?'"[34]

Ozzie Guillén, who has returned to the White Sox fold twice after departing, once called Reinsdorf "the greatest man I ever met, not because he's my boss. Because he's a straight man who will not lie to you."

"A lot of people should know Jerry the way I know him," Guillén continued. "Jerry means well for everybody, especially in this city. Jerry is treated so badly in this city. I think Jerry should be more loved, more respected."[35]

The time gained by hiring Getz, though, was one of agony. The fade continued and accelerated.

In 2005 every signing and trade seemed to go right. Now everything went wrong.

In Yoan Moncada's first eight years with the White Sox, he topped 130 games played only three times. His best year came in 2019, when he hit .315 with 25 homers. Moncada hit 93 homers for the White Sox through the end of the 2024 season, but making contact was a problem. He had five seasons of 100 or more strikeouts, topped by a league-leading 217 whiffs in 2018.

Eloy Jimenez played six years in Chicago before being dispatched in a trade to Baltimore. In no season did he top 130 games played. His best year also came in 2019 with 31 home runs.

Luis Robert, developed by the White Sox, had only one season in his first five where he reached 130 games played. In 2023 he hit 38 home runs. Tim Anderson, also a White Sox farmhand: batting champion at 26, All-Star at 28 and done as an effective player at 30.

Yasmani Grandal, signed in free agency to handle the catching duties, had only one year, out of four, when he played 100 or more games. In 2021 he hit 23 homers, more than his other three South Side years combined. Free agent Andrew Benintendi hit .273 for the Red Sox and .294 for the Royals, but less than .240 for Chicago in 2024. Benintendi's five-year, $75 million contract had been the richest in White Sox history.

Meanwhile, pitchers Chris Sale and Reynaldo López, both traded away, were All-Stars. Dylan Cease, Jose Quintana, and Michael Kopech, also traded from Chicago, were effective, as was Carlos Rodón. It was as if every estimate of talent had been wrong, and every possible injury had occurred.

Picking the worst possible timing, the White Sox announced plans for the new ballpark in February 2024. Located along the river between the South Loop and Chinatown, it would be part of a development called The 78. The ballpark alone would cost $1.1 billion, funded by a hotel tax, and there would be $900 million more needed in infrastructure.[36]

The new ballpark would be blended better into its surrounding community than Comiskey-Cellular-Guaranteed Rate. Parking would shrink. Skyline views would improve. More and better restaurants would arrive. Sodfather Roger

Bossard, the White Sox groundkeeper, has laid out a baseball diamond on The 78 site to give the public and the decision-makers a visual.

Guaranteed Rate is the eighth oldest ballpark in the majors. The three oldest, Fenway Park, Wrigley Field, and Dodger Stadium, are unlikely to be replaced. Only two ballparks, for the Braves in 2017 and the Rangers in 2020, have been built since 2012.

The 2023 season was marred by a shooting inside Guaranteed Rate Field, during an August 25 blowout loss to the As. Two women were injured; Neither injury was life-threatening.[37]

The White Sox drew some criticism for continuing to play the game, but reports indicated that that was a police decision to avoid panic. An ESPN reporter said the shot or shots were accidental and from a gun that was likely "snuck in." The police said that was the most likely scenario. Meanwhile the White Sox would not rule out the idea that the rounds came from outside the ballpark.

A lawsuit was filed against the White Sox and the Illinois Sports Facility Association. The entire incident seemed to reinforce the worst fears about the ballpark's location.

Yet fans have shown a willingness to attend. Fourteen times in the Reinsdorf years, attendance has topped 2 million. Most of those seemed to coincide with better teams, led by the 2,957,414 in the post-World Series year of 2006.

And today, as you walk inside the ballpark, the concourses are wide, with activities and lots of food choices. The audio and video systems are sharp. Colorful murals display team history. Statues of White Sox greats stand. Guaranteed Rate does not look or feel run-down.

Talking to *Crain's Chicago Business*, Reinsdorf left little doubt that the White Sox would depart without a new ballpark. The current lease runs through 2029. He told *Crain's* that when he's gone, his heirs would be obligated to do what's best for the other investors. "The big money" in the White Sox comes from out of town, he said.[38]

Son Michael, the Bulls' president, has been advised to hold onto that franchise, though.

The veiled threat to move the White Sox feels creepily like the pressure that built the current ballpark. As Yogi Berra might have said, "It's déjà vu all over again." Nashville is mentioned as the most likely suitor, and Reinsdorf did meet with Nashville's mayor.

But metropolitan Nashville is only 2 million people. It would be one of baseball's smallest markets, like Kansas City, Milwaukee, or Cleveland. Then again, franchise moves were frequent in earlier years. They are rare now. In the last half-century, there have been only two relocations: the A's now heading to Las Vegas and the 2005 Expos becoming the Washington Nationals.

Will the money for The 78 be found? Labeling it as a wise investment for taxpayers and a job creator is good. Both the mayor of Chicago and the governor of Illinois were lukewarm at best, expressing opposition to using tax money. And the current ballpark succeeded only because of the political pull of a popular governor.

But Baseball Commissioner Rob Manfred believes the White Sox will stay.

"Chicago is an anchor city for us," Manfred said. "I think that the White Sox are in a difficult situation. I think the location of the stadium is tough, but I have confidence that things are going to work out in Chicago and that we're going to continue to have two teams in Chicago."[39]

Putting the argument in the rearview mirror, at least temporarily, the White Sox became the team with the most losses in modern baseball history in 2024. They won five out of their last six, but still finished 41-121, worse than the 1962 expansion New York Mets, a team constructed of every other team's castoffs.

Grifol (28-89) was fired late in the 2024 season. So, just a few years after making the postseason in back-to-back years, they lost 100 in back-to-back years. They lost 12 in a row. They lost 14 in a row. They lost 21 in a row.

As the year 2024 drew to a close, Will Venable was hired as the new White Sox manager. Counting the interim hires, he becomes the sixth White Sox manager of the 2020s. He has been well-schooled under other excellent managers.

In a statement late in the 2024 season, Reinsdorf said everyone in the White Sox organization is extremely unhappy with the results. He called the year "painful," but saw a silver lining. "What impressed me is how our players and staff have continued to work and bring a professional attitude to the ballpark each day."[40]

How to evaluate the Reinsdorf era?

Of the 44 seasons under his ownership through 2024, two have been exactly at .500. There have been 21 winning seasons and 21 losing ones. Glass half-full or glass half-empty? There have been seven postseason years. Excluding the 2005 World Series run and the 2008 "Blackout" game won by Jim Thome's home run, all the others ended in first-round exits.

There have been peaks. Sustained success has been rare. There were back-to-back playoff appearances in 2020 and 2021. There would likely have been back-to-back ones again in 1993 and 1994 had not the latter season been canceled.

The tide right now is out rather than in. Of the 12 seasons counting back from 2024, nine have been losers. There has been one year at .500 and only two winners.

Criticism of Jerry Reinsdorf is nothing new. In 1992, *BusinessWeek* called him "The Toughest #&?!%* in Sports."[41]

Reinsdorf, the analysis said, "won't win any popularity contests." He challenges the rules of an old-boy network. He "didn't charm his way to the top." *BusinessWeek* called him the sports owner of the future, "an executive whose only business is sports, not a sport who is an executive in some other business."

Leigh Allan authored a totally negative column in 2022 for SouthsideSox, dwelling on Reinsdorf's use of tax law and calling him a "humongous liar."[42]

Detractors have grown in strength and vehemence as the team's play deteriorated in 2024.

"The Reinsdorf way is detached from the reality of modern baseball; it is feckless and loyal to everyone except the fans."[43]

A piece by The Athletic said that while Reinsdorf had once been viewed favorably, his opinions had "calcified" over the years. He reportedly has refused to invest in "cutting edge amenities."[44]

One anonymous source said: "I'm not sure if any owner loves baseball as much as Jerry. That's why he can't get out of his own way."

On a technical level, the story went on to explain that Chicago had fallen behind in its use and detail of analytics. At times it had two sets of analytic data competing against each other. At other times, the recommendations were vague and general, rather than being specific.

What would be fair in evaluating the White Sox in the Reinsdorf era? Are the White Sox a major-market team because they are in Chicago? There are four markets with two teams: Chicago, Los Angeles, New York, and (through 2024) San Francisco-Oakland. In each of the dual-team markets, the trailing team has won exactly one World Series since the time Reinsdorf acquired the White Sox. The list: Mets in 1986; A's in 1989; Angels in 2002; White Sox in 2005.

Although there are often numerous flip comments along the lines of cheapskate, the reality is that White Sox rank in the middle of the pack when it comes to payroll. *Statista* ranked the White Sox payroll on Opening Day in 2024 as 15th of the 30 teams. *Sportrac* compiled the 2024 White Sox payroll in 18th place.

USA Today put the White Sox 14th place in 2024 at $142,995,900.[45] The next five teams lower than the White Sox were Minnesota, Kansas City, Milwaukee, Baltimore, and Cleveland, all of which were markedly better than Chicago in the season.

No less a figure than Kenny Williams, fired by Reinsdorf, had this to say: "I always thought over the years it was a little unfair when people would say, 'All he cares about is making money.' I'm sitting in the office and he's saying, 'I'm going to give you what I got.'"[46]

There are, of course, different ways to look at team spending. MLB.com lists the most expensive player contracts for teams, counting both free-agent signings and extensions given to current players. The White Sox are one of only two teams to never have a $100 million player contract. The Oakland A's are the other team.

There are other teams that have paid $100 million or more to re-sign their own stars, but who have not paid $100 million for a free agent, as of 2024. That list includes the Rays, Reds, Pirates, Braves, Royals, and Guardians.

For Chicago perspective, the White Sox threw the World Series in 1919 and then went 40 years before the 1959 pennant, at a time when the American League was eight teams. The Chicago Bulls did not win a championship in the years before Reinsdorf. The Blackhawks have won six championships. The Bears have won nine titles. The Bears have not won since 1985. That team, like the '83 White Sox, remains beloved.

The Cubs and the White Sox have each won three World Series titles. The Cubs' drought, between 1908 and 2016, was a fan and media obsession. "Anyone can have a bad century."

Titles are also hard to come by. The Brooklyn Dodgers of the 1950s, subject of book-after-book-after-book, with Hall of Famers Duke Snider, Jackie Robinson, and Roy Campanella, won a World Series exactly once before moving to Los Angeles. It was the same situation for the Atlanta Braves of the 1990s. Greg Maddux, Tom Glavine, and John Smoltz together produced one World Series title.

The Milwaukee Brewers of Robin Yount and Paul Molitor had no World Series titles. The Seattle Mariners of Ken Griffey Jr. and Randy Johnson never reached the World Series. That is also true for the Montreal Expos of Gary Carter, Tim Raines, and Andre Dawson.

In 1994 the Expos, like the White Sox, likely paid a steep price for the cancellation of the World Series. Montreal had the best record in baseball that year at 74-40 and was represented by five players in the All-Star Game.

In the nonfield aspects of the franchise, the White Sox under Reinsdorf have done just fine.

The White Sox, purchased for $20 million in 1981, are now worth $2.05 billion.[47] Sports franchises of all kinds have escalated in price. The growing number of television channels demands more product. There are new revenue streams like the internet, alternative uniforms to sell and links to sports gambling – a real irony for a franchise where players threw a World Series. Mostly, though, it is supply and demand. The supply of franchises is limited. Demand is still there.

Founded in 2007, White Sox Charities has given away more than $47 million. Some 96 cents out of every dollar collected was given away. A car raffle, 50/50 drawings, scoreboard messages, selected bobbleheads and auctions of game-used material all benefit charity. There is a Sox Serve charity week. Among the projects helped is the Amateur City Elite athletes. Youths enrolled in the program graduate from high school at a 99 percent rate and 280 of them have earned college scholarships.[48]

The White Sox were also fairly out front with diversity. With Minnie Miñoso they were the sixth major-league team to integrate. Ted "Double Duty" Radcliffe, a legendary Negro League star, was tapped by the White Sox to throw out a ceremonial first pitch. Double Duty was past 100 at the time and lived to be 103. The team has a rich history of Latino players; and Ozzie Guillén was the first Latino manager to guide a team to a World Series victory.

Reinsdorf, along with Theo Epstein, Rick Hahn, and Bud Selig, is listed in the Owners, Front Office section of the Jewish Baseball Museum.

"I have always found Reinsdorf to be one of the most engaging, funny, thoughtful and honest people in sports," said Ed Sherman, interviewing Reinsdorf in 2018 for the museum.[49]

Reinsdorf has received the Order of Lincoln award in Illinois. He was the Chicago Park District Chicagoan of the Year and named a Guardian of Children by the Jewish Council of Youth Services. He was given an honorary degree by Illinois College and the Award of Merit from Northwestern University. [50]

Reinsdorf married Martyl Rifkin in 1956. They were a couple for 65 years. Reinsdorf remembered her working full-time and typing all his papers as he went to law school. He himself worked part-time making his way through law school.[51] A leader in charities and the designer of the Chicago Bulls championship rings, Martyl Reinsdorf died at age 85 in 2021. The couple had four children and nine grandchildren.

SOURCES

In addition to the sources cited in the Notes, the author consulted Baseball-Reference.com.

NOTES

1   Rich Westcott, "Philadelphia Phillies Team Ownership History," SABR.org. https://sabr.org/bioproj/topic/philadelphia-phillies-team-ownership-history/.

2   Bobby Nightengale, "Carl Pohlad and the Minnesota Twins: Four Decades of Highs and Lows," *Minnesota Star-Tribune*, October 10, 2024. https://www.startribune.com/carl-pohlad-history-selling-minnesota-twins/601160271.

3   *Chicago White Sox 2005 Media Guide*, 5.

4   Phil Rogers, "Jerry Reinsdorf Says New Stadium Is a Must to Keep White Sox in Chicago," Forbes.com, February 22, 2024. https://www.forbes.com/sites/philrogers/2024/02/22/jerry-reinsdorf-says-new-stadium-is-a-must-to-keep-white-sox-in-chicago/.

5   Phil Rosenthal, "Recalling Jerry Reinsdorf's Come-From-Behind Victory 40 Years Ago for Control of the Chicago White Sox: 'I've Never Celebrated Anniversaries of This Sort,'" Chicagotribune.com, January 29, 2021. https://www.chicagotribune.com/2021/01/29/recalling-jerry-reinsdorfs-come-from-behind-victory-40-years-ago-for-control-of-the-chicago-white-sox-ive-never-celebrated-anniversaries-of-this-sort/.

6   Ed Sherman, "Q/A with Jerry Reinsdorf: The Brooklyn Kid Who Grew Up to Own White Sox," Jewishbasecallmuseum.com, May 18, 2018. https://jewishbaseballmuseum.com/spotlight-story/q-a-with-jerry-reinsdorf-the-brooklyn-kid-who-grew-up-to-own-white-sox/.

7   Asinwreck, "Forty Years of Jerry Reinsdorf, White Sox Owner," Soxmachine.com, February 2, 2021. https://soxmachine.com/2021/02/forty-years-of-jerry-reinsdorf-white-sox-owner/.

8   "Jerry Reinsdorf," Thefamouspeople.com, https://www.thefamouspeople.com/profiles/jerry-reinsdorf-51457.php.

9   Bob Vorwald, *What It Means to Be a White Sox* (Chicago: Triumph Books, 2010), 310.

10   Richard C. Lindberg, *Total White Sox: The Definitive Encyclopedia of the Chicago White Sox* (Chicago: Triumph Books, 2011), 94.

11   Vorwald, 310.

12   Mark Liptak "The Legacy of SportsVision," SI.Com, May 13, 2020. https://www.si.com/mlb/whitesox/history/white-sox-the-legacy-of-sportsvision.

13   Vorwald, 310.

14   Vorwald, 310.

15   Vorwald, 310.

16   Vorwald, 310.

17   Jerome Holtzman and Peter Kendall, "Legislators Vote to Save Sox," Chicagotribune.com, August 8, 2021. https://www.chicagotribune.com/1988/07/01/legislators-vote-to-save-sox/.

18   The White Sox agreement with the Illinois Sports Facilities Authority can be found at https://www.isfauthority.com/assets/management-agreement-with-all-amendments2.pdf. The White Sox lease can be found in its entirety on the Websites of the Illinois Sports Facilities Authority. Go to Business, then Finance, then Management Agreement with All Amendments.

19   Lindberg, 411.

20   Steve Wulf, "For Him the Belle Tolls," *Time*, December 2, 1996.

21   Richard C. Lindberg, *Total White Sox: The Definitive Encyclopedia of the Chicago White Sox* (Chicago: Triumph Books, 2011), 411-412.

22   Bill King, "Jerry Reinsdorf: Staying True," *Sports Business Journal*, May 20, 2013.

23   Vorwald, 311.

24   Ted Keith, "Don Fehr Looks Back 30 Years Later on MLB Strike," *Sports Business Journal*, August 10, 2024.

25   Steve Wulf, "For Him the Belle Tolls." Also see Michael Haupert "MLB's annual salary leaders since 1874," Outside the Lines, SABR, Fall 2012. https://sabr.org/research/article/mlbs-annual-salary-leaders-since-1874/.

26   Lindberg, 154.

27   Vorwald, 311.

28   Vorwald, 314.

29   Vorwald, 314.

30   Vinnie Duber, "Reinsdorf on Rebuild: Always Knew Plan Was Going to Work," nbcsportschicago, September 21, 2021. https://www.nbcsportschicago.com/mlb/chicago-white-sox/reinsdorf-on-rebuild-always-knew-plan-was-going-to-work/183019/.

31   Jim Margalus, "Jerry Reinsdorf Gets His Man with Tony La Russa. The White Sox Are an Afterthought," Soxmachine, October 29, 2020. https://soxmachine.com/2020/10/jerry-reinsdorf-gets-his-man-with-tony-la-russa-the-white-sox-are-an-afterthought/.

32   Ryan Taylor, "How Did Jerry Reinsdorf Conclude on the Dismissal of Rick Hahn, Kenny Williams," nbcsportschicago.com, September 1, 2023. https://www.nbcsportschicago.com/mlb/chicago-white-sox/white-sox-news/how-did-jerry-reinsdorf-conclude-on-the-dismissal-of-rick-hahn-kenny-williams/504600/.

33   Ryan Taylor, "Jerry Reinsdorf Details Thought Process Behind Hiring Chris Getz as General Manager," Sports.yahoo.com, August 31, 2023. https://sports.yahoo.com/jerry-reinsdorf-details-thought-process-232339195.html?fr=yhssrp_catchall.

34   Vorwald, 314.

35   Chicago Tribune, *Believe It! The Story of Chicago's World Champions* (Chicago: Triumph Books, 2005), 30.

36   Bryan O'Neill, "Initial Plans Revealed for Purported New White Sox Park in The 78." southsidesox.com, February 8, 2024. https://www.southsidesox.

com/2024/2/8/24066466/initial-plans-revealed-for-purported-new-chicago-white-sox-park-in-the-78.

37   Associated Press, "Shooting at White Sox Game Likely Involved Gun Fired Inside Park," August 28, 2023. https://www.espn.com/mlb/story/_/id/38278821/shooting-white-sox-game-likely-involved- gun-fired-park.

38   Phil Rogers, "Jerry Reinsdorf Says New Stadium Is a Must to Keep White Sox in Chicago," Forbes, February 22, 2024. https://www.forbes.com/sites/philrogers/2024/02/22/jerry-reinsdorf-says-new-stadium-is-a-must-to-keep-white-sox-in-chicago/

39   R.J. Anderson, "Rob Manfred Weighs In on White Sox's Future in Chicago with Jerry Reinsdorf Reportedly Open to Selling Team," CBS Sports, October 23, 2024.

40   R.J. Anderson, "White Sox Owner Jerry Reinsdorf Has Noticed His Team's Historically Bad 2024 Season, Too: 'No One Is Happy,'" msn.com, September 13, 2024. https://ontapsportsnet.com/mlb/jerry-reinsdorf-statement-on-chicago-white-sox-2024-season-historically-bad

41   David Greising, "The Toughest #&?!%* in Sports," Bloomberg.com, June 14, 1992. https://www.bloomberg.com/news/articles/1992-06-14/the-toughest-no-and-percent-in-sports.

42   Leigh Allan, "Jerry Reinsdorf: The Man Who Called Baseball a Public Trust and Didn't Believe a Word of It," Southsidesox.com. March 3, 2022. https://www.southsidesox.com/2022/3/3/22958768/white-sox-jerry-reinsdorf-the-man-who-called-baseball-a-public-trust.

43   Besnik Zekiri, "Jerry Reinsdorf's Empty Rhetoric, Promises and Legacy of Failure Define a White Sox Franchise in Free Fall," msn.com, September 11, 2024. https://www.msn.com/en-us/sports/mlb/jerry-reinsdorf-s-empty-rhetoric-promises-and-legacy-of-failure-define-a-white-sox-franchise-in-freefall/ar-AA1qqkfw.

44   Brittany Ghiroli and Ken Rosenthal, "An Owner 'Who Thinks He Knows Everything' Led the White Sox to Historic Disaster," The Athletic, September 19, 2024. https://www.nytimes.com/athletic/5773947/2024/09/19/white-sox-failure-worst-season-history/.

45   Scott Boeck, "MLB Payrolls 2024: Full List of Every Baseball Team from Highest to Lowest," *USAToday*, April 3, 2024.

46   Ghiroli and Rosenthal.

47   Mike Ozanian and Justin Teitlebaum, "Baseball's Most Valuable Teams," Forbes.com, March 28, 2024. https://www.forbes.com/sites/mikeozanian/2024/03/28/baseballs-most-valuable-teams-2024/.

48   White Sox Website. https://www.mlb.com/whitesox/charities.

49   Ed Sherman, "Q/A With Jerry Reinsdorf: The Brooklyn Kid Who Grew Up to Own White Sox."

50   *Chicago White Sox 2005 Media Guide*, 6.

51   Interview with Reinsdorf for the Order of Lincoln award, found at IllinoisLincolnAcademy.org, laureates, 1997. https://www.youtube.com/watch?v=_6jN044d6os.

U.S. CELLULAR FIELD

By Ken Carrano

The saying "To retain respect for sausages and laws, one must not watch them in the making" is sometimes attributed to Otto von Bismarck, the Prussian statesman. He probably didn't say it,[1] but whoever did had a point. Anyone who observed the process that eventually led to the building of Guaranteed Rate Field (originally New Comiskey Park and then US Cellular Field) in 1988 would have confirmed the notion that politics in Illinois is a difficult watch. It took a governor and the heads of the Illinois Senate and House of Representatives, as well as some effective clock management, to strong-arm enough legislators to create the state agency that built the current home of the Chicago White Sox.

The partnership led by Jerry Reinsdorf and Eddie Einhorn took control of the White Sox from Bill Veeck in early 1981. In taking control of the team and Comiskey Park, built in 1910, the partnership relied on an engineering report on the ballpark that had been prepared when Veeck was attempting to sell the White Sox to Edward DeBartolo in 1980. The engineers concluded that there was "nothing substantially wrong" that couldn't be addressed with minor expenditures.[2] However, decades of deferred maintenance began presenting problems almost immediately. In building private skyboxes in the 1982-1983 offseason, the engineers hired to inspect the park concluded, "Had we not gotten into this project, within a very short period of time, the entire upper deck behind the plate would have collapsed."[3]

In the middle of the '80s, the owners decided to explore their options to leave Comiskey Park. Team owners held discussions with the City of Chicago to build a combined

More than a decade after the 2005 World Series win, the White Sox play their crosstown rival Cubs on a warm July 25 night in 2016. The Sox went on to win 5-4.

baseball/football stadium in the South Loop, but the Chicago Bears weren't interested. On December 23, 1985, the team received a letter from the American League president, Dr. Bobby Brown:

"I am writing to express interest and the concerns of the American League over your plans for Comiskey Park and/ or a new stadium. It has become apparent to all that despite the excellent job of continual maintenance that you afford Comiskey Park, the time is rapidly approaching where the structure will no longer remain viable as a big-league park."[4]

The letter set a one-year deadline for a decision to be made regarding the future of the White Sox home and set a 1992 deadline – seven years off – for being in a new facility, whether in metropolitan Chicago or perhaps being relocated.[5]

Negotiations ended with the City of Chicago in early 1986, and Reinsdorf and Einhorn visited potential relocation venues of Denver, Miami, Orlando, New Orleans, St. Petersburg, and Northern Indiana. The owners made their intentions clear at a press conference on July 8, 1986. The team announced that it had quietly purchased 140 acres of land in the western Chicago suburb of Addison, and that time has forced them to act, but that they would need help. "Owners of the White Sox conceded Tuesday that they will need a substantial state subsidy to move the team to Addison and warned that they will have a 'back-up deal' ready with another city in case their suburban plans fall through."[6] In a nonbinding referendum among residents in November on whether the stadium should be built in Addison, a slim margin of 43 votes separated the noes (3,787 votes) from the yeses (3,744). While the Addison Village president wanted to continue to work toward building the ballpark, Reinsdorf placed the parcel for sale in early 1987.

With the Addison White Sox no longer an option, the team returned to working with Chicago Mayor Harold Washington, who had rejected earlier attempts to find a solution for the White Sox and Bears. This time, Washington, a lifelong White Sox fan, agreed to a plan to keep the club in Chicago by building a baseball-only stadium in the South Armour Square neighborhood, across the street from Comiskey Park. This site, with limited need for additional infrastructure improvements, was ideal due to the limited number (116) of private properties that would be taken by the city and state through eminent domain.[7] There were other local options to building across 35th street. Architect Philip Bess designed a replacement just north of Comiskey Park. The design, called Armour Field (it would have been in the location of Armour Square Park), resembled some of the designs that came after New Comiskey Park, such as Camden Yards. A historic building located in Armour Square Park, as well as the local advocate Friends of the Parks, would have made approval on this site difficult.[8]

To build and finance the new ballpark, the team and city needed the state to create a stadium authority in order to issue the municipal bonds needed to raise the capital needed. The Illinois Sports Facility Authority (ISFA) was created in December 1986 after Governor Jim Thompson rallied support in the Illinois House. The seven-member body included three members appointed by Mayor Washington, three by the governor, and a final member (presumably the chairman of the ISFA) also by the governor, but with the approval of the mayor.[9]

When Thompson appointed a longtime friend, Thomas Reynolds, to lead the ISFA without gaining Washington's approval, a stalemate between the city and state delayed progress in getting final approval from the state legislature. It was during this time that Reinsdorf and Einhorn began negotiations with St. Petersburg, Florida, to potentially move the team to the new Florida Suncoast Dome (now Tropicana Field). Thompson, ever the politician, realized that these negotiations may have helped his chances to push the necessary legislation through. "But could I have sold the Sox stadium deal *without* St. Pete in the picture? As a politician I'd like to think I could have, but to tell you honestly, I just don't know," he said.[10]

Thompson, a Republican and Washington, a Democrat, had resolved their differences, but Washington's untimely death from a heart attack on November 25, 1987, delayed continued city/state/team negotiations. The ISFA held its first meeting in December 1987, a full year after its creation, and soon selected Hellmuth, Obata, and Kassabaum (HOK) of Kansas City, Missouri, as the architect for the new park. HOK had previously advised the White Sox on their Addison project and was the architect of the Suncoast Dome. The firm promised to build a ballpark that would fit into the fabric of the city.[11]

The White Sox continued to negotiate with the ISFA over the lease for the new ballpark, but also with St. Petersburg on their Plan B. Some of the ownership group of the White Sox privately told *Chicago Tribune* columnist Jerome Holtzman that they favored moving out of the South Side. "It's economics," one of the investors told Holtzman. "A new stadium would be an attraction, a curiosity for two or three years. Then what happens? What have we got? We're still in the same neighborhood. It'll be the same as before." The investor continued, "The sooner we move or sell the club to another city, the better. It's the only way we get our money back."[12]

Even White Sox fans were split on what was best. One organization, Save Our Sox (SOS), was more concerned about keeping Comiskey Park, seemingly convinced that a new team would occupy the old ballpark, and another, Sox Fans on Deck (SFOD), was committed to keeping the White Sox in Chicago. Mayor Washington's successor, Eugene Sawyer, finally committed the city to the South Armour Square location, and SFOD held a rally that produced 30,000 signatures to be presented to the legislators in Springfield in support of the deal. Some 300 SFOD members took a bus to Springfield to rally for the tax bill that would fund the ISFA, but at this point the White Sox had still not signed a lease with the agency.

The bill to authorize the funding of the ISFA was on the legislative docket on the final day of the legislative session, June 30, 1988. The bill would only need to be approved by a simple majority (60 votes) if approved by that date, but once the session ended at midnight, a super-majority (71 votes) would be needed to approve the legislation, and that was unlikely given the current climate. The state had already funded the rebuilding of Arlington Park racetrack after a fire destroyed the grandstand, as well as a new state building in Chicago. The White Sox and ISFA finally agreed to a lease on June 29, setting up the drama that would take place the next day. (A link to the lease is included in the notes to this article.) The lease was for 20 years, with the White Sox having up to four successive five-year extensions, potentially keeping the White Sox on 35th Street through the 2030 season. There would be no rent due if the White Sox failed to draw 1,200,000 in attendance through the 2020 season, and 1,500,000 thereafter. As the White Sox drew less than 1.2 million fans in both 1988 and 1989, this attendance clause favored the team.[13] Still, in St. Petersburg, Florida, White Sox T-shirts were selling for $10 each.

When June 30 arrived, Governor Thompson was told that he did not have enough votes in either the House or Senate to pass the bill. Thompson met with Senate President James "Pate" Phillip, a fellow Republican, and House Speaker Michael Madigan, a Democrat, and received their support to encourage the requisite number of legislators to vote in favor of the bill. The Senate roll call began after 11 P.M., and after convincing four members to change their votes to yes, the bill had enough support in the Senate to pass.

Thompson and his entourage rushed to the House, where approval was much less likely. A chorus of "Na Na Hey, Hey Kiss (Them) Goodbye" was sung by downstate Illinois House members, who often voted against anything that would benefit Chicago.[14] As the clock moved close to midnight, Madigan told James McPike, the House majority leader, that he would not gavel the session to an end until Madigan wanted it to end. Thompson and Madigan continued to work the room, cashing in favors and promising new ones, until the 60 votes needed to pass the bill were secured. The gavel ending the session was sounded at 11:59 P.M., or 12:03 A.M., depending on which side of the issue you fell on, and the deal to build New Comiskey Park was done.

With the funding now secured, the ISFA got to work on building the ballpark. Neighborhood residents were offered the appraised value of their homes plus $25,000, or a new home in a different location. Renters were given a moving allowance. The ISFA offered the Chicago Housing Authority an $8 million loan to renovate the Wentworth Gardens housing project, the site of the 39th Street Grounds (a/k/a Schorling Park), the original home of the White Sox, but the CHA turned down the loan, fearing it might not be able to repay it.[15] One of the casualties of the construction was the demolition of McCuddy's Saloon, which sat across 35th Street from the original Comiskey Park. McCuddy's was opened in May 1910; Comiskey Park opened in July. The legend that Babe Ruth frequented McCuddy's during games did not keep progress and a bulldozer, driven by John McCuddy's great-grandson, from knocking down the watering hole.[16] The official groundbreaking for the ballpark took place on May 7, 1989. Einhorn used the occasion to state, "The bottom line is we are here to stay. We are committed to the people, we are committed to Chicago, we are committed to winning."[17] Einhorn was booed by some in attendance.

Opening day for New Comiskey Park arrived on April 18, 1991. The total cost of the facility was $134,900,000, or about $2.1 million under budget. The White Sox paid tribute to their old ballpark by filming the passing of a baseball from the old ballpark to the new, which included Chicago's new Mayor Richard M. Daley, as well as White Sox legends Minnie Miñoso and Billy Pierce, as well as former groundskeeper Gene Bossard (whose son, Roger "The Sodfather" Bossard, succeeded him), and Nels Hendrickson, who at age 98 had seen the White Sox play at both the 39th Street Ground and Comiskey Park. Governor Thompson threw out the first pitch.[18]

Initial reviews of the new ballpark were very good. "Looks like a real ballpark," Sparky Anderson, the Detroit Tigers manager, told *Chicago Tribune* columnist Bob Verdi. "I hate domes. And Toronto, you feel like you're in a theater. This place is beautiful, but it's not gaudy. Everybody's going to want one of these now."[19] If Anderson's mood was lifted by his team's 16-0 victory over the White Sox that day, this is lost to history. A team record (only eclipsed in 2006) 2,934,154 fans crowded into New Comiskey Park in 1991. The opening in 1992 of Oriole Park at Camden Yards in Baltimore gave White Sox fans a glimpse of what they could have had, at least for another $100 million.[20] The primary criticisms were leveled at the upper deck, sloped at a 35-degree angle, and was uncovered aside from a small overhang at the very top of the ballpark. The slope at Old Comiskey Park was 27 degrees.[21] Paul Goldberger, in his book *Ballpark* (New York: Knopf Publishing, 2019), summarized the criticisms of the new ballpark succinctly:

> Its overall design bears a distant resemblance to the Royals stadium, but without the graceful curves of the Kansas City grandstand. The design of New Comiskey's enormous, wide, and steep upper-deck overhang that led to so many obstructed-view seats at the old Comiskey, meant that a vast number of seats were at a great distance from the field. It was a poor trade-off for getting rid of the columns that had supported old Comiskey's upper deck. The critic John Pastier observed that the seats in the first row of the upper deck in the new park are farther from the field than the seats in the last row of the old one.

GRINDERS AND GAMERS

The new Comiskey that HOK produced may have been built right next to the old Comiskey on Chicago's South Side, but it was in every other way a suburban stadium. By some measures it was worse, since it was a suburban stadium placed inside the city, and building it required the destruction of several blocks of original urban fabric.[22]

The unnamed White Sox investors' prediction from 1986 appeared to be becoming reality, though it took longer than three years. Attendance settled around 2.6 million during 1992 and 1993 (the latter a division championship year, the first since 1983). Attendance in 1994 was also strong, with the White Sox in first place again when the players strike began on August 12. When the 1995 season began, fans stayed away in droves.[23] Many White Sox fans blamed Reinsdorf for the strike that canceled what could have been a World Series year on the South Side.[24] Attendance at the new ballpark continued to decline, bottoming out in 1999 with only 1,338,851 fans attending. Fans and playoff baseball returned to the South Side in 2000, but attendance still did not eclipse the 2 million mark.

When New Comiskey Park opened in 1991, there was not much to remind the fans of the old ballpark aside from the pinwheels on the new exploding scoreboard, similar to the ones that Bill Veeck had installed when he owned the White Sox the first time, as well as a ballpark organ for legendary White Sox organist Nancy Faust. The first changes the team and ISFA made were throwbacks to the old yard – a bullpen bar with windows to the field was opened in 1996. This was similar to the left-field picnic area in the original. A shower was installed in left field in 1999, just like the one Veeck installed in center field in his second term as owner. It took the team and the ISFA 10 years to address some of the major issues. "The years after it opened to a mostly enthusiastic public, (New) Comiskey Park has become every stadium architect's nightmare," wrote the *Chicago Tribune*. "It is the place where other designers go to learn what not to do – and where the public, by and large, doesn't go."[25] Beginning in 2001, the ISFA and White Sox decided to add more seats in the lower deck. Seats were added along the foul lines beyond the dugouts, and the moat that had existed between the outfield wall and the stands was filled in, adding 1,900 seats. The funds for these and future renovations were provided by the ISFA, which had extra funding after being tasked with the renovations at Soldier Field, home of the Bears.

The ISFA continued its renovations, placing a fan deck in the center-field concourse and adding the first statue to the concourse, that of founder Charles Comiskey.[26] Over the years, additional statues were unveiled in the outfield, honoring White Sox legends Miñoso, Pierce, the double-play tandem of Luis Aparicio and Nellie Fox, Harold Baines, Carlton Fisk, Frank Thomas, and Paul Konerko. In 2003 the team sold the naming rights to US Cellular, a telecommunications company, for $68 million over 20 years ($3.4 million per year). At the same time, the White Sox exercised the first three of their four five-year options on their lease, which moved the expiration date of the lease through the 2025 season. Ten years later, US Cellular left the Chicago market for cell-phone service but retained the naming rights.[27]

Perhaps the most important renovation took place for the 2004 season, removing the top eight rows of the upper deck, and replacing the sloped roof over the upper deck with a flat roof. This reduced the ballpark's capacity from 47,098 to 40,615. This change did not solve the 35-degree pitch problem, but it seemed to make the slope not quite as steep as it used to.[28] A large area for children, the FUNdamentals Deck, was opened in left field before the 2005 season. Playoff baseball returned again to Chicago in 2005, but this time the tears at the end of the playoffs were of joy and not sorrow, as the White Sox went 11-1 in the postseason, winning their first World Series since 1917. Attendance crossed the 2 million level for the first time since 1993 and remained over this mark until 2012.

The playoff run featured one of the most controversial calls in American League Championship Series history, when in the ninth inning of Game Two, White Sox catcher A.J. Pierzynski reached first base on a dropped third strike call that may or may not have been dropped. "Customarily, a ball in the dirt for strike three, [the umpire] says, 'No catch, no catch, no catch,' and I didn't hear him say anything," Josh Paul, Angels (and former White Sox) catcher said.[29] Uncertain whether Paul had caught the third strike, Pierzynski took one step towards the Sox dugout before sprinting to first base to sell home-plate umpire Doug Eddings on the idea that Paul had dropped the ball.[30] Pablo Ozuna pinch ran for Pierzynski, stole second base, and scored the winning run on pinch-hitter Joe Crede's double. The Sox went on to win the next three games against the Angels and sweep the Houston Astros to win the flag.

Playoff baseball did not return to US Cellular Field until 2008, but the renovations continued at the ballpark. In 2006 the original blue seats from 1991 were replaced with dark green seats, reminiscent of the ballpark's predecessor. Only two seats remain blue – the landing locations of Konerko's grand slam and Scott Podsednik's walk-off home run in Game Two of the World Series. In 2008 the ballpark's outermost parking lot (Lot L) was refitted with permeable pavers to help reduce the amount of water entering the Chicago storm sewer system. In addition, a "Champions Plaza" was installed at the entrance to the ballpark, with a large statue commemorating the 2005 World Series victory.

Improvements in 2011 and 2012 included the first outside the ballpark itself. A restaurant, the ChiSox Bar and Grill, opened inside Gate 5, across the street from the ballpark (a pedestrian bridge takes fans into the park). It had indoor and outdoor seating and was open to the public during game days. In 2013 the Chicago Sports Depot a significantly larger merchandise shop than the primary shop at the lower

255

level opened, with access from both inside and outside the ballpark.

In 2016, three years after exiting the Chicago market, US Cellular ended its relationship with the White Sox, paying $13 million to exit the agreement early.[31] A local mortgage provider, Guaranteed Rate, purchased the naming rights for $20.4 million for 10 years, about $1 million less than the White Sox had received from US Cellular.[32] To many fans, the name US Cellular Field was bad enough (even though the nickname for the park – "The Cell" – had wide appeal), but the Guaranteed Rate Field name was worse, especially due to its corporate logo. The *Chicago Tribune* commented: "The corporate logo of mortgage lender Guaranteed Rate is a red arrow pointing downward. It suggests low rates for customers, which is a good thing for them. But when it comes to baseball, the symbol is more like an emoji for losing. Those red arrows will be all over Guaranteed Rate Field, which has already inspired nicknames like Guaranteed Loss Field or Low Interest Stadium."[33] Probably the most interesting addition to the park came in 2019, with the addition of "The Goose Island. Goose Island is a Chicago craft brewery, purchased by Anheuser-Busch in 2011. Sections 106 and 107 of the ballpark were replaced by a 326-seat section with water running along its sides giving the impression that the guest was on an island. Goose Island beer was served from two replica Chicago Transit Authority subway cars at the top of the section. Goose Island lost the rights to sell beer at Guaranteed Rate Field and the section was renamed the Miller Lite Landing.

In 2023 Guaranteed Rate Field became an unusual crime scene. At a game on August 25, two women were shot while seated in left-field Section 161. The police said it was unclear where the shots came from. Reinsdorf stated the opposite, telling NBC Chicago, "I don't want to influence the police's decision, but the fact is based upon the information available to us, I see virtually no possibility that the gunshots came from within the ballpark."[34]

The shooting invigorated the discussion that Guaranteed Rate Field is in a "bad area." But according to the web site crimegrade.org, the crime rate for the ZIP code that contains Guaranteed Rate Field is less (48.07 crimes per 1,000 residents) than that in the ZIP code for Wrigley Field (52.64).[35] Most White Sox fans express no concerns about crime in this area.

Guaranteed Rate Field was 34 years old in the 2024 season, probably having aged significantly during the season as the White Sox set the modern record for season losses (121), winning only 23 of their 81 home dates. Attendance of 1,380,733 was the lowest for the team since 1999, and the second lowest in the ballpark's history. Still, before the season started, the White Sox announced that they were in discussions with a developer to build a new ballpark on the South Loop, three miles north of Guaranteed Rate Field in an area known as "The 78." (It would become the city's 78th official neighborhood.) The developer, Related Midwest,

released renderings in February 2024 showing an open-air ballpark along the south branch of the Chicago River, with views of downtown.[36] The project's cost, estimated as high as $2 billion, would likely need, and struggle to get, governmental support. "I think I've been fairly clear about the fact that taxpayers' dollars are precious," Governor J.B. Pritzker said. "And the idea of taking taxpayer dollars and subsidizing the building of a stadium as opposed to, for example, subsidizing the building of a birthing center, just to give an example, does not seem like the stadium ought to have higher priority."[37] Some Illinois lawmakers agreed with Pritzker. "We say 'no' because we all want a shiny new car," said South Side Representative Marcus Evans. "Shiny new cars don't move me. It's all about the finance."[38]

Further complicating the potential move from Guaranteed Rate Field were revelations that Reinsdorf was in active discussions about selling the team. Reinsdorf is thought to own approximately 19 percent of the team, and the news is significant in that he has not expressed the potential of selling the team while he is alive. (Reinsdorf, born in 1936, was 88 years old in 2024.) He has said several times that he has advised his heirs to sell the White Sox and keep ownership of the Chicago Bulls, where his son is president.[39]

As of 2024 the future of Guaranteed Rate Field was in doubt. The White Sox could continue to use the ballpark past the lease expiration of 2029, move to The 78 as part of a grand neighborhood development, or look outside the city for greener pastures and more public money. What is certain is that the team, the City of Chicago, and the State of Illinois will continue their three-headed-monster relationship. Watching sausage being made will probably be easier on the eyes.

SOURCES

In addition to the sources cited in the Notes, the author consulted the following:

www.isfauthority.com

www.baseball-reference.com

www.soxmachine.com

Bauer, John. "A Ballpark as Political Football: Florida, Illinois, and New Home for the White Sox," in Gregory H. Wolf, ed., *The Baseball Palace of the World: Comiskey Park* (Phoenix: SABR, 2019).

Management Agreement between Illinois Sports Facilities Authority and Chicago White Sox, LTD – https://www.isfauthority.com/assets/management-agreement-with-all-amendments2.pdf

NOTES

1   https://quoteinvestigator.com/2010/07/08/laws-sausages/

2   Richard C. Lindberg, *Stealing First in a Two-Team Town* (Champaign, Illinois: Sagamore Publishing, 1984), 222.

3   Lindberg, 223-224.

4   Lindberg, 229.

5   Lindberg, 230.

6   John McCarron and David Young, "White Sox Owners: It's Addison or Adios," *Chicago Tribune*, July 9, 1986: 1.

7   Lindberg, 238.

8   https://www.cbssports.com/mlb/news/the-white-sox-ballpark-in-chicago-that-never-was-and-could-have-changed-history/.

9   Lindberg, 238.

10   Lindberg, 241.

11   Lindberg, 244.

12   Jerome Holtzman, "Sox Investors Cool to Staying in City," *Chicago Tribune*, Maech 29, 1988: 45.

13   While the calculation is based on numerous factors, the only season that White Sox attendance fell below the break point where no rent would be due was 2024.

14   Lindberg, xxvi.

15   Lindberg, 254.

16   Robert Davis, "Wreckers Leave Mccuddy's Down and Out on 35th St.," *Chicago Tribune*, March 28, 1989: 1.

17   William Recktenwald, "Sox Begin their Field of Dreams," *Chicago Tribune*, May 8, 1989: 9.

18   Alan Soloman, "Let the New Memories Begin," *Chicago Tribune*, April 18, 1991: 53.

19   Bob Verdi, "Well, the Ballpark Was Beautiful," *Chicago Tribune*, April 19, 1991: 51.

20   Oriole Park cost about $125 million to build, but site acquisition costs added another $100 million to the project. https://digitaledition.baltimoresun.com/tribune/article_popover.aspx?guid=2957dc23-3946-4545-9ec2-041be52dc0c0.

21   Lindberg, 259.

22   https://soxmachine.com/2019/07/considering-and-reconsidering-the-ballpark-after-ballpark/.

23   Average attendance in 1994 was 32,026. In 1995, attendance dropped 30 percent, to 22,358.

24   "Hoop Dreams," *Newsweek*, March 19, 1995. https://www.newsweek.com/hoop-dreams-180618.

25   Blair Kamin, "10 Years Later, Comiskey Still Has a Bad Reputation," *Chicago Tribune*, July 22, 2001: 111.

26   https://www.isfauthority.com/facilities/guaranteed-rate-field-renovations/.

27   Doug Padilla, "The Cell Not in Line for Name Change," ESPN.com, April 26, 2013. https://www.espn.com/blog/chicago/white-sox/post/_/id/14560/the-cell-not-in-line-for-name-change.

28   https://baseballparks.com/indepth/uscellular/.

29   Dave van Dyck, "The Play, the Goat, the Hero," *Chicago Tribune*, October 13, 2005: 7-4.

30   David Haugh, "Crede Doubles Fun at Finish," *Chicago Tribune*, October 13, 2005: 7-4.

31   Becky Yerak, "Deal to Drop Sox Park Naming Rights Early Costs US Cellular $13 Million," *Chicago Tribune*, November 4, 2016: 2-1.

32   Peter Thomas Ricci, "What Guaranteed Rate Paid for the White Sox Stadium Naming Rights," *Chicago Agent Magazine*, September 1, 2016. https://chicagoagentmagazine.com/2016/09/01/guaranteed-rate-paid-white-sox-stadium-naming-rights/.

33   Richard Sandomir, "One Guarantee for the Chicago White Sox' New Stadium Name: Derision," *New York Times*, August 25, 2016. B9.

34   Bennett Haeberle, "3 Weeks after Shooting at White Sox Game, Questions Remain Unanswered," NBC Chicago, September 15, 2023. https://www.nbcchicago.com/news/local/white-sox-shooting-chicago-police-department/3229319/.

35   Data pulled from www.crimerate.org on October 29, 2024.

36   Dan Lambert, "Developer Releases Renderings Showing New Riverfront White Sox Stadium at The 78," WTTW.com, February 8, 2024. https://news.wttw.com/2024/02/08/renderings-released-proposed-new-white-sox-stadium-78.

37   Amanda Vinicky, "Pritzker Says He's 'Reluctant' to Use Taxpayer Money to Help Build a New White Sox Stadium," WTTW, February 26, 2024. https://news.wttw.com/2024/02/26/pritzker-says-he-s-reluctant-use-taxpayer-money-help-build-new-white-sox-stadium.

38   Jeremy Gorner, "Legislators Say They're Still Skeptical About Public Funding for New White Sox stadium after Team-Sponsored Cruise," *Chicago Tribune*, September 18, 2024.

39   Brittany Ghiroli, "Jerry Reinsdorf Open to Selling White Sox: Sources," *The Athletic*, October 16, 2024. https://www.nytimes.com/athletic/5848339/2024/10/16/jerry-reinsdorf-chicago-white-sox-sale/?source=emp_shared_article.

KEN HARRELSON

By Alexander Edelman

Kenneth Smith Harrelson was born on September 4, 1941, in Woodruff, South Carolina. In the sixth grade, he moved to Savannah, Georgia, where he and his older sister would grow up. Harrelson was the youngest child of a single mother, Jessie, who was his biggest supporter, closest confidante, and best friend. Jessie worked hard to support her son, and she held a difficult and poor-paying job as a secretary in a meat-packing plant in order to provide for him. Fortunately, Ken had proved at a very young age that he was an extraordinary athlete, and when it came time for him to go to high school, the schools came to him, recruiting the athletic youngster by offering jobs, money, and financial support as incentives. Harrelson chose Benedictine Military School, because it was his mother's first choice. And despite Harrelson's strong aversion to the school's strict military code, he flourished as an athlete and obtained solid jobs through generous alumni.

By the time he was 17, Kenneth had matured into a street-smart young man and become the family's primary breadwinner.[1] While he was still in high school, Harrelson met his first wife, Betty Ann Pacifi, whom he married that year. Harrelson was an excellent baseball player who hit three home runs in the first Little League game ever played in Savannah, but was by nature a competitor who also played football, basketball, and golf. Ironically, he regarded baseball as his worst sport.

Despite being an excellent baseball player and a Basketball Schoolboy All-American, Harrelson was fondest of football and he accepted a scholarship to play at the University of Georgia. His mother, making $56.00 a week, asked him to reconsider, feeling that baseball would pay better, so her doting son decided instead to play baseball professionally.[2]

The two teams offering serious money were Kansas City and the Los Angeles Dodgers, and Los Angeles promised a larger bonus, but Harrelson signed with the A's because intrepid Kansas City scout Clyde Kluttz was able to convince him that he would be in the majors faster if he chose the Athletics.

Ken Harrelson and Hawk Harrelson are two very different sides of Kenneth Smith Harrelson, and, in a 1986 article for *Chicago Magazine*, he recounted the exact moment that the two sides met.[3] It was a Gulf Coast Instructional League game in Florida in 1959, and one of Harrelson's teammates, Dick Howser, had come up with a new name for him. Harrelson's nose, which had been broken several times and had started to take on a distinctly beak-like aspect, was a point of great amusement for Harrelson's teammates and childhood friends. Howser, who thought that Harrelson looked like a character in a popular comic strip, took to calling him "Henrietta Hawk" in a mocking manner.

Aggravating the matter was the fact that Harrelson, one of Kansas City's most touted prospects, "wasn't doing squat as far as hitting goes,"[4] and the usually thick-skinned teenager from Savannah began to take offense to Howser's name calling, dubbing him "Slick" in retaliation. One day, after another especially disappointing effort at the plate for Harrelson, Howser again poked fun at the frustrated rookie, causing the latter to lose his cool. "Hey Slick, why don't you lay off?"

"I'll lay off," Howser retorted, "when you get a hit."

Ken Harrelson

Disgruntled but inspired, Harrelson took the field the next day and hit two homers. "Okay," said Howser, "I'll drop the Henrietta."[5] The name "Hawk" stuck.

After two more or less average years in the minor leagues in 1959 and 1960, Harrelson started to show promise in 1961 with the Class-C California League's Visalia A's, where he hit 25 home runs, with 114 RBIs, and had a .301 average in 135 games. The next year, Harrelson exploded; in a magnificent season with Class-A Binghamton, he set Eastern League records with 38 homers and 138 RBIs. In 1963, Harrelson continued to improve, and his solid play with Portland of the Pacific Coast League, did not go unnoticed, as the Athletics promoted Harrelson to the majors, where he began to discover his more colorful side. In '64, Harrelson played only 49 games with the Athletics, who finished in 10th place. In 1965, the Hawk played 150 games and slug 23 homers — though the Athletics still finished in 10th again anyway.

Harrelson was a shrewd businessman and colorful hustler who always understood the value of a dollar, and, before long, he began to realize that the "Hawk" character was a persona that could make him lots of money. Harrelson was right, and as the outfielder began to hit home runs and grow more popular, "The Hawk" began to surface more often, and, almost overnight, his flashy alter-ego made Harrelson a fan favorite throughout the American League. After the 1964 season, Harrelson decided to play winter baseball in Venezuela, and it was there that he really discovered "The Hawk" personality.[6] "The Hawk was a character," says Harrelson's former Venezuela winter ball teammate Billy Bryan, "he was a hell of a pool shooter and arm-wrestler, and a fun roommate besides."[7]

Harrelson also learned some lessons about relating to fans during his early years in Kansas City. One day, after a tough day at the plate, Harrelson, who was in a hurry to get to a party, rebuffed a bunch of kids requesting his autograph. While he was shoving his way through the overeager youngsters, he felt a firm hand on the back of his neck, pulling him back towards the clubhouse. Harrelson, by now incensed and ready to fight, turned towards the person who the hand belonged to, but felt his anger melt away when he found himself face to face with his mother's favorite player and his own childhood hero, baseball legend Rocky Colavito. Colavito pulled Harrelson aside, and let him have it, telling the rookie on no uncertain turns that he should always take the time to sign autographs for the people who paid his salary. Harrelson never forgot the lesson, and from that point on would treat the fans with respect and courtesy.[8]

Though "The Hawk" would soon make a name for himself on the baseball field, what really would put him on the radar in professional baseball was his prowess on the golf course. In 1964, just a year after his major-league debut, Harrelson played in his first golf tournament for major leaguers. After he earned second place behind Albie Pearson, one of baseball's best golfers, many players, managers, and owners began to take notice of the sweet-swinging outfielder.[9] Golfing, besides being The Hawk's passion, would become part of his legacy: the popularization of the batting glove.

One day in 1963 after two long rounds of golfing with Athletics teammates Ted Bowsfield, Sammy Esposito, and Gino Cimoli, Harrelson developed painful blisters on his hands.[10] Arriving at the ballpark for that night's game, he found it would be easier to grip a bat if he wore the gloves he had used earlier that day to golf. When The Hawk stepped to the plate in the first inning against the New York Yankees, his teammates scoffed, but after Harrelson had a great night at the plate, both the Athletics and the Yankees showed up at the ballpark the next day wearing golf gloves. And thus, the batting glove was born.[11]

Growing up with little money, Harrelson could always sense when there was something to be earned. Raised in a rough-and-tumble area of Savannah, Harrelson chose his battles carefully and cautiously measured his actions. Despite his portrayal as an impulsive individual, the skinny baseball player learned how to maneuver his way out of unavoidable tight spots, using perceptive street smarts, the power of persuasion, and his extensive network of contacts and friends. Harrelson's autobiographical tome, *Hawk*, written with Al Hirshberg in 1969, describes the adventures of "The Hawk" in great detail. From pool hustling to golfing for money, dozens of anecdotes depicting shrewd play and smooth operating are contained in the book's 244 pages, and the stories, which start to pick up speed around 1964, show us the reluctant, slow emergence of the outspoken Hawk persona from the small-town Ken Harrelson, who took care of his mama and spoke with a Southern accent.

However, not everyone was a fan of the flashy façade, and The Hawk ruffled a few people's feathers and rubbed some the wrong way. Unfortunately, one such person bothered by the outfielder's flamboyance was Charles O. Finley, who owned the A's. Finley tried over and over again to irk The Hawk, and refused him a raise; Harrelson had to call his mother for financial support.[12] In 1966, after 63 games, a series of heated public arguments and angry private exchanges, Harrelson was traded to the Washington Senators, where he played for the remainder of the season and some of the next before he was reluctantly reunited with Finley, who bought him back in the early months of 1967. Harrelson had never seen eye to eye with the eccentric owner, but he liked Kansas City, and thus patiently put up with Finley's shenanigans. Harrelson had always been co-operative with Finley, even when he was asked to take part in one of the baseball mogul's more infamous pranks — a donkey named Charlie O. that Finley repeatedly forced Harrelson to ride.[13] Finley's antics were usually rash and impulsive, often causing more harm than good, and Harrelson bore them with tolerance. "Charlie had some good ideas and some bad ideas," Harrelson says, "but overall he was not a nice man."

After Finley suspended pitcher Lew Krausse on August 18, 1967, for what many viewed as a trumped-up offense, Krausse's teammates, led by Jack Aker, Harrelson and a half dozen other players, read a statement criticizing Finley. Manager Alvin Dark revolted, refusing to bench Krausse, instead choosing to voice his support for the pitcher.[14] Finley, not known for level-headed decisions, fired Dark, prompting Harrelson to publicly denounce the owner. On the morning of August 24, UPI reported wrote that Harrelson had called Finley a "menace to baseball."[15] Finley seethed, and all the extra effort The Hawk had employed to try to appease his boss was wasted when he was put on irrevocable waivers on August 25—because of his refusal to attend a press conference to apologize for a statement he says he never made.

Because Harrelson was having an excellent year (he had been hitting .273 at the time of his release), he found himself the subject of one of the first free agent bidding wars in modern baseball history. Among the bidders in the battle for Harrelson were the Boston Red Sox. The Red Sox were in the middle of a pennant race and had started the season with Tony Conigliaro as their right fielder. When Conigliaro, a popular and talented local sports hero, was tragically felled by a fastball on August 18, ending his season and curtailing a very promising career, the Sox began searching for a replacement. General Manager Dick O'Connell saw the release of Harrelson as an opportunity to fill the gap left by the injury to Conigliaro. After an intense struggle with several major-league teams (and even the Tokyo Giants), O'Connell and the Red Sox finally signed "The Hawk" for $150,000 on August 28—approximately a $138,000 increase in salary.

In many ways, the signing of Hawk Harrelson marked the end of the age where the owner was boss, and the beginning of the era in which players controlled their own destinies. Harrelson was someone the Red Sox desperately needed, and while O'Connell knew it, so did The Hawk. The end result, an incredibly lucrative contract by the standards of the time period, was what Bill Reynolds called "a sneak preview of free agency" in his book *Lost Summer*.[16]

The Red Sox and Hawk Harrelson were a perfect fit, and it was really in Boston that The Hawk took flight: the Red Sox needed a power-hitting right fielder, and Harrelson, who was having a great season, filled the bill perfectly. And not only did Boston love The Hawk, but The Hawk reciprocated that love.

"The Hawk was really a product of the fans of Boston," Harrelson says, "The Red Sox were a great team, but they didn't have any real personalities up there… after some success, The Hawk evolved, and that is really how it happened. For many reasons, one of them being that, Boston will always have a special place in my heart." To Harrelson, The Hawk wasn't just some false persona to utilize for monetary purposes — though that was a very nice side effect — The Hawk was something that gave Harrelson, someone who always thought of himself as an overachiever, support when he was behind or slumping. He credits the fans with "bringing The Hawk to the forefront," and maintains that he never could have been successful in baseball without The Hawk backing him up.

In 1967, the fans were behind Ken Harrelson — and The Hawk — all the way, and the now-happy outfielder helped the Red Sox take the pennant. Besides being a solid outfielder, he was also a great clubhouse influence who could take the strain of a pennant race off other players, players like Carl Yastrzemski. Especially Carl Yastrzemski. In 1967, Yaz was, as Harrelson wrote in his book, "the greatest ballplayer who ever lived, in fact or fiction. Compared to him [fictional sports hero] Frank Merriwell was a piker."[17] Harrelson provided a great help in taking the press load off the media-conscious Yaz. Like every other member of the 1967 team maintains, Harrelson recalls the Red Sox as having a great year, a magical, unbelievable, impossible year. Everyone did their part, even self-proclaimed Johnny-come-latelies like The Hawk. Harrelson did not have a good World Series, and the Red Sox lost in seven games.

In the clubhouse immediately after the final game, Harrelson finally lost his composure, sobbing uncontrollably as the victorious St. Louis Cardinals celebrated just down the hall. Harrelson had not played his best with the Red Sox, hitting just .200 with only 14 RBIs, and though Hawk had knocked out some clutch hits, including a key RBI in their October 1, pennant-clinching game, it was a definite possibility that his poor play would result in a trade.

Despite the rumored trade offers, by the spring of 1968, The Hawk was flying high. Harrelson had established himself as one of the baseball's best golfers, and won a number of golf tournaments in the offseason.[18] As soon as spring training started however, The Hawk totally dedicated himself to getting ready for a good year, and even gave away his clubs so he could focus on baseball.[19]

Red Sox fans, many of whom were initially upset at the thought of Harrelson replacing their beloved Conigliaro, had begun to open their arms to their flamboyant right fielder. Nonetheless, rookie Joe Lahoud was showing some promise in right, and with George Scott already at first base, Harrelson's second position, trade rumors regarding The Hawk abounded. Fortunately for Harrelson — and, as it would turn out, the Red Sox — Conigliaro's injury still prevented him from playing and Lahoud proved to still be too young. Shortly after Opening Day, it became clear that the Hawk would roost in right field at Fenway for at least one more season.

The 1968 season would become known as "The Year of the Pitcher," and in the American League, Detroit Tigers right-hander Denny McLain won 31 games and the MVP award. But despite the mastery of pitching that year, the Hawk excelled.[20] The Red Sox won no pennant in 1968, but Harrelson helped keep them competitive. He valued runs batted in above all other measures of individual success, and leading the majors in RBIs in 1968 with 109 is something he remained proud of more than 40 years later.

Again and again, The Hawk picked up the Sox, seemingly always getting a big hit when one was most needed. He hit 35 home runs during the season, 13 of them game-winners. Harrelson was enjoying Boston immensely and playing better than he ever had before, and his effusive, explosive alter-ego, The Hawk, was having the time of his life, earning more money then he ever had before — and spending that money just as quickly, which only helped build the "Hawk" persona.

The Hawk had become more than just a nickname, it was now a commodity, and lavish possessions proliferated. A lavender dune-buggy. A sandwich shop, an insurance company and travel agency. A song by a popular Boston band entitled "Don't Walk The Hawk."[21] The emblem "Hawk" embroidered on every piece of clothing, including his trademark Nehru jackets. He attended an Academy of Professional Sports Show that was televised from Hollywood — and, reportedly, his attire made the movie stars "look like rag pickers."[22] The Hawk loved the attention, but Harrelson was overwhelmed by it. Carl Yastrzemski, who was no stranger to endorsements himself, offered some helpful financial advice: Hire Bob Woolf.[23] Woolf, a Boston lawyer who had become one of the world's most well-known sports agents when he negotiated Larry Bird's contract with the Celtics in 1979, would manage The Hawk's finances for the rest of his career and serve as a voice of reason in times of trouble.

In the early stages of the 1969 season, in a shocking transaction, the Red Sox dealt Harrelson to the Cleveland Indians along with Juan Pizarro and Dick Ellsworth in exchange for Sonny Siebert, Joe Azcue, and Vicente Romo. George Scott and Dalton Jones split time at first base, and Tony Conigliaro tried to make a comeback in right field. The move came as a paralyzing blow to Harrelson, who loved Boston, and could not imagine leaving it. The previous season, Red Sox owner Tom Yawkey had announced in a newspaper article that he was thankful that the Red Sox had not traded Harrelson prior to spring training in 1968: "Often," Yawkey said, "the best deals are the ones you don't make."[24] Harrelson's Red Sox teammates were distraught, and the Hawk himself was inconsolable. Angry fans picketed the front office protesting the trade. Despite Harrelson's public displays of disappointment, when Harrelson announced that he would retire rather than play for another team, jaws dropped across the country, and chaos reigned.

How could The Hawk nest anywhere else but Boston? He was loved by the fans, loved by his teammates, loved by sponsors, endorsers, businessmen, and consumers. Harrelson simply could not leave Boston — he would rather not play. On the other hand, baseball meant too much to The Hawk to simply leave it behind. For Red Sox General Manager Dick O'Connell, Cleveland Indians president Gabe Paul, and Baseball Commissioner Bowie Kuhn, the situation was a nightmare. Azcue and Siebert had already said they would not go back to Cleveland, and the other three players involved in the transaction were caught in limbo — freshly dressed in their new uniforms but not eligible to play. Meanwhile, Harrelson waited, in the middle of the frenzy, exhausted from lack of sleep and emotionally in shambles, The Hawk lay mostly dormant throughout the entire solemn ordeal, but shone through briefly when Harrelson met Kuhn for the first time. Though the distressed Harrelson had a serious matter on his mind, his flashy alter-ego was distracted by the finely-dressed commissioner's attire, and, unable to help himself, The Hawk commented extensively on the sartorial elegance of Kuhn's suit.[25] On April 21, Harrelson and his agent, Wolff, met with the commissioner, AL President Joe Cronin, Paul, and O'Connell at the league offices in New York, and resolved the situation. Harrelson loved baseball "too much to hurt it," and he reported to Cleveland the next day, reunited with friend and former manager Alvin Dark.[26]

Despite Harrelson's reluctance to leave Boston, he was pleasantly surprised to be welcomed with open arms in Cleveland, and business deals abounded. He again endorsed products, and while in Cleveland his autobiography (written with Al Hirshberg) was published. The Hawk was huge again. But the style didn't lack substance, as Harrelson hit 30 homers and drove in 92 runs, en route to another productive year. He did, however, bat only .221, a 54-point drop from 1968. His OPS declined from 155 to 108.

In 1970, tragedy struck in the form of a debilitating injury. Playing in a spring training game on March 19 against his former team, the Oakland Athletics, Hawk slid into second base and immediately felt a shooting pain in his leg. It was broken. Harrelson was laid up for a long time, and while he was injured, rookie Chris Chambliss took his place. After the 1971 season, having played only 69 games since his injury, The Hawk felt an emotion that was entirely new to him. "I just lost my desire to play baseball," Harrelson said in his 2006 interview, "I was still a competitor, The Hawk was still there, but I didn't want to play baseball anymore." Harrelson sadly announced that he would quit the game he had loved for so long to pursue a professional golfing career. That pursuit ended badly, and Harrelson turned back to baseball once more in 1975, coming back to Boston—this time as an announcer. Harrelson grew up listening to Jack Buck and Harry Caray calling St. Louis Cardinals games and always felt that baseball was a perfect game for radio. He envisioned every home run, double play, and diving catch.[27] Many Boston fans have fond memories of Harrelson's work behind the mic with Dick Stockton.[28]

Harrelson was hired as the analyst for the Chicago White Sox in 1981, where he served with play-by-play announcer Don Drysdale[29] until 1986, when he moved from the broadcast booth to the front office, serving as the White Sox executive vice president of baseball operations for a year. He had no experience running a baseball team and was ill-equipped to do so. During his short lived time, he fired Tony LaRussa and Dave Dombrowski who would later build championship clubs elsewhere.[30] Jerrry Reinsdorf regretted it so much that he rehired LaRussa 34 years later in 2021. Carlton Fisk was also moved to left field in a controversial move but was back at catcher by mid-May.[31]

Harrelson returned to the broadcast booth for good in 1987, taking a similar position for the New York Yankees. He returned to the White Sox in 1991 as the lead play-by-play man and worked there for nearly three more decades teaming up with Tom "Wimpy" Paciorek and Steve Stone over that time.[32]

In his most recent book, *Hawk: I Did It My Way*, written with Jeff Snook, Harrelson recounted some of the 2005 White Sox championship season. During a late August swoon with the Cleveland Indians closing the gap, Harrelson paid a visit to Ozzie Guillén, saying "These players need you now more than ever."[33] Soon after Guillén ranted to the media, moving the focus from the struggling players onto him. The White Sox righted the ship and went on their magical postseason run. Harrelson was the MC of the championship celebration introducing the players, White Sox management, and local politicians such as Mayor Richard M. Daley.[34] The 2005 championship brought back memories of the 1967 Red Sox World Series loss. "I was not sure I felt real pain for losing that World Series with the Red Sox—until I experienced what the White Sox felt by winning it," Harrelson said.[35]

His Southern twang and enthusiastic catchphrases made him a fan favorite—and also led to some fans calling for his dismissal, claiming that his accent was unintelligible and his baseball phrases hackneyed. Some examples were, "You can put it on the board, yes!" when a White Sox hit a home run, and "Stretch!" when a fly ball didn't seem like it had enough to make it out as Harrelson was coaxing it over the fence. And "He gone!" when an opposing player made an out, as well "Grab some bench" when they struck out.[36] He had an uncanny talent for giving players nicknames that stuck: e.g. "The Big Hurt" for Thomas, "The Little Hurt" for Craig Grebeck, "The Deacon" for Warren Newson, "The Little Bulldog" for Greg Hibbard, and "Black Jack" McDowell.

Deep down, the competitive nature of The Hawk remained and whether he was defending Lew Krausse or Jerry Reinsdorf, he never shied away from an issue. In 2006, The Hawk's opponent wasn't an owner named Charlie Finley, but a journalist named Jay Mariotti. Mariotti, who constantly attacked Reinsdorf, and Harrelson. One verbal altercation between Mariotti and Harrelson almost came to blows in the press box in Minnesota,[37] and Mariotti later ripped Hawk on his radio show. Harrelson later called in and asked to speak with Mariotti, saying he was willing to drive to the station to settle the score once and for all: Mariotti wanted no part of that.[38] Hawk affectionately nicknamed Mariotti "The Hiney Bird," later explaining: "The Hiney Bird is a creature that flies in perfectly concentric circles over and over again until it flies up its own ass and disappears forever."

Harrelson also had several run-ins with umpires, usually related to missed calls against the White Sox. A famous on air outburst occurred on May 30, 2012 when umpire Mark Wegner tossed White Sox pitcher Jose Quintana and manager Robin Ventura from the game after Quintana threw a pitch behind the Tampa Bay Rays' Ben Zobrist. Several White Sox had been hit earlier in the game. Harrelson went berserk on the air, saying "What are you doing? What are you doing? This is absolutely brutal. This is unbelievable… Totally absurd…That just tells you that there is an umpire here in the American League who knows nothing about baseball…."[39] Afterward Harrelson received calls from both Commissioner Bud Selig and Joe Torre, who oversaw the umpires for Major League Baseball.[40]

Another long-time umpire foe of Harrelson was Joe West. Harrelson used to say there are two rules of baseball: "You've got to catch the ball; you can't give the other team 30 to 31 outs when you're getting 27. And the second rule is don't mess with Joe West."[41] Unbeknownst to Harrelson, West had throat cancer and continued to umpire games after recovering from cancer. Hawk immediately went to the umpire's locker room to see West after finding out. They patched things up, hung out, and eventually discovered a shared a passion for golf.[42] A foe had now become a friend.

Harrelson had the opportunity to call a perfect game—Mark Buehrle's on July 23, 2009 against the Tampa Bay Rays. Harrelson broke with normal baseball tradition about never mentioning a perfect game while it was in process. After the eighth inning Harrelson announced, "Call your friends, call your sons, call your daughters… Mark Buehrle has a perfect game heading into the ninth inning."[43] However, Harrelson was still very much old school in many aspects of how he saw the game. Most notably: his dislike of Sabermetrics. He felt that the modern way players were evaluated was overrated. The most important metric was what he called "TWTW," or "The Will To Win."[44]

Harrelson retired from broadcasting after the 2018 season.[45] The White Sox named the broadcast level of the stadium after Harrelson and placed a small plaque with his face on it, prominent nose protruding slightly was included.[46] He was honored with the Ford C. Frick Award for baseball broadcasting excellence in 2020 and participated in Induction Weekend ceremonies at the Baseball Hall of Fame in Cooperstown.[47] His baseball career spanned seven decades, beginning with his 13-year professional baseball career and ending with his 39 years in the broadcast booth.

Today, Harrelson resides in Granger, Indiana, about two hours outside of Chicago, with his wife, Aris. They are the proud parents of two children, Casey and Krista, and several grandchildren. Casey tried his hand at professional golf trying to make the PGA Tour, and also spent a year in professional baseball. The Hawk usually lies dormant, and for nearly four decades the Southern charm of Kenneth Smith Harrelson was what millions of White Sox fans heard every night when they tuned in to the White Sox games on WGN-TV. Harrelson claimed he loved the game "more than ever."

Hawk Harrelson summarizes how he says he viewed the game: "Our two rules were play your ass off, and have fun. … Sure, you wanted money … but that was third or fourth down the line."

An earlier version of this biography originally appeared in SABR's *The 1967 Impossible Dream Red Sox: Pandemonium On The Field* (Rounder Books, 2007), edited by Bill Nowlin.

Mark Morowczynski made additional contributions to the biography in October 2024 as part of *The World Champion 2005 Chicago White Sox: Grinders & Gamers.*

NOTES

1   Ken Harrelson interview with author on May 4, 2006. All quotations not otherwise attributed are from this interview.

2   Bill Reynolds, *Lost Summer: The 1967 Red Sox and the Impossible Dream* (New York: Warner Books, 1992), 170-171.

3   Steve Fiffer, "Interview: Ken 'Hawk' Harrelson," *Chicago Magazine*, April 1, 1986. https://www.chicagomag.com/Chicago-Magazine/April-1986/Interview-Ken-Hawk-Harrelson/

4   Harrelson interview with author.

5   Reynolds, 172.

6   Or "El Hawko," as Caracas fans referred to him. There are many stories about Harrelson's adventures in South America. For instance, once, when Harrelson was tossed from a game in Venezuela, he charged out of the dugout to argue with the umpire, who immediately struck him in the jaw. Harrelson fought back, punching the umpire repeatedly. A newspaper article commenting on the event remarked that Harrelson's jaw must have been a "prominent target." George Minot Jr., "Ken Harrelson Alters Senators' 'Character'," *Washington Post*, July 10, 1966: C4.

7   Author interview with Billy Bryan, May 23, 2006.

8   Harrelson interview with author.

9   Ken Harrelson and Al Hirshberg, *Hawk* (New York: Viking Press, 1969), 71.

10   Harrelson interview with author.

11   Harrelson interview with author.

12   Harrelson, *Hawk*, 178.

13   Harrelson says he was paid $25. Harrelson, *Hawk*, 145.

14   In *Hawk*, Harrelson claims that Krausse got a "bum rap," and wasn't even slightly disorderly. 182.

15   UPI, "Harrelson Fired, Aker Fined by Irate Finley," *Los Angeles Times*, August 22, 1967: C1.

16   Reynolds, 190.

17   Harrelson, *Hawk*, 207.

18   Harrelson, *Hawk*, op. cit. 67-81.

19   UPI, "Harrelson: The Hawk Flies High With Boston," *Los Angeles Times*, May 30, 1968: A13.

20   Harrelson won AL Player of the Year and came in third in the MVP race behind McLain and Bill Freehan of Detroit. He also made his only All-Star appearance in a game that seemed typical of the year — a 1-0 pitchers' duel in favor of the National League.

21   The Val Perry Trio's single was released on Stary Records. It can be heard at: https://www.youtube.com/watch?v=CozKHsmAEYI

22   Bob Addie, "The Lavender Hawk," *Washington Post*, February 27, 1969: C2,

23   Harrelson, *Hawk,* 220-221.

24   Dick Dew, "Harrelson No Longer On Block for Any Price," *Boston Record American*, May 22, 1968: 15.

25   George Vecsey, "Williams Joins Lombardi's Fan Club." *New York Times*, April 27, 1969: S3.

26   Harrelson, *Hawk,* 239-242.

27   Ken Harrelson and Jeff Snook, *Hawk: I Did It My Way* (Chicago: Triumph Books, 2018), 337.

28   Harrelson, *Hawk: I Did It My Way*, 343.

29   Harrelson, *Hawk: I Did It My Way*, 343.

30   John Snyder, *White Sox Journal: Year by Year and Day by Day with the Chicago White Sox Since 1901* (Cincinnati: Clerisy Press, 2009), 500.

31   Snyder, *White Sox Journal: Year by Year and Day by Day with the Chicago White Sox Since 1901*, 500.

32   Harrelson, *Hawk: I Did It My Way*, 343.

33   Harrelson, *Hawk: I Did It My Way*, 299.

34   Harrelson, *Hawk: I Did It My Way*, 301.

35   Harrelson, *Hawk: I Did It My Way*, 305.

36   Harrelson, *Hawk: I Did It My Way*, 341.

37   Harrelson, *Hawk: I Did It My Way*, 302.

38   Harrelson, *Hawk: I Did It My Way*, 303.

39   Harrelson, *Hawk: I Did It My Way*, 311.

40   Harrelson, *Hawk: I Did It My Way*, 312.

41   Phil Rosenthal, "Hawk no longer calling West 'a joke': Harrelson heaps praise on record-breaking ump," *Chicago Tribune*, May 26, 2021: 3.

42   Harrelson, *Hawk: I Did It My Way*, 317.

43   Harrelson, *Hawk: I Did It My Way*, 346.

44   Harrelson, *Hawk: I Did It My Way*, 357.

45   His retirement may not have been entirely voluntary he revealed several years later. See Karl Rasmussen, "Ex-White Sox Broadcaster Ken Harrelson Says He Was Forced to Retire," *Sports Illustrated*, March 28, 2023. https://www.si.com/mlb/2023/03/29/ken-hawk-harrelson-says-white-sox-forced-retirement See a special broadcast presented by the National Baseball Hall of Fame on YouTube at https://www.youtube.com/watch?v=7q0m7EWKteE

46   Harrelson, *Hawk: I Did It My Way*, 371.

47   The actual presentation was delayed by one years due to the COVID-19 pandemic. Scott Merkin, "Hawk finally receives '20 Ford C. Frick award," MLB.com, July 25, 2021. https://baseballhall.org/discover/awards/ford-c-frick/ken-harrelson

DARRIN JACKSON

By Don Zminda

Darrin Jackson has spent more than 40 years in professional baseball, first as a highly respected (and well-traveled) outfielder (1981-99) who overcame cancer and serious illnesses to have a productive career, and then as the longtime analyst for Chicago White Sox television (2000-08) and radio (2009-) broadcasts. In 2024 Jackson completed his 25th season as a White Sox broadcaster. Only Baseball Hall of Fame Ford C. Frick Award winners Bob Elson, Jack Brickhouse, and Ken "Hawk" Harrelson, along with Jackson's longtime partner Ed Farmer and Spanish broadcaster Héctor Molina, have spent more seasons broadcasting White Sox games.[1]

Darrin Jay Jackson was born in Los Angeles on August 22, 1963, to George and Sylvia (Nipper) Jackson. A talented athlete who excelled at both baseball and basketball, George Jackson had been scouted by the New York Giants, who were interested in signing him as a pitcher. Unfortunately for George, he only learned of the Giants' interest in him

Darrin Jackson

after he had enlisted in the Air Force. (He continued to excel at sports while in the service.) Sylvia, an Oklahoma native who had married for the first time at age 16, had four children from her previous two marriages, and two more with George, including Darrin, the baby of the family. The Jacksons separated when Darrin was 2, living on separate coasts: Sylvia in Los Angeles and George in Philadelphia, where he settled after being discharged from the Air Force on a disability. George, who suffered from injuries and alcohol problems and did not work after his discharge, "wasn't in my life that much," said Darrin; he and his five siblings (three brothers and two sisters) were primarily raised by Sylvia, who worked as a waitress to support the family.[2]

When Darrin was 2, Sylvia moved the family from central Los Angeles to the nearby suburb of Culver City. At his mother's insistence, Darrin began playing Little League baseball, but "I didn't like it. I stunk. There was just nothing fun about it. Well, after that year of stinking at baseball, I told my mom I didn't want to play, and she said, 'It's too bad. You're going to go back out and play again next year.' So I went back out to play, and I got a little better, and (the game) became a little more fun also." Sylvia, who Jackson said "protected her kids like she was Mama Bear," collected the baseball from Darrin's first Little League home run; on it, she wrote, "Keep hitting home runs all the way to the major leagues." Jackson still has the baseball.[3]

Jackson played both baseball and basketball at Culver City High; while admitting that he probably had more fun playing basketball, "I could have probably played junior college ball at best and that was it. Baseball was fun and it was also serious. It was business. When you get older, all of a sudden you're taking it seriously because you're hoping to play professionally."[4] As a senior, Jackson batted .460, stole 21 bases in 22 attempts, and was named the Most Outstanding Player in the Ocean League. He was selected by the Chicago Cubs in the second round of the June 1981 amateur draft, the 28th overall pick.[5]

Still only 17, Jackson batted .186 in 62 games for the Cubs' farm team in the short-season Gulf Coast League in 1981, though with 18 stolen bases. He improved markedly in 1982, batting .276 and stealing 58 bases for Class-A Quad Cities. After moving steadily up the Cubs' farm system the next few years, Jackson was called to the majors in June of 1985, after Cubs center fielder Bob Dernier went on the disabled list with a foot injury.[6] He made his major-league debut on June 17, starting in center field at New York's Shea Stadium against the Mets' Ron Darling. He went 0-for-2. The next day, Jackson got his first major-league hit, a seventh-inning single off Mets righty Ed Lynch, a future Jackson teammate who would later become general manager of the Cubs.

Jackson spent only about a week with the 1985 Cubs before returning to the minors. After hitting .267 with 15 home runs for Double-A Pittsfield in 1986 and .274 with 23 homers for Triple-A Iowa in 1987, he came back as a late-season call-up in September of '87. At that point the 24-year-old outfielder learned that he was dealing with a major medical issue. "I'd just been called to the big leagues in September of 1987 when I found out that I had testicular cancer," he recalled. "I had to have surgery here in Chicago at Northwestern Hospital, and then I went back to Southern California and had a bigger procedure to follow it up." During the second surgery, 54 lymph nodes were removed from his chest and stomach. The disease hadn't spread, but Jackson lost about 25 pounds while recovering. He reported to spring training in a very weakened condition.[7] "Don Zimmer, my manager, was awesome," Jackson recalled. "He knew I was recovering from surgeries and understood that I had a 12-inch scar in the middle of my stomach that probably wasn't quite healed yet. He was like, 'Kid, do what you can do. Don't overdo it.' The rest was up to me."[8] Jackson came through; when he made the Cubs' Opening Day roster, he was, according to baseball writer Bob Nightengale, the first player publicly known to have been diagnosed with cancer who was able to return to the major leagues.[9]

Jackson got into 100 games for the Cubs in 1988, though only 40 of them were as a starter. He batted .266 with six homers in that role, including his first major-league homer on May 21 against Reds lefty Danny Jackson (no relation) at Cincinnati's Riverfront Stadium. "Danny Jackson was really nasty," Darrin recalled. "He had great stuff, and he was having a great season [a National League-high 23 wins in 1988]. "I remember he just kept burying these little tight cutters and sliders, down and in, down and in. One of my processes as a hitter is, when you have a really good pitcher that's doing something to get you out, he's going to keep doing it. So you better take that away from him and look for that pitch. I stepped in the bucket and crushed it down the left-field line. He stopped throwing me that pitch after that."[10]

"D.J." (as he is popularly known) spent most of the 1989 season in a similar role – part-time outfielder, pinch-hitter, defensive sub. On August 30 the Cubs, who were contending for a playoff berth, traded Jackson, pitcher Calvin Schiraldi, and a player to be named later (Phil Stephenson) to the San Diego Padres for infielder Luis Salazar and outfielder Marvell Wynne. While Jackson missed playing in the postseason – not the first time this would happen to him – he was returning to Southern California, where he'd

grown up. With the Padres, Jackson got more of a chance to play regularly – especially in 1991-92, when he hit a total of 38 homers and was a four-plus-win player each year, according to Baseball-Reference WAR. Jackson filed for salary arbitration after the 1992 season; when he won his case and was awarded $2.1 million, the Padres, looking to cut salary, decided to trade him. On March 30, 1993, one week prior to the start of the season, they dealt Jackson to the Toronto Blue Jays for outfielder Derek Bell and minor leaguer Stoney Briggs.[11] "We're losing a first-class person," said Padres manager Jim Riggleman. "You hate to lose, to me, one of the best players in the league, period," said Jackson's Padres teammate and friend Tony Gwynn."[12]

Jackson opened the 1993 season as the starting right fielder for the defending World Series champion Blue Jays; however, he was far from healthy. Weakened first by a serious case of the flu and then a bout of food poisoning, he missed the last two weeks of spring training, resulting in a hospital stint as well as considerable weight loss. He felt unfocused, couldn't concentrate, and couldn't hit with his usual power. "A month into the season, I'm still weak," he recalled. "I can't focus. I don't feel good. My legs are shaking when I'm in the batter's box." He was concerned that his cancer had returned, but testing ruled that out; the Toronto team doctors simply did not know what was wrong with him. "They're like, this guy's making excuses," he said.[13] In June, with Jackson batting only .216, the Blue Jays traded him to the New York Mets for shortstop Tony Fernández. When he continued to feel weak and unfocused, more tests were ordered, and finally the cause was discovered: Jackson was suffering from hyperthyroidism, or Graves disease.[14] The disease is treatable with medication, and eventually Jackson was able to fully recover. However, 1993 was a lost season: he batted just .209 for the year, including a .195 mark in 31 games with the Mets.

A free agent after the season, Jackson drew considerable interest despite his struggles with the Blue Jays and Mets. Ultimately he signed a one-year, $750,000 contract (plus up to $800,000 for reaching plate-appearance benchmarks) with the White Sox, who had lost power-hitting outfielders Bo Jackson (no relation) and Ellis Burks to free agency over the winter.[15] Working with White Sox hitting coach Walt Hriniak, Jackson began using the whole field in 1994 much more than in the past; the result was career highs in batting average (.312) and OPS (.817) for the AL Central-leading White Sox. His previous full-season major-league high in batting average had been .266 for the 1988 Cubs.

Unfortunately, the season ended for Jackson and the White Sox in August, when major-league players went on strike. And despite his overall excellent numbers, Jackson struggled throughout the season with his medical condition. "The trainers and the team doctors were keeping me balanced with my thyroid medications," he recalled. "It was a constant 'Go in and then get your blood work done. See that your levels are okay.' So we kept adjusting my medicine. I can't focus again. I'm hitting like .351 one minute, down to .310 next minute. Gotta adjust your medicine.' So it was up and down throughout the year, and then the strike hits."[16]

The White Sox hoped to get Jackson to return in 1995,[17] but he had a different plan. With the strike still unsettled, he opted to sign a one-year, $3 million contract with the Seibu Lions of Japan's Pacific League. He was one of several major-league stars – others included Julio Franco, Shane Mack, and Kevin Mitchell – who signed with Japanese teams after the 1994 season.[18] "I'm a free agent," he recalled. "I have nearly seven years in the big leagues now, and I said, 'I am sick and tired of everything going this way. I'm not doing it anymore.' I ended up leaving because I was just tired of all the crazy things taking place in my career here." Jackson wound up playing two seasons in Japan, hitting .289 with 20 home runs in 1995 and .266 with 19 homers in 1996. "I loved it," he said about the experience. "I've always enjoyed traveling abroad, learning new cultures. So that was going to be a new chapter in my life. They treated me like a king over there. I've never been treated better."[19]

Nonetheless, Jackson opted to return to American baseball after the 1996 season. Several teams expressed interest, including the Pittsburgh Pirates, who were managed by Jackson's former White Sox skipper, Gene Lamont; the Pirates offered Jackson a major-league contract, with the likelihood that he would be the team's starting right fielder. But Jackson, who wanted to return to his California roots, instead signed a minor-league contract with the San Francisco Giants for a guaranteed $650,000 (plus incentives) if he made the Opening Day roster.[20] According to Jackson, the Giants verbally assured him that he would make their major-league roster no matter what. However, he missed a week of spring training with the flu and got off to a slow start in spring games. That seemed to sour the Giants on Jackson. They attempted to trade him, but when they did not receive an offer they found acceptable, they released him on March 31, the day before the start of the regular season. Jackson, who felt that the Giants had lied to him about making the team, was extremely upset. "They could have released me a week ago, two weeks ago," he said. "But they kept me until the last minute to serve their purposes, to try and get something for me. They couldn't, and now I'm in this situation."[21] He later described his experience with the Giants as "my worst chapter in major-league baseball."[22]

Released too late to land a major-league job at the start of the '97 season, Jackson spent some time in extended spring training with the Boston Red Sox, then signed a minor-league deal with the Triple-A Salt Lake Buzz, a Minnesota Twins farm team. The Twins recalled him in mid-May, and Jackson celebrated his return to the majors by getting three hits, including a grand slam, along with six RBIs in his first game.[23] After batting .254 with 3 home runs in 49 games with the Twins, he was traded to the Milwaukee Brewers on August 30 for a player to be named later (minor-league pitcher Mick Fieldbinder). "I told Minnesota, just trade me," said Jackson. "You're not playing me anymore. So get me out of here."[24] Jackson batted .272 in 26 games – 20 of them in the starting lineup – for the Brewers over the remainder of the season, then re-signed with Milwaukee for 1998.

After hitting .240 in 114 games – only 37 as a starter – for the Brewers in '98, Jackson was ready to retire. The team offered him a position as a minor-league manager or instructor. But at the urging of Chris Singleton, a young outfielder and workout buddy of Jackson's who had just been traded to the White Sox, he signed a one-year deal with the White Sox.[25] Jackson's .275 average in 75 games for the '99 White Sox was his major-league best since his .312 mark for the Sox in 1994. His 1999 season highlight came in the season-opening three-game series in Seattle: starting all three games, Jackson went 9-for-13 with two home runs. It was a nice homecoming for D.J., who had developed a good relationship with White Sox owner Jerry Reinsdorf and general manager Ron Schueler. He was ready to return as a player at age 36 in 2000, but Reinsdorf had a different idea: Tom "Wimpy" Paciorek, the White Sox' TV analyst since 1988, was leaving, and Reinsdorf offered Jackson a three-year contract to become Hawk Harrelson's TV partner. Jackson, who admitted that "I didn't even know that Tom had left," accepted the challenge.[26] He retired from baseball with a .257 career batting average and 80 home runs in 960 games over 12 major-league seasons.

Jackson, who was paired with Harrelson on White Sox television broadcasts from 2000 to 2008, has fond memories of the 2005 championship season. "I don't look back at that season and think of one particular game," he said. "What I do think of is a collective group of guys and how unbelievably talented they were. Watching them day in and day out, the consistency from all of those guys was amazing. I kept comparing them to the World Series champion '93 Blue Jays, who I played for; that Blue Jays team was really good, but when I realized that the White Sox were probably better due to that consistency, I just was blown away. It was fun to watch and talk with Hawk every day about what these guys were doing. It was just something to behold."[27]

In 2009 Jackson shifted to radio as the partner of Chicago native and ex-White Sox pitcher Ed Farmer, a fondly remembered and often irreverent pairing that continued until Farmer's death in April of 2020. "We are best friends," Jackson said about Farmer in 2019. "I look at us more like brothers. We go at each other all the time, whether it be at work or just in our time away, playing golf, having lunch, whatever. … I think our number-one priority is not only to give you the game and teach it, but also to make it fun. I want to be up here along with Ed and just have a great conversation."[28] Recalling the wide-ranging discussions that he and Farmer often had on the air, Jackson said, "We gave you baseball, but we also gave you a bunch of other stuff. Every now and then, I'd have to hold my phone out and show Ed. 'Just got a text from Jerry. He said, get back to baseball. Stop talking about that and get back to your jobs.' So we did."[29] Since Farmer's death, Jackson has worked with Andy Masur (in 2020), and then with Len Kasper.

Jackson has two children, Adian and Tatum, with his wife, Robin; he also has two (Alexandre and Adrianna) from his previous marriage. "I'm still there [working for the White Sox], Jackson said about his broadcasting career, "but that's because Jerry Reinsdorf is, you know, a very generous boss. So, 25 years later, I'm still up there."[30]

SOURCES

In addition to the references cited, the author utilized Retrosheet.com, Baseball-Reference.com, and the 2023 *Chicago White Sox Media Guide*.

NOTES

1   Longest White Sox broadcast tenures compiled from the White Sox chapter in Stuart Shea, *Calling the Game: Baseball Broadcasting from 1920 to the Present* (Phoenix: Society for American Baseball Research, 2015), 62-80.

2   Author interview with Darrin Jackson, November 18, 2024.

3   "Darrin Jackson reflects on his baseball roots (5/31/19)," Chicago White Sox video, https://www.youtube.com/watch?v=6yVkokO39yQ; accessed November 27, 2024.

4   Jackson interview.

5   Jim Thomas, "Culver's Jackson Has a Day," *Torrance* (California) *Daily Breeze*, June 9, 1981: 26.

6   Fred Mitchell, "Dernier Set for Surgery; Center-Fielder Called Up," *Chicago Tribune*, June 17, 1985: 24.

7   Bob Verdi, "Darrin Jackson Leads Cubs in 1 Category: Courage," *Chicago Tribune*, April 5, 1988: 41.

8   Jackson interview.

9   Bob Nightengale, "Jackson to Peers: You Can Beat It," *USA Today Baseball Weekly*, March 3-9, 1999: 6.

10   Jackson interview.

11   Buster Olney, "Padres Get Jays' Bell for Jackson; *San Diego Union-Tribune*, March 31, 1993: 28.

12   Buster Olney, "Padres React to the Trade," *San Diego Union-Tribune*, March 31, 1993: 30.

13   Jackson interview.

14   Tom Friend, "Finally, a Diagnosis; Now, the Road Back," *New York Times*, July 27, 1993: B11.

15   Alan Solomon, "Sox Sign Jackson (Darrin, not Bo) for RF," *Chicago Tribune*, December 29, 1993: 41.

16   Jackson interview.

17   Joseph A. Reaves, "Sox Ready to Offer Jackson a Deal," *Chicago Tribune*, January 14, 1995: 49.

18   Merrill Goozner, "Land of the Rising Salary," *Chicago Tribune*, April 5, 1995: 214.

19   Jackson interview.

20   Henry Schulman, "Giants Try to Re-Orient Center Field," *San Francisco Examiner*, December 21, 1996: 19.

21   Henry Schulman, "Ex-Giant Jackson Takes Release Hard," *San Francisco Examiner*, April 1, 1997: 57.

22   Jackson interview.

23   Patrick Reusse, "Stahoviak, Jackson Add Much-Needed Power to Lineup," *Minneapolis Star-Tribune*, May 17, 1997: 43.

24   Jackson interview.

25   Jackson interview.

26   Ed Sharman, "Jackson's Best Asset for TV Job: Honesty," *Chicago Tribune*, December 3, 1999: 69.

27   Jackson interview.

28   "Darrin Jackson Reflects on His Baseball Roots."

29   Jackson interview.

30   Jackson interview.

ED FARMER

By Besnik Zekiri

The Chicago White Sox' historic 2005 season can be told in many ways, but few shared it as personally as one of the teams radio voices, Ed Farmer. Born in Evergreen Park, Illinois, and raised on the South Side of Chicago, Farmer – affectionately known as "Farmio" – grew up watching and rooting for the White Sox.[1]

He eventually suited up for the team, but also spent nearly 30 years as a broadcaster, becoming a cherished voice of the franchise. He died on April 1, 2020, at the age of 70, leaving behind an indelible mark on baseball and the Chicago sports community.

Primarily a relief pitcher, Farmer played for the Cleveland Indians (1971-1973), Detroit Tigers (1973), Philadelphia Phillies (1974 and 1982-83), Baltimore Orioles (1977), Milwaukee Brewers (1978), Texas Rangers (1979), the White Sox (1979-1981), and the Oakland Athletics (1983).

Edward Joseph Farmer, the second of nine children, was born at Little Company of Mary Hospital in Evergreen Park,

Ed Farmer

a village bordering Chicago, on October 18, 1949, to Marilyn (Truesdale) and Edward Farmer, one of nine or 10 children in the family.[2] His father worked as an electrical contractor. Young Edward grew up at 79th Street and Francisco Avenue in the Wrightwood neighborhood on Chicago's South Side. He developed his passion for baseball early, impressing scouts as a hard-throwing 6-foot-5 right-hander and football player at St. Rita High School, where he became a multitime member of the Chicago Tribune Prep Baseball All-Stars. In his senior year, Ed Farmer led the Chicago Catholic High School League with an impressive 158 strikeouts and pitched the Mustangs to the league championship.

Despite Farmer's dominance on the mound, when he attended a White Sox summer camp, a scout told him to forget about pitching and try his luck as a catcher instead. Not everyone shared that opinion. Indians scout Benny Zientara saw something special in Farmer and recommended him as a pitcher to his bosses.

Dozens of colleges offered him scholarships, including Notre Dame, where his father hoped he'd play football. He wanted to study premed. However, at the urging of his ailing mother, Farmer pursued his dream of playing professional baseball, signing with the Cleveland Indians in 1967 for $10,000 after being selected in the fifth round.[3] He made his professional debut with the rookie-league Gulf Coast Indians, posting a 3-0 record and a 1.97 ERA in seven games. His transition into the professional ranks wasn't without its struggles – high ERAs marked his early seasons in the Indians system as a starting pitcher.[4]

By 1970, Farmer was pitching for the Triple-A Wichita Aeros, posting a 5-7 record and a 4.02 ERA. He was still only 20 years old but had already participated in three spring-training camps with the Indians. In June of 1971, after starting the season with the Aeros, Farmer was called up to the Indians.

Beginning a big-league career that saw him pitch primarily as a right-handed reliever for eight teams over 11 seasons, Farmer made his major-league debut on June 9 against the White Sox at Cleveland Stadium. He entered the game in the ninth inning with the Indians leading, 3-1, and runners at first and second. After throwing a wild pitch, Farmer earned the save by striking out Tom Egan. He made a total of 43 appearances in 1971, four of which were starts. He went 5-4 with four saves and a 4.35 ERA in 78⅔ innings pitched. On July 1 he earned his first win, against the

Baltimore Orioles, after he threw a perfect ninth inning, and Vada Pinson slammed a two-out walk-off homer off Eddie Watt. He started the first game of a doubleheader against the Detroit Tigers on August 31 and singled to center field off Joe Coleman in the third inning for his first career base hit.

In 1972 the 22-year-old logged 61⅓ innings in 46 games, making one start. He earned seven saves with a 4.40 ERA.

Cleveland dealt Farmer to the Tigers on June 15, 1973, for Tom Timmerman and Kevin Collins. Farmer had pitched only 17⅓ innings so far in the season and requested a trade. He made 24 appearances with the Tigers in 1973, never quite finding his stride, and finished with a 5.00 ERA for Detroit.

Before the 1974 season, on March 19, 1974, Farmer was traded to the Yankees in a three-team deal involving his former club, the Indians. Cleveland sent Rick Sawyer and Walt Williams to the Yankees, Detroit sent Farmer to the Yankees and Jim Perry to Cleveland, and the Yankees sent Jerry Moses to the Tigers. Two days later New York sold Farmer to the Philadelphia Phillies. The Yankees wanted to send him to the minor leagues, but Farmer affirmed that he would return to his premed studies at the University of Chicago. Much like his time in Detroit, he struggled with the Phillies. He had an ERA of 8.42 in 14 games.

Farmer found himself out of the big leagues for three years. The Phillies traded him on December 3, 1974, to the Brewers for minor leaguer Stephen McCartney. He spent 1975 pitching for their Triple-A affiliate, the Sacramento Solons. Farmer battled a sore arm through 14 appearances, and his performance suffered. He was released on June 13. A brief stop in Mexico followed, but after two rough outings, Farmer's career on the mound came to an abrupt halt. The Brewers released him in April of 1976. After surgery to remove a bone spur in his right shoulder, he did not pitch in professional baseball that season.

Farmer's path to becoming a White Sox legend wasn't a straight line – it was a roller coaster filled with setbacks, resilience, and a few near-misses. He started working in a warehouse in Southern California, his offseason home with his baseball future uncertain. It might've been the end of his baseball journey if it weren't for his resolve and the encouragement of his wife, Barbara, who urged him to keep pushing for another shot. While training for a tryout with the Orioles in 1977, Farmer was struck by a car while riding his bike – an accident that sent him through the windshield and knocked out his front teeth. But not even a brush with death kept him down for long.[5]

Even after the accident, Farmer impressed the Orioles scout and spent most of 1977 with their Triple-A affiliate in Rochester. A brief appearance in the majors didn't go as planned – he faced two batters, giving up a single to Lance Parrish, which loaded the bases, and then walking Ben Oglivie before being replaced – finishing the season with an infinite ERA. But he kept grinding.

Farmer bounced around again, making another stop with the Brewers when he signed with them as a free agent on

April 1, 1978. He spent most of the year in Triple A, making only three major-league appearances and surrendering just one run in 11 innings before landing with the Rangers in '79. Farmer's time in Texas is most remembered for a game in which he injured Frank White and Al Cowens by hitting them with pitches – White suffering a broken thumb and Cowens a fractured cheekbone. Farmer attributed his erratic pitching to nerves; it was his first major-league start in years. However, the Royals suspected the hits were intentional, and Cowens would later seek retribution.

Farmer's career finally clicked when he found his way home to the South Side thanks to a recommendation from Jerry Krause, a scout for the White Sox before his career as the general manager of the NBA's Chicago Bulls.

On June 15, 1979, Chicago acquired Farmer, Gary Holle, and cash from the Texas Rangers for third baseman Eric Soderholm. Despite spending most of his White Sox tenure as a reliever, Farmer debuted as a starter on June 20, 1979, taking the loss after surrendering four runs over 3⅓ innings in a 5-3 defeat.[6]

Farmer earned the first of his 54 saves with Chicago on July 10, 1979, after retiring six hitters in order, preserving a 6-3 win over the Rangers. Two days later, he made his eighth appearance with the South Siders, tossing a scoreless 3⅔ innings in the matinee of a doubleheader against the Tigers. The White Sox forfeited the nightcap of the twin bill after the infamous Disco Demolition Night festivities.

During an offday on August 2 of that year, White Sox owner Bill Veeck and general manager Roland Hemond fired player-manager Don Kessinger. Farmer recorded the final six outs of a 9-1 loss to the New York Yankees the day before, making him the last player as of 2025 to pitch for a player-manager in the American League. On August 3 Farmer earned the save in Tony La Russa's managerial debut.[7]

Farmer earned his lone All-Star nod in 1980 while earning 30 saves, the White Sox record at the time. (The record has been surpassed 17 times since then, most notably by Bobby Thigpen, who set the current mark with 57 saves in 1990.) Farmer had a 3.34 ERA over 99⅔ innings. He got his 30th save on October 4, in a game in which 56-year-old Minnie Miñoso pinch-hit, marking the record fifth decade he played in.

The three years Farmer spent on the South Side were his best seasons, from 1979 to 1981, when he recorded 54 of his 75 career saves. He was instrumental in nearly half of the White Sox' 70 wins in 1980, earning 30 saves and seven wins.

One of the most notable events of Farmer's White Sox career, a bizarre on-field fight with Al Cowens, occurred on June 21, 1980. Cowens hit a groundball but charged Farmer instead of running to first base. Cowens sought revenge for the broken jaw he suffered from a Farmer pitch the prior season. A wild brawl with Cowens and the Tigers ensued with Farmer on the bottom of a pile of players. Because of pressure from the weight on top of him, cysts on Farmer's kidney burst. White Sox owner Bill Veeck threatened to have Cowens arrested. The altercation resulted in an ejection, a seven-game suspension for Cowens, and even an arrest warrant. The two players later reconciled after Cowens apologized in a pregame lineup exchange, and Farmer dropped the charges.[8]

By the end of his White Sox career, Farmer had posted a 3.31 ERA in 148 appearances. He became a free agent after the 1981 season and re-signed with the Philadelphia Phillies.

His departure from the White Sox marked a historic moment in baseball. The White Sox were the first team to acquire a player from the newly established free-agent compensation pool, selecting Joel Skinner from the Pittsburgh Pirates.

Despite injuries throughout his career, including recurring elbow problems, Farmer's persistence and work ethic were undeniable. He continued to pitch with the minor-league affiliates of the Athletics, Philadelphia Phillies, and Pittsburgh Pirates until 1986. By the time he retired in 1986 after playing for the Hawaii Islanders, he had donned 22 different uniforms over his 19-year career.

He finished his major-league career with 75 saves.

Farmer's second brush with death came in August 1990, during a scouting trip to Boston. Working for the Orioles as a scout for a couple of seasons, he was there to evaluate Red Sox ace Roger Clemens in a game against the Angels. What began as a routine assignment turned into a pivotal moment that saved his life.

Farmer had been battling renal failure for nearly a year, and his declining health was becoming increasingly apparent. Angels manager Doug Rader noticed Farmer's unwell appearance. At the urging of the team's trainer, Farmer was taken to the Beth Israel Deaconess Medical Center. Doctors quickly determined that he was in critical condition and in desperate need of a kidney transplant, estimating that he had only three days to live without intervention.

Farmer, who had anticipated such a crisis after losing his father at 41 and his mother at 38, had already started preparing for the worst by transferring assets to his wife, Barbara, and their 10-year-old daughter, Shanda.

Farmer's brother Tom offered one of his kidneys for a transplant and it was determined to be a perfect match. Dr. Thoedore Steinman, a former wide receiver for the Green Bay Packers, performed the kidney transplant at Beth Israel on January 18, 1991.[9]

During his career as a scout, Farmer had also worked as a special assistant to Ron Schueler, his former White Sox pitching coach, who had become the team's general manager. Farmer quickly transitioned from his front-office position into broadcasting. In 1991 he joined the White Sox radio team, becoming a radio voice of the White Sox for 29 years until he died in 2020. The longevity of his broadcasting career with the White Sox is second only to that of Hall of Famer Bob Elson.

Farmer's distinctive broadcasting style, characterized by sharp, dry wit and insightful pitching analysis, resonated with White Sox fans. Partnering with broadcasters like John Rooney, Chris Singleton, Steve Stone, and Darrin Jackson, the latter of whom called Farmer "a competitor who was everyone's best friend." Farmer became a constant companion to White Sox fans, whether in the car, at home, or in the ballpark. He was approachable and kind, always making time for colleagues and fans. His long tenure in the booth was a testament to his deep connection to the team and the city of Chicago.[10]

Farmer's life off the field was defined by his advocacy for kidney disease awareness, shaped by his battle with polycystic kidney disease, a hereditary condition characterized by clusters of cysts forming around the kidneys. The disease took his 38-year-old mother's life when he was 17, the first year of his minor-league career.

Farmer spoke candidly about his health challenges, using his platform to promote organ donation and inspire others. For nearly 30 years, Farmer lived with his brother's kidney, managing medications and treatments, yet he remained steadfast in his career. He worked tirelessly to raise awareness about kidney disease and supported organizations like the Polycystic Kidney Disease Foundation, never allowing his health struggles to hinder his advocacy efforts.[11]

He supported various kidney health organizations, helping raise funds and awareness for the cause.

Farmer died on April 1, 2020, at 70, from idiopathic cardiomyopathy, a heart disorder. He broadcast one spring-training game for the White Sox in 2020 before returning home because of his failing health.

Farmer retired second all-time in saves among Illinois-born players, with John Wyatt holding the top spot at the time – a record later surpassed by Jason Isringhausen.

His excellence was honored when he was inducted into the Chicagoland Sports Hall of Fame and the Chicago Catholic League Hall of Fame, cementing his place as one of Chicago's sports icons.

Farmer was survived by his wife, Barbara, and daughter, Shanda.

SOURCES

In addition to the sources cited in the Notes, the author consulted Baseball-Reference.com and several other sites.

NOTES

1   "Ed Farmer Reflects on His Life In Baseball," YouTube.com, https://www.youtube.com/watch?v=SRWStLcvF9E.

2   Ed was reportedly the second of nine children, but another account said there were 10 children in the family.

3   Scott Merkin, "White Sox Announcer Ed Farmer, 70, Dies," MLB.com, April 2, 2020. https://www.mlb.com/news/ed-farmer-dies-at-70.

4   Sam Gazdziak, "Obituary: Ed Farmer (1949-2020)." https://ripbaseball.com/2020/04/03/obituary-ed-farmer-1949-2020/.

5   Daniel J. Lane, "Remembering the Greatness of Ed Farmer, On and Off the Field," *Northeastern Illinois University Independent*, April 5, 2020. https://neiuindependent.org/16144/sports/remembering-ed-farmers-greatness-on-and-off-the-field/.

6   Bruce Markusen, "Cooperstown Confidential: Thinking of Al Cowens," *Hardball Times*, March 23, 2012. https://tht.fangraphs.com/cooperstown-confidential-thinking-of-al-cowens/.

7   Andrew Seligman, "Ed Farmer, White Sox Reliever-Turned-Broadcaster, Dies at 70," *Washington Post*, April 4, 2020. https://www.washingtonpost.com/local/obituaries/ed-farmer-white-sox-reliever-turned-broadcaster-dies-at-70/2020/04/04/2c8530b6-7673-11ea-87da-77a8136c1a6d_story.html.

8   Scot Gregor, "Ed Farmer Tributes Come Pouring In," *Arlington Heights* (Illinois) *Daily Herald*, April 3, 2020. https://www.dailyherald.com/20200403/pro-sports/ed-farmer-tributes-come-pouring-in/.

9   Alan Solomon, "Ed Farmer enjoys life that was transplanted," *Chicago Tribune*, May 14, 1991.

JOHN ROONEY

By Don Zminda

On October 26, 2005, at Houston's Minute Maid Park, Chicago White Sox radio play-by-play broadcaster John Rooney was at his accustomed position behind the ESPN 1000 mic. It was Game Four of the World Series, and a victory over the Houston Astros would give the White Sox their first World Series championship in 88 years. With two out in the bottom of the ninth, the White Sox clinging to a 1-0 lead, and the potential tying run on second base, Astros pinch-hitter Orlando Palmeiro stepped up to face Chicago reliever Bobby Jenks. With the count at one ball and two strikes, Palmeiro swung. Rooney told his listeners what happened next:

> *Here's the one-two pitch to Palmeiro ... a ground-ball past Jenks up the middle of the infield. Uribe has it. He throws. Out! Out! A White Sox winner ... and a world championship! The White Sox have won the World Series and they're mobbing each other on the field! ... Enjoy the celebration, Chicago ... this is LONG overdue!*[1]

As it turned out, that World Series call was the last of John Rooney's 18-year White Sox broadcasting career. In 2006 he became the radio play-by-play voice of the St. Louis Cardinals ... and finished the season with another World Series championship. The back-to-back World Series titles were two of many highlights in the career of the award-winning broadcaster – one that has lasted more than five decades.

John Rooney was born in 1955 in Cameron, Missouri, a city of about 8,000 residents in the northwestern part of the state. When he was a child, the family moved to Richmond, another small Missouri town (population 6,000) about 50 miles south of Cameron. John's father, Patrick T. Rooney, owned the Rooney Trucking Company. Patrick and his wife, Lila, had three sons (Tom, Jim, and John), and a daughter (Mary); John was the youngest. Patrick was a St. Louis Cardinals fan, but Richmond was much closer to Kansas City than St. Louis, and as a child John's favorite major-league team was the Kansas City A's.[2]

Rooney's interest in a broadcasting career started early. During a childhood conversation – "I was probably in the in the fifth or sixth grade," Rooney said – his cousin Dennis told him that his ambition was to become a Top 40 disc jockey in St. Louis. "I said, you can do that?" Rooney recalled. When Dennis said yes, John responded, "Well, I want to be a baseball announcer." John Rooney, of course, lived to fulfill his ambition. Dennis Rooney went on to a long career as a news anchor in Kansas City prior to his death in 2016.

John Rooney's broadcasting career began while he was still in high school. "When I was 16," he recalled, "I went over to the radio station in Lexington, Missouri, and told [station manager] Ray Beckwith, 'I'm going to do sports for you.' And he hired me. I did a little bit of everything. I covered high school sports. I sold advertising. I played at record shows. I covered city council meetings, and I even covered a murder trial at 16. That was eye-opening." Rooney's work included conducting interviews with St. Louis Cardinals players for his sportscast. After graduation, Rooney said, "I attended the University of Missouri for a year. I ran out of money, so I went back to work in broadcasting, and I've been working ever since." Early gigs included broadcasting

John Rooney

GRINDERS AND GAMERS

University of Missouri basketball games. He was also the first sports director at Missouri Net in Lexington.

In 1980 Rooney began working at KMOX in St. Louis, the Cardinals' flagship station "as like the 10th guy on the support staff." A year later, he learned of an opening in Oklahoma City, and he took a cut in pay to broadcast baseball for the Triple-A Oklahoma City 89ers and basketball for Oklahoma City University. After two seasons in Oklahoma, he spent two years (1983-84) with the Louisville Redbirds, the Cardinals' Triple-A farm team. Rooney also broadcast several major-league baseball games during this period, filling in for Bob Uecker on Milwaukee Brewers radio after Uecker's mother died, and doing a Cardinals game in Cincinnati with future KMOX partners Jack Buck and Mike Shannon. "That was great," Rooney said. "I had the call on a George Hendrick double, and it sounded like a fast break in the Final Four. Jack said, "Slow down, you're gonna wear 'em out, kid. You've got 162 of these."

Rooney returned to KMOX as a sports reporter in 1984. He also began a long association with CBS Sports that year. By this time Rooney was a nationally-known basketball play-by-play broadcaster, and he was asked to work the 1984 NCAA Final Four in Seattle with Curt Gowdy. Rooney wound up doing at least one Final Four game for CBS for 19 years; his CBS Radio assignments also included college football bowl games, NFL *Monday Night Football,* baseball All-Star games, playoff games, World Series pre- and postgame, and baseball games of the week.[3] Rooney was the voice of University of Missouri football and basketball for 20 years. In later years, he also broadcast games for ESPN and FOX, and two seasons of Chicago Bulls NBA games (1989-90 and 1990-91).

In 1987 Rooney left KMOX to join the Minnesota Twins broadcast crew; he worked about 85 or 90 games for the Twins, a schedule that enabled him to continue his CBS work.[4] The Twins won the World Series that year, defeating the Cardinals in what turned out to be Rooney's only season with the club. During the 1987-88 offseason, veteran White Sox play-by-play broadcaster Don Drysdale left to work for the Los Angeles Dodgers, and the White Sox hired Rooney to replace him. In 1988, his first year with the club, Rooney worked White Sox television broadcasts along with Tom Paciorek.[5] A year later, he began his 17-year stint as the club's radio play-by-play man, first with Wayne Hagin (1989-91) and then with Ed Farmer, who was Rooney's radio partner for the remainder of his White Sox career.[6] "We had a good, good run together," said Rooney about working with Farmer.

Not surprisingly, the highlight of Rooney's White Sox broadcast career was the 2005 World Series championship. "One thing I remember is that just about everything that Ozzie Guillén wanted, Kenny Williams came through with," he said. "Ozzie needed some help the bullpen and in the outfield, they made the deal with Milwaukee that brought in Scott Podsednik and reliever Luis Vizcaíno. The starting pitching just lined up. The bullpen was really good. That team was solid. It had a chance right from the very beginning of the season to do something special, but it really came on when Bobby Jenks arrived. It was fabulous to have a closer who throws a fastball 100 miles an hour and a breaking ball in the low 90s. He was sensational."

Rooney's contract with the White Sox expired after the 2005 season, and he elected to return to KMOX as the Cardinals' lead radio broadcaster.[7] He was behind the mic for Cardinals' World Series championships in 2006 and 2011, another World Series appearance in 2013, and eight other postseason appearances. Rooney, who has two daughters (Rachel and Colleen) with his wife, Susan, was inducted into the Missouri Sports Hall of Fame in 2004. He also received the Tom Hammond National Media Award presented by the Kentucky Bluegrass Sports Commission in 2018 and was inducted into the Missouri Broadcasters Hall of Fame in 2021.

Rooney's trademark calls include "It's a goner!" after a home run and "That's a White Sox [or Redbirds] winner!" when his team is victorious. He began using the latter call while working at Louisville in 1984; it's Rooney tribute to Jack Buck, who punctuated Cardinals victories with "That's a winner!" Rooney is also celebrated for his ability to mimic the voices of other broadcasters. "When I was growing up, there was a guy [Vaughn Meader] who was good at imitating President [John F.] Kennedy," Rooney said. "I heard that and thought I could probably do Kennedy myself. After that I impersonated my football coach at a couple of assemblies in high school. I tried Jimmy Stewart a few times. In sports, I listened to Denny Matthews broadcasting Kansas City Royals games and started doing him, and then Jack Buck and Harry Kalas and Harry Caray. They weren't spot on, but they were close enough. And then I added imitations of the teams' radio broadcasters when we reported the out-of-town scores."[8]

Although Rooney has now broadcast Cardinals' games for more seasons than he worked for the White Sox, his years on the South Side remain special to him. "The interaction I had with Sox fans was always great," Rooney said. "And they were always so supportive of me. I can't thank them enough." He also has fond memories of working with Chicago writers like Jerome Holtzman, Joe Goddard, Tony Ginnetti, Bob Verdi, and Dave van Dyck, as well as his partners on radio and television broadcasts.

"The last time I talked to Vin Scully," Rooney said, "I said, 'Vin, you've been retired for a while now. Do you miss it?' And he said, 'I don't miss the games. But I do miss the people.' And when you think about it, that's what this business is all about. You're around people you really enjoy. People that make these games happen. The games are fun, and they're fine. But in the end, the people make it work. And that's what I enjoy the most."

SOURCES

Unless otherwise indicated, all quotes are from the author's interview with John Rooney on March 27, 2024.

A history of John Rooney's broadcasting career can be found at mlb.com/cardinals/team/broadcasters.

NOTES

1   "2005 World Series Game 4 Highlights Ed Farmer John Rooney Radio Call," YouTube.com, https://www.youtube.com/watch?v=yRf4N4peXC8. Accessed June 3, 2024.

2   Rooney's family information is based on his interview with the author on March 27, 2024.

3   Kent Pulliam, "Rooney Leaving Missouri Network for CBS Job," *Kansas City Star*, March 31, 1985: 219.

4   Jon Roe, "New Yorkers Join Twins Broadcasts," *Minneapolis Star-Tribune*, December 12, 1986: 65.

5   Skip Myslenski, "Sox Team Vet, Rookie in Booth," *Chicago Tribune*, April 3, 1988: 357.

6   Steve Nidetz, "Rooney Moves to Sox Radio's New Team," *Chicago Tribune*, December 25, 1988: 60.

7   Fred Mitchell, "Rooney Returns Home for Gig with Cardinals," *Chicago Tribune*, November 1, 2005: 3-1.

8   Rooney performed several of his broadcaster imitations at his induction speech for the Missouri Sports Broadcasters Hall of Fame in 2021. The speech can be seen at missouribroadcasters.org/hall-of-fame/john-rooney/.

HÉCTOR MOLINA

By Juan José Rodriguez

Horse racing and home run may start with the same letters, but not much more would seem to blend the excitement of the two. Unless Héctor Molina is involved.

Then it becomes the foundation for a voice known to Chicago sports fans for decades.

When the White Sox opened the 2025 season in celebration of the 20th anniversary of their 2005 World Series, Molina had called approximately 3,000 games in 23 seasons for the White Sox. His career in major-league baseball spans more than three decades, as he enters 2025 in his 24th season with the White Sox, first alongside legendary White Sox infielder Alfonso "Chico" Carrasquel – the first Latin American-born player selected as an American League All-Star – in the 1990s, and more recently alongside Billy Russo, who in 2024 completed his 12th season as the White Sox' Spanish radio color analyst while also serving on the team's media relations staff as Spanish communications manager and interpreter.

Molina was born in July 1944 in Barceloneta, Puerto Rico, approximately 35 miles west of the territory's capital city, San Juan. Before even becoming a teenager – let alone before calling a home run – Molina began showing off his voice as the morning DJ for Radio Borinquen (WBQN, 1160 AM), a local news and talk radio station in Barceloneta.

"The idea of working as a DJ never passed through my mind until a neighbor of mine, Juan Felix Ruiz, who was a Spanish teacher, bought a recorder and decided to try it out with the kids in the neighborhood," Molina said.[1]

Continuing to teach even outside of the classroom, Ruiz got the wheels turning in Molina's head, and the latter continued to ponder his interests. An avid horse-racing fan, Molina happened to wonder what his "call" of an imaginary horse race might sound like, and at 12 years old he recorded himself calling the photo finish that he visualized in his head.

Ruiz was captivated when he heard the clip, and asked Molina whether he would have any interest in a career in the radio industry. Molina responded that he would, but the conversation ended there. The ways in which he could use his vocal talents, though, kept expanding.

"If a Spanish teacher was surprised with the diction and creativity of a 12-year-old boy, the idea (of working in radio) was constantly turning in my head," Molina said. "In high school I belonged to the drama club, and that helped with

my diction and helped to eliminate my fears of speaking in front of an audience."

After Molina graduated from high school, he moved to New York with his uncle and 10 cousins, and his parents came the following year. Upon his arrival, Molina once again found himself infatuated with the urge to be performing for others. He began taking drama classes because he "had been bitten by the acting bug," he said. "I wanted to be an actor."

Shortly thereafter, though, he was bitten by a different bug: military recruitment, which led him overseas to Vietnam. Molina was drafted into the US Army and his connection to radio blossomed further; he spent 14 months as the radio operator for the lead sergeant.

After completing his service in Vietnam, he returned to Puerto Rico for his college education, enrolling at

Héctor Molina

Universidad Católica over St. Edward's University (Austin, Texas) and New York University. The choice was simple: going home.

"I wanted to study in my own language (Spanish) and return to the island," Molina said.

Molina volunteered with various local community-service programs, and once again he found a desire to continue speaking in public. This time he followed a slightly different path, accepting a role as the master of ceremonies for various community events. Through these events, his urge to pursue a career in radio grew steadily, although they were halted once again due to military service. After marrying his wife, Iraida, in 1972, he resumed military service for a brief period with the US Navy in Puerto Rico in 1973.

He completed his education at Interamerican University of Puerto Rico in San Germán, two hours southwest of Barceloneta, and graduated in 1977 with a degree in sociology, which he pursued in large part thanks to his military service in Vietnam.

"(My time in Vietnam) totally defined who I wanted to be in the future," Molina said. "My years in college, my experiences in Vietnam and [my major in] sociology changed my way of seeing the world and its inhabitants."

Now back in New York, Molina still had not pursued a formal career in broadcasting or the radio industry, but he continued inching closer. He added to his résumé with stops at the US Post Office, a nearby Puerto Rican high school, and the Department of Social Services. While in the final role, Molina's presence at a fundraising event for cancer patients – where he was noticed by the owner of a local radio station – was just the breakthrough he needed.

"The owner of the radio station suggested to me that I 'try out' as a DJ, and I accepted," Molina said. "He told me to go to the radio station when I had time to do some demos and record commercials. He liked me and suggested an unpaid 'internship' in which I would learn how to use the console and train on how to use the microphone.

"Finally, after a month, they offered me the shift from 6:00 P.M. to 10:00 P.M., which included assisting during the sports segment from 6:00 P.M. to 7:00 P.M. with the sportscaster and professional storyteller Luis Antonio Dávila. I learned a lot with him and with my trainer, Rafael Serrano – ironically also a Spanish teacher – who taught me what radio was and how to use it as an instrument for good."

Molina made the move upon receiving an offer for a permanent job with the radio station, which paid more and offered greater opportunities for adventure and more travel. After a brief stint as a social worker in Los Angeles during the crisis of the Mariel boatlift, a massive emigration of thousands of Cubans to the United States in the early 1980s, Molina realized that his career – and, quite frankly, his life – was reaching a pivotal inflection point.

He traveled to Chicago, where radio producer Elias Díaz y Pérez (who once offered Molina a job while the latter was in the midst of his radio work in Puerto Rico) was a well-known figure. With his sister already living in Chicago, Molina felt that the Windy City would be a good destination to prove himself behind the microphone, and he asked the producer to assist with finding such an opportunity. A morning news segment became available shortly thereafter, and Pérez offered to help Molina get started.

Just as in baseball, where the smallest of plays can blossom into the start of a rally, so too did the assistance from Elias Díaz y Pérez.

"Elias Díaz y Pérez was one of the people to whom I am most grateful for the opportunity he gave me," Molina said with gratitude. "After I had spent three months with the news, his morning DJ resigned for money reasons and I became the full-time morning announcer. I was able to bring my family, and the adventure and the trip began again."

Molina expressed plenty of gratitude for the support he has received along the way, but those he has worked with have happily reciprocated the appreciation. When Molina took his next position with a new 24-hour radio station in Chicago (WOJO-105 FM) to handle the news segments, he regretfully approached his boss to say goodbye, knowing the confidence that had been shown in him during his time at the station. Molina received a kind reassurance that he still remembers to this day: "I have never had a more responsible person working for me than you. You deserve (this new opportunity) and these doors will always be open for you."

With two more years of news and radio under his belt, Molina and his family moved to downtown Chicago, where he worked morning radio from 1987 to 1994, the latest step in the path bringing Molina increasingly closer to the diamond. That step proved to be instrumental: When Molina's news chief joined the executive ranks and thereby lost his side job as a Spanish baseball commentator with the station that had recently begun broadcasting Cubs games, he recommended Molina as his successor.

Molina's dream of breaking into the world of sports had finally become a reality.

While with WOJO, he spent the 1987 and 1988 seasons as an analyst for Bears games, an experience he believes helped to elevate his name and popularity among fans in Chicago. In 1992, the White Sox and the Chicago Bulls agreed to broadcast their games together for the next five years, and in 1994 Molina resigned from his role with the WOJO morning show to broadcast both teams' games on a more permanent basis, spanning both the regular season and the playoffs.

"I enjoyed the 'Beatles' experience when I did all the Chicago Bulls games (regular season and playoffs)," Molina said. "Four rings are the visual witness of that fabulous experience with Michael (Jordan), Scottie (Pippen), and the gang."

Having already called playoff games for the Bulls, Molina made his playoff debut in 1998 when the Caracol Network and ESPN joined forces to bring the broadcast of the World Series between the Yankees and the Padres to Latin America.

"I got the call from Armando Talavera in New York, and I couldn't believe it," Molina said.

He proceeded to call American League playoff games in 1999 and 2000, in addition to working as a reporter for the 2003 All-Star Game. After his eight seasons broadcasting White Sox games from 1992-99, Molina returned to the South Side of Chicago in 2005 as part of the team's one-year agreement with Univision Radio in which he would call 20 regular-season games, the first time since 1999 that the White Sox offered a Spanish-language radio broadcast.[2] Molina's time with the team continued into October, as he stayed on to cover the White Sox' magical playoff run – just the team's fourth postseason appearance since 1983 – culminating in the 2005 World Series championship, the third in franchise history and the first since 1917.

Upon meeting Molina, White Sox radio play-by-play broadcaster Len Kasper quickly noticed – and has since appreciated – Molina's approachability.

"I had met him a while ago, but didn't know a ton about him," Kasper said. "I just know that he loved baseball and people. … He's magnetic. He's got a magnetic personality and that's what always stuck out to me more than anything else."

Russo considered whether he could pick a favorite game or memory of his time alongside Molina, then replied, "I don't think I can pick just one. Every day with Héctor is entertaining. It can be because the game is a very exciting game, and even [when the game might not be] as good as we were expecting, there's always something in the booth with him that you know that you're going to enjoy that day. And it can be a comment about the game, it can be a comment about how his day is going, a comment about his family. … There's always something that makes you smile."

"He's got a ton of energy from the first pitch till the last, and I always appreciate – you can tell from the minute you meet him – that he loves baseball and he loves being at the ballpark," Kasper said, having often observed Molina from the neighboring booth. "I have so much fun at the ballpark that you want to be around people who feel the same way you do, and a lot of people do, but there are certain special people [for whom] you can tell: This is not a job. In Héctor's case, it's totally genuine. It's never forced – he loves being around the sport as much as I do — and that matters to me. I like him even more because of that – I feel like we're kindred spirits."

Kasper later added: "I love his voice and the energy of his calls, but for me it's more about the person – he's such a memorable person because he lights up a room everywhere he goes. He's just got this great laugh, and I could just hear him tell stories for hours. He's just one of those people – when he walks into a room, you just feel good, he makes you feel good about life."

Kasper was not alone in noticing the positive energy. Recalling the start of his partnership with Molina, Russo noted: "We didn't have that chemistry that you build through the years. So our first time working together, he had a particular style and I have a different style – he's been doing this here for a very long time and I was used to calling games in Venezuela, so it's a little different. And when you're doing this for the first time with a new person, you try to get to know him. Especially with him being the play-by-play, I was trying to figure out…how to mesh with his narrative. But he made that transition pretty easy, and we would talk during the breaks [to coordinate transitions]. It was an honest exchange on how to improve our work and how to make it very smooth and really professional."

Russo also observed a relationship with Molina that stretched beyond solely their occupation. "To me, not just because of the age gap, but he's like a relative – like an uncle or something like that. We have that kind of a relationship, and he brings that to the booth. There's always a teaching moment, because we always try to explain things to the audience and even sometimes to ourselves.

"And he did it just because that's the way that he is," Russo added. "He doesn't have an ego, and that's huge. And I think that's one of the things that made us click right away."

Molina's openness and engaging personality has been beneficial far beyond his own career and family. Molina has been an integral mentor for many, including the legendary White Sox manager Ozzie Guillén – who, as Russo noted, is "a guy that is loved in Chicago" – and his son Ozzie Jr., forming a close bond with both father and son when Molina would travel with the team.

Russo continued lauding Molina's mentorship abilities: "One of the first things I knew about Héctor, and this came from Ozzie Jr. He said, 'He was my teacher. He taught me how to call games, he taught me how to be on radio. And that was very good.' … Those two (Guillén Sr. and Guillén Jr.) hold Héctor in a really big regard. They really respect him, they really like the job that he does, and they listen to him. When Ozzie Jr. used to do games with Héctor, Héctor usually would give him advice about radio, work and sometimes even about life, and how to take advantage of the situation that he was in.

"And that's something that Ozzie Jr. would always remember."

From a broadcaster's standpoint, that sincere personality even transmitted across the radio waves. "This is what I like about every great broadcaster: He is himself on the air, and it's the same off the air – there's no act," Kasper said. "And I think the all-time greats generally are who they are all the time, and that's the best compliment I could ever give anyone. And when I can hear Héctor and see him and then I talk to him off the air, he's the same exact person."

Russo noted that Molina has been portrayed throughout his career as maintaining a "colorful" approach to his work.

In addition to his signature "Sayonara, baby" after a White Sox home run, one of Molina's best-known lines – "Lo retrataron de cuerpo entero" ("They portrayed him in full body") – would often illustrate a key strikeout.

"One of the things that makes Héctor a great play-by-play [broadcaster] is that he knows the story of the game, and then he knows when to mix that knowledge with the game situation," Russo said. "And those are things that get listeners excited."

The excitement from listening to Molina stems from more than just his popular one-liners. Having spent decades in the Windy City, Molina has built a familiarity with Chicago sports – and the market as a whole – which has fostered an overwhelmingly positive reception from White Sox fans.

"He knows what the listeners like to listen to, because he knows the market," Russo said. "I was new here, so there were some words that I would say that wouldn't connect with the audience. … Even during specific situations in games, we would discuss that "[t]his is called this way in Venezuela" or "[t]his is called this way in Puerto Rico" and then we would explain that situation on air, and that would add to the broadcast and make it more entertaining.

"It really didn't take us long to blend, and I think it was easy and that in a big measure was because of him."

Among fans, colleagues and players, the sentiment about Molina remains constant: happiness. Others feel it about Molina because they so often see it evident in him.

"He's just a very popular person at the ballpark because he always greets you with a smile on his face," Kasper said. "I was once told that you should broadcast with a smile on your face, and Héctor obviously learned that at a very young age because he does it to this day incredibly well."

Molina's relentless dedication to his craft earned him a trip to the plate; his voice and joyous spirit carried him the rest of the way. He had hit a home run in his first at-bat at the highest level, and his skills and personality kept shining forth with each new opportunity.

ACKNOWLEDGMENTS

Special thanks to Billy Russo, a partner of Molina in the broadcast booth as well as the White Sox' Spanish communications manager and interpreter, for his insights on Molina in addition to his coordination of interviews and contact with Molina in preparation of this article.

Much of the research for in this essay was originally conducted as part of a previous profile of Héctor Molina written for *Béisbol on the Air* (McFarland, 2024 – edited by Jorge Iber and Anthony R. Salazar).

NOTES

1   All comments attributed to Héctor Molina, Len Kasper, and Billy Russo are from the author's conversations with each in 2021.

2   Closing Bell, May 2, 2005," *Sports Business Journal*. May 2, 2005. https://www.sportsbusinessjournal.com/Daily/Closing-Bell/2005/05/02/Closing-Bell-May-2-2005.aspx.

A MAGICAL SEASON BEGINS (IN UNDER TWO HOURS)

APRIL 4, 2005: CHICAGO WHITE SOX 1, CLEVELAND INDIANS 0, AT US CELLULAR FIELD, CHICAGO

By Don Zminda

Sometimes a magical season begins with offensive thunder, other times more quietly. For the 2005 Chicago White Sox, the road to the franchise's first World Series championship in 88 years began *quickly*: with a 1-0 victory over the Cleveland Indians on April 4 in just an hour and 51 minutes. Credit White Sox starting pitcher Mark Buehrle, never a man to dawdle, and closer Shingo Takatsu, who worked a one-two-three ninth.

Buehrle, who retired the first 12 Cleveland batters to start the game, allowed only two hits and one walk in his eight innings of work, and – helped by two 5-4-3 double plays started by White Sox third baseman Joe Crede – faced only 25 batters, one over the minimum. He struck out five. The only hits he permitted were singles by Victor Martinez to lead off the fifth and Coco Crisp to open the seventh. Both were erased on double plays. "We have a good defense, so let them put the ball in play," Buehrle said after the game. "Buehrle was as good as I've ever seen him," said Cleveland manager Eric Wedge.[1]

Indians starter Jake Westbrook was excellent as well, pitching a complete game while permitting only four hits and one walk. "You've got to match him pitch for pitch," Westbrook said of Buehrle. "It's tough to go out and continue to put up zeroes. He one-upped me today."[2]

Buehrle's performance was a near-duplicate of his start against the Indians at Cleveland's Jacobs Field on July 21, 2004.[3] In that contest, a 14-0 White Sox victory, Buehrle had a perfect game for 6⅓ innings before finishing with a two-hit shutout in which he faced the minimum 27 batters, thanks to two double plays. Wedge felt that Buehrle's 2005 Opening Day performance surpassed the 2004 gem. "I really thought he was even better [than last season]," said Wedge. "He commanded the game. He didn't give in, and when he got behind he was still able to make pitches. You just have to tip your cap to him today."[4] Those two starts were not typical of Buehrle's career work against the

Indians. Overall, he was 16-18 against Cleveland for his career, with a 4.93 ERA that was his second highest against any American League opponent (6.03 vs. the Yankees).

The White Sox team that began the season at US Cellular Field featured a revamped roster with a greater emphasis on speed, defense, and pitching.[5] The White Sox front office felt that change was needed after the 2004 team finished only four games over .500 (83-79) despite slugging a franchise-record 242 home runs (tied with the New York Yankees for the most major-league home runs in 2004). Buehrle was making his fourth consecutive Opening Day start for the White Sox, but the other eight position players who took the field featured only three holdovers from the 2004 opener in Kansas City: first baseman Paul Konerko, center fielder Aaron Rowand, and Crede.

"The manner in which the Sox scored their only run was a victory in itself for general manager Ken Williams and manager Ozzie Guillén who had grown tired of watching the team fall short year after year despite a lineup stacked with sluggers," wrote *Chicago Tribune* reporter Mark Gonzales.[6] Leading off the bottom of the seventh, Konerko doubled to left field, then took third on a fly out to right by offseason free-agent signee Jermaine Dye. Indians shortstop Jhonny Peralta, the first player other than Omar Vizquel to start a season at shortstop for the Indians since 1993, then fumbled Rowand's grounder, allowing Konerko to score. "He started to run and I started to go into the ball. I couldn't catch the ball," said Peralta. Said the slow-footed Konerko, "If the guy throws the ball, I'm going to be out probably."[7]

After only one game, White Sox players seemed to sense that this was a different team from years past, and perhaps one heading for something special. "I like seeing the home run like anyone else," said Konerko. "[But] I enjoy this team because a lot of the guys are on the same wavelength, how they feel about their teammates and check everything at the door." On the fly out to right that allowed Konerko to advance to third, Dye commented that "you've got to get him over, somehow, some way. That's what Ozzie preached in spring training. Late in the ballgame, I know as a veteran player what it takes to get him over. I'm not trying to drive the ball." Rowand added praise for Ken Williams: "Hats off to Kenny for bringing in the guys who want to get it done. … We don't have anyone on this team who is selfish. …"[8]

Those glowing comments proved to be an accurate assessment of how the White Sox would perform in 2005. Though they were threatened by the Indians late in the season, the White Sox held first place in the American League Central Division for all 183 days of the season. The team was particularly strong early in the year. Chicago held a lead at some point in each of its first 37 games of the season, breaking a record of 25 straight games from the start of the season with a lead set by the 1955 Brooklyn Dodgers. The team also recorded three separate eight-game winning streaks prior to July 1, becoming only the fifth team since 1900 to accomplish that feat (1912 New York Giants, 1978 Boston Red Sox, 1998 New York Yankees, 2001 Seattle Mariners). As for the "small-ball" skills displayed in the Opening Day win, the White Sox postseason media guide reported that the 2005 team led the American League in sacrifice hits (53) and bunt hits (37), while ranking third in stolen bases (137).[9]

Buehrle finished the 2005 season with a 16-8 record, while posting a career-low 3.12 ERA. He led the American League in innings pitched (236⅔) for the second straight season. In addition, Buehrle was the winning pitcher for the American League in the 2005 All-Star Game at Detroit's Comerica Park. In his 2-1 victory over the Seattle Mariners in his third start of the season on April 16, Buehrle bettered even his Opening Day performance when it came to quick work: the game took just an hour and 39 minutes.

For Buehrle and the White Sox, the year culminated in a dominant postseason in which the team posted an 11-1 record, defeating the Houston Astros in four straight games for its first World Series championship since 1917. Fittingly, the White Sox year ended the way it began: with a 1-0 victory.

SOURCES

In addition to the sources cited in the Notes, the author consulted Baseball-Reference.com and Retrosheet.org.

The White Sox television broadcast of this game is available at https://www.youtube.com/watch?v=33FXCIiE8Mk'

NOTES

1   Associated Press, "Buehrle Shuts Out Indians with Two-Hit Gem," ESPN. com. espn.com/mlb/recap?gameId=250404104; accessed January 12, 2020.

2   "Buehrle Shuts Out Indians."

3   Jacobs Field was renamed Progressive Field in 2008.

4   Bolt Foltman, "Indians Baffled by the Same Old Stuff," *Chicago Tribune*, April 5, 2005: 4-4.

5   The White Sox ballpark was renamed Guaranteed Rate Field in 2017.

6   Mark Gonzales, "Small Ball Rules: Buehrle's Gem, 1 Run Just Enough to Top Cleveland," *Chicago Tribune*, April 5, 2005: 4-1.

7   "Buehrle Shuts Out Indians."

8   Gonzales.

9   Bob Beghtol, ed., *2005 Chicago White Sox Season in Review* (Chicago: Chicago White Sox: 2005), 3-5 (all statistics cited in this paragraph).

PIERZYNSKI'S "TWO-RUN, TWO-OUT, TWO-STRIKE SECOND-CHANCE HOMER" LIFTS WHITE SOX TO VICTORY ON TURN BACK THE CLOCK NIGHT

JUNE 18, 2005: CHICAGO WHITE SOX 5, LOS ANGELES DODGERS 3, AT US CELLULAR FIELD, CHICAGO

by Mike Huber

Almost midway through their season, the 2005 Chicago White Sox promoted "Turn Back the Clock Night" to honor the 1959 Go-Go White Sox. That team had won the American League pennant but had then lost the World Series to the Los Angeles Dodgers in six games. The Go-Go Sox roster had included six future Hall of Famers: Luis Aparicio, Larry Doby, Nellie Fox, Early Wynn, manager Al López, and owner Bill Veeck. Current White Sox skipper Ozzie Guillén told reporters, "I know they called them the Go-Go Sox and they were a better team than we are, because they won and we haven't."[1] Yet on June 18, 2005, Guillén's squad showed that they could also play like champions; they rallied in the bottom of the ninth inning for four runs, defeating the Los Angeles Dodgers 5-3 before a near-capacity crowd at US Cellular Field.

Eleven members of the '59 Go-Go Sox attended the pregame festivities: infielders Ron Jackson and J.C. Martin; outfielders Joe Hicks, Jim Landis, Jim McAnany, and Jim Rivera; and pitchers Rudy Árias, Barry Latman, Billy Pierce, Claude Raymond, and Bob Shaw.[2] Shaw threw out the ceremonial first pitch to current pitcher Mark Buehrle.

The 2005 White Sox had been in first place since Opening Day.[3] Winning 43 of their first 65 games, they entered a three-game series with the Dodgers (33-32) holding a 5½-game lead over the Minnesota Twins in the American League's Central Division. In the series opener, Buehrle had recorded his eighth victory and first shutout of the season as the White Sox blanked the Dodgers, 6-0. Buehrle also extended his scoreless-innings streak to 18⅓,[4] prompting Guillén to tell reporters, "This kid is the heart of the White

Sox. Every time he pitches, my bullpen will be fresh for the next day."[5]

Chicago started Freddy García. The Venezuelan-born right-hander had been traded to Chicago the previous season.[6] He had won his last three decisions and had pitched into the sixth inning in every one of his 13 starts to this point of the season.

Mexican native Elmer Dessens started for the Dodgers. The 34-year-old righty had been traded to Los Angeles the previous season and then signed with the Dodgers as a free agent in the offseason. He had begun his career in 1996 as a reliever, been a starter from 2001 to 2003 with the Cincinnati Reds and Arizona Diamondbacks, but reverted back to a primarily relief role with the Dodgers. Dessens had just returned from a rehab assignment at Triple-A Las Vegas, with the mission of halting the Dodgers' four-game losing streak.

García did not have his best stuff as the game began. He walked Antonio Pérez on four pitches to start the game. After Jayson Werth popped out, García uncorked a wild pitch, allowing Pérez to take second. After J.D. Drew flied out, Jeff Kent launched his 14th home run of the season, well beyond the left-field wall. García then walked the bases loaded before retiring Mike Edwards. García had walked more batters in the first inning than he had in any start in the season. After the game, he said, "I don't know what was going on. Maybe I was a little lazy. I threw the ball all over the place."[7] He walked another batter in the second but kept the Dodgers from scoring. Meanwhile Dessens retired the first six Chicago batters, throwing just 21 pitches in the first two frames.

García started throwing strikes in the top of third and Los Angeles went quietly. García's batterymate, catcher A.J. Pierzynski, said that his pitcher "got a little angry [after the second inning]. When he gets angry, he gets good. Maybe we should go punch him before the first pitch."[8]

In the bottom of the third, Pierzynski reached on an error by second baseman Kent. Joe Crede singled, putting runners at the corners. Juan Uribe then grounded a ball to shortstop Oscar Robles, whose only play was to first, and Pierzynski scored.

García still had a bit of wildness, giving up two singles, a wild pitch and a walk (loading the bases with just one out) in the fourth, but he retired Pérez and Werth to end the Dodgers threat. Los Angeles did not get another baserunner until the seventh.

Dessens struck out Frank Thomas to end the sixth, and his day was done. He had pitched well enough to win, allowing just two hits, a walk, and one unearned run in his quality start. Duaner Sánchez came on to pitch the seventh and eighth, and the right-hander put up a dominating performance. Meanwhile, the Dodgers added their third run in the top of the eighth. Kent led off with a double to left, moved to third on a groundout, and scored on García's third wild pitch of the game.

The clock was supposed to turn back to 1959, the last time the White Sox played in the World Series. Instead, according to the *Chicago Tribune*, "the White Sox almost dialed all the way back to the 'Hitless Wonders' days of 1906."[9] Until the final frame, Chicago had been held to only three hits and one unearned run.

Then came the excitement. Yhancy Brazobán entered in the ninth with a two-run cushion to preserve the Los Angeles win. Dodgers All-Star closer and former Cy Young Award winner Eric Gagné had been placed on the disabled list after his save performance on June 13,[10] and Brazobán was called on to fill the closer role. He had converted 11 of 13 save opportunities since Gagné went down at the start of the season.

Chicago's first batter in the ninth, Tadahito Iguchi, worked a full count and then walked. Thomas grounded out (Iguchi took second) and Paul Konerko flied out. Carl Everett singled on a 2-and-2 count to drive in Iguchi. Guillén inserted Willie Harris as a pinch-runner for Everett, and on Brazobán's first pitch to Aaron Rowand, Harris stole second base. According to the *Los Angeles Times*, "[catcher Jason] Phillips did not throw; he had no play because Brazobán's release time is so slow."[11] Rowand also had two strikes when he singled up the middle, plating Harris with the game-tying run. That brought Pierzynski to the batter's box. He worked a 3-and-1 count before fouling off three pitches. On Brazobán's eighth offering, Pierzynski popped the ball up, and believing he had made the game's final out, threw his bat in disgust. Fortunately, the ball landed on the

Dodgers' dugout, out of play. Pierzynski then made the most of his new life at the plate by crushing a "two-run, two-out, two-strike second-chance homer" to left-center, 414 feet from home plate.[12] Dessens' strong start had been wasted, and the Dodgers had lost their fifth straight game.

The 36,067 fans went wild. This was Chicago's 20th come-from-behind victory of the season (and their 10th in their last at-bat). Despite getting just six hits, Chicago had won in a walk-off, 5-3. In the dugout, Pierzynski told reporters, "This is my first walk-off anything."[13] This was only the fourth walk-off win of the season for the White Sox, and just the second time Chicago had won with a walk-off home run.[14]

Chicago swept Los Angeles in the series and continued to win, posting an eight-game winning streak from June 15 to 24. It was the White Sox' longest streak of the season (tied with eight-game stretches from April 18-25 and April 30-May 8). The White Sox ended the 2005 season with 38 comeback wins and five walk-off victories, en route to 99 wins and a World Series victory. In a 154-game schedule, the 1959 White Sox team won 94 games. This total included 45 comeback wins and 11 walk-off wins. Their longest winning streak was also eight games (May 9-16, 1959).[15] The Go-Go Sox would have been proud that the 2005 White Sox had beaten the clock for a last-minute victory.

SOURCES

In addition to the sources mentioned in the Notes, the author consulted Baseball-Reference.com, MLB.com, Retrosheet.org, and SABR.org.

https://www.baseball-reference.com/boxes/CHA/CHA200506180.shtml

https://www.retrosheet.org/boxesetc/2005/B06180CHA2005.htm

NOTES

1   Dave van Dyck, "White Sox Bits: Guillén Praises Talent of '59 World Series Sox," *Chicago Tribune*, June 19, 2005: 3-4. Only one Hall of Famer played on the 2005 White Sox: Frank Thomas.

2   "White Sox Bits: Guillén praises talent of '59 World Series Sox."

3   In early April Chicago spent five days tied for the first-place spot, but since April 18, the White Sox held the top spot in the standings on their own.

4   Buehrle ran the streak to 26 innings before yielding a run in the eighth inning of a game against the Kansas City Royals on June 22.

5   Mark Gonzales, "Sox Shutout Right Out of Hollywood," *Chicago Tribune*, June 19, 2005: 3-4. Buehrle, Chicago's 26-year-old left-hander, was the American League's starting pitcher in the 2005 All-Star Game and finished seventh in the 2005 AL Cy Young Award balloting.

6   On June 27, 2004, Garcia was traded by the Mariners with Ben Davis to the White Sox for Mike Morse, Miguel Olivo, and Jeremy Reed.

7   Dave van Dyck, "Pierzynski's 2-Out HR Caps 9th-Inning Rally," *Chicago Tribune*, June 19, 2005: 3-1.

8   "Pierzynski's 2-Out HR Caps 9th-Inning Rally."

9   "Pierzynski's 2-Out HR Caps 9th-Inning Rally." The 1906 White Sox won the American League pennant and the World Series despite having the fewest hits (1,133 – the league average was 1,256), home runs (7 – the league average was 17) and the lowest batting average (.230 – the league average was .249) in the AL.

10   Initially, Gagné went on the 15-day disabled list with a sprained ligament in his right elbow. This was the same problem that sidelined him for the first 35 games of the season. On June 21 the Dodgers announced that Gagné would undergo season-ending Tommy John surgery. See "Gagne Goes on DL With Elbow Injury," *Washington Post*, https://www.washingtonpost.com/archive/sports/2005/06/16/gagne-goes-on-dl-with-elbow-injury/a0239a90-8a8f-4a13-916f-e4711ef45035/. Accessed March 2024.

11   Bill Shaikin, "Dodgers Socked in Ninth," *Los Angeles Times*, June 19, 2005: D1, D11.

12   "Pierzynski's 2-Out HR Caps 9th-Inning Rally."

13   "Pierzynski's 2-Out HR Caps 9th-Inning Rally." In his career, Pierzynski had seven walk-off hits, including three home runs.

14   The White Sox finished the 2005 season with just five walk-off wins, and the last three were via the home run: Jermaine Dye on May 31 against the Los Angeles Angels of Anaheim, Pierzynski on June 18 against the Los Angeles Dodgers, and Crede on September 20 against the Cleveland Indians.

15   Comeback-win and walk-off-win stats are not available for the 1906 team. However, the "Hitless Wonders" had a 19-game winning streak (August 2-23, 1906).

GARCÍA DOMINATES AS WHITE SOX OFFENSE SLUGS WAY TO 50TH WIN

JUNE 24, 2005: CHICAGO WHITE SOX 12, CHICAGO CUBS 2, AT US CELLULAR FIELD, CHICAGO

By Bill Pearch

Ozzie Guillén understood Chicago's baseball rivalry. "And so that the Venezuelans understand what this series means," he wrote in his weekly column in *El Universal,* "imagine a Caracas-Magallanes game, and multiply the emotion by three."[1] Guillén knew, for decades, that fan bragging rights hung in the balance.

Both Chicago baseball fan bases' heightened emotions regarding intercity games was symptomatic of lengthy championship droughts. Starved for titles, they embraced anything – exhibition game wins, ballpark esthetics, and crowd sizes – to claim an advantage over their crosstown rivals. Chicago fans last experienced World Series energy when the White Sox won the 1959 American League pennant. The franchise's last World Series championship came 42 years before that. Cubs fans had waited even longer with the team's last National League pennant in 1945 and last World Series title in 1908.

Guillén, 41 years old and in his second season as the White Sox manager, was adamant. "We are going to take the Cubs the same way we take everybody," he said. "[The Cubs] were playing pretty good baseball."[2]

"The Cubs get most of the headlines in this city," said White Sox first baseman Paul Konerko, "so we like to show them we can play a little bit on the South Side."[3] Frank Thomas, a member of the White Sox since 1990 and nicknamed the Big Hurt, agreed. "The Cubs, they draw regardless of what type of team they put on the field," he said. "Over here, it's about winning. When we win here, we draw very, very well. When we don't play well over here, we don't draw well. That's just the way it's been."[4]

Despite sweltering temperatures that reached 95 degrees at first pitch, the White Sox boasted a season-high crowd and welcomed 39,610 fans to a sun-soaked ballpark at 35th and Shields.[5] The game was the third sellout of the season.[6] And bragging rights were not the only thing on the line.

"There's no shortage of excitement and energy," said Kenny Williams, the White Sox general manager. "And I like the midseason boost, to be honest with you. Coming from a guy who could use any extra dollars for payroll purposes. I like to see the ballpark filled."[7]

When Chicago's teams converged at Wrigley Field[8] earlier in the season, the White Sox claimed the first two games of the three-game set. As the series shifted south to US Cellular Field in June, both teams were headed in different directions. Guillén's White Sox (49-22, .690) maintained a comfortable 9½-game cushion over their nearest American League Central Division foes, the Minnesota Twins. They also enjoyed a seven-game winning streak, which included series sweeps of the Los Angeles Dodgers and Kansas City Royals. Manager Dusty Baker's second-place Cubs (36-35, .507) trailed the front-running St. Louis Cardinals by 8½ games in the National League Central Division. Compounding matters, they had dropped eight of their last 11 games.

Hall of Famer Luis Aparicio, the 1956 American League Rookie of the Year and a member of the 1959 pennant winners, started the celebration by throwing out the ceremonial first pitch. But for real mound duty, Guillén tapped 28-year-old right-hander Freddy García (6-3, 3.75 ERA) to be the starter, the 200th start of his career.

The White Sox had expressed interest in acquiring García, a two-time American League All-Star and Rookie of the Year (1999) from the Seattle Mariners during the 2004 season. "Who wouldn't want that kid?" Guillén said at the time. "He's one of the dominating pitchers in the game."[9] The White Sox sealed the deal in a five-player trade in June 2004.

García demonstrated why the White Sox wanted him in the starting rotation. He had not lost a game since May 14 against the Baltimore Orioles,[10] and his current winning streak began at Wrigley Field on May 20, when he pitched seven innings and defeated the Cubs yielding just five hits and surrendering one unearned run.[11] Dusty Baker countered with the 24-year-old right-hander, Sergio Mitre (2-2, 4.19 ERA).

From his first pitch, García seized control, retiring the first seven Cubs batters and 12 of the first 13. As he established his rhythm on the mound, designated hitter Frank Thomas provided offensive fireworks. Scott Podsednik opened the bottom of the first inning and worked a full count. After Podsednik drew a walk, Mitre caught him leaning too far off the bag. Mitre fanned Tadahito Iguchi, the team's Japanese rookie free agent, appearing to dodge an early jam. With two outs and the bases empty, Thomas, the two-time American League Most Valuable Player, put a charge in the crowd and secured his place in franchise history. His 428-foot blast moved Thomas past Dave Kingman into 29th place on the all-time home-run list.[12] When he crossed home plate, he scored his 1,319th career run, matching former shortstop Luke Appling's franchise record.[13] Mitre contained the damage when Konerko flied out to left.

Both pitchers matched zeros in the second, but the Cubs knotted the score with one down in their third. Left fielder Todd Hollandsworth hammered a high fastball deep into the right-field seats for a solo home run.

Pablo Ozuna and Podsednik opened the bottom of the third with singles. With runners on the corners, Iguchi's fly ball to deep right field scored Ozuna. Podsednik demonstrated why the White Sox had acquired the speedster from the Milwaukee Brewers in December. (In the 2003 and 2004 seasons, he had swiped 43 and 70 bases respectively.) Podsednik stole second and Thomas walked. With Konerko up, Podsednik swiped third. Mitre walked Konerko and with the bases loaded struck out Aaron Rowand looking. With Jermaine Dye at bat, Mitre's wild pitch skipped beyond catcher Michael Barrett. Podsednik scored, extending the White Sox' lead to two runs at 3-1, and Thomas and Konerko each advanced a base. Mitre coaxed Dye into hitting a grounder back to the mound, ending the inning.

García and Mitre blanked hitters in the fourth, but the Cubs threatened in the fifth. Cubs third baseman Aramis Ramírez singled to open the frame. Second baseman Todd Walker walked, then García fanned Barrett. Ramirez and Walker advanced as Hollandsworth grounded out. With two outs and two runners in scoring position, García struck out designated hitter Jason Dubois and squashed the rally.

The White Sox seized control in the bottom of the fifth. Podsednik walked. Iguchi singled, placing runners on the corners. Thomas's fly to right scored Podsednik and gave the White Sox a 4-1 lead. Konerko grounded to short, moving Iguchi to second. With two outs, Rowand singled off Ramírez's glove and scored Iguchi, making the score 5-1.

After Dye's single to center sent Rowand to third, Baker summoned reliever Todd Wellemeyer. With A.J. Pierzynski up, Rowand scored and Dye advanced to second on Wellemeyer's wild pitch. Then Pierzynski powered a

two-run opposite-field homer, giving the White Sox an 8-1 lead. Wellemeyer stopped the bleeding when Joe Crede flied out to center.

The Cubs failed to capitalize on Corey Patterson's single-handed attempt to spark a sixth-inning rally. After Patterson's leadoff single, Neifi Pérez struck out swinging. With Derrek Lee at the plate, Patterson swiped second. Lee grounded out to third, then right fielder Jeromy Burnitz popped out in foul territory.

Despite a one-out walk and single by Podsednik and Iguchi respectively, Wellemeyer shut down the White Sox in the sixth. García answered by retiring the side in the top of the seventh.

Rowand and Dye opened the bottom of the seventh with back-to-back singles. Pierzynski doubled to score Rowand and advance Dye to third. With two runners in scoring position and no outs, Crede connected against Wellemeyer with a slicing fly ball that struck the right-field foul pole for a three-run blast.[14] The White Sox now led 12-1.

Up 11 runs after seven innings, Guillén signaled for 25-year-old left-handed reliever Neal Cotts. He worked efficiently, needing 13 pitches but allowed a one-out solo homer by Dubois to complete the top of the eighth.

Trailing 12-2, Baker handed the ball to Joe Borowski to pitch the bottom of the eighth. Konerko grounded to shortstop Neifi Pérez. Borowski ended the inning with consecutive strikeouts of Rowand and Dye.

Maintaining a double-digit lead, Guillén tapped Luis Vizcaíno to secure the victory. Enrique Wilson, who replaced Lee at first, hit a ground-rule double. With Burnitz batting, Wilson took third on Vizcaino's passed ball. Burnitz walked. With no outs and runners at the corners, Macias struck out. Jerry Hairston Jr., a late-game replacement at second, ended the game by hitting into a 6-4-3 double play.

"For me, I don't do really good in this ballpark," García said. "It changed today."[15]

He added, "I was very aggressive. I cannot say it was my best game, but I felt great. I threw a lot of strikes and made pitches when I needed it."[16]

"First inning, first pitch," Pierzynski said when questioned about García's effectiveness. "He threw hard, worked the ball down. That's what we've been trying to get him to do all year."[17]

"[García] was mixing in a lot of breaking balls," Baker said. "He had great command. He was tantalizingly close to the strike zone and he threw very well."[18]

By beating the Cubs, the White Sox secured their 50th win of the season in just 72 games, becoming the quickest team in franchise history to reach that milestone. The victory gave the White Sox the team's third eight-game winning streak of the season. Since 1984, six teams have accomplished the same feat in fewer games:[19] the Detroit Tigers (1984), New York Mets (1986), Philadelphia Phillies (1993), Cleveland Indians (1995), New York Yankees (1998), and Seattle Mariners (2001). Each team reached the postseason with three winning the World Series (Tigers, Mets, Yankees).[20]

"When you play this team, you have to beat them in a big way," Guillén said. "I think we were very lucky."[21]

"We're playing the best team in baseball," said the Cubs' Todd Walker. "They're solid in every aspect of the game."[22]

SOURCES

In addition to the sources cited in the Notes, the author accessed Retrosheet.org, Baseball-Reference.com, and SABR.org.

https://www.baseball-reference.com/boxes/CHA/CHA200507240.shtml

https://www.retrosheet.org/boxesetc/2005/B07240CHA2005.htm

NOTES

1   Mike Debonis, "Ozzie Guillén, Man of Letters," slate.com, October 21, 2005. https://slate.com/culture/2005/10/ozzie-guillen-man-of-letters.html (accessed September 14, 2024).

2   "Neighborly Warfare," *Chicago Tribune,* June 24, 2005: 17.

3   Brian Mahoney, "White Sox and rest of AL Dominate NL," *Austin* (Texas) *American-Statesman*, June 24, 2005: 42.

4   "First-Place White Sox Trail Cubs in Attendance," *Knoxville News-Sentinel*, June 24, 2005: 37.

5   Mark Gonzales, "As Torrid as Weather, Sox Romp Over Cubs for 8th Straight Victory," *Chicago Tribune*, June 25, 2005: 1.

6   Associated Press, "Cubs Can't Cool Off White Sox," *Culpeper* (Virginia) *Star-Exponent*, June 25, 2005: 16.

7   Mark Gonzales, "Sox GM Williams Satisfied but Knows Work Isn't Done," *Chicago Tribune*, June 23, 2005: 4.

8   "Showdown Shifts to Cell," *Chicago Tribune*, June 24, 2005: 14.

9   Bob Foltman, "Guillen Hopes Sox Can Obtain His Pal García," *Chicago Tribune*, June 6, 2004: 4.

10   Mark Gonzales, "García at Best in Big Games," *Chicago Tribune*, June 25, 2005: 7.

11   "Showdown Shifts to Cell."

12   Mark Gonzales, "Thomas Does 'Homework,'" *Chicago Tribune*, June 25, 2005: 7.

13   Phil Rogers, "Just Look Who's Back in Sox's Mix," *Chicago Tribune*, June 25, 2005: 7.

14   Mark Gonzales, "As Torrid as Weather, Sox Romp Over Cubs for 8th Straight Victory."

15   Jeff Carroll, "No Sweat," *Hammond* (Indiana) *Times*, June 25, 2005: 21.

16   Mark Gonzales, "García at Best in Big Games."

17   Andrew Seligman (Associated Press), "White Sox Maul Cubs for Eighth Straight Victory," *Corpus Christi* (Texas) *Caller-Times*, June 25, 2005: 25.

18   Mark Gonzales, "City Series: Sox's Offense Pours It On," *Chicago Tribune*, June 25, 2005: 4.

19   Mark Gonzales, "As Torrid as Weather, Sox Romp Over Cubs for 8th Straight Victory."

20   Jenifer Langosch, "Cards Quickest to 50 Wins in a Decade," MLB.com, June 28, 2015 (accessed September 9, 2024).

21   Mark Gonzales, "As Torrid as Weather, Sox Romp Over Cubs for 8th Straight Victory."

22   Jeff Carroll, "No Sweat."

DOMINANT PITCHING COMPLETES WHITE SOX SWEEP OVER INDIANS

JULY 17, 2005: CHICAGO WHITE SOX 4, CLEVELAND INDIANS 0, AT JACOBS FIELD, CLEVELAND

By Steve Ginader

Entering the 2005 All-Star break, the Chicago White Sox held a sizable lead in the American League Central Division. They had catapulted to an early five-game margin by winning 16 of their first 20 games, and when the midseason hiatus began, the gap over the second-place Minnesota Twins had grown to nine games.

Much of Chicago's early success was due to the achievement of their top four starting pitchers. Homegrown hurlers Jon Garland and Mark Buehrle developed together in the White Sox system and were rotation stalwarts in their sixth season. Veterans Freddy García and José Contreras were acquired in 2004 midseason trades and were pitching their first full season with Chicago. Collectively, the four pitchers started 74 of Chicago's first 90 games, with a combined record of 40-15.

When games resumed after the break, the White Sox were in Cleveland to face the Indians in a four-game series. Coming off a sweep by Oakland at home before the break, Chicago was looking for improved results in its match-up with third-place Cleveland. "It's a division rival," said Garland, Sunday's scheduled starter. "The least you want to do is split so the standings stay the same."[1]

Chicago manager Ozzie Guillén arranged his rotation to have his top four pitchers face the Indians. In the first three contests, Contreras, García, and Buerhle each pitched seven innings, surrendering a total of three runs, as the White Sox won all three. In Sunday's finale, Garland was aiming for his league-leading 14th win and the White Sox were looking for the sweep.

As in the first three games, Chicago's offense struck early. Scott Podsednik drove Cleveland starter Scott Elarton's third pitch of the game into the left-center-field gap for a double. He took third on Tadahito Iguchi's fly ball to center field and scored on Frank Thomas's groundout.

Podsednik had been acquired by the White Sox in an offseason trade with Milwaukee for slugger Carlos Lee.

Chicago surrendered the power bat of Lee in the transaction but added the speed and defense of Podsednik. In his first year in Chicago, Podsednik was able to solidify the top of the White Sox lineup. "I can't imagine anyone doing a better job than what he's done this year," said White Sox hitting coach Greg Walker.[2]

Garland took the mound in the bottom of the first facing an Indians lineup that was missing its leading hitter, Travis Hafner. He sidelined with a cut lip and slight concussion after being hit by a pitch in Saturday's game. Leadoff hitter Grady Sizemore worked the count full before walking on Garland's ninth pitch. Coco Crisp grounded into a double play and Victor Martinez singled to center. Casey Blake, batting cleanup with Hafner sidelined, grounded out to end the inning.

In the top of the second, the White Sox expanded their lead by two. Jermaine Dye singled up the middle and scored on A.J. Pierzynski's long home run to center field. The blast was the Chicago catcher's 12th of the season. Elarton retired the next two batters, but the frame ended with the White Sox on top 3-0.

Chicago struck again in the top of the third. Podsednik flied out to center and Iguchi followed with his sixth homer of the season. "That's the one pitch I was most disappointed in throwing," said Elarton of Iguchi's home run. "Pierzynski put a good swing on what I thought was a good pitch, but the one to Iguchi was just a bad one by me."[3]

Garland retired the Indians in order in the bottom of the second, the only clean inning he threw. Cleveland had numerous baserunners in Garland's other five innings but went 0-for-7 with runners in scoring position.

Cleveland's best chance to score came in the fourth inning. Blake and Ben Broussard singled, putting runners at first and third with no outs. After Jhonny Peralta struck out, Ronnie Belliard hit a sharp grounder up the middle. White Sox shortstop Juan Uribe fielded the hot shot, stepped on second, and threw to first to complete the double play. "I hit the ball hard, but right at somebody," Belliard said.[4]

Elarton settled down after the two home runs. From the fourth inning through the seventh, the White Sox mustered only two singles and a walk. Podsednik led off the fifth with a bunt single and stole second. Iguchi walked, but Thomas hit into a double play and Paul Konerko flied out, ending the threat. In the sixth, Aaron Rowand singled, but was stranded.

The Indians had two more opportunities with multiple baserunners but could not push across any runs. In the bottom of the sixth, Garland's last inning, Martínez stroked a leadoff single and Peralta walked with two outs. Belliard lined a pitch to right that Dye snared, leaving the runners stranded. Neil Cotts relieved Garland in the seventh, then with one out in the eighth Cliff Politte took over for Cotts. He hit Blake with a pitch, Broussard flied to center, and Peralta walked. Belliard came to the plate for the third time with runners in scoring position. He popped out to shallow center and failed again to advance anyone. "I tried," Belliard said, "but didn't do the job. They have good pitching."[5]

After setting the White Sox down in order in the seventh, Elarton was finished, having surrendered four runs on eight hits. David Riske replaced him in the eighth and pitched two hitless, scoreless innings.

Politte completed the 4-0 shutout with a one-two-three ninth. "I never thought we'd sweep," said Guillén. I (came in) hoping we'd win the series."[6] The four straight wins secured Chicago's first four-game sweep in Cleveland in 42 years. The third-place Indians plummeted to 15 games behind the White Sox. Cleveland manager Eric Wedge acknowledged his team's dubious situation. "We're in a tough stretch now, but we can't put our heads down," he said.[7]

Garland secured his league-leading 14th win, tossing six effective innings. After the game he was asked about his performance and the state of his team. "We definitely like where we're sitting right now," he said. "But we don't want to get ahead of ourselves."[8]

Cleveland rebounded and gradually clawed its way back into the race. When the Indians defeated the Kansas City Royals on September 22, Chicago's division lead dwindled to 1½ games. That was the smallest gap Cleveland secured; the White Sox never surrendered the lead and won the division by six games.

The White Sox dominated the postseason with an 11-1 record, and gleefully captured their first World Series championship since 1917. The reliable quartet of Contreras, Buehrle, Garland, and García started all 12 postseason games. First baseman Konerko, who was named MVP of the AL Championship Series, gave credit to the four starters. "Those guys were the horses, and I was just along for the ride," he said. "Really, we all were."[9]

SOURCES

In addition to the sources cited in the Notes, the author consulted Baseball Reference and Retrosheet for information including the box score and play-by-play.

https://www.baseball-reference.com/boxes/CLE/CLE200507170.shtml

https://www.retrosheet.org/boxesetc/2005/B07170CLE2005.htm

NOTES

1 Associated Press, "White Sox Complete Sweep of Cleveland," *Bloomington* (Illinois) *Pantagraph,* May 18, 2005: B1.

2 Mark Gonzales, Podsednik Adds Hitting to Repertoire," *Chicago Tribune,* July 18, 2005: 3-3.

3 "White Sox Complete Sweep of Cleveland."

4 "White Sox Complete Sweep of Cleveland."

5 Burt Graeff, "It's Vibrant Hose, Pale Tribe," *Cleveland Plain Dealer,* May 18, 2005: C-1.

6 "White Sox Complete Sweep of Cleveland."

7 "It's Vibrant Hose, Pale Tribe."

8 Mark Gonzales, "Above All, It's Garland," *Chicago Tribune,* July 18, 2005: 3-1.

9 Phil Rogers, "10 Years Ago, White Sox Had Historic Run," MLB.com, October 26, 2015, https://www.mlb.com/news/white-sox-dominant-in-2005-world-series-run/c-155562852#:

ROWAND'S CENTER-FIELD DEFENSE IN YANKEE STADIUM STEALS SPOTLIGHT, SECURES SERIES

AUGUST 10, 2005: CHICAGO WHITE SOX 2, NEW YORK YANKEES 1 (10 INNINGS), AT YANKEE STADIUM, NEW YORK

By Jim Margalus

In 2005, the White Sox' Aaron Rowand finished tied for second among American League center fielders with 15 Defensive Runs Saved, one behind Tampa Bay's Joey Gathright at the top of the leaderboard.[1]

At the bottom of the leaderboard was Bernie Williams of the New York Yankees, whose total of negative-26 Defensive Runs Saved was 16 runs lower than the next-worst center fielder, Tampa Bay's Damon Hollins.

When the two teams met for the rubber match of a three-game series on Wednesday afternoon, August 10, at Yankee Stadium, this disparity decided the tightest of series between two eventual American League division winners.

On August 8 the White Sox entered the start of the series 13 games ahead of second-place Cleveland in the AL Central Division; the Yankees were 3½ games behind Boston in the East. All three games were decided by one run. The Yankees won the opener, 3-2, after which the White Sox knotted the series with a 2-1 victory behind seven scoreless innings by former Yankee José Contreras.

The finale followed suit, except it took a 10th inning to settle.

The game had been tied, 1-1, since Carl Everett's one-out double off Yankees starter Aaron Small scored Pablo Ozuna from first in the third inning. It answered the run the Yankees scored in the first on Gary Sheffield's one-out single off Chicago right-hander Freddy García, and the pitching duel carried into the late innings. Small completed seven innings, while García finished eight before turning it over to the White Sox bullpen.

Yankees manager Joe Torre called on his future Hall of Fame closer Mariano Rivera to keep the game tied in the ninth, which he did by retiring Rowand, Jermaine Dye, and Geoff Blum in order. Manager Ozzie Guillén responded by calling on lefty Neal Cotts to handle the heart of the New York lineup, and Bernie Williams had a chance to be the hero. He came to the plate with Hideki Matsui on first after a one-out single. A passed ball advanced Matsui to scoring position, but Williams flied out to right to send the game into extra innings.

An inning later, Williams was the goat.

Facing Rivera in his second inning of work with one out in the top of the 10th, Juan Uribe hit a line drive to right-center. With the option of taking a conservative route and holding Uribe to a single, Williams instead opted for a direct line. When he couldn't close the distance, the ball bounced past him to the wall, and Uribe beat the relay throw to third for a triple.

The extra bases loomed large. Scott Podsednik fouled off a squeeze attempt before hitting a 1-and-2 cutter to Robinson Canó at second base. Uribe broke for home on contact, and his feet-first slide beat Jorge Posada's tag for the go-ahead run. When the Yankees came to the plate in the bottom of the 10th, Tino Martinez came off the bench to draw a one-out walk off Cotts. That turned over the Yankees lineup, and Guillén called on closer Dustin Hermanson, who struck out Derek Jeter for the second out.

Canó came to the plate and launched a drive to deep center, but his bid for a walk-off homer died in the glove of Rowand, who flagged it down on the warning track to cap a series that was a triumph for both the White Sox and Rowand himself.

Rowand had already made waves in the Bronx by opening the series with a pair of sensational catches in each gap. He robbed Jeter of extra bases with a diving catch in left-center, followed by a full-sprint catch on the right-center warning track to do the same to Canó.

In the August 10 finale, Rowand made his mark with quantity. His game-clinching catch on the warning track was his seventh putout of the game, and his third in the further reaches of Yankee Stadium's outfield. He ran down Gary Sheffield's deep drive to end the third inning, and hauled in Matsui's bid for extra bases in the right-center gap for the final out of the sixth.

Rowand's ranging was the talk of the Yankees' clubhouse after the game, although despite his being in his fifth major-league season and third as a starting outfielder, not everybody knew his name.

"That center fielder over there put on an absolute clinic," said Álex Rodríguez, whose first guess at Rowand's last name ("Roland?") was off by a letter.[2] "He probably took seven or eight hits away."[3]

"He stole a lot of hits," Jeter said. "If he didn't make some of those catches, we probably score a few more runs."

"He was all over the place," Williams concurred. "He was a great part of their success during the whole series. It seemed like he was able to stop the offense at times."[4]

As for Williams, his faltering came at a sensitive juncture. A week earlier, the Yankees made an unusual in-season announcement that they had declined his $15 million option for the following season, which came after a trade deadline in which the Yankees reportedly tried and failed to acquire a center fielder.[5] At the same time, manager Torre was fielding questions about public criticism from Yankees owner George Steinbrenner, who ripped Torre for a late-game pitching decision in the second game of the series. ("I'm very displeased with my manager tonight.")[6]

For the White Sox, who won the series despite scoring only two runs in each of the three games, the series represented one of the formulas they had relied on to build their league-best 74-39 record.

"We can play under pressure," Guillén said after the game. "We can play 1-0 games, 2-1 games against anybody. We can compete against any team. We compete very well."

Rowand phrased it in a more self-effacing manner: "Just find a way to win, and don't score any more than you have to."[7]

The series loss knocked the Yankees to 5½ games back of the Boston Red Sox in the American League East at 60-52. After the White Sox left town, however, the Yankees rattled off five wins in a row to start a torrid stretch run. They won 35 of their final 50 games – including two of three against the White Sox at US Cellular Field on August 19-21 – to finish with the same record as the Red Sox at 95-67, but they clinched the division on the second-to-last day of the season when their 8-4 victory at Fenway Park on October 1 gave them the decisive 10th win in the head-to-head series.

Because the Yankees won the tiebreaker with Boston, they never faced the White Sox that October. Chicago swept Boston in three games to advance to the AL Championship Series, but the Yankees lost the Division Series to the Los Angeles Angels of Anaheim in five. The White Sox continued winning, dropping just one game to the Angels in the ALCS and sweeping the Houston Astros in the World Series.

SOURCES

In addition to the sources cited in the Notes, the author consulted Baseball-Reference.com.

https://www.baseball-reference.com/boxes/NYA/NYA200508100.shtml

NOTES

1   https://www.baseball-reference.com/leagues/AL/2005-specialpos_cf-fielding.shtml.

2   Joe Gergen, "Rowand Covers Ground," *Newsday* (Long Island, New York), August 11, 2005: A73.

3   Dom Amore, "Shoulders to Cry On," *Hartford Courant*, August 11, 2005: C1.

4   Julian Garcia, "Bernie, Yanks Playing Catch-Up to Rowand's Show," *New York Daily News*, August 11, 2005: 62.

5   "The Yankees Decline an Option on Williams," *New York Times*, August 3, 2005: D3.

6   George Vecsey, "Torre Finds There's No Magic Elixir," *New York Times*, August 11, 2005: D1.

7   Mark Gonzalez, "Legging It Out," *Chicago Tribune*, August 11, 2005: 4, 1.

RANDY JOHNSON STUNG WITH FOUR HOMERS IN THE FOURTH

AUGUST 21, 2005: CHICAGO WHITE SOX 6, NEW YORK YANKEES 2, AT US CELLULAR FIELD, CHICAGO

By Brian Jacoby

On Sunday, August 21, 2005, as the New York Yankees (67-54) took the field to play the White Sox (74-46), they were in second place, three games behind the Boston Red Sox in the AL East Division while the White Sox were in first place in the AL Central, 8½ games up on the Cleveland Indians. On this day, the White Sox not only got the best of the Yankees, winning 6-2, but they performed a feat that had never been done, and never would be, against future Hall of Fame pitcher Randy Johnson.

The Yankees' roster brimmed with talent. Their top four batters were Derek Jeter, Robinson Canó, Gary Sheffield, and Álex Rodríguez, who between them had 45 All-Star Game appearances. Pitching for the Yankees was the Big Unit, Randy Johnson, with an impressive 10 All-Star Game appearances. The White Sox boasted a lineup that focused offensively on Paul Konerko batting fourth with six All-Star Game appearances.

The skies were sunny and the temperature was 78 degrees. The attendance at US Cellular Field was 39,480.

The White Sox came into the game having lost seven straight games, their longest losing streak of the season. With only 42 games remaining, pressure was high.[1] Manager Ozzie Guillén was confident that the losing streak was going to end and "glad that his team had decided to get their losing streak out of the way now."[2]

The White Sox starting pitcher, José Contreras, threw 15 pitches in the first inning, leaving Gary Sheffield on base after his infield single to third base. In the bottom of the first, Randy Johnson allowed leadoff hitter Pablo Ozuna a groundball single into center field. Ozuna stole second on a 1-and-0 count on teammate Tadahito Iguchi, who eventually struck out on a 2-and-2 count. With one out, Ozuna was caught leaning between second and third. Johnson stepped off the rubber and threw to second baseman Robinson Canó, who eventually relayed to third baseman Álex Rodríguez for the tag out. Aaron Rowand popped out to left field,

allowing Johnson also to escape the inning throwing only 15 pitches.

It remained much of the same in the second. Both pitchers dominated, each facing only three batters. Contreras threw 12 pitches, striking out Hideki Matsui, forcing a popout to center field by Bernie Williams, and forcing a groundout to second base by Tino Martinez. Johnson threw nine pitches, striking out Paul Konerko and getting Jermaine Dye and Juan Uribe to ground out to shortstop.

Contreras gave up the first run of the day in the top of the third inning. After back-to-back singles from Tony Womack and Derek Jeter, Contreras attempted to pick off the speedy Womack at second but threw the ball into center field. The Yankees now had runners on second and third with one out. Canó's groundball to second base scored Womack. 1-0, Yankees.

In the bottom of the third, Randy Johnson continued his dominance, throwing only 11 pitches. He struck out Chris Widger and Brian Anderson and forced Geoff Blum to fly out to center field.

Through 3½ innings the game was straightforward, some might say, slowly unfolding like a long summer's day. However, Willie Mays once said of baseball, "For all its gentility, its almost leisurely pace, baseball is violence under wraps." This violence and unpredictability of baseball exploded all at once in the bottom of the fourth at US Cellular Field.[3]

Randy Johnson came into the bottom of the fourth having thrown only 35 pitches. With one out, Tadahito Iguchi came to the plate to start a team effort that not only broke the game open but was never repeated in Johnson's career. On a 2-and-0 count, Iguchi hit a line-drive home run to right field, tying the game at 1-1. Aaron Rowand, the number-three batter in the White Sox lineup, entered the batter's box and with a 2-and-2 count completed a carbon-copy home run of Iguchi's to right field. Johnson, visibly irritated, set to take on the cleanup power hitter of the White Sox, Paul Konerko. On a 0-and-2 count, Johnson attempted to strike out Konerko with a slider that hung over the plate. Konerko hit a towering 410-foot bomb to the deep left-field bleachers. For the third time in three batters, the White Sox play-by-play commentator, Ken "Hawk" Harrelson, belted, "You can put it on the boards, Yes!"[4]

The score now 3-1 and only one out, Johnson gave up line-drive singles to Dye and Uribe before taking on Chris Widger. Widger, who had hit only three home runs in the past five years, was able to cap off the unthinkable moment. On a 1-and-2 count, Johnson said later, he "fired a high fastball that was not meant to be a strike but to initiate a swing and miss."[5] However, Widger took the pitch and sent it into the bleachers. This was the fourth home run of the inning, making the score 6-1, White Sox. Widger later said, "Honestly, in this game, you get lucky sometimes, and sometimes it's better to be lucky than good."[6] This moment in the fourth inning was a head-scratching, once-in-a-lifetime moment not only for Randy Johnson but also for the White Sox fans erupting at US Cellular Field.[7]

With the snap of a finger, the game went back to the leisurely pace as seen prior to the bottom of the fourth. In the top of the sixth, Tino Martinez singled to right field, scoring Gary Sheffield and making the score 6-2, White Sox.

Johnson allowed back-to-back singles to Konerko and Dye in the bottom of the sixth inning. Juan Uribe's groundout to second base advanced the runners. However, Johnson closed the door and struck out both Widger and Brian Anderson.

The seventh and eighth innings saw only one baserunner, Robinson Canó, who singled on a line drive to center field in the top of the seventh.

José Contreras completed the eighth inning throwing 112 pitches and allowing no walks. This was the longest outing of his career to date without issuing a walk. In the ninth inning, Dámaso Marté came in and closed out the game, pitching to the minimum three batters, putting an

exclamation point on the game, beating Johnson and the Yankees and helping the White Sox end their losing streak at seven games.

The Yankees' Johnson settled down after the fourth inning and completed the game with 117 pitches. This was the only time in Johnson's Hall of Fame career that he gave up back-to-back-to-back home runs, and the only game in which he allowed four home runs in one inning.

SOURCES

In addition to the sources cited in the Notes, the author consulted Baseball-Reference.com, Restrosheet.org, and a YouTube video of the game.

https://www.baseball-reference.com/boxes/CHA/CHA200508210.shtml

https://www.retrosheet.org/boxesetc/2005/B08210CHA2005.htm

"White Sox go back-to-back-to-back off Unit in 2005," YouTube.com, uploaded by MLB August 21, 2005, https://youtu.be/OPkMVccOcig?si=wPTUKvF8QjVVoAC9

NOTES

1   "Yankees' Swoon in 2000 a Lesson for Sox," *Chicago Tribune*, August 22, 2005.

2   Riverside Sluggers, "August 21 Yankees vs White Sox," TalkSox.com, August 21, 2005. https://talksox.com/forums/topic/71942-august-21-yankees-vs-white-sox/. Retrieved on September 12, 2024.

3   "75+ Best Baseball Quotes From Players, Movies, & More," justtbats.com, May 8, 2024. https://www.justbats.com/blog/post/best-baseball-quotes-from-players-movies-more/. Retrieved August 10, 2024.

4   Robert Kuenster, "Across More Than 50 Years in Baseball, Ken 'Hawk' Harrelson Was an Entertainer," *Forbes*, September 20, 2018. Harrelson was a White Sox announcer from 1982 to 1985 and 1990 to 2018. He was known for his unique phrases like "You can put it on the boards, Yes!" and "He gone! Grab some bench!" referring to a White Sox pitcher striking out an opposing batter.

5   Tyler Kepner, "Fiasco in Fourth Sinks Johnson and Yankees," *New York Times*, August 22, 2005.

6   Kepner.

7   Chris Widger hit only four home runs in 2005. In 2006 Widger hit one home run with the White Sox.

JOSÉ CONTRERAS THROWS THE FIRST COMPLETE GAME OF HIS MAJOR-LEAGUE CAREER TO STOP WHITE SOX SKID

SEPTEMBER 23, 2005: CHICAGO WHITE SOX 3, MINNESOTA TWINS 1, AT US CELLULAR FIELD, CHICAGO

By Michael Marsh

For much of the 2005 season, the White Sox cruised in the American League Central Division race. Even with slugger Frank Thomas missing almost all of the season because of an injured left ankle, the team dominated the division with strong pitching, steady hitting, and strong defense. The White Sox had a 15-game lead over the second-place Cleveland Indians on August 1.

The team, however, began to slump. The White Sox won 22 games and lost 26 between August 2 and September 22. Meanwhile, the Indians got hot and closed the gap, going 35-12 during the same period. The White Sox' lead dropped to 1½ games.

During the White Sox slump, *Chicago Sun-Times* sports columnist Jay Mariotti compared them to the 1969 Chicago Cubs. That team led the former National League East division by 7½ games on August 19, 1969, before it suffered one of the most infamous collapses in major-league history. The team finished second in the division to the New York Mets, the eventual World Series champion. Mariotti wrote: "But when you see the Sox morph into a limp, feeble club that can't piece together a run, much less win a game – I mean, is it wrong to mention early similarities to 1969?"[1]

White Sox pitcher José Contreras gave his team a major boost. On September 23 Contreras threw the first complete game of his major-league career as the White Sox defeated the visiting Minnesota Twins 3-1 at US Cellular Field (later called Guaranteed Rate Field).

Contreras, a 6-4, 255-pound right-hander, improved to 14-7. He allowed six hits, struck out nine, and walked one batter in a brisk 2:19 before 28,003 raucous fans.

Contreras survived a shaky start in the top of the first inning. The Twins' Jason Tyner led off with a single to left field, then stole second base. Contreras walked Nick Punto.

Contreras faced Joe Mauer with two on and nobody out. Mauer grounded to Contreras, who threw to shortstop Juan Uribe to force out Punto at second base, and Uribe threw to Paul Konerko at first base to complete the double play. Tyner advanced to third. The Twins' Matt LeCroy flied to center fielder Aaron Rowand for the third out.

The White Sox scored all of their runs in the bottom of the first inning off losing pitcher Kyle Lohse, whose record fell to 9-13. Scott Podsednik led off with a double to left field. Tadahito Iguchi struck out and A.J. Pierzynski flied out to center field. After Konerko drew a walk, Jermaine Dye hit a three-run home run to left field. It was his 29th home run of the season.

Contreras retired the Twins in order in the second, third, and fourth innings. He started the top of the fifth inning by striking out the first two batters, Jacque Jones and Mike Ryan. (Ryan had replaced Michael Cuddyer in right field.) The third batter, Justin Morneau, doubled to left field. It was the only extra-base hit Contreras gave up in the game. Afterward, Contreras's fielding helped the White Sox again. The Twins' Terry Tiffee grounded back to him, and Contreras's throw to first retired the side.

Ryan drove in the Twins' only run in the top of the seventh inning. Mauer led off with a single to right field. He stole second after Matt LeCroy and Jones struck out. Ryan's single to right drove in Mauer. Ryan stole second during Morneau's at-bat, but Morneau fouled out to Konerko to end the inning.

The White Sox had a final scare in the top of the ninth. Punto led off with a single to right and went to second and third on groundouts by Mauer and LeCroy. Jacque Jones stepped to the plate. White Sox manager Ozzie Guillén walked to the pitcher's mound. The crowd, fearing Guillén wouldn't let Contreras complete the shutout, booed the manager. But Guillén left Contreras in the game, and he struck out Jones for the final out.[2]

Contreras gave up six hits, struck out nine, and walked just one batter. "It's one of the best games I've pitched in my whole career as a baseball player," Contreras said after the game. "And the best I've pitched in the US."[3]

The win gave the White Sox a much-needed lift. It preserved the team's thin lead and helped save the season. Cleveland beat host Kansas City 7-6 the same night. Starting with Contreras's win, the White Sox won 8 of their last 10 games and took the division. That included a season-ending three-game sweep of the Indians. The Indians finished 3-6 in their last nine games.

For Contreras, a 33-year-old Cuban defector, the game was part of a quest for vindication. Born in Las Martinas, Cuba, he had played seven years for the Cuban national team, He pitched well in international competition. Contreras often baffled hitters by throwing several different pitches, including a fastball and a forkball, from different angles.[4]

Although Contreras had achieved fame in his homeland, he craved to play in the US major leagues. He defected while the Cuban team was playing in Mexico in 2002.[5] He eventually was smuggled into the United States.

Contreras pitched for the New York Yankees in 2003 and part of 2004, finishing with records of 7-2 and 8-5 respectively. The Yankees traded him to the White Sox on July 31, 2004, for pitcher Esteban Loaiza. Baseball writer Phil Rogers speculated that Contreras's performances against the Boston Red Sox angered Yankees owner George Steinbrenner. Rogers wrote: "He had allowed 28 runs in 15⅓ innings over five career starts against Boston, an unforgivable sin in George Steinbrenner's world."[6]

After the trade, Contreras had a 5-4 record for the White Sox. The first half of the 2005 season did not go well for him. He was 4-5 with a 4.26 ERA at the All-Star break. White Sox general manager Ken Williams tried to trade him. A book about the White Sox, *The Pride of Chicago*, stated: "He was the weakest link on a strong pitching staff. One of Williams' midseason goals was to pull off a trade that would add a reliever or veteran bat to his lineup. He was willing – even eager – to package Contreras as the bait for any deal."[7]

Fortunately for the White Sox, Williams did not find any takers. Contreras emerged as the pitching staff's ace during the second half of the season. He won his last eight starts. Contreras finished the season 15-7, including 11-2 in the second half.

After the White Sox defeated the Twins, sportswriter Rick Gano wrote: "The second half of the season, Contreras has changed his arm angle and found his control, cutting down his walks and limiting his pitch count."[8]

Twins manager Ron Gardenhire complimented Contreras after the game, saying, "He was a little out of whack before, but he's not out of whack anymore."[9]

White Sox manager Guillén said: "Two months ago, everybody wanted to kill this kid and get him out of town because he was pitching horrible, and all of a sudden he's a Cy Young winner."[10]

Guillén told another writer, "Jose had always had the best arm on my team. It's a matter of time when he can use that. It's a matter of confidence. This kid won a big game for us and he showed the guys when you have confidence and throw strikes and attack the strike zone, you can win a lot of games."[11]

Sportswriter Vinnie Duber declared in a 2020 retrospective that Contreras's performance in September 2005, including the win over the Twins, greatly helped the White Sox. Duber wrote: "… [H]is biggest contribution was getting the White Sox to the postseason in the first place. From Sept. 7 to Sept. 23, the team went 6-10. But Contreras won all four starts he made during that stretch, preventing a true freefall out of the division race."[12]

SOURCES

In addition to the sources cited in the Notes, the author used the Baseball-Reference.com, Baseball-Almanac.com, and Retrosheet.org websites for box-score, player, team, and season pages, pitching and batting game logs, and other material.

NOTES

1   Jay Mariotti, "Gag Line Starting to form on 35th Street," *Chicago Sun-Times*, August 21, 2005: 118.

2   Mark Gonzales, "Complete Relief: Contreras Goes Distance for 1st Time, Gives Sox Major Lift," *Chicago Tribune*, September 24, 2005: Section 3: 1, 4.

3   Rick Gano (Associated Press), "Contreras to the Rescue – Sox Top Twins," *Ottawa* (Illinois) *Times*, September 24, 2005: B2.

4   Clemson Smith Muñiz, "Jose Contreras: A ChiSox Ambassador with Stories to Tell," La Vida Baseball, March 27, 2018. https://www.lavidabaseball.com/jose-contreras-cuba-journey/; Andrew Seligman (Associated Press), "Contreras Finally Displaying All His Talents on the Mound," *Pocono Record* (Stroudsburg, Pennsylvania), June 25, 2006. https://www.poconorecord.com/story/sports/2006/06/25/contreras-finally-displaying-all-his/53084139007/.

5   Smith Muñiz.

6   Phil Rogers, *Say It's So: The Chicago White Sox's Magical Season* (Chicago: Triumph Books, 2006), 60.

7   Chris De Luca, ed., *The Pride of Chicago: The White Sox's 2005 Championship Season* (St. Louis: Sporting News Books, 2005), 29.

8   Gano, "Contreras to the Rescue – Sox Top Twins."

9   "Twins Can't Solve Sox, 3-1," *St. Cloud* (Minnesota) *Times*, September 24, 2005: 1D.

10   Gonzales, "Complete Relief": 4.

11   Gano.

12   Vinnie Duber, "White Sox 2005 Rewind: Jose Contreras Went 'Ace Mode' to Save the Season," NBC Sports Chicago, May 14, 2020, https://www.nbcsportschicago.com/mlb/chicago-white-sox/white-sox-2005-rewind-jose-contreras-went-ace-mode-to-save-the-season/381271/.

WHITE SOX CLINCH AL CENTRAL CROWN EN ROUTE TO FIRST WORLD SERIES TITLE IN 88 YEARS

SEPTEMBER 29, 2005: CHICAGO WHITE SOX 4, DETROIT TIGERS 2, AT COMERICA PARK, DETROIT

By Chad Moody

Heading into the 2005 season, the Chicago White Sox had been consistent contenders in the American League Central Division since their last divisional title in 2000. Chicago, as was its wont during that period, constructed its 2004 squad to compete one-dimensionally via the long ball – much to the dismay of manager Ozzie Guillén. The outspoken first-year skipper (and the team's longtime former star shortstop) had "grown tired watching the team fall short year after year despite a lineup stacked with sluggers."[1] Instead, he sought strong pitching and a more balanced attack. "We hit a lot of home runs, but so what?" Guillén said. "We had no leadoff hitter, no speed, we had a lot of holes to fill."[2] Despite his managerial inexperience, Guillén helped persuade general manager Ken Williams to begin a major roster overhaul that would allow his team to "hit and run, bunt, steal bases [and] create action instead of wait for [home runs]."[3] Key midseason-2004 acquisitions included "professional hitter" Carl Everett along with starting pitchers Freddy García and José Contreras.[4]

Williams accelerated the rebuild in the offseason before the 2005 campaign. He offset the departure of sluggers Carlos Lee, Magglio Ordóñez, and José Valentín with the addition of a mix of speed, defense, and pitching that featured "low-maintenance, low-ego type guys, and hard workers."[5] Speedy left fielder Scott Podsednik, star Japanese import second baseman Tadahito Iguchi, power-hitting right fielder Jermaine Dye, and fiery catcher A.J. Pierzynski came aboard to become mainstays of the starting lineup. Incoming relievers Dustin Hermanson, Bobby Jenks, and Luis Vizcaíno helped revamp the bullpen. "We didn't try to reinvent the game when we set out to put this team together," Williams explained. "What we wanted to do was basically go back to what has worked in baseball history

and stand firm on those fundamentals: Catch the ball, pitch the ball, and give yourself a chance to be in and win every ballgame."[6]

The controversial "drastic" moves quickly proved successful, with the White Sox maintaining the division lead throughout the 2005 season – although not without some drama.[7] After enjoying a comfortable 15-game margin on August 1, the team fell flat over the final two months of the campaign and nearly squandered its divisional stranglehold. Nonetheless, the White Sox clutched a tenuous three-game lead over the Cleveland Indians as they headed into a September 29 road contest against the Detroit Tigers. A victory over the Tigers would guarantee the AL Central title for the White Sox.

Detroit had won two of the first three in the four-game set against its divisional foe. However, the woeful Tigers entered the contest a distant 24 games out of first place and were without the services of key regulars Iván Rodríguez and Carlos Guillén. "It's been a tough go," manager Alan Trammell said of the team's 12th consecutive losing season that ultimately resulted in his firing the day after the season ended.[8]

Making only his third appearance of the campaign, Jason Grilli took the mound for Detroit in his final big-league start before embarking on a lengthy career as a bullpen arm. The White Sox called upon the 13-8 workhorse García, who relished "high-profile games."[9] The crowd of 13,494 at Comerica Park endured brisk weather conditions during the afternoon tilt.

A bases-empty double by Dye kick-started a two-out rally for Chicago in the top of the first inning. After veteran slugger Paul Konerko walked to put two aboard, Everett tripled, scoring both runners. Everett remained stranded

295

on third when Grilli, who had started eight games for the White Sox a year earlier, retired his former teammate Aaron Rowand on a fly ball.

After García made quick work of Detroit in the bottom half of the inning, Chicago used its "small-ball tactics to manufacture a run" in the second frame.[10] Pierzynski led things off with a double and took third on a sacrifice by Juan Uribe. After a walk to Willie Harris put runners at the corners, Podsednik scored Pierzynski on a sacrifice fly to give the visitors a 3-0 lead. That score held until Grilli allowed a solo home run to Konerko in the sixth inning to give the White Sox a four-run advantage.

The Tigers' offense finally found some life in the bottom of the seventh. Craig Monroe and Brandon Inge led off with singles. Monroe moved to third on Vance Wilson's ground-out and scored on a wild pitch. García settled down to retire the next two batters and limit the damage to one run.

Detroit again chipped away at the deficit in the eighth after Tigers reliever Chris Spurling blanked Chicago in the top half of the frame. Plácido Polanco's leadoff single chased García from the game in favor of reliever Cliff Politte. After retiring the first batter he faced, the journey-man allowed a double to former White Sox star Ordóñez that scored Polanco. The inning's cavalcade of pitching changes continued with relievers Neal Cotts and Jenks being called upon from the bullpen; the two successfully held the score at 4-2 as the increasingly nerve-racking game headed into the final stanza.

After Detroit reliever Fernando Rodney narrowly escaped trouble in the top of the ninth, Guillén decided to leave the fate of Chicago's precarious two-run lead to the right arm of Jenks, whose last four appearances included two blown saves and a loss. The 6-foot-4, 275-pound rookie – promoted from Double-A ball in July – had recently supplanted an ailing Hermanson as the team's closer.

Inge's fourth single of the game led off the bottom of the ninth for Detroit. He moved to second on Wilson's bouncing ball that was booted by third baseman Joe Crede, who had just returned to the team that morning after visiting Missouri for the birth of his second child. After the "shaky" start, however, Jenks retired the next three Tigers on back-to-back strikeouts and a "scary" line drive to first that Konerko speared to end the game – and give the White Sox their first AL Central title in five years.[11] "I won't lie to you – my stomach dropped a little bit when the ball was hit," Jenks admitted after collecting his fourth save of the year. "It was an unbelievable catch."[12] After making his potentially game-saving grab, Konerko viewed the contest as being analogous to Chicago's campaign as a whole. "It was like our season," the All-Star first baseman said. "We cruised through seven innings, and then we got a little tight at the end and pulled it out."[13]

After the relatively mild on-field celebration among White Sox players moved into the clubhouse, a raucous party commenced. "At the height of the festivities, champagne and beer were being sprayed so fiercely it was as if an automatic sprinkler system had been activated," Chicago sportswriter Rick Morrissey wrote. "Cigar smoke hung over the scene. Salsa music throbbed. Grown men acted like boys."[14] The celebration validated the "feisty leadership of Guillén and foresight of Williams" from doubters who thought the team would fritter away its divisional lead.[15] However, the "only choke" on this day involved the manager and GM "choking back tears of joy."[16]

Curiously, not present during the merrymaking was longtime Chicago slugger and future Hall of Famer Frank Thomas, whose season ended in July when he fractured a foot. "Frank's not here because he chose not to be here," Guillén bluntly said.[17] Chicago sportswriter Chris De Luca deduced that Thomas's absence was a signal that his 16-season run with the team was "nearing its last chapter."[18] After two consecutive injury-plagued campaigns, Thomas indeed was not brought back by the White Sox in 2006, creating a years-long rift between the two parties.

Looking ahead despite being surrounded by the ongoing revelry, winning pitcher García declared that the team needed "to step up for the first round of the playoffs."[19] And while still in the midst of drying off from champagne baths, White Sox owner Jerry Reinsdorf, who had been a "basket case" down the tense stretch run, began wondering about the "mind-boggling" possibility of winning a championship for the city.[20] Even jubilant Chicago Mayor Richard M. Daley opined that the White Sox "can be in the World Series easily."[21]

Indeed, the "lunch-bucket" team took seven of eight games in the first two playoff rounds to win its first pennant in 46 years.[22] The White Sox then swept the Houston Astros to capture the World Series in "arguably the greatest postseason run in history."[23] The championship was the White Sox' first since 1917. Much of that year's squad subsequently became embroiled in the infamous Black Sox Scandal involving game-fixing in the 1919 fall classic that, as legend has it, cast a long-lingering malediction over the Windy City's South Siders. But Chicago's defeat of Detroit on a late September day 86 years after that ugly episode in baseball's annals was the first step toward finally exorcising the Curse of Shoeless Joe (Jackson).[24]

SOURCES

The author accessed Baseball-Reference.com and Retrosheet.org for box scores/play-by-play information, and other data.

https://www.baseball-reference.com/boxes/DET/DET200509290.shtml

https://www.retrosheet.org/boxesetc/2005/B09290DET2005.htm

In addition to the sources cited in the Notes, the author accessed GenealogyBank.com, NewspaperArchive.com, Newspapers.com, Paper of Record, Stathead.com, Weather Underground, and a recording of the game's television broadcast from Comcast SportsNet in Chicago posted on YouTube.

NOTES

1. Mark Gonzales, "Small Ball Rules: Buehrle's Gem, 1 Run Just Enough to Top Cleveland," *Chicago Tribune*, April 5, 2005: Section 4, 1.

2. *The Pride of Chicago: The White Sox's 2005 Championship Season* (St. Louis: The Sporting News, 2005), 18.

3. *The Pride of Chicago: The White Sox's 2005 Championship Season*, 14.

4. "D-Rays Offer Deal to Everett," *Lakeland* (Florida) *Ledger,* December 10, 2003, https://www.theledger.com/story/news/2003/12/10/d-rays-offer-deal-to-everett/26088026007/, accessed June 4, 2024.

5. Dave van Dyck, "Built From the Grind Up," *Chicago Tribune*, September 30, 2005: Section 4, 7.

6. Doug Padilla, "Williams Happy, but He Has a More Worldly View," *Chicago Sun-Times*, September 30, 2005: 151.

7. Van Dyck.

8. Gene Guidi, "Central Time for Chisox," *Detroit Free Press*, September 30, 2005: 7E.

9. Doug Padilla, "Celebration Central," *Chicago Sun-Times*, September 30, 2005: Red Streak, 19.

10. Mark Gonzales, "Weight Lifters," *Chicago Tribune*, September 30, 2005: Section 4, 3.

11. "Clinch Runners," *Chicago Tribune*, September 30, 2005: Redeye, 13; Mike Downey, "Sox's Gaze Extending Well Beyond Cleveland," *Chicago Tribune*, September 30, 2005: Section 4, 3.

12. Rick Morrissey, "An Amazin' Finish and a Fresh Start," *Chicago Tribune*, September 30, 2005: Section 1, 6.

13. Padilla, "Celebration Central."

14. Morrissey.

15. Chicago Sun-Times, *White Sox: 2005 World Series Champions* (Champaign, Illinois: Sports Publishing LLC, 2005), 125.

16. *White Sox: 2005 World Series Champions*, 54.

17. Chris De Luca, "Sox Stand Up to Test," *Chicago Sun-Times*, September 30, 2005: 157.

18. De Luca.

19. Doug Padilla, "Steady Freddy, Timely Hitting Return; 'Look Out' in Postseason, Konerko Warns," *Chicago Sun-Times*, September 30, 2005: 156.

20. Rick Telander, "The Way I See It," *Chicago Sun-Times*, September 30, 2005: 158.

21. Rummana Hussain, "Daley Rejoices: 'Happy, Happy Day,'" *Chicago Sun-Times*, September 30, 2005: 6.

22. Mark Gonzales, "Lunch-Bucket Sox Feast on Achievement," *Chicago Tribune*, September 30, 2005: Section 4, 6.

23. Phil Rogers, *Say It's So: The Chicago White Sox's Magical Season* (Chicago: Triumph Books, 2006), 263.

24. David S. Neft, Richard M. Cohen, and Michael L. Neft, *The Sports Encyclopedia: Baseball 2006* (New York: St. Martin's Griffin, 2006), 737.

WHITE SOX COMPLETE ALDS SWEEP OF RED SOX

OCTOBER 7, 2005: CHICAGO WHITE SOX 5, BOSTON RED SOX 3, AT FENWAY PARK, BOSTON (GAME THREE OF THE 2005 AMERICAN LEAGUE DIVISION SERIES)

By Eric Conrad and Mark Morowczynski

The last time the White Sox won a playoff series was also the last year they won the World Series, 88 years earlier, in 1917. They would need to overcome Boston in the Red Sox' home ballpark in an American League Division Series to do so in 2005. Boston had broken its 86-year World Series championship drought the previous year. Of the 22 teams to go down two games to none in a division series, only four had come back to win. The Red Sox had done so twice, in 1999 vs. Cleveland and in 2003 vs. Oakland.[1]

Catcher A.J. Pierzynski said, "That's the hardest one to win, the closing game. They know it could be the end of their year, and they'll give it all they can to try to get back in it. The last one is always harder. Each victory in a series gets harder. The last one was hard, but this one will be even harder."[2]

The Red Sox turned to Tim Wakefield, who had beaten the White Sox 7-4 at Fenway Park on August 13. The White Sox tapped Freddy García, who had been magnificent on the road during the season with a 10-3 record. One of those losses came on August 23, when he pitched a one-hitter vs. the Twins, giving up just a home run to Jacque Jones.

Scott Podsednik led off for the White Sox and was hit by a pitch, but was soon caught stealing at second with an excellent throw by Doug Mirabelli, who normally caught knuckleballer Wakefield. Wakefield then struck out Tadahito Iguchi and Jermaine Dye.

In the bottom of the first, Red Sox leadoff hitter Johnny Damon also reached base, with a walk, but was unable to score. Edgar Renteria popped out to third, and during a hit-and-run, David Ortiz lined into an unassisted double play to third baseman Joe Crede, who was playing the shift near second base.

The first runs of the game were scored in the top of the third. after a sliding catch in right field by Trot Nixon

and a deep-in-the-hole groundout to Renteria. Juan Uribe started the two-out rally with a double to left off the Green Monster. Podsednik followed with a double to the left-field corner, scoring Uribe. Iguchi singled up the middle to bring Podsednik around and made it 2-0. Jermaine Dye singled but Wakefield minimized the damage by getting Paul Konerko to fly out to right.

Heading into Game Three, the lack of offense from the Red Sox was a concern. After two games they had scored only six runs, were hitting .211 with runners in scoring position, and had no home runs. The White Sox had an offensive explosion of 19 runs, a .533 batting average with runners in scoring position, and six home runs. That changed in the bottom of the fourth.

David Ortiz led off the inning with a home run to center and Manny Ramirez followed with another homer, to right, to tie the game, 2-2. This was only the second time in 2005 that Ortiz and Ramirez hit back-to-back home runs; the first was 17 days before, on September 20 vs. the Tampa Bay Devil Rays. García eventually retired the next three batters to end the fourth.

The sixth inning proved the deciding inning of both the game and the Series as neither starting pitcher made it to the seventh. Wakefield started the sixth by walking Dye and then giving up a home run to Paul Konerko to give the White Sox a 4-2 lead. The last batter he faced was Carl Everett, who grounded out to first.

Manager Terry Francona, who was 4-0 in elimination games in his managerial career at the time, went to his bullpen for Chad Bradford and his submarine-style approach against Aaron Rowand. It didn't work and Rowand singled to center field. Bradford was replaced by Mike Myers to face Pierzynski. While Myers focused on attacking A.J., Rowand stole second. Myers ultimately walked Pierzynski.

Francona once again went to the bullpen – this time to bring in rookie Jonathan Papelbon to face Crede. The 24-year-old had never pitched above Class A before 2005.[3] Right fielder Trot Nixon benefited from familiarity with his home ballpark and caught Crede's foul popup reaching into the first row of the short right-field stands. Rowand tagged up on the play and took third base. With Uribe up, Pierzynski stole second, his first stolen base of the season. Papelbon stranded both runners by striking out Uribe.

García normally pitched deep into games during the 2005 season: Of his 33 starts, 26 were six or more innings and 22 were seven or more. However, he didn't record another out. Ramirez led off the bottom of the sixth by hitting his second home run of the game, making the score 4-3 and knocking García out of the game. White Sox manager Ozzie Guillén called for Dámaso Marté, who did not have it that night. Nixon – the first batter he faced – hit a line-drive single to right field. Marte then walked Bill Mueller and John Olerud to load the bases with nobody out. A rally was brewing.

Guillén then made a surprising choice and went to the veteran starter Orlando Hernández, who was making the 18th postseason appearance of his career. With Wakefield out, Francona had Jason Varitek bat for Mirabelli. Varitek was 3-for-8 in the first two games of the Series and the Red Sox would need a big inning here to extend this to a fourth game. Hernández got Varitek to pop out in foul territory on the first-base side to Konerko near the fungo circles.

Next came Tony Graffanino, looking to redeem himself from an earlier Game Two error. He battled through a 10-pitch at-bat before eventually popping out to shortstop Uribe on the infield grass for the second out of the inning.

Damon worked the count full but struck out on a close checked swing. "I was hoping we could get out of it with a run," White Sox owner Jerry Reinsdorf said.[4] The Red Sox were 4-for-19 with runners in scoring position heading into Game Three. After their best opportunity of the game, they couldn't convert and ended the series 4-for-24.

Both Papelbon and Hernández continued to hold the opposing offenses at bay. After Hernández retired eight batters in a row, Olerud singled to center field with two outs in the bottom of the eighth, but Hernández struck out Varitek swinging to end the inning. Hernández in his three shutout innings pitched gave up just one hit and struck out four.

Mike Timlin replaced Papelbon in the top of the ninth and the White Sox finally demonstrated some of their small ball/Ozzie ball that was so successful for them during the season. After Pierzynski led off with a double to left, Crede sacrificed him Pierzynski to third. The White Sox added an insurance run on a suicide squeeze with Uribe getting the bunt down – fielded by Timlin, but scoring Pierzynski and making it a 5-3 White Sox lead. Uribe ended up safe at first, but Timlin finished the inning without allowing any more runs.

For the bottom of the ninth, Guillén again turned to rookie Bobby Jenks. In Game Two, Jenks nailed down six outs to save a 5-4 White Sox win. He needed only 10 pitches to get the last three outs of the Series.[5] Facing Boston's ninth, first, and second hitters, Jenks got Graffanino to ground out to Crede at third and struck out Damon. The year before with the St. Louis Cardinals, Renteria made the last out of the World Series against the Red Sox. Now with Boston, it was up to him to try to extend their season. Jenks got the better of him and he grounded out to Iguchi at second, closing out the game and winning the Series for the White Sox.

"Don't get too high," Guillén said after the celebration started to subside. "We beat one of the best teams in baseball and continue to ride very low. Don't get too high. Don't get too excited. We'll wait for whoever we're playing and take it one day at a time."[6]

It had been 88 years since Clarence Henry "Pants" Rowland led the White Sox to a playoff series win and the Chicago fans were excited to celebrate. Hundreds of people waited several hours for the team's return at Chicago's Midway Airport the next day to cheer on the team.[7]

The next stop on the White Sox' march to their 2005 World Series championship was at home three days later, on October 11, vs. the Los Angeles Angels of Anaheim, playing their third game in as many days and cities after beating the New York Yankees in Anaheim in Game Five of the other AL Division Series.

SOURCES

In addition to the sources cited in the Notes, the authors consulted Baseball-Reference.com and Retrosheet.org.

https://www.baseball-reference.com/boxes/BOS/BOS200510070.shtml

https://www.retrosheet.org/boxesetc/2005/B10070BOS2005.htm

NOTES

1   Chris Snow, "For Starters, Several Options Being Weighed," *Boston Globe*, October 6, 2005: D4.

2   Mark Gonzales, "Won Two … Three?; Looking to Sweep Series, White Sox Take Aim at Knuckleballer Wakefield," *Chicago Tribune*, October 7, 2005: 4-1.

3   Chris Snow, "The Bottom Was Up at the Wrong Time," *Boston Globe*, October 8, 2005: F5.

4   Mark Gonzales, "1st-Round KO: White Sox Sweep Away World Series Champions; Next Stop, the ALCS; White Sox 5, Red Sox 3," *Chicago Tribune*, October 8, 2005: 6-3.

5   Tom Verducci, "Power and Fury," *Sports Illustrated*, October 17, 2005: 50.

6   Mark Gonzales, "Stakes, Reward Rise; Sox Stay Low-Key, Ride 8-Game Win Streak into ALCS," *Chicago Tribune*, October 9, 2005: 17-2.

7   Brendan McCarthy, "Sox Fans Are Flying High at Midway," *Chicago Tribune*, October 9, 2005: 17-2.

EXHAUSTED ANGELS OUTLAST CHISOX

OCTOBER 11, 2005: LOS ANGELES ANGELS OF ANAHEIM 3, CHICAGO WHITE SOX 2, AT US CELLULAR FIELD, CHICAGO (GAME ONE OF THE 2005 AMERICAN LEAGUE CHAMPIONSHIP SERIES)

By William M. Vines

In 2005 the White Sox put on one of the most dominating postseason performances in the history of major-league baseball. They won an astounding 11 out of 12 games. In the American League Division Series, the White Sox beat the Boston Red Sox in three straight. They won four out of five against the Los Angeles Angels of Anaheim in the American League Championship Series before going on to sweep the Houston Astros in the World Series. The only game the White Sox lost that postseason was Game One of the ALCS, played on Tuesday night, October 11, at US Cellular Field.

Before the start of Game One, White Sox fan Rod McKennell summed up the feelings of the Chicago fans:

> Give this city a championship. That's what we need, one baseball championship. And who better else than the White Sox? You know, we don't make excuses for losing, we don't have curses. We just go out and play and this is what it's all about. We got to win this right now.[1]

It had been an extraordinary season for the White Sox. Manager Ozzie Guillén was in his second season with the team. In his first season the team finished 83-79, second in the American League Central Division behind the Minnesota Twins. In 2005, the White Sox won 99 games, more than any other team in the American League. They were 52-29 on the road and 35-19 in one-run games (both the best in the majors). They had three pitchers with 15 or more wins (the first time for the White Sox since 1993).

The 2005 White Sox had seven hitters with 15 or more home runs, and they smashed 200 homers as a team (fourth in the American League). But the White Sox were not just a power-hitting team; they also knew how to play small ball. Only two other teams in the American League stole more bases than the White Sox in 2005 (Angels and Devil Rays).

The White Sox overpowered the Red Sox in the ALDS, outscoring them 24-9 on their way to a three-game sweep.[2]

The Angels' trip to the ALCS was a bit more difficult. They played a full, five-game series against the New York Yankees. The Angels won two of the first three in that series. Game Four was scheduled for October 8 in New York but was rained out. The game was played the next night and the Yankees won, 3-2. Both teams flew across the country for Game Five, which the Angels won in Anaheim, 5-3, to clinch the series. Since the ALCS started the next night in Chicago, the Angels had to immediately board another plane and travel to the Windy City. Thus, the Angels had to play three games in three different cities on three straight nights.

The travel did not seem to affect the celebratory attitude in the Angels clubhouse after Game Five, where the "beer and champagne flowed freely."[3] Star catcher Bengie Molina said, "This is unbelievable. … Don't think just because we win, it's easy. It hasn't been that way all year. We just keep finding a way."[4]

The White Sox and their fans were understandably confident going into Game One. The South Siders were playing at home on four days' rest. The Angels were worn out and playing on the road. And yet, as Phil Rogers of the *Chicago Tribune* noted, the ALCS should come with a "warning label" for White Sox fans: "Caution: Overconfidence can be bad for your health."[5]

The Sox started red-hot José Contreras, who was riding high on a nine-game winning streak. During the season the 33-year-old Cuban-born hurler had gone 15-7 with a 3.61 earned-run average. He pitched a career high of 204⅔ innings. Contreras had started and won Game One of the ALDS when the White Sox overwhelmed the Red Sox, 14-2.

Paul Byrd started for the Angels on three days' rest. The 34-year-old right-handed journeyman started 31 games for the Angels in his only season with the team. He went 12-11 and tied for second in the American League with 22 quality starts.

GRINDERS AND GAMERS

The Angels struck first when Garret Anderson led off the second inning by hitting a 2-and-0 Contreras pitch over the right-field wall. The Angels scored two more runs in the top of the third. Steve Finley, who had hit a measly .091 so far in the postseason, led off the inning by slicing a single into right field. The next batter, Adam Kennedy, hitting ninth in the batting order, slapped a single to left. That brought up Chone Figgins, who laid down a sacrifice bunt, advancing the runners. Shortstop Orlando Cabrera came up next and hit an infield single, scoring Finley. Vladimir Guerrero, the Angels' designated hitter, then grounded out to Contreras, allowing Kennedy to score. This was a classic case of "get 'em on, get 'em over, get 'em in." It was all the scoring the Angels would need to win Game One.

The White Sox tried to come back but ultimately fell short. In the bottom of the third, Joe Crede, who drilled 22 homers during the regular season, hit a one-out smash over the left-field wall. The next inning, Carl Everett poked a single to right, then advanced to second on a fielder's choice. A.J. Pierzynski then singled to right, driving in Everett. This was the final run scored in the game. The Angels won 3-2.

Contreras did his part. He went 8⅓ innings. And besides the third inning, when the Angels scored twice, he never really got in trouble. With one out in the eighth, he gave up a one-out hit to Bengie Molina that led Guillén to pull him. He had thrown 102 pitches.

The White Sox had their chances. Twice runners were caught trying to steal second. In the bottom of the fifth with two outs, Scott Podsednik attempted to steal on Byrd – but the Angels had called a pitchout, and a perfect throw by Molina to Cabrera caught him by a mile. On the Fox broadcast, Joe Buck quipped, "Ozzie Guillén just got his pocket picked."[6]

Two innings later, with reliever Scot Shields on the mound and A.J. Pierzynski on first, Joe Crede apparently missed a hit-and-run sign. As Pierzynski ran toward second, he looked back at Crede – who didn't swing – and Pierzynski was easily caught by another perfect strike by Molina. When Pierzynski got back to the dugout, he slammed his helmet onto the ground. Guillén just shook his head.

In the bottom of the eighth, with Juan Uribe on first and no outs, Scott Podsednik was unable to lay down a sacrifice bunt and ended up striking out. Later in the same inning, Paul Konerko came to the plate with two outs and runners on first and second, but he popped out to center field to end the inning.

The White Sox' last chance to score was in the bottom of the ninth. With pinch-runner Pablo Ozuna on first and no outs, Aaron Rowand tried to lay down a bunt, but it

The White Sox stand for the National Anthem on the third-base line at home before Game One of the ALCS, the only game they lost in the entire playoff run.

went directly to Chone Figgins at third, who threw out Ozuna at second. So much for small ball. It just wasn't the White Sox' night.

In the *Chicago Tribune* the next day, columnist Mike Downey seemed to speak for ChiSox Nation when he "addressed" the Angels, saying, "For a bunch of blood-shot-eyed, sleep-deprived, worn out, mixed-up zombies, you Los Angeles Angels of Anaheim sure did play a wide-awake game of baseball Tuesday night against our Chicago White Sox of Chicago."[7] Indeed they did.

But that was all the luck the Angels would have against the South Siders. In fact, that was all the luck *any* team would have against the White Sox that postseason. Chicago won the next four games against the Angels. White Sox pitchers threw complete games in all four wins, with Contreras winning Game Five. The White Sox then went on to dominate the Astros in a four-game sweep in the World Series, capping one of the most impressive postseason performances by any team in the history of the game. It was their first World Series championship since 1917. The day after the Series ended, Rick Morrissey concluded his column by reflecting, "Chicago, the big engine that couldn't, finally could. Don't wake us up. We're dreaming."[8]

SOURCES

In addition to the sources listed in the Notes, the author used data from Baseball-Reference.com.

https://www.baseball-reference.com/boxes/CHA/CHA200510110.shtml

NOTES

1   Cheryl Corley, "Angels Best White Sox in ALCS Game 1," National Public Radio *Morning Edition*, October 12, 2005, www.npr.org/2005/10/12/4955286/angels-best-white-sox-in-alcs-game-1. Fans of Chicago's other major-league team, the Cubs, had been waiting even longer for a championship – since 1908.

2   Boston was the reigning World Series champion, having ended its own 86-year drought just the year before, in 2004.

3   Mike DiGiovanna, "Angels Top the Yankees Again," *Los Angeles Times*, October 11, 2005: A18.

4   DiGiovanna.

5   Phil Rogers, "Don't Expect a Cakewalk," *Chicago Tribune*, October 11, 2005: Section 7, 3.

6   *Angels v. White Sox*, Game 1, 2005 ALCS, https://www.youtube.com/watch?v=3PowEiigv8I.

7   Mike Downey, "Angels Just Kept Going and Going," *Chicago Tribune*, October 12, 2005: Section 10, 2.

8   Rick Morrissey, "Special Team, Special Year for Chicago," *Chicago Tribune*, October 27, 2005: Section 7, 2.

IT WAS A TRAP GAME! JOE CREDE'S GAME-WINNING HIT EVENS THE ALCS SERIES, 1-1

OCTOBER 12, 2005: CHICAGO WHITE SOX 2, ANAHEIM ANGELS 1, AT US CELLULAR FIELD, CHICAGO (GAME TWO OF THE 2005 AMERICAN LEAGUE CHAMPIONSHIP SERIES)

By Joseph Wancho

Chicago White Sox fans were hoping for a better outcome in the 2005 American League Championship Series. The two previous trips to the ALCS were not kind to the Southside fans. The White Sox could muster only three combined wins in 1983 and 1993. Now in 2005, the Anaheim Angels eked out a 3-2 victory over Chicago in Game One.

Game Two was scheduled as a night game at the White Sox' US Cellular Field. Despite the loss in Game One, commuters on the Dan Ryan Expressway and the CTA Red Line were equally overflowing and boisterous.

Both teams chose a left-hander as their starting pitcher. The visiting Angels went with Jarrod Washburn (8-8, 3.20 ERA regular season) while the White Sox countered with Mark Buehrle (16-8, 3.12 ERA).

Washburn had been battling strep throat, which kept him off the pitching mound in the ALDS against the New York Yankees. "I felt like I let the team down in the last series and can't wait to get out there and help them out," he said.[1]

For Buehrle, the 2005 season was already memorable. Outside of his excellent regular season, Buehrle started for the AL in the All-Star Game at Detroit's Comerica Park. He was credited with the win in the AL's 7-5 victory. He also beat Boston in Game Two of the ALDS, helping Chicago sweep the reigning world champions.

A beautiful autumn day was forecast for the Windy City: high temperatures in the low 60s with a slight chance of rain in the evening.[2] Illinois US Senator Barack Obama strode to the pitcher's mound to deliver the ceremonial first pitch. The 41,013 fans in attendance were ready and anxious for Game Two.

The White Sox manufactured a run in the bottom of the first inning. Leadoff batter Scott Podsednik reached second base on a throwing error by Washburn. The Angels starter airmailed the ball over first baseman Darin Erstad's outstretched glove and into foul territory along right field.[3] Tadahito Iguchi sacrificed Podsednik to third, from where he scored on Jermaine Dye's groundout, short to first.

In the bottom of the second, Aaron Rowand doubled to right field. On an error by right fielder Vladimir Guerrero, Rowand kept running and might have scored but the throw from Guerrero to third base and then home enabled Angels catcher Jose Molina to tag out the sliding Rowand.

Anaheim did not record its first hit until the top of the fourth inning. A one-out double by Orlando Cabrera put a runner in scoring position. However, the Angels could not drive him in.

Robb Quinlan led off the top of the fifth with a solo home run off Buehrle. The score was tied, 1-1.

The White Sox had an opportunity to grab the lead back in the home half of the fifth inning. A.J. Pierzynski led off with a walk. After Joe Crede flied out, Juan Uribe singled Pierzynski to second base. Podsednik popped out to third baseman Quinlan and Iguchi was hit by a pitch to load the bases. Anaheim manager Mike Scioscia went to his bullpen, bringing in reliever Brendan Donnelly to replace Washburn. Donnelly struck out Dye to end the White Sox threat.

In the top of the eighth, Molina led off with a single to left field. Jeff DaVanon was sent in as a pinch-runner. However, he only moved up as far as third base before Buehrle retired the Angels.

Buehrle set the Angels down in order in the top of the ninth. Until this point in the game, there was not much scoring, or anything noteworthy except for both teams not being able to score more than one run, along with some blown opportunities. The complete-game effort by Buehrle was one of four thrown by Chicago starters in the ALCS.

This scenario was about to change.

Anaheim reliever Kelvim Escobar had entered the game in the bottom of the seventh inning. He was still hurling as the White Sox came up in the ninth to take their cuts. Carl Everett grounded out and Rowand struck out. It certainly looked as if extra innings were in the cards. Pierzynski stepped into the batter's box. The count went full. It appeared as if Escobar struck out Pierzynski on a split-finger fastball. Pierzynski swung wildly and missed Escobar's pitch. The Angels' catcher, Josh Paul, who had replaced Molina, backhanded the sinking pitch. Home-plate umpire Doug Eddings raised his right arm, his right fist balled up in the "You're out!" signal.[4] Paul rolled the baseball back to the pitching mound and the Angels headed to the first-base dugout. It appeared that extra innings would ensue.

But Eddings never called Pierzynski out. Pierzynski alertly ran to first base. He was ruled safe and suddenly the White Sox were still alive. Scioscia came out to protest, as did anyone wearing the Angels' grays. Eddings had doubts that Paul caught the ball cleanly, ruling that the catcher trapped the ball. However, he never made a safe signal. "Doug Eddings called him out, and somewhere along the line, because the guy ran to first base, he altered the call," said Scioscia.[5]

When the game resumed, Pablo Ozuna was inserted as a pinch-runner for Pierzynski. Ozuna stole second base. Crede lined a double into the left-field corner, scoring Ozuna. The White Sox won, 2-1, and tied the series at one win apiece.

The game may have been completed. But the controversy and overanalysis was just beginning. "That's my mechanism when it's a swinging strike," said Eddings. "I did not say 'No catch.' If you watch the replay (as I'm pumping my fist). I'm watching Josh Paul, so I'm seeing what he's going to do. I'm looking directly at him. That's when Pierzynski ran to first base."[6]

"I caught the ball," said Paul. "It was strike three. He was out. … It's not my fault. I take no responsibility for that whatsoever."[7]

"I didn't hear him call me out, so I thought – I thought for sure the ball hit the ground," said Pierzynski. "I watched the replay 50 times, and I still don't know. I think Josh thought he caught it, and I just ran, and luckily it worked out."[8]

Baseball likes to compare incidents that happen in games to previous history. Don Denkinger, the umpire noted for a blown call in the 1985 World Series, was now fielding questions about Eddings and his no-call. "I'm not saying he was wrong, but maybe his gestures were wrong," said Denkinger.[9] Whitey Herzog, the manager of the St. Louis Cardinals in 1985 and the recipient of Denkinger's blown call, thought that Scioscia should have protested the game and put the decision in the lap of Commissioner Bud Selig.[10]

Not to be forgotten: Brooklyn Dodgers catcher Mickey Owen dropped a third strike in Game Four of the 1941 World Series. The miscue triggered a three-run inning for the New York Yankees, who beat the Dodgers, 7-4, thus, edging closer to another championship.

The White Sox swept the Angels in the next three games in Anaheim to win their first ALCS. It was their first pennant since 1959. Chicago continued its hot streak, sweeping the Houston Astros in the World Series. It was the White Sox' first World Series championship since 1917.

SOURCES

In addition to the sources referenced in the Notes, the author consulted Baseball-Reference.com https://www.baseball-reference.com/boxes/CHA/CHA200510120.shtml and Retrosheet.org https://www.retrosheet.org/boxesetc/2005/B10120CHA2005.htm for pertinent information, including the box score and play-by-play.

NOTES

1   T.J. Simers "To Request, Anderson Will Sleep On It," *Los Angeles Times*, October 13, 2005: A21.

2   Tom Skilling, "Weather Report," *Chicago Tribune*, October 12, 2005: Section 2-12.

3   FOX broadcast, on YouTube Angels vs White Sox (2005 ALCS Game 2), accessed December 12, 2024.

4   Tim Brown, "Angels Lose Game in Bizarre Ending," *Los Angeles Times*, October 13, 2005: A1.

5   Bill Plaschke, "Umpire Is Charged With the Error," *Los Angeles Times*, October 13, 2005: A21.

6   Mike DiGiovanna, "Umpires Defend the Controversial Call That Leads to Chicago's 9th-Inning Win," *Los Angeles Times*, October 13, 2005: A21.

7   Brown, "Angels Lose Game in Bizarre Ending,"

8   DiGiovanna, "Umpires Defend the Controversial Call That Leads to Chicago's 9th-Inning Win."

9   David Haugh, "Ump Who Blew '85 Call Comes to Eddings' Aid," *Chicago Tribune*, October 14, 2005: 4-4.

10   Fred Mitchell "NLCS Bits," *Chicago Tribune*, October 14, 2024: 4-3.

CONTRERAS FIRES CHICAGO'S FOURTH STRAIGHT COMPLETE GAME, SENDS WHITE SOX TO WORLD SERIES

OCTOBER 16, 2005: CHICAGO WHITE SOX 6, LOS ANGELES ANGELS OF ANAHEIM 3, AT ANGEL STADIUM OF ANAHEIM

By Andrew Harner

On July 1, 2005, Chicago White Sox starter José Contreras took the loss at Oakland Coliseum after allowing four runs in 4⅓ innings. But even with a 3-5 record and a 4.34 ERA, manager Ozzie Guillén saw little reason to worry about the 33-year-old Cuban defector who joined his club through a midseason trade with the New York Yankees a year earlier.[1]

"... [Y]ou look at this guy, he should have a better record than what he has," said Guillén, a former White Sox shortstop in his second year as manager. "He has thrown the ball well. It doesn't seem like it because we don't score enough runs for him. But I think the consistency is a lot better. I'm happier with him right now than I was last year."[2]

And that happiness only grew in the second half of the campaign as Contreras played a pivotal role while the White Sox rolled up the American League's number-one playoff seed with their best season since 1983.[3]

After losing to the A's, Contreras went 12-2 as the White Sox ace. Half of those wins came away from US Cellular Field, and his "road warrior" status continued into the postseason when he took the hill on October 16 for Game Five of the AL Championship Series against the Los Angeles Angels of Anaheim looking to give the White Sox their first pennant since 1959.

On the heels of three straight complete-game victories from his rotation mates Freddy García, Jon Garland, and Mark Buehrle, Contreras also went the distance in a 6-3 victory at Angel Stadium of Anaheim. The group became the first quartet of pitchers to win four consecutive postseason games without a reliever since the 1928 New York Yankees[4] and pushed the White Sox into their fifth World Series.[5]

"I've never seen four horses like that come out of the gate and [pitch] so well," Angels manager Mike Scioscia said. "You might have to go back to Sandy Koufax, Don Drysdale, that group [with the Dodgers] or the group Baltimore had in 1966. These guys pitched tremendous baseball."[6]

Added White Sox catcher A.J. Pierzynski, who caught all 45 innings in the ALCS: "It has to be one of the best pitched series of all time."[7]

A Sunday night crowd of 44,712 fans watched through drizzle[8] and, at times, the hometown faithful had hope the Angels would break out of their offensive funk in a win-or-go-home scenario against the major leagues' best road team.[9] The Angels defeated Contreras and the White Sox 3-2 in Game One in Chicago but struggled over the next three games, collectively hitting .165 and scoring only five runs.[10]

After holding a team meeting following an 8-2 loss in Game Four, the Angels' Scioscia shuffled his lineup to alternate right-handed and left-handed batters against Contreras.[11] The Angels took a step forward offensively – although the White Sox still struck first for a fourth game in a row.[12]

In the top of the second, Chicago's Aaron Rowand dropped a ground-rule double just inside the right-field foul line and, after moving to third on Pierzynski's sacrifice bunt, he scored on Joe Crede's fly out to center. The Angels evened the score in the bottom of the third after Juan Rivera doubled on the first pitch of the inning, advanced to third on an errant pickoff throw, and scored on Adam Kennedy's single to left-center.[13]

Chicago reclaimed the lead in the fifth. Juan Uribe doubled to left past a diving Chone Figgins with one out, Scott Podsednik followed with a nine-pitch walk, and Jermaine Dye stroked a first-pitch double into left-center to chase

Los Angeles starter Paul Byrd, who had earned the win in Game One.

The Angels responded in the bottom of the inning to take their first lead since that Game One victory. Kennedy beat out a grounder to third, and on a hit-and-run play, Figgins launched a double into right field. A fan interfered with the ball in play and the umpires awarded Kennedy home plate to knot the game at 2-2. Orlando Cabrera grounded out to move Figgins to third, and Figgins scored on Garret Anderson's fly out to the warning track in right.

But from that point on, Contreras did not allow another baserunner.

Crede supported Contreras's brilliant effort by crushing Angels reliever Kelvim Escobar's second pitch for a game-tying home run to left to lead off the seventh.[14]

"Joe-Joe, sometimes it looks like he doesn't have a pulse out there," White Sox veteran Paul Konerko said of his 27-year-old teammate, who hit .368 during the ALCS. "That comes up big in big situations, because he doesn't get amped up, he doesn't try to overdo anything. He just stays within himself, and I'm just so happy for the guy."[15]

Despite allowing the homer, Escobar settled in and recorded the next five outs via the strikeout.   But he walked Rowand with two outs in the eighth and became involved in an unusual play that eventually led to the winning run.

Pierzynski lined a sharp shot that deflected off Escobar's body and to the first-base side of the mound. Escobar fielded the ball with his bare right hand, but as Pierzynski chugged to first, Escobar tagged him with his gloved left hand, while still holding the ball in his right hand. First-base umpire Ted Barrett initially ruled Pierzynski out, but after huddling with the other umpires, the call was reversed.

"I knew he had an empty glove," Pierzynski said. "That's why I was screaming right away."[16]

Scioscia did not put up much of an argument after the decision was overturned and acknowledged in postgame comments that the umpires made the correct call.[17] He pulled Escobar from the game in favor of closer Francisco Rodríguez, who led the AL with 45 saves during the regular season[18] but had not worked since Game One.

Crede battled back from a 1-and-2 count to hit a bouncer up the middle. Second baseman Kennedy made a diving stop but could not make a play because the runners had taken off on Rodríguez's 3-and-2 breaking ball. That allowed Rowand to score from second and gave the White Sox a 4-3 edge.

Tadahito Iguchi walked to open Chicago's ninth. He slid in safely on his first stolen-base attempt of the postseason because Kennedy could not field the throw cleanly, getting charged with his first error in 101 postseason chances. After Dye walked, Konerko ripped an RBI double off the top of the wall in right field, giving voters another reason to select him as the ALCS MVP.

"I'd like to split this [award] four ways among our pitchers," Konerko said after hitting .286 with 2 homers and 7 RBIs in the series. "They're the horses. I was just along for the ride. Really, we all were."[19]

The White Sox added their final run when Dye scored on Rowand's fly to right.

In the bottom of the ninth, Contreras threw only one ball among his 11 pitches to finish off the complete game with 15 straight outs.[20] His 114-pitch effort helped make the White Sox the 11th team to win three successive road games in a single postseason series.[21] Chicago's only reliever to appear in the ALCS was Neal Cotts, who pitched two-thirds of an inning in Game One.

"[Contreras] went from the last starter to being the [Number One] in the playoffs," said Guillén, the first foreign-born manager to lead his team into the World Series.[22] "If you told me in April [that] José Contreras was going to be my ace and Bobby Jenks was going to be my closer, I would tell you I don't think we're going to win."[23]

SOURCES

In addition to the sources cited in the Notes, the author consulted the Baseball-Reference.com, Stathead.com, and Retrosheet.org websites for pertinent material and box scores. He also used information obtained from news coverage by the Chicago Tribune, the Los Angeles Times, and the New York Times. The author also viewed the game on YouTube: https://www.youtube.com/watch?v=X5aIEBBG5bU&t=5112s.

https://www.baseball-reference.com/boxes/ANA/ANA200510160.shtml

https://www.retrosheet.org/boxesetc/2005/B10160ANA2005.htm

NOTES

1   On July 31, 2004, the New York Yankees traded Contreras to the White Sox for starting pitcher Esteban Loaiza.

2   Mark Gonzales, "Bay Area Blues Go On," Chicago Tribune, July 2, 2005: 3-1.

3   Chicago matched its 1983 record, finishing the season at 99-63 to win the AL Central Division title for the first time since 2000. The White Sox were in at least a tie for first place throughout the entire season. Only the NL's St. Louis Cardinals had a better record (100-62) in 2005.

4   In the 1928 World Series, New York swept the St. Louis Cardinals behind complete games from Waite Hoyt (Games One and Four), George Pipgras (Game Two), and Tom Zachary (Game Three). In 1956, Yankees starters hurled five straight complete games during the World Series, with Whitey Ford (Game Three), Tom Sturdivant (Game Four), Don Larsen (Game Five), Bob Turley (Game Six loss), and Johnny Kucks (Game Seven) contributing to New York's victory over the Brooklyn Dodgers. For the White Sox, the last time their starters fired four successive complete games was August 21-25, 1974, when Wilbur Wood (twice), Jim Kaat, and Bart Johnson all went the distance.

5   The White Sox won the World Series in 1906 and 1917 and took losses in 1919 and 1959. Chicago also won the first-ever AL pennant after the league declared major-league status in 1901, but the first World Series between the AL and NL was not played until 1903.

6   Phil Rogers, "Sox Pennant Win a Complete Work," Chicago Tribune, October 17, 2005: 7-7.

7   Mark Gonzales, "Wizards of Oz," Chicago Tribune, October 17, 2005: 7-3.

8   Rain and baseball rarely mixed in Anaheim. The last time the Angels had a rained-out home game was against the White Sox on June 16, 1995. The next

GRINDERS AND GAMERS

rainout at Angel Stadium did not occur until July 19, 2015 – a stretch of 1,635 home games.

9   The White Sox finished the regular season 52-29 on the road, which was two games better than the Cleveland Indians and St. Louis Cardinals and better than their record at home (47-34). During the postseason, Chicago won all six of its road games (one in the ALDS, three in the ALCS, and two in the World Series).

10   Overall in the Series, the Angels scored 11 runs in five games. That marked the lowest total for a team in the ALCS since the 1990 Boston Red Sox scored four runs while getting swept by the Athletics. No team had scored fewer runs in a five-game ALCS except the 1972 Detroit Tigers, who posted only 10 runs in a loss to the A's. LA's offensive struggles were punctuated by Vladimir Guerrero. The reigning AL MVP, who signed a five-year, $70 million contract with the Angels prior to the 2004 season, went 1-for-20 in the ALCS. (He had hit .333 in LA's five-game win over the Yankees in the ALDS.)

11   The Angels used four lineups throughout the Series. The only batters to hit in the same spot in all five games were Figgins (leadoff), Cabrera (second), and Kennedy (ninth). The most notable change to LA's lineup in Game Five saw Anderson move up from fourth to third and Guerrero drop from third to fourth in the order. Compared with Game One against Contreras, Bengie Molina and Darin Erstad flipped spots at fifth and sixth in the order, Rivera dropped from seventh to eighth, and Casey Kotchman played instead of Steve Finley.

12   During the first two rounds of the postseason, the White Sox went 5-0 when scoring first. In Game One of the ALCS, the Angels struck first with a run in the top of the second inning.

13   Prior to Kennedy's hit, the Angels had gone 2-for-16 with runners in scoring position during the eries.

14   In Game Two, Crede hit a walk-off double off Escobar on a similar pitch.

15   Paul Sullivan, "Cool Crede Delivers," *Chicago Tribune*, October 17, 2005: 7-4.

16   David Haugh, "He Was Everywhere," *Chicago Tribune*, October 17, 2005: 7-4.

17   Ronald Blum (Associated Press), "Windy City Wonders," *Oakland Tribune*, October 17, 2005: 33.

18   Rodríguez tied for the league lead in saves with Cleveland closer Bob Wickman and added 91 strikeouts over 67⅓ innings.

19   Rick Morrissey, "America, Here Come the Sox," *Chicago Tribune*, October 17, 2005: 7-3.

20   Contreras had only one complete game to his credit, coming against the Minnesota Twins on September 23 as part of eight successive victories to close out the season. Collectively, White Sox starters fired nine complete games during the regular season. (Buehrle and Garland each had three, and García added two.)

21   Teams to achieve the feat before the White Sox were the Boston Red Sox (1903), New York Yankees (1941, '49, '61, and '96), St. Louis Cardinals (1942 and '85), Baltimore Orioles (1983), Minnesota Twins (1991), and Arizona Diamondbacks (2001). Five other teams won at least three successive postseason games on the road but did so across multiple series: the Oakland Athletics (1972 and '74), Yankees (1999), San Francisco Giants (2002), and Florida Marlins (2003).

22   Guillén became the first Venezuelan native to manage in the AL or NL after the White Sox hired him before the 2004 season. Later that year, another Venezuelan, Al Pedrique, became the interim manager of the Arizona Diamondbacks.

23   Bob Buttitta, "Whiteout for Angels," *Ventura County* (California) *Star*, October 17, 2005: C4.

JOE CREDE SPARKS THE WHITE SOX ON OFFENSE AND DEFENSE IN THE FIRST GAME OF THE WORLD SERIES

OCTOBER 22, 2005: CHICAGO WHITE SOX 5, HOUSTON ASTROS 3, AT US CELLULAR FIELD, CHICAGO (GAME ONE OF THE 2005 WORLD SERIES)

By Michael Marsh

Game One of the 2005 World Series featured a matchup between two strong right-handers: José Contreras of the host Chicago White Sox and Roger Clemens of the Houston Astros. Contreras finished the regular season with a 15-7 record, including 11-2 after the All-Star break. He had found his control and baffled hitters, especially by using his fastball and forkball. Clemens, long known for his powerful fastball, had a 13-8 record in the regular season with a National League-leading 1.87 earned-run average. Both pitchers had won two games so far during the playoffs. At first glance, Game One figured to be a pitchers' duel.

Instead, White Sox third baseman Joe Crede stole the show. Crede hit a game-winning home run and made two stellar plays on defense. The White Sox, who were playing in their first World Series home game since 1959, defeated the Astros 5-3. The game took 3:13 on a cold, damp night before 41,206 fans at US Cellular Field.

Crede, a 6-3, 195-pound 27-year-old, had rebounded during the playoffs. Late in the regular season, the team placed him on the 15-day disabled list with an injured right middle finger. At the time, he was mired in an 0-for-21 batting slump.[1] He had only one hit in nine at-bats as the White Sox beat the Boston Red Sox in the American League Division Series. In contrast, Crede batted .368 as the White Sox defeated the Los Angeles Angels of Anaheim in the AL Championship Series. He went 7-for-19, including two home runs, and drove in seven runs.

As for World Series Game One, after Contreras shut down the Astros in order in the top of the first inning, the game turned into a back-and-forth offensive affair.

Clemens nearly matched Contreras in the bottom of the first inning. The White Sox' Scott Podsednik and Tadahito Iguchi grounded out. The third batter, however, Jermaine Dye, hit a solo home run to right field to give the White Sox a 1-0 lead.

Houston struck back in the top of the second. After Morgan Ensberg led off with a fly out to right field, Mike Lamb tied the game with a homer to center field.

The White Sox scored two more in the bottom of the second. Carl Everett singled and went to third on Aaron Rowand's single. Everett scored when A.J. Pierzynski's grounder forced Rowand out at second. Pierzynski moved to second on Crede's groundout. Pierzynski scored Juan Uribe's double to center field.

Clemens struck out Podsednik to end the inning. Afterward, Clemens left the game with a strained left hamstring. Wandy Rodríguez, a rookie left-hander with a 10-10 record in the regular season, replaced him.

Houston tied the game at 3-3 in the third inning. Brad Ausmus singled to right field. Ausmus was forced at second on Adam Everett's groundball. The next batter, Craig Biggio, singled to center field. Willy Taveras' sacrifice bunt moved Biggio and Everett to second and third. Both scored on Lance Berkman's double to right field. Ensberg grounded out to end the inning.

The White Sox broke the tie in the bottom of the fourth. Pierzynski led off with a groundout. Crede, the next batter, hit a solo home run to left-center field on a 0-and-2 pitch from Rodríguez. The shot gave the White Sox a 4-3 lead; they added one more run in the bottom of the eighth.

White Sox manager Ozzie Guillén praised Crede: "That's the Joe we expected. I think this kid really had a tough year. We expected a lot from him, and all of a sudden he started swinging the bat real good at the right moments. We were really struggling when he came back [September 10] from the [disabled list]. He had a broken finger for a little while, and all of a sudden he [came back] and started swinging the bat good, and he helped this team to be where we are."[2]

After Crede boosted the White Sox with his bat, he helped save the team with his glove in the top of the sixth inning. The Astros' Taveras led off with a double to left field. He took third on Berkman's groundout to first. The White Sox infielders drew in closer to the plate. Ensberg grounded sharply to third. Crede backhanded the ball, held Taveras, and threw out Ensberg at first. Mike Lamb grounded out to end the inning.

Said Crede after the game: "I was fortunate to get enough on the ball to make the play."[3]

He also bailed out the White Sox in the top of the seventh. Contreras hit leadoff batter Jeff Bagwell. The next batter, Jason Lane, popped out to first. Then Contreras hit Ausmus. Everett's grounder forced Ausmus at second as Bagwell took third. Biggio followed with a sharp grounder down the third-base line. Crede dived, snagged the ball, and threw out Biggio at first.[4] The play ended the Astros' scoring threat in a close game.

Contreras left the game after giving up a leadoff double to Taveras in the top of the eighth. He pitched seven-plus innings, allowing three runs on six hits. Guillén replaced Contreras with Neal Cotts, a left-hander with a good cutter. It was the first time the White Sox used a relief pitcher since Game One of the ALCS against the Angels. Berkman,

the next batter, singled to left, and Taveras went to third. After Cotts struck out Ensberg and Lamb, Guillén and Astros manager Phil Garner made strategic moves. Guillén replaced Cotts with Bobby Jenks, a hard-throwing right-hander, to face Bagwell. Garner sent Chris Burke to pinch-run for Berkman.

Jenks and Bagwell battled in a classic power vs. power showdown. Bagwell swung and missed on the first pitch, a 99-mph fastball. Bagwell fell behind 0-and-2 after he fouled the next pitch. Burke stole second as Jenks threw a high fastball that Pierzynski, the catcher, had to rise from a crouch to retrieve. The pitch count moved to 2-and-2 on another high fastball inside from Jenks. Bagwell fouled the next pitch. On the next pitch, Jenks fired a 100-mph fastball outside. Bagwell swung and missed to end the inning. The crowd erupted. Jenks and Pierzynski pumped their fists as they walked off the field.[5]

Bagwell afterward lamented the Astros' missed scoring opportunities. "It's tough. In those situations, you have to be able to get those guys in. We had the opportunities, we just need to do a better job with runners in scoring position."[6]

The White Sox got an insurance run in the bottom of the eighth. Pierzynski singled to right off reliever Russ Springer. Crede and Uribe flied out to right field and to left field. Pierzynski stole second during Podsednik's at-bat, and scored on Podsednik's triple to center field.

The first World Series game on the South Side since 1959. Attendance 41,206.

Jenks finished off the Astros in the top of the ninth. He retired Lane, Ausmus, and Everett in order to record the save and preserve Contreras's third victory in the postseason.

White Sox center fielder Aaron Rowand summed up Crede's role in the win, saying, "His home run was huge, but he saved a couple runs with those catches."[7]

SOURCES

In addition to the sources cited in the Notes, the author used the Baseball-Reference.com, Baseball-Almanac.com, and Retrosheet.org websites for box-score, player, team, and season pages, pitching and batting game logs, and other material. The telecast of the game can be seen on YouTube.

https://www.baseball-reference.com/boxes/CHA/CHA200510220.shtml

https://www.retrosheet.org/boxesetc/2005/B10220CHA2005.htm

https://www.youtube.com/watch?v=ArewsuEIzDk

NOTES

1   Mark Gonzales, "White Sox Bits: Crede's fractured Finger Passes an Important Test," *Chicago Tribune*, September 7, 2005: 4, 4.

2   Doug Padilla, "Joe, Pen and Shut: Mane Man Crede Attacks from Both Sides, Relievers Shine as Sox Take Game 1," *Chicago Sun-Times*, October 23, 2005: 2.

3   Toni Ginnetti, "Sox Agree Crede's Best Work Comes Infield," *Chicago Sun-Times*, October 23, 2005: 14.

4   Melissa Isaacson, "A Hit – at Plate, in Field," *Chicago Tribune*, October 23, 2005: 17, 3.

5   Mark Gonzales, "Chills, Thrills: It Gets Scary, but Sox Take Game 1," *Chicago Tribune*, October 23, 2005, 17, 3.

6   T.R. Sullivan, "Rocket Flames Out, but Jenks Flames On," *Fort Worth Star-Telegram*, October 23, 2005: 4C.

7   Ginnetti.

PODSEDNIK POWERS WHITE SOX TO A TWO-GAME LEAD

OCTOBER 23, 2005: CHICAGO WHITE SOX 7, HOUSTON ASTROS 6, AT US CELLULAR FIELD, CHICAGO

By Zac Petrillo

Stormy conditions in Chicago on October 23 threatened to wipe out Game Two of the World Series. With two of the league's premier workhorses, Andy Pettitte and Mark Buehrle, on the mound, it had the makings of a messy affair that might see little in the way of offense if the game got underway at all. Roughly three hours later, the game didn't limp but screamed into the bottom of the ninth inning, both teams' bats having delivered punches and counterpunches.

With the game knotted, 6-6, every hitter in the White Sox lineup had reached base … except Scott Podsednik.[1]

The temperature at game time was 45 degrees, and, as Fox broadcasters Joe Buck and Tim McCarver assured viewers, it felt even colder. Pettitte, a famously reliable big-game pitcher, was making the 11th World Series start of his career, tying him with Waite Hoyt and Christy Mathewson for second all-time.[2] He came into the game with a 3-4

Scott Podsednik hits a walkoff home run off Astros closer Brad Lidge.

record in World Series play and a 3.90 ERA. Buehrle, the 2005 All-Star Game starter, was 2-0 in the 2005 postseason with a 2.81 ERA.

The game didn't stay scoreless for long. Astros third baseman Morgan Ensberg hit the first pitch of the second inning for a home run to left field. Then right fielder Jason Lane lined a single and stole second. Brad Ausmus's infield hit gave the number-nine hitter, Adam Everett, a chance to break it open, but he struck out to end the threat. The White Sox grabbed the lead with three straight singles in the bottom of the second from Aaron Rowand, A.J. Pierzynski, and Joe Crede (which drove in Rowand). Juan Uribe's popup to shallow right field looked as though it would give Pettitte his second out, but instead the ball skipped off the top of veteran second baseman Craig Biggio's glove, allowing Pierzynski to score.

With his team down 2-1, the Astros' 23-year-old center fielder, Willy Taveras, laced a one-out triple down the first-base line. Next up, Lance Berkman brought Taveras in with a sacrifice fly. Knotted back at 2-2, the White Sox started their half with a single, but with the help of a spectacular diving stop by Ensberg, Pettitte got out of the inning with no additional damage.

The fifth inning began with a double by Ausmus. Three batters later, Taveras had his second hit of the night, moving Ausmus to third base with a single to left. Berkman knocked in his second and third RBIs of the game with a loud double past left fielder Podsednik.

Clinging to a 4-2 lead, Pettitte overcame a leadoff double by Uribe by making an excellent play off the mound to catch him as he tried to race to third base on a dribbler hit by Tadahito Iguchi. Pettitte then picked off Iguchi to end the inning.[3]

After a scoreless sixth, the Astros replaced Pettitte with Dan Wheeler, who had given up one earned run over seven innings so far in the 2005 postseason. Wheeler got Crede for the first out, but Uribe cracked a long double into left-center. After Podsednik struck out, Iguchi walked. Next up, Jermaine Dye was hit by a pitch on a ball that, upon replay, clearly hit the knob of his bat. "I'm not going to tell [the umpire] I fouled it off," Dye said after the game. "Just go to first and, hopefully, we get a big hit and we did."[4]

With the bases now loaded, the White Sox' best regular-season hitter, Paul Konerko, came to the plate. Astros manager Phil Garner replaced Wheeler with Chad Qualls, who had given up seven home runs over 79⅔ innings in the regular season.[5]

"I'll tell you, a home run was the last thing on my mind right there. I'm looking just for a base hit," Konerko said later.[6] The first pitch Qualls threw was a belt-high fastball in on Konerko's hands, but it caught enough of the plate that Konerko could barrel it up and belt it 13 rows into the left-field seats. The winds didn't keep this one back. As the crowd shook the foundation of US Cellular Field, fireworks erupted overhead. "I recall standing out in left field after

Paul had did what he did, thinking about, 'Man, what does that man feel like right now?'" Podsednik said.[7] The grand slam was the 18th in a fall classic, and it jumped the White Sox' chances of winning the game by 58 percent; the largest change off a slam in World Series history.[8] Earlier in the week, Konerko and his wife, Jennifer, had welcomed their first child. "It's the second-best feeling I've had all week," Konerko said. "The baby born Tuesday night, that's first for the week."[9]

The White Sox entered the eighth inning back on top, 6-4. Reliever Cliff Politte replaced Buehrle, who ended his night on precisely 100 pitches over seven gritty innings. Politte sat down the Astros' two-three-four hitters in order. Qualls and Mike Gallo combined to get the White Sox in order in their half of the eighth, sending the game to the ninth with the home team clinging to a two-run lead.

The big rookie and unlikely hero from the night before, Bobby Jenks, came in to close the door. He immediately surrendered a single to Houston's future Hall of Famer, Jeff Bagwell. Two batters later, he put another man on with a walk to Chris Burke. Ausmus's groundout sent runners to scoring position and José Vizcaíno came to bat with the White Sox just an out away from taking care of both games at home. Instead, Vizcaíno slashed a line drive to center field that dropped in front of Rowand. Bagwell scored, and Burke beat the throw at the plate. "I made a good pitch, and Vizcaíno did a good job taking his approach to the plate and going the other way with it," Jenks said after his blown save. Manager Ozzie Guillén swapped Jenks for Neal Cotts, who kept the game tied for the bottom of the ninth. "I think the closer's job is the toughest job in baseball," Guillén said. "You get paid to close, and then when you don't, people are all over your case."[10]

The Astros' All-Star closer, Brad Lidge, knew that sentiment too well. Lidge hadn't pitched since he gave up a ninth-inning home run to Albert Pujols in Game Five of the NLCS. Despite that, Garner returned to him against the White Sox. Lidge had 42 saves in the regular season thanks to 103 strikeouts over 70⅔ innings. "I was happy to get the opportunity to get in the game," Lidge said. "Anyone would want to get back in as fast as they can after a bad game."[11]

Lidge got the first batter in the bottom of the ninth, Uribe, on a harmless broken-bat fly ball to center field. Podsednik came to the plate, hoping to reach base for the first time in the game. He had 507 plate appearances during the regular season and zero home runs.[12] Lidge immediately delivered two balls off the plate, putting Podsednik ahead in the count. The closer then put one right down the middle that Podsednik didn't even consider swinging at.

Before the next pitch, Joe Buck asked McCarver if he thought Lidge should've pitched in Game Six to get the taste of the Pujols home run out of his mouth. McCarver remarked, "I don't think that taste is there."[13] Lidge then delivered the ball down the middle again, in the same exact spot. This time, Podsednik not only offered at it, but he propelled it deep into left-center field, where it sailed over the wall. Gone. McCarver quipped, "The taste might be there now."[14] As if in a flash, the game was over.

"You don't expect him to do that," Lidge said. "He's not a home run guy."[15] Just two innings earlier, Podsednik could only imagine what it might feel like to hit a huge home run; now he said, "To go out and hit one out of the ballpark for a game-winner is pretty much indescribable."[16]

After the series, Bagwell remarked, "We just didn't hit."[17] But that wasn't true of Game Two, when the Astros had nine hits and the game in the palm of their hands before lousy luck and two gutting homers. The White Sox proved the team of destiny with the ability to match the Astros every step of the way. As Murray Chass put it in his *New York Times* recap, "No save for the White Sox's closer, but no mercy for the Astros' closer."[18] Through the first two games, the Astros stranded 10 runners on base, including seven in scoring position with two outs.

The first White Sox World Series championship since 1917 ended in a sweep, but the difference in scoring over the four games was only six runs. Each game followed the same "movie-script"[19] tension of Game Two. Neither Konerko nor Podsednik took home the Series MVP,[20] but their two swings, separated by two innings, made them a pair of the most beloved players in White Sox history.[21] In 2014 the White Sox honored Konerko with a statue outside the ballpark, his bronze fist raised permanently in the air, just as it was when he rounded first on that cold night in 2005.[22]

SOURCES

In addition to the sources cited in the Notes, the author consulted Baseball-Reference.com and Retrosheet.org.

https://www.baseball-reference.com/boxes/CHA/CHA200510230.shtml

https://www.retrosheet.org/boxesetc/2005/B10230CHA2005.htm

A video of the full game is available on YouTube, at https://www.youtube.com/watch?v=278pqdhhwDw

NOTES

1   In Game One, Houston Astros ace Roger Clemens didn't have his best stuff, getting knocked around for three runs before exiting after two innings with a hamstring injury. It was the shortest outing of Clemens' postseason career. It was a back-and-forth contest early, with the Astros getting to White Sox starter José Contreras for three runs of their own. But things settled from there. The White Sox needed just a Joe Crede home run and a four-out save from "wide, tall" rookie Bobby Jenks to secure the 5-3 victory.

2   Pettitte passed Hoyt and Mathewson when he started his 12th World Series game in 2009. As of 2024, Whitey Ford held the record with 22 World Series starts.

3   Pettitte was known for his savvy move to first. This was his second successful pickoff of the 2005 postseason. He finished his career with 10 postseason pickoffs.

4   "Podsednik's Walk-Off Homer Lifts Chicago Past Houston," ESPN.com, October 25, 2005, https://web.archive.org/web/20121019110646/http://scores.espn.go.com/mlb/recap?gameId=251023104 (last accessed August 5, 2024).

5   Qualls was lights out in the prior series against the St. Louis Cardinals (zero earned runs over 4⅔ innings).

6   Tom Goldman, "White Sox Lead 2-0 in World Series," National Public Radio, October 24, 2005, https://www.npr.org/2005/10/24/4971020/white-sox-lead-2-0-in-world-series (last accessed August 5, 2024).

7   Goldman.

8   Ryan Potts, "World Series Gand Slams: Ranking the Best Five, Slam Station, March 23, 2023, https://slamstation.com/2023/03/18/world-series-grand-slams-top-5/ (last accessed August 5, 2024).

9   Rich Gano (Associated Press), "What's Next for Konerko?" *Spokane Spokesman-Review,* October 24, 2005.

10   "White Sox Jenks Faces Other Side of Being a Closer," *Uniontown* (Pennsylvania) *Herald-Standard,* October 25, 2005.

11   Jayson Stark, "Podsednik's Homer Can't Be Explained," ESPN.com, October 23, 2005, https://www.espn.com/mlb/playoffs2005/columns/story?columnist=stark_jayson&id=2202029 (last accessed August 5, 2024).

12   Podsednik did hit an improbable home run in the American League Division Series against the Boston Red Sox. As of 2024 he was the only major-league player to hit zero home runs in the regular season but two in the postseason.

13   John Quinn, "2005 World Series Game 2 Astros @ White Sox," YouTube, https://www.youtube.com/watch?v=k9Y1ZhKvMwA, May 16, 2020.

14   "2005 World Series Game 2 Astros @ White Sox."

15   Stark, "Podsednik's Homer Can't Be Explained."

16   After the game Podsednik edged out Konerko as Fox's Chevrolet Player of the Game.

17   Murray Chass, "There's Nothing Closed About Case of Missing Closers," *New York Times*, October 24, 2005.

18   Chass.

19   "2005 World Series," Baseball Almanac, https://www.baseball-almanac.com/ws/yr2005ws.shtml (last accessed August 5, 2024).

20   The MVP award went to Jermaine Dye and his .438 Series batting average.

21   A post-2005 renovation replaced all but two of the blue seats in the ballpark (called Guaranteed Rate Field since 2016) with green ones. The two? Section 159, row 7, seat 4, where Konerko's grand slam landed, and section 101, row 1, seat 13, where Podsednik's game-winner landed. As of 2024, the game's 41,432 fans made it the most attended White Sox home game since 2001, when significant renovations on the ballpark began.

22   "White Sox Honor Retiring Paul Konerko with a Statue," *USA Today,* September 28, 2014, https://www.usatoday.com/story/sports/mlb/2014/09/27/white-sox-honor-retiring-konerko-with-statue/16358271/ (last accessed August 26, 2024).

GEOFF BLUM, WHITE SOX BEAT ASTROS IN 14-INNING GAME THREE THRILLER

OCTOBER 25, 2005: CHICAGO WHITE SOX 7, HOUSTON ASTROS 5 (14 INNINGS), AT MINUTE MAID PARK, HOUSTON (GAME THREE OF THE 2005 WORLD SERIES)

By Roby Mammon

For the first time in World Series history, the fall classic was coming to the Lone Star State, Texas, but things weren't looking good for the team hosting the game. The National League champion Houston Astros came back to Minute Maid Park down two games to none to the American League champion Chicago White Sox.

The White Sox had seized the upper hand by rallying for a 7-6 win in Game Two on Paul Konerko's seventh-inning grand slam and Scott Podsednik's ninth-inning walk-off home run. This put Phil Garner's Astros in must-win territory while Ozzie Guillén's White Sox found themselves two wins away from their first title in 88 years, double the number of seasons that Houston had waited to even reach the fall classic for the first time. The team from Chicago's South Side had last played in the World Series in 1959, three years before the Astros' inaugural season.[1]

Both teams looked to end long streaks of misery and disappointment, sharing a combined 132 years without winning a championship and a combined 89 years without appearing in a World Series. (This record was broken in 2016, when the Cleveland Indians and the Chicago Cubs shared a combined 176 years without a championship and a combined 90 years without appearing in a World Series.)

Commissioner Bud Selig ordered the Astros to open the roof of Minute Maid Park at the game's start. The Astros objected, claiming they had a better record when playing with the roof closed.[2] Selig's office said the order was based on rules established by Houston and consistent with previous practice and the evening's weather forecast.[3]

For a starting pitcher, Houston sent the third arm of its starting rotation, Roy Oswalt, who had a 20-12 record and a 2.94 ERA in 35 starts during the regular season. Chicago countered with the third arm of its own dominant starting rotation that was one of the best in baseball, Jon Garland, who had an 18-10 record and a 3.50 ERA in 32 starts during the regular season.

In the early innings, all the momentum seemed to be on Houston's side as Lance Berkman drove in Craig Biggio in the bottom of the first with a double. The hit made Minute Maid Park come alive, and the train above the Crawford Boxes in left field took its celebratory ride, as it does every time the Astros add to their run total.[4]

The White Sox threatened in the top of the second by putting their first two men on base on a double by Konerko and a walk to A.J. Pierzynski, but a double play and a foul out put an end to that. In the bottom of the third, RBI singles by Biggio and Morgan Ensberg put the Astros ahead 3-0. The lead could have been greater, but the Astros left two men on base to end the inning.

Jason Lane added to Houston's lead in the fourth with a leadoff solo home run to left-center field, his drive striking the perpendicular yellow line where Minute Maid Park's wall juts out in left-center field and clearing the wall's parallel yellow home-run line.

In the fifth inning, the momentum suddenly shifted to the White Sox, who lived up to their "Win or Die Trying" mantra of 2005. Joe Crede led off the inning with a home run to put Chicago on the board. After singles by Juan Uribe and Podsednik, sandwiched around a strikeout by Garland, Tadahito Iguchi and Jermaine Dye hit back-to-back RBI singles to put the White Sox within one, 4-3. Catcher A.J. Pierzynski hit a double to Tal's Hill in deep center field to score Iguchi and Dye and give Chicago the lead.[5] In their five-run fifth inning, 11 White Sox came to the plate and Oswalt threw 46 pitches.

The score remained 5-4 in favor of the White Sox until the bottom of the eighth. The Astros' Ensberg and Mike Lamb drew two-out walks, and Guillen brought in his closer, Dustin Hermanson. But Jason Lane smashed a Hermanson pitch down the third-base line for a game-tying double; Uribe hustled over from shortstop to recover the carom off the left-field stands and hold pinch-runner Eric Bruntlett at third. That brought Minute Maid Park alive again, but Brad Ausmus took a called third strike to end the inning, stranding the runners on second and third.

In the bottom of the ninth, the Astros had Chris Burke on third after an error and a stolen base during Biggio's at-bat. With only one out, it looked as though Houston was about to win its first World Series game. But Orlando "El Duque" Hernández struck out Willy Taveras, gave an intentional walk to Lance Berkman, and fanned Ensberg to end the threat and send the game into extra innings.

Neither team scored in the first few extra frames. The White Sox stranded two runners in the 11th inning, while the Astros stranded two runners in the 10th and 11th and left a man on second in the 13th.

The tie was finally broken in the 14th inning. Former Astro Geoff Blum, batting after Konerko had extinguished a potential threat by hitting into a double play, hit a 2-and-0 pitch from Ezequiel Astacio into the right-field stands to give Chicago a 6-5 lead. The White Sox added another run with back-to-back infield hits from Aaron Rowand and Crede, followed by back-to-back walks to Uribe and Chris Widger. With two out and two on base in the bottom of the inning, the Astros attempted to make a comeback, but Adam Everett popped up to shortstop to end the game and give the White Sox a 3-0 lead in the World Series. Dámaso Marté earned the win, while Astacio took the loss and Mark Buehrle earned the save.

At the time, the game was tied with Game Two of the 1916 World Series (Red Sox vs. Brooklyn Robins) for the longest World Series game in innings.[6] It became the longest World Series game in length of time, at 5 hours and 41 minutes, until it was surpassed by Game Three of the 2018 World Series, which ran 18 innings and was 7 hours and 20 minutes long. Other World Series records broken in this game include the 17 combined pitchers used (nine by the White Sox, eight by the Astros), a total of 482 pitches thrown, and 21 bases on balls (12 by the White Sox, 9 by the Astros). Additionally, 43 players were used (22 by the White Sox and 21 by the Astros), and 30 men were left on base (15 by each team). Podsednik had eight at-bats.

The White Sox completed their sweep in Game Four in a defensive battle. They scored the only run of the game and Uribe made two amazing plays in the final inning to give Chicago's South Side its first moment of joy in 88 years. For Houston fans, it was disappointing to finally get to the World Series only to be swept.

Blum said of his home run: "It's the stuff that dreams are made of. I've had about 100 of these at-bats in the backyard with my younger brother."[7]

As of the end of the 2024 season, the White Sox have not returned to the World Series since and have made only three postseason appearances following their 2005 title. As for the Astros, 2005 turned out to be their final postseason run as a member of the National League. Within two years of reaching the World Series, two of the best players in franchise history, Jeff Bagwell and Biggio, had retired. Major League Baseball realigned Houston to the American League in 2013, at the same time that a franchise rebuilding effort saw the Astros lose at least 106 games in three consecutive seasons.

Houston has made the World Series four times since 2005, winning in 2017 against the Los Angeles Dodgers in seven games—a title tainted by subsequent revelations that the Astros had illegally used video technology to steal signs—and in 2022 against the Philadelphia Phillies in six games.[8]

Because of the Astros' league switch, the 2005 World Series is now one of only two World Series in baseball history where a rematch is impossible, as both teams are now in the same league.[9]

SOURCES

In addition to the sources cited in the Notes, the author consulted Baseball-Reference.com, Retrosheet.org, and a video of the game at YouTube.com.

https://www.baseball-reference.com/boxes/HOU/HOU200510250.shtml

https://www.retrosheet.org/boxesetc/2005/B10250HOU2005.htm

https://www.youtube.com/watch?v=IyEouya8164

NOTES

1   The Astros franchise was established in 1962 as the Houston Colt .45s. The team changed its name to Astros in 1965.

2   The Astros had a record of 40-18 with Minute Maid Park's roof closed, and went 15-11 with the roof open during the 2005 season. (This includes the postseason.)

3   Bill Shaikin and Tim Brown, "MLB Officials Force Astros to Open Roof," *Kitsap* (Washington) *Sun*, October 26, 2005. Accessed online March 19, 2021.

4   They're called the Crawford Boxes because they run parallel to Crawford Street, just outside the ballpark.

5   It was called Tal's Hill because it was named after former president of the Astros, Tal Smith, who proposed its inclusion. The hill was removed in 2016.

6   This game went 14 innings, tied for the longest in World Series history until Game Three of the 2018 World Series, which went 18 innings.

7   Mike Fitzpatrick, "Sox's Blum an Unlikely Hero," *Montreal Gazette*, October 27, 2005: 16.

8   The Astros also reached the World Series in 2019, losing to the Washington Nationals in seven games, and 2021, losing to the Atlanta Braves in six games.

9   The only other World Series where a rematch is impossible is the 1982 World Series between the Milwaukee Brewers and St. Louis Cardinals; the Brewers moved to the National League in 1998.

"DON'T STOP BELIEVIN'" — WHITE SOX COMPLETE SWEEP OF ASTROS TO WIN FIRST WORLD SERIES IN 88 YEARS

OCTOBER 26, 2005: CHICAGO WHITE SOX 1, HOUSTON ASTROS 0, AT MINUTE MAID PARK, HOUSTON GAME FOUR OF THE 2005 WORLD SERIES

By Will MacLean

People kept talking about the history. Eighty-eight years since the White Sox last won the World Series in 1917. Eighty-six since the Black Sox scandal "cursed" them to lose forever. One year after the Red Sox, whom the White Sox swept in the first round of the playoffs, swept the Cardinals to end their own 86-year championship drought and cured their own "curse."

They even threw some rock history into the mix. After winning the AL pennant over the Angels, catcher A.J. Pierzynski blasted Journey's 1981 hit, "Don't Stop Believin'," in the locker room. Then the team adopted it as a theme song and invited the vocalist and co-songwriter of the tune, Steve Perry, to join the scene for the World Series.[1]

As Tim McCarver framed it in the pregame telecast, "The White Sox have been playing a relentless brand of baseball in the postseason. It's been so good that a lot of people feel they can beat any team from any era."[2] He never said who "a lot of people" actually were.

Game Four of the World Series. Up three games to none over the Astros. On the verge of a sweep. A team that had long been the Second City's second team – where no fans figured they'd see a World Series championship in their lifetime. Chicago knew the stakes.

As Chris Myers said in the game telecast, "[Before the game] I talked to A.J. Pierzynski. He said, 'We have to take care of business. We don't wanna give them any life. We got 'em down. We wanna stomp on 'em. We wanna crush 'em.' I said, 'OK, I got the idea.'"[3]

The Astros had other plans. They fought hard. Both teams did. With neither team relenting, it was a fantastic game – a classic pitchers' duel. The starting pitchers had done well during the season. Both right-handers, the Astros' Brandon Backe was 10-8 for the season, and the White Sox' Freddy García was 14-8 with a 3.87 ERA.

And both starters threw masterfully that night. So many chances, so many zeros.

In the top of the first, with two out, White Sox right fielder Jermaine Dye hit a double. In the bottom of the first, Astros second baseman Craig Biggio singled, then moved to second on a sacrifice by center fielder Willy Taveras. In the top of the third, speedy White Sox left fielder Scott Podsednik stretched a double to a triple. In the bottom of the sixth, Taveras singled, then went to second on walk to Lance Berkman. They executed a double steal. An intentional walk to Mike Lamb loaded the bases. In the top of the seventh, Aaron Rowand singled, then went to third on a double by Joe Crede. Some scary moments to score on both sides and all of them failed to score. Neither team could pull the trigger – nothing but doughnuts.

For seven innings, Backe and García traded zeroes like baseball cards.

In the eighth, the Astros brought in closer Brad Lidge. The first White Sox batter he faced was Willie Harris, pinch-hitting for pitcher García. Harris singled. Podsednik sacrificed Harris to second. Carl Everett, pinch-hitting for Tadahito Iguchi, grounded out, moving Harris to third. Up came Dye, who with two hits already had twice as many as anyone else in the game. He singled to center, scoring Harris with the first run of the game. Paul Konerko struck out, ending the top of the eighth, but the damage was done: White Sox 1, Astros 0.

In the bottom of the eighth, right-hander Cliff Politte came in for García. The first batter, Biggio, grounded out. But Taveras was hit by a pitch. A bit unnerved, Politte threw a wild pitch to the next batter, home-run threat Lance Berkman, and Taveras took second. With first base empty, the White Sox walked Berkman. Morgan Ensberg flied out, and Taveras moved to third. Left-hander Neal Cotts relieved Politte and José Vizcaíno pinch-hit for Lamb. Vizcaíno grounded out to end the threat.

In the top of the ninth, Pierzynski led off with a double, but was left stranded as Lidge struck out Rowand and Crede, then got Uribe to ground out.

Bobby Jenks, with a 2.75 ERA and a 1.246 WHIP earning him the closer role at season's end, came in in the bottom of the ninth to finish the job. He gave up a leadoff single to center field by Astros right fielder Jason Lane. Lane went to second on a sacrifice by catcher Brad Ausmus. Chris Burke pinch-hit for shortstop Adam Everett and popped a foul down the third-base line almost out of play – but Uribe made a miracle catch, falling into the crowd, for out number two. Orlando Palmeiro pinch-hit for Lidge.

The final out, called by White Sox radio play-by-play voice John Rooney:

"From the stretch, with a runner at second, here's the 1-and-2 pitch to Palmeiro – a groundball past Jenks, up the middle of the infield. Uribe has it. He throws. OUT! OUT! A White Sox winner, and a World Series championship! The White Sox have won the World Series, and they're mobbing each other on the field!"[4]

As the mob ruled, celebrating on the mound, radio analyst, Southside Chicago native and 1980 White Sox All-Star closer Ed Farmer[5] continued, "This is as good as it gets. The Sox are world champions in Chicago. Go crazy! … Enjoy the celebration, Chicago! This is looong overdue."[6] Soon sports journalists wandered out onto the field, looking for interviews with whomever they could. And they found a team that kept coming back to the chemistry.

Bobby Jenks, on how the team welcomed him during his midseason call-up from Double-A ball: "That's what this team is all about all year long is just being one. It wasn't ever just one hero all season it was … just pick somebody out of this crowd now and that was the hero of some day of the season."[7]

General manager Ken Williams didn't really like being asked if he considered himself MVP for putting the team together, and gave all the credit to the players: "There's a whole bunch of MVPs and all of them are in the lineup … or coming off the bench."[8] When asked how they built the team, Williams replied, "For us, the foundation had to be the pitching. And Ozzie [Guillén] and I and the coaches, we just felt we wanted to be in more games. We've had a lot of talent here in the last few years, but we had to sacrifice a little bit on the talent end to get a lot of character people in here."[9]

Future Hall of Famer Frank Thomas, who was injured most of the season: "I gotta thank these guys, man. They put me on their back and carried me across the finish line."[10]

Steve Perry, co-author and singer of the Journey hit "Don't Stop Believin'," said, "You have no idea what these guys have done for me emotionally." He had stopped singing since leaving Journey, and was again feeling inspired.[11] World Series MVP Jermaine Dye, from up on the podium: "We don't have any egos on this team, I think what was what's really special about this club. Every got along with each other and everybody just wanted to win."[12]

Manager Ozzie Guillén, holding the World Series trophy in his hands, said: "I'm just happy for Jerry [Reinsdorf, team owner] and the Chicago fans. … They've been waiting for so long, so many years. … This is for Venezuela!"[13]

Both Guillen and Game Four winning pitcher García were from Venezuela. The major leagues had become more international – the 2005 White Sox also included two players from Cuba, six from the Dominican Republic, and two from Japan. The *Japan Times* wrote that second baseman Iguchi became the first Japanese to play on a World Series champion.[14]

And to everyone who celebrated around the world, as Pierzynski said, "I hope they lived it up and partied like it was 1917."[15]

SOURCES

In addition to the sources cited in the Notes, the author consulted Baseball-Reference.com and several YouTube videos containing copies of the original broadcast.

https://www.baseball-reference.com/boxes/HOU/HOU200510260.shtml

Fox Sports broadcast:
https://www.youtube.com/watch?v=HaAsMEN7qbA

NBC World Series Game Four postgame broadcast: https://youtu.be/HaAsMEN7qbA?si=Vw2L25qY2gO4IRSD

WMVP ESPN 1000 Radio World Series Game Four radio broadcast (partial): https://www.youtube.com/watch?v=yRf4N4peXC8

2005 Chicago White Sox World Series Documentary: https://www.youtube.com/watch?v=ZNkHOvPGIoo

NOTES

1   Terry Armour, "Don't Stop Believin' This," *Chicago Tribune*, October 18, 2005, https://www.chicagotribune.com/2005/10/18/dont-stop-believin-this/.

2   Fox Sports World Series Game Four broadcast, October 26, 2005.

3   Fox Sports World Series Game Four broadcast.

4   WMVP ESPN 1000 Radio World Series Game Four broadcast, October 26, 2005.

5   Phil Rosenthal, "White Sox Broadcasters John Rooney and Ed Farmer Call Game Action in the First Inning Against the Cubs at Wrigley Field on July 7, 2000," *Chicago Tribune*, April 2, 2020, https://www.chicagotribune.com/2020/04/02/ed-farmer-the-voice-of-the-chicago-white-sox-for-almost-30-years-dies/.

6   WMVP ESPN 1000 Radio World Series Game Four broadcast, October 26, 2005.

7   NBC World Series Game Four postgame broadcast, October 26, 2005.

8   NBC World Series Game Four postgame broadcast.

9   NBC World Series Game Four postgame broadcast.

10   *2005 Chicago White Sox World Series Documentary* DVD, MLB Productions, 2005.

11   NBC World Series Game Four postgame broadcast.

12   NBC World Series Game Four postgame broadcast.

13   NBC World Series Game Four postgame broadcast.

14   Kyodo, "Dream Come True for Iguchi as White Sox Win World Series," *Japan Times*, October 28, 2005, https://www.japantimes.co.jp/sports/2005/10/28/baseball/mlb/dream-come-true-for-iguchi-as-white-sox-win-world-series/.

15   Doug Padilla, *"Believe It!" White Sox: 2005 World Series Champions* (Chicago: *Chicago Sun-Times,* 2005), 117.

CONTRIBUTORS

A Chicago-area native, **Tom Alesia** wrote the book *Baseball Like It Oughta Be: How a Shoe Salesman's Madison Mallards and His Renegade Staff Became a Summer-Collegiate Sensation,* about the Madison Mallards' entertaining 25-year history. He also wrote the 2022 book, *Beauty at Short*, the bio of obscure Hall of Famer Dave Bancroft.

Malcolm Allen lives with his wife, Sara, and their daughters in Brooklyn, New York, where he manages an event production warehouse. He met Harold Baines at Memorial Stadium in Baltimore in the 1980s. More recently, on Maryland's Eastern Shore, he visited Harold Baines Way and Harold Baines Field.

Phil Angelo is the retired managing editor of the *Kankakee* (Illinois) *Daily Journal*. He wrote the newspaper's editorials for 30 years. A longtime White Sox fan, he takes an annual baseball road trip with his son, Alex. He also participates in Civil War Roundtables and Sherlock Holmes societies.

Doug Barker is a retired journalist who lives in Olympia, Washington, and follows the Seattle Mariners and San Francisco Giants. His baseball playing days effectively ended as a high-school sophomore when, as he describes it, he "forgot how to throw," an affliction shared with Mackey Sasser, Chuck Knoblauch, Jon Lester, Steve Sax, and all the other victims of the yips.

John Bauer resides with his wife and two children (although one is now at college) in Bedford, New Hampshire. By day he is general counsel of an insurance group headquartered in Manchester, New Hampshire, with specialties in corporate and regulatory law. By night, he spends many spring and summer evenings staying up too late to watch the San Francisco Giants, and he is a year-round avid reader of baseball, history, and baseball history. He is a past and ongoing contributor to various SABR projects.

Robert Bionaz is a retired history professor who has been a fan of the San Francisco Giants since 1958. Although he has written and taught on baseball and culture in the 1910s, his primary interests are in the game he grew up with – baseball in the '50s and '60s.

Alex Blair is an attorney and former sportswriter. He grew up in the Houston area and has been in love with baseball ever since he attended his first game at the Astrodome and stepped from the gloom into the vast interior to behold the tiers of multicolored seats, the faux-green field, and the soaring lamella roof. He lives in the Chicago area with his wife and two children. This is his first contribution to a SABR publication.

Ben Blotner is a financial professional and lifelong Boston Red Sox fan, thanks in part to his Massachusetts-raised father. The 2005 World Series was one of the first he followed as a child. In addition to contributing to the SABR *Games Project*, he has written for various publications including the *Wooster Voice*, the *Columbus Jewish News*, and his own writing website, *Brain of Benny Blot*. He hopes to soon release his debut novel, *Out of the Bassline*, which centers around baseball and music. Ben lives in the Columbus, Ohio area with his fiancée, Ingrid.

A lifelong White Sox fan now living in Cedarburg, Wisconsin, **Ken Carrano** works as the business operations manager for SABR. He has been a SABR member since 1992 and has contributed to several SABR publications and the SABR Games Project. Ken and his Brewers' fan wife, Ann, share two children, two golden retrievers, and a mutual disdain for the blue side of Chicago.

Alan Cohen has been a SABR member since 2011. He chairs the BioProject factchecking team, serves as vice president-treasurer of the Connecticut Smoky Joe Wood Chapter, and is a datacaster (MiLB stringer) with the Eastern League Hartford Yard Goats, the Double-A affiliate of the Colorado Rockies. He also works with the Retrosheet Negro Leagues project and served on SABR's Negro League Committee. His biographies, game stories, and essays have appeared in more than 70 baseball-related publications. He has four children, nine grandchildren, and one great-grandchild, and resides in Connecticut with wife Frances, their cats, Zoe and Ava, and their dog, Buddy.

Eric Conrad is a lifelong Red Sox fan, a SANS Institute Faculty Fellow, and co-owner of Backshore Communications, an internet security consulting company. He is author of several information security books, lives on Peaks Island, Maine, and can be reached at https://ericconrad.com.

Carter Cromwell was formerly a sportswriter for daily newspapers, covering a wide variety of athletics at all levels. In a later life, he was a public-relations professional in the high-tech world. Since 2019, he has worked with an independent-league professional baseball team, the San Rafael Pacifics, doing the play-by-play and coordinating the in-game statistics. A SABR member, he also writes baseball-related articles for various websites and has contributed to multiple book projects. When not doing that, he has a passion for world travel, photography, and rescue dogs.

Richard Cuicchi joined SABR in 1983 and is an active member of the Schott-Pelican Chapter. After his retirement as an information technology executive, Richard authored *Family Ties: A Comprehensive Collection of Facts and Trivia about Baseball's Relatives*. He has contributed to numerous SABR BioProject and Games Project publications. He does freelance writing and blogging about a variety of baseball topics on his website, TheTenthInning.com. Richard is a regular contributor to CrescentCitySports.com, where he writes about New Orleans baseball history. Richard lives in New Orleans with his wife, Mary.

Tim Deale is a SABR member and chairman of the Larry Doby Chapter of SABR. He is a native of Deale, Maryland, now residing in South Carolina. He is a contributor to the SABR BioProject and a member of the Nineteenth Century Research Committee. A former sports talk show host in Annapolis, Maryland, he currently writes books about baseball. Some of the things he enjoys are researching statistics, old-time baseball, and making lists of the top players and pitchers in various categories. Tim learned about baseball at an early age, listening to Baltimore Orioles games on the radio with his grandmother. Now, he says, "I want to help preserve baseball history and pass it on to other generations. I recently created a new statistic and would be glad to share it with SABR and baseball-reference.com and any other site that uses stats."

Alex Edelman was named one of *Time* magazine's 100 most influential people in 2024. SABR published his biography of Ken Harrelson in 2005 when he was a high-school student in the Boston area. He has since gone on to become a popular stand-up comedian, performing both in the United States and England. In 2024 he won an *Emmy* Award for Outstanding Writing for a Variety Special, recognizing his work in the Broadway solo play *Just for Us*, a comedy special about attending a White supremacist meeting in Queens, New York. He has also written for the *Atlantic,* the *New York Times*, and other publications.

Joseph "Joey" Elledge is the chair of the business department and an associate professor of sport management at Erskine College. As an avid baseball fan, Joey is a lifelong Chicago Cubs fan and a big supporter of minor league baseball. Joey became a baseball fan by attending Capital City Bombers (former Single-A affiliate for the New York Mets) ganes with his family. He holds partial season tickets to minor-league games in Columbia, South Carolina, with his mom, sisters, and his wife. He works with the Lexington County Blowfish (Coastal Plain League) in sales, A SABR member, he is a new contributor to SABR projects and studies the business side of baseball in his free time. Joey resides in Lexington, South Carolina, with his wife, Katie, and three dogs, Cookie, Sammy (named after Sammy Sosa), and Boone.

J.P. Garrett is a native Hoosier and marketing/communications executive who writes extensively about baseball in general and the Cincinnati Reds in particular.

Jeremy Gibbs is a high-school teacher from St. Peters, Missouri, with a passion for baseball history. A proud alumnus of Francis Howell North High School, he shares a unique connection with former major-league pitcher Mark Buehrle. Jeremy is the author of Buehrle's official SABR biography, blending his love of storytelling with his pride in their shared roots. He lives in St. Peters, Missouri, with his wife, stepson, and their cat, Stanley "Musial" Gibbs.

Steve Ginader is a former logistics manager residing in Green Valley, Arizona, with his wife, Julie. After retiring, he started writing game stories for the Games Project, including several articles for SABR published books. Steve plans to continue his research and writing using the many platforms of the SABR Research Collection.

A love of baseball was instilled in **Andrew Harner** from childhood, but since he had next to no athletic skills, he instead dived into the game's history and pored over box scores as often as he could. And because baseball history wasn't offered as a college major, he settled for the next best thing – a bachelor's degree in sports journalism with a minor in history. He graduated from Bowling Green State University in 2010 and spent nearly seven years as a sports editor before leaving the newspaper industry to pursue a career in hospitality management. Andrew has since published baseball research for HowTheyPlay and spent a little over a year producing online NFL content for *Sports Illustrated*. He has been married to his wife, Elizabeth, since 2011, and they have two daughters.

Jeff Howard is a lifelong resident of the Northwest Side of Chicago and a frequent contributor to the SABR Games Project with SABR journal and book articles as well. He attended Luther College in Decorah, Iowa, played Division III football, had a weekly sports column, and read news for the campus radio station. On graduation, he worked in the insurance industry and recently retired from a research analyst position handling claim appeals. He has organized multiple community baseball, softball, and basketball teams as a volunteer, teaching kids to appreciate and love the games they play.

Kenneth Huang grew up in New York but now is based in the United Kingdom. He spent a summer interning for the Yankees' ticket operations department working on their databases, aiding the ticket sales department, and contributing to growth initiatives before entering the world of sports consulting by joining Sportscorp Ltd., a consulting firm that specializes in international development for sports franchises and leagues. He now works closely with the British Baseball Federation to develop the sport in the United Kingdom.

Mike Huber has been a SABR member for almost 30 years. He enjoys writing for SABR's Games Project, concentrating on some of the rare events in the national pastime, such as pitching a no-hitter or hitting for the cycle. He has been rooting for the same American League team for over 55 years.

Brian Jacoby lives in Southern California with his wife and two daughters. He is an avid Arizona Diamondbacks fan surrounded by relentless Dodgers fans. He is a first-time contributor and has been a SABR member since 2021. Brian played baseball as a teenager and has spent most of his life building memories around baseball.

GRINDERS AND GAMERS

Ann S. Johnson is a career technology executive with a passion for the game of baseball. Her love of the game stretches back decades watching her beloved Mets win the 1986 World Series. Refusing to join the Cubs fandom upon moving to Chicago, she became a diehard White Sox fan and season-ticket holder. Witnessing the 2005 World Series in person was a dream come true, and the opportunity to write even a chapter about this team was an opportunity she could not refuse.

Christopher Kamka is an associate producer for Cubs baseball on Marquee Sports Network. He had previously worked in the same capacity for White Sox baseball on NBC Sports Chicago. Christopher and his wife, Janet, live in Addison, Illinois, with their son, Mateo.

Norm King (1957-2018) of Ottawa, Ontario, joined SABR in 2010 and became a prolific contributor to the SABR BioProject and Games Project until his untimely death from a rare form of bile duct cancer in 2018. He was the lead editor and author of *Au jeu/Play Ball: The 50 Greatest Games in the History of the Montreal Expos*, published in 2016, and wrote chapters for a number of other SABR books, including *Thar's Joy in Braveland: The 1957 Milwaukee Braves*; *Winning on the North Side: The 1929 Chicago Cubs*; and *A Pennant for the Twin Cities: The 1965 Minnesota Twins*. He was an active member of SABR's Quebec Chapter and a friendly face at the SABR national convention each year.

Sean Kolodziej, a SABR member since 2018, is a lifelong Cubs fan who has been known to take in a White Sox game or two. He was born, raised, and still lives in Joliet, Illinois, with his wife, Amy. His greatest moment at Comiskey Park II was watching Robin Ventura hit a walk-off grand slam to beat the Rangers on a beautiful night in July of 1991.

Gerard Kwilecki, a lifelong Atlanta Braves fan, was born and raised in Bainbridge, Georgia. He is a Valdosta State University alumnus and resides near Mobile, Alabama, with his family. He currently works for the University of South Alabama, where the Jaguars have a storied baseball program.

Bob LeMoine is a high-school librarian and adjunct professor. He lives in New Hampshire and has contributed to several SABR projects, including two as co-editor. Bob is the author of *When the Babe Went Back to Boston: Babe Ruth, Judge Fuchs, and the Hapless Braves of 1935* (McFarland & Co., 2023).

Len Levin is a longtime newspaper editor in New England, now retired. He lives in Providence with his wife, Linda, and an overachieving orange cat. He now (Len, not the cat) is the grammarian for the Rhode Island Supreme Court and copy-edits its decisions. He also copy-edits many SABR books, including this one. He is just down the interstate from Fenway Park, where he has spent many happy – and some not-so-happy – hours.

Will MacLean once interviewed for the role of director of software engineering, baseball systems for the Chicago Cubs. He didn't get the gig, but now he can joke he had a major-league tryout. He is actually a Southside fan anyway, so he signed up to write about the White Sox.

Roby Mammon is a student at Toronto Metropolitan University.

Jim Margalus is the managing editor of Sox Machine (soxmachine.com) and the co-host of the Sox Machine Podcast. He's been covering the White Sox since 2006 and has been a member of SABR since 2012. He lives in Nashville, Tennessee, with his wife and son, and is the vice president of the Nashville Curling Club.

Michael Marsh is a freelance writer based in Chicago. A former staff writer for the *Chicago Reader*, he also covered high-school sports for the *Chicago Sun-Times* and *Chicago Tribune*. At 10 years of age, he fell in love with the White Sox when the South Side Hitmen surprisingly contended for the crown of the old American League West in 1977.

Chad Moody is a nearly lifelong resident of the Detroit area, where he has been a fan of the Detroit Tigers from birth. An alumnus of the University of Michigan and Michigan State University, he has spent 30-plus years working in the automotive industry. Chad has contributed to numerous SABR and Professional Football Researchers Association projects. He and his wife, Lisa, live in Plymouth, Michigan, with their dog, Daisy.

Mark Morowczynski has been a SABR member since 2019 and, having grown up in Chicago, is a lifelong White Sox fan. He currently lives in Seattle and is an information security professional by day and has written several information security books. He can be reached at https://markmorow.com.

Bill Nowlin is a lifelong fan of the other Sox. He understood what it was like to wait decades and decades between World Series wins, and marveled at the Red Sox finally winning in 2004 and the White Sox winning the very next year, in 2005. A co-founder of Rounder Records and, more recently, Down the Road Records, he's in more than one Hall of Fame – but they're music-related ones. He has written more than 1,000 articles for SABR since the current century began.

Richard O'Connor is a lifelong Chicago White Sox fan and Chicago resident. He has been a member of SABR since 2024 and a member of the Emil Rothe Chapter to enrich his passion for baseball. Although a White Sox fan, he loves all aspects of baseball. His day job is as a firefighter and he also teaches at two colleges in the Chicagoland area.

Tony S. Oliver is a native of Puerto Rico currently living in Sacramento, California, with his wife and daughter. While he works as a project manager with a health company and teaches at three University of California campuses, his true love is baseball and he cheers for both the Red Sox and whoever happens to be playing the Yankees. He is fascinated by baseball cards and is currently researching the evolution of baseball tickets. He believes there is no prettier color than the vibrant green of freshly mown grass on a baseball field.

Bill Pearch is a lifelong Chicago Cubs fan and serves as secretary/newsletter editor for SABR's Emil Rothe Chapter (Chicago). In 2022 he helped establish SABR's Central Illinois Chapter. Bill has contributed to SABR's publications about Comiskey Park and Ebbets Field. His article "Boodle and Barnstorming: When Politics and the National Pastime Convened in Dwight, Illinois," published in *The National Pastime: Heart of the Midwest* (2023), told the story of semipro team owner Col. Frank L. Smith and how baseball factored into a scandalous pursuit of political office. Bill is happily married to a Milwaukee Brewers fan. Follow him on Bluesky: @billpearch.bsky.social.

Zac Petrillo holds a bachelor of arts from Hunter College and a master of fine arts from Chapman University's Dodge College of Film and Media Arts. His experience spans directing multiple short films and producing content for networks like Comedy Central and TruTV. In 2016 Zac played a pivotal role in the launch of Vice Media's 24/7 cable network, Vice TV. As an active member of the Society for American Baseball Research, he dedicates his research to exploring the realm of post-1980s baseball, particularly examining its intersection with the media industry. Currently, he serves as the director of technical operations at A+E Networks and imparts his knowledge in television studies as a lecturer at Marymount Manhattan College.

Bill Pruden has been a teacher of American history and government for over 40 years. A SABR member for over two decades, he has contributed to SABR's BioProject and Games Project as well as a number of book projects. He has also written on a range of American history subjects, an interest undoubtedly fueled by the fact that as a seven-year-old he was at Yankee Stadium to witness Roger Maris's historic 61st home run.

Carl Riechers retired from United Parcel Service in 2012 after 35 years of service. With more free time, he became a SABR member that same year. Born and raised in the suburbs of St. Louis, he became a big fan of the Cardinals. He and his wife, Janet, have three children and he is the proud grandpa of two.

Juan José Rodriguez is a content developer and data analyst for Burgundy Group Advertising in Nashville, Tennessee, a position he has held since 2023 after working for three years in Chicago as a consultant for EY. He graduated from the University of Notre Dame in 2019 with a degree in business analytics, along with a second major in film, television and theatre and a minor in journalism. While on campus, Juan José worked for Fighting Irish Media as a play-by-play announcer and color commentator for more than 200 live events on ESPN's and NBC's digital platforms. He also served on the editorial staff of *Scholastic* magazine, where he published 10 award-winning articles and led the staff as editor-in-chief during

his senior year. Juan José contributed to *¡Arriba! The Heroic Life of Roberto Clemente* (SABR, 2022) and *Béisbol on the Air: Essays on Major League Spanish-Language Broadcasters* (McFarland, 2024).

Jason Scheller is a professor of history at Vernon College in Wichita Falls, Texas. He is a graduate of Texas Tech University. His graduate work has been featured in the books *The Empire Strikes Out: How Baseball Sold U.S. Foreign Policy and Promoted the American Way Abroad*, by Robert Elias, and *The Boys Who Were Left Behind: The 1944 World Series Between the Hapless St. Louis Browns and the Legendary St. Louis Cardinals*, by John Heidenry and Brett Topel. He joined the Dallas-Fort Worth Banks-Bragan chapter of SABR in 2018. His interests are in World War II baseball, the Negro Leagues, the minor leagues, the Texas Rangers, the Los Angeles Dodgers, the Chicago White Sox, and the Boston Red Sox. He enjoys attending minor-league baseball games throughout the country with his wife and daughter each summer. A Red Sox fan since 1986, he follows them every season and relishes the opportunity to attend games at Fenway Park whenever he gets a chance.

Tom Shaer is a former television and radio sportscaster who worked in Boston (seven years) and Chicago (24 years). After a second career as a media consultant and government affairs specialist, he is semiretired and living in Scottsdale, Arizona, with his wife, Lisa. His two grown children and two grandchildren are big baseball fans, though the youngest grandchild doesn't yet know that because he is less than a year old.

Russ Speiller lives in Cincinnati with his incredible wife and two children. A SABR member for two years, he has contributed numerous stories to books, journals, and the online SABR BioProject. A Yankees fan, Russ welcomed the chance to write a bio on the man of mystery, pitcher Orlando "El Duque" Hernandez, for this 2005 White Sox book.

Bill Staples Jr. of Chandler, Arizona, is passionate about uncovering and sharing the untold stories of the "international pastime." A SABR member since 2006, he focuses his expertise on Japanese American and Negro Leagues baseball history, using these contexts to explore themes of civil rights, cross-cultural relations, and globalization. He serves as a board member of the Nisei Baseball Research Project and the Japanese American Citizens League-Arizona Chapter. Additionally, he is chairman of the SABR Asian Baseball Committee and an ambassador for the National Baseball Hall of Fame exhibit *YAKYU | BASEBALL: The Transpacific Exchange of the Game*. Learn more at zenimura.com.

Mark S. Sternman has attended only one home Chicago White Sox game in his life, a crazy 9-8 11-inning loss to Milwaukee on July 29, 1990. As a fan of the Expos, he appreciated Chris Widger (and Geoff Blum) contributing to a World Series win in 2005, but wished they could have also helped bring a championship to Montreal.

Ryan Van Der Karr is the owner of Tiered Real Estate of Minooka, Illinois. He likes to characterize himself as a boring realtor, but his love of baseball allows an occasional transformation into an optimistic fan of the Chicago White Sox. Ryan is one of the founders and former co-president of SABR's Central Illinois Chapter. A graduate of the University of Illinois-Chicago with a degree in electrical engineering, Ryan and his wife, Jennifer, strive to attend any sporting event with a giveaway (preferably a bobblehead).

William M. "Matt" Vines is a trial lawyer who has practiced in Jackson, Mississippi, since 1994. He is a life-long baseball fan and collector of baseball cards. His collection includes a 1955 Topps Roberto Clemente (rookie card), a 1933 Goudey Babe Ruth (#144), and a 1909-11 T206 Walter Johnson (hands at chest).

Joseph Wancho resides in Westlake, Ohio. He has been a SABR member since 2005 and he serves as co-chair of the Baseball Index Project. He is an occasional contributor to various SABR research committees.

Kirk Weber grew up in the Chicago suburbs rooting for the White Sox and now lives near Spokane, Washington, with his wife, Michelle. He has been a SABR member since 2020.

Bob Webster grew up in northwest Indiana and has been a Cubs fan since 1963. Bob moved to Portland, Oregon, in 1980 and now works on baseball research and writing and contributes to various SABR projects. Bob is the vice president of the Pacific Northwest Chapter of SABR and vice president of the Old-Timers Baseball Association of Portland.

Besnik Zekiri is a passionate baseball writer and co-author for Sox On Tap, where he delivers in-depth analysis and commentary on the Chicago White Sox. Drawn to baseball research by its rich history, evolving strategies, and endless data, he uncovers the narratives that shape the game. His work delivers fans stories and insights about players, team dynamics, and the trends defining modern baseball.

A SABR member since 1979, **Don Zminda** has been a devoted White Sox fan since he attended his first game at Old Comiskey Park in August of 1954. The director of publications for STATS, Inc. from 1988 to 2000, Don has authored numerous sports books, including *The Legendary Harry Caray: Baseball's Greatest Salesman*, a 2019 CASEY Award nominee, and *Justice Batted Last: Ernie Banks, Minnie Miñoso, and the Unheralded Players Who Integrated Chicago's Major League Teams* (2025). He also served as editor of the SABR publication *Go-Go to Glory: The 1959 Chicago White Sox* (2019).

Society for American Baseball Research

Become a SABR member today!

If you're interested in baseball — writing about it, reading about it, talking about it — there's a place for you in the Society for American Baseball Research.

SABR members include everyone from academics to professional sportswriters to amateur historians and statisticians to students and casual fans who merely enjoy reading about baseball history and gathering online or in person with other members to talk baseball.

We hope you'll join the most passionate international community of baseball fans!

Check us out online at SABR.org/join

SABR Membership Benefits

- Receive two e-book editions (spring and fall) of the Baseball Research Journal, our flagship publication
- Receive e-book edition of The National Pastime, our annual convention journal
- New e-books published by the SABR Digital Library, FREE to all members
- "This Week in SABR" e-newsletter, sent every Friday
- Regional chapter meetings, which can include guest speakers, presentations, and trips to ballgames
- Participate in research committees and online discussion groups

- Contribute to books, the Baseball Biography Project, and the SABR Games Project
- Collaborate with SABR researchers and experts
- Publish your research in peer-reviewed SABR journals
- Discount on registration to our annual conferences and National Convention
- FREE online access to Historical Black Newspapers Collection via ProQuest, the Newspapers.com World Collection, and The Sporting News via Paper of Record
- Discounts with other partners in the baseball community

SABR MEMBERSHIP FORM

Name _____

Email _____

Address _____

City _____ State _____ Zip _____

Phone _____

If you wish to pay by credit card, please contact the SABR office at (602) 496-1460 or sign up securely online at SABR.org/join.

We accept Visa, Mastercard & Discover.

	Standard	Young Pro.	Student
Annual:	☐$80	☐$55	☐$25
3 Year:	☐$215		
Monthly:	☐$7.95	☐$5.95	

Members who wish to be mailed a printed copy of the Baseball Research Journal should add $7 per issue (U.S.) or $11 per issue (international). Two (2) issues of the BRJ are delivered each year.

SABR memberships are available on an annual, multi-year, or monthly subscription basis. Memberships auto-renew for your convenience. Young Professional memberships are for ages 30 and under. Student memberships are available to currently enrolled middle/high school or full-time college/university students. Monthly subscription members are eligible for SABR event discounts after 12 months.

Mail to: SABR, PO Box 1715, Milwaukee, WI 53201

The SABR Digital Library

Available wherever books are sold

The First Negro League Champion: The 1920 Chicago American Giants

Edited by Frederick C. Bush and Bill Nowlin

Paperback $29.95 244 pages • Ebook $9.99

This book chronicles the team which won the title of champion in the Negro National League's inaugural season. Rube Foster, a Hall of Famer, and his White business partner John Schorling are featured along with biographies of every player on the team include Cristóbal Torriente, a member of both the National Baseball Hall of Fame and the Cuban Baseball Hall of Fame, as well as early Blackball stalwarts Dave "Lefty" Brown, Bingo DeMoss, Judy Gans, Dave Malarcher, Frank Warfield, and Frank Wickware. A comprehensive timeline of the 1920 season and a history of the founding of the Negro National League are included.

We Are, We Can, We Will: The 1992 World Champion Toronto Blue Jays

Edited by Adrian Fung and Bill Nowlin

Forewords by Buck Martinez and Dave Winfield

Paperback US $34.95/Canada $41.95 394 pages • Ebook $9.99

The 1992 Toronto Blue Jays will always be remembered as the first World Series-winning club from Canada. After a near miss in 1991, the 1992 club confidently adopted "We Are, We Can, We Will" as their team motto. This book features biographies of every player who played for the 1992 Toronto Blue Jays including Hall of Famers Dave Winfield, Jack Morris, and Roberto Alomar. Manager Cito Gaston, Hall of Fame general manager Pat Gillick, and radio broadcaster Tom Cheek are also included, as well as a "ballpark biography" of SkyDome. Ten reports describe significant games from the 1992 season illustrating Toronto's championship journey from Opening Day to the last game of the World Series.

From Shibe Park to Connie Mack Stadium: Great Games in Philadelphia's Lost Ballpark

Edited by Gregory H. Wolf
Paperback $39.95 398 pages • Ebook $9.99

This collection evokes memories and the exciting history of the celebrated ballpark through stories of 100 games played there and several feature essays. The games included in this volume reflect every decade in the ballpark's history, from the inaugural game in 1909, to the last in 1970.

Shibe Park was the home of the Philadelphia A's from 1909 until their relocation to Kansas City and the Philadelphia Phillies from 1938 until the ballpark's closure at the end 1970. In 1953 it was renamed Connie Mack Stadium. The ballpark hosted big-league baseball for 62 seasons and more than 6,000 games—over 3,500 games by the A's and 2,500 by the Phillies—and was home to Frank Baker, Del Ennis, Chief Bender, and Robin Roberts.

¡Arriba!: The Heroic Life of Roberto Clemente

edited by Bill Nowlin and Glen Sparks

Paperback $34.95 338 pages • Ebook $9.99

2022 marks the 50th anniversary year of Roberto Clemente's passing. This book celebrates his life and baseball career. Named to 15 All-Star Game squads, Clemente won 12 Gold Gloves, four batting titles, and was the National League's Most Valuable Player in 1966. The first Latino inducted into the National Baseball Hall of Fame, Clemente played 18 seasons for the Pittsburgh Pirates and became the 11th player to reach the 3,000-hit milestone, hitting number 3000 on the season's last day. At the time no one knew he would never play baseball again. Clemente was known for his charitable work. He lost his life on the final day of 1972 while working to provide relief for victims of an earthquake in Nicaragua.

The Stars Shone on Philadelphia: The 1934 Phila. Stars
ISBN 978-1-960819-04-8 $9.99 ebook
ISBN 978-1-960819-05-5 $29.95 paperback
Biographies of Ed Bolden's 1934 Negro National League champions, including Biz Mackie and Jud Wilson.

Yankee Stadium: America's First Modern Ballpark
ISBN 978-1-960819-16-8 $9.99 ebook
ISBN 978-1-960819-21-5 $39.95 paperback
Essays about the history of Yankee Stadium and recaps of over 50 historic games and other events there, including papal visits, football, and more.

Ebbets Field: Great, Historic, and Memorable Games at Brooklyn's Lost Ballpark
ISBN 978-1-960819-16-1 $9.99 ebook
ISBN 978-1-960819-17-8 $39.95 paperback
Relive Jackie Robinson's and Sandy Koufax's debuts, and over 90 other heartbreaks and triumphs in Brooklyn, plus essays on the ballpark.

Nichibei Yakyu: Volume II: 1960-2019
ISBN 978-1-960819-14-7 $9.99 ebook
ISBN 978-1-960819-15-4 $34.95 paperback
Fascinating recaps of the exhibition tours and MLB games by US baseball teams in Japan.

Sox Bid Curse Farewell: The 2004 Boston Red Sox
ISBN 978-1-960819-18-5 $9.99 ebook
ISBN 978-1-960819-19-2 $34.95 paperback
Biographies of every player and coach on the 2004 World Championship team, as well as essays about the season, effects of the win on fans, and more.

Dodger Stadium: Blue Heaven on Earth
ISBN 978-1-960819-20-8 $9.99 ebook
ISBN 978-1-960819-21-5 $29.95 paperback
Essays about the history of Dodger Stadium and recaps of over 50 historic games there, from Fernandomania to Vin Scully's bow.

One-Win Wonders
ISBN 978-1-960819-13-0 $39.95 paperback
ISBN 978-1-960819-12-3 $9.99 ebook
Biographies of 78 players whose entire major league pitching record consisted of just one win, from the tragic, like Nick Adenhart, to the improbable, like catcher Brent Mayne.

Willie Mays: Five Tools
ISBN 978-1-960819-02-4 $9.99 ebook
ISBN 978-1-960819-03-1 $29.95 paperback
Twenty essays on Mays' life and career, plus recaps of 30 historic games.